Restaurant
La
Jadouine
☎ 51 24 61 50

FLAVORS OF FRANCE
THE BEAUTIFUL
COOKBOOK

AUTHENTIC RECIPES FROM THE REGIONS OF FRANCE

SWISS CHARD PIE (top, recipe page 238), PASTRY PUFFS (right, recipe page 247) AND LEMON TART (bottom, recipe page 238)

AUTHENTIC RECIPES FROM THE REGIONS OF FRANCE

FLAVORS OF FRANCE
THE BEAUTIFUL
COOKBOOK

RECIPES
THE SCOTTO SISTERS

TEXT
GILLES PUDLOWSKI

PHOTOGRAPHY
PIERRE HUSSENOT
PETER JOHNSON
LEO MEIER

HarperCollins*Publishers*

Flavors of France: The Beautiful Cookbook
Copyright © 2004

President: John Owen
General Manager: Stuart Laurence
Co-editions Director: Derek Barton
Publisher: Jane Fraser
Indexer: Jo Rudd
Production: Mick Bagnato
Design and Art Direction: John Bull,
The book Design Company
Map: Mike Gorman
Illustrations: Yolande Bull
Food Stylists: Janice Baker, Laurence Mouton

© 1989 Weldon Owen Pty Limited
© 1990 Weldon Owen Inc., San Francisco

ISBN 0-06-757593-5 (pbk.)

Copyright © 1993 Weldon Owen Inc., San Francisco

Library of Congress Cataloging-in-Publication Data:

Provence, the beautiful cookbook : authentic
    recipes from the regions of Provence / recipes
    and food text Richard Olney; regional text
    Jacques Gantié; food photography by Peter
    Johnson; styled by Janice Baker; scenic
    photography by Michael Freeman.
            p.   cm.
        Includes index.
        ISBN 0-00-255154-3 : $45.00
        1. Cookery, French—Provençal style.
    2. Cookery—France—Provence.   3. Provence
    (France)—Description and travel.
    I. Olney, Richard   II. Grantié, Jacques.
    TX719.2.P75P76   1993
    641.59449—dc20   93–55
                                        CIP
        ISBN 0-06-757598-6 (pbk.)

Printed by Toppan in China

BOUILLABAISSE (top right, recipe page 110) AND BOURRIDE (recipe page 109), PHOTOGRAPHED IN PROVENCE

CONTENTS

THE REPUBLICAN *TRICOLORE*, SYMBOL OF FRANCE, REPLACED
THE *FLEUR-DE-LIS* AS THE FRENCH NATIONAL FLAG AFTER
THE REVOLUTION IN 1789.

INTRODUCTION

A particular approach to eating and drinking

France, this magnificent, many-hued country! A stroll along its narrow country lanes, a ramble through the woods by forest paths, yield the rewards of armfuls of perfumes, the scents of fresh grass, a thousand aromas. Nowhere else in the whole world, from arid deserts to luxuriant gardens, from golden beaches shaded by palm trees to vast untouched landscapes where the horizon appears infinite, can be found this sense of the exotic which takes the traveler directly from the countryside to the table.

In France, every road leads to a splendid food. From Flanders (Flandres) to the Basque country (Pays Basque), from Normandy (Normandie) to Nice, from the Ardennes to southernmost Bigorre, the worthy hexagon is unequaled in its flavors. But more than that, it is a store of fine ingredients which produce not only thousands of good recipes, but also the rich fragrances steaming from a simmering pot in a homely country inn, the aroma of sausages and hams hanging in a corner of an alpine chalet in winter, the characteristic iodine and seaweed scents in a bustling seaside port.

Without the piles of oysters, without *cassoulet*, without *hochepot*, without *bourride*, without the curly green Savoy cabbage, and without the wines and beers that go with them, France would not be France. It is no use denying its postcard image.

This book simply bears witness to an infinite richness, a richness that embraces ancient regional traditions (zealously retained in spite of new administrative boundaries), the landscape, the flavors of its foods and the methods of preparation particular to each small area.

FRANCE DIVIDED: OIL VS BUTTER
Do not protest if someone expresses it in a single word: "France." Just smile. And chant after me the lilting names of Rouergue and Auvergne, of Berry and Quercy, of Aunis and Saintonge. Small or large, each province is a piece in a huge jigsaw puzzle, to be divided like a cake.

And why not? Because throughout history, throughout administrative divisions and boundary changes, each region has maintained the originality of its culinary traditions. In truth, there is nothing unusual in this: culinary traditions very often correspond to a climate.

So beer and charcuterie predominate in eastern France, fresh vegetables and garden herbs in the south. It is easy to discern two faces in France: the domain of butter and the domain of oil, which correspond, more or less, to north and south. Butter cuisine is heavier; fresh oil is lighter, more digestible. *Andouillettes* and poultry sizzle in butter; oil — from the olive in the southeastern region, the wal-

THIS DELIGHTFUL OLD WOODEN SHOP SIGN AND SCULPTURES
BELONG TO THE *PATISSÉRIE ROLLAND* IN QUIMPER, BRETAGNE, WHERE
LOCAL SPECIALTIES SUCH AS *KOUIGH AMANN* ARE A MUST TO SAMPLE.
LEO MEIER

PREVIOUS PAGES: DUCK WITH OLIVES (left, recipe page 138), FRESH FOIS GRAS
WITH GRAPES (right, recipe page 140) AND BREAST OF DUCK WITH GARLIC
SAUCE (center, recipe page 135), PHOTOGRAPHED IN LANGUEDOC
PIERRE HUSSENOT/AGENCE TOP

nut in the southwest — caresses the fish of the Mediterranean. And one can go further, to discover a France of potatoes, of the artichoke, of the beet, of the cabbage in all its forms — cauliflower, Savoy cabbage, green cabbage, red cabbage, Brussels sprouts, sauerkraut. A France that links together in a tightly packed crown the regions of the north, from Brittany (Bretagne) to Alsace, its tip directed towards northern Flanders, and in contrast, another France, with vegetables of bright, vibrant colors and robust flavors: garlic, sweet red and green peppers, pumpkin, tomato, zucchini and eggplant. And yet again one could divide France into rings and circles: a marine France, obligingly abundant in fish, and an earthy France, rich in poultry and charcuterie; or find common roots in Brittany and southern France, in the northern stretch of the Opal Coast and Le Touquet and its southern rival, the Basque coast. The same ingredients, microclimates born of the high and low tides: nothing better to bring together peoples who imagined themselves to be separated by thousands of kilometers.

From mountain to mountain, the roots meet, entwine and marry. Are not the cheeses of Auvergne, with their fresh, wholesome perfume of milk from alpine pastures, close cousins of the cheeses of Savoy (Savoie)? Are there not a few family ties between the Munster of Val d'Orbey and of Lapoutroie in the Vosges mountains of Alsace, and the Tamié cheese fabricated in the abbey of the same name by reclusive monks? Are

BOTH BUYERS AND SELLERS SEEM TO ENJOY THE ATMOSPHERE OF THE OPEN-AIR FOOD MARKETS — THE OLDEST AND SIMPLEST FORM OF RETAILING IN FRANCE, AND PERHAPS THE MOST PLEASANT.

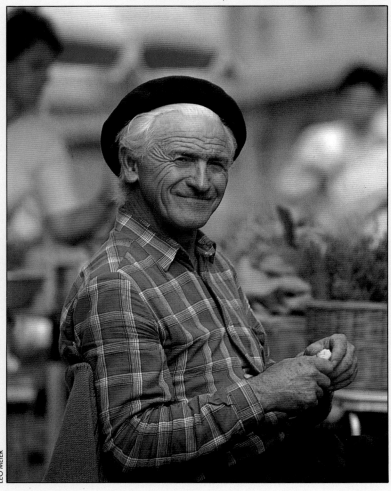

LEO MEIER

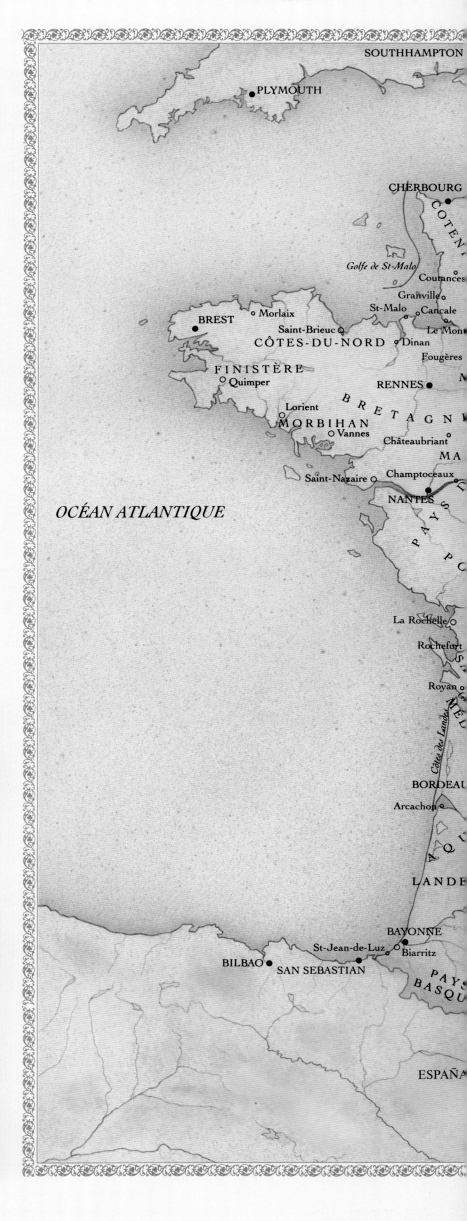

OCÉAN ATLANTIQUE

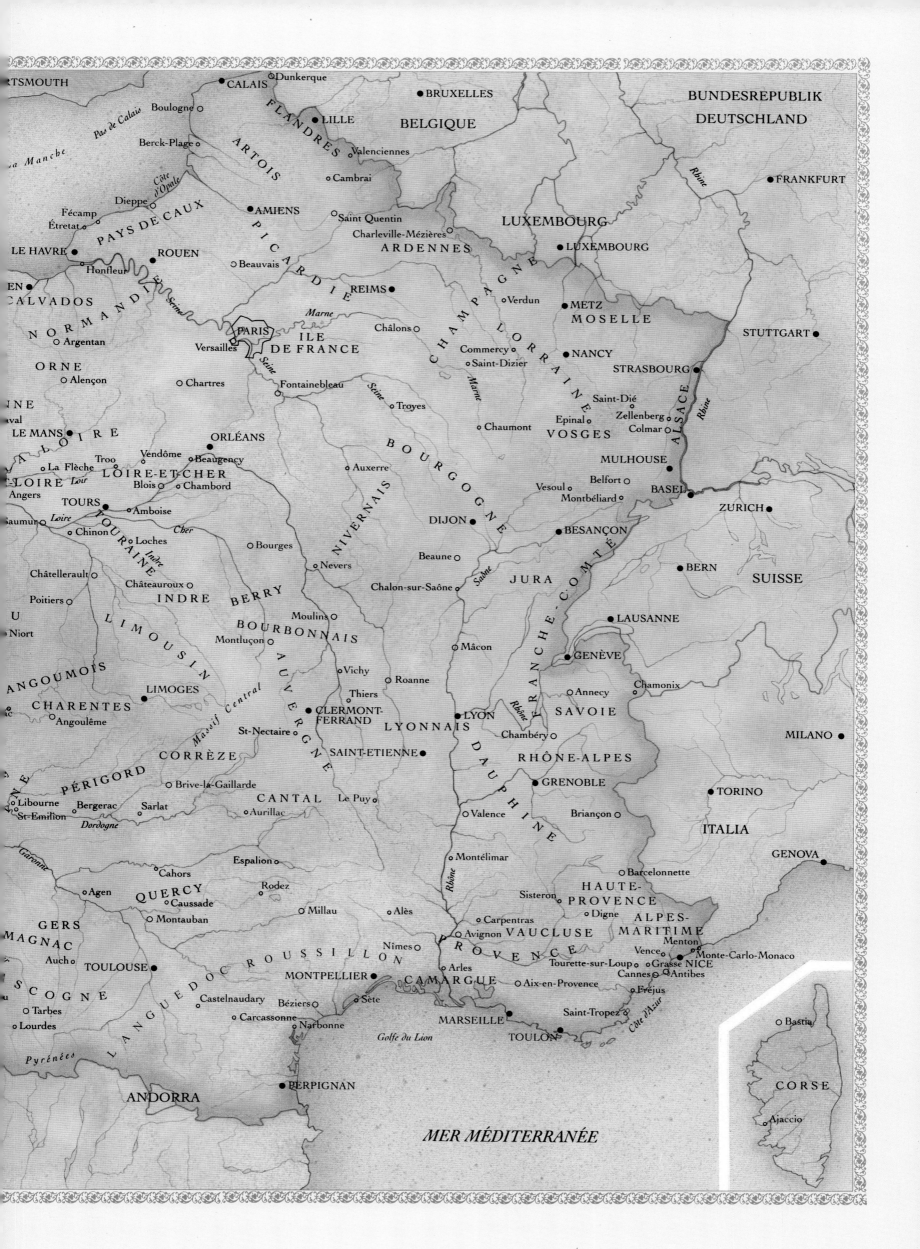

LEO MEIER

FRANCE IS FAMOUS FOR ITS *PÂTISSÉRIES*, AND IN EVERY VILLAGE OR TOWN
YOU CAN BE SURE TO FIND A SELECTION OF THE MOST POPULAR TARTS,
PASTRIES, CAKES AND COOKIES AS WELL AS THE REGIONAL SPECIALTIES.
HERE IN DINAN, BRETAGNE, *GALETTES BRETONNES* ARE ON DISPLAY.

ENJOYING A MOMENT TOGETHER
WHILE PICKING GRAPES IN CHAMPAGNE.

LEO MEIER

not the lambs of Haute-Provence related — however distantly — to the sheep of the Pyrenees? Could not the free-range veal known as *broutard* in Corrèze descend from the red cattle of the Charolais mountains? In appearance, France may be sectioned and subdivided, but between its diverse blocks is woven a close fabric.

THE TRIUMPH OF THE NATURAL

The French predilection for fine cooking has never faltered. Spices were highly esteemed in the Middle Ages, but rejected at the start of the Renaissance, when the flavors of exotic seasonings were replaced by those of indigenous herbs: onions, shallots, garlic, *rocambole*. Mushrooms were honored, truffles worshiped. The acidic, spicy medieval sauces eventually gave way to more subtle flavors, smoother textures, as butter entered into the cuisine.

Thus the French discovered the resources of their own country, but mostly kept them for themselves. The classic texts written around the end of the seventeenth century — such as *Le Cuisinier François* — advocate the selection of natural ingredients and the use of crunchy vegetables — asparagus for example — with an *al dente* style of

WITH TWO MONASTERIES, THE TOWN OF ST-EMILION IN BORDEAUX OFFERS A WEALTH OF RELIGIOUS AND MEDIEVAL ARCHITECTURE, AND IT COULD EASILY BE FORGOTTEN THAT THESE BUILDINGS ARE ACTUAL HOMES.

cooking. Taste was becoming more refined. The prodigious quantities characteristic of medieval banquets were succeeded by a sense of elegance, which shines through such classics as the *Cuisinier Royal et Bourgeois*. The nineteenth century, the boomtime of the great Parisian restaurants (Café de Foy, Véry, Café Français), was also the century of rich and ornate cuisine: cleverly concocted dishes, all too often embellished, always highly sauced. No one hesitated to hide a food's natural taste by sophisticated preparations intended to benefit the eye more than the palate. Hence the vogue for dishes flamed in the dining room, and for *chartreuses* — elaborately fashioned preparations designed to hide the meats under a mass of vegetables — which served as counterparts to the pastrycook's *pièces montées*.

There was as little regional cuisine in the restaurants of Paris, or in the homes of the well-to-do, as there were tourists in the countryside. The twentieth century, from the decade of the '30s, is the era of the return to nature and, first of all, to regional virtues. The enemy — according to La Mazille who, in 1929, penned *La Bonne Cuisine du Périgord* — was Paris, which would accept nothing but a butter-based cuisine, which banished garlic and other strong flavors, and which rejected the traditional recipes of yesteryear.

It was Curnonsky, the elected Prince of Gastronomes, otherwise known as Maurice-Edmond Saillant, who decreed the proper and honorable principle according to which good cuisine means that "things have the taste of what they are." In 1946 he founded the magazine *Cuisine et Vins de France* which attempted to identify and promote regional specialties — recipes, quality ingredients, good restaurants. This insistence on the return to nature goes hand in hand with the rediscovery of the ancient treasure trove of French regional gastronomy.

Thirty years later, Henri Gault and Christian Millau, launching the slogan *nouvelle cuisine*, extolled the return to nature and issued a series of rules that have become a hallmark of modern cuisine: short cooking times, reduced sauces, elimination of unnecessary fats and flour, a ban on the roux that is fatal to digestion, *al dente* cooking of vegetables (as in the sixteenth century) and the marriage of sweet and savory flavors (as in medieval times). In addition, they initiated regional awards — *lauriers du terroir* — for the upholding of certain gourmand traditions.

LEO MEIER

AZAY-LE-RIDEAU IS CONSIDERED BY MANY TO BE THE MOST FEMININE OF THE LOIRE VALLEY CHATEAUX.
THE RIVER FORMS A WIDE MOAT AROUND THIS EPITOME OF RENAISSANCE GRACE AND PERFECTION.

In parallel fashion, top chefs were innovating, imaginatively creating new dishes based on the traditional recipes and products of their regions. Pike-perch with sauerkraut, from Emile Jung at Strasbourg; snails with nettles, from Bernard Loiseau in Burgundy (Bourgogne); peppers with cod, from Firmin Arrambide in the Basque country — all are illustrations of a regional cuisine reinterpreted. No longer satisfied simply to copy, or to combine goat cheese and cabbage, or duck and kiwifruit, these chefs are returning to the old framework and the time-honored products to give them a new savor.

"Rediscover yesterday's flavors with today's techniques": this could be the motto of the cuisine of the present era. While the regional renovation shakes the provinces, the capital and its leading chefs — most of whom have their roots in the country — amuse themselves by imitating a homely style of cuisine. The dish which was all the rage in Paris in the 1980s was a "common" pig's head simmered with sage and served with "simple" mashed potatoes. But it was prepared with impeccable style and subtle perfection. As if at all costs one had to return to the splendid taste of simple things.

So it seems that now, at the end of the twentieth century, all the traditions of France have been thoughtfully brought together: the diverse regional cuisines, the bourgeois cuisine restoring to honor the old, slow-simmered dishes (*blanquette, daube, navarin, pot-au-feu*), preserving with jealous care the great classics of the country. The *bouillabaisse* of Marseilles, the *aïoli* of Provence, the *bourride* of southern France, the *cassoulet* of the southwest — as well as the preserved goose and foie gras of Périgord, the *choucroute* of Alsace, the *potée* of Lorraine, the tripe of Normandy and the *aligot* of Auvergne — are but a few of the unique culinary masterpieces which the year 2000 should preserve and promote as supreme examples of French genius.

If French cuisine is today thought of as a major art — a daily art, constantly being renewed — it owes this status to the enormous riches of its countryside. Each generation has a duty of conservation and adaption. The last decades of the twentieth century will be seen as the era of a lighter cuisine, and at the same time as a period of authenticity. The genius of French cuisine will be seen as knowing how to adapt to new technologies (preserving, freezing, vacuum packaging) without in any way betraying its principles. Now will you believe me when I say that, from the gastronomic point of view, France has never been so rich, so thoroughly in control, as in the 1980s?

RIGHT: ONE OF THE MANY NARROW MEDIEVAL STREETS OF DINAN IN
BRETAGNE WHERE THE TINY SHOPS SEEM TO COMPETE FOR ATTENTION.

LEO MEIER

NORMANDIE, BRETAGNE

Gateways to the sea

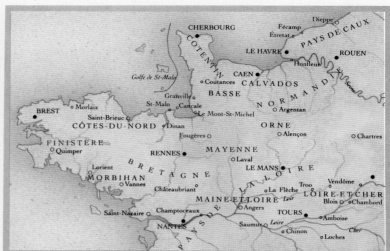

NORMANDIE, BRETAGNE

Gateways to the sea

Two regions facing the sea but still agricultural, still strongly tied to the soil; two sovereign provinces for seafood, yet both endowed with incomparable treasures from the land: how to explain it?

By the beauty of grassy meadows, of crooked white fences, and picturesque dwellings. Half-timbered Norman houses, Breton granite, handsome churches, tormented calvaries, wild hills running down to the sea, marshes: from Normandy through to Brittany, the beauty of the French countryside continues. It is noble, proud, even imperial, like Mont-Saint-Michel, adored by the Bretons but separated from them by the thin stream of the Coesnon and belonging to Normandy. As the Breton saying goes:

"The Coesnon in its folly
Placed the Mount in Normandy."

And there is Coutances, in the region of Cotentin situated between solemn Brittany and traditional Normandy and pointing towards Ireland and England. Norman it is, but the buildings of grey stone, the rough and jagged coast, the serenity of its wooded wilderness make it appear more Breton.

And again, Rouen, so happily Norman, devastated by the last war like so many other little villages in Normandy, has been able to retain its wonderful medieval quarter — with its street named after the ancient clock, the *Gros Horloge*; its Gothic houses with their wooden facades; its superb cathedral; the Saint-Maclou cemetery, where plague victims were buried; and the city has even reconstructed the site where Joan of Arc was burned. In the same way, Rouen has kept alive the

LEFT: ONE OF THE BEST PRESERVED TOWNS IN BRETAGNE, DINAN BOASTS MANY BEAUTIFUL HALF-TIMBERED HOUSES AND COBBLESTONE STREETS.

PREVIOUS PAGES: NESTLED IN THE BAIE DU MONT-ST-MICHEL, CANCALE, LIKE MANY OF THE COASTAL VILLAGES OF BRETAGNE, IS FAMOUS FOR ITS OYSTERS.
LEO MEIER

LEO MEIER

ENJOYING THE AMBIANCE OF THE LOCAL RURAL FAIR AT
LANDÉVANT, NEAR LORIENT.

house origin, it is typically extra dry, and goes very well with savory dishes — like pork tripe cooked in the Caen style, stewed for hours in a special pot with carrots and onions; sole in the style of Dieppe (with mussels) or of Fécamp (with shrimp); turbot with sorrel; or chicken cooked with calvados and cream.

Distillation of the fermented apple juice, followed by its aging in wood, produces calvados, with its aroma of ripe apples, soft and mature; it is the best Norman digestive. The valleys of the Auge and the Orne are favored for its production, and the picturesque villages of Beuvron, Pierre-fitte, Beaumont — all qualified by the suffix "en Auge" — indicate that this is the heart of the traditional farmland.

But good cider and fine apples are also found on the farms of the windy plateau of the Caux district, to the north of Rouen, near Etretat and Fécamp. This is also the realm of the chalky white cliffs and of the sea. Sole, turbot, John Dory, and shellfish — oysters, clams, shrimp — all go so well with thick farmhouse cream and orchard-fresh apples.

Exactly the same varieties are found in Brittany, though there the countryside is more reserved. Too often the milk is pasteurized, converted to industrial cheeses that are distributed over the whole of France. But this is where the great kingdom of the sea opens up. Its character is determined in the Cotentin, the Norman boundary next to the the lands of Brittany. There are white, sea-smelling oysters from Saint-Vaast-la-Hougue, scallops from Érquy, and shrimp from the waters off Granville.

Further inland, the landscape is somewhat harsher, its charm more on the wild side, like the wind that blows relentlessly around the point of Penmarch, situated at the country's far western tip. Here the Atlantic Ocean marks the end of Brittany, and this most maritime department of France bears the name Finistère which, in the Breton tongue, means "the end of the earth." Guilvinec offers squirming shrimp; the huge nurseries of Audierne provide lobsters and crayfish, and an abundance of fish is brought into Saint-Guénolé — mackerel, mullet, sardines, tuna, as well as sea bass, sole large and small, salmon and sea trout. It is easy to imagine Brittany as a huge bowl of salt water where only fishermen have rights of citizenship — and yet this is a region which, together with its Norman neighbor, produces the world's best cider, at Forêt-Fouesnant in the sunny south of the Finistère. It is also an agricultural region, famous for its artichokes, potatoes and cauliflower. To the north are Finistère-nord, Côtes du Nord, and the Léon — a vast market garden, where once again the tides bring in the bounty of the sea.

nineteenth-century tradition of the *canard à la rouennaise,* reproduced in Paris under the name *canard au sang* by Frédéric Delair, the famous chef of the Tour d'Argent. The bird is roasted, then carved, after which the carcass is crushed in a special press to extract all its juices; they become the starting point for a smooth and fragrant sauce, thickened with cream and enriched with cognac. The authentic Rouen duck, its flesh fine-textured and reddish, should come from the village of Duclair.

Butter, cream and cheese: this is the holy trinity of the Normandy pasturelands. One need only detour into the hinterland of the Mother-of-Pearl coast, just behind the splendid resorts of Cabourg, Deauville, Trouville and Honfleur, to discover a picture-postcard Normandy, still virtually as it was during the last century: the old villages with their plaster-and-wood houses and ancient churches, the unforgettably green meadows with their grazing cows, the manors that watch over docile and agile horses.

Some fine cheeses reign there: camembert, invented by a young peasant girl, Marie Harel, whose memory remains very much alive around Vimoutiers; Livarot, choice and strong, found around the commune which bears its name, and also known as "colonel" because of the five bands of woven rushes that surround its red form; and Pont-l'Evêque, the most delicate, still made in the traditional craftsman style throughout the valley of the river Touques. The superb butter, golden yellow, churned on the farms of Isigny, Sainte-Mère-Eglise, Gournay, Neufchâtel-en-Bray or Valognes, and the pale cream, so thick you can cut it with a knife; these treasures can hardly be found elsewhere.

It is here, too, in the heart of the Pays d'Auge, this most Norman part of Normandy, nurtured by orchards of apple trees that blossom in the month of May, that the sparkling cider is produced, the best of which comes from Cambremer. Of farm-

Like that of Normandy, Breton cuisine is constantly bringing together the land and the sea, the harvest of one with that of the other. Oysters from the bay of Quiberon and the gulf of Morbihan served with crisp-cooked lettuce, or with shallot juice and vinegar; lobster with artichokes; turbot with potatoes; these are the ingredients of some happy marriages. Cotriade — which is the local version of bouillabaisse — combines conger eel, halibut, anglerfish and whiting with carrots and onions, all cooked in stock and white wine — muscadet, the only wine of Brittany, which comes from the region around Nantes (already almost the Loire).

The art of charcuterie, country-style, is highly regarded in Brittany — pork pâtés described as "Breton," the highly flavored *andouilles* which, in both Brittany and Normandy, are prepared in distinctive and characteristic styles. The Norman *andouille,* known as "Vire," is made from finely chopped pork tripe, whereas for the Breton *andouille* — labeled "of Guéménée" — the lengths of tripe are wound around one another and finally wrapped in a piece of beef membrane. A real craftsman's job! Today the farmers of both Normandy and Brittany, proud of their skills and of their rich, fertile territory, have begun to produce their own foie gras, starting with geese and ducks imported from the Gers *département*, raised in their grassy meadows, fattened with the customary corn, then slaughtered in the traditional way. To differentiate between the products of the two regions is impossible.

On the other hand, there are some treasures that really belong to only one particular province. One such treasure is the salt-meadow lamb from pastures bathed by the sea breeze where the grass itself has a faint salty taste, by right belonging to the Bay of Mont-Saint-Michel. It was here, on Mont-Saint-Michel, that Mère Poularde, who ran a celebrated inn, invented the omelette that still bears her name: eggs beaten long and rhythmically, then cooked in plenty of butter in a long-handled iron pan over an open fire, and finally served, thick, warm and creamy, to revive the weary traveler who has arrived late, and on foot, to this miracle of a mountain in a watery land.

Butter shows the dividing line betwen the two provinces; it is invariably salted in Brittany, unsalted in Normandy. In the Breton region, it goes into the caramels of Morbihan as well as the brioches and regional cakes, like the butter cake or *quatre-quarts*, *kouign amann*, and lacy pancakes or crêpes-dentelles, all of which are characterized by their fresh, buttery flavor. The two regions come together again around their common assets: crêpes, made with wheat flour if sweet, with buckwheat flour if savory. With either type, the proper drink is cider, with its distinctive aroma of ripened apples, its deep golden color and its head of light foam. A fair and friendly way to celebrate the union of two neighbors, rivals, each jealously guarding its own fame, and yet cousins.

BUILT FROM THE ELEVENTH TO THE SIXTEENTH CENTURIES BY BENEDICTINE MONKS,
MONT-ST-MICHEL, ONE OF THE GREATEST RELIGIOUS BUILDINGS IN EUROPE, IS AN INSPIRING AND AUSTERE SIGHT.

LEO MEIER

FIRST COURSES

To excite the appetite

THE CHARCUTERIE TOURON, IN THE TOWN OF CAUSSADE, DISPLAYS TYPICAL GASCOGNE
SPECIALTY MEATS, SAUSAGES, PÂTÉS AND *PLATS CUISINE*.

FIRST COURSES

To excite the appetite

A typical meal in France today would consist of a first course, a main dish, cheese (which is eliminated by those in a hurry or considered as the final course by those on a diet) and dessert. For a special occasion, three dishes would be served before the cheese — generally a cold hors d'oeuvre, a hot first course and then the main dish. The great chefs very skilfully manage both the hot and the cold. Soup, for example, is reputed to have a beneficial effect on digestion, whether it be a hot consommé or chicken broth, or a creamy vegetable soup that is served cold.

Likewise, soup makes an excellent first course when it helps the diner to understand the region in which he is eating. Emile Jung, the famous chef of Le Crocodile at Strasbourg, likes to serve a goose soup with pearl barley, whose basic components — meat and cereal — are strongly representative of both the originality and the variety of the products of Alsace. The pale, garlic-flavored *tourain* (or *tourin*) in the Landes, the Provençal *soupe au pistou* from the inland regions and the *soupe de poissons* of the coast from Marseilles to Nice, fulfil the same introductory functions; you learn about where you are, while you experience the aromas and flavors of the region that welcomes you.

Hot first courses often take the form of *tourtes*, quiches, pâtés, *hures* and soufflés: all of which rely on forcemeats, pastries, jellies and other components designed to enrich an ingredient which the land offers au naturel. These are rich, contrived dishes that typically demand a complicated, or at least elaborate, preparation. It is a mark of respect to one's guests to offer them such a dish, to which much care and attention will have been devoted in the kitchen well before their arrival.

First courses are not necessarily based on meat and fish, but they often depend heavily on such ingredients. Eggs, too, are treated in a multitude of styles, according to region: with peppers in the Basque country, as *pipérade*; as truffle omelettes in Provence and Tricastin; poached in red wine as *oeufs en meurette* in Burgundy or *couilles d'âne* in the Berry. These dishes are perfect examples of the diversity of preparations which the richness of the French countryside allows for a single ingredient.

Often it is vegetables which make the difference, either as one component of a recipe, or as a complete dish. Tomatoes, zucchini, olives, peppers and eggplant from the Midi are opposed to the cabbage, beets and potatoes of the north and east. Mediterranean artichokes, which might be stewed in oil, *à la barigoule*, contrast with Breton artichokes, which are simply eaten with a vinaigrette sauce. Asparagus, whether from the Vaucluse, the Loire Valley or Alsace, here slender and green, there large and white, is always served with the same accompaniments — mousseline sauce, mayonnaise or vinaigrette. Yet in the east it will be accompanied by ham, and in the Midi it will be served as a vegetable, nobly accompanying a main dish. In general, the first courses offered north of the Loire — the line which divides France both climatically and gastronomically — are more substantial,

PREVIOUS PAGES: STUFFED VEGETABLES OF PROVENCE (bottom right, recipe page 50), NIÇOISE SALAD (bottom left, recipe page 50, VEGETABLE SOUP WITH BASIL (center front, recipe page 40), AND ANCHOVY SPREAD (top, recipe page 33), PHOTOGRAPHED IN PROVENCE
PIERRE HUSSENOT/AGENCE TOP

more robust, richer than in the south. But it is all a matter of the weather, and therefore of the season. Naturally, summer dishes are often cold, and their wintertime counterparts are usually intended to be served hot — even if both furnish exactly the same amount of energy to the body.

A few first courses have become quite separate dishes, like the foie gras that is served cold as an hors d'oeuvre, but which might be pan-fried and served warm, accompanied by fruits which also have been tossed in butter. Similarly a meat-filled pasta like ravioli, which might become the centerpiece of the meal when servings are substantial.

Contrarily, and with the help of fashion, certain dishes that might otherwise have been served as the main course have been accepted as light first courses: like marinated raw fish, either Scandinavian- or Tahitian-style, or raw meats prepared in the manner of the Italian *carpaccio*. Such relative newcomers prove that in gastronomy nothing is ever fixed. According to individual appetites, tastes and habits, a first course will or will not be effectively considered as such.

It is all a question of era and custom. Some regions have a reputation for abundant first courses, as prelude to a rich and copious meal. This is equally true of the Périgord and of Alsace, both of which share a love of foie gras — and both claim

LEO MEIER

EVERY FRENCH VILLAGE AND TOWN HAS A RESIDENT *BOULANGER* WHO PRODUCES THE STRAIGHT AND NARROW *BAGUETTE* THAT APPEARS ON THE TABLE AT EVERY MEAL.

TO TEMPT THE PASSING SHOPPER, THIS STALL IN THE MARKETS OF NICE OFFERS A RANGE OF POPULAR FRENCH CHEESES. THEY INCLUDE CANTAL AND COMTÉ, AS WELL AS SOME ITALIAN SPECIALTIES FROM ACROSS THE BORDER.

LEO MEIER

LEO MEIER

THE FRENCH ARE CONVINCED THAT GARLIC, LIKE WINE, IS GOOD FOR YOU.
GARLIC STALLS ARE PROMINENT IN EVERY MARKETPLACE, AND FEATURE THE THREE
MAIN VARIETIES, WHITE, VIOLET AND ROSE.

MUSHROOM PÂTÉ IS EVIDENTLY POPULAR
IN THE VILLAGE OF DIGNE IN HAUTE PROVENCE.

to have created it. Could this be related to the fact that many Alsatians emigrated to the southwest in 1940, just before the German annexation of their region?

On the other hand, certain regions in France have retained a tradition of light, fresh-tasting first courses. Often these are the maritime regions, where salads — such as the *salade niçoise* at Nice — or seafood (oysters, shellfish, mussels, alone or in combination) constitute the most natural of preludes to a meal.

Actually, in any self-respecting French meal, the first course has one single role: to inspire in the diner the desire to pursue his pleasant task. And everyone knows that there are a thousand and one ways of doing it.

LEO MEIER

Provence

ANCHOÏADE
Anchovy Spread

12 anchovies preserved in salt
6 cloves fresh, young garlic, finely chopped
3 fresh, young French shallots, finely chopped
1 tablespoon red wine vinegar
¾ cup (6 fl oz/200 ml) extra virgin olive oil
6 sprigs parsley, stemmed and finely chopped
slices of baguette (French bread), toasted
raw vegetables: celery, cauliflower, radishes, fennel,
    artichokes, peppers (capsicums)...

❖Rinse the anchovies under cold running water and rub them to remove all traces of salt. Separate into fillets, removing the head and backbone. Cut each fillet into small pieces.
❖Combine the chopped anchovies, garlic and shallots in a food processor. Add the vinegar and blend until smooth. With machine running, pour in the oil in a thin stream, then add the parsley and blend for 10 seconds longer. Serve the *anchoïade* spread on toasted slices of bread or as a dip for raw vegetables.

SERVES 6   *Photograph pages 28 – 29*

ANCHOVY DIP

PETER JOHNSON

Provence

BAGNA CAUDA
Anchovy Dip

Bagna cauda *is very similar to* anchoïade*, but as its Provençal name indicates (*bagna cauda *means hot bath), it is served hot.*

12 anchovies preserved in salt
4 cloves fresh, young garlic
2½ oz (75 g) butter
3 tablespoons extra virgin olive oil
slices of baguette (French bread), toasted
raw vegetables: celery, cauliflower, radishes, fennel,
    artichokes, peppers (capsicums)...

❖Rinse the anchovies under cold running water and rub them to remove all traces of salt. Separate into fillets, removing the head and backbone. Cut each fillet into small pieces.
❖Force the garlic through a garlic press into a small saucepan. Add the anchovies, butter and oil and stir over very gentle heat until the mixture forms a smooth, homogeneous paste. Serve immediately, on slices of toast or as a dip for raw vegetables.

SERVES 6

Bourgogne

OEUFS EN MEURETTE
Poached Eggs with Red Wine Sauce

The term meurette *in Bourgogne applies to any preparation based on red wine, whether it is for use with fish, meat or eggs.*

2 cups (16 fl oz/500 ml) red Burgundy
3 French shallots, finely chopped
2 carrots, each about 3 oz (100 g), peeled and finely chopped
5 oz (150 g) butter, cut into small pieces
1 generous cup (300 ml) red wine vinegar
12 eggs
salt and freshly ground pepper

❖Pour the wine into a nonaluminum saucepan, add the shallots and carrots and bring to boil. Reduce by boiling over high heat for 5 minutes.
❖Reduce heat to very low and whisk in the pieces of butter one or two at a time. Strain the sauce into a small saucepan and keep warm over hot water.
❖Combine 2 qt (2 l) water and the vinegar in a skillet and bring to a gentle simmer. Break the eggs into a bowl, one after the other. As soon as the water begins to bubble, delicately slide in the eggs. Carefully turn the eggs over with a skimming spoon to bring the white over the yolk. Poach for 4 minutes.
❖When the eggs are cooked, remove them with the skimming spoon and transfer to a clean cloth. Trim the ragged edges of each egg to give a nice oval shape. Divide the sauce among six warm plates and arrange 2 eggs in the middle of each. Season with salt and pepper and serve immediately.

SERVES 6   *Photograph page 35*

Bourgogne

JAMBON PERSILLÉ
Parsleyed Ham

This is the traditional Easter Sunday dish in Bourgogne.

2 lb (1 kg) unsmoked raw ham
2 calf's feet
10 oz (300 g) veal knuckle
2 French shallots, halved
1 clove garlic, halved
1 sprig dried thyme
1 bay leaf
2 sprigs tarragon
3 sprigs chervil
10 sprigs flat-leaf parsley
salt and freshly ground pepper
3 cups (24 fl oz/750 ml) white Burgundy
2 tablespoons white wine vinegar

❖In a large bowl, cover the ham with cold water and soak for 12 hours to remove excess salt.
❖Blanch the calf's feet in boiling water to cover for 5 minutes, then drain. Drain the ham and rinse under running water. Combine the calf's feet, ham and veal knuckle in a large pot; add the shallots, garlic, thyme, bay leaf, tarragon, chervil and 3 sprigs of parsley. Season lightly with salt and pepper, and pour in the wine. Bring to boil over gentle heat and simmer slowly for 2 hours, stirring from time to time.
❖Snip the leaves from the remaining parsley. Drain the ham and the veal knuckle meat and roughly crush the meat with a fork. Strain the cooking liquid and stir in salt, pepper and the vinegar. Let cool until the stock is thick and viscous.
❖Pour a layer of the stock into a mold just large enough to accommodate the meat and liquid. Let cool, then refrigerate until firmly set. Cover with a layer of meat, then sprinkle with parsley. Pour more stock over and again refrigerate to set. Repeat the layers until all ingredients have been used, ending with a layer of stock. Cover the mold and refrigerate for 12 hours before unmolding. Serve in slices, accompanied by salad.

SERVES 8

Lyonnais/Ile de France

GRATINÉE À L'OIGNON
French Onion Soup

In days gone by, this thick, fragrant soup, invigorating and robust, was enjoyed late at night and into the small hours of the morning at the old markets of Les Halles, in Paris. The recipe is thought to have originated in Lyon.

3 oz (100 g) butter
1 lb (500 g) large onions, thinly sliced
1 tablespoon all purpose (plain) flour
1½ qt (1.5 l) beef or chicken stock
salt and freshly ground pepper
12 slices of baguette (French bread)
3 oz (100 g) grated Emmenthaler cheese

❖Melt the butter in a heavy 4-qt (4-l) saucepan. Add the onions and cook over low heat, stirring constantly, for 20 minutes or until they become soft and golden. Sprinkle in flour and stir for 2 minutes. Pour in the stock, season with salt and pepper and bring to boil. Cover and cook over very low heat for 45 minutes, stirring from time to time.
❖Toast the slices of bread on both sides under the broiler (griller). Divide them among four flameproof soup bowls and sprinkle with the cheese. Pour the soup into the bowls and slide the bowls under the broiler, close to the heat source; broil just long enough to melt and lightly brown the cheese. Serve immediately.

SERVES 4

BOUILLON DE VOLAILLE
Chicken Stock

For approximately 4¾ cups (1.2 l) stock:
4 lb (2 kg) chicken carcasses and bones
1 small onion (about 2 oz/50 g)
1 clove
8 cups (2 qt/2 l) cold water
1 carrot (about 3 oz/100 g), peeled
1 celery stalk
1 leaf of leek
1 sprig dried thyme
1 bay leaf
½ teaspoon sea salt
12 black peppercorns

❖Wash carcasses and bones under running water. Stud the onion with the clove. Place the carcasses and bones in a large pot. Add the cold water and bring to boil over low heat, skimming off the first brown scum. Add the vegetables, thyme, bay leaf, salt and pepper and simmer gently, half covered, for 2 hours or until reduced to about 4¾ cups (1.2 l). Strain.
❖This delicate, aromatic stock is used in the preparation of many dishes. It may be frozen in small containers for future use.

FRENCH ONION SOUP (top) AND OLIVE SPREAD (recipe page 36)

PETER JOHNSON

RIGHT: PARSLEYED HAM AND POACHED EGGS
WITH RED WINE SAUCE (recipe page 33)

PIERRE HUSSENOT/AGENCE TOP

Provence

TAPENADE
Olive Spread

The name of this dish derives from the word tapeno, *which is the Provençal equivalent of* câpres (capers). *In fact Toulon capers are an indispensable ingredient of this wonderfully flavored sauce.*

6 anchovies preserved in salt
13 oz (400 g) black olives in brine, pitted
1 small clove fresh, young garlic, coarsely chopped
3 tablespoons capers, rinsed and drained
2 teaspoons strong mustard
2 tablespoons cognac
freshly ground pepper
⅔ cup (5 fl oz/150 ml) extra virgin olive oil
For serving:
country bread or rye bread

❖Rinse the anchovies under cold running water and rub them to remove all traces of salt. Separate into fillets, removing the head and backbone. Cut each fillet into small pieces.
❖Combine the anchovies, olives, garlic and capers in a food processor. Add the mustard, cognac, pepper and half the oil and blend to a thick paste; while continuing to blend, pour in the rest of the oil. When the *tapenade* is smooth and homogeneous, transfer it to a serving bowl.
❖Serve as an appetizer with slices of country bread or rye bread, plain or toasted. *Tapenade* may be kept for several days in a sealed container.

SERVES 6   *Photograph page 34*

Touraine

RILLETTES
Pork Spread

The origins of rillettes *are shared by Le Mans, Tours and Angers. Some goose is also generally added to the basis of pure pork. In Orléans,* rillettes *made with wild rabbit are served in fall with fresh walnuts.*

2 cloves garlic
4 French shallots, quartered
2 sprigs fresh thyme, crumbled
2 bay leaves, crumbled
4 cloves
2 lb (1 kg) fresh pork belly
1 lb (500 g) pork fat
¾ cup (6 fl oz/200 ml) water
1 heaping teaspoon fine sea salt
½ teaspoon *quatre-épices* (see glossary)
½ teaspoon cayenne pepper

❖Flatten the garlic cloves with the side of the hand. Wrap garlic, shallots, thyme, bay leaves and cloves in a square of cheesecloth and tie with kitchen thread.
❖Remove rind and bones from the pork belly; cut the meat into 1¼-in (3-cm) cubes. Melt the pork fat in a heavy 4-qt (4-l) saucepan over low heat. Add the pieces of meat and brown them, turning constantly with a wooden spoon.

PORK SPREAD (top) AND HERBED CHEESE SPREAD

Remove the browned meat with a slotted spoon and strain the fat through a sieve into a small bowl. Set aside.
❖Return the meat to the pan. Add the cheesecloth bag and the water and cook over very low heat for 4 hours, stirring from time to time and adding a little more water if the mixture seems too dry.
❖Remove the bag of seasonings. Stir in the salt, *quatre-épices* and cayenne pepper and cook for another 30 minutes. Remove from the heat and let cool to lukewarm, then remove meat from the pan and shred using two forks. Add the reserved fat and mix well.
❖Turn the spread into one large container, or divide it among several smaller ones, and cover. Store in the refrigerator and serve within two weeks, spread on slices of country bread or crusty baguette (French bread).

SERVES 6

FIRST COURSES

Lyonnais

CERVELLE DE CANUT
Herbed Cheese Spread

This is a dish traditionally served in the máchons — *the bistros of Lyon. The name* máchon *originally referred to a small meal that was eaten mid-morning. It is also known as* claqueret, *from the expression "claquer le fromage," meaning to beat or whisk the cheese.* Canut *was the name of the silk workers who for a long period represented a true gourmet tradition.*

8 oz (250 g) fresh *fromage blanc* or ricotta cheese
¼ cup (2 fl oz/60 ml) olive oil
3 tablespoons white wine vinegar
3 tablespoons dry white wine
¾ cup (6 fl oz/200 ml) chilled cream
2 French shallots, finely chopped
6 sprigs flat-leaf parsley, leaves only, finely chopped
6 sprigs chervil, leaves only, finely chopped
10 chive stalks, finely chopped
salt and freshly ground pepper

❖Set the cheese to drain, in the container or a colander, 12 hours before commencing preparations. Turn the drained cheese into a bowl and mash with a fork. Mix in the oil, vinegar and wine.
❖Whip the cream until stiff and fold into the cheese mixture. Mix in the shallots, herbs, salt and pepper. Chill thoroughly. Serve the cheese with whole-grain country bread or rye bread.

SERVES 6

Provence

SOUPE DE POISSONS
Fish Soup

Saffron and fennel are the indispensable seasonings for this thick broth with its characteristic flavor. It is served all along the coast of the Mediterranean, and particularly in Marseille.

3 lb (1.5 kg) small white-fleshed fish of several types
1 green bell pepper (capsicum) (about 7 oz/200 g)
¼ cup (2 fl oz/60 ml) olive oil
1 onion (about 3 oz/100 g), finely chopped
4 cloves garlic, coarsely chopped
1 leek, white part only, washed and sliced
1 lb (500 g) ripe tomatoes, quartered
2 sprigs dried fennel
1 sprig dried thyme
2 pinches of saffron threads
3 sprigs parsley
1 bay leaf
2 qt (2 l) water
salt and freshly ground pepper
5 oz (150 g) vermicelli or 18 slices bread from a baguette (French bread)
grated Emmenthaler cheese
For the *rouille* sauce:
3 cloves garlic, coarsely chopped
2 to 3 fresh red chili peppers, halved and seeded
½ teaspoon coarse sea salt
1 slice of bread, crusts trimmed (from a sandwich loaf, about 3 oz/100 g)
¾ cup (6 fl oz/200 ml) extra virgin olive oil

❖Scale and gut the fish; wash and pat dry. Cut the green pepper into quarters. Remove the stem, seeds and white ribs, then slice the pepper thinly.
❖Heat the oil in a heavy 6-qt (6-l) saucepan. Add the onion, garlic, pepper and leek and cook, stirring, over low heat for 2 minutes. Add the tomatoes, fennel, thyme, saffron, parsley, bay leaf and fish and stir for 1 minute. Cover and cook over low heat for 10 minutes.
❖Bring 2 qt (2 l) water to boil in a saucepan and add to the fish mixture. Season the soup with salt and pepper. Cover and let simmer for 20 minutes over low heat.
❖Prepare the *rouille* sauce: combine the garlic, chilies and salt in a food processor or blender and grind to a smooth paste. Crumble in the bread and blend again. With machine running, pour in the oil in a thin stream; blend until the sauce is thick and smooth.
❖Strain the cooked soup through a sieve, pressing down well to extract all the flavor of the fish. Rinse the pan and return the soup to it, straining through a fine sieve. If you are using vermicelli, bring the soup to boil, add the pasta and cook until *al dente*. If you prefer to use bread, lightly toast the slices on both sides and offer them separately.
❖Pour the soup into a tureen and serve it immediately, with the *rouille* and cheese passed around separately.

SERVES 6

INGREDIENTS FOR FISH SOUP

PETER JOHNSON

Flandres

SOUPE DE POTIRON
Pumpkin Soup

2 tablespoons (50 g) butter
4 leeks, white parts only, washed and thinly sliced
1½ lb (750 g) peeled pumpkin, cut into 1-in (2-cm) cubes
3 cups (24 fl oz/750 ml) chicken stock
salt and freshly ground pepper
1 cup (8 fl oz/250 ml) milk

❖ Melt half the butter in a heavy 4-qt (4-l) saucepan and cook the leeks until soft and golden, about 5 minutes, stirring constantly with a wooden spoon. Stir in the pumpkin cubes, stock, salt and pepper and simmer for about 30 minutes, or until the pumpkin is very soft.
❖ Transfer the mixture to a food processor and blend to a smooth puree. Reheat gently, adding the remaining butter and the milk. Stir well and remove from heat. Pour the soup into a tureen and serve immediately.

SERVES 6

Picardie/Ile de France

POTAGE CRÉCY
Carrot Soup

The towns of Crécy-en-Brie in Picardie and Crécy-en-Ponthieu in Ile de France both claim credit for the creation of this soup, and indeed both are famous for the quality of their carrots. The rice is sometimes replaced by 9 oz (300 g) of potatoes, peeled, cut into small cubes and cooked in the same way.

2 oz (50 g) butter
1 onion (about 3 oz/100 g), finely chopped
2 leeks, white parts only, washed and thinly sliced
2 qt (2 l) water
2 lb (1 kg) small, young carrots, peeled and cut into ¼-in (5-mm) slices
salt and freshly ground pepper
⅓ cup (2 oz/50 g) long-grain rice
6 tablespoons (3 fl oz/100 ml) heavy (double) cream or crème fraîche

❖ Melt half the butter in a heavy 4-qt (4-l) saucepan. Add the onion and leeks and cook, stirring, for about 3 minutes or until golden. Pour in the water and bring to boil. Add the carrots and season with salt and pepper. Cover and cook over low heat for 30 minutes or until the carrots are very soft.
❖ Pour the contents of the pan into a food processor and blend at high speed for 1 minute or until the mixture is smooth and creamy. Return to the saucepan and bring to boil. Stir in the rice and simmer gently for 20 minutes or until the rice is cooked. Stir in the cream and the remaining butter. Pour the soup into shallow soup bowls and serve immediately.

SERVES 4

Languedoc

TOURAIN
Bread and Garlic Soup

Tourains, or tourins, are prepared all over the Languedoc and the recipes for these hearty soups — based on foie gras, garlic, onion or tomatoes *— vary from one place to another. This recipe comes from Toulouse.*

⅓ cup (2½ oz/75 g) goose fat
8 cloves fresh young garlic, finely chopped
2 qt (2 l) boiling water
bouquet garni: 1 sprig thyme, 1 bay leaf, 2 sprigs sage (tied together)
salt and freshly ground pepper
6 bread slices
3 oz (100 g) grated Emmenthaler cheese
3 eggs

❖ Melt the goose fat in a heavy 4-qt (4-l) saucepan. Add the chopped garlic and stir over low heat until golden, about 2 minutes. Add the boiling water, bouquet garni, salt and pepper. Return to boil, then cover and simmer gently for 30 minutes.
❖ Meanwhile, toast the slices of bread and lay them in a soup tureen. Add the grated cheese.
❖ Separate the eggs into two bowls. Discard the bouquet garni. Beat the egg whites with a fork until foamy, then whisk them into the boiling soup until they coagulate. Remove 2 tablespoons of soup and beat into the yolks with a fork. Quickly stir this mixture back into the soup and remove from heat; the yolks should not cook, but serve simply to thicken the soup. Pour the boiling soup into the tureen and serve immediately.

SERVES 6

MILK SOUP (top, recipe page 40), CARROT SOUP (right)
AND BREAD AND GARLIC SOUP (bottom)

Ardennes

SOUPE AU LAIT
Milk Soup

8 oz (250 g) baking potatoes
1 tablespoon (25 g) butter
1 onion (about 3 oz/100 g), finely chopped
3 leeks, white parts only, washed and thinly sliced
  diagonally
1 qt (1 l) milk
salt and freshly ground pepper
4 pinches of freshly grated nutmeg
8 slices baguette (French bread)

❖ Peel and wash the potatoes; slice into thin rounds.
❖ Melt the butter in a heavy 4-qt (4-l) saucepan and cook the onion and leeks over low heat, stirring with a wooden spoon, for about 5 minutes or until soft and golden. Pour in the milk and bring to boil. Add the potatoes, salt, pepper and nutmeg, cover the pan and cook over gentle heat for about 20 minutes or until the potatoes are tender.
❖ Divide the slices of bread among four shallow soup plates. Pour in the boiling soup and serve immediately.

SERVES 4   *Photograph page 38*

Provence

SOUPE AU PISTOU
Vegetable Soup with Basil

In the Provençal dialect, pistou *means not basil, but* pilé — *the Italian* pesto *of Genoese origin — a paste that includes ground basil and garlic, bound with olive oil. This soup is made all along the Mediterranean coast in summer, when the fresh haricot beans arrive at the markets. Each family has its favored recipe, and different vegetables are often used. But they all have in common that light paste with its incomparable flavor which is added to the soup before serving.*

2 lb (1 kg) fresh haricot beans or 1 lb (500 g) dried
  haricot beans, soaked overnight and drained
8 oz (250 g) fresh broad beans or 4 oz (125 g) dried
  broad beans, soaked overnight and drained
4 oz (125 g) green beans
8 oz (250 g) small zucchini (courgettes), trimmed
2 cloves fresh, young garlic
8 oz (250 g) boiling potatoes
8 oz (250 g) ripe tomatoes
2 onions, about 3 oz (100 g) each, chopped
1 sprig basil
salt
3 oz (100 g) soup pasta or small macaroni
3 oz (100 g) Emmenthaler or Parmesan cheese,
  freshly and finely grated
For the *pistou:*
8 oz (250 g) ripe tomatoes
1 large bunch of basil, about 3 oz (100 g), stems
  removed
4 cloves fresh, young garlic, quartered
6 tablespoons fruity olive oil

❖ Shell the haricot and broad beans, if fresh, and remove the soft green skin that covers them. String the green beans (if necessary); wash and pat dry. Quarter the zucchini lengthwise, then cut into ¼-in (5-mm) slices. Crush the garlic with a blow of the hand or with the side of a cleaver. Peel and wash potatoes; cut into ½-in (1-cm) cubes. Drop the tomatoes into boiling water for 10 seconds, then cool under running water. Peel, halve and squeeze out the seeds; coarsely chop the flesh.
❖ Combine all the vegetables with the garlic, onions and basil in a 4-qt (4-l) saucepan and cover with cold water. Bring to boil over gentle heat. Season with salt, cover and let simmer very slowly for 1 hour.
❖ When the soup is cooked, remove the garlic and basil. Add the pasta and cook until *al dente*.
❖ Meanwhile, prepare the *pistou:* drop the tomatoes into boiling water for 10 seconds, then cool under running water. Peel, halve and squeeze out the seeds; coarsely chop the flesh and let drain in a colander.
❖ Combine the basil, garlic, oil and tomatoes in a food processor or blender and blend to a smooth puree. When the pasta is cooked, pour the soup into a tureen. Add the *pistou*, stir well and serve immediately, passing the cheese separately.

SERVES 6   *Photograph pages 28 – 29*

MUSHROOM SOUP

PETER JOHNSON

Poitou/Charentes

POTAGE AUX CÈPES
Mushroom Soup

1 lb (500 g) fresh cèpes or *porcini* (boletus) mushrooms
1 tablespoon (25 g) butter
1 level tablespoon all purpose (plain) flour
1 qt (1 l) chicken stock
salt and freshly ground pepper
4 pinches of freshly grated nutmeg
6 tablespoons heavy (double) cream or crème
    fraîche

❖Trim the ends of the mushroom stems. Rinse the mushrooms quickly under running water, pat dry and slice thinly. Melt the butter in a heavy 4-qt (4-l) saucepan and cook the mushroom slices until they are golden and have stopped giving out moisture. Add the flour and mix, stirring, for 1 minute.
❖Stir in the stock and return to the boil. Add salt, pepper and nutmeg, cover and cook for 30 minutes over gentle heat, stirring from time to time.
❖Pour the contents of the saucepan into a food processor and blend at high speed for 1 minute to produce a smooth puree. Return to the pan and bring to boil. Add the cream and boil the soup for 1 minute. Pour into a tureen and serve immediately.

SERVES 4

Alsace

TARTE FLAMBÉE
Alsatian Tart

This tart used to be baked in the ovens of bakeries, where it would be licked by the flames — hence its name. There is another version in which fromage blanc *(fresh cheese) and eggs are added to the cream filling.*

2 tablespoons peanut oil
1 onion (about 3 oz/100 g), finely chopped
1 cup (8 fl oz/250 ml) heavy (double) cream or crème
    fraîche
salt and freshly ground pepper
4 pinches of freshly grated nutmeg
3 oz (100 g) streaky bacon
13 oz (400 g) bread dough (recipe this page)

❖Heat half the oil in a nonstick 10-in (26-cm) skillet. Add the onion and cook, stirring, over low heat for 5 minutes or until golden.
❖Combine the cream, salt, pepper and nutmeg. Stir in the onion. Remove the rind from the bacon and cut bacon into thin matchsticks. Heat the remaining oil in the skillet and fry the bacon until lightly browned, about 3 minutes, stirring constantly. Drain on paper towels and set aside.
❖Heat the oven to 450°F (230°C). Oil a 14 x 9-in (35 x 22-cm) baking sheet. Roll out the bread dough until slightly smaller than the baking sheet; place it on the sheet. Spread the onion mixture over the dough and dot with the bacon. Bake for 20 minutes or until the tart is lightly browned. Serve hot.

SERVES 6

PETER JOHNSON

EGGS WITH TOMATO AND PEPPERS (top, recipe page 42)
AND ALSATIAN TART

PÂTE À PAIN
Bread Dough

For approximately 1½ lb (750 g) dough:
1 teaspoon superfine (caster) sugar
6 tablespoons (3 fl oz/100 ml) lukewarm water
1 envelope (½ oz/15 g) dry yeast
1 lb (500 g) all purpose (plain) flour
1½ teaspoons salt
⅔ cup (5 fl oz/150 ml) lukewarm milk

❖Place the sugar in a teacup. Add the lukewarm water and stir until the sugar is dissolved. Sprinkle the yeast over, stir in, and let rise in a warm place for about 10 minutes, or until the mixture reaches the edge of the cup.
❖Sift the flour onto a work surface and sprinkle with salt. Mix the two together and make a well in the middle. Pour in the milk and the yeast mixture.
❖Mix all ingredients together, using the fingertips in a quick movement from the center to the edges, then roll the dough into a ball. Knead it by stretching out the dough in front of you, then folding it in two, giving it a quarter turn in a counterclockwise direction and repeating the operation. Continue to knead the dough in this way for about 10 minutes, or until it is smooth, elastic and no longer sticky.
❖Place the dough in a floured bowl and cover with a clean, damp towel. Let rise in a warm draft-free area until doubled in volume, about 1½ hours.
❖Turn the risen dough onto a floured work surface and flatten with the palm of the hand, then knead as before for about 3 minutes. The dough is then ready for use.

Pays Basque

PIPÉRADE
Eggs with Tomatoes and Peppers

The pipérade is traditionally made with the very fine-skinned small, sweet green peppers, shaped like little horns, that are found in the markets in summer and fall.

2 red bell peppers (capsicums), each about 5 oz (150 g)
2 green bell peppers (capsicums), each about 5 oz (150 g)
3 oz (100 g) onions
2 lb (1 kg) perfectly ripe tomatoes
4 tablespoons extra virgin olive oil
2 cloves garlic, finely chopped
1 fresh red or green hot (chili) pepper, seeded and
    coarsely chopped
salt and freshly ground pepper
pinch of sugar
6 eggs
6 medium-size slices of raw ham, such as Bayonne

❖Preheat broiler (griller). Place the peppers on the broiler rack and grill, not too close to the heat source, for about 20 minutes or until the skins are black, turning often.
❖Meanwhile, peel and thinly slice the onions. Drop the tomatoes into boiling water for 10 seconds, then cool them under cold running water. Peel, halve and squeeze out the seeds; coarsely chop the flesh.
❖When the peppers are charred, place them in a bowl, cover and cool to lukewarm. Peel away blackened skin; discard the stem, seeds and white parts. Rinse peppers briefly, then slice into fine strips.
❖Heat 3 tablespoons oil in a nonstick 10-in (26-cm) skillet. Add the onions and cook, stirring, for 5 minutes or until golden. Add the garlic, hot pepper and pepper strips and cook, stirring, for a further 2 minutes. Add the tomatoes and season with salt, pepper and sugar. Cover and cook over gentle heat for 30 minutes, stirring from time to time. Break the eggs into a bowl, season with salt and pepper and beat with a fork until blended. Pour into the skillet and cook, stirring, until the eggs have set. Keep warm.
❖Heat the remaining oil in another nonstick 10-in (26-cm) skillet and cook the ham slices over high heat for 30 seconds on each side.
❖Turn the *pipérade* into a shallow serving dish, arrange the slices of ham on top and serve immediately.

SERVES 6   *Photograph page 41*

Picardie

PÂTÉ DE CANARD D'AMIENS
Duck Pâté, Amiens-style

In Amiens, pâtés have a tradition going back to the Middle Ages, and duck pâté is certainly the most representative and the most authentic recipe of all. Reference to this pâté was made by Madame de Sévigné in her Letters, *written in the seventeenth century.*

1 duck, about 2½ lb (1.2 kg), with its liver
3 oz (100 g) fresh pork belly
8 oz (250 g) pork fillet

8 oz (250 g) boneless rabbit or chicken meat
8 oz (250 g) mushrooms
1 oz (25 g) butter
1 onion (about 3 oz/100 g), finely chopped
2 French shallots, finely chopped
2 tablespoons juniper eau-de-vie or gin
3 eggs
salt and freshly ground pepper
½ teaspoon *quatre-épices* (see glossary)
3 oz (100 g) shelled unsalted pistachio nuts
1 lb 6 oz (700 g) short (shortcrust) pastry (page 50)
1 tablespoon milk
1 calf's foot, split in two

❖Ask the butcher to bone the duck completely, without cutting through the skin; reserve the bones. After the tail and wing tips are removed, what should remain is a large pocket.
❖Cut the pork belly and fillet and the rabbit (or chicken) into ½-in (1-cm) cubes. Trim the duck liver and cut into large cubes. Trim the mushroom stalks, then wash and thinly slice the mushrooms.

DUCK PÂTÉ, AMIENS-STYLE AND LEEK TART (recipe page 44)

❖Melt the butter in a nonstick 10-in (26-cm) skillet. Add the onion and shallots and cook, stirring, over moderate heat for 2 minutes or until golden. Add the mushrooms and cook over high heat until they have rendered all their liquid and it has evaporated. Add the three meats and the duck liver and cook, stirring, for 5 minutes or until lightly browned. Pour in the eau-de-vie and ignite, shaking the pan gently until the flames subside.

❖Turn the contents of the pan onto a chopping board and chop finely. Transfer to a bowl and mix in 2 whole eggs and 1 egg white (reserve remaining yolk), salt, pepper, *quatre-épices* and the pistachios. Fill the duck with ⅔ of this mixture.

❖Preheat oven to 400°F (200°C). Divide the short pastry in half. On a work surface, roll out half of the pastry into an oval shape somewhat larger than the duck. Spread half the reserved filling on the pastry to within ¾ in (2 cm) of the edges. Moisten the edges with a pastry brush dipped in cold water. Place the duck on top of the filling and spread the remaining filling over the duck. Roll the remaining pastry into an oval and lay it over the duck, reserving any pas-

try trimmings. Firmly press the pastry edges together to seal. Roll the edges towards the center and crimp with the tines of a fork. Whisk the reserved egg yolk with the milk and brush this mixture over the entire surface of the pâté. Cut three small holes in the top of the pâté and insert small "chimneys" of aluminum foil or waxed paper. Decorate the pâté with the pastry trimmings, cut into leaf shapes.

❖Bake the pâté for 2½ hours, reducing the oven temperature to 375°F (190°C) after 1 hour when the pâté is nicely colored.

❖Meanwhile, place the duck bones and the split calf's foot in a saucepan, cover with cold water and bring to boil. Season with salt. Simmer for 2 hours, then strain the resultant stock. When the pâté is cooked, remove it from the oven and pour the stock into the pâté through one of the chimneys; remove chimneys. Pour any leftover stock into a shallow dish to a depth of ½ in (1 cm) and refrigerate until set. Cut this jelly into small cubes and use to garnish the pâté. Let the pâté cool overnight before serving.

SERVES 8

Picardie

FLAMICHE AUX POIREAUX
Leek Tart

The word flamiche *(formerly* flamique*) is of Flemish origin and means a savory or sweet cake. In Picardie,* flamiches *are also made with pumpkin and onions, and the puff pastry may be replaced by the short pastry known as* pâte brisée.

2 oz (50 g) butter
1 lb (500 g) leeks, white parts only, washed and thinly sliced diagonally
salt and freshly ground pepper
2 tablespoons water
8 oz (250 g) puff pastry (recipe this page)
3 egg yolks
¾ cup (6 fl oz/200 g) heavy (double) cream or crème fraîche
6 pinches of freshly grated nutmeg
1 egg yolk
1 tablespoon water

❖Melt the butter in a nonstick 10-in (26-cm) skillet. Add the leeks, season with salt and pepper and cook, stirring, over low heat for 5 minutes or until the leeks begin to turn golden. Add 2 tablespoons water, cover and cook over very low heat for 30 minutes or until the leeks are very soft and transparent.
❖Meanwhile, divide the pastry into two portions, ⅔ and ⅓. Roll out the larger portion into an 11-in (28-cm) circle. Brush a straight-sided 8-in (20-cm) tart pan with water and line with the pastry, leaving ½ in (1 cm) overlapping the sides.
❖When the leeks are cooked, remove from heat and let cool. Beat 3 egg yolks in a medium bowl with a fork until blended. Add the cream, salt, pepper and nutmeg. Stir in the leeks.
❖Preheat oven to 400°F (200°C). Roll out the remaining third of the pastry into an 8-in (20-cm) circle. Pour the leek mixture into the pastry case and cover with the pastry circle, pressing the edges together to seal. Roll the edges of the pastry back over the pastry lid and crimp the edges of the roll with the tines of a fork.
❖Beat 1 egg yolk and 1 tablespoon water with a fork in a small bowl. Brush over the whole surface of the pastry. Cut out a small circle from the center of the pastry lid and insert a "chimney" of aluminum foil or waxed paper to keep it open. Bake the tart for 40 minutes or until golden brown. Serve hot or lukewarm.

SERVES 6   *Photograph page 43*

PÂTE FEUILLETÉE
Puff Pastry

For approximately 2 lb 6 oz (1.2 kg) pastry:
1 lb (500 g) soft butter
4 cups (1 lb/500 g) all purpose (plain) flour
1 teaspoon salt
about 1 cup (8 fl oz/250 ml) water

❖Remove the butter from the refrigerator 1 hour before using. In a large bowl, cream the butter until smooth and soft.

Sift the flour onto a work surface. Make a well in the center and add the salt and ¾ of the water. Blend the flour and water together with the fingertips of one hand, while the other hand gradually pushes the flour from the edges towards the center. Working with the fingertips, gradually blend in just enough of the remaining water to make a dough of the same consistency as the creamed butter; this dough is called *détrempe*. Roll it into a ball and let rest for 15 minutes.
❖Roll out the *détrempe* on a floured work surface to form a circle ¾ in (2 cm) thick and 6 in (15 cm) in diameter. With moistened fingers, spread the butter, in a layer again about ¾ in (2 cm) thick, in the center of the circle. Fold the edges of the dough over the butter, allowing an overlap of ¾ in (2 cm). You will now have a kind of envelope enclosing the butter; this is called the *pâton*. Dust both the *pâton* and the rolling pin with flour and roll out the *pâton* to a rectangle approximately 12 x 4 in (30 x 10 cm); apply only light pressure to the *pâton* so that it rolls out smoothly and the butter is not squeezed out.
❖ Now the operation known as *tourage* begins. Lift the lower edge of the pastry and fold it over to 4 in (10 cm) from the opposite edge. Press down this fold lightly with the rolling pin. Fold the remaining third of the pastry over the two layers and again lightly press down with the rolling pin: the pastry has just been given its first *tour*, or turn. The *tours* are done two at a time, but the *pâton* must always be turned a quarter of a circle, in a clockwise direction, so that the folds are no longer at the top and bottom, but on the left and right. Once more, roll out the *pâton* and fold it in thirds; it has now been given another turn. With the thumb and index finger, make two small indentations on the surface of the rectangle to indicate that the pastry has had two turns. Cover with a tea towel and refrigerate for 20 minutes.
❖Give the pastry two more turns as before, making four indentations with the fingers to show that the pastry has had four turns. Classic puff pastry is given six turns, but it is preferable to give the last two just before the pastry is to be used. After four turns, the pastry should rest for at least another 20 minutes; it may be kept in the refrigerator for 48 hours before use.
❖After the sixth turn, roll out the pastry and cut as required. When cutting the pastry, the knife should be kept vertical to avoid breaking the fine layers and allow maximum rise during baking. Puff pastry is always baked on a moistened, not buttered, baking sheet.

Savoie

SOUFFLÉ AU COMTÉ
Comté Cheese Soufflé

3 egg yolks
4 egg whites
salt
1 cup (8 fl oz/250 ml) milk
1½ oz (40 g) butter
¼ cup (1½ oz/40 g) all purpose (plain) flour
1 tablespoon heavy (double) cream or crème fraîche
freshly ground pepper
2 pinches of freshly grated nutmeg
3 oz (100 g) finely grated Comté cheese (or Emmenthaler)

PETER JOHNSON

COMTÉ CHEESE SOUFFLÉ

❖Preheat oven to 425°F (215°C). Generously butter a 6-in (16-cm) ovenproof porcelain soufflé dish. Place the egg yolks in one bowl, the whites in another. Sprinkle 2 pinches of salt over the whites. Bring the milk to boil in a small saucepan.

❖Melt the butter in a medium saucepan, add the flour and stir for 1 minute over low heat. Pour in the boiling milk in a thin stream, stirring constantly. Cook the mixture over low heat, stirring constantly, for 5 minutes or until it is the consistency of heavy cream. Remove from heat and whisk in the yolks one at a time. Blend in the cream, salt, pepper and nutmeg.

❖Beat the egg whites until firm but not too stiff. Whisk ¼ of the whites into the mixture in the saucepan, then pour this mixture back into the remaining egg whites. Gently fold together with a spatula, at the same time incorporating the cheese a spoonful at a time. Pour the mixture into the prepared soufflé dish, which should be about ¾ full. Bake for 30 minutes or until the soufflé has risen and is golden brown on top. Bring to the table immediately, in the dish, and serve with a large spoon.

SERVES 3-4

Corse/Côte d'Azur

RAVIOLIS
Ravioli

Traditionally, the filling for this ravioli is prepared from leftover daube (beef stewed in tomato sauce). It can also be made with veal that has been browned briefly in oil and ground.

For the pasta:
2½ cups (10 oz/300 g) all purpose (plain) flour
4 pinches of salt
2 eggs
2 tablespoons olive oil

For the filling:
1½ lb (750 g) cooked beef, finely chopped
1 egg
2 oz (50 g) Parmesan cheese, freshly and finely grated
1 lb (500 g) beet greens, Swiss chard or spinach
salt and freshly ground pepper
For serving:
tomato sauce
freshly and finely grated Parmesan cheese

❖Prepare the pasta: sift the flour and salt onto a work surface. Make a well in the center and add the eggs and oil. Combine all ingredients, using the fingertips in a quick movement from the middle towards the edges. When the dough is homogeneous, knead by pushing it out and then bringing it back into a ball, working it until it is elastic and comes away from the fingers. Roll out the dough into a ball, wrap in plastic and let rest for at least 30 minutes in a cool place.

❖Meanwhile, prepare the filling: combine the meat, egg and cheese in a bowl and mix well. Drop the greens into boiling water for 30 seconds, then drain and squeeze dry. Let cool slightly, then chop finely with a sharp knife. Stir into the meat mixture with salt and pepper.

❖Divide the pasta dough in half; roll out into equal-size rectangles. Place level teaspoons of the filling in small mounds on one rectangle, spaced 1 in (2 cm) apart. Moisten the dough between the mounds, using a pastry brush dipped in water, then cover with the second rectangle of dough. Seal the two sheets of dough together along the edges and around each mound of filling, pressing firmly. Cut out the ravioli using a sharp knife or a smooth-edged or crimped pastry wheel. Arrange the ravioli on a clean tea towel, taking care that they do not overlap.

❖Bring a large pot of water to boil. Add salt, then drop in the ravioli and cook for 5 minutes. Drain and turn the ravioli into a shallow dish. Cover with tomato sauce and toss lightly, then sprinkle with a little grated Parmesan. Serve immediately, with more Parmesan offered separately.

SERVES 6

PETER JOHNSON

RAVIOLI

PETER JOHNSON

POTATO OMELETTE, AUVERGNE-STYLE (top)
AND CHEESE AND WALNUT OMELETTE

Auvergne

OMELETTE BRAYAUDE
Potato Omelette, Auvergne-style

This recipe comes from the town of Riom in the Auvergne. It is also popular in the Bourbonnais, where it is sometimes served without cream and sometimes without cheese. Bacon may be used in place of ham.

13 oz (400 g) baking potatoes
1 tablespoon lard
1 thick slice raw ham (7 oz/200 g), cut into small cubes
10 eggs
salt and freshly ground pepper
2 oz (50 g) Cantal cheese or aged cheddar
3 tablespoons cream

❖Peel and wash the potatoes; pat dry. Cut into ½-in (1-cm) cubes. Melt the lard in a nonstick 10-in (26-cm) skillet. Add the potatoes and cook, stirring, for 2 minutes or until lightly browned. Cover the pan and cook over very low heat until the potatoes are tender, about 15 minutes, stirring from time to time. Stir in the ham and cook for 2 minutes.
❖Break the eggs into a bowl, season with salt and pepper and beat with a fork until blended. Pour the beaten eggs into the skillet and stir for 1 minute. Cover and cook the omelette over low heat for 5 minutes or until the bottom is just set. Turn and cook the other side.
❖Meanwhile, grate the cheese using a coarse grater. When the omelette is cooked, pour the cream over and sprinkle with cheese. Slide onto a plate and serve immediately.

SERVES 6

Quercy

OMELETTE QUERCYNOISE
Cheese and Walnut Omelette

10 eggs
salt and freshly ground pepper
2 teaspoons armagnac
12 walnuts, coarsely grated
4 oz (120 g) Roquefort cheese, crumbled
1 tablespoon goose fat

❖Break the eggs into a bowl and beat with a fork until blended, adding salt, pepper and armagnac. Mix in the walnuts and crumbled Roquefort.
❖Melt the goose fat in a nonstick 10-in (26-cm) skillet. Pour in the egg mixture and cook the omelette over low heat, delicately stirring the surface, until it is firm on the bottom. Turn it over and cover the skillet until the other side is cooked. Slide the omelette onto a plate and serve immediately.

SERVES 5-6

Côte d'Azur

PISSALADIÈRE
Pissaladière

The name comes from the Niçoise dialect word pissalat *meaning a puree of anchovies flavored with thyme, cloves, fennel and a dash of olive oil. But this remains strictly a local combination and is usually replaced by anchovy fillets.*

5 tablespoons extra virgin olive oil
4 lb (2 kg) large onions, thinly sliced
4 cloves fresh, young garlic, finely chopped
2 tablespoons water
salt
13 oz (400 g) bread dough (see page 41)
16 anchovy fillets in olive oil
4 oz (125 g) black Niçoise olives

❖Heat 4 tablespoons olive oil in a nonstick 10-in (26-cm) skillet. Add the onions and garlic and cook, stirring, over low heat for 10 minutes or until the onions are golden. Add the water and season with salt. Cover and cook gently for 30 minutes or until the onions are transparent and very soft, adding a little more water if necessary during cooking.
❖Preheat oven to 425°F (215°C). Lightly oil a 14 x 9-in (35 x 22-cm) baking sheet or a 12-in (30-cm) round tart pan. Gently roll out the bread dough to fit and lay it in the pan. Spread the cooked onion mixture on the surface. Arrange the anchovy fillets in a lattice pattern on top, placing an olive in the center of each square. Sprinkle with the remaining oil. Bake for 30 minutes or until the crust is golden.
❖Serve the pissaladière hot or warm, cut into large squares or wedges.

SERVES 6

PISSALADIÈRE (top), ALLYMES TART (bottom left, recipe page 48)
AND HERB PIE (bottom right, recipe page 48)

PETER JOHNSON

Lyonnais

TÂTRE DES ALLYMES

Allymes Tart

The tâtre *(a regional word for tart) is a specialty of the village of Allymes. It may also be made with* pâte brisée.

2 tablespoons peanut oil
1 lb (500 g) large onions, thinly sliced
½ cup (4 oz/125 g) well-drained *fromage blanc* or ricotta cheese
salt and freshly ground pepper
4 pinches of freshly grated nutmeg
½ cup (4 fl oz/125 ml) heavy (double) cream or crème fraîche
2 eggs
13 oz (400 g) bread dough (page 41)

❖Heat the oil in a nonstick 10-in (26-cm) skillet. Add the onions and cook, stirring, over low heat for 10 minutes or until golden. Set aside.
❖Beat the cheese in a bowl with a fork, adding salt, pepper, nutmeg and cream. Break the eggs into a separate bowl and beat with a fork until blended, then add to the cheese mixture and beat until smooth. Stir in the onions.
❖Preheat oven to 425°F (215°C). Lightly oil a 16 x 9-in (35 x 22-cm) baking sheet. Roll out the bread dough to the same size and lift the dough onto the sheet. Spread the onion mixture over the dough. Bake for 30 minutes or until the tart is lightly browned. Serve hot.

SERVES 6   *Photograph page 47*

Val de Loire

TOURTE AUX HERBES

Herb Pie

This is a specialty of Tours.

1 lb (500 g) fresh spinach
8 oz (250 g) sorrel
8 oz (250 g) beet greens or spinach
1 lettuce heart
2 oz (60 g) butter
salt and freshly ground pepper
1 lb (500 g) boiling potatoes
4 sprigs parsley
4 sprigs tarragon
2 cloves garlic, finely chopped
1 lb (500 g) puff pastry (page 44)
1 egg yolk
1 tablespoon water
1 cup (8 fl oz/250 ml) heavy (double) cream or crème fraîche

❖Wash the spinach and sorrel and trim the stalks; drain. Wash and drain the beet greens and lettuce. Coarsely chop all four greens. Melt half the butter in a nonstick 10-in (26-cm) skillet and gradually add the vegetables. Season with salt and pepper and cook over high heat, stirring constantly, for 5 minutes or until all liquid has evaporated. Turn vegetables out onto a plate and set aside.

❖Peel and wash the potatoes, pat dry and slice into ¼-in (5-mm) rounds. Rinse and dry the skillet. Melt the remaining butter in the skillet, add the potato and cook, turning often, for 15 minutes or until golden.
❖Finely chop the parsley and tarragon leaves. Add the chopped herbs and garlic to the potatoes, season with salt and pepper and cook, stirring, for 2 minutes. Remove from heat.
❖Preheat the oven to 425°F (215°C). Divide the pastry into two portions, ⅔ and ⅓. Roll out the larger portion into a 12 x 6-in (30 x 15-cm) rectangle and transfer it to a greased baking sheet. Spread half the potato mixture on the pastry to within 1 in (2 cm) of the edges. Cover with half the green vegetable mixture, then the remaining potatoes and finally the remaining green vegetable mixture. Roll out the remaining pastry into a 12½ x 6¾-in (32 x 17-cm) rectangle and place it over the filling. Press the two edges of the pastry together to seal.
❖To gild the pastry, beat the egg yolk and water with a fork in a small bowl. Brush this mixture over the entire surface of the pastry, using a pastry brush. Cut two small holes in the center of the pastry lid and insert small "chimneys" of aluminum foil or waxed paper to keep them open. Bake the pie for 45 minutes or until the pastry is golden brown.
❖Meanwhile, season the cream with salt and pepper. When the pie is baked, pour in the cream through the two chimneys. Let rest for 10 minutes before serving.

SERVES 6   *Photograph page 47*

Bourgogne

CORNIOTTES

Cheese Pastry "Hats"

8 oz (250 g) *fromage blanc* or ricotta cheese, drained
salt and freshly ground pepper
½ cup (4 fl oz/125 g) heavy (double) cream or crème fraîche
7 oz (200 g) Emmenthaler cheese, coarsely grated
2 eggs
1 lb (500 g) short (shortcrust) pastry (page 50)
1 egg yolk
1 tablespoon water

❖Turn the cheese into a bowl and mash it with a fork, adding salt, pepper and cream. Mix well. Add the Emmenthaler and eggs and mix well.
❖Preheat oven to 425°F (215°C). Roll out the pastry to a thickness of ⅛ in (3 mm). Cut out 26 circles, each 4 in (10 cm) in diameter.
❖Dip your finger in cold water and moisten the edges of the first pastry circle. Place a walnut-size mound of filling in the center of the pastry and turn up the edges of the circle on three sides to make a three-cornered "hat". Press the edges of the pastry firmly together at the corners so that the filling is enclosed. Repeat with the other pastry circles, arranging the *corniottes* on two nonstick baking sheets.
❖Beat the egg yolk and water and brush this mixture over the surface of the *corniottes*. Bake for 25 minutes or until the pastries are nicely browned. Arrange on a platter and serve hot or lukewarm.

SERVES 6

CHEESE PASTRY "HATS" (left) AND HERBED CHEESE
SPREAD (right, recipe page 37)
PIERRE HUSSENOT/AGENCE TOP

PÂTE BRISÉE
Short (Shortcrust) Pastry

For approximately 8 oz (250 g) pastry: *
1¼ cups (5 oz/150 g) all purpose (plain) flour
3 oz (100 g) soft butter
1½ tablespoons water
½ teaspoon salt

❖If possible, prepare the pastry the day before, so that it loses all elasticity and is easy to roll out.
❖Place the flour, butter, water and salt in the bowl of a food processor. Mix for 30 seconds, or until the pastry comes together into a ball. Wrap the ball of dough in plastic wrap, without further kneading, and chill thoroughly. Remove the pastry from the refrigerator 1 hour before it is to be used, and let rest at room temperature.
❖Roll out pastry on a lightly floured surface according to instructions in recipe; transfer to pan. If possible, return pan to the refrigerator for an hour before baking; although this is not absolutely necessary, the pastry will cook better if prechilled.
* Makes enough to line one 9- to 10-in (24- to 26-cm) pan.

Provence

SALADE NIÇOISE
Niçoise Salad

This typically southern dish is made with raw vegetables, tuna, garlic, basil and olive oil. Neither cooked vegetables nor potatoes should be included.

6 eggs
1 lb (500 g) fresh broad beans
1 red bell pepper (capsicum), (about 5 oz/150 g)
2 small artichokes
½ lemon
1 clove garlic
1 lb (500 g) firm-ripe tomatoes, cut into eighths
1 small cucumber, thinly sliced
3 green (spring) onions, thinly sliced
2 tender celery stalks, strings removed, cut into fine strips
12 anchovy fillets in olive oil, halved lengthwise
1 can (6½ oz/195 g) tuna in olive oil, drained and coarsely flaked
2 oz (50 g) black Niçoise olives
12 large basil leaves
salt
6 tablespoons extra virgin olive oil

❖Place the eggs in a saucepan of cold water, bring to boil over low heat and simmer for 10 minutes. Drain the eggs and cool under running water. Shell them and cut into quarters.
❖Shell the broad beans and remove the green outer skins. Halve the red pepper and remove the stem, seeds and white ribs, then slice the pepper into fine slivers. Remove the outer leaves of the artichokes and trim the points of the remaining leaves. Cut each artichoke into quarters and rub the surfaces with lemon.
❖Rub a shallow bowl with the peeled clove of garlic. Arrange in it the tomatoes, pepper, cucumber, artichokes, onions, celery and broad beans. Garnish with anchovies, tuna, olives and hard-cooked eggs. Using scissors, snip the

basil leaves over the salad. Sprinkle lightly with salt. Drizzle with olive oil and serve immediately.

SERVES 6   *Photograph pages 28 – 29*

Provence

PETITS FARCIS PROVENÇAUX
Stuffed Vegetables of Provence

3 eggplants (aubergines), 7 oz (200 g) each
3 zucchini (courgettes), 3 oz (100 g) each
6 firm-ripe tomatoes, 5 oz (150 g) each
6 onions, 3 oz (100 g) each
salt and freshly ground pepper
3 tablespoons extra virgin olive oil
2 cloves garlic, finely chopped
1 lb (500 g) boneless veal from the neck or shoulder, trimmed of fat and finely chopped
3 oz (100 g) fresh pork belly, finely chopped
10 sprigs flat-leaf parsley, stemmed and chopped
3 tablespoons boiled rice
2 oz (50 g) Parmesan cheese, freshly and finely grated
2 eggs
2 sprigs thyme

❖Wash the eggplants and zucchini and pat dry. Cut in half lengthwise and remove most of the flesh, leaving ¼ in (5 mm) next to the skin. Cut off the top quarter of each tomato and hollow out the inside with a small spoon. Peel the onions, cut off the top quarter and scoop out a hollow in the center. Season the insides of all the vegetables with salt and pepper and brush lightly with oil. With a sharp knife, finely chop the flesh removed from the vegetables.
❖Heat 1 tablespoon oil in a nonstick 10-in (26-cm) skillet. Add the garlic, chopped vegetables and meat and cook, stirring, over moderate heat for 5 minutes or until lightly browned. Transfer to a bowl and let cool.
❖Preheat oven to 400°F (200°C). Using 1 teaspoon oil, brush the inside of a shallow baking dish large enough to hold all the vegetables side by side.
❖Add the parsley to the bowl with the rice, Parmesan, eggs, thyme, salt and pepper and mix well. Divide the filling among the vegetables and arrange them in the prepared dish. Sprinkle with the remaining oil and pour ¼ cup (2 fl oz/60 ml) water into the dish. Bake for 45 minutes or until the vegetables are tender, basting them from time to time with the pan juices and adding a little more water if the liquid evaporates too quickly.
❖When the vegetables are cooked, arrange them on a platter, spoon over the remaining cooking juices and serve immediately.

SERVES 6   *Photograph pages 28 – 29*

Languedoc

PETITS PÂTÉS DE BÉZIERS
Little Pies from Béziers

It is said that in 1766 Lord Clive went to Pézenas to convalesce, and had these little pies made by his Indian cook. The original ownership of the recipe has been disputed ever since by Pézenas and Béziers; the version made in Pézenas does not contain currants.

For the pastry:
2½ tablespoons (50g) lard
2 cups (8oz/250g) all purpose (plain) flour
2 pinches of fine sea salt
3 tablespoons water
For the filling:
grated rind of 1 lemon
1 egg
2oz (50g) dried currants
1 tablespoon brown sugar
salt and freshly ground pepper
3oz (100g) veal kidney fat or suet, coarsely chopped
10oz (300g) lamb shoulder or loin, finely chopped
1 egg yolk
1 tablespoon water

❖First prepare the pastry: melt the lard in a small saucepan and let cool to lukewarm. Sift the flour and salt onto a work surface. Make a well in the center and pour in the melted lard and 3 tablespoons water. Combine all together with the fingertips to make a smooth homogeneous dough. Roll into a ball and wrap in plastic. Refrigerate for 30 minutes.

❖Meanwhile, prepare the filling: wash and dry the lemon and grate its peel into a bowl. Add the egg, currants, sugar, salt and pepper and mix well.

❖Place the fat in a nonstick 10-in (26-cm) skillet and melt over low heat. Add the meat and cook, stirring, for 5 minutes or until well browned. Remove meat with a slotted spoon and add to the currant mixture, mixing well. Preheat the oven to 425°F (215°C).

❖Lightly butter six small custard cups or brioche tins 1½in (4cm) in diameter and 1¼in (3cm) high. Roll out the pastry thinly and cut out six 3-in (8-cm) circles and six 2-in (5-cm) circles. Line the cups or tins with the larger circles, then add the filling. Brush the edges of the pastry with water and cover with one of the smaller circles. Press the edges together to seal and make a few slits in the top of each pie with the blade of a knife to allow the steam to escape.

❖Beat the egg yolk and 1 tablespoon water with a fork in a small bowl. Brush this mixture over the surface of the pies. Bake for 20 minutes or until golden. Remove from tins and serve hot.

SERVES 6

PETER JOHNSON

LITTLE PIES FROM BÉZIERS (top) AND EGG AND BACON QUICHE

Lorraine

QUICHE LORRAINE
Egg and Bacon Quiche

The word quiche comes from the German küche, *meaning cake. The origins of* quiche lorraine *go back to the seventeenth century, but today the name quiche is used for savory tarts that are served warm.*

8oz (250g) short (shortcrust) pastry (page 50)
8oz (250g) thinly sliced streaky bacon
2oz (50g) butter
3 eggs
1 cup (8floz/250ml) heavy (double) cream or crème fraîche
salt and freshly ground pepper
6 pinches of freshly grated nutmeg

❖Heat the oven to 425°F (215°C). Lightly butter a deep 9- to 10-in (24-cm) tart pan. Roll out the pastry and line the tin, crimping the edge. Refrigerate until needed. Remove rind from the bacon and cut the bacon into small pieces. Drop these into a small saucepan of boiling water and blanch for 1 minute. Drain, rinse under cold running water and pat dry. Melt half the butter in a nonstick 8-in (20-cm) skillet and lightly fry the bacon, stirring constantly with a wooden spoon. Drain on paper towels.

❖Break the eggs into a bowl and beat with a fork until blended, adding the cream, salt, pepper and nutmeg.

❖Remove the tart pan from the refrigerator. Scatter bacon over the bottom of the pastry. Pour in the egg mixture and dot with the remaining butter. Bake for about 30 minutes or until the quiche is lightly browned. Serve hot.

SERVES 6

Lorraine

FOIE GRAS EN TERRINE
Cooked Whole Duck Liver Terrine

The much sought-after delicacy, foie gras, *whether of goose or duck, is traditionally made in two regions, the Landes and Alsace, according to recipes dictated by fashion or by the region. At one time, for example, it used to be served at the end of the meal instead of at the beginning, as we know today.*

1 uncooked duck *foie gras,* about 1¼ lb (600 g)
1 teaspoon fine sea salt
1 teaspoon crushed pepper
scant ½ cup (100 ml) cognac

❖Carefully separate the two lobes of the liver and, using a small, sharp-pointed knife, remove the fine outer membrane, the blood vessels and other filaments. Place the two lobes, side by side, in a shallow dish just large enough to hold them. Season with salt and pepper and sprinkle with cognac. Cover the dish and refrigerate for 12 hours, turning the liver once or twice.

❖Remove the liver from the refrigerator and let stand at room temperature for 1 hour. Preheat the oven to 350°F (180°C). Pat the liver dry and arrange the pieces in a covered baking dish just large enough to hold them. Top with the lid.

❖Place the dish in a pan of hot, but not boiling, water and bake for 40 minutes.

❖Place the two lobes of liver in a stainless steel colander resting over a bowl; let drain for about 15 minutes.

❖In a small container just large enough to hold them, rearrange the two lobes into the original form of the liver. Press down to firm, using the back of a spoon. Cover with a sheet of waxed paper, then with a board or a sheet of cardboard. Top with a 1-lb (500-g) weight and let stand for 1 hour.

❖Remove the weight, the board and the paper. Cover the liver by ¼ in (5 mm) with the fat collected in the bowl. Let the fat set, then cover the dish and refrigerate.

❖Chill the liver for 2 to 3 days before serving, in slices, accompanied by toasted country bread.

❖This terrine may be kept for a week in the refrigerator.

SERVES 6

COOKED WHOLE DUCK LIVER TERRINE
PIERRE HUSSENOT/AGENCE TOP

VAL DE LOIRE

A gentle garden

VAL DE LOIRE

A gentle garden

How soft and sweet it is, the garden of France! Following the length of the seemingly endless and capricious river, dotted with friendly colors: it is a cameo of grey, blue and green, tricking the eye with its contrasts, resisting clear definitions. It would be fascinating to follow its course.

Yet the Loire has become useless. No longer does it convey the flat-bottomed river barges, nor those sailing ships which once transported cargo to Nantes, the former "ebony" port, port of the Antilles. It gives an impression of indolence, but in reality it is frolicsome and reckless, forever swirling feverishly.

It is impossible to speak of the Loire Valley without first invoking the landscape. The bridge of Beaugency, the roofs of Blois, the levee banks that go as far as Tours, the tributaries — the Cher, the Indre, the lazy Cosson, the warm Sauldre — lapping at manors and châteaux. Back at Beaugency, behind the high-humped bridge, a dungeon watches over nothing more than the flights of birds. At Orléans, an island is lost in the middle of the river. Further on, towards Nantes and the sea, Champtoceaux, the promenade of Champalud, forms a panorama that spreads out and goes on and on. And then, the colors of the Loire, soft and muted, and of the fields . . . a garden of beauty! No matter whether you take leave of the river near Loché or near Ouchamps, whether you reach the low forests of Sologne or the high hedges of the park at Chambord, with its hundred bell turrets, or whether you wander towards the nearby Berry, awaiting, from across the flat green expanse of the countryside, the sight of the spire of the tower of Bourges cathedral; or whether you traverse the

LEFT: IN THE CALM OF TWILIGHT THE ENTRANCING FOURTEENTH-CENTURY CHÂTEAU DE SAUMUR IS REFLECTED IN THE WATERS OF THE LOIRE.

PREVIOUS PAGES: THE LOIR, A TRIBUTARY OF THE FAMOUS LOIRE RIVER, FLOWS THROUGH THE TINY VILLAGE OF LES ROCHES-L'ÉVÊQUE.

LIKE THE BUILDINGS IN TROO, THE ARCHITECTURE THROUGHOUT THE
LOIRE VALLEY EVOKES FAIRY-TALE IMAGES.

savored, they are forgotten. But it is only right to
begin with the fruits of the vine, which accompany to perfection the fruits of the earth.

The white asparagus and the green endive
grown between the Loire and the Sologne are the
most delicate in the world. The miniature
tomatoes, in the form of tiny cherries and minipears, are common. There are innumerable garden
herbs, credited with medicinal virtues: balm,
camomile, tarragon, wild and cultivated thyme,
basil, chives, savory and simple parsley.
Everywhere, charcuterie reigns supreme, from the
rillons of Vouvray and the *rillettes* of Maine and
Anjou, to the *andouillette* of Jargeau and crumbed
pig's trotters, to chicken liver terrine and a variety
of sausages.

A few pâtés are based on game, since this is
hunting country: red deer and roe deer gallop
across fields, partridge and pheasant thread their
way through the heather of the moors, hares start
up and streak away along the roadsides, and wild
mallard ducks, or *cols verts*, fly over the ponds
between Bracieux and Romorantin. The vast,
gentle Sologne, with its expanses for hunting on
horseback; the flat Berry, where the châteaux
stand out on the horizon like spurs; the region of
Orléans with sandy soils and immense forests
wedded to the canals: these are the companions
of the river Loire.

WHILE CHINON IS WELL-KNOWN FOR ITS WHITE WINE (CELEBRATED IN
THE SIXTEENTH-CENTURY WORK *GARGANTUA AND PANTAGRUEL* BY FRANÇOIS
RABELAIS), FISHING REMAINS A POPULAR PASTIME.

deserted terrain of the Nivernais, which flirts with
the strict architecture of the château of Serrant . . .
behind the verdant serenity of a landscape shaped
by man beams an innocent appeal to the appetite.

If, once upon a time, the kings of France abandoned Paris for Chinon, where they established
their court, where they awaited the faltering steps
of the maid of Orléans on the smooth-worn
stones of the Grand-Carroi, it was because they
were certain of finding fine foods, fine wines and
festivity in the Loire Valley. Is it the richest region
of France? If so, it is also the most modest, for it
does not boast — except perhaps that the French
spoken here is the purest in the country and is free
of any provincial *patois*.

And here the miracle of wine occurs. After the
pleasant muscadets of Nantes come the fullbodied Chaume of Anjou; the honorable Layons,
which improves with age, splendidly deep in
flavor in good years; the proud Savennières, with
a nose of almond and linden, of verbena and
acacia; the fresh red wine from Chinon, made
from the Cabernet Franc grape, smelling of green
peppers and pea pods; and its first cousins, from
Saumur-Champigny and Bourgueil, the mellow
Vouvray with enormous aging potential, the likeable Montlouis, the light Gamay, the easy-drinking Sauvignon, the fruity Sancerre and its flintyflavored cousins from Menetou-Salon and Reuilly.
All these wines are nurtured religiously in the region's white limestone caves, which become even
more white with age. They are drunk, they are

THE CHÂTEAU CHENONCEAUX IS PERHAPS THE MOST ELEGANT OF THE LOIRE VALLEY JEWELS. ITS BEAUTIFUL GARDENS AND SURROUNDING BUILDINGS MAINTAIN A STYLE FAITHFUL TO THE TIME OF HENRI II, WHEN THE CHÂTEAU WAS BUILT.

And here gambol the goats from which come such fine cheeses: the pyramids of Valençay and of Pouligny-Saint-Pierre, the cylindrical forms of Sainte-Maure-de-Touraine, the ash-covered loaves of Selles-sur-Cher. All make admirable marriages with the white wine pressed from the Sauvignon grape. Start with the *crottin* of Chavignol, firm to the touch, sandy-textured in the mouth, with a grassy, curdy taste, a product of the Sancerre region, where it finds its natural ally in the wine of the same name. All these cheeses make a fine prelude to the fruits harvested in this gentle climate: pears primarily, but also greengage plums, raspberries, strawberries and peaches. The sandy soils on either side of the river support a natural orchard, its offspring the quince or apple jelly known as *cotignac*, the caramelized upside-down apple tart invented by the Tatin sisters in their hotel (situated in the Sologne town of Lamotte-Beuvron), and the pancakes from Anjou, flavored with the locally produced, orange-scented liqueur, Cointreau.

Would these make us forget the other riches of the countryside? The Loire's tender fish include beautifully pink salmon, the pike with its estimable flesh but plentiful bones, the shad, the eel that is typically prepared with the red wine of Chinon *en matelote* or accompanied with a white butter sauce flavored with white wine, vinegar and shallots and said to be a specialty of Nantes. The eels were thought to have vanished long ago, eagerly seized by the few odd fishermen along the canals, but mostly chased away by pollution. But the opposite has occurred: they are proliferating in the river, now warmed by the discharge water of the nuclear power stations at Saint-Laurence-des-Eaux (near Beaugency) and Avoine (near Chinon).

Nor should we forget the diversity of mushrooms cultivated in underground caves. The grey *pleurotes* are of vaguely rubbery appearance, and the little cultivated mushrooms known as *champignons de Paris* are grown easily in the natural vaults found in the wine region of Saumur and along the banks of the Cher; pale in appearance, they take on flavor when fried with garlic. Poultry, too, has a high reputation here. Tender-fleshed guinea fowl, flavorful rabbit, and the succulent hen-chicken called *géline*, are still prepared in the same way as they were in the days of François I in the châteaux of Chambord and Ussé, when the art of combining sweet and salty flavors was highly esteemed. They are served with local heather honey or combined with the orchard-fresh fruits, lightly fried or roasted like choice vegetables.

Two typical dishes that epitomize this ancient sweet-sour style (which has nothing to do with the fad of *nouvelle cuisine*, but rather represents an underlying influence persisting since the Middle Ages) are noisette of pork with prunes and hindquarter of rabbit with honey. Here ingredients which would otherwise clash are gently and judiciously married. Is not the Loire Valley, after all, the land of soft colors, of subdued and apparently fragile landscapes, of bold wines and peaceful digestion?

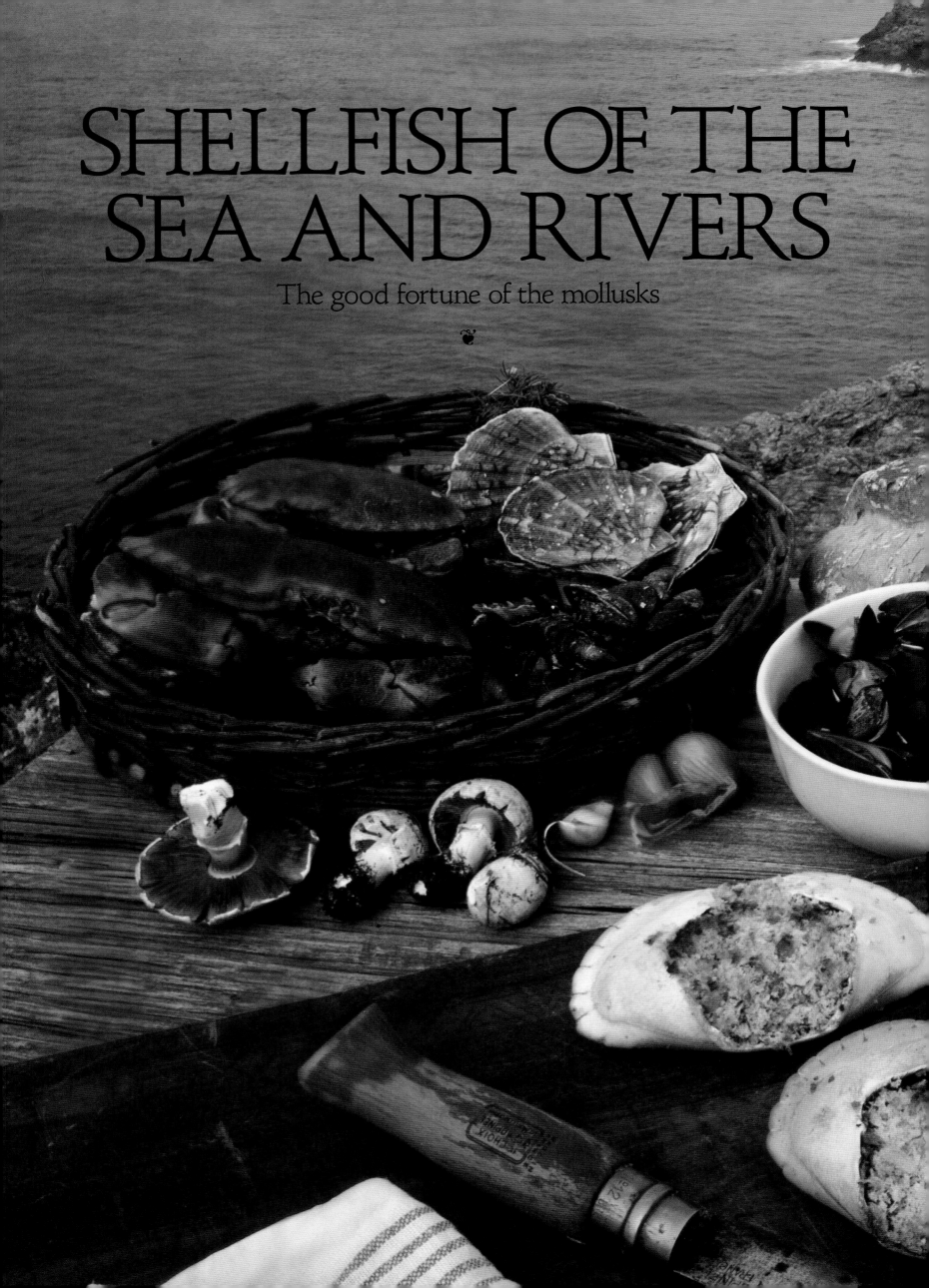

SHELLFISH OF THE SEA AND RIVERS

The good fortune of the mollusks

CULTIVATED IN THE BAIE DU MONT-ST-MICHEL, *MOULES DE BOUCHOT*,
SMALL HIGHLY-PRIZED MUSSELS, ARE GROWN ON STAKES DRIVEN
INTO THE SEDIMENT OF ITS SHALLOW COASTAL BEDS.

SHELLFISH OF THE SEA AND RIVERS

The good fortune of the mollusks

It is an utter mystery. Why on earth does the gourmet, and in particular the French gourmet, rave so much about white-fleshed mollusks? In the nineteenth century there were clubs and oyster-eating competitions at which honest, bourgeois citizens would be encouraged to overindulge in chorus, stuffing themselves with seafood.

Oysters from Cancale, from the bay of Morbihan, from Belon, from Saint-Vaast-la Hougue, from Marennes-Oléron: to say that they do not all have the same flavor is not enough. The flat oyster, which gave Cancale its fame, has almost disappeared as the result of an epidemic known as *bonamia*. The deep-shelled oyster, or *huître creusé*, although also decimated, was better able to survive than its more highly reputed neighbor. The Portuguese oyster, or *portugaise*, so named because a Portuguese ship once tipped its copious cargo of shellfish onto the Atlantic coast, has been replaced by a species of Japanese origin, the *gigas*. Apart from all this, the oyster has a solid reputation, and even dieters appreciate it.

The texture of the oyster can be deceptive. During the "R" months — in other words, from September to April — the mollusks are fresh and lively. In July and August, the period of egg-laying and reproduction, they are plump and milky — but should not be confused with those oysters that are naturally fatter because they are older (called *spéciales* by the vendors), in contrast to the *claires* which are younger and thinner in flavor.

Mussels are generally cultivated on fixed wooden stakes in the waters off Oléron and La Rochelle; these are the best. Others are grown in special "parks" at Croisic or, in the Mediterranean, on ropes, as are those from Bouzigues, on the Etang de Thau. Their tender, orange-red, flavorful flesh lends itself to many cooking variations: *marinière* style, or with cream, or in the preparation known as *éclade*, where a quick fire directly on top of the mussels causes them to open, or *mouclade*, which is nothing more or less than a mussel stew with white wine and cream.

It is no mystery why shellfish are well treated in cuisine: over-complicating the recipes entails a risk of losing their prime freshness. Scallops, firm-fleshed and delicate, and their baby sisters the *pétoncles*, white-fleshed mollusks with an almost-sweet flavor, can take only a very brief cooking, which preserves their iodine and their savor.

Lobster and crayfish, which are the kings — albeit rare — of the Breton coasts (the true Mediterranean crayfish are scarcely found any more) and which are trapped in pots, are served in a way that is both attractive and simple: grilled, with *beurre blanc* sauce. Spices and strongly flavored sauces should be used sparingly. The old ways which involved flaming, or outdated preparations such as "Thermidor" (covered with a white wine- and mustard-flavored sauce, then topped with grated cheese and grilled), or "Newburg" (cooked in a creamy, American-style sauce) have

PREVIOUS PAGES: STUFFED CRAB (left, recipe page 80), MUSSELS IN CREAM (center, recipe page 66) AND SCALLOPS ÉTRETAT-STYLE (right, recipe page 68),
PHOTOGRAPHED IN NORMANDIE
PIERRE HUSSENOT/AGENCE TOP

BARGAINING FOR FRESHLY HARVESTED MUSSELS AND OYSTERS AT
VIVIER-SUR-MER ON THE BAIE DU MONT-ST-MICHEL.

A VARIETY OF SHELLFISH FOR SALE AT LES HALLES IN QUIMPER, BRETAGNE.
DELIGHTS INCLUDE *TOURTEAUX* (LARGE CRABS), *BOUQUET CUITS* (COOKED SHRIMP),
LANGOUSTINES CUITS (COOKED CRAYFISH), *HOMARDS* (LOBSTER), AND
ARAIGNÉES (SPIDER CRABS).

the effect of masking the shellfish's natural flavor.
Perhaps the reason that certain restaurateurs persist
with them is that such preparations hide the lack
of flavor of an inferior product.

Shrimp — the tiny ones, *grises*, and the larger
ones, *bouquèts* — make excellent first courses,
whether as a salad, lightly fried, or cold with *sauce
verte* or mayonnaise. Langoustines, which resemble baby lobsters in shape, are easily cooked —
but watch the time! A few seconds too long, and
a firm, crisp-textured flesh becomes soft and
stringy. Only the tail is used, pan-fried. The great
chef Joël Robuchon used to serve them as an
extremely elegant salad which was all the rage in
Paris in the early '80s; he would pan-fry them just
before serving, then dress them with a small
amount of goose fat.

There is a whole family of crabs, all hiding soft,
pinkish flesh under a hard red shell. The *tourteau*
(common crab) is the most hardy; the *étrille* (swimmer) is smaller and more delicate; the *araignée*
(spider crab) is the most fragile of all, but also the
rarest and tastiest. All are rich in vitamins, low in
calories and exquisite served cold with a lemony
mayonnaise.

To complete this diverse range of marine
shellfish, mention should be made of the sea
cockle, which must be cleaned of sand before
being eaten raw or cooked; the *palourdes*, or clams,
translucent and delicate, with their lightly striped
shell, excellent served raw with a dash of lemon;

the *praires*, or warty venus, which are usually stuffed and grilled with garlic butter or made into a soup.

Freshwater crustaceans are gradually disappearing from French rivers as a result of pollution. The crayfish, or *écrevisses*, that were once plentiful in small streams, lakes and reservoirs, now usually come from other countries (Turkey, in particular). The most highly reputed are the *pattes rouges*, the red-legged variety. It should be added, however, that in spite of the attraction of their delicate, firm-textured flesh, the taste depends more on their mode of presentation, which often involves extracting the flavor of the crushed shells to make a sauce or soup.

Contrary to popular opinion, squid (*calamars*, *calmars* or *chipirons*, to give them their Basque name, and the larger *encornets*) and small cuttlefish (*supions* in the Mediterranean) are not fish but mollusks. According to region, they may be stuffed, cooked with sweet peppers or tomatoes, or served with a sauce, their firm flesh retaining its distinctive taste and appearance regardless of recipe.

LEO MEIER

BUSINESS IS BRISK IN THE OPEN MARKETPLACE AT BLOIS WITH BOTH LOCAL FRESH AND OCEAN SEAFOOD FOR SALE.

THIS ENTICING DISPLAY OF LOCAL MEDITERRANEAN SEAFOOD IN NICE INCLUDES MUSSELS, CLAMS, SEA-URCHINS AND SPINY CRAYFISH.

LEO MEIER

lightly cook the shallots, stirring constantly, for 2 minutes or until they are golden. Add the mussel liquid and bring to boil; boil for 1 minute.

❖Strain the contents of the small saucepan back into the pot used for cooking the mussels, add the curry, cayenne and ⅔ of the cream and boil for 1 minute. Beat the egg yolks in a small bowl with the remaining cream. Whisk 2 tablespoons of the hot liquid into the beaten yolks, then pour into the large saucepan. Add the mussels and reheat for 1 minute, stirring, over very low heat; do not allow the sauce to boil.

❖Ladle the mussels into shallow soup bowls, pour the sauce over and serve immediately.

SERVES 4

Provence

MOULES AUX ÉPINARDS
Mussels with Spinach

3 tablespoons milk
2 oz (50 g) fresh bread, crusts trimmed
2 lb (1 kg) spinach, washed and drained
1 lb (500 g) small mussels
2 lb (1 kg) large mussels
salt and freshly ground pepper
1 lb (500 g) ripe tomatoes
2 tablespoons olive oil
2 onions, each about 3 oz (100 g), finely chopped
pinch of sugar

❖Warm the milk in a small saucepan and crumble in the bread. Let cool.

❖Place the spinach in a large saucepan with the water clinging to its leaves. Cook over high heat for 4 minutes or until tender. Drain very well and squeeze dry, then chop finely.

❖Wash the mussels. Scrape the small ones and remove the beards, then transfer them to a large saucepan and place over high heat just until opened, turning them over constantly with a wooden spoon. Drain, reserving the cooking juices, and let the mussels cool. Discard any unopened mussels.

❖Open the large mussels by pulling on the beard, but do not separate the two halves of the shell. Reserve the juices, remove the small mussels from their shells and chop coarsely with a knife. Strain the cooking liquid, as well as the juices from the large mussels. Add the bread mixture and the spinach and mix well, mashing with a fork. Add the chopped mussels with a little salt and pepper and mix well. Fill the raw mussels with this mixture and tie the two halves of the shells together to retain the stuffing.

❖Drop the tomatoes into boiling water for 10 seconds, then cool under running water. Peel, halve and squeeze out the seeds; mash the flesh with a fork.

❖Heat the oil in a nonstick 11-in (28-cm) sauté pan. Add the onions, stirring, and cook for 2 minutes or until golden. Add the tomatoes, salt, pepper and sugar and cook, stirring, for 2 minutes. Add the stuffed mussels and cook for 5 minutes, turning over once. Remove the strings and arrange the mussels in a shallow soup dish. Pour the tomato sauce over and serve immediately.

SERVES 6 *Photograph page 67*

PETER JOHNSON

MUSSELS IN WINE AND CREAM SAUCE

Charentes

MOUCLADE
Mussels in Wine and Cream Sauce

In Charentes, the mouclade *is made with the same basic ingredients as in Aunis and Saintonge: cultivated mussels, wine, French shallots, cream and egg yolk. The flavors vary, however: the curry powder may be replaced by saffron, and sometimes* Pineau des Charentes *is added. This is a delicious fortified wine made from grape must and cognac.*

5 lb (2.5 kg) mussels
1½ cups (12 fl oz/400 ml) dry white wine (in Charentes, Muscadet or Gros-plant would be used)
1 sprig thyme
1 bay leaf
6 sprigs parsley
1 oz (25 g) butter
3 French shallots, finely chopped
1 teaspoon curry powder
pinch of cayenne pepper
⅔ cup (5 fl oz/150 g) heavy (double) cream or crème fraîche
3 egg yolks

❖Scrape the mussels and remove the beards. Wash mussels in several changes of water, then drain.

❖Pour the wine into a large nonaluminum saucepan. Add the thyme, bay leaf and parsley, bruising them between the fingers. Bring just to boil over high heat and add the mussels, moving them around in the liquid with a slotted spoon. Remove them with the slotted spoon as soon as they open, and set aside in a bowl. Boil the mussel cooking liquid over high heat until reduced by half, then strain it into a bowl. Discard any unopened mussels.

❖Meanwhile, melt the butter in a small saucepan and

Normandie/Bretagne

MOULES MARINIÈRE
Mussels in White Wine

This is a traditional dish served all over France. It is usually made with a local white wine.

6 lb (3 kg) mussels
bouquet garni: 1 bay leaf, 1 sprig thyme, 6 sprigs parsley
2 oz (50 g) butter
6 French shallots, finely chopped
1 clove garlic, finely chopped
2 cups (16 fl oz/500 ml) dry white wine such as Muscadet
freshly ground pepper
2 tablespoons chopped flat-leaf parsley

❖Scrape the mussels and remove the beards. Wash in several changes of water and drain. Tie together the herbs for the bouquet garni.
❖Melt the butter in a saucepan large enough to hold all the mussels. Add the chopped shallots and garlic and cook over low heat, stirring, for 1 minute or until softened. Pour in the wine, add the bouquet garni and season with pepper; bring to boil. Boil for 2 minutes, then add the mussels and stir with a slotted spoon. As soon as they open, remove them with the slotted spoon and keep warm in a large bowl. Discard any unopened mussels.
❖Boil the cooking liquid over high heat until reduced by half, then return the mussels to the pan and add the chopped parsley. Mix all together just long enough to reheat the mussels, about 30 seconds. Remove the bouquet garni.
❖Divide the mussels and liquid among four large shallow soup plates and serve immediately.

SERVES 4

Normandie

MOULES À LA CRÈME
Mussels in Cream

Mussels are cultivated in different ways in different regions. The best known are those grown in Charentes on wooden stakes or bouchots, to which they attach themselves in clusters. In Bretagne mussels are cultivated like oysters — flat, in beds. In the south they are grown hanging, and in the Etang de Thau the famous Bouzigues mussels live permanently submerged, but without contact with the bottom of the lagoon.

8 lb (4 kg) mussels
2 cups (16 fl oz/500 ml) dry cider
4 French shallots, finely chopped
¾ cup (6 fl oz/185 g) heavy (double) cream or crème fraîche
salt and freshly ground pepper
3 egg yolks
1 tablespoon chopped parsley

❖Scrape the mussels and remove the beards. Wash in several changes of water and drain.
❖Pour the cider into a pot large enough to hold the mussels and place over high heat. Add the shallots and boil for 2 minutes. Add the mussels and stir with a slotted spoon. As soon as they open, remove the mussels with the slotted spoon and keep warm in a large bowl.
❖Pour half the cream into the pot and cook over high heat until the sauce is smooth and slightly thickened. Strain into a small saucepan and keep warm. Season with salt and pepper.
❖Beat together the remaining cream and the egg yolks with a fork. Pour this mixture into the small saucepan and whisk over low heat until the sauce becomes thick and creamy; take care that the sauce does not boil and become grainy. Stir in the parsley. Divide the mussels among four warm plates and pour the sauce over. Serve immediately.

SERVES 4   *Photograph pages 60 – 61*

Charentes

HUÎTRES EN BROCHETTES
Grilled Oysters on Skewers

Whether they originated in Charentes or the kitchens of Queen Victoria, these delectable "angels on horseback" are equally popular in England and France, and bear the same name in both countries.

24 large oysters
6 slices of white sandwich bread
24 paper-thin slices of bacon
1 oz (40 g) butter
4 tablespoons dry breadcrumbs
2 pinches of cayenne pepper

❖Open the oysters, pouring their juices into a large saucepan through a fine sieve lined with dampened cheesecloth. Remove the oysters from their shells.
❖Place the saucepan over low heat. As soon as the liquid begins to bubble, add the oysters. Poach them for 7 seconds, then drain in a sieve.
❖Preheat broiler (griller). Trim the crusts from the bread and lightly brown the slices on both sides under the broiler. Cut each slice into 4 squares. Place in a baking dish, in 4 rows of 6 squares.
❖Remove the rind from the bacon and cut each slice in half crosswise. Wrap each oyster in a piece of bacon and thread 6 onto each of 4 wood or metal skewers, not too closely together. Arrange the skewers in the baking dish so that each oyster rests on a square of bread. Broil until the bacon is nicely crisp, about 2 minutes, turning after 1 minute.
❖Meanwhile, melt the butter in a nonstick 8-in (20-cm) skillet, over low heat. Add the breadcrumbs and fry, stirring constantly with a wooden spoon, until golden. Turn into a fine sieve to drain.
❖Carefully withdraw the oysters from the skewers. Sprinkle the oysters with cayenne and breadcrumbs and serve immediately.

SERVES 4

MUSSELS WITH SPINACH (top left, recipe page 65), GRILLED OYSTERS ON SKEWERS (top right) AND MUSSELS IN WHITE WINE (bottom)
PETER JOHNSON

Bretagne

COQUILLES SAINT-JACQUES AU BEURRE BLANC

Scallops with Beurre Blanc

Beurre blanc sauce is a reduction of French shallots and vinegar with butter incorporated into it. In Anjou, and in the Nantes area where it is a specialty, it is made with unsalted butter, which has a delicious nutty flavor, and accompanies pike or shad. In Bretagne it is made the same way, but with a semi-salted butter that has a subtle taste of iodine and is used to coat crustaceans and fish.

1 lb (500 g) scallops (without their coral)
salt and freshly ground pepper
4 French shallots, finely chopped
6 tablespoons dry white wine
3 tablespoons white wine vinegar
7 oz (200 g) butter

❖Rinse the scallops and pat dry. Cut each in half, into 2 thinner discs. Season with salt and pepper.
❖Combine the shallots, wine, vinegar and salt and pepper in a small saucepan. Simmer gently over low heat until only 2 teaspoons of liquid remain.
❖Meanwhile, cut the butter into ¾-in (1.5-cm) cubes; set aside ¾ oz (20 g). Over a very low heat, vigorously whisk the butter into the saucepan, piece by piece. When all the butter has been incorporated and the *beurre blanc* is light and foamy, set it aside and keep warm.
❖Melt the remaining butter in a nonstick 10-in (26-cm) skillet and cook the scallops over very low heat for 20 seconds on each side. Divide among four hot plates and pour the sauce over. Serve immediately.

SERVES 4

SCALLOPS, LANDES-STYLE (top) AND SCALLOPS WITH BEURRE BLANC

PETER JOHNSON

Aquitaine

COQUILLES SAINT-JACQUES À LA LANDAISE

Scallops, Landes-style

2 oz (50 g) pine nuts
1 lb (500 g) scallops, with their coral
salt and freshly ground pepper
2 tablespoons vegetable oil
1 tablespoon wine vinegar
1 tablespoon water
2 oz (50 g) butter
1 tablespoon chopped flat-leaf parsley

❖Lightly brown the pine nuts over low heat in a dry skillet. Set aside in a bowl.
❖Rinse the scallops and pat dry. Cut the white parts horizontally in half making two thin discs; season both the white parts and the coral with salt and pepper.
❖Heat the oil in a nonstick 10-in (26-cm) skillet. Lightly brown the scallops and coral over moderate heat for 1 minute on each side. Set aside and keep warm.
❖Discard the cooking oil. Add the vinegar and water to the pan and boil until reduced by half. Add the butter and whisk over low heat until it softens and becomes incorporated into the sauce. Add the parsley and pine nuts and stir again. Pour this sauce over the scallops and serve immediately.

SERVES 4

Normandie

COQUILLES SAINT-JACQUES D'ÉTRETAT

Scallops Étretat-style

With its shingle and tall cliffs making it one of Normandie's prettiest "postcards," Etretat is also a gastronomic mecca, famous for its shellfish and crustaceans.

1 lb (500 g) scallops, with their coral
salt and freshly ground pepper
8 oz (250 g) mushrooms
6 tablespoons heavy (double) cream or crème fraîche
2 egg yolks
2 oz (50 g) butter
2 French shallots, finely chopped
1 tablespoon calvados
1 cup (8 fl oz/250 ml) dry white wine

❖Rinse the scallops and pat dry. Season with salt and pepper. Trim the stems of the mushrooms; wash them, pat dry and chop finely. Beat the cream and egg yolks together with a fork in a small bowl.
❖Melt the butter in a nonstick 10-in (26-cm) skillet and cook the chopped shallots and mushrooms over very low heat, stirring, for 5 minutes. Add the scallops and cook for 30 seconds on each side. Sprinkle in the calvados and ignite, shaking the pan gently until flames subside. Remove the scallops and set aside in a warm place.

STUFFED SQUID (top) AND SQUID COOKED IN THEIR OWN INK (bottom, recipe page 70)

❖Pour the wine into the skillet and boil over high heat until the sauce is syrupy and reduced by ⅔. Add the egg yolk mixture and stir until the sauce thickens; do not allow it to boil.

❖Preheat the broiler (griller). Divide the scallops among four individual broilerproof dishes and cover with sauce. Slide under the broiler, close to the heat source, for about 30 seconds or until lightly browned. Serve immediately in the same dishes.

SERVES 4   *Photograph pages 60 – 61*

Provence

CALMARS FARCIS
Stuffed Squid

2 squid, about 11 oz (350 g) each
2 lb (1 kg) ripe tomatoes
2 onions, about 3 oz (100 g) each, finely chopped
1 tablespoon olive oil
salt and freshly ground pepper
1 teaspoon sugar
For the stuffing:
5 tablespoons milk
2 oz (50 g) stale bread, crusts trimmed
1 tablespoon dried currants
1 tablespoon chopped flat-leaf parsley
salt and freshly ground pepper
1 tablespoon olive oil
1 onion, about 3 oz (100 g), finely chopped
1 clove garlic, finely chopped
3 oz (100 g) prosciutto or other raw ham, finely chopped
2 eggs, beaten

❖Place one squid on a work surface. Hold the body with

one hand and pull away the tentacles with the other. Discard the insides and the internal quill. Cut the tentacles off the head at the level of the eyes and reserve, discarding the rest of the head. Wash the tentacles and body; if the latter contains eggs or roe, leave them, as they have an excellent flavor. Prepare the second squid in the same way. Finely chop the tentacles.

❖Prepare the stuffing: heat the milk in a small saucepan over low heat. Crumble in the bread and stir. Remove from heat and let cool. Rinse the currants under warm water. Combine the soaked bread, currants, parsley, salt and pepper in a bowl.

❖Heat the oil in a nonstick 10-in (26-cm) skillet. Add the chopped onion and garlic and cook, stirring, for 2 minutes or until golden. Add the ham and chopped tentacles and continue to cook over low heat, stirring, for 5 minutes. Add the soaked bread mixture and eggs and cook, stirring, for 1 minute or until the eggs begin to set. Stir until smooth and remove from heat. Loosely fill the squid bodies with the stuffing; sew the opening closed with kitchen thread.

❖Drop the tomatoes into boiling water for 10 seconds. Cool under running water, then peel, halve and squeeze out the seeds. Finely chop the flesh.

❖Place the squid in an enameled saucepan over low heat and turn with a wooden spoon until they give out no more liquid. Add the onions and cook, stirring, until any liquid has evaporated. Pour in the oil and continue to cook, still turning the squid, for 3 minutes or until lightly browned. Stir in the tomatoes, salt, pepper and sugar and bring to boil. Cover and cook over low heat for 2 hours, turning the squid from time to time.

❖Remove the squid from the pan and slice into ¾-in (1.5-cm) rounds. Pour the sauce into a shallow serving plate and arrange the slices of squid on top. Serve immediately.

SERVES 4

CHIPIRONS EN SU TINTA
Squid Cooked in Their own Ink

Chipirons is the regional Basque name for squid.

2½ lb (1.2 kg) small squid
8 oz (250 g) ripe tomatoes
3 tablespoons olive oil
1 onion, about 3 oz (100 g), finely chopped
1 clove garlic, finely chopped
1 cup (8 fl oz/250 ml) dry white wine
salt and freshly ground pepper
4 pinches of cayenne pepper
For the stuffing:
2 oz (50 g) stale bread, crusts trimmed
1 tablespoon olive oil
1 onion, about 3 oz (100 g), finely chopped
1 clove garlic, finely chopped
salt and freshly ground pepper

❖Place one squid on a work surface. Hold the body with one hand and pull away the tentacles with the other. Discard the insides, except for the ink sac, and the internal quill. Cut the tentacles off the head at the level of the eyes and reserve, discarding the rest of the head. Wash the tentacles and body. Prepare the remaining squid in the same way. Finely chop the tentacles.

❖Prepare the stuffing: grind the bread to coarse crumbs in a blender or food processor. Heat the oil in a nonstick 8-in (20-cm) skillet. Add the chopped onion and garlic and cook over low heat for 5 minutes, stirring, without allowing them to color. Add the chopped tentacles, season with salt and pepper, stir well and cook for 5 minutes. Stir in the breadcrumbs and remove from heat. Stuff the squid bodies with this mixture and secure the opening with a toothpick. Drop the tomatoes into boiling water for 10 seconds. Cool under running water, peel, halve and squeeze out the seeds; finely chop the flesh. Empty the squid ink sacs, straining the liquid through a small sieve into a bowl.

❖Heat the oil in a nonstick 10-in (26-cm) sauté pan. Add the stuffed squid, chopped onion and garlic and cook over low heat for 5 minutes, turning frequently. Pour in the wine and evaporate it over high heat. Add the tomatoes, salt, pepper and cayenne and cook, stirring, until the tomatoes give out no more liquid. Stir in the squid ink and simmer for 30 minutes. Serve hot.

SERVES 4   *Photograph page 69*

LES BAISERS
Kisses

The Provençal name for these is lei poutoun. *It is the delicious kissing sounds made by the diners as they savor this dish that gives it its name.*

4 lb (2 kg) fresh spinach
1 tablespoon olive oil
1 onion, about 3 oz (100 g), finely chopped
salt

4 lb (2 kg) clams
For the *aïoli*:
1 clove garlic, coarsely chopped
1 egg yolk
2 pinches of salt
3 tablespoons peanut oil
3 tablespoons olive oil

❖Prepare the *aïoli*: combine the garlic, egg yolk and salt in a blender or food processor and mix for 10 seconds. With machine running, pour in the peanut oil and then the olive oil, blending to make a thick emulsion. Set aside.

❖Trim the stalks from the spinach; wash and drain the leaves. Cut the leaves into strips ⅜ in (1 cm) wide.

❖Heat the oil in a large nonstick sauté pan. Add the onion and cook over low heat, stirring, for 3 minutes or until golden. Add the spinach and season with salt. Mix well and cook, covered, for 5 minutes or until the spinach is very soft.

❖Wash the clams in several changes of water; drain. Transfer to a large pot and cook over high heat, turning constantly, until all have opened. Discard any unopened clams. Remove the clams with a slotted spoon and keep warm; discard the shells.

❖Strain the clam cooking liquid into a small saucepan and boil until reduced by half. Blend into the *aïoli*. Turn this mixture into the spinach and stir well. Add the clams, stir and serve immediately.

SERVES 4

CALMARS AU RIZ
Squid with Rice

The name calmar *comes from the old French* calamar, *an eighteenth-century word for a desk. Like a desk, squid contains all that is necessary for writing: ink and a pen (the name given to its small transparent bone).*

2½ lb (1.2 kg) medium squid
8 oz (250 g) ripe tomatoes
2 onions, about 3 oz (100 g) each, finely chopped
3 cloves garlic, finely chopped
3 tablespoons olive oil
4 pinches of saffron threads
1 teaspoon *herbes de Provence* (see glossary)
1 teaspoon fennel seeds
salt and freshly ground pepper
2 pinches of cayenne pepper
2 cups (10 oz/300 g) Camargue (long-grain) rice
3 cups (24 fl oz/750 ml) water

❖Place one squid on a work surface. Hold the body with one hand and pull away the tentacles with the other. Discard the insides and the internal quill. Cut the tentacles off the head at the level of the eyes and reserve, discarding the rest of the head. Wash the tentacles and body; if the latter contains eggs or roe, leave them, as they have an excellent flavor. Cut both the tentacles and the body into ⅜-in (1-cm) crosswise slices. Prepare the remaining squid in the same way.

❖Drop the tomatoes into boiling water for 10 seconds. Cool under running water, then peel, halve and squeeze out the seeds; chop the flesh finely.

❖Cook the squid in a 6-qt (6-l) enameled pot over low

KISSES (front) AND SQUID WITH RICE (rear), PHOTOGRAPHED IN PROVENCE

heat, stirring with a wooden spoon, until they give out no more liquid. Add the chopped onions and garlic, stir again and cook until no more liquid remains. Add the oil, saffron, herbs, fennel seed, salt, pepper, cayenne and rice and cook, stirring, until everything is lightly browned.

❖ Add the tomatoes and water to the pot and bring to boil. Cover and cook until the rice is tender, about 25 minutes. Serve hot, directly from the pot.

SERVES 6

Bretagne/Normandie

CREVETTES AU CIDRE
Shrimp (Prawns) in Cider

This dish is made with small, live shrimp which are caught all year round using a special fine-meshed shrimping net, that is shaped like a pocket about three feet (one meter) deep.

3 cups (24 fl oz/750 ml) dry cider
2 tablespoons coarse sea salt
2 lb (1 kg) small, live shrimp (prawns)
freshly ground pepper
For serving:
whole-grain bread
butter

❖Pour the cider into a large saucepan and bring to boil. Stir in the salt. Add shrimp, return to boil and cook for 1 to 2 minutes.
❖Drain the shrimp and arrange them in a shallow dish. Season with pepper and serve immediately, accompanied by bread and butter.

SERVES 4

Bretagne

LANGOUSTINES DE GUILVINEC
Langoustines, Guilvinec-style

The little port of Guilvinec near Quimper is famous for its fish market. Each day in the late afternoon the fishermen bring in their live catch of fish, shellfish and crustaceans, including tender Norway lobsters of incomparable quality and flavor.

12 langoustines (king prawns or yabbies), just under 3 oz
    (80 g) each
5 oz (150 g) butter
1 tablespoon chopped fresh tarragon
salt and freshly ground pepper
2 pinches of cayenne pepper
4 pinches of sweet paprika
6 tablespoons lemon juice

❖Preheat oven to 450°F (230°C). Halve the langoustines lengthwise and remove the grainy sac from the head. Arrange the halves in a baking dish just large enough to hold them.
❖Melt 1 oz (25 g) butter in a small saucepan over low heat. Remove from heat and add the tarragon, salt, pepper, cayenne and paprika. Drizzle over the langoustines and bake for 5 minutes.
❖Meanwhile, boil the lemon juice in a small non-aluminum saucepan over high heat until reduced by ⅔. Remove from heat and whisk in the remaining butter, cut into small pieces, until the sauce becomes a thick emulsion. Pour into a sauceboat.
❖Arrange the langoustines on four plates and serve immediately with the lemon butter sauce.

SERVES 4

PHOTOGRAPHED IN BRETAGNE: SHRIMP IN CIDER (top left), COCKLES WITH GARLIC AND PARSLEY (top right, recipe page 74), LOBSTER FOR *HOMARD AU CURRY* (bottom left, recipe page 74) AND LANGOUSTINES, GUILVINEC-STYLE (bottom right)

Bretagne

COQUES À LA FAÇON DE ROZ-SUR-COUESNON
Cockles with Garlic and Parsley

4 lb (2 kg) cockles or pipis
2½ oz (75 g) stale bread, crusts trimmed
2 cloves garlic, finely chopped
4 French shallots, finely chopped
4 tablespoons chopped flat-leaf parsley
2 oz (50 g) butter
freshly ground pepper

❖Wash the cockles in several changes of water, then drain. Grind the bread to coarse crumbs in a blender or food processor. Combine the crumbs with the garlic, shallots and parsley.
❖Transfer the cockles to a large saucepan and place over high heat. Add the butter and pepper and cook the cockles just until they open, turning often with a slotted spoon and regularly sprinkling with the breadcrumb mixture. When all the cockles are open, spoon them with their sauce onto heated plates and serve immediately. Discard any unopened shells.

SERVES 4   *Photograph page 73*

Bretagne

HOMARD AU CURRY
Lobster in Curry Sauce

Bretagne's major ports, such as Saint-Malo, Brest and Lorient, have always been centers for trade with the Indies and America. Curry powder (which in French is sometimes written cari *or* kari) *came into use very early with fish and shellfish, and local curry mixtures were soon developed and sold in small sachets under the name of* cari lorientais. *These were used in the preparation of lobster—then called* le rouge (the red) *—and also Norway lobster, anglerfish, skate, clams, John Dory, chicken and lamb.*

1 live lobster, about 1½ lb (800 g)
2½ oz (75 g) butter
2 tablespoons vegetable oil
salt and freshly ground pepper
1 teaspoon curry powder
1 onion, chopped
3 cloves garlic, chopped
bouquet garni: 1 bay leaf, 1 sprig thyme, 6 sprigs parsley
3 tablespoons calvados
1¼ cups (10 fl oz/300 ml) dry white wine

❖Cook the lobster in boiling water for 3 minutes then cut it in half, separating head from tail and catching the juices in a small saucepan. Split the head in half lengthwise and remove the entrails and stomach; take out the coral and creamy parts and add to the saucepan with the butter. Cut the tails into medallions according to the natural divisions of the shell.
❖Heat the oil in a nonstick 10-in (26-cm) sauté pan over high heat. Add the lobster medallions and cook until they turn red, about 3 minutes, turning constantly. Add salt, pep-

per, curry powder and chopped onion and cook over low heat, stirring, for 3 minutes; do not allow the onion to brown. Add the garlic and bouquet garni and cook, stirring, for 1 minute. Sprinkle in calvados and let it evaporate. Pour in the wine and cook until it is reduced by half, mixing well to obtain a smooth sauce. Transfer the medallions of lobster to a heated plate.
❖Place the small saucepan of butter, coral and creamy parts over low heat and whisk until the butter is melted and foamy. Strain the contents of the sauté pan into the saucepan.
❖Pour this sauce over the lobster and serve immediately.

SERVES 2   *Photograph page 73*

Languedoc

CIVET DE LANGOUSTE AU BANYULS
Rock Lobster in Banyuls Wine

Banyuls is the name of a vin doux naturel, *a wine produced in the cantons of Banyuls, Collioure, Port-Vendres and Cerbère, which is served chilled as an aperitif or a dessert wine. It is made in sweet, demi-sec and brut styles.*

1 lb (500 g) ripe tomatoes
2 live rock lobsters (crayfish), about 2 lb (1 kg) each
3–6 tablespoons vegetable oil
salt and freshly ground pepper
1 carrot, about 3 oz (100 g), peeled and finely chopped
2 onions, about 3 oz (100 g) each, finely chopped
2 French shallots, finely chopped
3 cloves garlic, finely chopped
5 oz (150 g) prosciutto or other raw ham, cut into fine matchsticks
2 pinches of cayenne pepper
3 tablespoons cognac
1 bottle (750 ml) dry Banyuls wine, dry sherry or Madeira

❖Drop the tomatoes into boiling water for 10 seconds. Cool under running water, then peel, halve and squeeze out the seeds. Finely chop the flesh.
❖Drop lobsters in boiling water for 3 minutes then cut them in half, separating the head from the tail and catching the juices in a bowl. Split the heads in half lengthwise, and remove the entrails and stomach; set aside the coral (green when uncooked) and the creamy parts in a bowl. Cut the tails into medallions according to the natural divisions of the shell.
❖Heat the oil in a nonstick 10-in (26-cm) sauté pan over high heat. Lightly brown the lobster medallions for 5 minutes, moving them around in the pan constantly. Season with salt and pepper. Add the chopped vegetables, ham and cayenne and cook for 5 minutes, stirring. Pour in the cognac and let it evaporate over high heat.
❖Remove the lobster medallions from the sauté pan and keep warm. Add the tomatoes and wine to the pan, bring to boil and cook over high heat until reduced by half. Return the lobster to the sauté pan, together with the reserved juices, coral and creamy parts of the lobster, and simmer for 3 minutes. Pour into a shallow serving dish and serve immediately.

SERVES 6

ROCK LOBSTER IN BANYULS WINE (top right), CRAYFISH
LIMOUSIN-STYLE (center left, recipe page 76)
AND GRATIN OF CRAYFISH (bottom right, recipe page 76)
PETER JOHNSON

Limousin

LIMOUSINE D'ÉCREVISSES
Crayfish, Limousin-style

24 live crayfish (small yabbies)
bouquet garni: 1 bay leaf, 1 sprig thyme, 6 sprigs parsley
1 oz (25 g) butter
2 French shallots, finely chopped
salt and freshly ground pepper
2 tablespoons cognac
2 cups (16 fl oz/500 ml) dry white wine
3 tablespoons tomato paste (puree), optional
6 tablespoons heavy (double) cream or crème fraîche
2 egg yolks
2 pinches of cayenne pepper
2 tablespoons chopped fresh tarragon

❖Prepare the crayfish: lift up the central tail fin and twist it to remove the small black vein which runs through the center of the tail. Rinse and drain the crayfish. Tie together the herbs for the bouquet garni.
❖Melt the butter in a nonstick 11-in (28-cm) sauté pan. Add the crayfish, cover and cook for 5 minutes. Add the shallots, season with salt and pepper and cook, stirring, over low heat for 2 minutes. Pour in the cognac and ignite, shaking the pan gently until flames subside. Add the wine, tomato paste and bouquet garni and cook over high heat, stirring, for 2 minutes. Remove the crayfish with a slotted spoon and keep warm.
❖Boil the cooking liquid until syrupy, about 5 minutes. Add half the cream and cook for 2 more minutes. Remove the bouquet garni.
❖Beat the egg yolks with a fork; beat in the remaining cream. Pour into the sauté pan and remove from heat; stir with a wooden spoon until the sauce is smooth and thickened. Add the crayfish and cayenne and reheat, stirring, for 30 seconds.
❖Turn the crayfish and sauce onto a large platter, sprinkle with chopped tarragon and serve immediately.

SERVES 4   *Photograph page 75*

Savoie/Lorraine

GRATIN DE QUEUES D'ÉCREVISSES
Gratin of Crayfish

There are innumerable varieties of this little freshwater crustacean. Of all the types that are cooked and enjoyed throughout France, the best is undoubtedly the "red-footed" river crayfish.

1 onion, about 2 oz (50 g)
2 cloves
2 cloves garlic, peeled and halved
1 carrot, about 2 oz (50 g), peeled and sliced
1 celery stalk
1 sprig thyme
1 bay leaf
4 sprigs parsley
6 peppercorns
2½ qt (2.5 l) water
salt
6 lb (3 kg) live crayfish (yabbies)
8 oz (250 g) mushrooms
1 oz (25 g) butter
freshly ground pepper
1 teaspoon cornstarch (cornflour)
6 tablespoons heavy (double) cream or crème fraîche
2 egg yolks
2 tablespoons dry breadcrumbs
2 tablespoons grated Emmenthaler cheese

❖Peel the onion and stud with cloves. Place the onion, garlic, carrot and celery in a large saucepan with the thyme, bay leaf, parsley and peppercorns. Pour in the water and bring to boil. Season with salt and let simmer 15 minutes.
❖Meanwhile, prepare the crayfish: lift up the central tail fin and twist it to remove the small black vein which runs through the center of the tail. Rinse and drain the crayfish.
❖Add the crayfish to the stock, cover and cook for 5 minutes. Drain, reserving the stock, and let the crayfish cool to lukewarm.
❖Shell the crayfish, setting aside in a bowl the tail meat, the coral and the creamy parts from the heads. Roughly crush the shells and return them to the stock. Cook over high heat for 10 minutes.
❖Meanwhile, trim the mushroom stalks; wash the mushrooms, drain and slice thinly. Melt half the butter in a nonstick 10-in (26-cm) skillet and cook the mushrooms until they no longer exude moisture and are golden. Add to the crayfish.
❖Strain the stock into a saucepan and boil until reduced to about 3 cups (24 fl oz/750 ml). Season with salt and pepper if necessary.
❖Preheat broiler (griller). Combine the cornstarch with half the cream, using a small whisk. Beat the egg yolks with a fork and beat in the remaining cream. Pour the cornstarch mixture into the reduced stock and simmer until thickened, about 3 minutes, stirring constantly with a wooden spoon. Remove from heat and blend in the egg yolk mixture. Keep the sauce warm over low heat without allowing it to boil.
❖With the remaining butter, grease a shallow broilerproof dish just large enough to hold the crayfish, mushrooms and sauce. Spread the crayfish and mushrooms evenly over the base and cover with sauce. Combine the breadcrumbs and cheese and sprinkle over the surface. Broil until crumbs are lightly browned. Serve immediately.

SERVES 6   *Photograph page 75*

Champagne

ÉCREVISSES AU CHAMPAGNE
Crayfish in Champagne

36 live crayfish (small yabbies)
2 oz (50 g) butter
3 French shallots, finely chopped
salt and freshly ground pepper
1 tablespoon *marc de champagne* or cognac
¾ cup (6 fl oz/200 ml) dry champagne
¾ cup (6 fl oz/200 ml) heavy (double) cream or crème fraîche
2 pinches of cayenne pepper
1 tablespoon chopped fresh tarragon

INGREDIENTS FOR CRAYFISH IN CHAMPAGNE

❖Prepare the crayfish: lift up the central tail fin and twist it to remove the small black vein which runs through the center of the tail. Rinse and drain the crayfish.

❖Melt the butter in a 10-in (26-cm) sauté pan. Add the shallots and cook, stirring, for 3 minutes or until softened. Add the crayfish and cook for 5 minutes, stirring constantly. Season with salt and pepper, then pour in the *marc* and ignite, shaking the pan gently until flames subside. Add the champagne, bring to boil, cover and simmer for 5 minutes.

❖Transfer the crayfish to a serving platter with a slotted spoon and keep warm. Boil the cooking liquid over high heat until reduced by half. Stir in the cream and cook over high heat for 2 to 3 minutes or until the sauce is slightly thickened. Season with cayenne pepper and strain over the crayfish. Sprinkle with chopped tarragon and serve immediately.

SERVES 4

Bretagne

PALOURDES FARCIES À LA LORIENTAISE
Stuffed Clams Lorient-style

2 oz (50 g) salted butter
2 onions, about 3 oz (100 g) each, finely chopped
freshly ground pepper
24 clams
coarse sea salt
4 tablespoons dry breadcrumbs

❖ Melt the butter in a nonstick 9-in (22-cm) skillet. Add the onions, season with pepper and cook over low heat until soft, about 5 minutes, stirring from time to time with a wooden spoon.

❖ Preheat broiler (griller). Wash the clams in several changes of water; drain. Transfer to a large pot, cover with water and cook over high heat, turning constantly, until all have opened. Remove the clams with a slotted spoon and discard any unopened shells. Strain the cooking liquid into the onions, stir, and boil until reduced by half.

❖ Pour a layer of coarse sea salt onto each of four individual gratin dishes or snail plates. Arrange 6 clams on each. Sprinkle with some of the onion mixture, then the breadcrumbs.

❖ Broil close to the heat source for 3 minutes or until the breadcrumbs are lightly browned. Serve immediately in the same dishes.

SERVES 4   *Photograph page 105*

Pays Basque

SALADE D'ARAIGNÉE
Salad of Spider Crab

In spring and winter the spider crabs are delicious. They have fine, delicate-tasting flesh, a triangular, convex shell and long pitted claws. The females, with their plentiful coral, are the most flavorsome. Spider crabs are abundant in the Atlantic and are also found in the Mediterranean and the English Channel.

bouquet garni: 1 bay leaf, 1 sprig thyme, 6 sprigs parsley
2 tablespoons coarse sea salt
2 tablespoons wine vinegar
4 live spider (Blue Swimmer) crabs, about 1½ lb (800 g) each
4 eggs
1 teaspoon strong mustard
salt and freshly ground pepper
⅔ cup (5 fl oz/150 ml) extra virgin olive oil
2 tablespoons chopped mint
1 teaspoon lemon juice
2 pinches of cayenne pepper

❖ In a large pot, bring 3 qt (3 l) water to boil. Tie together the herbs of the bouquet garni and add to the water with the sea salt and vinegar. Plunge in the spider crabs and return to boil, then cook 15 minutes.

❖ Drain the cooked crabs and let cool, then shell. Roughly shred and set aside the meat, the coral and the creamy parts from the shells. Scrub the shells under running water; set aside.

❖ Place the eggs in a saucepan and cover with cold water. Bring to the boil, then cook for 6 minutes. Shell the eggs and cut in half. Turn the yolks into a bowl, add the mustard, salt and pepper and mix well with a fork. Whisk in the oil in a thin stream until the sauce becomes a thick emulsion. Stir in the mint, lemon juice and cayenne. Cut the egg whites into small dice and add to the bowl.

❖ Add the sauce to the crab mixture and toss carefully. Divide among the shells and serve immediately.

SERVES 4

Pays Basque

ARAIGNÉE FARCIE
Stuffed Spider Crab

2 tablespoons coarse sea salt
4 live spider (Blue Swimmer) crabs, about 1½ lb (800 g) each
1 lb (500 g) ripe tomatoes
2 tablespoons vegetable oil
1 onion, about 3 oz (100 g), finely chopped
1 leek, white part only, washed and finely chopped
2 French shallots, finely chopped
1 carrot, about 3 oz (100 g), peeled and finely chopped
1 tender celery stalk with leaves, finely chopped
1 fresh chili pepper, finely chopped
3 tablespoons dry sherry
6 tablespoons chicken stock
salt and freshly ground pepper
1 tablespoon chopped flat-leaf parsley
1 tablespoon dry breadcrumbs
1 tablespoon freshly and finely grated Parmesan cheese

❖ In a large pot, bring 3 qt (3 l) water to boil. Add the sea salt, plunge in the spider crabs and return to boil, then cook 15 minutes.

❖ Drop the tomatoes into boiling water for 10 seconds, then cool under running water. Peel, halve and squeeze out the seeds; chop the flesh finely.

❖ Drain the cooked crabs and let cool, then shell. Roughly shred and set aside the meat, the coral and the creamy parts from the shell. Scrub the shells under running water; set aside.

❖ Preheat oven to 450°F (230°C). Heat the oil in a nonstick 10-in (26-cm) sauté pan. Add the chopped vegetables and cook, stirring, over moderate heat for 5 minutes or until golden. Add the sherry and cook until evaporated, stirring constantly. Stir in the tomatoes and chicken stock; season with salt and pepper. Cook over high heat until all liquid is evaporated, about 5 minutes. Add the crab mixture and cook, stirring, for 2 minutes. Remove from heat and stir in the parsley.

❖ Divide the filling among the crab shells. Combine the breadcrumbs and cheese and sprinkle over the surface. Bake until lightly browned, about 15 minutes. Serve hot.

SERVES 4

STUFFED SPIDER CRAB (left), SALAD OF SPIDER CRAB (bottom right), AND SQUID COOKED IN THEIR OWN INK (top right, recipe page 70)
PIERRE HUSSENOT/AGENCE TOP

Normandie

CRABE FARCI
Stuffed Crab

These large crabs, or tourteaux, *are caught all along the coasts of Normandie and Bretagne. They have two huge and fleshy pincers, and are also known by other names:* dormeurs *(sleepers),* endormis, pouparts, clos-poing ...

bouquet garni: 1 bay leaf, 1 sprig thyme, 6 sprigs parsley
2 tablespoons coarse sea salt
2 tablespoons wine vinegar
2 large live crabs, about 2 lb (1 kg) each
3 tablespoons milk
3 oz (100 g) fresh bread, crusts trimmed
2 tablespoons calvados
1 tablespoon vegetable oil
1 onion, about 3 oz (100 g), finely chopped
2 French shallots, finely chopped
2 cloves garlic, mashed or pressed
2 tablespoons chopped flat-leaf parsley
salt and freshly ground pepper
2 pinches of cayenne pepper
4 pinches of freshly grated nutmeg
1 tablespoon dry breadcrumbs
1 oz (30 g) butter

❖In a large pot, bring 3 qt (3 l) water to boil. Tie together the herbs of the bouquet garni and add to the water with the salt and vinegar. Plunge the crabs into the boiling liquid and return to boil. Reduce heat and simmer gently for 20 minutes.
❖Bring the milk to boil in a small saucepan. Remove from heat and crumble in the bread. Drain the cooked crabs and let cool, then shell. Set aside the crabmeat, the coral and the creamy parts from the shell. Scrub the shells under running water; set aside. Remove the meat from the claws. Roughly shred the crabmeat, the coral and the creamy parts and add the calvados.
❖Preheat oven to 450°F (230°C). Heat the oil in a nonstick 10-in (26-cm) skillet. Add the chopped onion and shallots and cook over low heat, stirring, for 3 minutes or until golden. Add the garlic and cook, stirring, for 1 minute longer. Remove from heat and add the milk mixture, parsley, salt, pepper, cayenne and nutmeg. Add the crab-meat mixture and mix well.
❖Divide the stuffing evenly between the two shells. Sprinkle with breadcrumbs and dot with butter. Bake until lightly browned, about 15 minutes. Serve hot.

SERVES 2   *Photograph pages 60 – 61*

Ile de France

HOMARD À L'AMERICAINE
Lobster, American-style

There is always some confusion over whether this dish should be called lobster "à l'américaine" or "à l'armoricaine." In 1854 a French cook from Sète, by the name of Pierre Fraisse, after a long career on the other side of the Atlantic opened a restaurant in Paris. The story goes that he named this lobster dish for his American

clients, when improvising with a sauce of white wine, champagne and tomatoes reminiscent of his Mediterranean home. The "armoricaine" version of the dish, reputed to have been created by a cook from Bretagne, has not yet been found.

1 live lobster, about 2 lb (1 kg)
3 oz (100 g) butter
12 oz (400 g) ripe tomatoes
1 clove garlic
bouquet garni: 1 bay leaf, 1 sprig thyme, 6 sprigs parsley
1 tablespoon vegetable oil
salt and freshly ground pepper
4 French shallots, finely chopped
1 celery stalk, strings removed, finely chopped
1 carrot, about 3 oz (100 g), peeled and finely chopped
3 tablespoons cognac, preferably *fine champagne*
1¼ cups (10 fl oz/300 ml) dry white wine
2 pinches of cayenne pepper

❖Cook the lobster in boiling water for 3 minutes then cut it in half, separating head from tail and catching the juices in a small saucepan. Split the head in half lengthwise and remove the entrails and stomach; take out the coral and creamy parts and add to the saucepan with half the butter. Cut the tails into medallions according to the natural divisions of the shell.
❖ Drop the tomatoes into boiling water for 10 seconds. Cool under running water, then peel, halve and squeeze out the seeds. Finely chop the flesh and set aside in a colander. Crush the clove of garlic with the side of a cleaver. Tie together the herbs of the bouquet garni.
❖Heat the oil in a nonstick 10-in (26-cm) sauté pan. Add the remaining butter and, when melted, the lobster medallions. Cook over high heat until the lobster turns red, about 3 minutes, turning constantly. Season with salt and pepper. Add the shallots, celery, carrot, bouquet garni and garlic and cook, stirring, over low heat for 3 minutes; do not allow the vegetables to brown. Pour in the cognac and let it evaporate. Transfer the medallions of lobster to a plate. Pour the wine into the pan and let it evaporate. Add the tomatoes and cayenne and mix well to obtain a smooth sauce. Return the lobster to the sauté pan and simmer for 5 minutes.
❖Meanwhile, place the small saucepan of butter, coral and creamy parts over low heat and whisk until the butter is melted and foamy. Remove the bouquet garni from the sauté pan. Add the contents of the small saucepan, stirring with a wooden spoon. Pour the lobster and its sauce into a shallow dish and serve immediately.

SERVES 2

THE NORTH, ALSACE, LORRAINE

Solid, rugged, joyful

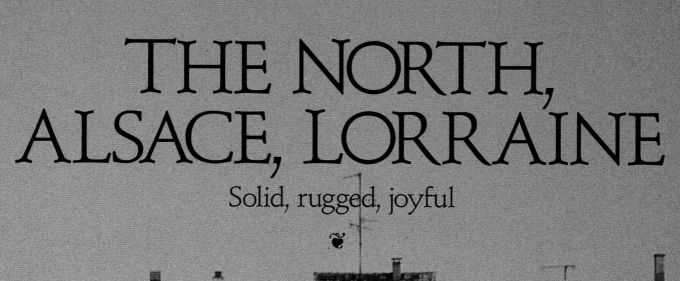

LEO MEIER

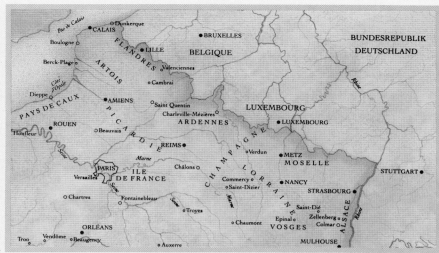

THE NORTH, ALSACE, LORRAINE

Solid, rugged, joyful

The north of France: a cold country, an industrialized country; even in France, people have a wrong impression of the warm-welcoming north, with its stretches of sandy dunes, its fields as green as those of Kent or Sussex in nearby England, its little cottages of red or whitewashed brick with glazed tile roofs, its substantial and copious meals. Who knows that the best cheesemaker in France — Philippe Olivier — lives at Boulogne-sur-Mer, where he ripens not only the best Bries, Comtés, Beauforts, but more than these, the strong cheeses of the north: the *Gris* from Lille, otherwise known as *Vieux Puant* (Old Smelly); the *Boulette* from Cambrai or Avesnes; the *Larron* from Ors and, above all, the Maroilles, reputedly the finest of the strong cheeses. It is the product of the sinuous green Thiérache, a region of woodlands, orchards, cider-apple trees, fresh butter, thick cream and rabbits hopping in the meadows; this Normandy of the north is a fresh, green pastureland that supplies Paris with milk.

But which north are we talking about? In reality, Flanders is divided in two — the French part and the Belgian part. The two capitals, on either side of the border, testify to its splendid treasures: Gothic mansions, brick houses, gabled roofs, the great square and belfry in Lille and in Anvers. The *waterzoï*, a kind of pot-au-feu made either with freshwater fish or with chicken, is common to both regions. So, too, the *potjevfleish* — a "pot of meat" consisting of veal, bacon and rabbit. But the Flemish cuisine is so rich that you would be afraid of leaving out something if you tried to list all the specialties: soups made with beer or with beets, *andouillettes* from Cambrai, *craquelots* from Dun-

PICKING GRAPES NEAR CHÂTEAU-THIERRY IN THE CHAMPAGNE REGION.

kirk, *flamiche, goyère, carbonnades*. It is a litany that expresses itself in solid dishes.

The northerner is a worker, his climate harsh; he needs foods that will help him resist it, but they do not preclude sophistication. The typical regional drink is beer, which turns up in various dishes — chicken cooked in beer, eel cooked in beer — and accompanies them all, starting with the charcuterie, and the *flamiches* or *flamiques*. These latter vary between Flanders and Picardy — in other words, between the north and the south of the north. In Flanders the *flamiche* is made with the runny Maroilles cheese and in Picardy with leeks, but in both cases it takes the form of a thick, savory tart. The charcuterie products are legion: the traditional *andouillette* of Cambrai, the smoked tongue of Valenciennes, and the country-style sausages, *andouilles* and black puddings that are specialties of the region bounded by Berck-Plage, Calais and Aire-sur-la-Lys (and which have English counterparts on the other side of the Channel). Next to these are the *hochepot*, which is nothing other than a pot-au-feu, and the Flemish *carbonnade*, a dish of beef and chopped onions cooked in beer.

But it must not be forgotten that the north is primarily a maritime region. Sole, eel, salmon, herring, and the fish soup called *caudière* at Berck are the pride of the Artois region and of Flanders. Likewise the seafoods from the shores of Dunkirk: oysters, *tourteaux* (a species of crab), lobsters that are prepared *au gratin* in the same way as scallops.

All blend sagely with the local vegetables: boiled or fried potatoes, beets, red and green cabbages, cauliflowers that are firm and tender at the same time. All are proper precedents to the desserts and sweets of the region: the sugar tarts (*tartes au sucre*), *couques* and, above all, the celebrated *bêtises* of Cambrai. These are nothing more than mint-flavored boiled sweets, slightly puffed and hollow. They are said to have been invented by chance, thanks to a blunder by an apprentice sweetmaker in the firm of Afchin, who simply mixed up his ingredients.

Sweets are the glory of Lorraine, a proud country, by its own wish austere and industrial, which has suffered in all wars. But the wars have also left sweet specialties in each village. The trenches of Verdun, the ossuary of Douaumont, the souvenirs of the Great War: they are here. But right beside these you will discover the famous madeleines of Commercy, the cream-filled puffs of Pont-à-Mousson. *Bergamotes* — pulled candy flavored with bergamot, which has the fragrance of a Sicilian lemon — are the pride of Nancy, the capital, together with the gold-colored wrought iron gates of the Place Stanislas, one of the most harmonious squares in the world.

It was Stanislas Leczinsky, exiled king of Poland, and father-in-law of Louis XV, who brought aid and prosperity to the region. The arts have always flourished around Nancy, which has lent its name to the French school of Art Nouveau. Majorelle (who was responsible for the woodwork of the restaurant Lucas-Carton in Paris), Daum (whose crystal has lost none of its sparkle), Gruber, Gallé...all had their beginnings here and all have the right to have their work displayed in the museum. Baccarat crystal, fashioned into some of the most prestigious glasses and carafes in France, is produced only a few kilometers away. Also of nearby origin are a genial local wine, the *Gris de Toul*, and above all a spirit distilled from the mirabelle plum that is the most highly reputed in the whole country. The local orchards are prolific (mirabelle and quetsch plums, cherries); they contour around the inspired hill of Sion-Vaudémont, beloved of Maurice Barrès, the great nationalist writer whose roots were in Lorraine. The Meuse and Moselle rivers still offer carp, pike and trout to be nurtured in ponds.

The local charcuterie is no less prolific. Here pig is king, and jellied suckling pig, a specialty of Metz — the great neighbor and rival of Nancy — is his representative. From the pig come blood puddings, smoked hams and the smoked bacon that gives *tourte* and quiche lorraine their flavor.

Even if one adds to the list of gastronomic riches of Lorraine the macaroons of Nancy, the gingerbread of Remiremont in the Vosges, the kirsch of Fougerolles, the classic *potée lorraine* (a kind of pot-au-feu with cabbage and sausage) — it is still not complete. Lorraine presents itself as hard-working, strict, more discreet than frivolous; and yet it hides in its pocket more than a few treasures to delight the gourmet.

Contrasting with the unknown north and the modest Lorraine is exuberant, exceptionally affluent Alsace. Eating in Alsace is virtually a religious experience; it is impossible to be a well-brought-up Alsatian and not do honor to the table. Helpings in Alsace are two or three times bigger than anywhere else — but the people of Alsace will tell you that these are "normal" size.

If Alsace has a good appetite, it is because — so they say — it has swung between France and Germany for so long and to such an extent that it no longer knows which side it belongs to. Even in Strasbourg, the capital of the region, food holds a royal position: the patisseries and tea salons are monuments, the charcuterie windows are works of art and bistros are institutions.

Besides, they are not really bistros, but rather places where wine is sold — *winstubs*, established long ago by wine merchants who wanted to pass off their surplus production to the citizens of the towns. These *winstubs* are an expression of the gourmet soul of Alsace, marked by conviviality, familiarity and a respect for traditions, and here you discover the simple marvels of the region. First of all, pork, in all forms: jellied (parsleyed brawn, or *presskopf*), smoked shoulder (*wadele*) or fillet (*kasler*), stuffed belly (*saumawen*) or smoked hocks to go with sauerkraut.

Today the snails often come from China, the freshwater crayfish from Yugoslavia, the frogs from Egypt or the Vendée. But traditions persist in spite of the pollution that has decimated the river catches. In Sundgau, the most southerly region of Alsace, right next to the Swiss Jura, fresh lake carp can still be found to be served fried. Along the Rhine, restaurants still offer the *matelote*, a dish that combines perch, pike and eel in a sauce made with cream and the local white wine — even if the fish often come from Holland. The Kockersberg is the region of hops, used for beer, but the hop shoots — asparaguslike in flavor — make a dish for a king. South of Strasbourg, from Geispolsheim to Krautergersheim (literally "Cabbage-town"), stretch fields of cabbages for sauerkraut. This is the territory of the sauerkraut that is so closely identified with Alsace; it is washed and gently stewed, flavored with bacon and eaten with all kinds of local charcuterie, from smoked and fresh sausages to smoked shoulder and black puddings. Never ask someone from Alsace which is the best sauerkraut; they will always reply that it is their mother's.

Another family dish that is emblematic of Alsace is the *baeckeoffe*, a celebrated casserole of three different meats (beef, veal and pork) layered with potato and moistened with white wine. It is placed in the oven before Sunday Mass and is ready to eat, piping hot, when the family returns from the service.

We should not forget that foie gras originated in Alsace, since it was invented by Jean-Pierre Clause, cook to the marshal of Contades, military governor of the town of Strasbourg from 1762 to 1788. Nor that the goose is here a privileged bird and can be paired with the most sublime accompaniments. Nor that the game (roe deer and red

PRACTICING FIDDLE SOLOS ON THE BANKS OF THE RIVER SEINE.

deer, fawns and does, wild boar, pheasants, partridges, mallard ducks) frolic and fly above the prolific forests of the Vosges and the fertile plains along the Rhine, known as the Ried.

Alsatian patisserie? It is one of the best endowed in the world, heiress of the traditions of Vienna and *Mitteleuropa* — and not only for the traditional (and dry) *kugelhopf*, which is served for Sunday breakfast. In Strasbourg, the patisseries are still full of the classic French *mille-feuilles*, *éclairs* and *religieuses*, in addition to German-style Black Forest cake (with chocolate and cherries), cheesecakes, walnut cakes and apple fritters. And the tea salons are legion, their cozy, welcoming, wood-paneled interiors offering, according to the season, plum, cherry or rhubarb tarts.

One could hardly conclude this gourmet's tour of Alsace without listing the wines, sprightly and serious, that the fair province produces, along a ribbon of road that stretches for some one hundred and fifty kilometers from Marlenheim to Thann, with a small enclave in the north at Cleebourg. The fresh Muscat, with its aroma of fresh-picked grapes; the smooth, honest Pinot Blanc; the light, joyous Sylvaner; the elegant, well-bred Riesling; the smoky-flavored Tokay-Pinot Gris, well-made and powerful; the Gewürztraminer, velvety, spicy, rose-scented; the Pinot Noir, which can produce anything from an unpretentious rosé to a classy, oak-aged red. And then the sparkling wine, prepared in the traditional style according to methods practiced in Champagne. And again, the classic spirits: raspberry, plum, pear, elderberry, holly, and wild serviceberry. Not to mention the *marc* distilled from grapes.

Now, after all this, try to tell a gourmand that bountiful Alsace is not the most privileged region!

FISH

The sea's great bounty

QUAINT DECORATIONS LIKE THIS ONE IN CANCALE REVEAL THE BRETON AFFINITY
WITH THE SEA AND ITS BOUNTY.

FISH

The sea's great bounty

Oh, the magnificent coasts! From Dunkirk to Menton, France has four coasts: on the North Sea, the Channel, the Atlantic Ocean and the Mediterranean. This last-mentioned, tideless, has seen its catches diminish. In the north, however, the herring and mackerel that are the mainstay of the port of Boulogne are still plentiful. They are smoked immediately, in the port, before being exported to all parts of the globe. Sardines, which do very nicely in Brittany, are the success story of the port of Quiberon. The two important local canning concerns — the Quiberonnaise and the Belle-Iloise — have even developed a reputation among gastronomes for their tinned sardines in oil, which are turned over periodically and which, like wine, appear to improve with age. An abundance of tuna is fished at Saint-Jean-de-Luz, in the Basque country, and anchovies are the pride of Collioure, on the Mediterranean close to the border.

Although they still form the basis of some superb regional dishes, these are popular, everyday fish rather than gourmet specialties. But to tell the truth, the ways of dealing with fish have changed. Less and less often is the flavor of the fish hidden by complex sauces. Simple treatments — pan-frying, grilling, steaming and oven-baking — are often sympathetically paired with flavored butters, or vegetable-based sauces, or a reduced fish stock (*fumet*). The sole, a worthy flatfish whose cousins include the dab, the lemon sole, the plaice and the flounder, is frequently caught in the North Sea and the Atlantic; it has a delicate, firm flesh which comes away easily from its bones. The ideal method of preparation is *à la poêle*, in the frying pan (also known as *au plat*), dressed with melted butter, and this is the sensible principle behind the renowned *sole meunière*.

But each region takes care to complement its fish with its own particular aromas — peppers in the south, cider in Normandy, muscadet in the region of Nantes, garlic around Nice and in Provence, a Riesling sauce in Alsace, aromatic fennel around the Mediterranean, as in the classic grilled bass. And of course it should be remembered that the hazards of geography change the names of some fish. After leaving the shores of the Mediterranean, sea bass is no longer *loup* but *bar* in the ocean and *louvine* in the Gulf of Gascony. Similarly, the *baudroie* or anglerfish of the southern coasts becomes the *lotte* of the north.

PREVIOUS PAGES: AÏOLI FEAST (recipe page 93), PHOTOGRAPHED IN PROVENCE
PIERRE HUSSENOT/AGENCE TOP

LA ROCHELLE, ONE OF FRANCE'S LOVELIEST PORTS, HAS BEEN INHABITED SINCE THE TWELTH CENTURY WHEN IT WAS A FISHING VILLAGE SET ATOP A ROCKY PLATFORM IN THE MIDDLE OF THE EXPANSIVE SALT MARSHES.

THE FRESHEST FISH, USED TO CREATE THE TASTY DISHES UNIQUE TO EACH REGION, ARE ALWAYS AVAILABLE THROUGHOUT FRANCE.

Are the fish so different from one coast to another? Here again, each region leaves its mark. Brill, sole, the delicate red mullet and the coarser gurnard, cod, hake, whiting, sea bass and John Dory may all be simply grilled, with a sprinkling of herbs in the south or combined in more complex preparations in the north. Once more, it is a question of climate: in the one, the dish is kept light; in the other, it is enriched.

Take the soup of little rockfish, served as simply as possible in Corsica and around the Mediterranean, with bones, tails and heads to provide the aroma that encompasses the total flavor and essence of the sea. On the other hand, the *caudière berckoise*, prepared in the north between Berck-Plage and Dunkirk, is enriched with potatoes, onions, white wine, garlic and cream. *Ttoro*, the soup of the fishermen of Saint-Jean-de-Luz, combines oil, pimento, tomatoes and small red peppers in the Basque style. The *chaudrée* of Aunis and Saintonge, prepared in the Charentes, combines eel with fish from the sea and local butter. Potatoes turn up again in the Breton *cotriade* in company with sorrel, salted butter and vinegar. These are five different versions of one dish: five versions in which the sea and the coast marry with the countryside of the immediate hinterland.

At one time, freshwater fish were plentiful in the rivers, but these have been polluted by industry, devastated by petrochemicals, and literally ruined. But fish farming has restored to honor the carp, tench, pike, shad, even the salmon, which once more are swimming up the rivers.

The Loire salmon are surrounded by an almost mythical aura. Their delicate pink flesh, at the same time solid and substantial, has as its standard accompaniment butter flavored with shallot, vinegar and white wine — the celebrated *beurre blanc* or *beurre nantais*, which pairs equally well with turbot and pike. But farmed salmon is easier to find than river salmon. In the lakes of Savoy and the Auvergne fine fish still abound, especially in winter: trout, *fera*, perch and the esteemed but rare *omble-chevalier*.

If the pike-perch often come from Holland, the carp, which enter into Jewish cuisine either cold or stuffed, are reappearing in the lakes of Berry and in Alsace, where they are simply fried, and in Sologne, where it is customary to cook them with red wine and small cubes of salt pork. But freshwater fish are often prepared as a mousse, or a forcemeat, or in quenelles — like the pike quenelles that sealed the reputation of the *mères* of Lyons. Such a compact presentation solves the problem of their many bones and coarse white flesh.

Those dishes that pay due homage to fish, considering it the centerpiece of the dinner, do not hesitate to combine several more or less delicate species, accompanied by a *sauce rouille*, or garlic (*aïoli*), or with red or white wine.

For fish lovers, the special treats often depend on rare species like the *pibales* or *civelles*, eel fingerlings which the fishermen of the Basque, Aquitaine and Charentes regions haul in during rough weather. They are cooked with garlic, vinegar, olive oil and dried red pepper — these are the simple ingredients which enhance the eels' natural flavor without losing the freshness and vitality of the open sea.

OBLIVIOUS TO THEIR IDYLLIC SURROUNDINGS, FISHERMEN FROM SAUMUR ARE INTENT ON CATCHING LOIRE RIVER SALMON.

LEO MEIER

Provence

GRAND AÏOLI

Aïoli Feast

The word aïoli *is Provençal, derived from* ail *(garlic) and* huile *(oil). The sauce gives its name to this dish which in Provence is traditionally served on Good Friday.*

4 lb (2 kg) salt cod fillets
2 lb (1 kg) shellfish (large sea snails, whelks, clams or cockles)
salt and freshly ground pepper
10 small artichokes
2 lb (1 kg) small carrots, peeled
2 lb (1 kg) small leeks, trimmed
1 lb (500 g) small green beans
10 medium boiling potatoes, peeled
1 cauliflower, separated into small florets
10 eggs

For the *aïoli*:
6 cloves garlic
2 teaspoons strong mustard
3 egg yolks
salt
2 cups (16 fl oz/500 ml) extra virgin olive oil

❖Soak the salt cod in a large bowl of cold water, skin side up, for 12 hours, changing the water 3 times.
❖Rinse the shellfish and place in a saucepan. Cover with cold water and bring to boil. Remove the scum during the first 5 minutes of cooking, then season liberally with salt and simmer gently for 45 minutes. Drain the shellfish and either leave them in their shells or remove them and keep warm.
❖Discard the bruised outside leaves of the artichokes and trim the heart, cutting off the spiky tips. Cook all the vegetables separately in boiling salted water until slightly crisp. Drain and keep warm. Hard-cook the eggs for 10 minutes, then cool and shell.
❖Drain the salt cod and transfer to a large pot of cold water, skin side down. Bring to boil over low heat, then reduce heat and cook at the barest simmer for 10 minutes. Drain and cool to lukewarm.
❖Meanwhile, prepare the *aïoli*: force the garlic through a press into a shallow bowl. Add the mustard, egg yolks and salt and stir well. Set aside for 1 minute, then add the oil in a thin stream, whisking until the mixture is quite firm. (The *aïoli* may also be prepared in a food processor.)
❖Arrange the lukewarm salt cod, shellfish and vegetables on a large platter. Add the hard-cooked eggs, and offer the *aïoli* separately: each diner takes a little *aïoli* and dips the pieces of salt cod, shellfish and vegetables into it before eating them.

SERVES 8–10 *Photograph pages 88 – 89*

Bretagne

SOLE MEUNIÈRE

Sole Meunière

*Before the days of nonstick pans, fish had to be floured before being pan-fried in butter, which accounts for the origin of the name of this dish (*la meunière *is a miller's wife or female owner of a flour mill). The name still applies to any fish cooked in butter.*

4 sole, about 6 oz (200 g) each
salt and freshly ground pepper
5 oz (150 g) salted butter
1 tablespoon fresh lemon juice
For serving:
2 tablespoons chopped flat-leaf parsley

❖Ask the fishmonger to clean and skin the sole. Rinse them and pat dry. Season with salt and pepper.
❖Using two nonstick 10-in (26-cm) skillets, melt half the butter and cook the sole for 4 minutes on each side. Transfer them to 4 heated plates. Discard the cooking butter in one of the skillets and add the remaining butter. Add the lemon juice and let the butter melt over very low heat. Pour this sauce over the sole, sprinkle with parsley and serve immediately.

SERVES 4

PETER JOHNSON

SOLE MEUNIÈRE

Normandie

SOLE À LA NORMANDE
Sole with Shrimp and Mushrooms

This dish is thought to have been created in 1838 by Monsieur Langlais, chef of a restaurant called Le Rocher de Cancale in the Les Halles quarter of Paris. Its name derives from the fact that M. Langlais used only ingredients typical of Normandie — cream, shrimp and mussels — and almost certainly cider rather than white wine.

4 sole or gemfish, about 8 oz (250 g) each
salt and freshly ground pepper
bouquet garni: 1 bay leaf, 1 sprig thyme, 6 sprigs parsley
1 carrot, peeled and thinly sliced
1 onion, thinly sliced
2 cloves garlic
¾ cup (6 fl oz/200 ml) dry white wine
2 cups (16 fl oz/500 ml) water
1 tablespoon butter

For the garnish:
2 lb (1 kg) mussels
4 French shallots, finely chopped
6 tablespoons dry white wine
4 oz (125 g) small shrimp (prawns)
5 oz (150 g) small mushrooms
1 tablespoon fresh lemon juice

For the sauce:
2 egg yolks
¾ cup (6 fl oz/200 ml) heavy (double) cream or crème fraîche

❖Ask the fishmonger to fillet the fish and to keep the heads and bones. Rinse the fillets and pat dry. Season with salt and pepper. Tie together the herbs for the bouquet garni.
❖Place the heads and bones of the fish in a pot and add the carrot, onion, bouquet garni and whole garlic cloves. Pour in the wine and water and bring to boil. Simmer for 20 minutes to obtain a rich and flavorful stock, or *fumet*.
❖Meanwhile, prepare the garnish. Scrub the mussels under running water and remove the beards. Place them in a large saucepan with the shallots and wine and cook over high heat, turning often, until they open. Discard any unopened shells. Drain and remove the mussels from their shells. Strain the cooking liquid into a saucepan and set aside. Plunge the shrimp into simmering salted water for 1 minute, then drain and shell. Trim the mushrooms, rinse and pat dry; cut into quarters. Place in another saucepan and add the lemon juice. Season with salt and pepper and cook over high heat until the mushrooms give out no more liquid. Combine the mushrooms, mussels and shrimp in one saucepan and keep warm.
❖Preheat oven to 425°F (215°C). Strain the fumet. Using 1 tablespoon butter, grease a baking dish. Lay the fillets of sole in the dish. Pour the fumet over, cover the dish with waxed paper or aluminum foil and bake for 10 minutes.
❖Lift out the fillets with a slotted spoon and arrange on 4 heated plates. Surround with the mixture of mushrooms, shrimp and mussels.
❖Strain the fish cooking liquid into the saucepan of mussel liquid. Boil over high heat until reduced to a syrupy consistency, about 5 minutes. Beat the egg yolks and cream in a

PETER JOHNSON

SOLE WITH SHRIMP AND MUSHROOMS

bowl and blend in 2 tablespoons of the hot liquid. Pour the mixture back into the saucepan, remove from heat and beat until the sauce is thick and smooth. Pour over the fish and serve immediately.

SERVES 4

Pays de Loire

BROCHETS GRILLÉS AUX NOIX
Grilled Pike with Walnuts

2 small pike or gemfish, about 1½ lb (800 g) each
salt and freshly ground pepper
4 French shallots, finely chopped
1 sprig thyme, crumbled
1 bay leaf, crumbled
6 sprigs parsley
4 sprigs tarragon
1 tablespoon walnut oil
1 tablespoon fresh lemon juice
24 walnuts
5 oz (150 g) butter

❖Ask the fishmonger to scale and gut the fish; rinse and pat dry. Season with salt and pepper, and lay the fish in a shallow dish.
❖In a small bowl combine the shallots, thyme and bay leaf with salt and pepper. Wash the parsley and tarragon, strip off the leaves and add the bruised stems to the bowl. Mix in the oil and lemon juice and pour over the fish. Marinate in the refrigerator for 6 hours, turning several times.
❖Preheat broiler (griller). Drain the fish, reserving marinade. Broil for 15 minutes, turning once after 7 to 8 minutes and basting frequently with the marinade.
❖Coarsely chop the walnuts in a blender or food processor. Finely chop the parsley and tarragon leaves. Melt the butter in a small saucepan. Add the herbs and walnuts; season with salt and pepper. Pour into a sauceboat. Serve the fish as soon as they are cooked, passing the sauce separately.

SERVES 4

MARINATING INGREDIENTS FOR GRILLED PIKE WITH WALNUTS
PETER JOHNSON

Bretagne/Charentes

MAQUEREAUX MARINÉS
Marinated Mackerel

Caught by the line fishermen from the Gulf of Saint-Malo to the Gulf of Gascogne, the little mackerel used in this recipe are known as lisettes.

12 small mackerel, about 3 oz (100 g) each
salt
1 lemon
bouquet garni: 1 bay leaf, 1 sprig thyme, 6 sprigs parsley
2 cups (16 fl oz/500 ml) dry white wine
1 onion, about 3 oz (100 g), thinly sliced
2 carrots, about 2 oz (50 g) each, peeled and thinly sliced
2½ tablespoons white wine vinegar
2 cloves
1 teaspoon peppercorns
1 dried red chili pepper (bird pepper) or pimento, crumbled

❖Ask the fishmonger to gut the fish; rinse them, pat dry and season with salt. Wash and dry the lemon; cut into thin rounds. Tie together the herbs for the bouquet garni.
❖Pour the wine into a 10-in (26-cm) sauté pan. Add the onion, carrots, lemon, vinegar, bouquet garni, cloves, salt, peppercorns and dried pepper. Bring to boil and simmer for 10 minutes. Add the fish and simmer for 5 minutes.
❖Remove the fish and drain well. Boil the stock until slightly reduced, about 5 more minutes. In a rectangular terrine, alternate the fish with slices of onion, carrot and lemon. Strain the stock; pour over the fish and let cool. Cover the terrine and refrigerate for 12 hours before serving.

SERVES 4

Pays Basque

ANCHOIS AU TXAKOLI
Anchovies in Txakoli Wine

2 lb (1 kg) fresh anchovies
1 chili pepper
2½ oz (75 g) butter
8 oz (500 g) onions, finely chopped
4 cloves garlic, finely chopped
6 tablespoons txakoli (dry white) wine
salt and freshly ground pepper

❖Remove the heads from the anchovies and gut them. Rinse and pat dry with paper towels. Halve the pepper; remove stem and seeds and mince the flesh. Melt the butter in a nonstick 10-in (26-cm) sauté pan. Add the chopped onion, garlic and pepper and cook, stirring, for 2 minutes. Add the anchovies and wine and cook for 10 minutes over high heat, turning the anchovies so that they cook on both sides. Season with salt and pepper. Remove from heat, cover and let rest for 10 minutes before serving.

SERVES 4

PIERRE HUSSENOT/AGENCE TOP

PHOTOGRAPHED IN THE PAYS BASQUE:
ANCHOVIES IN TXAKOLI WINE (left), MARINATED MACKEREL (center front),
TTORO (bottom right, recipe page 98) AND CHAUDRÉE (top right, recipe page 98)

Pays Basque

TTORO
Ttoro

1 pollack or gemfish, about 2 lb (1 kg)
2 rock cod or trevally, about 1 lb (500 g) each
2 red gurnard or white-fleshed fish, about 1 lb (500 g) each
1 lb (500 g) monkfish (anglerfish) or blue-eye cod
8 oz (250 g) mussels
6 uncooked langoustines (Dublin Bay prawns) or yabbies
1 small fresh chili pepper
6 tablespoons extra virgin olive oil
2 cloves garlic, peeled and halved
1 onion, about 3 oz (100 g), thinly sliced
8 oz (250 g) ripe tomatoes, coarsely chopped
1 sprig thyme
1 bay leaf
2 cups (16 fl oz/500 ml) dry white wine
salt and freshly ground pepper

For serving:
croutons
cloves of garlic, halved

❖ Ask the fishmonger to scale and gut the fish and remove the heads. Reserve the heads and bones. Cut the monkfish into ¾-in (2-cm) slices, and the others into 1½-in (4-cm) chunks.
❖ Scrub the mussels in several changes of water and remove the beards. Drain well. Rinse the langoustines. Halve the chili, remove the seeds and chop the flesh.
❖ Heat half the oil in an enameled 4-qt (4-l) pot. Add the fish heads and bones and cook, stirring, over low heat for 5 minutes. Add the garlic, chili and onion and cook, stirring, for 5 minutes or until the vegetables are golden. Add the tomatoes, thyme and bay leaf and cook, stirring, for 1 minute. Pour in the wine and simmer gently for 45 minutes.
❖ Strain the liquid into a shallow baking dish.
❖ Preheat the oven to 425°F (215°C). Wipe out the pot and pour in the remaining oil. Cook the fish for 3 minutes on each side, then transfer to the baking dish. Add the langoustines and mussels and bake for 5 minutes to reheat the broth and cook the langoustines and mussels.
❖ Remove the dish from the oven and serve hot, accompanied by croutons rubbed with garlic.

SERVES 6   *Photograph page 97*

Charentes

CHAUDRÉE
Chaudrée

As popular in Charentes as the bouillabaisse *is in Provence, the* chaudrée *contains one invariable ingredient: the white part of the squid. Sometimes it includes potatoes.*

4 lb (2 kg) mixed fish: skate, sea eel, dogfish (rock salmon), turbot or gemfish, sole, blue-eye cod...
1 lb (500 g) cleaned squid, bodies only
salt and freshly ground pepper
12 oz (400 g) onions, thinly sliced
8 cloves garlic, peeled

2 tablespoons oil
2 cups (16 fl oz/500 ml) dry white wine
2 cups (16 fl oz/500 ml) water
3 oz (100 g) butter

For serving:
croutons

❖ Ask the fishmonger to scale and gut the fish and remove the heads. Cut the largest fish into 1½-in (4-cm) chunks and leave the others whole. Wash them and pat dry. Rinse the squid and pat dry; cut into strips ¾ in (2 cm) wide. Season with salt and pepper.
❖ Transfer the strips of squid to an enameled 6-qt (6-l) pot and place over low heat. Cook, stirring with a wooden spoon, until the squid have given out all their liquid. Add the onion and garlic and stir until all the liquid is absorbed. Add the oil and cook, stirring, until the squid is lightly browned all over. Pour in the wine and water and bring to simmer.
❖ Add the fish to the simmering liquid, beginning with those with the firmest flesh (skate, eel, dogfish), then adding those with softer flesh (sole, turbot) and letting the liquid return to simmer after each addition. Season with salt and pepper and simmer for 15 minutes.
❖ Add the butter to the pot and let it melt. Serve the chaudrée immediately, accompanied by croutons.

SERVES 6   *Photograph page 97*

Bretagne

DAURADE AU MUSCADET
Baked Bream in Muscadet

1 bream or carp, about 2 lb (1 kg)
salt and freshly ground pepper
1 lb (500 g) ripe tomatoes
2 lb (1 kg) small new potatoes
2 onions, about 3 oz (100 g) each, thinly sliced
8 cloves garlic, finely chopped
2 cups (16 fl oz/500 ml) Muscadet wine
3 oz (100 g) salted butter

❖ Ask the fishmonger to scale and gut the fish. Rinse it and pat dry. Season with salt and pepper.
❖ Preheat oven to 450°F (230°C). Drop the tomatoes into boiling water for 10 seconds. Cool under running water, then peel, halve, squeeze out the seeds and coarsely chop the flesh. Peel the potatoes, wash them and pat dry. In a bowl mix together the potatoes, onions, garlic and tomatoes; season with salt and pepper.
❖ Lightly butter a baking dish large enough to hold the fish. Place it in the center of the dish and surround it with the tomato mixture. Pour in the wine and dot with butter. Bake for 40 to 45 minutes, turning the potatoes several times and basting the fish frequently with the cooking liquid.
❖ By the end of the cooking time there should be very little liquid left. Serve the fish immediately, directly from the dish.

SERVES 4

BAKED BREAM IN MUSCADET (top), MULLET IN RAÏTO (center right, recipe page 100)
AND BOURRIDE OF MONKFISH, SÈTE-STYLE (bottom, recipe page 100)

PETER JOHNSON

Provence

MUGE EN RAÏTO
Mullet in Raïto

Muge is the Provençal name for mullet. Coated with raïto, *a sauce whose origins go far back in time, it is one of the traditional dishes served for the* gros souper, *the grand Christmas supper served on the evening of 24 December, before midnight Mass.*

1 mullet, about 2½ lb (1.2 kg)
salt and freshly ground pepper
8 oz (250 g) ripe tomatoes
bouquet garni: 1 bay leaf, 1 sprig thyme, 6 sprigs parsley
¼ cup (2 fl oz/60 ml) extra virgin olive oil
1 onion, about 3 oz (100 g), finely chopped
2 cloves garlic, finely chopped
¾ cup (6 fl oz/200 ml) light red wine
2 tablespoons capers, drained
24 small black Niçoise olives

❖Ask the fishmonger to scale and gut the fish and to cut it into slices about 1¼ in (3 cm) thick. Rinse and pat dry; season with salt and pepper.
❖Drop the tomatoes into boiling water for 10 seconds. Cool under running water, then peel, halve and squeeze out the seeds. Finely chop the flesh. Tie together the herbs for the bouquet garni.
❖Heat half the oil in a nonstick 10-in (26-cm) sauté pan and brown the slices of fish for 2 to 3 minutes each side. Remove and set aside.
❖Pour off the oil from the sauté pan and wipe the pan with paper towels. Add the remaining oil and place the pan over low heat. Add the chopped onion and garlic and cook, stirring, until golden, about 3 minutes. Pour in the wine and evaporate it over high heat. Add the tomatoes, bouquet garni, salt and pepper and stir for 1 minute. Return the fish to the pan, cover and simmer for 10 minutes, turning the fish once. Add the capers and olives and simmer for 5 minutes longer.
❖Arrange the slices of fish on a shallow plate and cover them with sauce, discarding the bouquet garni. Serve hot.

SERVES 4   *Photograph page 99*

Languedoc

BOURRIDE DE LOTTE À LA SÉTOISE
Bourride of Monkfish, Sète-style

This recipe is a specialty of the charming little fishing port of Sète, where it features on the menu of all the restaurants along the sea front. It is often accompanied by croutons rubbed with garlic and fried in butter, or by steamed potatoes.

¼ cup (2 fl oz/60 ml) olive oil
1 carrot, peeled and finely chopped
10 celery leaves, finely chopped
2 leeks, white parts only, well washed and finely chopped
1 large beet leaf (silverbeet), finely chopped
salt and freshly ground pepper
4 sections of monkfish (anglerfish) or blue-eye cod, each about 2 in (5 cm) thick and weighing 8 oz (250 g)

For the sauce:
1 clove garlic
½ teaspoon strong mustard
1 egg yolk
salt
6 tablespoons extra virgin olive oil

❖Heat the oil in a sauté pan large enough to hold the pieces of fish in a single layer. Add the chopped vegetables and cook over very low heat, stirring occasionally with a wooden spoon, for 10 minutes; do not let the vegetables brown. Season with salt and pepper and add the fish. Cover and cook over low heat for 10 minutes on each side.
❖Meanwhile, prepare the sauce: force the garlic through a press into a shallow bowl. Add the mustard, egg yolk and salt and stir well. Set aside for 1 minute, then add the oil in a thin stream, whisking until the mixture is quite firm; this *aïoli* will thicken the sauce.
❖Transfer the cooked fish to a platter and keep warm. Off the heat, add the *aïoli* to the contents of the sauté pan and mix well. Coat the pieces of fish with this sauce and serve immediately.

SERVES 4   *Photograph page 99*

Provence

LOUP AU FENOUIL
Grilled Sea Bass with Fennel

1 sea bass, snapper or silver bream about 3 lb (1.5 kg)
salt and freshly ground pepper
¼ cup (2 fl oz/60 ml) olive oil
10 stalks dried fennel
For the sauce:
1 clove garlic
½ teaspoon strong mustard
1 small egg yolk
salt and pepper
6 tablespoons extra virgin olive oil
1 teaspoon white wine vinegar
3 cornichons (small French sour pickles or gherkins), finely chopped
1 tablespoon capers, drained and finely chopped
2 tablespoons chopped flat-leaf parsley
1 tablespoon chopped chives

❖Ask the fishmonger to scale and gut the fish; rinse it and pat dry. Season inside and outside with salt and pepper. Stuff the fish with some of the dried fennel and brush the skin with olive oil.
❖Preheat broiler (griller). Place the remaining fennel in the broiler pan, place the rack over the fennel and lay the fish on the rack. Broil for about 25 minutes, turning the fish after about 12 minutes.
❖Meanwhile, prepare the sauce: force the garlic through a press into a shallow bowl. Add the mustard, egg yolk and salt and stir well. Set aside for 1 minute, then add the oil in a thin stream, whisking until the mixture is quite firm. Add the vinegar and whisk for 30 seconds more, then blend in the cornichons, capers, parsley and chives. Pour the sauce into a sauceboat.
❖Arrange the cooked fish on a platter and serve immediately, passing the sauce separately.

SERVES 4

Provence

ROUGETS À LA NIÇOISE
Red Mullet, Nice-style

Redfish liver is particularly tasty, so take care not to discard it when you are gutting the fish. It can be left to cook in the fish or pureed raw and mixed into anchovy butter, which is used as a sauce for grilled fish.

8 red mullet, about 6 oz (180 g) each
salt and freshly ground pepper
1 lb (500 g) ripe tomatoes
¼ cup (2 fl oz/60 ml) extra virgin olive oil
1 onion, about 3 oz (100 g), finely chopped
3 cloves garlic, finely chopped
8 anchovy fillets in oil
2 oz (50 g) small black Niçoise olives

❖Ask the fishmonger to scale and gut the fish, leaving the livers intact. Rinse the fish and pat dry; season with salt and pepper. Drop the tomatoes into boiling water for 10 seconds. Cool under running water, peel, halve and squeeze out the seeds.
❖Heat half the oil in a nonstick 10-in (26-cm) sauté pan and cook the chopped onion and garlic until soft and golden. Stir in the tomatoes, season with salt and pepper and cook over high heat for 5 minutes.
❖Heat the rest of the oil in a nonstick 10-in (26-cm) skillet and cook the fish for 4 minutes each side. Drain and arrange on a heated serving platter. Cover with the tomato sauce and garnish with anchovy fillets and olives. Serve immediately.

SERVES 4   *Photograph page 101*

Provence

DAURADE À LA PROVENÇALE
Baked Bream, Provençal-style

1 bream or carp, about 2½ lb (1.2 kg)
1 lb (500 g) ripe tomatoes
¼ cup (2 fl oz/60 ml) extra virgin olive oil
2 cloves garlic, finely chopped
1 tablespoon chopped flat-leaf parsley
salt and freshly ground pepper
1 lemon

❖Ask the fishmonger to scale and gut the fish; rinse it and pat dry.
❖Preheat oven to 450°F (230°C). Drop the tomatoes into boiling water for 10 seconds. Cool under running water, then peel, halve, squeeze out the seeds and coarsely chop the flesh.
❖Heat half the oil in a nonstick 10-in (26-cm) skillet. Add the garlic and parsley and cook, stirring, until the garlic is soft and golden. Stir in the tomatoes and season with salt and pepper. Cook over moderate heat until the liquid from the tomatoes has almost entirely evaporated, about 5 minutes.
❖Lay the fish in a baking dish just large enough to hold it. Sprinkle with the remaining oil and turn so that all the surfaces are coated with oil. Bake for 5 minutes.

❖Meanwhile, wash and dry the lemon and cut into thin rounds. Cover the fish with the tomato sauce. Arrange the lemon slices over the fish and bake for 30 minutes longer. Serve directly from the dish.

SERVES 4   *Photograph page 101*

Languedoc

THON À LA LANGUEDOCIENNE
Tuna, Languedoc-style

1 slice fresh tuna, about 2½ lb (1.2 kg) and ¾ in (2 cm) thick
salt and freshly ground pepper
3 lemons
¼ cup (1 oz/25 g) all purpose (plain) flour
3 tablespoons extra virgin olive oil
10 cloves garlic, peeled
2 cups (16 fl oz/500 ml) dry white wine

❖Rinse the tuna and pat dry. Season with salt and pepper. Wash the lemons and thinly slice two of them. Squeeze 1 tablespoon of juice from the third lemon.
❖Sprinkle the flour into a shallow bowl and coat the fish on both sides, shaking off excess.
❖Heat the oil in a sauté pan just large enough to hold the slice of tuna. Lightly brown it for 4 minutes on each side, then remove and keep warm. Add the garlic cloves and cook until golden, about 2 minutes. Set aside with the fish. Stir the wine and lemon juice into the sauté pan and boil until reduced by half. Return the tuna and garlic to the pan and cook, covered, over low heat for 10 minutes, turning the fish after 5 minutes.
❖Arrange the tuna and garlic on a shallow plate and keep warm. Reduce the cooking liquid over high heat to a smooth consistency and pour over the fish. Serve immediately.

SERVES 6

TUNA, LANGUEDOC-STYLE

PETER JOHNSON

Normandie

BARBUE À L'OSEILLE
Brill with Sorrel

1 brill, Petrale sole, flounder or other flatfish,
  about 3 lb (1.5 kg)
1 onion, about 3 oz (100 g)
2 cloves
bouquet garni: 1 bay leaf, 1 sprig thyme, 6 sprigs parsley
1 carrot, about 3 oz (100 g), peeled and sliced
2 cups (16 fl oz/500 ml) dry cider
2 cups (16 fl oz/500 ml) water
salt and freshly ground pepper
2 lb (1 kg) sorrel
¾ cup (6 fl oz/185 ml) heavy (double) cream or crème
  fraîche

❖Ask the fishmonger to clean and fillet the fish, but keep the head and all the trimmings.
❖Peel the onion and stud with cloves. Tie together the herbs for the bouquet garni. Place the bouquet garni, onion and carrot in a large saucepan and add the fish head and trimmings, cider and water. Bring to boil, season with salt and pepper and simmer gently for 20 minutes.
❖Meanwhile, wash the sorrel, drain it and cut into very fine strips. In a nonstick 10-in (26-cm) sauté pan combine the sorrel, cream, and salt and pepper. Cook over low heat, stirring often, until reduced to a thick sauce, about 5 minutes; keep warm.
❖Rinse and pat dry the fish fillets. Strain the stock, return to the saucepan and bring to simmer over low heat. Add the fish and poach gently for 10 minutes, then drain.
❖Divide the fish among four plates, coat with sauce and serve immediately.

SERVES 4

Alsace

BROCHET DE L'ILL À LA CRÈME
Pike in Cream Sauce

1 pike or gemfish, about 3½ lb (1.75 kg)
salt and freshly ground pepper
4 oz (125 g) butter
4 French shallots, finely chopped
¾ cup (6 fl oz/185 ml) heavy (double) cream or
  crème fraîche
1 cup (8 fl oz/250 ml) Riesling
1 tablespoon fresh lemon juice

❖Ask the fishmonger to scale and gut the fish, then rinse it and pat dry. Season with salt and pepper.
❖Preheat oven to 450°F (230°C). Using a scant tablespoon of the butter, grease a baking dish large enough to hold the fish. Scatter the chopped shallots over the bottom. Place the fish in the dish and dot with a generous tablespoon of butter. Bake for 15 minutes.
❖Combine the cream and wine in a small bowl and pour over the fish. Bake for 20 minutes longer, basting the fish often with the pan juices.
❖Transfer the cooked fish to a serving platter and keep warm. Add the lemon juice to the sauce and boil over mod-

BRILL WITH SORREL (center left), PIKE IN CREAM SAUCE (top)
AND BRILL IN CIDER (right)

erate heat until thickened, then strain into a small saucepan. Gradually whisk in the remaining butter over low heat to obtain a thick, smooth sauce. Pour the sauce into a sauceboat. Serve the fish hot, accompanied by its sauce.

SERVES 4

Normandie

BARBUE AU CIDRE
Brill in Cider

1 brill, Petrale sole, flounder or other flatfish,
  about 3 lb (1.5 kg)
salt and freshly ground pepper
2 oz (50 g) butter
3 French shallots, finely chopped
8 oz (250 g) mushrooms, coarsely chopped
6 tablespoons heavy (double) cream or crème fraîche
2 cups (16 fl oz/500 ml) dry cider

❖Ask the fishmonger to clean and prepare the fish, trimming the fins. Rinse it, pat dry and season with salt and pepper.
❖Preheat oven to 425°F (215°C). Using half the butter, grease a baking dish just large enough to hold the fish. Scatter half the chopped shallots and mushrooms over the bottom. Place the fish on top and cover with the remaining shallots and mushrooms.
❖Combine the cream and cider, season with salt and pepper and pour this mixture into the dish. Dot the fish with the remaining butter. Bake for 30 to 35 minutes or until the sauce thickens and coats the fish. Serve hot, directly from the dish.

SERVES 4

Provence

GRATIN DE SARDINES AUX ÉPINARDS

Baked Sardines with Spinach

1¼ lb (600 g) fresh medium sardines
2 lb (1 kg) spinach
salt
1 small egg
1 oz (30 g) freshly and finely grated Emmenthaler or
    Parmesan cheese
¼ cup (2 fl oz/60 ml) extra virgin olive oil
freshly ground pepper
½ teaspoon dried thyme
¼ cup (1 oz/30 g) dried breadcrumbs

❖Scale the sardines and remove the heads; gut and rinse the fish. Split them along the belly and separate the two fillets, removing the row of bones beneath the dorsal fins and tail. Pat the fillets dry using paper towels.

❖Wash and stem the spinach. Cut the leaves, with the water clinging to them, into strips ¾ in (2 cm) wide and place in a large saucepan. Season with salt and cook, covered, over high heat for 5 minutes. Drain the spinach and turn into a bowl. Beat the egg; mix in half the cheese and season with salt and pepper. Blend this mixture into the spinach.

❖Preheat oven to 450°F (230°C). Using some of the olive oil, lightly oil a baking dish just large enough to hold the fillets in a single layer. Spread the spinach mixture over the bottom, then arrange the sardine fillets on top, skin side down. Season with salt and pepper, sprinkle with thyme and pour the remaining oil over. Combine the breadcrumbs with the remaining cheese and sprinkle over the fish. Bake until lightly browned, about 15 minutes. Serve hot, directly from the baking dish.

SERVES 4–5

Provence

SARDINES FARCIES

Stuffed Sardines

2 lb (1 kg) fresh medium sardines
salt and freshly ground pepper
8 oz (250 g) spinach
4 tablespoons extra virgin olive oil
2 green onions (scallions or spring onions), finely chopped
2 cloves garlic, finely chopped
1 egg
8 oz (250 g) ewe's milk cheese, *Brousse de brebis*
    or ricotta
2 tablespoons flat-leaf parsley, chopped
¼ cup (1 oz/30 g) dried breadcrumbs
6 pinches of freshly grated nutmeg

❖Scale the sardines and remove the heads; gut and rinse the fish. Split them along the belly and open out without separating the fillets. Remove the backbone, breaking it off at the tail. Pat the fish dry with paper towels. Season inside and out with salt and pepper.

❖Wash and stem the spinach. Place the leaves, with the water clinging to them, in a saucepan. Season with salt and cook, covered, over high heat for 3 minutes. Drain the spinach and chop finely with a knife.

❖Heat 1 tablespoon oil in a nonstick 10-in (26-cm) skillet. Add the onion and cook, stirring, over low heat for 3 minutes or until golden, then add the garlic and cook for 1 minute longer.

❖Beat the egg in a bowl, add the cheese and mash with a fork. Add the spinach, parsley, the contents of the skillet and half the breadcrumbs. Season with salt, pepper and nutmeg and stir well.

❖Preheat the oven to 450°F (230°C). Using some of the remaining oil, lightly oil a baking dish large enough to hold half the sardines in a single layer. Arrange half the sardines in the dish and spread each one with a spoonful of the stuffing mixture. Cover each sardine with a second one and pour the rest of the oil over. Sprinkle with breadcrumbs and bake for 20 minutes. Serve hot, warm or cold, directly from the baking dish.

SERVES 6

BAKED SARDINES WITH SPINACH (top) AND STUFFED SARDINES

PETER JOHNSON

ESCABÈCHE OF RED MULLET

Provence

ROUGETS EN ESCABÈCHE
Escabèche of Red Mullet

Escabèche is a vinegar marinade of Spanish origin created for preserving little fried fish from which the heads have been removed: hence the name, which comes from cabeza, *the Spanish word for head. Today, whole fish such as redfish, mackerel and whiting, and cutlets of tuna, bonito, swordfish or hake are also prepared in this manner.*

8 red mullet, about 6 oz (200 g) each
salt and freshly ground pepper
6 tablespoons extra virgin olive oil
6 tablespoons red wine vinegar
3 oz (100 g) fresh mint leaves

❖Ask the fishmonger to scale and gut the fish, leaving the livers intact. Rinse the fish and pat dry; season with salt and pepper.
❖Heat the oil in a nonstick 10-in (26-cm) skillet and cook the fish for 4 minutes on each side. Drain on paper towels and lay in a shallow dish. Transfer 4 tablespoons of the cooking oil to a small saucepan.
❖Pour the vinegar into a second small nonaluminum saucepan and add the mint leaves. Bring to boil, stir and remove from heat. Pour this mixture into the reserved oil and boil for a few seconds, then pour over the fish.
❖Allow the fish to cool. Let stand for at least 4 hours before serving.

SERVES 4

Bretagne

ANCHOIS GRILLÉS À LA MOUTARDE ET À L'ESTRAGON
Grilled Anchovies with Mustard and Tarragon

24 fresh medium anchovies
salt and freshly ground pepper
6 sprigs tarragon, leaves only
3 oz (100 g) low-salt butter
2 tablespoons strong mustard
½ cup (2 oz/50 g) dry breadcrumbs

❖Remove the heads from the anchovies and gut them. Rinse and split along the ventral fin; open out without separating the fillets. Remove the backbone, breaking it off near the tail. Dry the fish with paper towels and season with salt and pepper. Scatter the tarragon over the fish, then fold the fillets together to enclose the tarragon.
❖Melt the butter in a small saucepan. Add the mustard and stir well, then let cool.
❖Preheat broiler (griller). Arrange the fish on a rack over the broiler pan. Sprinkle with breadcrumbs and spoon half the mustard butter over. Broil for 10 minutes, not too far from the heat source, turning the fish several times and sprinkling with mustard butter.
❖When the anchovies are cooked, arrange them on a serving plate. Sprinkle with the remaining butter and serve.

SERVES 4

GRILLED ANCHOVIES WITH MUSTARD AND TARRAGON (top)
AND STUFFED CLAMS, LORIENT-STYLE (recipe page 78)

Bretagne

BAR FARCI
Stuffed Sea Bass

1 sea bass, sea bream or snapper, about 3 lb (1.5 kg)
8 oz (250 g) fresh spinach
6 oz (200 g) sorrel
8 oz (250 g) mushrooms
3 oz (100 g) stale bread, crusts trimmed
4 oz (125 g) salted butter
6 French shallots, finely chopped
salt and freshly ground pepper
¾ cup (6 fl oz/185 ml) heavy (double) cream or crème
    fraîche
6 tablespoons dry white wine

❖Ask the fishmonger to scale and gut the fish and to open it along the belly, without separating the two fillets, in order to remove the backbone. Rinse and pat dry the opened fish.
❖Wash and drain the spinach and sorrel; trim the stalks and cut the leaves into very fine strips. Rinse the mushrooms and pat dry, then chop finely. Grind the bread to coarse crumbs in a blender or food processor.
❖Melt half the butter in a nonstick 10-in (26-cm) sauté pan. Add the shallots and cook, stirring, for 2 minutes over low heat. Add the mushrooms, spinach and sorrel and cook until the vegetables give out no more liquid, about 10 minutes. Season with salt and pepper, mix in the breadcrumbs and remove from heat. Cool to lukewarm.
❖Preheat oven to 450°F (230°C). Season the inside of the fish with salt and pepper, then fill with the stuffing. Tie the fish together with string. With half the remaining butter, grease a shallow baking dish just large enough to hold the fish; lay the fish in the dish. Combine the cream and wine, season lightly with salt and pepper, and coat the fish with this mixture. Dot with the remaining butter and bake for 45 minutes, turning the fish after 20 to 25 minutes.
❖Transfer the cooked fish to a serving platter. Boil the sauce until reduced to a thick, creamy consistency and pour over the fish. Serve hot.

SERVES 6

Bretagne

COTRIADE
Cotriade

This soup, based on potatoes, onions and lard, includes a wide variety of fish. It is prepared all along the coast of Bretagne, and there are as many versions as there are fishing ports.

4 lb (2 kg) mixed fish: whiting, mackerel, smelt or red fish,
    monkfish or blue-eye cod, skate, sole, deep sea bream…
2 lb (1 kg) baking potatoes
⅓ cup (2½ oz/80 g) lard
8 oz (250 g) onions, thinly sliced
salt and freshly ground pepper

For serving:
toasted slices of country bread
red wine vinegar

❖Ask the fishmonger to scale and gut the fish and remove the heads. Cut the largest fish into 1½-in (4-cm) chunks and leave the others whole; wash and pat dry. Peel the potatoes, wash and cut into 1¼-in (3-cm) cubes.
❖Melt the lard in an enameled 6-qt (6-l) pot and cook the onions until golden, about 5 minutes, stirring with a wooden spoon. Stir in the potatoes, salt and pepper, then add cold water to cover. Bring to simmer, then cook for 15 minutes.
❖Add the fish to the simmering liquid, beginning with those with the firmest flesh (skate, monkfish, mackerel), then adding those with softer flesh (bream, sole, whiting, smelt) and letting the liquid return to simmer after each addition. Season with salt and pepper and simmer for 15 minutes.
❖Remove the cooked fish and potatoes with a slotted spoon and arrange in a shallow dish. Pour a little of the broth over and keep warm. Pour the broth into a tureen and serve immediately, with the toasted slices of country bread. Serve the fish and potatoes dressed with a dash of vinegar.

SERVES 6

Bretagne

MERLANS DE LORIENT
Whiting in Mustard Cream Sauce

4 French shallots, finely chopped
2 tablespoons chopped flat-leaf parsley
salt and freshly ground pepper
2½ oz (80 g) butter
1½ lb (750 g) whiting fillets, skin and bones removed
6 tablespoons Muscadet
1 tablespoon strong mustard
1 tablespoon fresh lemon juice
6 tablespoons heavy (double) cream or crème fraîche

❖Preheat oven to 425°F (215°C). Mix the shallots and parsley and season with salt and pepper. Using 1 tablespoon of the butter, grease a baking dish just large enough to hold the fillets of fish in a single layer. Spread the shallot mixture over the bottom.
❖Rinse the fish fillets and pat dry. Season with salt and pepper and arrange in the dish. Blend the wine and mustard and pour over the fish. Dot with 1 tablespoon butter. Bake for 10 minutes.
❖Transfer the fish fillets to a heatproof serving platter. Pour the cooking liquid into a small saucepan, add the lemon juice and boil until the sauce is reduced to a syrupy consistency. Stir in the cream and boil until thick enough to coat the fish. Remove from heat and whisk in the remaining butter in small pieces.
❖Preheat broiler. Coat the fish with the sauce, then place under the broiler, close to the heat source, for 2 minutes. Serve immediately.

SERVES 4

WHITING IN MUSTARD CREAM SAUCE *(left),*
COTRIADE *(center)* AND STUFFED SEA BASS *(right)*
PIERRE HUSSENOT/AGENCE TOP

SALT COD WITH BEET GREENS AND CURRANTS (top left),
PUREE OF SALT COD (bottom left) AND SALT COD, BREST-STYLE (right)

Using the remaining butter, grease a shallow 9x13-in (22x32-cm) pan or gratin dish. Arrange the potatoes and cod in layers, finishing with a layer of cod. Sprinkle with chervil, then pour the leek mixture over. Bake until lightly browned, about 10 minutes. Serve hot, directly from the pan.

SERVES 6

Corse

MORUE AUX BLETTES ET AUX RAISINS SECS

Salt Cod with Beet Greens and Currants

2 lb (1 kg) salt cod fillets
2 oz (50 g) dried currants
1 lb (500 g) ripe tomatoes
1 lb (500 g) boiling potatoes
1 lb (500 g) beet greens or Swiss chard
3 tablespoons extra virgin olive oil
1 onion, about 3 oz (100 g), finely chopped
2 cloves garlic, finely chopped
1 bay leaf
salt and freshly ground pepper

❖Soak the salt cod fillets in a large bowl of cold water, skin side up, for 12 hours, changing the water 3 times.
❖Drain the cod and cut it into 1½-in (4-cm) squares. Rinse the currants in hot water and drain. Quarter the tomatoes and puree in a food mill, using the plate with medium-size holes. Peel the potatoes, wash and pat dry; cut into ¾-in (2-cm) cubes.
❖Rinse the beet greens, drain and slice into ¾-in (2-cm) strips. Place in a saucepan with the water clinging to the leaves and cook, covered, over high heat for 4 minutes. Drain.
❖Heat the oil in a nonstick 10-in (26-cm) sauté pan. Cook the chopped onion and garlic, stirring constantly, for 2 minutes or until golden. Add the tomato pulp, bay leaf and potatoes. Season with salt and pepper and cook, covered, over low heat for 15 minutes.
❖Add the cod, greens and currants and cook for 15 minutes, covered, over very low heat. Turn into a shallow dish and serve hot.

SERVES 6

Bretagne

MORUE BRESTOISE

Salt Cod, Brest-style

Time was when the fishermen of Bretagne caught the species of fish called gadidae, *and among them fresh cod. When it deserted their coasts, they were obliged to pursue it as far as Terre-Neuve — as they still do today.*

2 lb (1 kg) salt cod fillets
2 lb (1 kg) boiling potatoes
2 oz (60 g) butter
8 oz (250 g) leeks, white parts only, well washed and
    thinly sliced
4 tablespoons water
½ teaspoon arrowroot
2 tablespoons chopped chervil

❖Soak the salt cod fillets in a large bowl of cold water, skin side up, for 12 hours, changing the water 3 times.
❖Drain the cod and transfer it to a large pot of cold water, skin side down. Bring to boil over low heat, then reduce heat and cook at the barest simmer for 10 minutes. Remove from heat and let cool.
❖Place the potatoes in a saucepan of cold salted water and bring to boil. Cook for about 25 minutes or until the potatoes are easily pierced with the point of a knife. Drain, peel and slice into ⅛-in (3-mm) rounds.
❖Melt 1 oz (30 g) butter in a saucepan and cook the leeks until soft and golden, stirring constantly with a wooden spoon. Add 2 tablespoons water. Blend the arrowroot with the remaining 2 tablespoons water and add to the saucepan. Cook over moderate heat, stirring constantly, until the sauce thickens.
❖Preheat oven to 450°F (230°C). Drain and flake the fish.

Languedoc

BRANDADE DE MORUE

Puree of Salt Cod

The name of this dish comes from the Provençal word brandar, *to stir. A specialty of the town of Nîmes, it is a puree of cod mixed with olive oil and milk. In Marseille and Toulon it is flavored with crushed garlic and spread on croutons that have been rubbed with more garlic. When a puree of potatoes is added, it becomes a* parmentière de morue.

2 lb (1 kg) salt cod fillets
1 cup (8 fl oz/250 ml) milk

1 cup (8 fl oz/250 ml) extra virgin olive oil
For serving:
croutons

❖Soak the salt cod fillets in a large bowl of cold water, skin side up, for 12 hours, changing the water 3 times.
❖Drain the cod and transfer it to a large pot of cold water, skin side down. Bring to boil over low heat, then reduce heat and cook at the barest simmer for 10 minutes.
❖Meanwhile, heat the milk in a small saucepan. Pour half the oil into a large saucepan.
❖Drain the fish and remove skin and bones. Flake the flesh and add to the oil in the saucepan. Over very low heat, and turning and mashing the mixture with a wooden spoon, gradually add the remaining oil and the hot milk, blending until the mixture is a very smooth puree; this will take about 15 minutes.
❖Turn the *brandade* into a shallow dish and serve immediately, accompanied with croutons.

SERVES 6

QUENELLES

PETER JOHNSON

Lyonnais

QUENELLES
Quenelles

Pike quenelles are a specialty of the Lyonnais region. They are sometimes served coated in Nantua sauce (which originated in the town of the same name), a cream sauce that includes écrevisses (freshwater crayfish) among its ingredients.

1 lb (500 g) pike fillets, skin and bones removed
4 eggs
1¼ cups (10 fl oz/310 ml) heavy (double) cream or crème fraîche
salt and freshly ground pepper
4 pinches of cayenne pepper
4 oz (125 g) butter
For serving:
beurre blanc (page 68) or melted butter

❖Place the fish in a blender or food processor and blend to a fine puree. With the machine running, add the eggs, cream, salt, pepper and cayenne. Add the butter in small pieces, blending until the puree is very smooth. Refrigerate the puree for 12 hours before preparing the quenelles.

❖On a lightly floured work surface, shape large spoonfuls of the mixture into smooth sausage shapes. Half-fill a large saucepan with salted water and bring to simmer. Drop in the quenelles, a few at a time, and simmer for 15 minutes. Drain on a clean cloth, then transfer to a warmed platter. Serve immediately, coated with *beurre blanc* or sprinkled with melted butter.

SERVES 6

Provence

BOURRIDE
Bourride

The link between the bourride de lotte *of Languedoc and the Provençal* bourride *is aïoli. But whereas the first is made only with anglerfish and includes a very thick sauce, the second is a true thick soup, containing every variety of white-fleshed fish.*

4 lb (2 kg) mixed white fish: monkfish (anglerfish) or blue-eye cod, sea bass, John Dory, turbot or flounder...
bouquet garni: 1 bay leaf, 1 sprig thyme, 1 sprig dried fennel, 6 sprigs parsley, 1 strip dried orange peel
1 medium carrot, peeled and coarsely chopped
1 onion, about 3 oz (100 g), coarsely chopped
2 leeks, white parts only, well washed and coarsely chopped
6 cloves garlic, peeled
2 cups (16 fl oz/500 ml) dry white wine
3 cups (24 fl oz/750 ml) water
salt and freshly ground pepper
For the sauce:
3 cloves garlic
1 teaspoon strong mustard
2 egg yolks
salt
1 cup (8 fl oz/250 ml) extra virgin olive oil
For serving:
slices of toasted baguette (French bread)
cloves of garlic, halved

❖Ask the fishmonger to scale and gut the fish and remove the heads, reserving the heads and bones. Cut the fish into 1½-in (4-cm) chunks.
❖Tie together the herbs for the bouquet garni. Place the fish heads and bones in a large saucepan. Add the carrot, onion, leeks, garlic, bouquet garni, wine and water and bring to simmer. Season with salt and pepper and simmer for 20 minutes.
❖Meanwhile, prepare the sauce: force the garlic through a press into a shallow bowl. Add the mustard, egg yolk and salt and stir well. Set aside for 1 minute, then add the oil in a thin stream, whisking until the mixture is quite firm; this *aïoli* will thicken the sauce.
❖Strain the broth into another saucepan. Bring to simmer over low heat and add the fish. Simmer, covered, for 10 minutes.
❖Remove the cooked fish from the broth with a slotted spoon and keep warm in a tureen. Blend half the *aïoli* into the broth, off the heat. Pour this sauce over the fish and serve immediately, accompanied by toasted bread rubbed with garlic and spread with the remaining *aïoli*.

SERVES 6   *Photograph page 10*

Provence

BOUILLABAISSE
Bouillabaisse

Bouillabaisse was invented by Mediterranean fishermen who, when they returned from a fishing trip, would cook their more modest fish with a few shellfish in a huge cauldron over a wood fire using olive oil, a piece of dried orange peel and some saffron.

Gradually it became a highlight of the cuisine of the Midi region, each cook adding his or her own individual touch. The common factor in all the recipes is the use of as many white-fleshed rockfish as possible, to which may be added small crabs, mussels, squillfish, and even cuttlefish with their ink.

6 lb (3 kg) of a mixture of fish and crustaceans: rock cod, John Dory, monkfish (anglerfish), blue-eye cod, eel, sea bass, snapper, red mullet, cuttlefish, sole, brill (Petrale sole), small crabs, lobster, crayfish…
¼ cup (2 fl oz/60 ml) extra virgin olive oil
1 lb (500 g) ripe tomatoes, coarsely chopped
2 medium carrots, peeled and thinly sliced
1 leek, well washed and thinly sliced
1 celery stalk, thinly sliced
1 onion, about 3 oz (100 g), thinly sliced
1 sprig dried thyme
1 sprig dried rosemary
1 sprig dried fennel
1 bay leaf
1 strip dried orange peel
10 cloves garlic, peeled
10 sprigs parsley
6 pinches of saffron threads
salt and freshly ground pepper
2 cups (16 fl oz/500 ml) dry white wine

For serving:
slices of toasted baguette (French bread)
cloves of garlic, halved

❖Ask the fishmonger to scale and gut the fish and remove the heads. Reserve the heads, bones and shells. Cut the largest fish into 1½-in (4-cm) chunks and leave the others whole. Wash all the fish and pat dry. If crayfish or lobster is included, cut it in half to separate the head from the tail and remove the grainy sac from the head. Clean the cuttlefish, keeping only the body and tentacles; wash and pat dry.

❖Heat the oil in a 6-qt (6-l) saucepan. Add the heads, bones and shells of the fish and crustaceans and cook over low heat, stirring, for 5 minutes. Add the tomatoes, carrots, leek, celery and onion and cook, stirring, for 5 minutes or until the vegetables are lightly colored. Add the thyme, rosemary, fennel, bay leaf, orange peel, garlic, parsley, saffron, salt and pepper and stir for 1 minute. Add the wine and simmer gently for 45 minutes.

❖Remove the fish trimmings, thyme, rosemary, fennel, bay leaf, orange peel, garlic and parsley. Puree the tomato mixture in a blender or food processor until smooth.

❖Wipe the saucepan and return the pureed mixture to it. Bring to boil over low heat. Add the fish, beginning with those with the firmest flesh (cuttlefish, eel, monkfish, rock cod, red mullet) and later adding those with softer flesh (John Dory, sea bass, sole, brill), letting the mixture return to boil between additions. Finally add the crustaceans. Sim-

mer for 10 minutes, then remove the seafood with a slotted spoon and arrange on a plate. Keep warm.

❖Pour the soup into a tureen and serve hot, over slices of bread rubbed with garlic. Follow with the seafood as a separate course.

SERVES 6–8   *Photograph page 10*

Alsace

MATELOTE AU RIESLING
Matelote of Freshwater Fish in Riesling

4 lb (2 kg) mixed river fish: eel, pike, tench or Murray cod, perch or bass, trout…
bouquet garni: 1 sprig thyme, 1 bay leaf, 6 sprigs parsley, 2 sprigs tarragon
2 medium carrots, peeled and sliced
2 leeks, well washed and sliced
2 onions, about 3 oz (100 g) each, sliced
2 cups (16 fl oz/500 ml) Riesling
2 cups (16 fl oz/500 ml) water
4 pinches of freshly grated nutmeg
salt and freshly ground pepper
3 egg yolks
¾ cup (6 fl oz/200 ml) heavy (double) cream or crème fraîche

❖Ask the fishmonger to scale and gut the fish and remove the heads. Reserve the heads and bones. Cut the fish into 1½-in (4-cm) chunks.

❖Tie together the herbs for the bouquet garni. In a large saucepan, combine the carrots, leeks, onions, fish heads and bones, bouquet garni, wine, water, nutmeg, salt and pepper. Bring to simmer, then simmer for 20 minutes.

❖Strain the broth into a clean pot and bring to simmer. Add the fish in the order listed, letting the liquid return to simmer each time before adding the next fish. Simmer for 25 minutes, then remove from heat. Remove the fish with a slotted spoon and keep warm in a shallow dish.

PETER JOHNSON

MATELOTE OF FRESHWATER FISH IN RIESLING

❖Boil the cooking liquid until reduced by half. Beat the egg yolks and cream together in a small bowl, using a fork. Beat 2 tablespoons of the broth into the egg yolk mixture. Return this mixture to the broth, off the heat, and whisk until thickened. Pour this sauce over the fish and serve immediately.

SERVES 6

Bourgogne

POCHOUSE

Fish and Onion Stew

4 lb (2 kg) river fish: eel, carp, tench, perch, pike…
5 oz (150 g) lightly salted pork fatback
2½ oz (75 g) butter
25 tiny pickling onions, peeled
salt and freshly ground pepper
3 cups (24 fl oz/750 ml) white Burgundy
6 cloves garlic, peeled
¼ cup (1 oz/25 g) all purpose (plain) flour

For serving:
croutons

❖Ask the fishmonger to scale and gut the fish and remove the heads. Cut the fish into 1½-in (4-cm) chunks, rinse and pat dry.
❖Rinse the fatback. Remove the rind and cut the fat into fine matchsticks. Blanch for 1 minute in boiling water, then drain, rinse and drain again.
❖Melt 1½ oz (50 g) of the butter in a 6-qt (6-l) pot. Add the onions and fatback and cook, stirring, over low heat for 5 minutes or until lightly golden. Season lightly with salt and pepper. Pour in the wine and bring to simmer. Add the garlic and fish and simmer for 20 minutes. Remove the fish and keep warm in a tureen. Discard the garlic.
❖Mix together the flour and the remaining butter in a small bowl to form a soft ball. Blend in 3 tablespoons of the broth, then return the mixture to the pot and cook over low heat, stirring, for 5 minutes or until the sauce thickens to a creamy consistency. Pour over the fish and serve immediately, accompanied by croutons.

SERVES 6

INGREDIENTS FOR FISH AND ONION STEW

PETER JOHNSON

TROUT IN RIESLING (top) AND TROUT WITH ALMONDS

Alsace

TRUITES AU RIESLING
Trout in Riesling

4 trout, about 6 oz (200 g) each
salt and freshly ground pepper
2½ oz (75 g) butter
4 French shallots, finely chopped
⅔ cup (5 fl oz/150 ml) Riesling
5 oz (150 g) small mushrooms
6 tablespoons heavy (double) cream or crème fraîche

❖Ask the fishmonger to clean the fish. Rinse them and pat dry; season with salt and pepper.
❖Preheat oven to 425°F (215°C). Using 1 tablespoon of the butter, grease a baking dish just large enough to hold the fish. Scatter the chopped shallots over the bottom and lay the fish on top. Pour the wine into the dish and cover with a sheet of waxed paper or aluminum foil. Bake for 20 minutes.
❖Meanwhile, trim the mushroom stems; wash the mushrooms, pat dry and cut into quarters. Melt 1 tablespoon butter in a nonstick 10-in (26-cm) skillet and cook the mushrooms until they are golden and give out no more liquid. Keep warm.
❖Skin the trout and arrange on a serving platter. Surround with mushrooms and keep warm.
❖Strain the trout cooking liquid into a small saucepan and boil over high heat until reduced to a syrupy consistency. Add the cream and cook until the sauce is thick and creamy. Briskly stir in the remaining butter with a wooden spoon. Coat the fish and mushrooms with the sauce and serve immediately.

SERVES 4

PETER JOHNSON

Champagne

TRUITES AUX AMANDES
Trout with Almonds

4 trout, about 6 oz (200 g) each
salt and freshly ground pepper
5 oz (150 g) butter
4 oz (120 g) flaked almonds

❖Ask the fishmonger to clean the fish. Rinse them and pat dry; season with salt and pepper.
❖Melt half the butter in a nonstick 10-in (26-cm) skillet and cook the trout for 6 minutes each side. Transfer to a serving platter and keep warm.
❖Discard the butter from the skillet and wipe out the pan. Add the almonds and toast lightly over low heat, stirring often. Add the remaining butter and let it melt over low heat. Pour over the trout and serve immediately.

SERVES 4

Bourgogne

CARPE FARCIE
Stuffed Carp

1 carp, about 3 lb (1.5 kg)
5 oz (150 g) stale bread, crusts trimmed
3 oz (100 g) thinly sliced streaky bacon
2 tablespoons butter
1 clove garlic, finely chopped

PETER JOHNSON

3 French shallots, finely chopped
salt and freshly ground pepper
1 tablespoon chopped flat-leaf parsley
1 egg
6 tablespoons (100 ml) dry white wine
¾ cup (6 fl oz/185 ml) heavy (double) cream or
  crème fraîche

❖ Ask the fishmonger to scale and gut the fish and to open it along the belly, without separating the two fillets, in order to remove the backbone. If the fish contains any roe, set this aside and chop coarsely. Rinse the fish and pat dry on all surfaces.

❖ Grind the bread into coarse crumbs in a blender or food processor. Trim the rind from the bacon and finely chop the meat with a knife.

❖ Melt 1 tablespoon butter in a nonstick 10-in (26-cm) sauté pan. Add the chopped garlic and shallots and cook over low heat, stirring, for 2 minutes. Add the bacon and cook, stirring, for 2 more minutes. Season with salt and pepper. Stir in the roe, parsley and breadcrumbs, then remove from heat. Mix in the egg and let cool.

❖ Preheat oven to 450°F (230°C). Season the inside of the fish with salt and pepper and spread with the stuffing. Fold the fillets together and tie the fish at intervals.

❖ Use the remaining butter to grease a baking dish large enough to hold the fish; lay the fish in the dish. Add the wine and bake for 45 minutes, basting often with the cooking juices.

❖ Transfer the cooked fish to a serving platter. Boil the sauce until reduced to a syrupy consistency. Add the cream and cook, stirring, until it thickens, about 2 more minutes. Pour sauce over the fish and serve.

SERVES 6

STUFFED CARP

PETER JOHNSON

EELS IN GREEN SAUCE

Picardie

ANGUILLES AU VERT

Eels in Green Sauce

2 lb (1 kg) medium eels
salt and freshly ground pepper
3 oz (100 g) sorrel
3 oz (100 g) fresh spinach
10 sprigs flat-leaf parsley
4 sprigs chervil
4 sprigs sage
2 sprigs tarragon
1 sprig mint
1½ oz (40 g) butter
3 French shallots, finely chopped
6 tablespoons dry white wine
2 sprigs thyme
1 bay leaf
2 egg yolks
6 tablespoons heavy (double) cream or crème fraîche

❖ Skin and gut the eels, wash them and slice into chunks 1½ in (4 cm) thick. Pat dry with paper towels and season with salt and pepper.

❖ Remove the stalks from the sorrel, spinach, parsley, chervil, sage, tarragon and mint. Wash, pat dry and chop the leaves.

❖ Melt the butter in a nonstick 10-in (26-cm) sauté pan. Add the chunks of eel and the shallots and cook over low heat, stirring, for 5 minutes or until the eel is just lightly browned. Discard the butter from the pan and stir in the wine. Add thyme and bay leaf and bring to boil. Cover and simmer for 5 minutes over low heat.

❖ Remove the thyme and bay leaf and add the remaining herbs, sorrel and spinach. Mix well and simmer, covered, for 5 minutes.

❖ Meanwhile, beat the egg yolks and cream with a fork in a small bowl. Stir in 2 tablespoons of the cooking liquid, then return the mixture to the sauté pan. Remove from heat and stir until the sauce thickens and coats the chunks of eel. Turn into a shallow dish and serve immediately.

SERVES 4

FROM FRANCHE-COMTÉ TO DAUPHINÉ

From one mountain to another

LEO MEIER

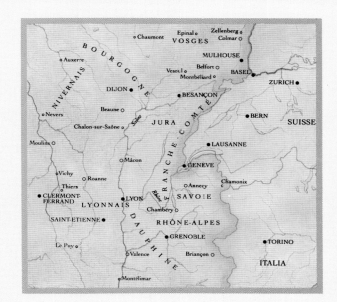

FROM FRANCHE-COMTÉ TO DAUPHINÉ

From one mountain to another

The appearance of Franche-Comté's landscape provides its name — the *reculées*, or recesses, as one plateau comes after the other, then withdraws behind the valley. The Jura mountains have many of these. This gentle, soft, green mountain range, rarely exceeding 1000 meters in height, shoulder to shoulder with Switzerland, belongs entirely to the free county that was for so long disputed between the Kings of Spain and the Dukes of Burgundy. It was once the land of the *gaude*, but this thick gruel, enriched with fresh butter, is now hardly ever made. Nor is the *bresi*, salted beef dried by the hearth.

This is the kingdom of small mountains, of fresh air, of pure wines — light, fruity reds from Poulsard and Trousseau grapes, whites from the Chardonnay and, especially, the distinctively colored Savagnin, rosy-tinged and golden yellow. The wine from this grape, left in barrels for six years during which time one-third of its volume is lost through evaporation, becomes *vin jaune*, or yellow wine. The real treasure of the region, it takes its flavor and scent from walnuts, resin and dried flowers, delicately mixed.

The reason for insisting on the particular quality of the Jura wines, the best of which are found between Arbois — the city of Pasteur — and the belvedere of Château-Chalon, is that they marry admirably with the dishes of the Franche-Comté: sausages, *côti du Sauguais* (the smoked pork chop that is a standard dish of Arbois), chicken with *vin jaune* and morels, veal sweetbreads with cream and wine sauce, walnut cakes and, naturally, the cheeses of the region.

There are the Comté and the Morbier of the local dairies, the Vacherin from Mont d'Or and

LEFT: GRAPEVINES ADORN THIS FARMHOUSE NEAR CHALON-SUR-SAÔNE IN BOURGOGNE, A REGION PROUD OF ITS RED WINES.

PREVIOUS PAGES: SHROUDED IN MIST, MONT BLANC IS THE HIGHEST MOUNTAIN IN EUROPE, BREATHTAKINGLY BEAUTIFUL AND DESERVEDLY FAMOUS.
LEO MEIER

117

again, but more commercial, the Cancoillotte from Besançon or Haute-Saône, a runny cheese made from skim milk. The Comté, which bears the name of its province, is a splendid Gruyère-type cheese made from unpasteurized cow's milk, with an aroma of grassy meadows. It demonstrates that the Franche-Comté, so aptly named, has in no way abdicated its characteristic frankness, nor the natural qualities of the pastures of its plateaus.

At the foot of the plateaus, the beautiful valley of the Loue produces the kirsch of La Marsotte. The valley has hardly changed since the time when Gustave Courbet, a native of Ornans — the town has established a museum in his studio — painted it from the viewpoint of a wide-eyed observer. Brook trout and river fish are still plentiful in the clear waters that abound in the vicinity of Lods and Mouthier-Haute-Pierre.

Right next door is Burgundy — another wine region, and famous in a different way. From Dijon to Chagny, an expanse of vineyard: the Côtes de Nuits from Fixin to Corgoloin, the Côtes de Beaune from Ladoix to Cheilley-les-Maranges. Here are found some of the world's most celebrated wine appellations: Clos Vougeot, Chambertin, Vosne-Romanée, Pommard, Meursault, Montrachet. A region of fine wines, exquisite fare and joyous revelry.

Henri Vincenot, the incomparable Burgundian writer, used to tell the story of the "three-man wine," the *vin de trois* — which, it seems, needed three people to appreciate it: "an obliging taster and two men to carry him." Burgundian humor.

There is no other region more serious, however, about the art of dining. Old traditions persist in spite of the increasing rarity of old-fashioned ingredients — the snails of Burgundy, known as *gros gris* or "large greys"; the *pochouse verdunoise*, a fricassée of freshwater fish cooked in white wine. Wine has always played an important part in the cuisine: *civet* with red wine, marinades based on white wine or, again, "verjuice" from freshly crushed grapes.

There are other festive products as well, and all seem to converge at Dijon, the splendid capital of the former duchy — a town of old dwellings, historic churches and cobbled streets where the old palace of Charles the Bold now houses a magnificent art museum. Dijon is the home of mustard; its gingerbread, or *pain d'épices*, is equally famous. Blackcurrant liqueur — *crème de cassis* — made from the tiny berries picked around Arcenant, a sleepy village high above the Côtes de Nuits, has known an illustrious career thanks to Canon Kir, mayor of Dijon, who mixed it with white wine to create the drink which now bears his name.

Mushrooms, pike, freshwater crayfish and *sauce nantua*, prepared with a puree of the same crayfish, belong to the shared assets of Burgundy and the Franche-Comté, the destinies of which were once intertwined. But Burgundy, which at the height of its glory was greater than the kingdom of France,

LEO MEIER

LIKE MOST ALPINE RESORTS, CHAMONIX REMAINS AN OLD-FASHIONED MOUNTAIN TOWN, WITH CHARMING CHALETS LIKE THIS ONE THAT ATTRACT A SOPHISTICATED INTERNATIONAL CLIENTELE.

LEO MEIER

THE BORDER TOWN OF CHAMONIX, HIGH IN THE FRENCH ALPS, IS A POPULAR TOURIST RESORT ALL YEAR ROUND.

has been able to appropriate the riches of its smaller neighbors: the Charolais, renowned for its beef; the Morvan, for its ham; the Bresse, for its highly esteemed white poultry. Thus dishes such as ham in cream sauce, chicken in white wine, *coq au vin*, Burgundian beef and slow-simmered stews, are all evidence of the enormous wealth of the province.

The cheeses of Epoisses and Chambertin, both strong, soft and made from cow's milk, are perfect mates for the powerful, well-structured red wines of the Côte de Nuits. *Oeufs en meurette* (eggs poached in red wine), *gougères* (little cheese puffs, traditionally served at the start of a meal) and various charcuterie products, like parsleyed ham set in a clear, wine-flavored jelly enlivened with fresh thyme, chervil and tarragon: these add the finishing touch to a festive spread.

Lyons could easily pass for the natural daughter, or elder sister, of Burgundy. For years writers have overflowed with praise for this ex-capital of ancient Gaul — the "capital of fine food" — claiming it to be, in the words of Curnonsky, "world capital of gastronomy." Or as Henri Clos-Jouve put it, "Lyons is a larder."

In fact, Lyons and its surrounding regions hold a trump hand when it comes to attracting the gourmet: pears from the Rhône valley, nougat from Montélimar, the wines of Hermitage, Condrieu, Cornas, Château-Grillet and Saint-Joseph; more wines from the Côte-Rôtie, violet-scented reds made from the Syrah grape, the amiable red and white wines of Mâcon, the great Pouilly-Fuissés, the seductive Saint-Verans; the modest wines from Crozes-Hermitage. And then the Beaujolais, which is a whole saga in itself. "Lyons," wrote Léon Daudet, "is watered by three rivers: the Rhône, the Saône and the Beaujolais."

More than just a city of good living, Lyons is a symbol. It is the great gastronomic crossroads where all routes meet: a bridge to the Côte d'Azur from Paris, a link with Switzerland and eastern Europe, touching the Charolais, Bresse and Auvergne region, making the most of its important strategic situation and benefiting from the unsurpassed reputation it has enjoyed since it was known by the Romans as Lugdunum.

It used to be said that Lyons is a city that makes you hungry. At one time it was the women, the *mères*, who set the gastronomic standards. Mère Charles, Mère Guy, Mère Blanc and the most famous of all, Mère Brazier, have now been replaced by men who do not always have descendants. So is Lyons stagnating, resting on the good fortune of its location? No: in truth, Lyons is still a capital of good eating and good living, even if it is left to Paris, or indeed to the other provinces, to set the styles.

There are plenty of good charcutiers, those kings of the *rosette*, the preserved sausage, the *andouillette*, the *sabodet*, the boiling sausage, the tripe known as *gras double* and the little bundles of pork rind. They provide the superb products on which is based the popular cuisine of Lyons, the cuisine served in the *bouchons* — familiar little bistros where the wine comes in jugs — and in the most characteristic of the large restaurants of the town, Léon de Lyons. Here, too, you can eat poached sausage accompanied by potatoes cooked in oil; or *tablier de sapeur* (the fireman's apron), made from beef mesentery that is cut into pieces, then crumbed and fried; or perhaps brains cooked with capers.

The cheese called *cervelle de canut* owes its name to the silk weavers from the mills of Lyons, the *canuts*. It is a blend of fresh cheese beaten until smooth with salt and pepper, finely chopped shallot and fresh herbs, white wine and a dash of oil, and it epitomizes the honest, simple character of the food of Lyons. Other typical dishes? Spit-roasted chickens, served simply with cardoons (a vegetable of the same family as the artichoke) or a gratin of macaroni; veal liver fried with onions and vinegar; pike quenelles cooked in beef fat; *andouillette*, prepared from pork and veal mesentery and pan-fried with onions and white wine or vinegar, sometimes with mustard as well; chicken with slices of truffle slipped under the skin, said to be *en demi-deuil* (in half-mourning); or chicken poached in a pig's bladder filled with vegetable stock, with cream added later; chicken flavored with vinegar; the savory tart (called *tartre*) of Les Allymes; the sugar-topped *galette*, or cake, from Pérouges; the *bugnes*, or fritters, from Bresse — all these are just as much part of the repertoire of Lyons, which makes the most of all the resources of the orchards, the valleys, the lakes, the pastures and the vineyards that surround it.

The mountains encircling Lyons bring a breath of fresh air from their intoxicating heights, and are hardly mean with their riches. *Gratin dauphinois*, so popular in Lyons but also throughout the whole of France, consists of layers of thinly sliced potatoes, cooked in the oven with cream. The *ravioles* of Romans, in the Drôme, are small pasta shapes stuffed with goat cheese. The sharp, satisfying flavor of Saint-Marcellin cheese — soft, medium-sized, made with cow's milk — makes a pleasant ending to a cozy dinner. The various charcuterie items — which rejoice in such names as *boudins farçons*, *mursons*, *caillettes* (small pâtés of liver combined with spinach) — are some of the assets of the Dauphiné, although they are also found on the other side of the Rhône, on the rugged slopes of the Ardèche.

Savoy, with its expansive mountainside pastures, its wooded farms, its flower-bedecked chalets, its huge barns, its forest fruits and its dairy traditions, offers unexpected wealth; even the French have little idea of the diversity of its products. The lakes of Bourget, Annecy and Léman produce magnificent fish: trout, perch, carp, eel and a local specialty, the *féra*, but best of all the superb, rosy-fleshed *omble-chevalier*, which is cooked simply *à la meunière* or served with foaming butter.

The local cheeses, which must be included among the finest in France, are often seen at their best in the modern market of Lyons at La Part-Dieu. They include the Reblochon, produced in the region between Thônes and the Grand-Bornand from unpasteurized, unfermented milk, its rind washed frequently during two weeks of aging in a cool cellar; the Beaufort, pride of the Beaufortin region, a land of steeples, *clochers à bulbe* and undulating pastures — the "prince of Gruyères," according to Brillat-Savarin, made only during a period of 100 days in summer when cows graze on the mountain pastures, from warm milk that smells of both grass and curds; the Tamié, which is a strong-flavored, Reblochon-type cheese, made by monks in the abbey of the same name; the Tomme des Bauges, with its rich, powdery white

THE TRANQUIL BARRAGE DE ROSELAND,
ONE OF MANY ALPINE DAMS, WILL TURN TO ICE IN THE WEEKS TO COME.

LEO MEIER

LEO MEIER

VEGETABLE GARDENS SURROUND THE TINY SHINGLE-TOPPED HOMES OF
ST-PIERRE-DE-CHARTREUSE IN DAUPHINÉ.

rind; the *Persillé* cheese, made from slowly heated goat's milk that takes on a musty flavor: are these not enough to demonstrate the great wealth of cheeses from Savoy? More significantly, many of the traditional dishes of the region rely on this variety of cheeses — like the *pela des Aravis*, which is a simple dish of melted cheese on boiled potatoes, or the renowned *fondue* based on melted Gruyère, with white wine and sometimes kirsch and nutmeg.

Are these traditional dishes tending to disappear for reasons of health and diet? On the farms between Megève and Chamonix they still prepare the *farcement savoyard* (a cake made with grated raw potato to which are added prunes, dried pears, raisins, eggs and flour), the *farçon* (a potato puree enriched with eggs and chopped herbs), and the *caïon*, a dish of pork cooked in red wine, which is accompanied by polenta. And you still find — not only in Savoy — the *matafan* or *mate-faim*, a thick, substantial potato pancake which in Burgundy and the Jura is made with apples and sugar. The pastries here — like the sponge known as *biscuit de Savoie*, whose basic ingredients are eggs and sugar — are as delicate as snow. Another find is the brioche of Saint-Genix, originally from the Pâtisserie Debeauve at Yenne: a hand-shaped brioche, filled with praline and covered with brown sugar.

Savoy wines include the Roussette and the Chignin, made from Roussette grapes (smooth, elegant, distinctive); the Bergeron, from the Roussane (full-bodied and structured); and the Apremont or Abymes, from the Jacquère grape (lighter, more diuretic); it is all too easy to think of them as uncomplicated, après-ski wines, but the two first mentioned improve greatly with age. The most typical local red comes from the Mondeuse, a grape brought to the region long ago by the Allobroges. The wine has a heady perfume of mountain fruit and a considerable aging potential.

From local fruits and berries are made jams, jellies, syrups and spirits. *Génépi*, which results from the distillation of an indigenous Savoy plant, is the local digestive *par excellence*. But how many know that it was in Chambéry that French vermouth was born, in 1821, at the Routin distillery? The recipe calls for macerating whole plants, roots, bark and mountain flowers in the local dry white wine. Here, too, *Chambéry fraise* was launched, to become a favorite apéritif for Americans in France in the postwar years: a simple beverage, made from alpine strawberries and white wine.

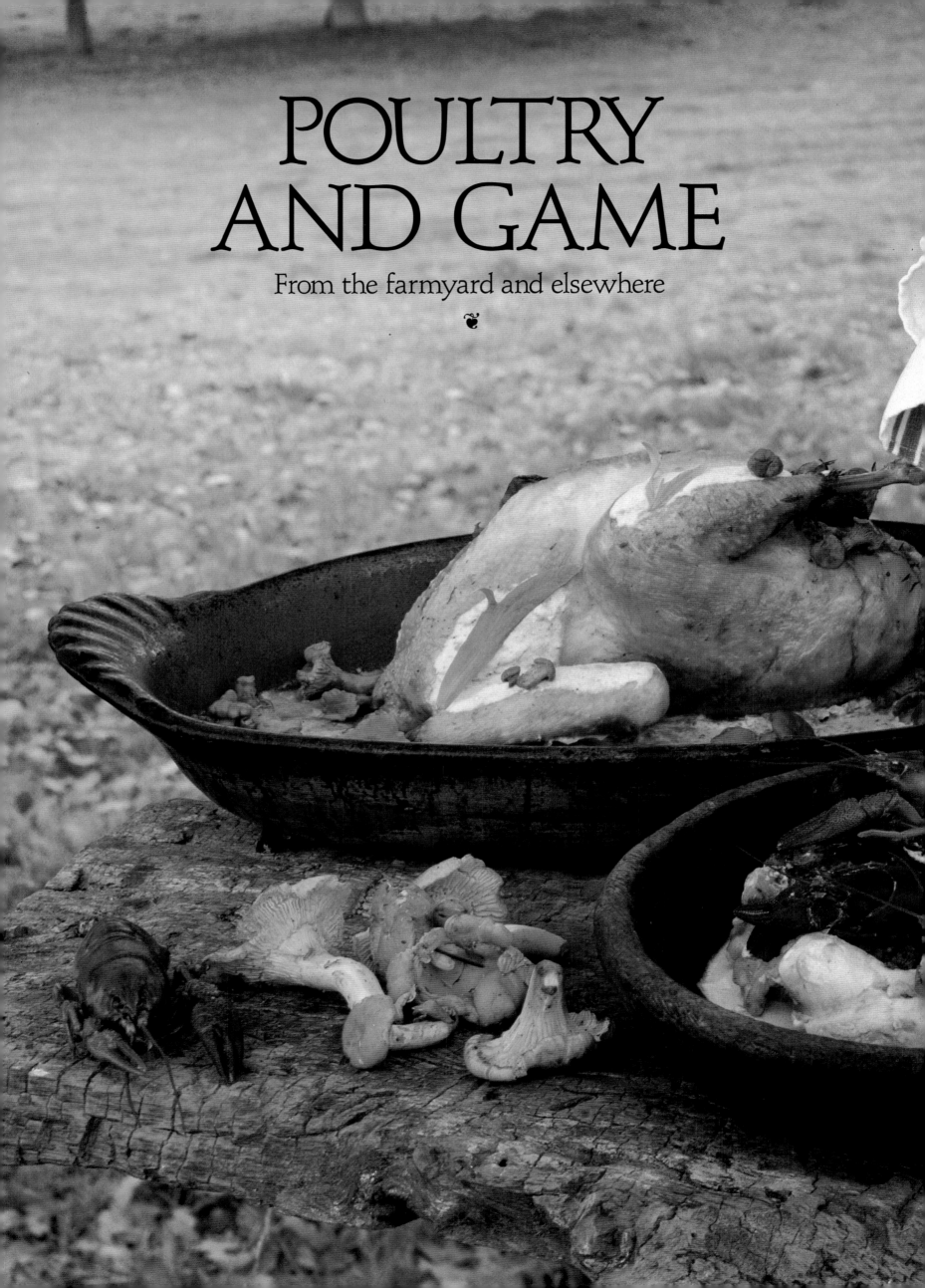

POULTRY
AND GAME

From the farmyard and elsewhere

FOIE GRAS, THE ENLARGED LIVER OF A FORCE-FED DUCK OR GOOSE, IS ONE OF THE
MOST ANCIENT FRENCH DELICACIES. THE BEST *FOIE GRAS* COMES FROM ALSACE
AND PÉRIGORD, AND IS PRODUCED BETWEEN OCTOBER AND APRIL.

POULTRY AND GAME

From the farmyard and elsewhere

It all began with the Sunday *poule au pot* which Henri IV, much-beloved king of France, wished to provide as festive fare for all his subjects. Over five centuries, many changes have taken place: chicken has become an economical dish, even an everyday one. So much for the exceptional, the special-occasion dish; the so-called "battery" chicken is mass-produced.

As a reaction against the raising of poultry not in farmyards but in closed, cramped quarters, practitioners of the traditional system have grouped together to defend their "label," granted in accordance with the extent of the pasture area and of the liberty allowed the bird. The finest of all, the greatest luxury, is the Bresse chicken: white-feathered, blue-clawed, allowed 10 square meters space each, fed on grain. The poultry is superb, with tender, juicy and tasty flesh, the gentle and soothing reflection of a fertile earth. In Bresse, chickens are treated like children.

The chickens of Loué, in the Landes of Chalosse, are also of top quality, raised in the open air and fed on grain. The best way of eating them? Spit-roasted, or gently pot-roasted, or cooked *en vessie*, in a pig's bladder. Their fatty skin becomes deliciously crisp when cooked, the feet — grilled — are eaten in a salad, and the tender, delicate white meat can be made into scallops or marinated.

If the truth be known, poultry appeals to all palates, lends itself to all kinds of preparations and all vegetables, adapts to all traditions. With cream, with tarragon, with vinegar, with wild mushrooms from the forest, with rich *vin jaune*, with freshwater crayfish (*écrevisses*), with garlic, with cider, with butter, with mustard, stuffed, poached in stock, cooked with rice, with a cream sauce known as *suprême*, with peppers, with truffles, with beer, with champagne, with Riesling: every region has its own recipe. Indeed, poultry is the lowest common denominator of the French.

The *coq*, or rooster (typically a bird at least one year of age, its reproductive duties already past), which is traditionally cooked *au vin*, either red, white or *jaune*, in order to tenderize its somewhat tough flesh, is becoming rare. The situation is similar for the hen. Both are being profitably replaced by year-old chickens. The *ne plus ultra* is the capon, a specialty of Bresse and of the Landes of Upper

PREVIOUS PAGES: GUINEA FOWL STUFFED WITH GIROLLES (top left, recipe page 130), SADDLE OF HARE IN CREAM SAUCE (top right, recipe page 128), CHICKEN WITH CRAYFISH (bottom left, recipe page 131), AND CHICKEN WITH VINEGAR (bottom right, recipe page 127), PHOTOGRAPHED IN LYONNAIS.

PIERRE HUSSENOT/AGENCE TOP

THE FRENCH HAVE LONG BEEN KEEN HUNTERS. IN EARLY FALL THE HUNTING SEASON BEGINS, AND THIS FARMER WASTES NO TIME TRAMPING THROUGH HIS FIELDS OF LETTUCE IN SEARCH OF HARE OR PHEASANT.

MANY OF THE HALF-TIMBERED HOUSES IN DINAN, BRETAGNE, ARE OCCUPIED BY ARTISANS. THIS ONE IN THE *CENTRE VILLE* IS A RESTAURANT WHERE THE POULTRY AND GAME DISHES ARE SURE TO BE SUPERB.

Gascony: male chickens are castrated at six weeks, fattened from the age of six months, and weigh four to five kilos by the time they are killed and sold for Christmas. This plump and succulent bird, with meltingly tender flesh, is a real delight; as a festive treat, it is unsurpassable.

Among poultry one must also include the guinea fowl; the turkey, which is eaten with chestnuts at Christmas in what has become an international tradition, and which also, in the form of breaded slices or *escalopes*, is beginning to replace veal; and the pheasant, which might come from either the poultry farm or the wild. Certain birds that used to exist only in the wild state have now been domesticated.

Amongst the many forests of the Sologne, partridge, quail and mallard ducks are bred and released at the start of the hunting season. But domestic pigeons, fattened on grain, are not to be confused with the wood pigeon (*pigeon ramier*), of darker, denser flesh and flavor. From the lakes to the copses, from the forests to the thickets, there is still fine game to be found in France.

As for the duck, it is one of those ingredients

that give rise to some of the great French dishes. Its special quality is a firm, substantial flesh, which can be cooked rare like steak and which lends itself to sweet-sour combinations, to the flavor of the orange, to sauces enriched with liver, or foie gras, and other offal, and with the juices extracted from the carcass by means of a silver duck press. The finest breed is the Challans, from the region of Nantes. The *Mulard* breed produces excellent foie gras. The Barbary duck, however, is equally appreciated and rather more common.

More and more often, the fillets of the fattened duck, called *magrets* or *maigrets*, are cooked rare, following a fashion initiated in the Gers by the chef of Auch, André Daguin. In effect, they are duck "steaks." The tradition of preserving the duck in *confits*, by cooking it in its fat and storing the product in earthenware pots, goes back to the Moors, who passed through the southwest of France. The method is equally applicable to the more stringy meat of the goose, which is highly appreciated in Alsace, especially among the Jewish community.

The rabbit, for many years disregarded and relegated to everyday fare, has made a triumphant return to the table. But regional traditions never abandoned the rabbit, accompanying it with prunes, mustard or cider and inviting gourmets to partake of its plump thighs and also its saddle (the meaty part from the end of the ribs to the tail), which might be pan-fried, roasted, cooked *en gibelotte* or *en civet*, or stuffed. It can truly be considered part of the *grande cuisine*, as long as it is not overcooked to the extent that it becomes insipid. The best rabbits often come from the Gâtinais, the flat region around Orléans to the south of Paris. If you cross the Loire, you come to the Sologne with its forests and its hunting lands, where you can still find the hare (a type of wild rabbit). Its dark meat retains the flavor of the forests, the moss and the heather that it brushes aside as it flees the hunter. As a *civet* or *à la royale*, stuffed with foie gras and served with a sauce flavored with its offal, with pan-fried fruits such as quinces and pears, with a chestnut puree or with fresh pasta, it represents the tastiest of autumn fare.

AN OLD BRETAGNE BARN HAS AN AIR OF PEACEFUL RUSTICITY, CHARACTERISTIC OF THE MONT-ST-MICHEL REGION.

LEO MEIER

Lyonnais

POULET AU VINAIGRE
Chicken with Vinegar

2 ripe medium tomatoes
1 chicken, about 3 lb (1.5 kg), cut into 8 serving pieces
salt and freshly ground pepper
1 tablespoon vegetable oil
1 oz (25 g) butter
6 cloves garlic, peeled
6 tablespoons tarragon vinegar
⅔ cup (5 fl oz/150 ml) dry white wine
2 pinches of sugar
⅔ cup (5 fl oz/150 ml) heavy (double) cream or crème fraîche
1 teaspoon strong mustard

❖Drop the tomatoes into boiling water for 10 seconds. Cool under running water, peel, halve and squeeze out the seeds; finely chop the flesh.

❖Season the chicken with salt and pepper. Heat the oil in a nonstick 10-in (26-cm) sauté pan and add the butter. As soon as it has melted, add the chicken pieces and garlic cloves and cook until golden brown, about 10 minutes. Pour in the vinegar and let it evaporate. Stir in the wine and tomatoes and season with salt, pepper and sugar. Cook for 45 minutes, stirring from time to time.

❖While the chicken is cooking, combine the cream and mustard in a small bowl. Remove the cooked chicken from the pan and keep warm. Strain the cooking juices through a fine sieve into a saucepan, crushing the garlic to a paste. Boil over high heat until syrupy, about 5 minutes. Add the mustard mixture and boil over high heat for 2 minutes to produce a thick, creamy sauce. Pour over the chicken pieces and serve immediately.

SERVES 4 – 6   *Photograph pages 122 – 123*

Auvergne/Bourgogne

COQ AU VIN
Chicken Casserole

This dish was originally made with Chanturgues, a red wine from Auvergne. This has become rare and is now replaced by red wine from Bourgogne. However, every province in France claims to have invented the dish, and indeed similar preparations based on red or white wine are found almost everywhere.

1 chicken, about 4 lb (2 kg), cut into 10 serving pieces
salt and freshly ground pepper
6 tablespoons all purpose (plain) flour
bouquet garni: 1 bay leaf, 1 sprig thyme, 1 sprig rosemary,
    8 sprigs parsley
1 slice streaky bacon, about 3 oz (100 g)
24 small (button) mushrooms
1 tablespoon vegetable oil
2 oz (50 g) butter
24 small pickling onions, peeled
2 tablespoons cognac
3 cups (24 fl oz/750 ml) red Burgundy, such as Chambertin
3 cloves garlic, peeled

CHICKEN CASSEROLE

4 pinches of freshly grated nutmeg
1 teaspoon sugar
For serving:
croutons

❖Season the chicken with salt and pepper. Spread the flour on a plate and roll the chicken pieces in it, shaking off excess.

❖Tie together the herbs for the bouquet garni. Cut the bacon into fine matchsticks, removing the rind. Trim the mushrooms, wash and pat dry.

❖Heat the oil in a 6-qt (6-l) pot and add the butter. Cook the onions, bacon and mushrooms until softened, then remove and set aside. Brown the chicken pieces on all sides for about 10 minutes. Sprinkle in the cognac and ignite, shaking the pot gently until flames subside. Pour in the wine and stir in the bouquet garni, garlic, salt, pepper, nutmeg and sugar. Bring to simmer and cook for 1 hour, stirring from time to time.

❖Add the mushroom mixture and cook for 30 minutes longer.

❖Remove the cooked chicken pieces from the pot and arrange on a serving platter. Remove the bouquet garni and let the sauce boil over high heat for 2 minutes or until thickened. Pour over the chicken and serve immediately, accompanied by croutons.

SERVES 6

RABLE DE LIÈVRE À LA CRÈME
Saddle of Hare in Cream Sauce

This dish is also popular in Alsace, where it is served with spätzele *(noodles) and sautéed wild mushrooms.*

2 saddles of hare, halved crosswise
salt and freshly ground pepper
2 tablespoons cognac
¾ cup (6 fl oz/200 ml) chicken stock (recipe page 34)
1 tablespoon vegetable oil
1 onion, about 3 oz (100 g), sliced
1 carrot, peeled and sliced
2 cloves garlic, peeled and quartered
1 sprig thyme
1 bay leaf
6 sprigs parsley
⅔ cup (5 fl oz/150 ml) heavy (double) cream or crème fraîche

❖Rinse the meat and pat dry; season with salt and pepper. Pour the cognac, stock and oil into a bowl. Add the onion, carrot, garlic, thyme, bay leaf and parsley, crushing the herbs between the fingers. Place the pieces of hare in this marinade, turn them to coat and marinate in the refrigerator for 12 hours, turning several times.
❖Remove the pieces of hare and pat dry. Strain the marinade, discarding herbs and flavorings.
❖Preheat oven to 450°F (230°C). Place the pieces of hare in a baking dish just large enough to hold them. Brown the hare in the oven for 10 minutes on each side, then roast for 30 minutes longer, frequently pouring a little of the marinade into the bottom of the dish and basting the hare with the pan juices.
❖Transfer the hare pieces to a plate and keep warm. Pour the pan juices into a small saucepan and skim the fat from the surface. Boil until reduced to a syrupy consistency, about 2 minutes. Add the cream and boil until the sauce is thick and creamy, 3 to 4 minutes longer. Pour the sauce over the hare and serve immediately.

SERVES 4   *Photograph pages 122 – 123*

POULET AUX QUARANTE GOUSSES D'AIL
Chicken with Forty Cloves of Garlic

In Provence, where it is called the poor man's truffle, garlic is the basis of the local cuisine. Braised en chemise *("in a shirt" — in other words, unpeeled), the garlic cloves become soft and creamy, making a delicious puree that enhances the flavor of poultry.*

1 chicken, about 3½ lb (1.75 kg)
salt
2 sprigs fresh thyme
2 sprigs fresh rosemary
2 sprigs fresh sage
2 tender celery stalks, with their leaves
2 sprigs flat-leaf parsley
40 cloves of fresh, young garlic, unpeeled
3 tablespoons olive oil
freshly ground pepper
For serving:
toasted slices of country bread

❖Preheat oven to 400°F (200°C). Sprinkle the chicken with salt inside and out. Stuff the chicken with half the thyme, rosemary, sage and celery; add the parsley and 4 cloves of garlic. Place the remaining herbs and celery in an oval earthenware or enameled pot just large enough to hold the chicken. Add the oil, salt, pepper and remaining garlic cloves. Roll the chicken in the oil to coat on all sides. Cover the pot and bake for 1¾ hours.
❖Transfer the cooked chicken to a serving platter and surround it with the cloves of garlic. Skim the fat from the cooking juices and pour into a sauceboat. Serve the chicken hot, accompanied by its sauce and toasted slices of bread. Each diner crushes the garlic slightly to remove the skin and spreads the wonderful fragrant puree that is left onto a slice of bread.

SERVES 5 – 6

LAPIN EN PAQUETS
Rabbit Parcels

It is the method of preparation that gives this dish its name: each piece of rabbit is enclosed in a "packet" of bacon. Rabbit is cooked this way throughout Provence, and sometimes fried eggplant (aubergine) slices are used instead of the tomatoes.

8 oz (250 g) ripe tomatoes
2 tablespoons olive oil
salt and freshly ground pepper
2 pinches of sugar
1 rabbit, about 3¼ lb (1.6 kg), cut into 8 serving pieces
8 very thin slices streaky bacon
8 small sprigs thyme
2 cloves garlic, peeled and finely slivered

❖Preheat oven to 400°F (200°C). Drop the tomatoes into boiling water for 10 seconds. Cool under running water, then peel, halve, squeeze out the seeds and coarsely chop the flesh. Combine the tomatoes and 1 tablespoon olive oil in a nonstick 10-in (26-cm) sauté pan. Add salt, pepper and sugar and cook over high heat, stirring constantly, until reduced to a thick puree.
❖Using the remaining oil, grease a shallow baking dish large enough to hold the rabbit pieces in a single layer. Pour in the tomato puree.
❖Rinse the rabbit and pat dry; season with salt and pepper. Place one piece of rabbit in the center of a slice of bacon. Season with a sprig of thyme and a few slivers of garlic. Wrap the bacon around the rabbit and secure with a toothpick. Repeat with the remaining ingredients.
❖Arrange the rabbit "parcels" on the tomato puree and bake for 1 hour, turning the parcels after 30 minutes.
❖Remove the toothpicks and arrange the rabbit parcels on a serving platter. Cover with the tomato sauce and serve immediately.

SERVES 4

RABBIT PARCELS (left) AND CHICKEN WITH FORTY CLOVES OF GARLIC (right), PHOTOGRAPHED IN PROVENCE.
PIERRE HUSSENOT/AGENCE TOP

BOILED CHICKEN, TOULOUSE STYLE

PETER JOHNSON

Languedoc

POULE AU POT À LA TOULOUSAINE

Boiled Chicken, Toulouse-style

1 chicken, about 4 lb (2 kg), with liver, gizzard, heart and
  neck
salt and freshly ground pepper
3 tablespoons milk
3 oz (100 g) fresh bread, crusts trimmed
4 cloves garlic
6 oz (200 g) prosciutto or other raw ham
2 eggs
1 tablespoon chopped flat-leaf parsley
4 pinches of freshly grated nutmeg
2 onions, about 3 oz (100 g) each
4 cloves
bouquet garni: 1 bay leaf, 1 sprig thyme, 6 sprigs parsley
2 medium carrots, peeled and thickly sliced
2 tender celery stalks, cut into large chunks
10 peppercorns, white and black mixed
For serving:
slices of toasted bread

❖Season the chicken inside and out with salt and pepper.
❖Heat the milk in a small saucepan and crumble in the
bread. Mix to a smooth paste, then remove from heat and
let cool.
❖Finely chop 2 cloves of garlic. Chop the ham and chicken
liver finely in a food processor.
❖Break the eggs into a bowl and beat with a fork to blend.
Add the garlic, chopped ham and liver, soaked bread,

parsley, salt, pepper and nutmeg and mix with a wooden
spoon until smooth. Stuff the chicken with this mixture
and sew the opening with kitchen thread.
❖Peel the onions and stud with cloves. Tie together the
herbs for the bouquet garni. Pour 3 qt (3 l) water into a pot
large enough to easily hold the chicken. Add the chicken
innards and neck, onions, carrots, celery, remaining 2 cloves
of garlic, peppercorns and bouquet garni. Bring to boil and
add the chicken. Season with salt. Cover and simmer
gently for 3 hours.
❖Remove the chicken, carve, sprinkle with a little stock
and keep warm. Strain the cooking liquid into a tureen.
Serve the soup with toasted bread, followed by the chicken
and its stuffing.

SERVES 8

Savoie

PINTADE FARCIE AUX GIROLLES

Guinea Fowl Stuffed with Girolles

1 guinea fowl, about 2½ lb (1.2 kg), with liver
salt and freshly ground pepper
1 lb (500 g) fresh *girolles* or 1 oz (30 g) dried mushrooms,
  soaked in tepid water for 10 minutes
2 oz (50 g) chicken livers
1 tablespoon chopped fresh parsley
2 tablespoons chopped fresh tarragon
2 oz (50 g) butter
2 French shallots, finely chopped
2 tablespoons port
6 tablespoons heavy (double) cream or crème fraîche

❖Season the guinea fowl inside and out with salt and pepper.
❖Prepare the stuffing: wash 6 oz (200 g) *girolles* and pat dry
(or pat dry a little less than half the soaked dried mushrooms). Chop finely. Rinse the chicken livers and the guinea
fowl liver, pat dry and chop finely. Combine the mushrooms,
livers and herbs in a bowl. Melt half the butter, season with
salt and pepper and cool to lukewarm. Add to the liver mixture and blend well. Fill the cavity of the guinea fowl with
the stuffing and secure the opening with kitchen thread.
❖Preheat oven to 425 °F (215 °C). Melt the remaining butter
in a pot large enough to hold the guinea fowl. Brown it on
all sides over low heat, then remove it and discard the butter.
Lightly brown the shallots in the same pot, stirring constantly. Return the guinea fowl to the pot, cover and bake
for 45 minutes.
❖Meanwhile, wash the remaining mushrooms and pat
dry. After 35 minutes cooking, scatter them around the
guinea fowl and cook for 10 minutes, stirring after 5
minutes. When both guinea fowl and mushrooms are
cooked, arrange them in a serving dish and keep warm.
Boil the cooking liquid until reduced to a syrupy consistency. Add the port and cream and boil until the sauce is
thick, about 2 minutes longer, then stir in the remaining
tarragon and pour into a sauceboat.
❖To serve, carve the guinea fowl into portions; surround
with slices of stuffing and mushrooms. Pass the sauce separately.

SERVES 4 – 6   *Photograph pages 122 – 123*

Lyonnais

POULET AUX ÉCREVISSES

Chicken with Crayfish

24 crayfish
8 oz (250 g) ripe tomatoes
1 chicken, about 3 lb (1.5 kg), cut into 8 serving pieces
salt and freshly ground pepper
3 tablespoons vegetable oil
2 oz (50 g) butter
1 cup (8 fl oz/250 ml) dry white wine
2 cloves garlic, quartered
1 carrot, peeled and thinly sliced
1 onion, about 2 oz (50 g), chopped
2 French shallots, chopped
2 pinches of dried thyme
2 tablespoons cognac
6 tablespoons heavy (double) cream or crème fraîche

❖ To prepare the crayfish, twist and pull the central tail fin to remove the black vein. Rinse and drain the crayfish. Drop the tomatoes into boiling water for 10 seconds. Cool under running water, peel, halve and squeeze out the seeds.

❖ Season the chicken with salt and pepper. Heat the oil in a nonstick 10-in (26-cm) sauté pan with half the butter. Lightly brown the chicken pieces on all sides. Pour in half the wine and let it evaporate over high heat. Stir in the tomatoes and garlic, season with salt and pepper and cook over low heat for 45 minutes.

❖ Meanwhile, melt the remaining butter in a 9-in (22-cm) sauté pan. Add the carrot, onion, shallots, thyme and crayfish and cook for 3 minutes, turning the crayfish constantly. Sprinkle in the cognac and let it evaporate. Add the remaining wine and mix well over high heat. Cook for 5 minutes longer, then remove the crayfish from the pan and let cool. Shell the crayfish, reserving 6 as a garnish; set aside.

❖ Transfer the cooked chicken from the sauté pan to a serving dish. Pour the contents of the crayfish cooking pan into the chicken cooking pan and cook over high heat for 5 minutes or until the sauce is syrupy. Add the cream and boil until the sauce is thick and creamy, 3 to 4 more minutes. Strain it through a fine sieve, pressing down on the vegetables to extract all their flavor.

❖ Return the sauce to the larger sauté pan. Add the chicken and crayfish and reheat for 1 minute. Arrange the chicken and crayfish on a platter, garnish with the reserved whole crayfish and serve immediately.

SERVES 4 – 6   *Photograph pages 122 – 123*

Pays Basque

POULET BASQUAISE

Basque Chicken

4 small green peppers (capsicums)
1 lb (500 g) ripe tomatoes
1 chicken, about 3 lb (1.5 kg), cut into 8 serving pieces
salt and freshly ground pepper
3 tablespoons vegetable oil
2 onions, about 3 oz (100 g) each, finely chopped

CHICKEN WITH RICE (top, recipe page 132), BASQUE CHICKEN (bottom left) AND CHICKEN WITH COMTÉ CHEESE (bottom right, recipe page 132)

3 cloves garlic, finely chopped
1 slice prosciutto or Bayonne ham, about 5 oz (150 g), cut into small cubes
1 fresh chili pepper, seeded and finely chopped
⅔ cup (5 fl oz/150 ml) dry white wine

❖ Cut the green peppers in half and remove the stems, seeds and white ribs. Cut the flesh into fine strips. Drop the tomatoes into boiling water for 10 seconds. Cool under running water, peel, halve and squeeze out the seeds; finely chop the flesh.

❖ Season the chicken with salt and pepper. Heat the oil in a nonstick 10-in (26-cm) sauté pan and lightly brown the chicken pieces on all sides. Remove from the pan. Add the onions and garlic and stir for 1 minute. Add the ham, peppers and chili and cook over low heat, stirring, for 5 minutes or until the vegetables soften and are lightly browned.

❖ Return the chicken pieces to the pan, pour in the wine and let it evaporate over high heat. Add the tomatoes and season with salt and pepper. Cover and cook over low heat for 45 minutes, stirring from time to time.

❖ Transfer the chicken to a shallow dish. Boil the cooking liquid over high heat until thick. Pour over the chicken and serve immediately.

SERVES 4 – 6

Savoie

POULET AU COMTÉ
Chicken with Comté Cheese

This delicious dish is equally good whether it is made in Savoie, in Franche-Comté or in the Lyonnais region, where it is simply called poulet au fromage. *Sometimes half the Comté cheese is replaced by Emmenthaler.*

1 chicken, about 3¼ lb (1.6 kg), cut into 8 serving pieces
salt and freshly ground pepper
1 tablespoon vegetable oil
¾ cup (6 fl oz/200 ml) dry white wine, preferably from Savoie
2 tablespoons strong mustard
3 oz (100 g) finely and freshly grated Comté cheese

❖ Preheat oven to 425°F (215°C). Season the chicken with salt and pepper. Heat the oil in a nonstick 10-in (26-cm) sauté pan and lightly brown the chicken pieces on all sides. Remove the chicken from the pan and discard the oil. Pour in the wine and deglaze the pan, using a wooden spoon to scrape up the browned bits. Blend the mustard into the wine.
❖ Arrange the chicken pieces in a baking dish large enough to hold them in a single layer. Pour over the sauce from the pan. Bake for 40 minutes, turning the chicken from time to time.
❖ Sprinkle the chicken with grated cheese and cook for 5 minutes longer or until the cheese melts and starts to brown. Serve hot, directly from the dish.

SERVES 6   *Photograph page 131*

Bourgogne

POULE AU RIZ
Chicken with Rice

This simple, invigorating family dish is prepared in every French home. Sometimes the rice is sprinkled with finely grated Emmenthaler.

1 chicken, about 4 lb (2 kg), with liver, gizzard, heart and neck
salt and freshly ground pepper
8 oz (250 g) carrots
bouquet garni: 1 bay leaf, 1 sprig thyme, 6 sprigs parsley
1 tablespoon vegetable oil
1 oz (25 g) butter
8 oz (250 g) onions, finely chopped
2 cups (16 fl oz/500 ml) white Burgundy
1¼ cups (10 fl oz/300 ml) water
2 cups (11 oz/350 g) long-grain rice

❖ Season the chicken inside and out with salt and pepper. Peel the carrots and quarter them lengthwise, then cut into ¼-in (.5-cm) fan-shaped slices. Tie together the herbs for the bouquet garni.
❖ Heat the oil in a 4-qt (4-l) pot and lightly brown the chicken on all sides. Remove from the pot and discard the oil. Place the butter, carrots and onions in the pot and soften over low heat, stirring constantly with a wooden spoon. Add the chicken liver, gizzard, heart and neck and cook

for a further minute. Return the chicken to the pot, add the wine and water and bring to simmer. Add the bouquet garni, salt and pepper. Turn the chicken onto its side, cover the pot and cook over very gentle heat for 1 hour.
❖ Turn the chicken over to its other side and simmer gently for a further hour.
❖ Place the chicken on its back and sprinkle the rice around it. Cover and cook for 30 minutes longer over low heat, without stirring.
❖ Remove the chicken and place it on a serving platter. Discard the chicken innards and neck and the bouquet garni; stir the rice with a fork. Surround the chicken with the rice and serve.

SERVES 6   *Photograph page 131*

Normandie

POULET VALLÉE D'AUGE
Chicken with Mushroom Sauce

This recipe takes its name from the Vallée d'Auge in Normandie, which is renowned for its apples. It includes butter, cream and calvados, all basic ingredients of the cuisine of Normandie.

1 chicken, about 3 lb (1.5 kg), cut into 8 serving pieces
salt and freshly ground pepper
1 tart apple
1 tablespoon vegetable oil
2 oz (50 g) butter
2 tablespoons calvados
1 tablespoon water
1 lb (500 g) mushrooms
⅔ cup (5 fl oz/150 ml) heavy (double) cream or crème fraîche

❖ Season the chicken with salt and pepper. Peel and core the apple and cut into ½-in (1-cm) cubes.
❖ Heat the oil in a nonstick 10-in (26-cm) sauté pan. Add half the butter and, as soon as it has melted, lightly brown the chicken pieces on all sides, turning them with a wooden spoon. Add the apple and mix for 1 minute. Pour in the calvados and ignite, shaking the pan gently until flames subside. Stir in the water, cover and cook over very low heat for 45 minutes.
❖ Meanwhile, trim the mushrooms, rinse and pat dry. Slice thinly. Melt the remaining butter in a nonstick 10-in (26-cm) skillet and cook the mushrooms over high heat until they are golden and give out no more liquid.
❖ Remove the cooked chicken pieces from the pan and keep warm on a platter. Boil the cooking liquid until reduced to a syrupy consistency. Add the cream and boil over high heat for about 2 minutes, stirring with a wooden spoon, until the sauce is thick and smooth. Add the mushrooms and stir for 1 minute. Pour the sauce over the chicken pieces and serve immediately.

SERVES 4 – 6

RABBIT IN CIDER (top left, recipe page 140), CHICKEN WITH MUSHROOM SAUCE (top right), AND CHICKEN WITH CREAM AND TARRAGON (bottom, recipe page 134), PHOTOGRAPHED IN NORMANDIE.
PIERRE HUSSENOT/AGENCE TOP

Normandie

POULET À LA CRÈME À L'ESTRAGON

Chicken with Cream and Tarragon

1 chicken, about 3½ lb (1.75 kg)
salt
10 sprigs fresh tarragon
1 oz (25 g) butter
¾ cup (6 fl oz/200 ml) chicken stock
¾ cup (6 fl oz/200 ml) heavy (double) cream or crème
  fraîche

❖Season the chicken inside and out with salt. Place 8 sprigs of tarragon inside the cavity of the chicken.
❖Melt the butter in a pot just large enough to hold the chicken. Brown the chicken on all sides for about 10 minutes. Remove from the pot and discard the butter. Pour in the stock and deglaze the pot, scraping up browned bits with a wooden spoon. Return the chicken to the pot, cover and cook over low heat for 1 hour and 20 minutes.
❖Meanwhile, strip the leaves from the reserved tarragon and chop finely. Remove the cooked chicken from the pot and keep warm. Boil the cooking juices until reduced to a syrupy consistency, then add the cream and boil for 2 minutes longer. Stir in the chopped tarragon and remove from heat.
❖Carve the chicken into portions and arrange on a serving plate. Pour the cream sauce over and serve immediately.

SERVES 4 – 6   *Photograph page 133*

Alsace

FAISAN EN CHARTREUSE

Pheasant Carthusian

The term en chartreuse *refers to a combination of meat (generally game birds) and vegetables which are layered in a round or oval mold. At one time it consisted only of vegetables, and the name referred to the vegetarian diet of the Carthusian monks.*

1 pheasant, about 3 lb (1.5 kg)
salt and freshly ground pepper
3 oz (100 g) butter
5 oz (150 g) carrots, peeled
5 oz (150 g) turnips, peeled
5 oz (150 g) small green beans
1 green cabbage, heart only
6 tablespoons chicken stock
2 tablespoons madeira
3 oz (100 g) ground (minced) veal
1 egg white
⅔ cup (6 fl oz/150 ml) heavy (double) cream or crème fraîche

❖Season the pheasant inside and out with salt and pepper. Melt half the butter in a pot large enough to hold the pheasant. Brown it on all sides for about 15 minutes, then cover and cook over low heat for 30 minutes.
❖Meanwhile, cut the carrots and turnips into strips about the same size as the beans. Cook each of the three vegetables separately in boiling salted water until slightly crisp.

PHEASANT CARTHUSIAN

Drain. Core the cabbage heart; cut into quarters, then into ½-in (1-cm) strips. Melt 1 oz (25 g) butter in a nonstick 10-in (26-cm) sauté pan and cook the cabbage strips for 1 minute, stirring constantly. Add the stock, season with salt and cook, covered, over low heat until the cabbage is very tender, about 20 minutes.
❖Remove the pheasant from the pot and set aside; discard the butter. Add the madeira and boil for 1 minute, then transfer to a bowl and set aside.
❖Remove the meat from the pheasant. Cut the thigh and breast meat into neat strips and set aside; finely chop all remaining meat, including the parts very close to the bone. Mix the finely chopped meat with the veal. Beat the egg white in a bowl until foamy. Add the meat mixture, cream, salt and pepper and blend until smooth. Refrigerate until needed.
❖Preheat oven to 400°F (200°C). Set aside a small amount of butter; use the rest to grease a 2-qt (2-l) soufflé dish. Arrange the carrot and turnip sticks and the beans on the bottom and around the sides, alternating colors. Cover with a layer of half the meat mixture, then half the cabbage. Arrange the strips of pheasant on the cabbage. Cover with the remaining cabbage, then with a smooth layer of the remaining meat mixture. Coat a sheet of waxed paper with the reserved butter and use it to cover the dish, buttered side down. Place the soufflé dish in a shallow pan of simmering water and bake for 40 minutes.
❖Remove the *chartreuse* from the oven and let rest for 10 minutes. Unmold it onto a serving plate. Reheat the reserved cooking juices and pour around the *chartreuse*. Serve immediately.

SERVES 4 – 6

Languedoc

CANARD AUX NAVETS DU PARDAILHAN

Duck with Glazed Turnips

This extraordinary turnip grows on the Minervois plateau. It is elongated in shape, snow white with a covering of black skin, and firm-textured with a slightly pungent taste.

1 duck, about 3 lb (1.5 kg)
2 oz (50 g) goose fat or butter
2 tablespoons cognac
1 tablespoon juniper berries
6 tablespoons dry white wine
2 lb (1 kg) long, slender turnips, peeled
salt and freshly ground pepper
1 tablespoon sugar

❖Season the duck inside and out with salt and pepper. Melt half the goose fat in an oval pot large enough to hold the duck and brown it on all sides for 15 minutes. Sprinkle with cognac, scatter around the juniper berries and pour in the wine. Bring to boil, then cover and simmer for 45 minutes.
❖Meanwhile, cut the turnips into 1½ x ½-in (4 x 1-cm) sticks. Melt the remaining goose fat in a nonstick 10-in (26-cm) sauté

DUCK WITH GLAZED TURNIPS

PETER JOHNSON

pan and lightly brown the turnips, turning them over in the hot fat for about 5 minutes. Sprinkle with sugar and salt, season lightly with pepper and turn carefully until the turnips are covered with a sticky, caramelized glaze. Cover and cook the turnips until just tender, about 8-10 minutes. Keep warm.
❖Remove the cooked duck from the pot and keep warm. Skim the fat from the cooking juices. Boil the juices until syrupy, about 2 minutes. Add the turnips to the pot and turn them in the hot liquid for 1 minute.
❖Carve the duck and arrange on a serving dish. Surround with turnips and serve immediately.

SERVES 4

Languedoc

MAGRETS GRILLÉS SAUCE AILLADE

Breast of Duck with Garlic Sauce

Sauce aillade, which is particularly appreciated in Toulouse, may be made using equal amounts of olive oil and walnut oil. Breast of duck served with this fragrant sauce is excellent accompanied with sautéed cèpes.

2 cloves garlic, coarsely chopped
3 tablespoons armagnac
1 sprig thyme, crumbled
salt and freshly ground pepper
2 fresh duck breasts, 12 oz (350 g) each
24 fresh walnuts, shelled and peeled
3 cloves garlic, peeled and halved
2 tablespoons water
6 tablespoons extra virgin olive oil

❖Combine the chopped garlic, armagnac and thyme in a bowl and season with salt and pepper. Add the duck breasts and turn to coat. Let marinate at room temperature for 1 hour, turning often.
❖Combine the walnuts, halved garlic cloves and water in a food processor and blend to a thick paste. Season with salt and pepper. With the machine running, pour in the oil in a thin stream to produce an emulsified sauce. Transfer to a sauceboat and set aside.
❖Drain the duck breasts, reserving marinade. Pat them dry and wipe off the garlic. Heat an enameled 4-qt (4-l) pot over moderate heat and lay the duck breasts on the bottom, skin side down. Cook for 8 minutes, basting the meat with the fat given out during cooking. Discard the fat, turn the breasts over and cook for 5 minutes longer, pricking the skin with a fork to allow some of the fat to escape. Remove the duck from the pot and discard all fat. Strain the reserved marinade into the pot and boil for 1 minute, then remove from heat. Return the duck breasts to the pot skin side down, cover and let rest for 15 minutes.
❖Remove the duck from the pot and slice thinly. Divide slices among four heated plates. Add to the pot any juices that have escaped during slicing. Pour this sauce over the duck and serve immediately, accompanied by the garlic sauce.

SERVES 4 *Photograph pages 12 – 13*

Orléanais

CANARD À L'ORANGE
Duck with Orange

1 duck, about 3 lb (1.5 kg)
salt and freshly ground pepper
1 tablespoon vegetable oil
6 medium oranges
1 lemon
¼ cup (2½ oz/75 g) sugar
2 tablespoons water
3 tablespoons red wine vinegar
6 tablespoons dry white wine
1 teaspoon arrowroot
3 tablespoons curaçao
1 tablespoon red currant jelly

❖Preheat oven to 425°F (215°C). Season the duck inside and out with salt and pepper. Place the duck in a greased roasting pan and roast for 1 hour, basting regularly with the pan juices.
❖Meanwhile, prepare the fruits: wash and dry the oranges and lemon. Carefully remove the zest from the lemon and two of the oranges with a zester. Squeeze the juice of these three fruits into a bowl. Peel the remaining oranges so that no trace of white pith is left, collecting any juice in the bowl. Separate the oranges into segments.
❖Heat the sugar and water in a saucepan over low heat until the sugar caramelizes to a light golden color. Add the vinegar and citrus juices and boil for 1 minute.
❖Remove the cooked duck from the oven, tilting it so that any juices inside the bird will run into the pan. Keep warm on a plate.
❖Skim the fat from the roasting juices. Add the wine and deglaze the pan over high heat, scraping up browned bits with a wooden spoon. Boil until the liquid is reduced by half. Transfer to a small saucepan and return to boil. Blend the arrowroot and curaçao in a small bowl, then pour into the boiling sauce with the red currant jelly. Boil, stirring constantly, until the sauce thickens, about 2 minutes. Stir in the zest and the orange segments and remove from heat.
❖Carve the duck and arrange it on a serving plate. Remove some of the orange segments from the sauce with a slotted spoon and arrange around the duck. Pour the sauce into a sauceboat and serve immediately.

SERVES 4

Ile de France

CANARD MONTMORENCY
Duck with Cherries

Montmorency is the name of a variety of small cherry — a bitter-sweet morello that is excellent for cooking. It is used in a number of dishes, both savory and sweet.

1 duck, about 3 lb (1.5 kg)
salt and freshly ground pepper
1 lb (500 g) Montmorency cherries
⅔ cup (5 fl oz/150 ml) dry white wine
1 teaspoon sugar
1 teaspoon arrowroot
3 tablespoons cherry brandy

❖Preheat oven to 425°F (215°C). Season the duck inside and out with salt and pepper. Place in roasting pan and roast for 1 hour, basting frequently with the cooking juices. Meanwhile, pit the cherries, catching all juices.
❖Remove the cooked duck from the oven, tilting it so that any juices inside the bird will run into the pan. Transfer to a plate and keep warm. Skim the fat from the juices in the roasting pan. Place the pan over high heat, pour in the wine and deglaze the pan, scraping up browned bits with a wooden spoon. Boil until the liquid is reduced by half. Transfer to a small saucepan and add the cherry juice and sugar.
❖Bring the contents of the saucepan to boil. Blend together the arrowroot and cherry brandy and pour into the boiling sauce. Boil, stirring constantly, until the sauce thickens, about 2 minutes. Add the cherries and remove from heat.
❖Carve the duck and arrange on a serving plate. Surround it with a few cherries. Pour the remaining sauce and cherries into a sauceboat and serve immediately.

SERVES 4

DUCK WITH CHERRIES

DUCK WITH ORANGE
PIERRE HUSSENOT/AGENCE TOP

PETER JOHNSON

PRESERVED DUCK

Languedoc

CONFIT DE CANARD
Preserved Duck

Confits of goose or duck are made all over Languedoc. Every family has its terrines or special wide-mouthed jars in which the homemade confit is kept, ready for an impromptu feast.

1 duck, about 3 lb (1.5 kg), cut into 6 pieces
2 cloves garlic, peeled and halved
2 sprigs dried thyme
¼ cup (2 oz/60 g) coarse sea salt
2 tablespoons coarsely ground pepper
2½ lb (1.2 kg) duck or goose fat, or more

❖Rub the pieces of duck all over with garlic. Crumble the thyme into a shallow dish; mix with the coarse salt and pepper. Roll the duck pieces in this mixture, then place in a bowl. Cover and refrigerate for 12 hours.
❖Pat the duck dry. Melt the fat in a large pot over low heat. Add the duck pieces and turn them over in the fat. Make sure they are well covered; if necessary, add more fat. Cover the pot and cook for 2 hours over very low heat; the fat should barely simmer.
❖Remove the duck pieces from the pot. Cool the fat to lukewarm, then strain. Pour the melted fat into a terrine to a depth of ½ in (1 cm). Arrange the pieces of duck on top. Cover with the remaining fat and let cool. Cover the terrine and store in the refrigerator, where it will keep for several months.
❖To serve, remove the duck pieces from the fat and either grill or cook in a nonstick skillet to remove as much fat as possible. They may be served hot, accompanied by fried potatoes or mushrooms. When cool, the duck is excellent with a salad of chicory or dandelion, dressed with walnut oil and served on garlic-flavored croutons.

SERVES 6 – 8

Languedoc

CANARD AUX OLIVES
Duck with Olives

The classic recipe for duck with olives used all over France contains only green olives. Languedoc cooks mix black and green olives, which gives an unexpected and richer flavor.

10 oz (300 g) green olives in brine, pitted
1 duck, about 2½ lb (1.2 kg)
salt and freshly ground pepper
1 tablespoon vegetable oil
3 tablespoons white vermouth
1 cup (8 fl oz/250 ml) chicken stock
3 oz (100 g) black olives in olive oil, pitted

❖Rinse the green olives in warm water, then soak them for 1 hour in warm water to cover, changing the water once.
❖Season the duck inside and out with salt and pepper. Heat the oil in a round or oval pot just large enough to hold the duck. Brown on all sides for about 15 minutes, then discard the fat. Sprinkle the duck with vermouth, then turn it over in the pot and allow the vermouth to evaporate. Pour in the stock and bring to boil. Cover and simmer for 45 minutes, turning the duck two or three times.
❖Remove the duck from the pot and keep warm. Skim the fat from the pan juices, then boil the juices for 2 minutes or until syrupy. Drain the green olives and add them to the pot with the black olives; simmer for 1 minute.
❖Carve the duck and arrange it on a serving platter. Surround it with the olives. Pour the sauce into a sauceboat and serve immediately.

SERVES 4   *Photograph pages 12 – 13*

Lorraine

CANARD À TOUTES LES HERBES
Duck with Herbs

5 oz (150 g) sorrel
5 oz (150 g) fresh spinach
5 oz (150 g) small leeks, white and tender green parts only
1 lettuce heart
3 tender celery stalks, with leaves
4 sprigs flat-leaf parsley
3 sprigs tarragon
3 sprigs chervil
2 sprigs mint
1 duck, about 4 lb (2 kg), cut into 10 serving pieces
salt and freshly ground pepper
1 oz (25 g) lard
1 tablespoon all purpose (plain) flour
¾ cup (6 fl oz/200 ml) dry white wine
1 bunch chives, chopped
6 tablespoons heavy (double) cream or crème fraîche

❖Wash, dry and stem the sorrel and spinach. Cut the leeks, lettuce and celery into ½-in (1-cm) strips. Strip the leaves from the parsley, tarragon, chervil and mint and chop finely.
❖Season the duck with salt and pepper. Melt the lard in a

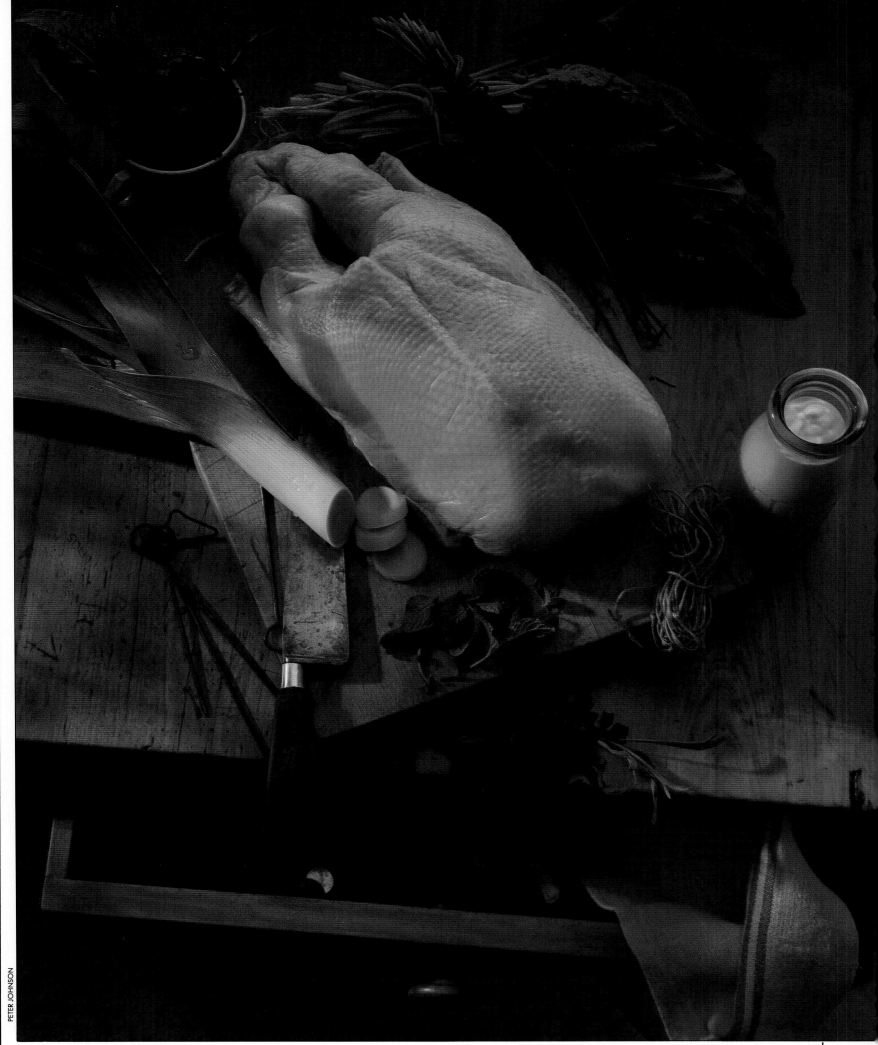

INGREDIENTS FOR DUCK WITH HERBS

4-qt (4-l) round or oval pot and brown the pieces of duck on all sides for about 10 minutes. Discard the cooking fat. Sprinkle the duck pieces with flour and stir for 1 minute. Pour in the wine and bring to boil. Add the vegetables and herbs and mix well. Cover and cook over low heat for 1 hour, stirring from time to time.

❖Stir in the cream and cook for 30 minutes longer, again stirring from time to time. When the duck is cooked, it will be surrounded by a thick, aromatic green sauce. Turn it into a shallow dish and serve immediately.

SERVES 6

Languedoc

FOIE GRAS FRAIS AUX RAISINS
Fresh Foie Gras with Grapes

This version of the classic dish in the grand tradition of French cuisine has been simplified so that only the true taste of the fresh foie gras comes through.

5 oz (150 g) white muscat grapes
4 slices fresh duck foie gras, about 3 oz (80 g) each and ½ in (1 cm) thick, chilled
salt and freshly ground pepper
1 tablespoon armagnac

❖Peel the grapes and remove the seeds, working over a plate to catch the juice.
❖Heat a nonstick skillet over moderate heat. Season the slices of foie gras with salt and pepper. Cook them for 40 seconds on each side or until a crusty surface forms. Arrange them on 2 heated plates.
❖Discard the fat in the pan and pour in the armagnac and grape juice. Boil the liquid until reduced by half. Add the grapes to the pan and mix for 30 seconds. Surround the slices of foie gras with grapes, pour the sauce over and serve immediately.

SERVES 2   *Photograph pages 12 – 13*

Quercy/Périgord

LAPIN AUX PRUNEAUX
Rabbit with Prunes

The delicious Enthe plum, dried to become a prune, is used in as many savory dishes as sweet ones.

¾ cup (6 fl oz/200 ml) red wine
1 tablespoon sugar
16 "Agen" prunes
1 rabbit, about 3¼ lb (1.6 kg), cut into 8 serving pieces
salt and freshly ground pepper
2 tablespoons vegetable oil
1 sprig fresh thyme
1 onion, about 3 oz (100 g), finely chopped
2 cloves garlic, finely chopped
2 French shallots, finely chopped
2 tablespoons armagnac
⅔ cup (5 fl oz/150 ml) heavy (double) cream or crème fraîche

❖Combine the wine and sugar in a saucepan and bring to boil. Stir until the sugar has dissolved. Add the prunes and simmer for 10 minutes, stirring. Remove from heat, cover and let stand for 10 minutes, then strain off and reserve the liquid, leaving the prunes in the saucepan.
❖Rinse the rabbit and pat dry; season with salt and pepper. Heat the oil in a nonstick 11-in (28-cm) sauté pan and lightly brown the rabbit pieces on all sides for about 10 minutes. Crumble in the thyme and add the onion, garlic and shallots. Cook, stirring, until the rabbit pieces are well browned, about 5 minutes longer.
❖Pour in the armagnac and ignite, shaking the pan gently until flames subside. Stir in the wine reserved from the prunes and bring to boil. Cover and simmer for 40 minutes.

PETER JOHNSON

RABBIT WITH PRUNES

❖Remove the rabbit pieces to a heated plate and keep warm. Boil the liquid in the pan over high heat until reduced to a syrupy consistency. Add the cream and boil until the sauce is smooth, about 3 minutes. Return the rabbit to the pan, add the prunes and reheat for 2 minutes, stirring.
❖Arrange the rabbit and prunes in a shallow dish. Coat with sauce and serve immediately.

SERVES 4

Bretagne/Normandie

LAPIN AU CIDRE
Rabbit in Cider

1 rabbit, about 3¼ lb (1.6 kg), cut into 9 pieces (reserve liver)
salt and freshly ground pepper
1 slice streaky bacon, about 3 oz (100 g)
3 oz (100 g) small fresh cèpes (*porcini* mushrooms)
1 tablespoon vegetable oil
1 oz (25 g) butter
4 French shallots, finely chopped
2 tablespoons calvados
1 cup (8 fl oz/250 ml) dry cider
1 egg yolk
1 tablespoon strong mustard
6 tablespoons heavy (double) cream or crème fraîche

❖Rinse the rabbit and pat dry; season with salt and pepper. Cut the bacon into small strips, removing the rind. Trim, wash, dry and quarter the mushrooms. Heat the oil in a nonstick 11-in (28-cm) sauté pan. Add the butter and gently cook the shallots, bacon and mushrooms, stirring constantly with a wooden spoon. Scrape this mixture from the pan, add the rabbit pieces and brown on all sides for 10 minutes. Pour in the calvados and let it evaporate. Stir in the cider and bring to boil, then cover and cook over low heat for 30 minutes, turning two or three times. After 30 minutes, return the bacon, mushrooms and shallots to the pan and simmer for 15 minutes longer.

❖In a bowl beat the egg yolk, mustard and cream. Add the uncooked rabbit liver, pushing it through a sieve, and mix well.

❖Remove the cooked rabbit from the sauté pan with a slotted spoon and arrange in a serving dish with the mushrooms and bacon. Boil the cooking liquid over high heat until reduced to a syrupy consistency. Pour the mustard mixture into the pan and stir for 30 seconds, then remove from heat. Whisk the sauce until smooth and creamy. Pour it over the rabbit and serve immediately.

SERVES 4   *Photograph page 133*

Alsace

CIVET DE LIÈVRE AUX SPÄTZELE
Hare in Red Wine with Egg Noodles

The word civet *in France is indicative of the culinary procedure whereby game, furred or feathered, is simmered in red wine and served with a sauce cooked with the animal or bird's blood.*

3 cups (24 fl oz/750 ml) red wine
3 tablespoons cognac
1 onion, about 3 oz (100 g), sliced
1 medium carrot, peeled and sliced
2 cloves garlic, peeled and quartered
1 sprig thyme
1 bay leaf
1 sprig rosemary
1 teaspoon coarsely ground pepper
1 hare, about 4 lb (2 kg), cut into 9 serving pieces, (reserve liver)
8 oz (250 g) streaky bacon
3 tablespoons vegetable oil
18 small pickling onions, peeled
1 tablespoon all purpose (plain) flour
salt and freshly ground pepper
8 oz (250 g) small (button) mushrooms
For the noodles:
2¾ cups (11 oz/350 g) all purpose (plain) flour
3 eggs
3 tablespoons cold water
salt and freshly ground pepper
4 pinches of freshly grated nutmeg
2 oz (50 g) butter

❖Pour the wine and cognac into a bowl. Add the onion, carrot, garlic, thyme, bay leaf and rosemary, crumbling the herbs between the fingers, and the pepper. Add the pieces of hare to this marinade, turn them to coat and marinate for 12 hours in the refrigerator, turning several times.

❖Remove the pieces of hare from the marinade and pat dry. Strain the marinade, discarding the herbs and flavorings. Cut the bacon into matchsticks, removing the rind.

❖Heat the oil in a heavy 4-qt (4-l) pot and lightly brown the pieces of hare on all sides for about 10 minutes. Add the bacon and pickling onions and cook, stirring, until the pieces of hare are well browned, about 5 minutes. Sprinkle with flour and stir for 1 minute longer. Pour the marinade into the pot and bring to boil, then cover and cook for 2 hours over very low heat, stirring occasionally. Season with salt and pepper.

❖Meanwhile, trim the mushrooms; wash, pat dry and cut into quarters. Add them to the pot after the 2 hours' cooking time; stir and cook for 30 minutes longer.

❖While the hare is cooking, prepare the egg noodles: sift the flour into a bowl. Beat the eggs in a separate bowl with the water, salt, pepper and nutmeg. Pour this mixture into the flour and mix vigorously with a wooden spoon to make a soft, smooth dough which comes away from the sides of the bowl. Roll out the dough on a wooden board, in several separate batches.

❖Bring a large saucepan of salted water to boil. Using a moistened palette knife, cut off small strips of the dough and drop them into the boiling water. As soon as they come to the surface, lift them out with a slotted spoon and transfer them to a dish of cold water. Repeat this process until all the dough is cooked.

❖Melt the butter in a nonstick 10-in (26-cm) skillet and add the noodles. Turn them over in the hot butter for 5 minutes, keeping them moving constantly. Keep warm.

❖Remove the pieces of hare with a slotted spoon and arrange on a shallow dish. Press the raw hare liver through a sieve into a bowl and mix in ¼ cup (2 fl oz/60 ml) of the sauce from the hare. Return the mixture to the pot and stir for 30 seconds over low heat, without allowing the liver to cook. Pour this sauce over the pieces of hare and serve immediately with the noodles.

SERVES 6

HARE IN RED WINE WITH EGG NOODLES

PETER JOHNSON

STUFFED HARE

Périgord

LIÈVRE EN CABESSAL

Stuffed Hare

Cabessal is the name of a napkin tied into a crown shape, which women used to place on their heads so they could carry heavy weights. The hare bound into a ring shape suggests the cabessal.

6 tablespoons chicken stock
3 oz (100 g) stale bread, crusts trimmed
10 oz (300 g) veal, knuckle or shoulder, boned
3 oz (100 g) *pancetta,* fresh pork belly or rindless streaky bacon
3 oz (100 g) prosciutto or other unsmoked ham
2 cloves garlic, finely chopped
2 French shallots, finely chopped
1 tablespoon chopped parsley
salt and freshly ground pepper
6 pinches of freshly grated nutmeg
1 sprig thyme
1 egg
1 hare, about 4 lb (2 kg)
6 oz (200 g) fresh pork rind
1 onion, about 3 oz (100 g), finely chopped
3 cups (24 fl oz/750 ml) dry red wine, such as Cahors
3 tablespoons armagnac

❖Heat the chicken stock in a small saucepan and crumble in the bread. Stir, remove from heat and leave the bread to absorb the stock. Using a food processor, grind (mince) together the veal, pork and ham.
❖In a bowl mix together the meats, garlic, shallots, parsley, bread, salt, pepper, nutmeg and the thyme, crumbled between the fingers. Add the egg and mix well.
❖Season the hare with salt and pepper. Spread the stuffing mixture inside the hare and sew up the opening with kitchen thread. Bend the hare into a circle by bringing the front and hind legs together and tying them with kitchen thread.
❖Oil a round or oval pot just large enough to hold the hare. Rinse the pork rind, roll it into a cylinder and secure with string. Drop it into boiling water for 1 minute; rinse and drain. Slice the roll into strips ½ in (1 cm) wide and spread these on the bottom of the pot, together with the onion. Place the hare on top.

❖Cook the hare for 15 minutes over moderate heat, then turn and cook for 15 minutes on the other side. Pour in the wine and armagnac and bring to simmer. Cover and cook over very low heat for 5 hours, without disturbing it.
❖Carefully transfer the hare to a serving plate. Boil the cooking liquid until reduced to a syrupy consistency. Pour into a sauceboat and serve immediately. The hare is very tender and the meat falls away from the bones; it is traditionally "carved" with a spoon.

SERVES 6

Corse

LAPIN À L'ISTRETTU

Rabbit, Corsican-style

1 rabbit, about 3¼ lb (1.6 kg), cut into 9 serving pieces (reserve the liver)
salt and freshly ground pepper
14 black olives in brine
2 tablespoons olive oil
1 sprig dried thyme
1 sprig dried rosemary
1 bay leaf
6 cloves garlic, peeled and halved
8 oz (250 g) onions, thinly sliced
⅔ cup (5 fl oz/150 ml) dry white wine
3 tablespoons tomato paste (puree)
2 tablespoons capers, drained

❖Rinse the rabbit pieces and pat dry; season with salt and pepper. Rinse the olives and pat dry. Slice thickly, discarding the pits.
❖Heat the oil in a nonstick 11-in (28-cm) sauté pan and lightly brown the rabbit pieces on all sides for about 10 minutes. Crumble in the thyme and rosemary. Add the bay leaf, the halved cloves of garlic and the onions and cook, stirring, until the rabbit pieces are well browned, about 5 minutes longer. Stir in the wine and tomato paste and bring to boil, then cover and cook for 30 minutes over low heat.
❖Add the rabbit liver, olives and capers and simmer, stirring often, until the sauce thickens and coats the rabbit pieces, about 15 more minutes.
❖Turn the rabbit into a shallow dish and serve immediately.

SERVES 4

Bourgogne

LAPIN À LA MOUTARDE

Rabbit with Mustard Sauce

1 rabbit, about 3 lb (1.5 kg)
salt and freshly ground pepper
1 tablespoon vegetable oil
4 tablespoons strong mustard
1 sprig fresh thyme
1 oz (25 g) butter
6 tablespoons dry white wine
⅔ cup (5 fl oz 150 ml) heavy (double) cream or crème fraîche

RABBIT, CORSICAN STYLE (top) AND RABBIT WITH
MUSTARD SAUCE (bottom)

❖Preheat oven to 425°F (215°C). Rinse the rabbit and pat dry; season with salt and pepper. Oil a shallow oval baking dish large enough to hold the rabbit. Spread the entire surface of the rabbit with 3 tablespoons mustard and place it in the dish. Strip the thyme leaves from the stalk and sprinkle over the rabbit. Dot with thin slivers of butter. Bake for 50 minutes, basting the rabbit regularly with the pan juices and wine.

❖Arrange the cooked rabbit on a serving platter and keep warm. Pour the cream and the remaining mustard into the baking dish and scrape up browned bits with a wooden spoon. Pour this mixture into a saucepan and boil for 2 to 3 minutes.

❖Coat the rabbit with the sauce and serve immediately.

SERVES 4

PROVENCE, CORSE, LANGUEDOC-ROUSSILLON

Sun-drenched dishes

PROVENCE, CORSE, LANGUEDOC-ROUSSILLON

Sun-drenched dishes

The road threads inland, sidles in between the plateaus, changes sides as it follows the dry banks of the Durance, forgets the Luberon to the left, and at last enters a totally new country. It is not yet the mountains, but a foretaste of their heights, which here reach to around five hundred meters. At Forcalquier, a belvedere dominates the highest part of the village, indicating the directions to Vienna, St. Petersburg and Constantinople. In other words, the region is far-seeing, and has been for a very long time. The eagle's aerie of Lurs, patiently undergoing renovation, has a stations-of-the-Cross path that takes in the whole horizon: on one side the Lure mountain, a remnant of snow still on its highest peaks; on the other, the plateau of Valensole, from where one's gaze drops to the lavender-colored fields below.

Everything here seems to be built to man's proportions. Reach the high priory of Ganagobie, with its panoramic view, and Haute-Provence is spread before you, still an Eldorado. Here men protect their crops, replant, kill weeds and honor the vine; they also produce lavender honey and almond nougat, breed the best lambs in the world (those known as *Sisteron*), uphold the tradition of the Banon cheeses made from goat's milk, harvest wild mushrooms and truffles, crush splendid black olives for oil. Their links: the products of the soil.

Further towards the south and west are the Alpilles: a mountainous mass which scoffs at geography, turns away on one peak and playfully meets the desert mass of La Crau. At the handsome village of Les Baux, the wind blows so strongly one might think it would run out of breath. Vineyards squeeze themselves between

LEFT: EARLY MORNING SUNLIGHT FILTERS THROUGH THE NARROW STREETS OF NICE AS LOCAL RESIDENTS GO ABOUT THEIR DAILY BUSINESS.

PREVIOUS PAGES: IN THE HILLS BEHIND NICE, TOURETTE-SUR-LOUP PERCHES HIGH UP ON THE CRAGGY CLIFFS WHICH HAVE BEEN PAINSTAKINGLY TERRACED TO ALLOW SPACE FOR HOME GARDENS AND PATHWAYS INTO THE VALLEY.
LEO MEIER

LEO MEIER

TUCKED AWAY BEHIND THE BUSY MARKET STALLS IN DIGNE, HAUTE-PROVENCE, A SMALL BOY PLAYS WITH HIS TWO-MONTH-OLD KITTEN WHILE WAITING FOR A SYMPATHETIC PASSER-BY TO OFFER IT A HOME.

cooked, then the fish themselves: wrasse, *rascasse* or red rock cod, gurnard, weaver, *blavier*, anglerfish or *baudroie*, tiny cuttlefish, bream. Then, too, bass (called *loup* in the Mediterranean) is paired with fennel — although the infidels, chasing the custom of tourists, also add pastis, and even go so far as to flame it. The crayfish that is said to be Mediterranean often comes from somewhere else. But the soup made from *favouilles* — little crabs found along the coast — is a real treat, and tiny *supions*, or baby cuttlefish, are an absolute delicacy.

Provence is a store of fine products, tempting aromas and good dishes, and the Côte d'Azur is its display window. Here is sold what is produced elsewhere. The local cuisine is more economical, less luxurious: fish, properly prepared, and the local vegetables, spiced and seasoned, that make up *ratatouille*. Light and fresh, they are the kings of the kitchen in summer: zucchini, red and green peppers, eggplant, cucumbers.

Does "niçoise" salad really belong to Nice? With its tomatoes, broad beans, cucumbers, baby artichokes, green peppers, onions, hard-cooked eggs, anchovies, tuna and black olives, it is the very image of the region — although now it seems to be reserved for the visiting foreigner, for it is hardly ever found in the bistros of old Nice.

Here a Mediterranean gastronomy dominates, recalling the history of the county of Nice, for many years Italian territory. The ravioli filled with silverbeet, the stuffed sardines, the stockfish or *stoficado* (a stew of dried cod), the pizza and the *pissaladière* (the former garnished with tomato, the latter with onion marinated in olive oil, both with bases of bread dough), the hearty beef stew called *daube* or *estouffade*, the preparations of tripe: all these, as aromatic as the flowers in the market on the Cours Saleya, already have a faintly trans-alpine flavor. Likewise the *panisse* or *socca*, a gruel of chickpea flour boiled in salted water, spooned into dishes to set, then unmolded, cut into smaller pieces and fried. These are the "chips" of the southerners!

The real Provence is the one that protects her hinterland — its herbs, its markets, its lamb, for example, which is the best in the world. Which lamb has the juiciest meat, the most succulent flavor, the least fat? That of Sisteron. Its origins: the lower Alps. Its diet: aromatic thyme, rosemary, sage and savory. The Sisteron lamb lives its life in the fresh air; it is a *broutard*, a lamb that browses in the meadows, and is fattened on corn — not a milk-fed lamb. "In the lamb, everything is good," declares the enthusiastic Robert Lombard, known as "Bichette," a butcher in Château-Arnoux in Haute-Provence. The rack of lamb, with its combination of fat and lean, is the tastiest. But the leg, the shoulder and the cheeks all have their own particular qualities. A traditional dish of the region is the *pieds paquets*, little parcels made from the stomach of the lamb, stuffed with finely chopped mesentery with ham, tomatoes and herbs.

the two villages of Saint-Etienne-du-Grès and Eygalières. The olive reigns supreme. Lambs frolic in liberty, feeding on the pastures, as do the goats which seem to make the most of the blue sky.

All sing the praises of the landscape of Provence, with its clear blue skies, its old houses of yellowed stone, and its holy trinity of lamb, goat and olive tree. Alpilles and Haute-Provence: two faces of the same land, where the cuisine always has a hint of garlic and a scent of sunshine. It is undoubtedly for this reason that it best symbolizes the oft-envied French subtlety.

In every village, between Aix and Apt, Manosque and Carpentras, from Sorgues to Saint-Didier, from the top of Provence to the bottom, the markets are gardens of fragrance. The stalls are redolent of herbs — thyme, lavender and rosemary, tarragon and mint, chervil, savory and chives. They burst with wild asparagus, purple artichokes, *roquette* with its hazelnutlike flavor; with *cébettes*, the local onion; with *mesclun*, with *trévise*, with chicory and endive. Not to mention the squashes that become *petits farcis provençaux* (stuffed vegetables) and the tasty zucchini flowers that are cooked as fritters.

For the fish which accord so comfortably with the olive oil of the region, one must look further afield — to Cannes, for example, which has the finest market of its kind, at Forville, where are arrayed all Mediterranean products that go into a bouillabaisse. This dish, which has become largely identified with Marseilles, is also found at Cap d'Antibes and Golfe Juan. It is always served as two courses, first the broth in which the fish were

The other treasure of the region is its olives — black, almost dry, without any trace of bitterness. The secret? It is simply a matter of letting them suffer the cold in order to sweeten the flavor, then gently frying them in a little oil and cooling them before they are eaten. The local oil is also a miracle of freshness and clarity. The authentic olive oil of Provence, such as that produced at Maussane-des-Alpilles, is the result of the first cold pressing. There is nothing but the oil and aroma of the fruit — no grinding, which crushes the kernel inside the stone and so contributes a bitter tinge, and no "criminal" centrifuge.

The third of the progeny of Provence: the goat cheese called Banon, after a village of the same name. But the appellation refers chiefly to a method: the cheese is dried, brushed with water, dipped in *marc*, then wrapped in a chestnut leaf and tied with raffia. In this form, it can be aged in a cool cellar until it has developed its characteristically strong flavor, and it can be kept for a long period of time.

Garlic is always a part of Provençal cuisine — above all, in that most characteristic sauce, *aïoli*, a garlic mayonnaise which accompanies cold poached fish, hard-cooked eggs or meats. The name *grand aïoli* designates a festive dish for which boiled meat, poached cod, hard-cooked eggs, snails and cooked vegetables are arrayed around the sacred sauce: a kind of *pot-au-feu* in the Provençal style.

Bread in Provence takes on a particular appearance, and is prepared in a particular way. The prime example is *fougasse*; it is a bread of irregular shape cooked *à la volée*, speedily, in an open oven and therefore in a dry atmosphere. The bakers may choose to flavor it with garlic, or anchovies, or orangeflower water. It should not be forgotten that Provence also has a sweet tooth and makes magnificent glacé fruits, nor that it is a lover of the almond, so essential to the famous *calissons* of Aix-en-Provence, made with almond paste and glacé fruits. The special sweetmeat which has become the glory of Montélimar is its nougat, which needs only sugar syrup, honey, almonds and pistachio nuts. The *nougat noir*, or black nougat, contains lavender honey, caramelized sugar and Provençal almonds — although Spanish almonds, supposedly coarser in flavor, are creeping into the kitchens of almost all the craftsmen-confectioners.

THE ARCHEOLOGICAL SITE OF FILITOSA, SOUTH OF AJACCIO IN CORSE, WHERE HUGE STONE MONOLITHS CARVED WITH HUMAN FACES GAZE OUT TO SEA.

THE ATTRACTIVE COASTAL TOWN OF MENTON WAS, UNTIL 1914, THE HOME OF A LARGE BRITISH COLONY. APART FROM BEING A POPULAR BEACH RESORT, IT IS ALSO FAMOUS FOR ITS CONSTANTLY FLOWERING AND FRUIT-BEARING LEMON TREES.

Corsica is solitary, high-minded and readily censorious. Austere? Yes, a little. It struggled for its independence for a long time before deciding to become French. Its gastronomy might appear unworldly and even fairly insignificant, but it has the merit of remaining original, rooted in the soil, defining its territory.

Corsica's traditions are those of an island, but one very much attached to the soil. In the first place, they reflect its mountainous nature: the kid, which is usually spit-roasted; the *brousse* or *bruccio*, a fresh goat cheese which might be sprinkled with *grappa* and which accompanies the local desserts, such as *fiadone* cake, or fritters known as *fritelle*.

Italy's proximity is seen in the cannelloni, ravioli and lasagne made by the local *mammas*. Charcuterie reigns supreme, whether it depends on tripe and offal (blood pudding or *sangue*, pork liver sausages or *figatelle*), or is based on game (blackbird pâté), or borrows from transalpine traditions (*coppa*, raw ham).

The local fruits come from the forests: chestnuts, figs, *arbousiers* (strawberry trees), olives. The principal Corsican fish are mountain trout, but there are also those from the sea, in the vicinity of Bonifacio, Bastia or Cargèse — bream, mullet, red mullet, red rock cod. All go well with the local vintages, the fiery red wine from Toraccia or the softer, sweeter types like the muscat from Saint-Florent or from Patrimonio.

An amphitheater, its cultivated terraces opening wide onto the Mediterranean: this is the traditional image of the Languedoc. This vast southwestern part of the Midi has an undeniable accent, a result of its intermediate position between the olive groves of Provence and the Landes of Gascony, between garlic and foie gras, adopting certain dishes of the one and of the other.

The coast is close by — which means fish. And at Bouzigues are found oysters, mussels, scallops and clams that are eaten with chopped garlic, shallots and parsley. The *bourride* of Sète is made with anglerfish; it is the sister of the Provençal bouillabaisse, with its broth strained at the end of cooking and thickened with *aïoli*. The *brandade* of Nîmes, a puree combining salt cod with a mixture of oil and milk, is almost the little sister of similar dishes belonging to Marseilles and Toulon, where crushed garlic is also added.

But crossing the Gard and heading towards Montpellier, the cuisine of the Languedoc quickly turns to the southwest. The little pies (*petits pâtes*) of Pézenas and Béziers are made with mutton and mutton fat, raisins, brown sugar and grated lemon rind, which already gives a hint of Gascony. This is confirmed by the *cassoulet*, of which three versions are known.

The first, the most simple and pure, from Castelnaudary, is of course made with white haricot beans, but also with pork in varied guises (hock, ham, loin, fat, rind, sausage) and a little preserved goose. More subtle, perhaps, is that of Carcassonne, which adds leg of mutton and also, in the hunting season, partridges. Finally, the most urbane *cassoulet*, from the great city of Toulouse, includes preserved goose or duck, mutton, Toulouse sausage, plus the ingredients already listed for the Castelnaudary version, although in smaller quantities.

The Languedoc cares for its traditions. This is not a region where fats are frowned on. Olive oil, walnut oil, pork fat and the fatty liver are generally preferred to butter. Pâtés of foie gras, of game, of wild rabbit, of thrush — tiny birds cooked with a dash of port — and of ortolans, which are eaten whole, head and bones included, while one pulls a napkin over one's head in order to enjoy the tantalizing aromas to the full: these are what unite the Gascon southwest and the Périgord.

But Spain is not far away. You think you have caught a glimpse of it between the rocky vineyards of Corbières, the Minervois, Maury; and the terraces of Banyuls already give a foretaste of Catalonia. The vines cling to the sturdy, mountainous ravines, yielding a wine that is almost black, with an aroma of chocolate and roasted coffee — you would swear that it is almost a French port.

This rich, generous Banyuls, which comes from the area around the picturesque port of Collioure and near Cerbère, next to Spain, demonstrates that the borders here have been unstable. The people are dark-skinned, black-haired. Crayfish *civet*, anglerfish in the Catalan style, anchovy pâtés, cod cooked in a spicy mixture of eggplant, peppers and tomato: this is the Roussillon, which has been French only since the time of Richelieu. Shoulder of mutton *en pistache*, garnished with whole cloves of garlic, or pigeon cooked in *rancio* (a sweet, aged, fortified wine): these are some more of the robustly flavored dishes which turn up on the other side of the frontier. And come to think of it, this deep red wine from Collioure, with its hints of purple, goes quite well with a paella ... but that takes us into another country.

THE DUSKY PINK HUES AND CASCADING FLOWER BOXES TYPIFY THE ROMANTIC BEAUTY OF GRASSE, A TOWN WHICH HAS INSPIRED MANY ARTISTS, AND IN PARTICULAR, JEAN-HONORÉ FRAGONARD OR "LE PETIT FRAGO".

LEO MEIER

MEATS
Gang of Four

A SELECTION OF LOCALLY PRODUCED SALAMIS FROM DIGNE IN THE
ALPES-DE-HAUTE-PROVENCE TEMPTS SHOPPERS AT THE MARKET.

MEATS

Gang of four

The French adore meat. They may well claim to have a passion for fish, reputedly lighter, more healthy and more sympathetic to the chef's culinary fantasies, but as soon as they venture into a foreign country, they cannot stop thinking about good old *steack-frites* — steak and fries — which have been all around the world. But there is steak, and there is steak.

Let's start with beef. Beef comes from a bovine animal, castrated, raised and fattened for the production of meat. The French herd numbers about 25 million, spread among various breeds: Limousin, Salers, Aubrac, Maine Anjou, Blonde Aquitaine, and above all the Charolais, whose reputation is the most acclaimed.

Beef is said to be "marbled" when it has fine white threads between the muscle fibers, indicating an optimum degree of fattening. This is the meat, nicely fat and flavorful, that is most prized by beef lovers. As a rule it should not be eaten too fresh, but rather aged in a cool room for at least two to three weeks. In this way the meat develops its full flavor and acquires a good texture: it becomes perfectly matured.

But there is, as I have noted, steak and steak. The best cuts for an authentic *bifteck* come from the loin, the rump, the flank, the sirloin and the fillet, which is the most tender but least flavorful part of the animal, and which furnishes the thick cut known as chateaubriand. The sirloin is highly suitable for *tournedos*.

Braised, boiled or pan-fried, beef is robust and handsome. The entrecôte, tender and with a nice cover of fat, is a cut worthy of a king, much appreciated when pan-fried and served with a sauce based on shallots and red wine (known as Bercy or *marchand de vin* sauce). Red wine and beef also combine in Burgundian-style beef, in the *daube* or with beef cooked as a *civet*. Or the beef might be braised (*estouffade*), or cooked in a consommé, lowered into the liquid and taken out by means of a string (*ficelle*) — hence the name *boeuf à la ficelle*. When all is said and done, there is nothing more adaptable nor more varied than magnificent beef.

Veal comes from a young, unweaned calf — that is, one that has been nourished solely on milk, natural or reconstituted, then slaughtered at between one and four months. The best and the worst coexist under this name: the milk-fed calf, raised by its mother, with tasty, tender, succulent flesh, and hormone-added veal for which the calves are fed a chemical diet and raised in a small enclosure, to produce a tough meat which shrinks and

PREVIOUS PAGES: BEEF BRAISED WITH CALVADOS (bottom right, recipe 165), VEAL POT ROAST, ANJOU-STYLE (top, recipe page 173) AND VEAL MARENGO (bottom left, recipe page 176), PHOTOGRAPHED IN THE PAYS DE LOIRE.
PIERRE HUSSENOT/AGENCE TOP

LEO MEIER

THE ROMANS DEVELOPED THE ART OF PORK BUTCHERY AND INTRODUCED IT TO
THE FRENCH WHO PRESERVED THE TRADITION DURING THE MIDDLE AGES. IN 1476
CHARCUTERIES WERE GRANTED THE MONOPOLY OF SELLING PORK MEAT.

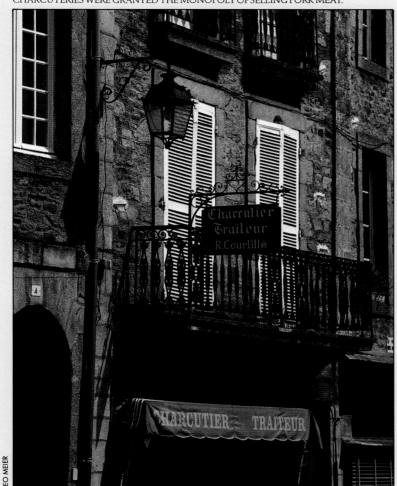

LEO MEIER

exudes moisture during cooking. The former is prized; the latter can only be condemned. Fortunately, it seems that the situation is changing as veterinary controls are now in force.

Racks of veal cut between the ninth and thirteenth rib make the tender, juicy cutlets that, like their sister the *escalope* (often replaced by more economical turkey in everyday French cuisine), are gently pan-fried, simmered in their juices with cream and mushrooms, or breaded. The family-style *blanquette de veau*, which calls for tender cuts from the breast, shoulder and neck, is customarily accompanied by rice. It is the perfect example of a bourgeois dish.

But the most prized parts of the animal — excluding the offal (superb liver, or *foie de veau*, sliced thickly and cooked until just pink, along with kidneys which, preferably, are served whole and still red at the center) — are the *grenadins* or slices of fillet, perhaps the most delicate cut but not necessarily the most tasty. Veal is still a luxury, but there are certain economical and tasty cuts — such as the knuckle, which will happily simmer in a thousand different ways, marrying equally well with fried potatoes as with Belgian endive. Aromatic and savory, it's enough to make you remember the fine veal of yesteryear.

A COW HERD LEADS HIS COWS TO PASTURE AT A LEISURELY PACE ALONG THE HEAVILY WOODED ALPINE ROADS.

AN ABUNDANCE OF GOOD-QUALITY PRODUCE HAS LED TO THE CREATION OF NUMEROUS REGIONAL SPECIALTIES IN PROVENCE SUCH AS *GAYETTES*, A SAUSAGE PATTY MADE WITH PIG'S LIVER, AND *SOU-FRASSAM*, MEAT-STUFFED CABBAGE SIMMERED IN STOCK WITH VEGETABLES.

And how about lamb as the queen of meats? Aged from one to six months and weighing between 30 and 50 lb (15 and 25 kg), lamb provides meat that is more tender and delicate than that of older sheep. The most highly ranked, preferred by gourmets, is that from Sisteron, in Upper Provence; its flavor reflects the animal's diet of wild thyme, rosemary, savory and sage. Thus a "simple" Provençal roast of lamb, which might be studded with garlic, scents the air with the perfume of the land where it lived.

Milk-fed lamb, six weeks old, is valued more for its tenderness than for its flavor. The leg, or *gigot*, makes the most agreeable of dishes; it is a favorite among the French, often served on Sundays accompanied by flageolet beans. *Pré salé* lamb, which has grazed on the salty pastures around the peninsula of Mont-Saint-Michel, is also highly regarded. But there is excellent lamb from other regions as well: from the Texel breed in the Ardennes and Ile de France, from the Berrichonne breed in the Cher, the Vendée and the Pyrenees.

Every cut of lamb is flavorful: chops, rack, neck, saddle, shoulder (often neglected, and cheaper than the leg) and breast, which may be simply grilled. Whether a slow-simmered dish in a *daube* or *navarin*, or simply spit-roasted, lamb remains a royal dish — one of the few things about which the French always seem to agree.

Pork has a bad reputation. Said to be vulgar, blamed for illnesses resulting from tapeworms, pork — more commonly called *le cochon*, "the pig," — is, however, a well-flavored meat. Prized by the people of eastern France, it goes very well with beer and cabbage, is the starting point for charcuterie (ham, terrines, pâtés), and indeed is the natural accompaniment (in the form of sausages, salted shoulder or knuckle) of the traditional sauerkraut. The tender *échine* or shoulder cut, the suckling pig slaughtered in its youth, the *travers* or chops which are salted, the salted and smoked belly, or again the tender *filet mignon*, not to mention the royal suckling pig, roasted on the spit: here are a thousand reasons to come to terms with the pig.

In Alsace, in the north, in Lorraine, the marriage of the gourmet and the pig has always been celebrated in traditional dishes. In the Loire Valley, as in the southwest and in Picardy, *noisettes* of pork are often paired with prunes. The trotters, the tongue, grilled pig's ears, smoked bacon: these make for brasserie-style dishes called *canailles*, because they offer a good excuse to the Parisian bourgeois to *s'encanailler* — to mix with the lower classes, to change his style of food at after-theater suppers. Glass or mug in hand, the pig thus regains his pedigree on both the plate and the palate of the most civilized gourmet.

LEO MEIER

THE SPARSE ROCKY TERRAINE OF HAUTE-PROVENCE IS UTILIZED AS GRAZING GROUNDS FOR GOATS AND SHEEP. THE GOATS' MILK IS USED IN A VARIETY OF LOCAL CHEESES AND THE SHEEPS' MEAT IS PREPARED FOR REGIONAL DISHES SUCH AS *GIGOT FARCI* (STUFFED LEG OF LAMB).

A COOK'S PALETTE OF SPICES ON DISPLAY AT A LOCAL MARKET IN TROYES, ONCE THE CAPITAL OF CHAMPAGNE. MORE THAN OTHER REGIONS, CHAMPAGNE IS AN AREA WHERE MEAT IS PARTICULARLY POPULAR, ESPECIALLY LAMB, AND THE CENTURY-OLD PENCHANT FOR SPICES FEATURES IN NUMEROUS REGIONAL SPECIALTIES FROM FLEMISH GINGER WAFERS TO BREADS, POULTRY AND OF COURSE MEAT.

LEO MEIER

Ile de France

POT-AU-FEU ET MIROTON
Boiled Beef and Miroton

The principle of a pot-au-feu is always the same, but the ingredients vary from one region to another. In Auvergne, for example, stuffed cabbage leaves are added; in Bourgogne, oxtail; in Champagne, chicken and rabbit; in Provence, veal knuckle, and so on. Miroton or mironton is one of the many ways of preparing the leftovers of meat cooked in the pot-au-feu.

For the *pot-au-feu:*
bouquet garni: 1 bay leaf, 1 sprig thyme, 6 sprigs parsley,
  2 celery stalks with leaves
1 small onion, about 2 oz (50 g)
3 cloves
4 lb (2 kg) beef, such as chuck, neck, topside or brisket
1 large carrot, peeled and cut into 4 chunks
2 teaspoons coarse sea salt
1 teaspoon mixed peppercorns (black and white)
3 cloves garlic, peeled
For the vegetables:
18 small carrots, peeled
12 small turnips, peeled
12 leeks, white parts only, washed
12 small potatoes, peeled
3 celery hearts
For the *miroton:*
1 lb (500 g) boiled beef, left over from the *pot-au-feu*
1 oz (25 g) butter
8 oz (250 g) onions, finely chopped
salt and freshly ground pepper
1 tablespoon red wine vinegar
6 tablespoons stock from the *pot-au-feu*
2 tablespoons dried breadcrumbs

❖Prepare the *pot-au-feu:* tie together the herbs of the bouquet garni. Peel the onion and stud it with the cloves. Place the meat in a large pot. Add the carrot, onion, bouquet garni, salt, peppercorns and garlic cloves. Pour in cold water to cover generously. Bring slowly to boil, then cook at the barest simmer for 4 to 5 hours or until the meat is very tender, skimming the liquid for the first half hour.

❖Remove the meat, vegetables and flavorings and let the stock cool for about 30 minutes, then remove the layer of fat from the surface with a spoon. If you have time, allow the stock to cool for several hours; all the fat will rise to the surface and all particles will settle to the bottom, leaving a perfectly clear stock.

❖Prepare the vegetables: bring a large saucepan of water to boil. Add the vegetables and cook for 10 minutes, then drain. Transfer to a nonstick 11-in (28-cm) sauté pan and half-cover with degreased stock. Cover and cook over low heat until the vegetables are tender and no more liquid is left in the sauté pan, about 15 to 20 minutes. Reheat the stock and meat. Serve the broth in cups and the meat on a platter, carved into slices and surrounded by vegetables, reserving ¼ of the meat for the *miroton.*

❖Prepare the *miroton:* preheat oven to 450°F (230°C). Finely crumble the meat from the *pot-au-feu*. Melt the butter in a nonstick 10-in (26-cm) sauté pan and stir the onions over low heat until golden, about 10 minutes. Season with salt and pepper. Add the meat and cook, stirring, for 5 minutes

BOILED BEEF AND MIROTON

or until the meat is lightly browned. Sprinkle with vinegar and allow the vinegar to evaporate over high heat. Add the stock and simmer uncovered, stirring from time to time, for 10 minutes or until the stock evaporates.

❖Spread the mixture in a baking dish in a layer ¾ in (2 cm) thick. Sprinkle with breadcrumbs and bake for 5 minutes or until the surface of the *miroton* is lightly browned. Serve immediately.

SERVES 6

Ile de France

BOEUF À LA FICELLE
Poached Beef on a String

The name of this dish undoubtedly comes from the phrase pelican à la ficelle. *The pelican is an atrophied muscle on the heart side of the animal which the butchers kept for themselves.*

When their work was finished they would go to a restaurant in the Villette quarter of Paris and cook this piece of meat in a large pot of boiling salted water. In order to recognize his piece, each butcher would attach it to a length of string carrying his number. This pelican was eaten with coarse salt as soon as it was cooked.

4 pieces of beef, rump, fillet or tenderloin, each about 5 oz
  (150 g) and 1¼ in (3 cm) thick
salt and freshly ground pepper
3 qt (3 l) beef stock (from Pot-au-Feu, recipe this page)
For serving:
coarse salt
a variety of mustards
cornichons (small French sour pickles or gherkins)

❖Tie the pieces of beef with string as you would a parcel, leaving a loop 2½ in (6 cm) long at the center. Season with salt and pepper.

❖Pour the stock into a 4-qt (4-l) pot and bring to boil. Slip the handle of a wooden spoon under the string loops so that the pieces of meat are suspended from it. Rest the spoon on the sides of the pot. Poach 4 minutes for steaks that will be pink at the center, or more or less to taste. Remove the meat from the stock and place one piece on each of 4 warmed plates. Serve immediately, accompanied by coarse salt, mustards and cornichons.

SERVES 4

POACHED BEEF ON A STRING (top), LAMB WITH SPRING VEGETABLES (bottom right, recipe page 172) AND VEAL IN WHITE SAUCE (bottom left, recipe page 174), PHOTOGRAPHED IN THE ILE DE FRANCE.
PIERRE HUSSENOT/AGENCE TOP

PROVENÇAL BRAISED BEEF

PETER JOHNSON

Provence

BOEUF À LA GORDIENNE
Provençal Braised Beef

1 lb 10 oz (1.8 kg) beef suitable for braising, such as topside, neck or chuck steak
1 onion, about 3 oz (100 g)
2 cloves
bouquet garni: 1 sprig thyme, 1 sprig sage, 1 bay leaf, 2 celery stalks, 2 strips orange rind
3 cups (24 fl oz/750 ml) red wine, such as Côtes du Rhône
3 tablespoons red wine vinegar
4 cloves garlic, peeled and quartered
5 oz (150 g) fresh pork rind, trimmed of all fat
3 tablespoons olive oil
8 oz (250 g) medium carrots, peeled and cut into ¼-in (.5-cm) slices
salt and freshly ground pepper
4 pinches of freshly grated nutmeg
7 oz (200 g) bacon

❖Cut the meat into 2-in (5-cm) cubes. Peel the onion and stud with cloves. Tie together the ingredients for the bouquet garni. Place the cubes of meat in a large bowl and cover with the wine and vinegar. Add the bouquet garni, garlic and onion, cover and refrigerate for 12 hours.
❖Preheat oven to 350°F (180°C). Cut the pork rind into ¾-in (2-cm) squares. Drop into boiling water for 2 minutes, then drain. Scatter ⅔ cup of the squares over the bottom of a 4-qt (4-l) enameled pot.
❖Heat the oil in a nonstick 11-in (28-cm) sauté pan. Add the carrots and cook over high heat until lightly browned and caramelized, 7 to 8 minutes. Sprinkle with salt, pepper and nutmeg. Remove with a slotted spoon and set aside.
❖Drain the cubes of meat and pat dry. Cut the bacon into thin matchsticks. Lightly brown the meat and the bacon in the same pan used for the carrots, for about 5 minutes.
❖Place the meat and bacon in the pot and surround with carrots. Cover the meat with the remaining squares of pork rind and pour the marinade over. Add the bouquet garni, garlic and onion. Season with salt and pepper. Cover the

pot with a sheet of oiled waxed paper or parchment paper and place the lid on top. Bake for 5 hours.
❖Remove the onion, garlic and bouquet garni from the pot. If desired, boil the cooking juices over high heat for several minutes to reduce to a syrupy consistency. Serve the meat with the carrots, bacon, pork rind and sauce.

SERVES 6

Ile de France

BOEUF MODE
Aromatic Braised Beef with Vegetables

4 lb (2 kg) beef (round steak, neck, topside, chuck, etc.) in one piece, larded and tied by the butcher
salt and freshly ground pepper
½ teaspoon *quatre-épices* (see glossary)
6 tablespoons cognac
3 cups (24 fl oz/750 ml) dry white wine
2 calf's feet, halved
3 oz (100 g) fresh pork rind, trimmed of all fat
1 large onion
3 cloves
bouquet garni: 1 bay leaf, 1 sprig thyme, 6 sprigs parsley
3 tablespoons vegetable oil
1 oz (25 g) butter
1 large carrot, peeled and sliced
3 cloves garlic, peeled
30 small pickling onions
10 small carrots

❖Wipe the meat. Combine salt, pepper and *quatre-épices* and sprinkle over the meat. Place in a deep bowl just wide enough to hold it and pour the cognac and wine over; the meat should be completely immersed. Cover and refrigerate for 12 hours, turning the meat from time to time.
❖Remove the meat from the marinade and pat dry; reserve the marinade. Bring a large saucepan of water to boil. Drop in the calf's feet and pork rind and boil for 5 minutes. Drain them and cool under running water. Cut the rind into large squares. Peel the large onion and stud with cloves. Tie together the herbs for the bouquet garni.
❖Heat 2 tablespoons oil and the butter in an oval flameproof casserole large enough to hold the meat. Brown the meat on all sides for about 10 minutes. Add the sliced carrot and cook, stirring, for 2 minutes. Add the calf's feet, pork rind, bouquet garni, onion studded with cloves, and the whole cloves of garlic. Pour in the wine; the meat should be covered, but if not, add more wine, water or beef stock. Season with salt and pepper and bring to simmer. Simmer very gently for 5 hours.
❖Meanwhile, peel the small onions and the small carrots. Cut the carrots into ¼-in (1-cm) slices. Heat the remaining oil in a nonstick 11-in (28-cm) sauté pan and add the butter. When it is melted, lightly brown the onions and carrots for about 5 minutes, stirring constantly with a wooden spoon. Add salt and pepper and cook, stirring, for 2 minutes longer, until the vegetables caramelize. Add 6 fl oz (200 ml) stock from the beef and cook for 20 minutes over low heat, until tender.
❖When the meat has cooked for 5 hours, remove the pot from the heat. Remove the meat from the bones of the calf's feet and cut into ¼-in (1-cm) squares. Similarly cut

PETER JOHNSON

AROMATIC BRAISED BEEF WITH VEGETABLES

the pork rind into small squares. Transfer the meat from the pot to a serving platter. Surround it with the veal, pork rind, glazed carrots and onions. Keep hot.

❖Strain the cooking liquid — it will be reduced, highly aromatic and syrupy — and pour it into a sauceboat. Serve immediately; each diner takes a slice of beef, a few cubes of the veal and pork rind, and some glazed vegetables and pours over some of the reduced sauce.

SERVES 8–10

Provence

ALOUETTES SANS TÊTES

Beef Rolls

The shape of these little meat rolls is reminiscent of tiny birds with the heads removed: hence the name of the recipe (literally "larks without heads").

3lb 10oz (1.8kg) rump steak, cut into ⅜-in (1-cm) slices
18 slices prosciutto, each weighing about ½oz (15g)
2oz (60g) soft white bread, crusts trimmed
2 cloves garlic, finely chopped
4 tablespoons chopped flat-leaf parsley
6 pinches of freshly grated nutmeg
freshly ground pepper
3 tablespoons olive oil
1oz (25g) butter
3oz (100g) carrots, peeled and finely chopped
5oz (150g) onions, finely chopped
2 tender celery stalks, chopped
¾ cup (6floz/200ml) red wine
8 cups (2qt/2l) tomato puree
salt
½ teaspoon sugar

❖Cut each slice of meat into rectangles weighing about 3oz (100g). Cut the slices of prosciutto in half crosswise. Using a food processor, grind the bread to crumbs. Combine the crumbs with the garlic, parsley and nutmeg; season well with pepper.

❖Place a rectangle of meat on a work surface and cover with two half-slices of prosciutto. Spread a portion of the bread-crumb mixture to within ⅜in (1cm) of the edge. Starting at a narrow end, roll the meat and secure by tying with kitchen thread. Repeat with the remaining ingredients to form about 18 rolls.

❖Heat the oil in a 6-qt (6-l) pot. In two or three batches, quickly sear the rolls, turning them with two wooden spoons, but do not allow them to brown all over. Remove and set aside.

❖Add the butter to the pot and let melt. Stir in the carrots, onions and celery, cover and cook over very low heat until very soft but not browned, about 10 minutes. Return the beef rolls to the pot and pour the wine over. Boil until the liquid is reduced to a syrupy consistency, about 15 minutes. Add the tomato puree; if the beef rolls are not completely covered, add water to cover. Season with salt, pepper and sugar. Cover and cook over very low heat for 3 hours, stirring several times.

❖Transfer the beef rolls to a shallow dish and keep warm. Boil the sauce over moderate heat until smooth and thickened, about 10 minutes.

❖Meanwhile, remove the thread from the beef rolls. Reheat them for 5 minutes in the sauce, then return rolls and sauce to the dish and serve.

SERVES 8

BEEF ROLLS

PETER JOHNSON

Flandres

CARBONNADES FLAMANDES
Beef Braised in Beer

*In Flandres most meats are served with fried potatoes, and
carbonnades are no exception — but you could also serve them
with steamed or mashed potatoes.*

3 lb 10 oz (1.8 kg) beef suitable for braising, such as round
  steak, brisket, neck or chuck steak
salt and freshly ground pepper
bouquet garni: 1 sprig thyme, 1 bay leaf, 6 sprigs parsley
1 slice whole-grain country-style bread, about 3 oz (100 g)
2 tablespoons strong mustard
1 tablespoon vegetable oil
1 oz (25 g) butter
12 oz (400 g) onions, thinly sliced
1 tablespoon firmly packed brown sugar
2 tablespoons red wine vinegar
16 fl oz (500 ml) dark beer

❖Ask your butcher to cut the meat into slices ½ in (1 cm)
thick and then into 2 x 2½-in (5 x 6-cm) rectangles. Season
with salt and pepper. Tie together the herbs of the bouquet
garni. Cut the crusts from the slice of bread and spread it
with the mustard.
❖Preheat oven to 350°F (180°C). Heat the oil in a nonstick
10-in (26-cm) sauté pan and quickly seal the slices of meat
over high heat for 2 minutes each side. Set aside. Melt the
butter in the sauté pan. Add the onions and cook, stirring,
for 5 minutes or until golden brown. Add the brown sugar
and cook until the onions are lightly caramelized. Pour in
the vinegar and evaporate it over high heat.
❖Arrange alternating layers of meat and onions in an ovenproof 4-qt (4-l) casserole, inserting the slice of bread and
the bouquet garni in the middle. Pour the beer into the
sauté pan and heat it over high heat. Transfer it to the casserole, adding more if necessary to just cover the meat.
Cover and braise in the oven for 4 hours without disturbing.
❖Transfer the meat to a shallow dish and keep warm.
Puree the bread, onions and cooking juices through the fine
holes of a food mill or in a food processor to make a smooth
sauce. Reheat the sauce over high heat, then pour over the
meat. Serve immediately.

SERVES 6

Corse

STUFATU
Corsican Stew with Pasta

*Stufatu is the Corsican word for stew. The term is applied to
numerous dishes cooked by simmering.*

2½ lb (1.25 kg) beef suitable for braising, such as neck or
  chuck
8 oz (250 g) raw smoked ham
bouquet garni: 1 bay leaf, 1 sprig thyme, 1 sprig rosemary,
  6 sprigs parsley

1 lb (500 g) ripe tomatoes
¼ cup (2 fl oz/60 ml) olive oil
8 oz (250 g) onions, thinly sliced
6 cloves garlic, finely chopped
1 cup (8 fl oz/250 ml) dry white wine
salt and freshly ground pepper
4 pinches of freshly grated nutmeg
1 oz (30 g) dried cèpes (*porcini* mushrooms)
For serving:
12 oz (375 g) fresh pasta, or 10 oz (315 g) dried pasta
2 oz (50 g) butter
4 oz (100 g) freshly grated Corsican sheep's milk cheese or
  Parmesan

❖Cut the beef and the ham into ¾-in (2-cm) cubes. Tie
together the herbs for the bouquet garni. Drop the
tomatoes into boiling water for 10 seconds. Cool under running water, peel, halve and squeeze out the seeds; coarsely
chop the flesh.
❖Heat the oil in a 4-qt (4-l) pot and cook the meat, ham,
onions and garlic for 5 minutes, stirring constantly with a
wooden spoon. Add the tomatoes, wine and bouquet garni
and mix well. Season with salt, pepper and nutmeg and
bring to simmer. Cover and simmer for 1 hour.
❖Meanwhile, place the mushrooms in a bowl, cover with
2 cups warm water and leave them to swell.
❖Add the mushrooms to the pot with the strained soaking
liquid and simmer for 2 hours longer.
❖Prepare the pasta: drop the pasta into a large pot of boiling salted water and cook until *al dente*. Drain, place in a
shallow dish and toss with the butter. Pour over half the
sauce from the meat and mix well. Season with pepper and
serve immediately, the meat in its sauce accompanied by
pasta; pass the grated cheese separately.

SERVES 6

Languedoc

BROUFADO
Braised Beef with Anchovies

3 lb 10 oz (1.8 kg) rump steak
¼ cup (2 fl oz/60 ml) olive oil
¼ cup (2 fl oz/60 ml) red wine vinegar
2 cups (16 fl oz/500 ml) dry white wine
3 tablespoons cognac
2 onions, 3 oz (100 g) each, thinly sliced
bouquet garni: 1 sprig thyme, 1 bay leaf, 6 sprigs parsley
2 cloves garlic, halved
salt and freshly ground pepper
3 anchovies preserved in salt
3 tablespoons capers, rinsed and dried
4 cornichons (small French sour pickles or gherkins), thinly
  sliced
1 teaspoon arrowroot
2 tablespoons cold water

❖Cut the meat into 2-in (5-cm) cubes. Pour 2 tablespoons
oil, the vinegar, wine and cognac into a large bowl. Add
the onions and meat and combine. Cover and refrigerate
for 12 hours.

PETER JOHNSON

CORSICAN STEW WITH PASTA (bottom), BRAISED BEEF WITH
ANCHOVIES (center) AND BEEF BRAISED IN BEER (top)

❖Preheat oven to 350°F (180°C). Tie together the herbs for the bouquet garni. Pour the contents of the bowl into a 4-qt (4-l) pot. Add the garlic, bouquet garni, salt and pepper and bring to simmer. Cover and braise in the oven for 4 hours.
❖Rub the salt off the anchovies under cold running water. Lift off the fillets and cut in fourths. Add the capers and cornichons to the pot and braise for 1 hour longer.

❖Transfer the pieces of meat to a warmed plate using a slotted spoon. Blend the arrowroot with the cold water and pour into the sauce. Boil until the mixture thickens, about 2 minutes. Stir in the anchovies, then return the meat to the pot and simmer for 5 minutes. Serve directly from the pot.

SERVES 6

Bourgogne

BOEUF BOURGUIGNON
Burgundy Beef

8 oz (250 g) pork belly
1 tablespoon vegetable oil
2 oz (50 g) butter
36 small pickling onions, peeled
3 lb 10 oz (1.8 kg) beef suitable for braising, such as round, topside or chuck steak
3 tablespoons *marc de Bourgogne* or brandy
3 cups (24 fl oz/750 ml) red Burgundy
36 small (button) mushrooms
1 tablespoon fresh lemon juice
salt and freshly ground pepper
2 teaspoons arrowroot
2 tablespoons cold water

❖Rinse the pork belly under running water, then cut into thin strips. Drop into boiling water and blanch for 5 minutes; drain and rinse.

❖Heat the oil in a 6-qt (6-l) pot and cook the strips of pork belly over low heat until golden brown, about 5 minutes, stirring constantly. Remove from the pot with a slotted spoon and set aside.

❖Add a little less than half the butter to the pot and cook the onions over very low heat until golden, turning frequently, about 10 minutes. Remove with a slotted spoon and add to the pork.

❖Cut the meat into 2-in (5-cm) cubes. Cook in the pot in batches until lightly browned, about 5 minutes, turning frequently. Set aside.

❖Discard the fat from the pot. Add the *marc* and, 1 minute later, the wine, scraping up browned bits with a wooden spoon. Ignite the wine and wait until flames subside. Return the meat to the pot and bring to simmer. Cover and cook over very low heat for 3 hours.

❖Meanwhile, trim the mushroom stems, rinse the mushrooms and pat dry. Melt the remaining butter in a nonstick 10-in (26-cm) sauté pan. Add the mushrooms and lemon juice, season with salt and pepper, and cook the mushrooms until they are golden and have stopped giving out any liquid.

❖Add the pork, onions and mushrooms to the pot and cook over low heat, covered, for 1 hour longer.

❖Remove the meat, pork, onions and mushrooms with a slotted spoon and set aside. Bring the sauce to boil. Blend the arrowroot and cold water, add to the boiling sauce and boil over high heat for 1½ minutes or until the sauce is thickened and smooth. Return the meat and other ingredients to the pot and reheat for 2 minutes. Transfer to a shallow dish and serve.

SERVES 8

BURGUNDY BEEF

PETER JOHNSON

Maine

POTHINE DE BOEUF
Beef Braised with Calvados

Pothines of meat are typical of Maine. The pothine, *or* pothin, *is the heavy cast-iron casserole in which the meats are simmered, either over an open fire or on the edge of the stove.*

3 lb 10 oz (1.8 kg) beef, such as round, neck, topside or chuck steak, in one piece
3 oz (100 g) raw smoked ham
3 oz (100 g) *pancetta* or fresh pork belly
bouquet garni: 1 sprig thyme, 1 bay leaf, 6 sprigs parsley
1 onion, about 3 oz (100 g)
2 cloves
1 calf's foot, halved
3 oz (100 g) fresh pork rind, trimmed of all fat
2 tablespoons vegetable oil
2 cloves garlic, halved
1 cup (8 fl oz/250 ml) beef stock
6 tablespoons calvados
1 cup (8 fl oz/250 ml) dry white wine
salt and freshly ground pepper

❖ Ask the butcher to lard the piece of meat with the ham and pork belly and to tie it securely. Tie together the herbs for the bouquet garni. Peel the onion and stud with cloves.
❖ Bring a large saucepan of water to boil. Add the calf's foot and pork rind and boil for 5 minutes. Drain and refresh under running water, then cut the rind into large squares.
❖ Preheat oven to 350 °F (180 °C). Heat the oil in an oval pot large enough to hold the meat, and brown the meat on all sides. Add the calf's foot, pork rind, bouquet garni, onion and garlic. Pour in the stock, calvados and wine; the meat should be completely covered, but if not, add more wine or stock. Season with salt and pepper, cover and bring to simmer. Braise in the preheated oven for 5 hours.
❖ Extract the meat from the calf's foot and cut it into ½-in (1-cm) squares. Cut the pork rind into similar squares. Remove the beef with a slotted spoon and transfer to a serving platter. Surround with the squares of veal and pork rind and keep warm.
❖ If necessary, boil the cooking liquid over high heat until aromatic and syrupy in consistency. Pour into a sauceboat and serve.

SERVES 8   *Photograph pages 152 – 153*

Lyonnais

GRILLADE DES MARINIERS
Boatman's Grill

This dish is called a grillade *because the meat is thinly cut — as it would be for a grill. As for the boatmen, this is a reference to the bargemen who plied the Rhône, and who would carry this dish with them already prepared so they had only to heat it when they were ready to eat.*

3 lb 10 oz (1.8 kg) rump steak
5 tablespoons olive oil
2 tablespoons red wine vinegar

PETER JOHNSON

BOATMAN'S GRILL

1 bay leaf, crumbled
1 strip orange rind, about 2 in (5 cm) long
2 cloves
salt and freshly ground pepper
4 pinches of freshly grated nutmeg
4 cloves garlic, peeled
2 lb (1 kg) onions, thinly sliced
4 anchovies preserved in salt

❖ Ask the butcher to cut the meat into slices about ¼ in (.5 cm) thick and weighing about 3 oz (100 g).
❖ In a bowl combine 3 tablespoons of the oil, the vinegar, bay leaf, orange rind, cloves, salt, pepper and nutmeg. Whisk with a fork until well blended, then add the meat and stir to coat well. Cover and refrigerate for 12 hours.
❖ Preheat oven to 350 °F (180 °C). Crush 3 cloves of garlic through a garlic press into another bowl. Add the onions, season with salt and pepper and mix well.
❖ Oil a 4-qt (4-l) casserole or baking dish with a lid, using 1 tablespoon oil. Spread a layer of onion mixture over the bottom. Cover with a layer of meat. Continue to alternate the ingredients, finishing with a layer of onions. Discard the orange rind, then pour the marinade over the onions and meat. Cover and braise in the oven for 4 hours.
❖ Wash the anchovies under cold running water, rubbing off the salt. Lift off the fillets and place them in a food processor. Add the remaining clove of garlic, the last tablespoon of oil and ¼ cup (2 fl oz/60 ml) of the liquid from the baking dish and blend to a smooth paste. Pour this paste into the baking dish, stir carefully and simmer for 3 minutes. Serve immediately, straight from the baking dish.

SERVES 6

Bretagne

KIG-HA-FARZ
Buckwheat Pudding with Meat and Vegetables

This traditional Breton dish was once served at family celebrations. The woman of the house carefully kept the white linen bags in which the farz was enclosed, boiling and drying them in the sun after each use. They were then put away in the linen cupboard until the next occasion.

3 lb (1.5 kg) beef suitable for braising, such as top round (topside), neck or chuck
bouquet garni: 1 bay leaf, 1 sprig thyme, 6 sprigs parsley, 3 celery stalks
1 onion
3 cloves
1 lb (500 g) fresh pork belly
1 tablespoon coarse sea salt
1 teaspoon mixed black and white peppercorns
½ teaspoon coriander seeds
3 leeks
1 green cabbage
6 carrots, peeled
6 turnips, peeled
1 celery heart
1 oz (30 g) butter
salt and freshly ground pepper
For the *farz:*
2 oz (60 g) butter
2 cups (8 oz/250 g) buckwheat flour
6 tablespoons milk
6 tablespoons heavy (double) cream or crème fraîche
1 egg
1 teaspoon superfine (caster) sugar
3 oz (100 g) raisins

❖Pour 4 qt (4 l) water into a large pot and bring to boil. Add the piece of beef and simmer gently for 15 minutes, skimming the surface regularly. Tie together the herbs of the bouquet garni. Peel the onion and stud with cloves. Add the pork belly, bouquet garni, onion, coarse salt, peppercorns and coriander to the pot, cover and simmer gently for 2 hours.
❖Trim off the deep green parts of the leeks. Wash the leeks and halve crosswise, separating the white part from the tender green part; tie together in two bundles. Quarter and core the cabbage.
❖Prepare the *farz:* transfer ¾ cup (200 ml) of the cooking liquid from the pot to a small saucepan. Add 2 oz (60 g) butter and allow it to melt. Sift the flour into a bowl. Add the butter mixture, milk, cream, egg and sugar and mix to a smooth paste using a wooden spoon. Blend in the raisins. Wrap the mixture in a square of white cotton cloth and tie the two ends with kitchen thread, taking care not to compress the *farz* too much.
❖Add the leeks, carrots, turnips and celery to the pot and return to boil. Add the *farz* and simmer gently for another 1½ hours.
❖Meanwhile, parboil the cabbage in water to cover for 5 minutes. Drain and transfer to a nonstick 10-in (26-cm) sauté pan with the butter. Season with salt and pepper. Cover and cook over very low heat for 1 hour or until very

tender. Keep warm. Remove the cooked vegetables, meats and *farz* from the pot and strain the stock into a soup tureen. Slice the meats and arrange on a plate; surround with vegetables. Remove the *farz* from its cloth covering and coarsely crumble it around the vegetables. Have guests help themselves to some of each, pouring a little of the stock over before eating.

SERVES 6

Ile de France

STEAK AU POIVRE
Pepper Steak

Invented around 1920 in the kitchens of the Trianon Palace at Versailles, steak au poivre *has become one of the classic dishes of French cuisine. In order to give a lift to some very tender but rather tasteless beef from Argentina, the chef, Emile Lerch, had the idea of covering it with crushed peppercorns before cooking it.*

Today, mignonette *or coarse ground pepper is also referred to as* poivre à steak.

1 porterhouse or rump steak, about 13 oz (400 g) and 1 in (3 cm) thick
salt
1 tablespoon cracked peppercorns
2 oz (60 g) butter
2 tablespoons cognac
3 tablespoons heavy (double) cream or crème fraîche

❖Ask the butcher to trim the meat and to cut it into two equal-size steaks. Pat dry and season with salt. Spread the peppercorns on a plate and roll the steaks over them to coat each side lightly.
❖Melt half the butter in a 10-in (26-cm) skillet. Cook the steaks over high heat for 2 to 3 minutes on each side, according to taste. Pour the cognac over and ignite. When the flames subside, remove the steaks from the pan and keep warm on a plate.
❖Discard the butter from the pan and add the cream. Boil for 1 minute over high heat, then whisk in the remaining butter.
❖Pour this sauce over the steaks and serve immediately.

SERVES 2

PEPPER STEAK

OPPOSITE PAGE: BUCKWHEAT PUDDING WITH MEAT AND VEGETABLES (top left) AND LEG OF LAMB, BRITTANY-STYLE (bottom right, recipe page 170), PHOTOGRAPHED IN BRETAGNE
PIERRE HUSSENOT/AGENCE TOP

PETER JOHNSON

Flandres

HOCHEPOT
Oxtail Stew

The word pot *indicates that different meats and vegetables are cooked together in the same pot. Sometimes this Flandres pot-au-feu is enriched by the addition of some pig's tail and bacon.*

2 lb (1 kg) oxtail
1½ lb (750 g) beef spareribs (flank)
1½ lb (750 g) lamb shoulder
8 oz (250 g) lightly salted pork belly
1 pig's ear
8 leeks
1 onion, about 3 oz (100 g)
3 cloves
2 cloves garlic
bouquet garni: 2 bay leaves, 1 sprig thyme, 10 sprigs parsley
8 small carrots, peeled
8 small turnips, peeled
1 celeriac (celery root), peeled
1 bunch celery, washed
10 juniper berries
10 peppercorns, black and white mixed
8 medium-size boiling potatoes
1 green cabbage
salt
1 unsmoked kielbasa (boiling sausage)
For serving (optional):
toasted bread
grated Emmenthaler cheese

❖Ask the butcher to cut the oxtail into 1½-in (4-cm) sections. Rinse the meats and pat dry. Place the oxtail, spareribs, lamb shoulder, pork belly and pig's ear in a large pot and cover with plenty of cold water. Bring to boil and cook for 5 minutes, then drain the meats, discarding the liquid. Return the meats to the pot and cover again with plenty of cold water. Bring to boil over low heat.
❖Clean the leeks and tie together in 2 bunches. Peel the onion and stud with cloves. Peel the cloves of garlic and crush them with the hand or the side of a cleaver. Tie together the herbs for the bouquet garni.
❖Add the carrots, turnips, celeriac, celery, leeks, garlic, bouquet garni, juniper berries and peppercorns to the pot and simmer gently for 2 hours.
❖Meanwhile, peel and wash the potatoes. Core and quarter the cabbage. Blanch the cabbage in boiling water to cover for 5 minutes, then transfer to a nonstick 10-in (26-cm) sauté pan with the potatoes. Season with salt. Add 6 tablespoons stock from the meat and cook over low heat, covered, for 20 minutes, or until cabbage and potatoes are tender, adding more liquid from time to time as necessary.
❖About 45 minutes before the end of the cooking time, prick the sausage with a fork and add to the pot with the meats.
❖Drain the meats and carve into ¾-in (2-cm) slices. Arrange on a platter and surround with the boiled vegetables, cabbage and potatoes, moistening them with a little stock. Strain the remaining stock into a soup tureen. Serve the broth hot, either as is or with toasted bread and grated cheese, followed by the meats and vegetables.

SERVES 8   *Photograph pages 6 – 7*

Ile de France

ENTRECÔTES BERCY, POMMES FRITES
Rib Steaks, Bercy-style, with French Fries

The Bercy quarter of Paris, which for a long time was home to the most important wine market of Europe, gave its name to a method of cooking with wine and shallots that was fashionable in Parisian restaurants around 1820.

This was also the era of the traveling marchands de frites *or* friteurs *who operated around the Pont-Neuf selling potatoes fried in sizzling hot oil called* pommes Pont-Neuf.

Gradually these merchants spread all over Paris and their fried potatoes became known simply as frites *or* pommes frites.

2 lb (1 kg) boiling potatoes
about 2 qt (2 l) peanut (groundnut) oil
2 entrecôtes, rib steaks or Scotch fillets, 1¼ lb (600 g) each, trimmed
salt and freshly ground pepper
3 oz (100 g) beef marrow
1 tablespoon vegetable oil
3 oz (100 g) butter
4 French shallots, finely chopped
6 tablespoons dry white wine
1 tablespoon chopped flat-leaf parsley

❖Peel the potatoes, wash them and cut them into pieces 2 to 2½ in (5 to 6 cm) long and ½ in (1 cm) wide. Rinse under cold water and dry in a tea towel.
❖Heat the oil in a deep fryer to 350°F (180°C). As soon as it starts to bubble, add the potatoes in a frying basket, in batches if necessary, and fry until a pale straw color. Remove the basket from the oil and set the fries aside; maintain the oil at 350°F (180°C).
❖Pat the steaks dry and season with salt and pepper. Cut the beef marrow into ¼-in (.5-cm) cubes. Drop into a saucepan of simmering water and poach for 3 minutes. Drain in a sieve.
❖Heat the oil in a nonstick 10-in (26-cm) skillet. Add 1 oz (25 g) butter. As soon as it melts, add the steaks and cook for 1½ to 2½ minutes on each side, according to taste. Remove from the pan and keep warm; discard the fat from the pan. Add the shallots and wine and cook over high heat, scraping up browned bits with a wooden spoon, until the liquid is reduced to 1 tablespoon. Remove the pan from the heat and whisk in the remaining butter in small pieces to make a light, foamy sauce. Add the parsley and pour over the steaks. Reheat the marrow in the skillet for 30 seconds and scatter over the meat.
❖Plunge the basket of potatoes back into the hot oil and fry until crisp and golden brown. Drain on paper towels. Sprinkle with salt and turn onto a plate. Serve the steaks immediately, accompanied by the potatoes.

SERVES 4

RIB STEAKS, BERCY-STYLE, WITH FRENCH FRIES
PETER JOHNSON

Bretagne

GIGOT D'AGNEAU À LA BRETONNE

Leg of Lamb, Brittany-style

Haricot beans, one of the best known vegetables from Bretagne, are the main ingredient of any dish called à la bretonne. *The beans may be left whole or pureed.*

1 onion, about 3 oz (100 g)
2 cloves
6 cloves garlic
bouquet garni: 1 bay leaf, 1 sprig thyme, 6 sprigs parsley
3 lb (1.5 kg) fresh haricot (white) beans, shelled
5 oz (150 g) carrots, peeled and coarsely chopped
1 leg of lamb, about 3½ lb (1.7 kg), trimmed
2 tablespoons peanut (groundnut) oil
salt and freshly ground pepper
1 oz (25 g) butter

❖Peel the onion and stud with cloves. Peel and halve 4 cloves of garlic. Tie together the herbs for the bouquet garni.
❖Combine the beans, onion, carrots, bouquet garni and halved garlic cloves in a large saucepan and cover with plenty of water. Bring to boil over low heat. Simmer gently for 1½ hours, seasoning with salt after 1 hour.
❖When the beans have been cooking for 30 minutes, pre-heat oven to 475°F (245°C). Peel the remaining 2 cloves of garlic and cut each into 6 slivers. Make incisions in the leg of lamb with the point of a knife and slip a sliver of garlic into each. Rub the lamb with oil and season with salt and pepper. Oil a large roasting pan and rack and place the leg of lamb on the rack, curved side down.
❖Roast the lamb for 20 minutes, then turn it over, reduce heat to 450°F (230°C) and roast for 25 minutes longer, checking that the juices in the pan do not burn; they should only caramelize. If the juices begin to burn, add a few spoonfuls of water to the pan from time to time.
❖A leg of lamb of this weight will be roasted to the rosy-pink stage in 45 minutes. Turn off the oven, turn the lamb over and let rest for 10 minutes.
❖When the beans are cooked, drain them and discard the bouquet garni, onion and garlic. Discard the fat from the roasting pan and add the butter. Turn the beans into the pan and stir to coat with the butter and pan juices. Transfer to a serving dish. Place the leg of lamb on a platter and serve with the beans.

SERVES 6   *Photograph page 167*

Savoie

ÉPAULE D'AGNEAU À LA BOULANGÈRE

Shoulder of Lamb with Potatoes

Large pieces of meat were once cooked in the baker's oven, and the expression à la boulangère *has remained. This method is used for shoulder or leg of lamb, and for "roasts" of fish such as cod.*

1 shoulder of lamb, about 3 lb (1.5 kg)
salt and freshly ground pepper
2 oz (50 g) butter
2 lb (1 kg) boiling potatoes
8 oz (250 g) onions, thinly sliced
3 tablespoons water

❖Ask the butcher to bone the lamb and trim off the fat. Season the meat with salt and pepper on both sides. Roll up and secure with string.
❖Preheat oven to 425°F (215°C). Spread half the butter over the outside of the meat. Place in a dish which will easily hold it.
❖Roast the lamb for 20 minutes, turning frequently so that it browns lightly all over.
❖Peel the potatoes, wash and pat dry. Cut into quarters lengthwise. Melt the remaining butter in a nonstick 10-in (26-cm) sauté pan and lightly brown the onions and potatoes for 10 minutes, turning with a wooden spoon and seasoning with salt and pepper.
❖Arrange the onion-potato mixture around the meat and drizzle with the water. Roast for 45 minutes or until both meat and vegetables are cooked.
❖Remove the string from the meat and carve into slices. Arrange them on a serving platter. Surround with vegetables and serve.

SERVES 6

SHOULDER OF LAMB WITH POTATOES (bottom) AND AVIGNON LAMB STEW (top)

PETER JOHNSON

Provence

DAUBE D'AVIGNON
Avignon Lamb Stew

Although the word daube *refers to a method of cooking in which meat or poultry is simmered for several hours in white or red wine and seasoned with herbs, there are an amazing number of variations of the dish in different towns and villages.*

This is the fragrant, mellow version served in the charming town of Avignon. It is usually accompanied by lightly buttered noodles coated with the juices of the daube *and sprinkled with grated cheese — Emmenthaler or Parmesan, or a mixture of the two.*

3 lb (1.5 kg) lamb from the leg, boned and trimmed of fat
2 onions (3 oz/100 g each) finely chopped
4 cloves garlic, finely chopped
1 sprig thyme, crumbled
1 bay leaf, crumbled
2 tablespoons chopped flat-leaf parsley
2 cloves
6 tablespoons olive oil
1 cup (8 fl oz/250 ml) red wine, such as Côtes du Rhône
2 tablespoons cognac
salt and freshly ground pepper
1 slice pork belly, about 7 oz (200 g)
5 oz (150 g) fresh pork rind
1 strip dried orange rind

❖Cut the meat into 1½-in (4-cm) cubes and place in a large bowl. Add the onion, garlic, thyme, bay leaf, parsley, cloves, oil, wine and cognac. Season with salt and pepper. Stir well, then marinate for 2 hours at room temperature.
❖About 20 minutes before the end of the marinating time, bring a large saucepan of water to boil. Add the pork belly and rind and boil for 5 minutes. Drain, rinse and drain again. Cool to lukewarm, then cut the pork belly into thin strips and the rind into ⅜-in (1-cm) squares. Stir the strips of belly into the marinating mixture.
❖Preheat oven to 350°F (180°C). Scatter the squares of pork rind on the bottom of a 4-qt (4-l) earthenware or enameled casserole. Pour in all the marinating mixture and meat and add the orange rind. Seal the pot airtight by putting waxed paper between casserole and lid, and bake for 5 hours without disturbing the contents.
❖Serve the stew very hot, directly from the casserole.

SERVES 6

Provence

GIGOT FARCI
Stuffed Leg of Lamb

This method of cooking a leg of lamb is found in many parts of France, but the stuffings vary considerably according to the region.

8 oz (250 g) wild mushrooms
1 tablespoon butter
2 oz (50 g) lean smoked bacon, finely chopped
1 heart of fennel, about 3 oz (100 g), chopped
4 tablespoons chopped parsley and fresh chervil, mixed
2 pinches dried thyme

PETER JOHNSON

STUFFED LEG OF LAMB

salt and freshly ground pepper
3 pinches of freshly grated nutmeg
1 oz (25 g) white sandwich bread, crusts trimmed
1 clove garlic
1 leg of lamb, about 3 lb 10 oz (1.8 kg), trimmed and boned
1 teaspoon peanut oil
For the potatoes:
3½ lb (1.7 kg) boiling potatoes
3 oz (80 g) butter
½ teaspoon dried thyme
1 clove garlic

❖Trim the mushroom stems. Wash the mushrooms quickly under cold water and pat dry; chop. Melt 1 tablespoon butter in a nonstick 9-in (22-cm) sauté pan and lightly brown the bacon for 2 minutes, stirring with a wooden spoon. Add the fennel, cover and cook for 2 minutes longer. Add the mushrooms, the parsley mixture, thyme, salt, pepper and nutmeg and cook, half-covered, until the fennel is very tender and all liquid has evaporated.
❖Grind the bread to coarse crumbs in a food processor. Remove the sauté pan from heat. Mix in the crumbs and the crushed garlic.
❖Stuff the leg of lamb with this mixture and sew the opening with kitchen thread. Coat the lamb with oil and season with salt and pepper. Make very shallow crisscross cuts over the surface of the leg. Preheat oven to 450°F (230°C). Peel the potatoes, rinse and pat dry. Slice into very thin rounds. Melt the butter in a 13 x 9-in (32 x 22-cm) baking dish. Add the thyme and the garlic, crushed in a garlic press. Toss the potatoes in this flavored butter to coat well. Spread the slices in the pan and smooth the surface.
❖Place the leg of lamb on the bed of potatoes, rounded side down. Roast for 30 minutes. Turn the lamb and potato slices over and roast 25 minutes longer. Turn off the oven and let the leg of lamb rest in the oven for 10 minutes before serving.

SERVES 8

PETER JOHNSON

ROAST LAMB OF PAUILLAC

squeeze out the seeds and finely chop the flesh. Tie together the herbs for the bouquet garni.

❖Heat the oil in a 4-qt (4-l) flameproof casserole, add half the butter and lightly brown the cubes of meat on all sides. Sprinkle with flour and cook, stirring, for 1 minute. Stir in the tomatoes, stock, bouquet garni and garlic. Cover and cook over low heat for 1½ hours.

❖Meanwhile, prepare the vegetables: shell the peas. Peel the carrots and turnips. Peel the onions and cut off the green stalks. Remove the strings from the beans, if necessary. Blanch in a large quantity of boiling water for 5 minutes, then drain.

❖Melt the remaining butter in a nonstick 11-in (28-cm) sauté pan. Add the carrots, turnips and onions and cook over low heat until lightly golden, about 5 minutes, stirring frequently. Add the beans and peas and sprinkle with sugar, salt and pepper. Cook until the vegetables are golden, about 2 minutes longer. Add ¾ cup (6 fl oz/200 ml) of the veal cooking liquid and simmer over low heat for 15 minutes.

❖After the meat has cooked for 1½ hours, add the vegetables and cook over low heat, stirring, for 5 minutes. Remove the meat and vegetables with a slotted spoon, transfer to a shallow dish and keep warm. Boil the cooking liquid until thickened, then remove the garlic and bouquet garni. Stir in the chervil. Pour the sauce over the meat and vegetables and serve.

SERVES 6 *Photograph page 159*

Ile de France

NAVARIN PRINTANIER
Lamb with Spring Vegetables

On October 20, 1827, the French, English and Russian armies together defeated the Egyptian and Turkish fleet at Navarin in Greece in the course of the Greek War of Independence. It is thought that this dish of lamb stewed with vegetables was christened navarin *in honor of the war. Or perhaps the name comes from the* navet *(turnip) which was once the main vegetable used. The mystery remains unsolved.*

3¼ lb (1.6 kg) lamb shoulder, neck and breast, mixed
salt and freshly ground pepper
6 oz (200 g) ripe tomatoes
bouquet garni: 1 bay leaf, 1 sprig thyme, 6 sprigs parsley
1 tablespoon vegetable oil
2 oz (50 g) butter
1 tablespoon all purpose (plain) flour
2 cups (16 fl oz/500 ml) chicken stock (recipe page 34)
2 cloves garlic, halved
1 lb (500 g) fresh peas, in the shell
1 lb (500 g) very small carrots
1 lb (500 g) small turnips
18 small green (spring) onions
6 oz (200 g) slender green beans
1 teaspoon sugar
1 tablespoon chopped fresh chervil

❖Cut the meat into 2-in (5-cm) cubes and season with salt and pepper. Drop the tomatoes into boiling water for 10 seconds. Cool under running water, then peel, halve,

Languedoc

AGNEAU RÔTI DE PAUILLAC
Roast Lamb of Pauillac

2½ oz (75 g) stale bread, crusts trimmed
8 cloves garlic
2 oz (50 g) butter
salt and freshly ground pepper
8 tablespoons chopped flat-leaf parsley
1 leg of lamb, about 3½ lb (1.7 kg), trimmed
2 tablespoons peanut (groundnut) oil

❖Preheat oven to 450°F (230°C). Grind the bread to coarse crumbs in a food processor. Finely chop 6 garlic cloves and cut the remaining two into fine slivers. In a bowl, combine the butter, salt, pepper, breadcrumbs, parsley and chopped garlic and mix with a fork to produce a smooth paste.

❖Make slits in the leg of lamb with the point of a knife and insert slivers of garlic in the slits. Season the lamb with salt and pepper and spread the garlic paste over the surface. Coat the lamb with oil and season with salt and pepper.

❖Oil a large baking dish. Place the leg of lamb on a roasting rack in the dish, rounded side down. Roast for 20 minutes, then turn the lamb over and reduce the heat to 425°F (215°C), checking that the juices in the pan are not burning; they should just caramelize. If the juices start to burn, add a few spoonfuls of hot water to the dish from time to time. After 45 minutes of cooking, turn off the oven, turn the leg of lamb over and let it rest for 10 minutes in the oven. Carve in slices, sprinkle over the pan juices and serve.

SERVES 6

Anjou

CUL DE VEAU À L'ANGEVINE
Veal Pot Roast, Anjou-style

Cul de veau is another name for quasi de veau, the chump end of veal taken from above the thigh of the animal. This Anjou dish is served with sautéed wild mushrooms, glazed carrots or a puree of celeriac.

3 oz (100 g) fresh pork rind, trimmed of all fat
bouquet garni: 1 bay leaf, 1 sprig thyme, 6 sprigs parsley
¾ cup (200 ml) dry white wine
¾ cup (200 ml) chicken stock (recipe page 34)
2 oz (50 g) butter
3½ lb (1.75 kg) veal rump
2 medium carrots, peeled and thinly sliced
2 onions, about 3 oz (100 g) each, thinly sliced
salt and freshly ground pepper

❖Blanch the pork rind in boiling water to cover for 2 minutes; drain. Cut into ¾ x ¼-in (2 x .5-cm) strips. Tie together the herbs for the bouquet garni.
❖Preheat oven to 350°F (180°C). Pour the wine and the stock into a saucepan and boil over high heat until reduced by half. Melt the butter in a pot large enough to hold the piece of veal and lightly brown it on all sides. Remove the meat and set aside. Add the carrots and onions to the pot and cook, stirring, for 5 minutes, then return meat to the pot. Pour in the wine mixture and turn the meat over. Season with salt and pepper; add the pork rind and the bouquet garni. Cover and braise in the oven for 3 hours.
❖Remove the meat from the pot and transfer to a serving plate. Surround with the pork rind, onions and carrots. Boil the cooking liquid until reduced to a syrupy consistency and pour over the meat. Serve immediately.

SERVES 6   *Photograph pages 152 – 153*

Normandie

CÔTES DE VEAU À LA NORMANDE
Veal Chops, Normandy-style

4 Golden Delicious apples, about 7 oz (200 g) each
2½ oz (75 g) butter
4 veal chops (cutlets), about 7 oz (200 g) each
salt and freshly ground pepper
2 tablespoons calvados
¾ cup (6 fl oz/200 ml) heavy (double) cream or crème fraîche

❖Peel, core and quarter the apples; cut each quarter into 3 slices. Melt half the butter in a nonstick 11-in (28-cm) skillet. Add the apple slices and cook over moderate heat for 10 minutes, turning after 5 minutes.
❖Meanwhile, melt the remaining butter in a nonstick 10-in (26-cm) skillet. Sauté the veal over moderate heat for 5 minutes on each side, seasoning with salt and pepper.
❖Arrange the veal and apples on a serving platter and keep warm. Pour the calvados into the pan used for cooking the veal and boil until evaporated, scraping up browned bits

with a wooden spoon. Add the cream and boil until reduced by half, stirring constantly. Pour this sauce over the veal and serve immediately.

SERVES 4

Lyonnais

FOIE DE VEAU À LA LYONNAISE
Calf's Liver, Lyons-style

À la lyonnaise is the term used for any dish cooked with onions that have been chopped and softened in butter with vinegar and chopped parsley added. Among the foods prepared in this way are cardoons and calf's head.

4 slices calf's liver, ⅝ in (1.5 cm) thick and 5 oz (150 g) each
salt and freshly ground pepper
2 oz (50 g) butter
8 oz (250 g) onions, thinly sliced
1 tablespoon red wine vinegar
2 tablespoons chopped flat-leaf parsley

❖Pat the slices of liver dry. Season with salt and pepper. Melt ⅓ of the butter in a nonstick 10-in (26-cm) skillet. Cook the slices of liver over moderate heat for 2 minutes on each side. Remove and keep warm.
❖Melt the remaining butter in the same skillet. Add the onions and cook over low heat, stirring frequently, for 15 minutes or until very soft. Add the vinegar and the juices which have escaped from the liver. Season with salt and pepper and cook, stirring, for 1 minute longer. Divide the onion mixture among four heated plates.
❖Reheat the slices of liver in the skillet for 30 seconds on each side, then arrange them on the plates. Sprinkle with chopped parsley and serve immediately.

SERVES 4

VEAL CHOPS, NORMANDY-STYLE (top)
AND CALF'S LIVER, LYONS-STYLE (bottom)

PETER JOHNSON

CREAMED KIDNEYS AND SWEETBREADS

Touraine

BEUCHELLE
Creamed Kidneys and Sweetbreads

The origin of this very old Touraine dish is not known. We only know that it was brought back into fashion by a chef named Edouard Nignon at the Larue restaurant in Paris at the beginning of this century.

2 veal kidneys
salt and freshly ground pepper
2 veal sweetbreads
1 lb (500 g) fresh cèpes (*porcini* mushrooms)
3 oz (100 g) butter
1 cup (8 fl oz/250 ml) heavy (double) cream or crème fraîche
2 oz (50 g) Parmesan cheese, freshly and finely grated

❖Ask the butcher to remove the fat from the kidneys and to cut them into slices ¼ in (.5 cm) thick. Season the kidneys with salt and pepper.
❖Bring a large saucepan of water to boil. Drop in the sweetbreads and blanch for 2 minutes. Drain, then soak for 15 minutes in ice water. Drain, pat dry and cut into slices ¼ in (.5 cm) thick.
❖Trim the stems of the cèpes. Wash quickly under running water, pat dry and cut into slices ¼ in (.5 cm) thick.
❖Melt half the butter in a nonstick 10-in (26-cm) skillet and cook the kidney slices for 2 minutes or until lightly browned, turning with a wooden spoon. Remove from the pan and keep warm. Cook the sweetbread slices in the same way and set aside with the kidneys.
❖Wipe out the skillet, then melt the remaining butter in it. Add the cèpes and cook over high heat until they are golden and do not give out any more liquid. Add the cream and boil, stirring, for 3 minutes or until it thickens and coats the cèpes. Season with salt and pepper.

❖Preheat broiler (griller). Butter a broilerproof dish large enough to hold the meat and cèpes in a 1¼ in (3 cm) layer.
❖Add the sweetbread and kidney slices to the skillet and cook, stirring, for 30 seconds. Pour the mixture into the buttered dish and sprinkle with Parmesan. Broil close to the heat for 2 minutes. Serve immediately from the same dish.

SERVES 6

Ile de France

BLANQUETTE DE VEAU
Veal in White Sauce

3 lb (1.5 kg) veal, on the bone: ⅓ breast, ⅓ shoulder, ⅓ forequarter
1 onion, about 3 oz (100 g)
2 cloves
bouquet garni: 1 bay leaf, 1 sprig thyme, 6 sprigs parsley, 2 celery stalks, white part of 1 leek
1 medium carrot, peeled and cut into 4 chunks
¾ cup (6 fl oz/200 ml) dry white wine
⅔ cup (5 fl oz/150 ml) heavy (double) cream or crème fraîche
2 egg yolks
4 pinches of freshly grated nutmeg
1 tablespoon fresh lemon juice
salt and freshly ground pepper
To garnish:
24 small pickling onions
8 oz (250 g) small (button) mushrooms
2 oz (50 g) butter
6 tablespoons water
1 tablespoon fresh lemon juice

❖Cut the meat into 2-in (5-cm) cubes. Peel the onion and stud with cloves. Tie together the herbs for the bouquet garni. Place the meat in a flameproof casserole and add the carrot, onion and bouquet garni. Pour in the wine and water just to cover. Bring to boil, skimming the surface for the first 10 minutes, then cover and simmer very gently for 2½ hours.
❖About 45 minutes before the meat is ready, prepare the garnish: peel the pickling onions. Trim the mushroom stems; wash the mushrooms and pat dry. Melt half the butter in a nonstick 10-in (26-cm) skillet and cook the onions until golden, about 5 minutes, stirring frequently. Add the water, season with salt and pepper and cook, covered, for 20 minutes or until tender. Melt the remaining butter in a second skillet and add the mushrooms and lemon juice. Season with salt and pepper and cook until mushrooms are golden and no longer give out any liquid. Add to the onions and keep warm.
❖Remove the meat with a slotted spoon and transfer to a heated plate. Surround with the mushrooms and onions.
❖Strain the cooking liquid into a saucepan and boil over high heat until reduced to about 1 cup (250 ml). In a bowl beat the cream and egg yolks; blend in 3 tablespoons of the hot stock. Return to the saucepan and cook, stirring constantly, until slightly thickened; do not boil. Remove from heat and whisk the sauce to a smooth, velvety consistency. Add the nutmeg, lemon juice, salt and pepper and whisk for 30 seconds longer. Pour this sauce over the meat and vegetables; serve immediately.

SERVES 6   *Photograph page 159*

PETER JOHNSON

VEAL WITH GARLIC (top left), STUFFED BREAST OF VEAL
(bottom) AND VEAL ROLLS (top right, recipe page 176)

Aquitaine

AILLADE GASCONNE
Veal with Garlic

The large quantity of garlic used in this recipe is responsible for the name of the dish, which is very popular in the southwest.

2 lb (1 kg) veal shoulder, boned and trimmed of all fat
1 oz (25 g) goose fat
10 cloves garlic
⅓ cup (2 oz/50 g) untoasted dried breadcrumbs
1 lb (500 g) ripe tomatoes, quartered
½ teaspoon sugar
salt and freshly ground pepper

❖Cut the meat into 1½-in (4-cm) cubes. Melt the goose fat in a nonstick 10-in (26-cm) sauté pan and lightly brown the veal over moderate heat for about 5 minutes, stirring constantly. Remove with a slotted spoon and set aside. Add the garlic and breadcrumbs to the sauté pan and cook, stirring, until golden brown. Add the tomatoes, sugar, salt and pepper. Return the meat to the sauté pan, stir well and bring to simmer. Cover and cook over low heat for 2 hours, stirring two or three times.
❖Remove the meat with a slotted spoon and transfer to a shallow dish; keep warm. Puree the sauce through the medium holes of a food mill, or use a processor. Pour over the meat and serve immediately.

SERVES 4

Auvergne

FALETTE
Stuffed Breast of Veal

A specialty of Auvergne, this dish is delicious served hot with braised cabbage or sautéed potatoes, or cold with a dandelion and walnut salad. It can also be made from breast of pork, in which case it is called fraude.

1½ lb (750 g) beet greens, Swiss chard or silverbeet
6 tablespoons milk
2 oz (50 g) stale bread, crusts trimmed
5 oz (150 g) fresh pork belly, finely chopped
1 clove garlic, finely chopped
1 tablespoon chopped flat-leaf parsley
1 tablespoon chopped fresh chervil
2 tablespoons cognac
salt and freshly ground pepper
6 pinches of freshly grated nutmeg
2 eggs
3½ lb (1.75 kg) breast of veal, boned and trimmed of all fat
3 oz (100 g) fresh pork rind, trimmed of all fat
bouquet garni: 1 bay leaf, 1 sprig thyme, 10 sprigs parsley
2 tablespoons vegetable oil
1 oz (25 g) butter
1 onion, about 3 oz (100 g), thinly sliced
1 medium carrot, washed and thinly sliced
6 tablespoons dry white wine
¾ cup (6 fl oz/200 ml) chicken stock (recipe page 34)

❖Wash the beet greens and place in a pot with the water clinging to the leaves. Cover and cook over high heat for 4 minutes. Drain the greens and chop finely with a knife.

Bring the milk to boil in a small saucepan. Crumble in the bread. Remove from heat and stir to form a smooth paste. In a bowl, mix the pork belly, garlic, parsley, chervil, cognac, bread paste and beet greens. Season with salt, pepper and nutmeg. Blend in the eggs.
❖Season the veal with salt and pepper. Spread on a work surface and arrange the stuffing lengthwise down the middle. Roll the meat around the stuffing and tie at intervals with kitchen thread.
❖Blanch the pork rind in boiling water to cover for 2 minutes. Drain and cut into ¾-in (2-cm) squares. Tie together the herbs for the bouquet garni.
❖Heat the oil in a heavy pot just large enough to hold the rolled veal. Add the butter and brown the meat on all sides. Remove the meat and discard the cooking fat. Add the onion and carrot to the pot and cook, stirring, for 5 minutes. Return the meat to the pot and pour in the wine and stock. Add the pork rind and bouquet garni; season with salt and pepper. Cover and cook over very low heat for 2 hours.
❖Transfer the meat to a serving plate. Surround it with the pork rind, onion and carrot. Boil the cooking liquid until reduced to a syrupy consistency and pour over the meat. Serve immediately.

SERVES 6–7

Provence

PAUPIETTES
Veal Rolls

The term paupiette *originally referred to a thin slice of veal rolled around some kind of stuffing and tied with string. It was subsequently applied to slices of beef, cabbage leaves or fillets of fish used in the same way.*

12 veal scallops (escalopes), 3 oz (80 g) each
salt and freshly ground pepper
7 oz (200 g) black olives, pitted
7 oz (200 g) cooked ham, finely chopped
2 cloves garlic, finely chopped
2 tablespoons chopped flat-leaf parsley
4 pinches of freshly grated nutmeg
2 tablespoons olive oil
1 oz (25 g) butter
¾ cup (6 fl oz/200 ml) dry white wine

❖Pound the veal scallops until very thin. Season with salt and pepper.
❖Drop the olives into boiling water and blanch for 2 minutes. Refresh them under running water and drain. Finely chop half the olives; halve the remainder.
❖In a bowl mix the ham, chopped olives, garlic, parsley, pepper and nutmeg. Lay one veal scallop on a work surface and spread ¹⁄₁₂ of the mixture to within ⅜ in (1 cm) of the edges. Roll up starting from a narrow end. Tie the roll with kitchen thread. Repeat with the remaining ingredients to produce 12 *paupiettes*.
❖Heat the oil in a heavy 4-qt (4-l) pot. Add the butter and let it melt. Brown the rolls on all sides in two or three batches. Return all the rolls to the pot. Pour in the wine and boil for 1 minute to evaporate the alcohol. Cover and cook over very low heat for 1½ hours, stirring several times.
❖Remove the rolls from the pot and keep warm. Add the remaining olives to the pot and cook for 2 minutes.
❖Remove the strings from the rolls. Reheat the rolls for 5 minutes in the sauce, then arrange on a serving platter. Pour the olive sauce over and serve immediately.

SERVES 6   *Photograph page 175*

Ile de France

VEAU MARENGO
Veal Marengo

On the evening of June 14, 1880, Napoleon defeated the Austrians at Marengo. As the Emperor's cook, Dunand, was organizing the provisions, he improvised a chicken dish, dressing the bird with white wine, garlic, tomatoes and cognac and thus inventing Chicken Marengo. The recipe has since been adapted to shoulder of veal.

2½ lb (1.2 kg) veal shoulder, trimmed of bones and fat
bouquet garni: 1 bay leaf, 1 sprig thyme, 6 sprigs parsley
1 tablespoon vegetable oil
1 oz (30 g) butter
1 medium carrot, peeled and finely chopped
2 onions, about 3 oz (100 g) each, finely chopped
1 tablespoon all purpose (plain) flour
2 cloves garlic, halved
¾ cup (6 fl oz/200 ml) dry white wine

¾ cup (6 fl oz/200 ml) chicken stock (recipe page 34)
¾ cup (6 fl oz/200 ml) tomato puree
salt and freshly ground pepper
1 lemon
1 tablespoon chopped fresh parsley
1 tablespoon chopped fresh tarragon
To garnish:
24 small pickling onions
8 oz (250 g) small (button) mushrooms
1 oz (25 g) butter

❖Cut the meat into 2-in (5-cm) cubes. Tie together the herbs of the bouquet garni.
❖Heat the oil in a nonstick 11-in (28-cm) sauté pan. Add the butter and let melt. Add the meat, carrot and onions and cook over high heat, stirring, for 5 minutes or until lightly browned. Sprinkle with flour and cook, stirring, for 1 minute longer. Add the garlic and bouquet garni, then the white wine. Boil over high heat until reduced by half, then pour in the stock and the tomato puree (the meat should be covered with liquid; if necessary, add a little more stock or water). Season with salt and pepper and bring to boil. Cover and cook over low heat for 1 hour.
❖Meanwhile, prepare the garnish: peel the pickling onions. Trim the mushroom stems, wash the mushrooms and pat dry. Melt the butter in a nonstick 10-in (26-cm) skillet and cook the onions until golden, about 5 minutes, stirring frequently. Remove with a slotted spoon and set aside. Add the mushrooms to the pan and cook until they are golden and give out no more liquid. Set aside with the onions.
❖Wash the lemon and wipe dry. Finely grate half the rind. Halve the lemon and squeeze 1 tablespoon of juice. Stir the onion-mushroom mixture and grated lemon rind into the sauté pan. Cover and cook gently for 45 minutes longer.
❖When the meat is cooked, stir in the lemon juice, parsley and tarragon. Discard the bouquet garni. Remove from heat and turn into a shallow dish. Serve immediately.

SERVES 6   *Photograph pages 152 – 153*

Bourgogne

ROGNONS À LA MOUTARDE
Veal Kidneys in Mustard Sauce

The seeds of a Mediterranean plant are used to make mustard. The vinegar-and-mustard makers guild was formed in Orléans at the end of the sixteenth century, and in Dijon in 1630, to establish rules for its manufacture. Today, verjuice and white wine are added to Dijon mustard; in Meaux, the seeds are coarsely crushed; in Orléans vinegar is added; and in Bordeaux grape must is used.

2 veal kidneys
salt and freshly ground pepper
6 tablespoons heavy (double) cream or crème fraîche
2 tablespoons strong mustard
1 tablespoon vegetable oil
1 oz (25 g) butter
2 French shallots, finely chopped
⅔ cup (5 fl oz/150 ml) dry white wine

❖Ask the butcher to remove the fat from the kidneys. Season them with salt and pepper. Mix the cream and mustard in a bowl.

VEAL KIDNEYS IN MUSTARD SAUCE

PETER JOHNSON

❖Heat the oil in a nonstick 10-in (26-cm) sauté pan. Add the butter and let melt. Add the shallots and kidneys and brown the kidneys on all sides, about 5 minutes. Pour in the wine, cover and simmer for 10 minutes, turning the kidneys over after 5 minutes.

❖Remove the kidneys and keep warm. Strain the cooking juices into a saucepan and boil until reduced to 3 tablespoons.

❖Meanwhile, thinly slice the kidneys and divide among 4 heated plates. Pour the juices that escape during slicing into the saucepan. Add the mustard mixture and boil over high heat until the sauce becomes thick and creamy, about 1 minute. Pour over the kidneys and serve immediately.

SERVES 4

Picardie

Porc aux Deux Pommes

Pork with Potatoes and Apples

2 lb (1 kg) pork fillet or shoulder, boned and trimmed of fat
salt and freshly ground pepper
1 tablespoon vegetable oil
2 oz (50 g) butter
1 lb (500 g) very small new potatoes, peeled
¾ cup (6 fl oz/200 ml) water
1 lb (500 g) Golden Delicious apples

❖Ask the butcher to tie the meat at intervals. Season with salt and pepper. Heat the oil in an oval pot in which the meat will fit comfortably. Add half the butter and brown the meat on all sides. Remove the meat, add the potatoes to the pot and sauté until golden, about 3 to 4 minutes, turning them over from time to time. Return the meat to the pot, add the water and bring to simmer. Cover and simmer for 1½ hours, turning the meat and potatoes several times.

❖About 20 minutes before the end of the cooking time, peel, quarter and core the apples. Cut each quarter into 3 slices. Melt the remaining butter in a nonstick 11-in (28-cm) skillet and cook the apple slices until golden, about 8

minutes, turning them over after 4 minutes. Keep warm.
❖When the meat is cooked, transfer it to a serving platter. Surround with the potatoes and apple slices and serve.

SERVES 4

Bretagne

Porc au Lait

Pork Cooked in Milk

1 pork fillet, about 3 lb (1.5 kg), boned and trimmed of fat
salt and freshly ground pepper
4 cloves garlic
1 oz (25 g) butter
1 qt (1 l) whole milk
2 sprigs thyme
1 bay leaf, cut into 4 pieces
4 sprigs parsley, lightly crushed
6 pinches of freshly grated nutmeg

❖Ask the butcher to tie the meat at intervals. Season with salt and pepper. Peel 2 cloves of garlic and cut into fine slivers. Make slits all over the meat and insert the slivers of garlic.

❖Melt the butter in an oval pot just large enough to hold the pork fillet. Brown the meat on all sides. Remove the meat, discard the cooking fat and wipe out the pot. Return the fillet to the pot and cover with milk. Surround it with the thyme, the bay leaf pieces, the parsley and 2 whole garlic cloves, lightly bruised. Season with salt and pepper and add the nutmeg. Bring to the boil over low heat and cook for 2 hours, covered, at a slow simmer, turning the meat over several times.

❖After this time, the meat should be very tender and covered with a golden sauce, reduced and slightly curdled. Transfer to a heated plate. Remove the herbs and garlic from the sauce and puree the sauce in a blender until smooth. Pour into a sauceboat and serve immediately.

SERVES 6

PORK WITH POTATOES AND APPLES (top) AND PORK COOKED IN MILK (bottom)

PETER JOHNSON

Lorraine

ÉCHINE À LA BIÈRE

Pork Cooked in Beer

The north and the east, being the two greatest beer-producing areas of France, use beer in their cuisine just as wine is used by the Bordelais. It gives excellent results, producing some very tasty dishes.

2 lb (1 kg) chine of pork or pork shoulder, boned and trimmed of fat
salt and freshly ground pepper
bouquet garni: 1 bay leaf, 1 sprig thyme, 6 sprigs parsley
1 oz (25 g) butter
1½ lb (750 g) onions, thinly sliced
½ teaspoon sugar
½ cup (2 oz/50 g) dried white breadcrumbs
2 cups (16 fl oz/500 ml) beer

❖Ask the butcher to tie the piece of pork with string to secure it in one piece. Season with salt and pepper. Tie together the herbs for the bouquet garni.
❖Melt the butter in an oval pot large enough to hold the meat comfortably. Add the meat and brown on all sides, then remove it and set aside. Add the onions to the pot and cook until golden, about 3 to 4 minutes. Stir in the sugar and breadcrumbs and cook, stirring, for 2 minutes longer or until the mixture is golden brown. Place the meat on the bed of onions, pour in the beer and bring to boil. Cover and simmer for 1¾ hours, turning the meat over several times.
❖Transfer the meat to a serving dish and surround with onions. Boil the cooking juices over high heat until syrupy, then pour over the onions. Serve immediately.

SERVES 4   *Photograph pages 6 – 7*

Languedoc

CASSOULET

Toulouse Casserole

The word cassoulet *comes from* cassole, *the name of the glazed earthenware dish in which the* cassoulet *is gratinéed. The main ingredient is haricot beans (originally brought to France from Spain in the sixteenth century), which must be local — either from Cazères or from Pamiers — and must have been picked within the year. To these are added different meats, according to the area.*

This version is the simplest, and perhaps the oldest, and originated in Castelnaudary. Carcassonne cooks add leg of lamb, and partridge when it is in season; Toulouse cooks add Toulouse sausage, leg of lamb and confit; *pigs' tails are added in Limoux, chitterlings in Mas d'Azil, and stuffed goose neck and* confit *in Périgord.*

1½ lb (750 g) dried haricot (white) beans
1 lb (500 g) lightly salted pork belly
8 oz (250 g) fresh pork rind, trimmed of all fat
1 lb (500 g) Toulouse (coarse-textured) sausage
1 unsmoked kielbasa (boiling sausage)
8 cloves garlic
1 teaspoon dried thyme
salt and freshly ground pepper

1½ lb (750 g) fresh pork tenderloin (fillet), bones removed and reserved
bouquet garni: 1 bay leaf, 1 sprig thyme, 6 sprigs parsley
13 oz (400 g) ripe tomatoes
8 oz (250 g) onions
2 cloves
2 leeks, white and tender green parts only, washed and thinly sliced
6 oz (200 g) goose fat
3 tablespoons dried white breadcrumbs

❖Place the beans in a pot and cover with plenty of cold water. Let soak for 4 hours.
❖Parboil the pork belly and pork rind in water to cover for 5 minutes, then rinse and drain. Cut the pork rind into strips 1¼ in (3 cm) wide. Roll the strips over themselves and secure with kitchen thread. Prick the sausages with a fork to keep them from bursting during cooking.
❖Peel 2 cloves of garlic and cut each into 6 slivers. Mix the thyme, salt, pepper and garlic slivers. Make 12 slits in the surface of the pork tenderloin and slip a piece of garlic into each. Tie together the herbs for the bouquet garni.
❖Drop the tomatoes into boiling water for 10 seconds. Cool under running water, peel, halve and squeeze out the seeds; coarsely chop the flesh. Peel 4 cloves of garlic and chop finely. Peel the onions; stud one with cloves and finely chop the remainder.
❖Drain the beans, discarding the soaking water. Return them to the pot and cover with 3 qt (3 l) of cold water. Add the pork belly, leeks, clove-studded onion, bouquet garni, pork rind and the bone from the pork tenderloin and bring to boil over very low heat. Simmer for 1½ hours.
❖Meanwhile, melt 3 oz (100 g) goose fat in a heavy pot large enough to hold the tenderloin, and brown it on all sides. Remove and set aside. Add the chopped onions to the pot and cook over low heat until golden, about 5 minutes, stirring with a wooden spoon. Add the chopped garlic and cook, stirring, for 2 minutes. Add the tomatoes and cook for 3 minutes longer. Season with salt and pepper. Return the meat to the pot, cover and cook over low heat for 1 hour.
❖Remove the meat and add it with the cooking liquid to the beans. Add the sausages and cook for 30 minutes longer.
❖Preheat oven to 375°F (190°C). Remove the meats from the pot and carve into ¼-in (.5-cm) slices. Remove the thread from the rolls of pork rind and cut them into 1¼ x ¼-in (3 x .5-cm) strips. Discard the onion and bouquet garni.
❖Halve the remaining 2 cloves of garlic and rub over the inside of a large casserole. Spread a layer of beans on the bottom; cover with a layer of mixed meats. Continue to layer the ingredients, finishing with a layer of beans. Melt the remaining goose fat and pour over the surface. Sprinkle with the breadcrumbs and bake for 1½ hours. Serve directly from the casserole.

SERVES 8 – 10

TOULOUSE CASSEROLE, PHOTOGRAPHED IN LANGUEDOC
PIERRE HUSSENOT/AGENCE TOP

Alsace

BAECKEOFFE
Baked Meat and Potatoes

The word baeckeoffe *in the dialect of Alsace means baker's oven, and in fact this tasty mixture of meat and vegetables used to be cooked in the baker's oven.*

Once a week, on washing day, the women of Alsace would carry their stewpots to the bakery, and when he had finished making bread for the day the baker would leave their marvelous stews to simmer for many hours in his oven.

1½ lb (750 g) pork shoulder, without bones
1½ lb (750 g) lamb shoulder, without bones
1½ lb (750 g) beef flank, without bones
10 oz (300 g) onions, thinly sliced
8 oz (250 g) carrots, thinly sliced
2 cloves garlic
1 sprig fresh thyme, leaves only
1 bay leaf, broken in half
10 sprigs fresh parsley, bruised
2 cloves
10 peppercorns
salt
2 cups white wine, preferably Riesling or Sylvaner
3 lb (1.5 kg) baking potatoes
⅔ cup (2½ oz/75 g) all purpose (plain) flour

❖Cut the meats into 1½-in (4-cm) cubes and place in a large bowl with the onions and carrots. Peel the garlic cloves and crush with the hand or the side of a cleaver. Add to the bowl with the thyme leaves, bay leaf, parsley, cloves, peppercorns and salt. Pour the wine over and stir. Cover and refrigerate for 12 hours, turning the meats often.
❖Preheat oven to 375°F (190°C). Peel and wash the potatoes; cut into ¼-in (.5-cm) slices. Drain the meat, reserving the vegetable marinade.
❖Arrange a layer of potatoes in a 2-qt (2-l) flameproof earthenware pot with tight-fitting lid. Scatter some of the vegetables from the marinade over the potatoes, then add a layer of meat. Continue alternating layers of meat and potatoes, finishing with potatoes. Pour the marinade over the potatoes.
❖In a small bowl, mix the flour with enough water to produce a smooth, thick paste. Roll into a long, thin sausage shape and lay it around the edge of the pot. Place the lid firmly on the pot, pressing down to ensure a perfect seal. (This operation, called *lutage*, seals the lid so that no evaporation can take place.) Bake for 3 hours.
❖Remove the pot from the oven and break the circle of pastry. Remove the lid and carry the pot straight to the table. Serve hot.

SERVES 8   *Photograph pages 6 – 7*

Alsace

CHOUCROUTE
Sauerkraut with Pork and Sausages

The word comes from the Alsatian dialect term sûrkrût, *which in turn is derived from the German* sauerkraut, *meaning sour herb.*
Choucroute *is white cabbage that has been shredded, salted and fermented and put into wooden barrels or large stone pots. It is served in Alsace and Lorraine, and in some parts of Germany, and is used in stews containing potatoes, salted and smoked pork, and regional* charcuterie *products.*

1½ lb (750 g) lightly salted pork shoulder, without bone
2 lb (1 kg) raw sauerkraut
3 cloves garlic
1 bay leaf
3 cloves
1 tablespoon juniper berries
1 teaspoon mixed black and white peppercorns
3 oz (100 g) lard
1 onion, about 3 oz (100 g), finely chopped
2 cups white wine, preferably Riesling or Sylvaner
1 cup (8 fl oz/250 ml) chicken stock (recipe page 34)
1 lb (500 g) smoked bacon
1 lb (500 g) fresh pork belly
1 smoked kielbasa (boiling sausage), about 1 lb (500 g)
6 Strasbourg sausages or frankfurters
1½ lb (750 g) boiling potatoes

❖Parboil the pork shoulder in water to cover for 5 minutes, then cool under running water and drain. Thoroughly wash the sauerkraut under running water and drain. Crush the cloves of garlic with the hand or the side of a cleaver and tie in a square of cheesecloth with the bay leaf, cloves, juniper berries and peppercorns.
❖Melt the lard in a heavy 6-qt (6-l) pot and cook the onion until golden, about 3 minutes, stirring with a wooden spoon. Add the sauerkraut and cook for 5 minutes longer, separating the strands with two forks. Pour in the wine and stock and mix well. Bury the pork shoulder and spice bag in the middle of the sauerkraut. Cover and cook over very low heat for 1½ hours.
❖Add the bacon and pork belly to the sauerkraut, burying them as well, and cook for 1 hour longer.
❖Meanwhile, prick the boiling sausage with a fork to keep it from bursting during cooking. Boil the Strasbourg sausages for 1 minute; let stand in the hot water. Peel and wash the potatoes.
❖Add the boiling sausage to the pot. Place the potatoes on top, cover and cook for 1 hour. About 10 minutes before the end of the cooking time, lay the Strasbourg sausages on top of the potatoes to reheat.
❖Arrange a mound of sauerkraut on a platter and surround with the meat, sausages and potatoes. Serve very hot.

SERVES 6   *Photograph pages 6 – 7*

Périgord

PORC AUX CHÂTAIGNES
Pork with Chestnuts

1 pork fillet, about 2 lb (1 kg), boned and trimmed of fat
salt and freshly ground pepper
1 tablespoon vegetable oil
1 oz (25 g) butter
4 cloves garlic, peeled
3 tablespoons white vermouth
½ teaspoon sugar
6 tablespoons water
1½ lb (750 g) chestnuts

❖Ask the butcher to tie the pork fillet at intervals. Season with salt and pepper.

❖Heat the oil in an oval pot in which the meat will fit comfortably. Add half the butter and the garlic, and brown the meat on all sides.

❖Remove the meat and garlic and discard the cooking fat. Add the vermouth and sugar, and boil over high heat until slightly reduced, scraping up browned bits with a wooden spoon. Return the meat to the pot and turn it over in the liquid. Add the garlic and water and bring to simmer. Cover and cook over low heat for 45 minutes, turning the meat over twice.

❖Meanwhile, make a slash on the flat side of each chestnut. Bring a large saucepan of water to boil. Drop in the chestnuts and boil for 5 minutes. Drain, then shell and remove the brown skin that covers each chestnut.

❖Add the chestnuts to the pot and cook for 45 minutes longer, turning both meat and chestnuts several times.

❖When the meat is cooked, transfer it to a serving plate and surround with chestnuts. Add the remaining butter to the sauce in the pot and stir until it melts. Pour sauce over the chestnuts and serve immediately.

SERVES 4

Périgord/Picardie

PORC AUX PRUNEAUX

Pork with Prunes

1 pork fillet, about 2 lb (1 kg), boned and trimmed of fat
salt
1 bay leaf, crushed

30 prunes
8 walnuts
3 oz (100 g) lean bacon
2 French shallots, finely chopped
4 leaves dried sage
4 tablespoons dry white wine
freshly ground pepper
1 tablespoon vegetable oil

❖Ask the butcher to tie the pork fillet at intervals. Rub the salt and the bay leaf over the pork. Remove the pits from 10 prunes and chop them. Coarsely grate the nuts, using a cylindrical grater with large holes. Remove the rind from the bacon. Finely chop the bacon and cook with the shallots in a nonstick 9-in (22-cm) skillet, stirring often, until lightly browned, about 5 minutes. Remove from heat. Crumble in the sage leaves and add the pepper, grated walnuts, 1 tablespoon wine and the chopped prunes.

❖Pit the remaining 20 prunes, making a single slit in the side. Fill each with a small mound of the stuffing and close the prune over the stuffing. To stuff the roast, make two cuts through the center in the shape of an "X" and make shallow crisscross cuts over the whole surface of the meat. Stuff the meat with the remaining prune mixture, pushing it well in so that the stuffing is not visible from the outside.

❖Lightly oil an oval baking dish just large enough to hold the pork surrounded by the stuffed prunes. Oil the meat and place it in the dish. Place the dish in the oven. Heat the oven to 425°F (215°C) and roast the pork for 30 minutes, then surround the meat with the prunes and pour the remaining wine over them. Reduce the heat to 375°F (190°C) and roast for 1 hour longer. Transfer the roast to a platter, surround with prunes and serve.

SERVES 4

PETER JOHNSON

PORK WITH CHESTNUTS (bottom) AND PORK WITH PRUNES (top)

FROM CHARENTES TO THE BASQUE COUNTRY

A joyous accent

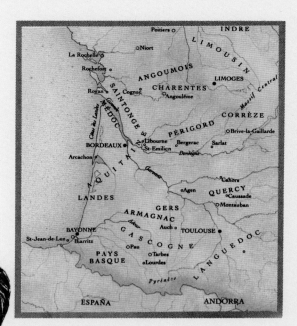

FROM CHARENTES TO THE BASQUE COUNTRY

A joyous accent

This is a country that sings and dances. It is green, undulating, isolated behind its high forests or modest in the shadow of its châteaux. In the southwest there are many reminders of its rich history: separated from the kingdom of France, for three centuries ruled by the Plantagenet dynasty from the time of the marriage of Eleanor of Aquitaine with Henry II, the future king of Great Britain. The provinces of Guyenne, Gascony, Périgord and Saintonge were its vassals; thus were woven enduring ties with England. At Bordeaux, on the wharves of Les Chartrons, oak barrels full of "claret" leave for the port of London. In the Charente, the names of the cognac houses have English connotations. In Périgord, the *bastides* — villages transformed into fortresses — had, by the thirteenth century, become props for the English crown in the Capetian kingdom.

The cuisine amongst all this? It is a solid inheritance, artful, proud of its assets. Almost everywhere, but principally in the Landes of Upper Gascony, in the Périgord and the adjacent Quercy, one is in the kingdom of foie gras, of duck "steaks" (*magrets*), of preserved goose and duck — the birds, fattened on corn, disport themselves in liberty on the fertile soil.

And the whole region is the domain of noble wines and spirits — not only the great vintages of the Gironde, Médoc, Graves, Pomerol and Saint-Emilion, but also *eaux de vie*, distilled in copper alembics by a system of double distillation known as the *double repasse charentaise*. The Saint-Emilion

LEFT: ARTISANS MAKING WINE BARRELS AT THE TONNELLERIE DEMPTOS IN ST-EMILION.

PREVIOUS PAGES: BEYNAC-ET-CAZENAC, A THIRTEENTH-CENTURY CHÂTEAU ON THE DORDOGNE RIVER, COMMANDS A SPECTACULAR VIEW OVER THE TOWN OF LA ROQUE-GAGEAC.

LEO MEIER

THE MAIN SEAPORT OF CHARENTES-MARITIMES, LA ROCHELLE BOASTS ONE OF THE MOST PICTURESQUE HARBORS ON THE ATLANTIC COAST.

them slowly and lovingly in their own fat, then storing them in earthenware pots, is applied to the goose and duck, and also to chicken and even pork. The custom is said to date from the time of the Moorish invasions, but just as important as its historic character is its tenderizing effect, giving the meat a more subtle taste. Potatoes cooked in the style of Sarlat, with garlic, are the standard accompaniment.

Pâté of foie gras is only one of the many forms — a privileged one, to be sure — of the local pâtés, which might equally be based on partridges or chicken livers. The old guard of the Périgord like the traditional way of preparing foie gras, believing that it matures very well in its shiny tins. The truffle is also used in many of the variously shaped terrines. This "black diamond" belongs to a rare variety of fungi, concealed beneath the shady oak trees, which produces a network of white threads — the mycelium —at the soil's surface, so that it can be recognized. People have attributed aphrodisiacal qualities to the truffle, and it must be said that its perfume is one of the most intoxicating imaginable. And this perfume enhances countless dishes in the form of truffle juice, or thin shavings, or more substantial portions. In scrambled eggs or a simple salad, the truffle (supposedly from Périgord, but those found in Provence, and sold at the markets of Tricastin, share the same name) works wonders.

It is difficult to separate the riches of the Périgord from those of its near neighbor, the Quercy. The handsome dwellings of the Périgord seem to confront the more dilapidated houses of Quercy. But the Black Périgord, which follows the course of the Vézère through its snakelike meanderings, encircling belvederes (like that of Domme) alongside the Dordogne, is not to be confused with the Quercy of the *causses*, chalky plateaus of which the best known is that of Gramat.

Here, as there, are high-perched villages of brown stone which take on golden tones from the setting sun; and olive-tinted roofs; and flocks of geese and ducks parading through the fields. The villages of Autoire and Loubressac, of Carennac and Fénélon, in Quercy, are the distant cousins of those others, more splendid, of Beynac-et-Cazenac, la Roque-Gageac and, above all, Sarlat, the proud and high-born city of Périgord.

Périgord, like Quercy, is the realm of the walnut; here ancient mills produce a velvety, pure and aromatic oil. In both regions, the queen of the pâtisserie is the *pastis*, made from a paper-thin pastry and flavored with apples and Armagnac. It has a strong similarity to the Moroccan *bstilla* — demonstrating, in the same way as does the *confit*, the influence of the passage through the region by the Moors. The method is simple: a noodle dough, made with flour, vanilla sugar, salt, eggs and water, is kneaded the night before, then very gently stretched out over long tables to produce the thinnest pastry possible.

grape is used in the Charentes, the Colombard at Cognac, the Folle blanche or the Ugni blanc in Armagnac. These "waters of life," aged in oak barrels encircled by bands of iron, have a soft, silky texture and the wonderful fragrance of mature plums.

Of all the regions of the Southwest, the Périgord is undoubtedly the one which has best preserved its traditions. One sees history itself in the golden stone of the villages of the region known as the Black Périgord, centered on Sarlat; the chalky white stone of Nontron, at Bourdeilles; the rustic charm of the "green" Périgord, from the waters of the Dronne which laps Bourdeilles, the ancient town of Saint-Jean-de-Cole; the markets of Bergerac and Thiviers; the noble mansions of Trémolat, Saint-Léon-sur-Vézère; the countless caves of Les Eyzies-de-Tayac, world capital of prehistory; the châteaux of Beynac, Castelnaud, and Puyguilhem; the abbeys of Saint-Cyprien, Cadouin and Brantôme.

The older people here wear berets, and walk with canes; they sit in their armchairs beside the fire and shell chestnuts and walnuts. Traditional ingredients abound, and end up in dishes that bring the aroma of the whole country to the tastebuds: stuffed goose neck, preserved goose and duck *confits*, foie gras and truffles. The time-honored practice of preserving meats by cooking

EAST OF BORDEAUX IS THE VILLAGE OF ST-EMILION WITH BEAUTIFUL CLOISTERS AND
A SPECTACULAR VIEW OF THE REGION'S FAMOUS VINEYARDS.

From Quercy, above all, come the little goat cheeses called *cabécou*, in the form of flat cylinders about 2 ½ in (60 mm) in diameter and ¾ in (16 mm) thick. They are customarily made on the plateaus of Rocamadour, and have a pronounced flavor — of milk, of grass and of Nature —and a firm texture, especially after aging, when the *cabécou* crumbles away like the chalk of the *causse*.

Here, too, one finds plum brandies aged in wood; snails and mushrooms, such as the *cèpes* of the underbrush. And from both regions, wine: reds and whites from Bergerac, the more noble wine from Pécharmant in the Périgord, and the sweet and velvety Montbazillac, perfect accompaniment to foie gras. In Quercy, the red wine of Cahors, made from the Cot grape, is highly perfumed, harsh when young but becoming rounder and smoother with age. It is produced along the whole length of the Lot valley, only a stone's throw away from the ancient hunting grounds of the truffle gatherers.

The Landes of Chalosse, fertile, undulating and rounded, is also a region of good eating, enjoying the lesser-known wines of Tursan and Armagnac, foie gras, preserved goose and duck: in short, it has everything that is found further on, in the Gers, around the capital of Auch. Contrasting with the vast forests of the Landes, where the pines stretch down to the sea, are the lush, green, tranquil hillside meadows, dotted with sheep.

The province of Gascony, won back from the English, was reincorporated into the kingdom of France in the middle of the fifteenth century. It brings together several *départements* and a variety of reliefs: the Gers, Hautes-Pyrénées, a part of the Landes, fractions of Ariège, Haute-Garonne, Tarn-et-Garonne and Lot-et-Garonne. To these might be added Bordeaux, the Gironde and the former county of Guyenne.

They share the same traditions and the same ingredients: foie gras, which is produced in massive quantities around Auch, and *magret* or *maigret*, the breast meat of the fattened duck which is pan-fried like a steak and accompanied either by garlic-flavored potatoes or by yellow peaches, gently cooked in butter. *Confits*, too, which abound in the Landes of Chalosse, and then there are the fish of the Gironde. Salmon is becoming scarce, but it appears that the sturgeon, whose caviar was once so highly prized, is returning to the estuary.

For the time being, the sovereign fish of the Aquitaine — Eleanor's former province, of which Bordeaux is the capital — is the lamprey, a large eel, with a fine-textured and fatty flesh; it is cooked in red wine, *en matelote*. So numerous are the specialties of Bordeaux and its region that they

DINERS AT THE RESTAURANT DOMINIQUE IN ST-EMILION WILL ENJOY NOT ONLY
THE REGIONAL FOOD SPECIALTIES, BUT ALSO THE WINES. THERE ARE OVER
TWENTY-NINE WINE-PRODUCING CHÂTEAUX IN THE AREA THAT BEAR THE MARK OF
HIGHEST DISTINCTION — *GRAND CRUS.*

could almost be plucked as if from an enormous edible necklace: oysters from Marennes, which are accompanied by tiny grilled sausages (the truffled *crépinettes*); *piballes*, tiny eels which are either fried or grilled; *entrecôte à la bordelaise*, a thick steak served with a shallot and red wine sauce. Any dish that includes red wine plus *cèpes*, beef marrow and chopped onions, parsley, shallots or even garlic can, it seems, be considered *à la bordelaise*. The term covers a vast multitude of dishes, each subject to various interpretations.

To the north, the Charentes: this popular name refers to the former provinces of Aunis and Saintonge. Its prime treasure is cognac, but one must not neglect *pineau*, a blend of cognac and grape must. The region's gastronomy reflects both the proximity of the sea and the expanse of flat plains where the people are as slow-moving as their animal confrères, the snails known as *cagouilles* — hence the local nickname of *cagouillards*.

The specialties here include the oysters of Marennes, Oléron and La Rochelle; *mouclade*, a dish of mussels with cream, white wine and shallots; *éclade*, peculiar to Saintonge, for which the mussels are arranged on a plank of wood and covered with a layer of dry pine needles, which

are then set alight; the *chaudrée* of Aunis, a fish soup made with skate, sole, little cuttlefish and chunks of eel, cooked in white wine and flavored with thyme, butter, bay leaf and garlic; *gigourit charentais*, a stew of pork offal, cooked with the blood; *lumas* or *cagouilles* prepared *à la vigneronne*, snails cooked in red wine; *palourdes*, or clams, eaten *au naturel*; *daube*, or beef stew; the tripe of Angoulême; and finally, the broad beans from the market gardens, known locally as *mojettes*, which are eaten in a stew.

Charentais butter is reputed to be one of the best in France. It appears in every dish, but more particularly in celebrated pastries such as the almond-flavored *tarte à la frangipane*, the *biscottes* of Pons, the brioches of Taillebourg and all the Charentais cakes that are flavored with either pineau or cognac.

The Basque region deserves a separate section. It is undoubtedly the most captivating of the regions of the southwest, certainly the most original. Its language, traditions and vigor extend to the other side of the border with Spain, its origins remain a mystery and its identity rests intact.

The Basque country means more than just the black beret worn by the men, the game of handball known as *pelote*, and the *makila*, a pointed staff much used by shepherds. It is above all the pure, uncontaminated air found in the area around the summit of the Rhûne, the sacred mountain of the Basques, and continuing on to the mountain of

IN PORT CITIES LIKE LA ROCHELLE, DINERS LOOKING FORWARD TO A *PLATEAU DE FRUITS DE MER*, A PLATTER OF RAW AND COOKED SHELLFISH, CAN BE ASSURED OF ITS FRESHNESS. IT IS NOT UNCOMMON TO FIND FISHERMEN WANDERING IN AT LUNCHTIME WITH BUCKETS OF FRESHLY-CAUGHT FISH AND SHELLFISH.

LEO MEIER

PLAYING *BOULES*, WHERE THE AIM IS TO TOSS A HEAVY METAL BALL AS CLOSE AS POSSIBLE TO THE SMALL CENTRAL BALL. FAVORED BY FRENCHMEN OF ALL AGES, INCLUDING THIS GROUP IN BERGERAC, *BOULES* IS WITHOUT A DOUBT FRANCE'S MOST POPULAR GAME.

Soule, in the middle of the Pyrenees, past the green hills of Labourdine, with their white cottages with green and red painted wood panels and high-pitched roofs.

The air of the region is also the salty air of the old fishing port of Saint-Jean-de-Luz, where the boats unload their cargoes of tuna, baby eels, shad, hake and *louvines*, the local species of bass; of the waterfalls near the fresh waters of the Nive; and of the alleys of Saint-Jean-Pied-de-Port, capital of the interior.

Adding to the Basque country's allure is Bayonne ham, raw, salted, dried and rubbed with red peppers; *tourons*, tiny treats of delicately tinted and decorated almond paste; macaroons; chocolate caramels known as *kanouga*; pure chocolate originally imported by the Spanish Jews; the local *gâteau basque*, made with eggs, sugar and flour, flavored with rum and enriched with fruits such as black cherries or dried apricots.

The flavor of the region? It comes from the pimento, or red pepper. Grown in the charming village of Espelette, this sweet red pepper turns up in every dish: the black pudding called *tripoxa*, peppers stuffed with cod, the *pipérade*, which is nothing other than eggs scrambled with cooked peppers and tomatoes. And also in the sauces that accompany shrimp and fish from the gulf of Saint-Jean-de-Luz, and in the fish soup, the slow-cooked *ttorro* of the fishermen.

And more again: bull beef, very red and very tough, which is eaten in Bayonne on the evenings of the *corridas*; the *palombes*, or ring-doves, that are hunted in autumn in the valley of the Aldudes, in a totally preserved landscape, green and mountainous, dotted with little cabins called *palombières*; Pyrenees lamb, naturally raised, its flesh aromatic and juicy; the salmon which returns to the river of the Adour, and which is simply grilled and accompanied by a bearnaise sauce; the *piballes*, the baby eels that are caught in bad weather and cooked with garlic and peppers, *à la basquaise*; the strong wine of Irouléguy; the fruit spirits made from plums and pears from the orchards around Saint-Etienne-de-Baïgorry; the robust green Izarra or the softer, yellow version, resulting from the maceration of mountain herbs; ewe's milk cheese, with a grassy, hazelnut flavor.

Perhaps you've had enough — but now you will believe anyone who tells you how exciting it is, this Basque country, the most southerly of the small regions of the great southwest.

VEGETABLES

A garden of Eden

NO OTHER VEGETABLE IS USED SO OFTEN IN FRENCH REGIONAL CUISINE AS THE POTATO, AND IT
APPEARS MOST OFTEN IN NORTHERN AND CENTRAL FRENCH COOKING.

VEGETABLES

A garden of Eden

France is one large garden, lavishly planted from north to south. Large-scale farming, glasshouse culture, market gardens: these are the sources of some splendid ingredients.

There is nothing more agreeable than to choose one's vegetables at the Marché d'Intérêt National, situated at Rungis. To the great regret of those who enjoy strolling around the capital, Rungis has replaced the old and venerated market of Les Halles, with its decorative ironwork designed by the architect Baltard. In this world of concrete and galvanized iron, the professional — restaurateur or wholesaler of fruit and vegetables — comes in search of the best of the best. Purple artichokes from Provence, cabbages from Alsace and the Auvergne, endives from Flanders, beans from Poitou, broad beans from Aquitaine, peas from Vendée, potatoes from Ile-de-France: all are here, according to season, and they do not even begin to exhaust the enormous richness of the French vegetable garden.

Each vegetable speaks for a region. The zucchini, pepper and olive evoke the markets of Provence and the Côte d'Azur. The market of Forville, at Cannes, bears witness to the prodigality of this land of sunshine. Brittany has elected as king and queen the artichoke and the potato. The sweet pepper is the glory of the Basque village of Espelette. And if beets belong to the north, cardoons — fine-flavored but stringy cousins of the artichoke that are eaten as a gratin and with beef marrow — are part of the territory of Lyons.

The noble asparagus is found as readily in Sologne, at Vineuil, as it is in the Lubéron at Pertuis, in Alsace at Village-Neuf or Hoerdt, in the Val de Loire near Chinon. Anyone willing to trade it for the "common" leek would be delighted to discover that the latter is, in fact, just as rich in possibilities as its better-born neighbor.

Behind one vegetable is often hidden another. Cabbage, Savoy cabbage, white cabbage, red cabbage, green cabbage, Brussels sprouts, sauerkraut cabbage: a vegetable with a thousand uses. Artichokes — stewed *à la barigoule*; in vinaigrette, first the leaves savored and finally the heart; the bases, or *fonds*, garnishing a pâté de foie gras. Or a combination of vegetables — a bouquet of peas, baby carrots, onions, turnips and green beans epitomizing spring, ratatouille and exquisitely stuffed vegetables symbolizing Provence. Vegetables to be eaten as fritters, pan-fried, flavored with onion, garlic, fresh herbs, butter or oil; vegetables to be fried, roasted, simmered, braised — in a bain-marie, in a cast-iron casserole, in the oven.

PREVIOUS PAGES: BRAISED ARTICHOKES (left, recipe page 204),
RATATOUILLE (center, recipe page 195), AND TOMATOES, PROVENÇAL-STYLE
(right, recipe page 195), PHOTOGRAPHED IN PROVENCE.
PIERRE HUSSENOT/AGENCE TOP

SHOPPING FOR FRESH VEGETABLES AND FRUIT IN FRANCE IS NOT A SOLITARY STROLL
DOWN A SUPERMARKET AISLE, IT IS A RITUAL OF DAILY LIFE.

A CAREFULLY TENDED GARDEN LIKE THIS ONE IN THE LOIRE VALLEY WILL YIELD THE MOST BEAUTIFUL FLOWERS AND SUCCULENT VEGETABLES.

THE IDEAL WAY TO PREPARE *LACTAIRES DÉLICIEUSES*, THE MOST COMMON MUSHROOM IN PROVENCE, IS TO SAUTÉ THEM *À LA PROVENÇAL* — IN OLIVE OIL WITH CHOPPED GARLIC, PARSLEY AND A SQUEEZE OF LEMON.

What fine and wholesome vegetables they are! Alone, they might constitute a whole meal: witness the *aligot* of the Aubrac, a creamy-smooth potato puree flavored with garlic and blended with the fresh local cheese, which is turned over and over, drawn out with the spoon, and is enough in itself; the *truffade* of Auvergne; a dish of lentils enriched with cubes of salt pork; cabbage filled with a succulent stuffing. In countless traditional dishes, vegetables are the central element; they give the dish its flavor, its unity, its *raison d'être*. In the Middle Ages they were somewhat neglected, and the nineteenth century practically stifled them under a heap of over-refined sauces. Nouvelle cuisine has restored vegetables to a position of honor, recommending cooks to make the most of their healthful variety.

Some chefs abused the craze for baby vegetables and for mousses more appropriate to infants. Other chefs have been able to extract new accents from beets, snow and sugar-snap peas, celery, turnips (exquisite when served as *confits*, coated with a sweet glaze), endive with its hint of sweetness, even the simple potato, which give an unexpected lift to the most classical preparations of meat and fish. Indeed, if today we had to do without these fine fresh vegetables, we would be wondering what was happening to the *grande cuisine française*.

TOMATES À LA PROVENÇALE
Tomatoes, Provençal-style

6 large, firm-ripe tomatoes, about 7 oz (200 g) each
2 cloves garlic, finely chopped
2 tablespoons chopped flat-leaf parsley
5 tablespoons olive oil
salt and freshly ground pepper
1 tablespoon sugar

❖Preheat oven to 425 °F (215 °C). Wash the tomatoes and halve horizontally. Remove the seeds with a small spoon. Combine the garlic and parsley.
❖Lightly oil a baking dish large enough to hold the tomato halves in a single layer. Arrange the tomatoes in the dish, cut side up. Drizzle with the remaining oil and sprinkle with the garlic mixture, salt, pepper and sugar.
❖Bake the tomatoes for 1 hour. Serve hot.

SERVES 4   *Photograph pages 190 – 191*

Provence

RATATOUILLE
Ratatouille

Although it is often called ratatouille niçoise*, this is a summer favorite not only in the Nice area but all along the Mediterranean coast.*

2 red peppers (capsicums), about 7 oz (200 g) each
10 oz (300 g) small eggplants (aubergines)
2 lb (1 kg) small zucchini (courgettes)
2 lb (1 kg) ripe tomatoes
12 tablespoons peanut (groundnut) oil
1 lb (500 g) onions
4 tablespoons olive oil
1 bay leaf
2 sprigs fresh thyme
4 cloves garlic
salt and freshly ground pepper
1 teaspoon sugar
6 sprigs fresh basil

❖Broil the peppers until the skins are blackened, about 25 minutes, turning frequently. Place in a dish, cover and let cool.
❖Cut the eggplants and zucchini into ¾-in (2-cm) cubes. Drop the tomatoes into boiling water for 10 seconds, then cool under running water. Peel, halve and squeeze out the seeds; coarsely chop the flesh.
❖Peel the skins from the broiled peppers. Halve them and remove the seeds and veins. Cut the flesh into ¾ x 1½-in (2 x 4-cm) rectangles.
❖Heat 2 tablespoons peanut oil in a nonstick 10-in (26-cm) skillet. Add the peppers and cook for 2 minutes. Transfer to a colander and discard the cooking oil.
❖Add 4 tablespoons peanut oil to the skillet and lightly brown the onions. Drain and add to the peppers.
❖Add another 3 tablespoons peanut oil to the skillet and lightly brown the zucchini. Drain and add to the other vegetables in the colander.

❖Pour the last 3 tablespoons peanut oil into the frying pan and lightly brown the eggplant cubes. Drain and add to the other vegetables in the colander.
❖In a nonstick 11-in (28-cm) sauté pan combine the tomatoes, olive oil, bay leaf, thyme and the garlic crushed in a garlic press. Bring to boil and add salt, pepper and sugar. Transfer the other vegetables to the sauté pan and return to boil. Cover and cook over moderate heat for about 30 minutes or until very tender, turning the ingredients from time to time.
❖Meanwhile, strip the basil leaves from the stems and chop coarsely. Remove the thyme and bay leaf from the ratatouille. Stir in the chopped basil. Serve hot, lukewarm or cold.

SERVES 4   *Photograph pages 190 – 191*

Bourgogne

PETS DE NONNE
Cheese Beignets

1 scant cup (3 oz/100 g) all purpose (plain) flour
¾ cup (6 fl oz/200 ml) water
½ teaspoon salt
2½ oz (80 g) butter
3 oz (100 g) Comté cheese, freshly and finely grated
5 eggs
1 qt (1 l) peanut oil

❖Prepare a choux pastry according to the recipe on page 247, omitting the sugar and adding the cheese just before the eggs.
❖Heat the oil in a small deep-fryer to 325 °F (160 °C). Drop in small spoonfuls of the mixture, pushing them off with a second lightly oiled teaspoon so that they drop into the oil in the shape of little balls. They will puff up as soon as they are in the oil and will rotate so that all sides are cooked. Fry until golden brown, about 5 minutes, then remove with a slotted spoon. Drain on paper towels and serve immediately as a side dish.

SERVES 6

CHEESE BEIGNETS

PETER JOHNSON

GNOCCHI

Provence

GNOCCHI
Gnocchi

2 lb (1 kg) baking potatoes
1 egg
2 tablespoons olive oil
about 2 cups (8 oz/250 g) all purpose (plain) flour, sifted
salt and freshly ground pepper
For serving:
tomato sauce, or the sauce from a beef *daube* combined
   with cream and butter to taste
freshly and finely grated Parmesan cheese

❖Scrub the potatoes under running water and place in a saucepan. Cover with plenty of cold salted water. Bring to boil and cook for about 25 minutes or until the potatoes are very tender and easily pierced with a knife.
❖Drain the potatoes and refresh under running water. Peel them and puree through the finest holes of a food mill. Add the egg, oil, flour, salt and pepper and stir with a wooden spoon until well blended, then work the mixture with your hands to produce a smooth dough that comes away from the fingers. (Depending on the type of flour used, you may need more or less than 2 cups.)
❖Roll the dough into sausage shapes ⅜ in (1 cm) diameter, then cut into ¾-in (1.5-cm) chunks. Dip a fork in flour. Place the rounded side of the fork on a work surface and roll each chunk of dough over the fork, from the tips of the tines towards the handle, using a floured finger. Place each formed gnocchi on a tea towel.
❖Bring a large pot of salted water to boil. Drop in the gnocchi. As soon as they float to the surface, in about 2 to 3 minutes, remove with a slotted spoon and transfer to a serving dish. Mix in the desired sauce and serve with grated Parmesan.

SERVES 8

Corse

POLENTA DE CHÂTAIGNES
Chestnut-flour Polenta

salt
2 cups (8 oz/250 g) chestnut flour
For serving:
fresh *broccio* cheese, ricotta or lightly salted feta cheese
olive oil
freshly ground pepper

❖Pour 1 qt (1 l) water into a saucepan and bring to boil. Season with salt. Pour in the chestnut flour and cook, stirring with a wooden spoon, until the mixture thickens into a solid mass that comes away from the sides of the saucepan, about 15 minutes.
❖Pour the polenta out onto a moistened tea towel. Cut into portions using a knife dipped in cold water. Serve immediately, accompanying with the cheese. Drizzle each slice with olive oil and season to taste with pepper.
❖Any leftover polenta may be browned in olive oil and eaten with a seasonal salad.

SERVES 6

Corse

COURGETTES AU BROCCIO
Corsican-style Stuffed Zucchini

10 small round zucchini (courgettes), about 2½ lb (1.2 kg)
2 tablespoons olive oil
1 clove garlic, finely chopped
1 tablespoon chopped fresh basil
salt and freshly ground pepper
1 slice white bread, crusts trimmed
8 oz (250 g) fresh Corsican *broccio* cheese or ricotta
½ oz (15 g) finely grated Parmesan cheese
1 tablespoon dried currants
1 tablespoon pine nuts

❖Scrub the zucchini under running water and trim the ends. Halve lengthwise and steam for 15 minutes. Using a small teaspoon, hollow out the flesh, leaving a shell ⅜ in (1 cm) thick. Coarsely chop the pulp removed. Let the shells cool.
❖Heat 1 tablespoon oil in a nonstick 10-in (26-cm) skillet and cook the chopped zucchini for 3 minutes, stirring constantly with a wooden spoon. Add the garlic and basil and cook, stirring, for 2 minutes longer. Remove from heat and season with salt and pepper.
❖In a blender or food processor, grind the bread to crumbs. Crush the cheese with a fork and mix in the breadcrumbs, Parmesan, currants and pine nuts. Add the contents of the skillet and stir well.
❖Preheat oven to 425 °F (215 °C). Pat the insides of the zucchini shells dry with paper towels. Fill with the cheese mixture, piling it into a dome shape. With the remaining tablespoon of oil, grease a shallow baking dish large enough to hold the zucchini in a single layer. Arrange them in the dish. Bake for 45 minutes or until the stuffing is puffed and browned. Serve hot or warm.

SERVES 5

STEWED BROAD BEANS

Aquitaine

FÈVES EN RAGOÛT
Stewed Broad Beans

4 lb (2 kg) fresh broad beans
2 oz (50 g) goose fat
6 small carrots, peeled and thinly sliced
8 green onions (scallions or spring onions), trimmed
3 oz (100 g) streaky bacon, finely chopped
1 sprig fresh thyme, leaves only
⅔ cup (5 fl oz/150 ml) chicken stock (recipe page 34)
salt and freshly ground pepper

❖Shell the beans and peel off the green skin covering each bean. Melt the goose fat in a nonstick 10-in (26-cm) sauté pan. Add the carrots, onions, bacon and thyme and cook over low heat, stirring often, for 5 minutes or until the vegetables are golden. Add the beans and stock, season lightly with salt and pepper, cover and cook for 10 minutes or until the beans are tender.
❖Turn the beans into a shallow dish and serve immediately.

SERVES 4

Ile de France

POMMES ANNA
Potatoes Anna

This dish was invented by Adolphe Dugléré in honor of Anna Deslions, a "lioness" of the Second Empire. In restaurants it is cooked in a special little copper dish with a tight-fitting lid to ensure that the potatoes cook perfectly.

5 oz (150 g) butter
1½ lb (750 g) boiling potatoes
salt

❖Preheat oven to 400°F (200°C). To clarify the butter, melt it in a saucepan and let cool to lukewarm. Skim off the froth from the surface, then carefully pour the clear liquid into a bowl, discarding the white milk solids at the bottom of the saucepan.
❖Peel and wash the potatoes and pat dry. Cut into ⅛-in (3-mm) slices.
❖Butter a 9-in (22-cm) round pan and layer the potato slices in it, seasoning each layer with salt and adding some of the clarified butter to each layer. Cover with aluminum or waxed paper and bake for 1 hour. Let rest at room temperature for 5 minutes before unmolding onto a plate. Serve immediately.

SERVES 4

Dauphiné

GRATIN DAUPHINOIS
Dauphiné-style Potato Gratin

1 clove garlic
¾ cup (6 fl oz/200 ml) milk
6 tablespoons heavy (double) cream
1 lb (500 g) boiling potatoes
salt and freshly ground pepper
2 pinches of cinnamon
4 pinches of freshly grated nutmeg

❖Preheat oven to 375°F (190°C). Peel the garlic and crush in a garlic press into a large saucepan. Add the milk and cream and bring to boil over low heat.
❖Meanwhile, peel the potatoes, wash and pat dry. Using the shredder attachment of a food processor, slice them very thinly. Add to the saucepan with salt, pepper, cinnamon and nutmeg. Cook for 5 minutes, turning the potatoes carefully.
❖Butter a 10x7-in (26x18-cm) baking dish. Add the potatoes and smooth the surface with a wooden spoon. Bake until golden brown, about 50 minutes. Serve hot from the baking dish.

SERVES 4

Bretagne

POMMES DE TERRE À LA BRETONNE
Potato Casserole

2 lb (1 kg) boiling potatoes
13 oz (400 g) ripe tomatoes
2 oz (50 g) butter
7 oz (200 g) onions, thinly sliced
3 cloves garlic, finely chopped
1 sprig thyme
1 bay leaf
salt and freshly ground pepper
2 cups (16 fl oz/500 ml) chicken stock (recipe page 34)

POTATOES ANNA (left), DAUPHINÉ-STYLE POTATO GRATIN (bottom right)
AND POTATO CASSEROLE (top right)

❖Preheat oven to 375°F (190°C). Peel the potatoes, wash and pat dry. Cut into ¾-in (1.5-cm) cubes. Drop the tomatoes into boiling water for 10 seconds. Cool under running water, peel, halve and squeeze out the seeds; coarsely chop the flesh.

❖Use half the butter to grease an 8 x 12-in (20 x 30-cm) baking dish. Add the potatoes, onions, garlic, herbs, tomatoes, salt and pepper and stir gently to mix. Pour in the stock and dot the surface with the remaining butter.

❖Bake for about 1 hour or until the potatoes are tender and golden brown and the stock has been absorbed. Serve hot, directly from the dish.

SERVES 4

Provence

FLEURS DE COURGETTE FARCIES
Stuffed Zucchini Flowers

18 large zucchini (courgette) flowers
8 oz (250 g) fresh sheep's milk cheese
grated rind of 1 lemon

⅓ cup (1½ oz/40 g) dried breadcrumbs
2 oz (50 g) freshly and finely grated Parmesan cheese
2 tablespoons chopped flat-leaf parsley
salt and freshly ground pepper
2 egg whites
1½ oz (40 g) butter

❖Preheat oven to 425°F (215°C). Butter a 13 x 9-in (32 x 22-cm) baking dish. Remove the stamens from the zucchini flowers without destroying their shape or separating the petals. Wipe the flowers with a dampened cloth and set aside. Using a fork, mash the fresh cheese in a bowl. Add the lemon rind, breadcrumbs, half the Parmesan and the parsley. Season liberally with salt and pepper and mix well.

❖Beat the egg whites to stiff peaks and fold into the breadcrumb mixture. Fill each flower with a portion of this mixture and roll up tightly to seal.

❖Arrange the stuffed flowers in the baking dish. Melt the butter in a small saucepan and pour over the flowers. Sprinkle with the remaining Parmesan. Bake for 15 minutes or until the flowers have puffed up and become golden. Serve immediately.

SERVES 6   *Photograph pages 8 – 9*

Vendée

EMBEURRÉE DE CHOU
Buttered Cabbage

1 white cabbage, about 2 lb (1 kg)
3 oz (100 g) butter
salt and freshly ground pepper

❖Remove the large outside leaves of the cabbage, then cook the cabbage in a large pot of boiling water for 10 minutes. Drain, cut into quarters and remove the hard core. Cut each quarter into very fine strips, cutting away the hard ribs.
❖Melt half the butter in a nonstick 11-in (28-cm) sauté pan. Add the cabbage, season with salt and pepper and cook for about 20 minutes or until the cabbage is very soft. Remove from heat, add the remaining butter and stir well, mashing the cabbage slightly.
❖Turn the buttered cabbage into a shallow plate and serve immediately.

SERVES 4

Provence

HARICOTS VERTS À L'AIL
Green Beans with Garlic

1½ lb (750 g) young, very slender green beans
2 tablespoons extra virgin olive oil
6 cloves garlic, minced
2 tablespoons dried white breadcrumbs
2 tablespoons chopped flat-leaf parsley
salt and freshly ground pepper
1 oz (25 g) butter

❖Drop the beans into a large pot of boiling salted water and cook uncovered over high heat for about 6 to 8 minutes or until slightly crisp. Drain the beans in a colander, then drop them immediately into a large quantity of very cold water so that they retain their bright green color. Drain.
❖Heat the oil in a nonstick 10-in (26-cm) sauté pan over low heat. Add the garlic, breadcrumbs, parsley and salt and pepper and cook, stirring, for 1 minute. Add the butter and, when it has melted, add the beans and stir to reheat. Serve immediately.

SERVES 4

Flandres

ENDIVES À LA FLAMANDE
Endives, Flemish-style

The endive is a vegetable from Belgium which first appeared in France in 1879. It also goes under the names "Brussels chicory" and chicon.

2 lb (1 kg) medium-size Belgian endives (witloof or chicory)
2 oz (50 g) butter
1 tablespoon sugar
salt and freshly ground pepper
¼ cup (2 fl oz/60 ml) fresh lemon juice

❖Pull off the outside leaves of the endives and the bitter part of the heart. Rinse the endives and pat dry.
❖Preheat oven to 400°F (200°C). Using a small amount of the butter, grease a baking dish large enough to hold the endives in a single layer. Arrange them in the dish, season with sugar, salt and pepper, and sprinkle with lemon juice. Dot with the remaining butter.
❖Bake for 45 minutes or until soft and caramelized, turning the endives over halfway through cooking. Arrange on a platter and serve immediately.

SERVES 4

Provence

BEIGNETS DE LEGUMES
Vegetable Fritters

For the batter:
1¼ cups (5 oz/150 g) all purpose (plain) flour
salt
⅔ cup (5 fl oz/150 ml) milk
1 tablespoon olive oil
2 eggs, separated
For the vegetables:
1 eggplant (aubergine), about 5 oz (150 g)
1 zucchini (courgette), about 5 oz (150 g)
6 zucchini (courgette) flowers
2 artichokes, about 4 oz (125 g) each
½ lemon
For cooking:
3 cups (24 fl oz/750 ml) peanut (groundnut) oil

❖Prepare the fritter batter: sift the flour into a bowl. Whisk in the salt, milk and oil, then the egg yolks, whisking until the batter is smooth and homogeneous. Cover and let rest for 2 hours.
❖After this time, prepare the vegetables: cut the eggplant and zucchini diagonally into ¼-in (.5-cm) slices. Remove the stamens from the zucchini flowers and cut each flower into 2 or 3 pieces, according to size. Break off the stalk of the artichokes level with the heart. Remove the tough outside leaves and cut off the tips of the tender leaves to within ½ in (1 cm) of the heart. Remove the chokes and rub the hearts with the lemon half to keep them from discoloring. Slice each artichoke vertically and sprinkle with lemon juice.
❖Beat the egg whites to stiff peaks and fold into the batter. Heat the oil in a small deep fryer or saucepan to 375°F (190°C). Dip the artichoke, eggplant and zucchini slices and the zucchini flowers into the batter, then drop into the hot oil a few at a time and fry for 1 to 2 minutes or until golden brown.
❖Remove the fritters with a slotted spoon and drain on paper towels. Arrange on a plate and serve immediately.

SERVES 4   *Photograph pages 8 – 9*

BUTTERED CABBAGE (top right), GREEN BEANS WITH GARLIC (top left)
AND ENDIVES, FLEMISH-STYLE (bottom)
PETER JOHNSON

Périgord

CÈPES FARCIS
Stuffed Mushrooms

12 large fresh cèpes (*porcini* mushrooms)
3 tablespoons olive oil
3½ oz (100 g) prosciutto or other raw ham, finely chopped
3½ oz (100 g) *ventrèche, pancetta* or rindless bacon, chopped
2 cloves garlic, finely chopped
2 French shallots, finely chopped
2 tablespoons chopped flat-leaf parsley
salt and freshly ground pepper
2 eggs, beaten

❖Remove the stems of the mushrooms and trim off the base. Quickly wash the caps and stems under cold running water and pat dry. Finely chop the stems.
❖Heat 1 tablespoon oil in a nonstick 10-in (26-cm) skillet and cook the ham and *ventrèche* for 2 minutes, stirring. Add the garlic and shallots and cook for 2 more minutes, stirring. Add the chopped mushroom stems and parsley and cook until golden. Remove from heat. Season lightly with salt and pepper. Add the eggs and mix well.
❖Preheat oven to 400°F (200°C). Lightly oil a baking dish large enough to hold the mushroom caps in one layer. Arrange the caps upside down in the dish and fill with the stuffing. Sprinkle with the remaining oil. Bake for 25 minutes or until the mushrooms are tender and the stuffing is golden brown. Arrange on a platter and serve immediately.

SERVES 4   *Photograph page 207*

Languedoc

MILLAS
Cornmeal Mush

This corn galette is sometimes served as a dessert, sprinkled with sugar.

1 qt (1 l) water
2½ oz (75 g) lard
salt and freshly ground pepper
1½ cups (8 oz/250 g) cornmeal

❖Pour the water into a large saucepan. Add the lard, salt and pepper and bring to boil. Pour in the cornmeal and cook, stirring with a wooden spoon, for 15 minutes or until the mixture forms a solid mass which comes away from the sides of the saucepan.
❖Turn the mixture onto a dampened linen towel; it will spread out of its own accord. Cut it with a knife dipped in cold water and serve hot. When cold, it may be cut into slices and fried.
❖*Millas* is served hot as an accompaniment to beef stews (*daubes*) and similar dishes. When cold, it is fried in lard, then served warm with a garlic-seasoned salad. It can also be sprinkled with cheese and baked until crusty.

SERVES 6

Périgord

HARICOTS À LA PÉRIGOURDINE
Haricot Beans, Périgord-style

7 oz (200 g) fresh pork rind, trimmed of fat
1 lb (500 g) ripe tomatoes
4 lb (2 kg) fresh haricot beans (or flageolet beans), shelled
1 onion, about 3 oz (100 g), finely chopped
20 sprigs parsley
4 cloves garlic, finely chopped
7 oz (200 g) fresh pork belly, finely chopped
salt and freshly ground pepper

❖Boil the pork rind in water to cover for 5 minutes, then cool under running water and cut into ⅜-in (1-cm) squares. Drop the tomatoes into boiling water for 10 seconds. Cool under running water, peel, halve and squeeze out the seeds; coarsely chop the flesh.
❖Place the beans in a large saucepan and cover with plenty of water. Add the pork rind, onion and tomatoes and bring to boil. Cook for 1 hour over low heat, stirring from time to time.
❖Meanwhile, wash and dry the parsley. Remove the stalks and finely chop the leaves. Combine with the garlic and pork belly.
❖Add the parsley mixture to the beans and cook for 30 minutes longer, stirring from time to time and adding a little water if necessary. Season with salt and pepper, turn the beans into a shallow dish and serve immediately.

SERVES 6

Poitou

HARICOTS BLANCS À LA CRÈME
Haricot Beans in Cream Sauce

1 medium onion
2 cloves
bouquet garni: 1 bay leaf, 1 sprig thyme, 6 sprigs parsley, 2 celery stalks
4 lb (2 kg) fresh haricot beans (or flageolet beans), shelled
1 medium carrot, peeled and cut into 6 pieces
2 cloves garlic, halved
1 cup (8 fl oz/250 ml) heavy (double) cream or crème fraîche
1 oz (25 g) butter
salt and freshly ground pepper
4 pinches of freshly grated nutmeg

❖Peel the onion and stud with the cloves. Tie together the herbs for the bouquet garni.
❖Place the beans in a pot and cover with plenty of cold water. Add the carrot, onion, garlic and bouquet garni and bring to boil. Cook over low heat for 1½ hours, stirring from time to time and adding a little extra water if necessary.
❖When the beans are cooked, pour the cream into a large saucepan. Add the butter, salt, pepper and nutmeg and place over low heat. Drain the beans and discard the carrot, onion, garlic and bouquet garni. Add the beans to the cream and stir to coat well. Turn into a shallow dish and serve immediately.

SERVES 6

PETER JOHNSON

HERB RISOTTO FROM LES BAUX

Provence

RISOTTO DES BAUX
Herb Risotto from Les Baux

1 clove garlic, finely chopped
2 French shallots, finely chopped
1 sprig thyme
1 sprig rosemary
1 bay leaf
2 sage leaves
3 oz (80 g) butter, softened
1 tablespoon olive oil
2 cups (10 oz/300 g) long-grain or Camargue rice
salt and freshly ground pepper
6 tablespoons dry white wine
3¼ cups (26 fl oz/800 ml) water
12 sprigs basil, leaves only

❖In a 4-qt (4-l) enameled pot combine the garlic, shallots, thyme, rosemary, bay leaf and sage. Add half the butter and oil and cook for 2 minutes over low heat, stirring constantly with a wooden spoon. Add the rice, season with salt and pepper and cook over low heat, stirring, for 3 minutes.
❖Sprinkle the wine over the rice and let it evaporate. Add 1¾ cups (14 fl oz/400 ml) water, cover and cook for 10 minutes. Add ¾ cup (6 fl oz/200 ml) more water, cover and cook for 5 minutes. Again add ¾ cup water and cook until the rice has absorbed all the liquid, about 25 minutes total; do not stir the rice during cooking.
❖Coarsely chop the basil. When the rice is cooked, remove the thyme, rosemary, bay leaf and sage. Add the remaining butter and the basil and season with pepper. Stir well and serve immediately from the pot.

SERVES 6

Aquitaine

CÈPES À LA BORDELAISE
Cèpes, Bordelaise-style

1½ lb (750 g) small fresh cèpes (*porcini* mushrooms)
¼ cup (2 fl oz/60 ml) olive oil
2 cloves garlic, finely chopped
3 tablespoons chopped flat-leaf parsley
salt and freshly ground pepper

❖Cut off the stalks of the cèpes at the level of the cap. Quickly wash the caps under running water and pat dry.
❖Heat the oil in a nonstick 10-in (26-cm) sauté pan over high heat. Add the cèpes; they will immediately give out a lot of liquid. Cook over very high heat, stirring constantly, until all liquid evaporates. Remove the cèpes. Add the garlic and parsley to the pan and cook, stirring, for 2 minutes, then turn out of the pan onto a plate.
❖Return the cèpes to the pan, rounded surface up. Sprinkle with the garlic and parsley and season with salt and pepper. Cover and cook over low heat for 30 minutes.
❖Arrange the cèpes on a serving plate. Boil the pan juices until reduced to a syrupy consistency. Pour over the cèpes and serve immediately.

SERVES 4

Provence

ARTICHAUTS À LA BARIGOULE
Braised Artichokes

Artichokes came to France with Catherine de' Medici. At first they were served simply grilled, like mushrooms. Barigoulo, the name of a mushroom in the Provençal dialect, is a recipe that has evolved into this fragrant sauté which still goes by the original name.

12 young artichokes, about 4 oz (125 g) each
1 lemon, halved
¼ cup (2 fl oz/60 ml) olive oil
4 large onions, finely chopped
3 small carrots, peeled and thinly sliced
3 cloves garlic, cut into fine slivers
1 sprig thyme, crumbled
1 bay leaf
6 tablespoons dry white wine
6 tablespoons water
salt and freshly ground pepper

❖Trim the artichoke stalks ¾ in (2 cm) from the heart and strip off the tough leaves. Cut off the tips of the tender leaves to within ¾ in (2 cm) of the heart. Pare the heart and stalks and rub with lemon.
❖Heat the oil in an enameled pot just large enough to hold the artichokes. Add the onions and carrots and cook for 5 minutes without allowing them to color. Add the garlic and cook, stirring, for 1 minute longer. Rinse the artichokes and pat dry. Add to the pot with the thyme and bay leaf and cook, stirring, for 2 minutes. Add the wine and water and season with salt and pepper. Cover and cook over very low heat for about 1 hour or until the artichokes are easily pierced with a knife and are coated with a reduced sauce. Serve warm.

SERVES 4

CÈPES, BORDELAISE-STYLE (top) AND BRAISED ARTICHOKES (bottom)
PETER JOHNSON

Auvergne

CHOU FARCI
Stuffed Cabbage

1 Savoy cabbage, about 3 lb (1.5 kg)
1 tablespoon vegetable oil
2 cloves garlic, finely chopped
2 French shallots, finely chopped
6 tablespoons milk
2 oz (50 g) soft bread, crusts trimmed
12 oz (400 g) beef round steak (top round) or porterhouse
12 oz (400 g) fresh pork shoulder, boned and trimmed of fat
6 oz (200 g) fresh pork belly, boned
1 egg
2 tablespoons finely chopped mixed fresh parsley and
   chives
½ teaspoon dried thyme
½ teaspoon *quatre-épices* (see glossary)
salt and freshly ground pepper
1 sheet pork caul fat (*crépine*)
bouquet garni: 1 bay leaf, 1 sprig thyme, 10 sprigs parsley
1 oz (25 g) butter
6 oz (200 g) onions, thinly sliced
6 oz (200 g) carrots, peeled and thinly sliced
1 cup (8 fl oz/250 ml) chicken stock (recipe page 34)

❖Remove the tough outer leaves from the cabbage and parboil the cabbage for 10 minutes in water to cover. Drain and let cool.

❖Heat the oil in a nonstick 8-in (20-cm) skillet and cook the garlic and shallots until golden. Pour the milk into a small saucepan and bring to boil. Crumble in the bread, remove from heat and stir to form a smooth paste. Let cool.

❖Grind (mince) the three meats in a grinder or food processor. Add the garlic and bread mixtures, egg, herbs, *quatre-épices*, salt and pepper and mix well.

❖To stuff the cabbage, stand it on its base and delicately spread the outside leaves, taking care not to tear them; as each leaf is spread out, cut away the thick white stalk from the base with a small knife. Continue in this way to the heart of the cabbage. Place half the stuffing in the heart. Fold the leaves back over the heart, adding a few spoonfuls of stuffing between the leaves. Use the last layer of leaves to cover the whole cabbage. Rinse the caul fat under cold water, drain and use it to wrap the cabbage.

❖Preheat oven to 425°F (215°C). Tie together the herbs of the bouquet garni. Melt the butter in a heavy pot just large enough to hold the cabbage. Cook the onions and carrots until golden, stirring with a wooden spoon, about 5 minutes. Add the bouquet garni, salt, pepper and stock. Place the cabbage on top and cover. Bake for 1½ hours undisturbed.

❖Transfer the cabbage to a serving platter. Strain the cooking liquid into a sauceboat. Quarter the cabbage, pour the sauce over and serve.

SERVES 8

STUFFED CABBAGE (top right), STUFFED MUSHROOMS (center right, recipe page 203), POTATO CREAM PIE (bottom right, recipe page 212), AND AUVERGNE-STYLE LENTILS (left, recipe page 214), PHOTOGRAPHED IN PÉRIGORD.

PIERRE HUSSENOT/AGENCE TOP

TOMATO AND EGGPLANT CASSEROLE

Provence

BOHÉMIENNE

Tomato and Eggplant Casserole

This dish is served throughout the summer in the town of Avignon.

4 tablespoons olive oil
6 tablespoons water
2 lb (1 kg) eggplants (aubergines), peeled and cut into ¾-in (2-cm) cubes
1½ lb (750 g) ripe tomatoes
6 cloves garlic
1 teaspoon sugar
salt and freshly ground pepper
1 bay leaf
¼ cup (2 fl oz/60 ml) milk
6 anchovy fillets in oil
2 oz (50 g) freshly and finely grated Parmesan cheese

❖Heat 2 tablespoons oil in a nonstick 10-in (26-cm) sauté pan. Add the water and eggplant cubes, cover and cook over low heat, stirring frequently, for 1 hour or until the eggplant is very tender.
❖Drop the tomatoes into boiling water for 10 seconds. Cool under running water; peel, halve and squeeze out the seeds. Chop the flesh into small pieces.
❖Heat the remaining oil in a nonstick 10-in (26-cm) skillet. Add the garlic, forced through a garlic press. Stir in the tomatoes, sugar, salt, pepper and bay leaf and cook over high heat for 20 minutes or until all liquid has evaporated. Add the milk and the anchovies and cook, stirring, for 5 minutes or until the anchovies dissolve.
❖Preheat oven to 400°F (200°C). Discard the bay leaf. Add the tomato sauce to the eggplant and mix well. Pour into a 10-in (26-cm) oval baking dish. Sprinkle with Parmesan and bake for 20 minutes. Serve hot from the baking dish.

SERVES 4

Provence

EPINARDS AUX PIGNONS

Spinach with Pine Nuts

2½ oz (75 g) dried currants
3 lb (1.5 kg) fresh spinach
3 tablespoons olive oil
salt and freshly ground pepper
2½ oz (75 g) pine nuts
6 drops orangeflower water

❖Cover the currants with warm water in a small bowl. Trim the stalks from the spinach; wash the leaves and dry in a salad spinner.
❖Heat 2 tablespoons oil in a nonstick 11-in (28-cm) sauté pan and cook the spinach in batches over high heat, turning constantly, for 5 minutes. Season with salt and pepper and keep hot.
❖Heat the remaining oil in a nonstick 8-in (20-cm) skillet. Add the drained currants and pine nuts and cook, stirring, for 2 minutes or until the pine nuts are golden. Add the pine nuts, currants and orangeflower water to the sauté pan with the spinach and stir for 30 seconds, then remove from heat. Arrange the spinach on a serving plate and serve immediately.

SERVES 4

Poitou

PALETS DE MARRONS

Chestnut Patties

2 lb (1 kg) fresh chestnuts
2 tender celery stalks, with leaves, chopped
3 oz (100 g) butter
6 tablespoons water
salt and freshly ground pepper
3 egg yolks, beaten

❖Make a small incision on the flat face of each chestnut. Bring a large saucepan of water to boil and drop in the chestnuts. Boil for 5 minutes, then drain and remove both the outside shells and the inner skins.
❖Combine the chestnuts, celery and 2 oz (60 g) butter in a nonstick 10-in (26-cm) sauté pan over low heat. Add the water and cook, stirring often, for about 1 hour or until the chestnuts are very soft. Season with salt and pepper during cooking.
❖Puree the chestnuts through the finest holes of a food mill into a bowl. Add the egg yolks and refrigerate for 2 hours.
❖Shape the mixture into rounds 2 in (5 cm) in diameter and ⅜ in (1 cm) thick. Melt the remaining butter in a nonstick 11-in (28-cm) skillet and fry the patties for 2 minutes on each side. Arrange on a platter and serve immediately.

SERVES 6

SPINACH WITH PINE NUTS (top) AND CHESTNUT PATTIES (bottom)

Languedoc

POMMES SARLADAISES

Potatoes, Sarlat-style

1½ lb (750 g) boiling potatoes
2 oz (50 g) goose fat
4 cloves garlic, finely chopped
2 tablespoons chopped flat-leaf parsley
salt and freshly ground pepper

❖Peel the potatoes, wash and slice into ⅛-in (3-mm) rounds.
❖Melt the goose fat in a nonstick 10-in (26-cm) skillet. Add the potatoes and turn them over in the hot fat for 10 minutes. Add the garlic and parsley, season with salt and pepper and stir again. Cover and cook over low heat for 20 minutes or until the potatoes are tender, turning them several times.
❖Transfer the potatoes to a shallow dish and serve hot.

SERVES 4

Savoie

GRATIN SAVOYARD

Potato Gratin, Savoy-style

1¼ cups (10 fl oz/300 ml) chicken stock
salt and freshly ground pepper
6 pinches of freshly grated nutmeg
1¼ lb (625 g) boiling potatoes
1½ oz (40 g) butter
4 oz (125 g) Beaufort or Emmenthaler cheese, freshly and
  finely grated

❖Preheat oven to 375°F (190°C). Bring the chicken stock to boil over low heat. Add salt, pepper and nutmeg and remove from heat.
❖Peel the potatoes, wash them and pat dry. Using the shredder attachment of a food processor, slice the potatoes very thinly.
❖Using a small amount of the butter, grease a 10x7-in (26x18-cm) baking dish. Spread a layer of potatoes over the bottom, then a layer of cheese. Continue layering the remaining potatoes and cheese, ending with cheese. Pour the hot stock over and dot with the remaining butter.
❖Bake until golden brown, about 50 minutes. Serve hot from the baking dish.

SERVES 4

Provence

BARBOUIADO DE FÈVES ET D'ARTICHAUTS

Braised Broad Beans and Artichokes

3 lb (1.5 kg) fresh broad beans
3 oz (100 g) streaky bacon
5 small artichokes, about 4 oz (125 g) each

PETER JOHNSON

½ lemon
2 tablespoons olive oil
1 green onion (scallion or spring onion), finely chopped
1 sprig thyme
1 sprig savory
3 tablespoons water
salt and freshly ground pepper

❖Shell the broad beans and peel off the soft green skin from each bean. Remove the rind from the bacon and cut the meat into thin matchsticks.
❖Trim each artichoke stalk at the base of the heart. Remove the tough outside leaves. Cut off the tips of the tender leaves to within ¼ in (½ cm) of the heart. Trim the hearts and rub with the cut surface of the lemon. Cut each heart into quarters and remove the choke. Cut each quarter into 3 slices.
❖Heat the oil in a 4-qt (4-l) pot. Add the onion, bacon, thyme and savory and cook gently for 2 minutes, stirring with a wooden spoon. Add the artichokes and cook over moderate heat, stirring constantly, until light golden and almost tender, about 7 to 8 minutes.
❖Add the water and beans and season with salt and pepper. Mix well. Cover and cook for 5 minutes longer. Remove from heat and discard the thyme and savory. Turn into a shallow dish and serve immediately.

SERVES 4

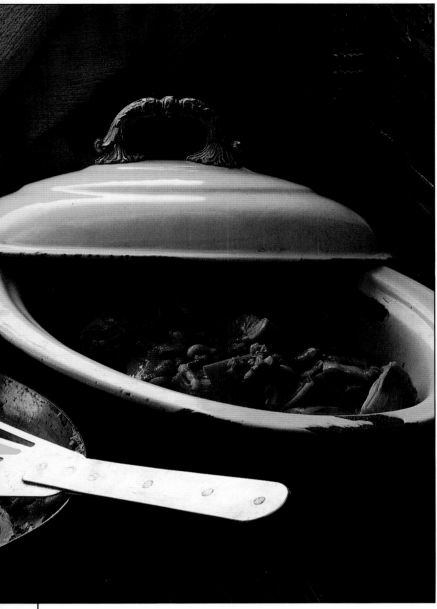

POTATOES, SARLAT-STYLE (bottom), POTATO GRATIN, SAVOY-STYLE (top left)
AND BRAISED BROAD BEANS AND ARTICHOKES (right)

Franche-Comté

MORILLES À LA CRÈME

Morels in Cream Sauce

1 lb (500 g) fresh morels
1 tablespoon fresh lemon juice
6 tablespoons heavy (double) cream or crème fraîche
2 oz (50 g) butter
2 French shallots, finely chopped
salt and freshly ground pepper

❖Trim the ends of the morel stalks. Wash and dry the morels. Place in a saucepan with the lemon juice and cook over low heat for 15 minutes.
❖Remove the morels with a slotted spoon, add the cream to the saucepan and mix well.
❖Melt the butter in a nonstick 10-in (26-cm) skillet and cook the shallots until golden, about 3 minutes, stirring with a wooden spoon. Add the morels, season with salt and pepper, then add the cream sauce from the saucepan. Increase heat and cook until the mixture reduces to form a thick, creamy sauce to coat the morels, about 2 to 3 minutes.
❖Turn them into a shallow dish and serve immediately.

SERVES 4

Provence

TIAN DE COURGETTES

Baked Zucchini with Tomatoes and Onions

Tian is the name of the square or rectangular glazed earthenware dish in which vegetable, meat or fish dishes are baked. Because of this, all Provençal gratins have taken the name of tians.

1 lb (500 g) green (spring) onions
1 lb 10 oz (800 g) medium zucchini (courgettes)
1½ lb (750 g) firm-ripe tomatoes
6 tablespoons olive oil
2 cloves garlic, finely chopped
salt and freshly ground pepper
1 sprig fresh thyme, leaves only
1 sprig fresh savory, leaves only (optional)

❖Cut the onions into ¼-in (.5-cm) slices, including the green stalk. Cut the zucchini diagonally into ¼-in (.5-cm) slices; cut the tomatoes into similar-size slices.
❖Preheat oven to 400°F (200°C). Heat 4 tablespoons oil in a nonstick 10-in (26-cm) skillet and cook the onions over low heat, stirring frequently, until soft and transparent, about 8 minutes. Add the garlic, salt and pepper and cook, stirring, for 2 minutes longer.
❖Transfer the mixture to a 10 x 7-in (26 x 18-cm) baking dish and smooth the surface. Arrange 4 lengthwise rows of tomato and zucchini slices on top of the onions. Sprinkle with thyme and savory. Pour the remaining oil over and season with salt and pepper.
❖Bake until the vegetables are very soft and slightly browned, about 1 hour. Serve directly from the baking dish, hot or lukewarm.

SERVES 4 – 5   *Photograph pages 8 – 9*

MORELS IN CREAM SAUCE

PETER JOHNSON

Bourbonnais

TRUFFAT

Potato Cream Pie

2½ cups (10 oz/300 g) all purpose (plain) flour
5 oz (150 g) butter
¼ cup (2 fl oz/60 ml) water
salt
5 oz (150 g) smoked bacon
1 tablespoon peanut (groundnut) oil
1 onion, about 4 oz (125 g), finely chopped
1 lb 10 oz (800 g) boiling potatoes
freshly ground pepper
6 pinches freshly grated nutmeg
1 egg yolk
1 tablespoon milk
⅔ cup (5 oz/150 ml) heavy (double) cream or crème fraîche

❖Sift the flour onto a work surface and make a well in the center. Add the butter, water and 3 pinches of salt. Combine the ingredients with the fingertips to produce a smooth dough. Roll it into a ball and refrigerate for 1 hour.
❖Meanwhile, remove the rind from the bacon and chop the meat finely with a knife. Heat the oil in a nonstick 9-in (22-cm) skillet and cook the onion and bacon over low heat until golden, stirring with a wooden spoon. Remove from heat.
❖Wash the potatoes and slice thinly. Turn into a bowl and add salt, pepper, nutmeg, and the mixture from the skillet. Combine carefully so that the potato slices do not break.
❖Preheat oven to 425°F (215°C). Cut the pastry into two portions, one slightly larger than the other. Roll out the larger portion to a 12-in (30-cm) circle. Butter a 10-in (26-cm) cake pan and line with pastry. Turn the potato mixture into the pastry case and smooth the surface. Roll out the second portion of pastry into a 10-in (26-cm) circle for the lid. Place on top of the filling and press the edges together firmly to seal.
❖Beat together the egg yolk and milk and brush the surface of the pastry with this mixture. Bake for 1¼ hours or until the pastry is light golden. Cut a ¾-in (2-cm) circle of pastry from the center of the lid and pour the cream through this opening. Replace the circle of pastry and return the *truffat* to the oven for 10 minutes longer. Serve hot.

SERVES 6   *Photograph page 207*

Provence

PAPETON D'AUBERGINES

Eggplant Charlotte

This is a specialty of Avignon, once the city of the Popes. In the old days it was baked in a mold shaped like a papal tiara. It is sometimes called "aubergines of the Popes."

3 lb (1.5 kg) eggplant (aubergine), the long oval variety
4 tablespoons olive oil
6 tablespoons water
2 sprigs fresh thyme, leaves only
1 clove garlic, finely chopped
salt and freshly ground pepper
5 eggs

2½ oz (75 g) freshly and finely grated Parmesan
For serving:
fresh tomato sauce flavored with basil

❖Wash the eggplant and wipe dry. Cut into 2-in (5-cm) cubes. Heat 3 tablespoons oil in a nonstick 11-in (28-cm) sauté pan. Add the water, thyme and garlic and cook for 1 minute, then add the eggplant. Season with salt and pepper. Cover and cook over low heat, stirring from time to time, until the eggplant is tender, about 30 minutes.
❖Preheat oven to 400°F (200°C). Puree the cooked eggplant through the medium holes of a food mill. Beat the eggs with a fork. Add the eggs and cheese to the eggplant puree and mix well. Oil a charlotte mold 7 in (18 cm) in diameter. Turn the eggplant mixture into the mold and smooth the surface. Bake for 40 minutes or until the surface is golden brown.
❖Let the *papeton* rest for 10 minutes at room temperature, then unmold. Serve hot or lukewarm with tomato sauce.

SERVES 6

Aquitaine

COUSINAT

Cousinat

This dish is a specialty of the town of Bayonne.

1 lb (500 g) fresh broad beans
1 red bell pepper (capsicum), about 7 oz (200 g)
7 oz (200 g) ripe tomatoes
4 small artichokes, about 4 oz (125 g) each
1 oz (25 g) goose fat
2 slices prosciutto or other raw ham, ½ in (1 cm) thick, diced
12 green onions (scallions or spring onions), trimmed
7 oz (200 g) small carrots, peeled and thinly sliced
4 oz (125 g) slender green beans
6 tablespoons dry white wine
salt and freshly ground pepper

❖Shell the broad beans and peel off the soft green skin from each bean. Quarter the pepper, remove the seeds and veins and cut into thin strips.
❖Drop the tomatoes into boiling water for 10 seconds. Cool under running water, peel, halve and squeeze out the seeds; coarsely chop the flesh. Cut off the stalk of each artichoke at the base of the heart. Remove the tough outside leaves. Cut off the tips of the tender leaves to within ¾ in (2 cm) of the heart; trim the heart.
❖Melt the goose fat in a 4-qt (4-l) pot and lightly brown the cubes of ham for 3 minutes, stirring with a wooden spoon. Add the onions, pepper, artichokes and carrots and cook, stirring, for 2 minutes. Add the tomatoes and beans and cook for 10 minutes, stirring often. Pour in the wine and boil for 5 minutes. Season with salt and pepper, cover and cook over very low heat for 1 hour, stirring from time to time; the vegetables should be tender and coated with a syrupy glaze. Turn into a shallow dish and serve.

SERVES 4

EGGPLANT CHARLOTTE (top) AND COUSINAT (bottom)
PETER JOHNSON

PETER JOHNSON

GREEN PEAS, VENDÉE-STYLE

Vendée

PETITS POIS À LA VENDÉENNE
Green Peas, Vendée-style

1 sprig thyme
1 sprig hyssop
1 sprig savory
1 sprig flat-leaf parsley
2 oz (50 g) butter
16 fresh green onions (scallions or spring onions)
3 lb (1.5 kg) green peas, shelled
2 lettuce hearts, quartered
salt and freshly ground pepper
1 teaspoon sugar

❖Strip the leaves from the thyme, hyssop, savory and parsley.
❖Melt the butter in a nonstick 10-in (26-cm) sauté pan. Add the onions and herbs and cook over low heat, stirring, for 3 minutes or until the onions are golden. Add the peas and cook, stirring, for 2 minutes longer. Add the lettuce hearts, season with salt, pepper and sugar and add cold water just to cover.
❖Cover the pan and cook for 1 hour, stirring from time to time. Turn the peas into a shallow dish and serve immediately.

SERVES 4

Auvergne

LENTILLES À L'AUVERGNATE
Auvergne-style Lentils

10 oz (300 g) carrots
10 oz (300 g) onions
2 cloves

bouquet garni: 1 bay leaf, 1 sprig thyme, 6 sprigs parsley
2 cloves garlic
1 lb (500 g) lentils
7 oz (200 g) smoked bacon, in one piece
1 oz (25 g) lard
1 tablespoon chopped flat-leaf parsley
1 tablespoon chopped fresh chives
salt and freshly ground pepper

❖Cut the carrots into ¼-in (.5-cm) slices. Peel the onions; stud one onion with cloves and finely chop the remainder. Tie together the herbs of the bouquet garni. Crush the cloves of garlic with your hand or the side of a cleaver.
❖Rinse the lentils, then place them in a large pot. Add the bacon, whole onion, garlic, carrots and bouquet garni. Cover with plenty of cold water and bring to boil over low heat. Cook for 45 minutes.
❖Lift out the bacon, remove the rind and fat and break the lean meat into small pieces. Melt the lard in a nonstick 10-in (26-cm) skillet and cook the chopped onions until golden, about 3 minutes, stirring with a wooden spoon. Add the bacon and cook, stirring, for 2 more minutes. Drain the lentils and discard the whole onion, garlic and bouquet garni. Stir in the contents of the skillet with the parsley and chives. Season with salt and pepper. Turn the lentils into a shallow dish and serve immediately.

SERVES 6   *Photograph page 207*

Ile de France

POMMES SOUFFLÉES
Puffed Potatoes

The date of the inauguration of the railway line between Paris and St Germain-en-Laye, August 26, 1837, apparently marked the entirely accidental creation of this dish.

When someone told the chef at the celebration banquet that the guests were arriving, he plunged the prepared potatoes into the frying oil; but alas, the guests had been held up. The same thing happened a second time: another frying, and still no guests. At the third attempt, the chef was astonished to see his potatoes puffing up in the hot oil. When they were drained, they remained light and golden, and were praised by all who tasted them.

So a new recipe was born, and for a long time it bore the title pommes soufflées de Saint-Germain-en-Laye.

1½ lb (750 g) boiling potatoes
2 qt (2 l) peanut (groundnut) oil
salt

❖Peel the potatoes and trim them to a roughly rectangular shape. Rinse, pat dry and slice each potato into ⅛-in (3-mm) slices. Pour 1 qt (1 l) oil into each of two deep fryers or large saucepans. Heat one to 212°F (100°C) and the second to 425°F (220°C).
❖Place the potatoes in a frying basket and plunge into the fryer with the 212°F oil. Cook until they are just beginning to color, then lift out the basket and immediately plunge it into the second fryer; the potatoes will puff up. Drain immediately on paper towels and transfer to a serving plate. Season with salt and serve at once.

SERVES 4

PUFFED POTATOES
PHOTOGRAPHED IN THE ILE DE FRANCE
PIERRE HUSSENOT/AGENCE TOP

BOURBONNAIS, ROUERGUE

Cheeses, mountains and plateaus

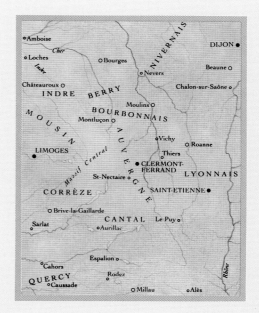

AUVERGNE, BOURBONNAIS, ROUERGUE

Cheeses, mountains and plateaus

"The Auvergne," wrote Alexandre Vialatte, "produces government ministers, cheeses and volcanoes." As far as cheeses go, he is absolutely right. Together with those of Savoy, they are the kings of the French mountains. Their taste of natural pastures, their undeniable wholesomeness, their genuine flavor — in sum, their authenticity and the vigor of their aroma, all the result of good-quality cow's milk, give them pride of place in the cheese-lover's heart: the grassy Saint-Nectaire, with its handsome grey or purplish crust, which seems to come directly from the pasturages where it was born — not to be confused with the Murol, similarly shaped but with a hole in the center, a commercial cheese, of plastic appearance and neutral flavor; the solid and powerful Cantal, whose reputation is not eclipsed by that of its near cousins from Laguiole-en-Aubrac and Salers, with their distinctive flavor of pressed curds and dried hazelnuts; the Fourme d'Ambert, with its light veining and slightly bitter aftertaste, a cheese as fine as English Stilton and which goes well with a good port. But also the *bleu d'Auvergne*, the *Tomme de Brach*, the *Brique de Livradois*, the *Galette de la Chaise-Dieu* — all local cheeses which amply justify the local saying that the Auvergne is one immense cheese platter.

With its southern appendage of the Rouergue, which produces Roquefort, the Auvergne is the very symbol of the tourist's eternal France, peaceful and cheese-producing. Roquefort is the star of

LEFT: A SHEPHERD FROM ST-BERAIN NEAR LE PUY STARTS HIS DAY.

PREVIOUS PAGES: LE PUY'S BEAUTIFUL ROMANESQUE CATHÉDRALE NÔTRE-DAME IS STILL AN IMPORTANT PILGRIMAGE SITE, AND IT TOWERS OVER THE RED-TILED ROOFS AND NARROW COBBLESTONE STREETS OF THE TOWN.

the Rouergue Midi. Made from the milk of sheep of the Lacaune breed, the cheese is handsomely veined, soft-textured and moist-crusted, containing a minimum of 52% fat. It comes from the village of Roquefort-sur-Soulzon in the *département* of Aveyron, in the south of the Auvergne, wrapped in foil that is stamped with the name of the producer. Somewhat acidic, Roquefort marries admirably with sweet white wines like those of Sauternes or Montbazillac. The *Bleu des Causses*, made from cow's milk, is its first cousin. These are the cheeses of this splendid country, the Auvergne.

But the volcanoes? They are a source of pure air and sparkling water (the many brands of mineral water bottled in the region are renowned for their purifying properties) and of open pastures. To crisscross from the Bourbonnais to Clermont-Ferrand, which dominates the landscape of Puy de Dôme, then to turn towards the charming village of Salers, with its old houses of black lava, its Renaissance-style former bailey and its Templars' House, is to experience a rich and self-contained land, closed around its treasures — which are, first of all, a group of extinct volcanoes unique in France.

Puy de Sancy, Puy Mary, Puy de Montchal, the deservedly famous Puy de Dôme, which offers a spectacular view over the nearby craters and a green and grassy landscape that looks more like the moon. On this rich, lush, ancient earth the flocks graze without risk. The cattle give a juicy, flavorful, marbled beef — Charolais in the north, Salers in the south, the long-horned Aubrac on the plateau of the same name. Cattle with a smooth, orange-red coat, which have never eaten anything but tender grass.

In the Auvergne, the cuisine is generous, rustic, country- rather than city-style. The traditional dish is *aligot*: a potato puree mixed with fresh *tomme* cheese and a hint of garlic. In the Aubrac mountains in summer it is prepared in the open air in front of the *burons*, small shepherds' huts made of stone. It will be accompanied by some good sausages, dried or grilled, or by pig's trotters or *andouillette*. The star of local vegetables is the green lentil from Le Puy, jokingly called the "caviar of the poor," since in appearance it recalls those small, luxurious black pearls. The *gigot brayaude* is a leg of lamb cooked in a closed pot, very gently, for seven hours, with salt pork, garlic cloves, onions and carrots. It is a true peasant dish, appetizingly aromatic, the meat so soft and tender that it can be eaten with a spoon. *Mourtayrol* is the plentiful pot-au-feu of feast days. *Falette* is a boned breast of veal, stuffed with ham, bacon, veal, onions and garlic, which is slowly cooked over gentle heat and served with braised cabbage. The *potée auvergnat* calls for cabbage and salted pork, in particular the head and knuckle. Mountain trout are cooked *au bleu*, in a court bouillon, and enhanced with melted butter. The *omble-chevalier*, a highly esteemed, pink-fleshed trout which is the glory of the Savoy lakes, is equally the pride of

ROSINE MAZIN/AGENCE TOP

IN THE HEART OF FRANCE, AUVERGNE'S CHARACTERISTIC MOUNTAINS ARE EXTINCT VOLCANOES, AND THE ONCE-FIERY CRATERS ARE NOW INVITING BLUE LAKES LIKE LAC CHAMBON, SOUTH OF CLERMONT-FERRAND.

Lake Pavin. Mushrooms come in infinite variety — *chanterelles, girolles, lactaires, morilles, gyromitres*. In Velay, and also in Combrailles and Aubrac, they make for a real treasure hunt.

The *truffade* or *truffado* makes use of the "truffle" of the Auvergne, otherwise known as a potato, which is cut into thick slices and fried with cubes of salt pork and slivers of cheese — certainly solid fare, but what flavor! But then, the whole of Auvergne is a land of substantial flavors, of powerful aromas. Its liqueurs come from the plants of its mountains: the verveine, which is the glory of the Velay, and which also serves to make soothing infusions, and the deep-rooted gentian, yellow-flowered, herbaceous, bitter and sweet at the same time, from which results one of the best of the bitter aperitifs, Suze. The red wines, from Gamay grapes, are light: Chanturgue and Châteaugay around Clermont-Ferrand, Côtes du Forez and Roannaise between Roanne and Saint-Etienne. In the Bourbonnais, the light, fresh Saint-Pourçain wine, made from Gamay, Pinot noir, Sauvignon and Chardonnay grapes, comes in white, red and rosé styles.

The Bourbonnais in the northeast is another region that could very well stand on its own. On the edge of the Auvergne, renowned for such spa resorts as Vichy and Bourbon-l'Archambault, it borders with the Nivernais, the Berry and the

ROSINE MAZIN/AGENCE TOP

IN THE TINY TOWN OF ESPALION IN THE AVEYRON REGION OF AUVERGNE, AN
ANCIENT BRIDGE SPANS THE RIVER LOT.

Loire. As in Auvergne, this is still the territory of the cabbage, which goes into the *potée* — the pot-au-feu of the region — and the celebrated *soupe aux choux*, aromatic and restorative. But at the same time it enriches this heritage with its own original dishes: *pâté de tartouffes*, a potato pie with cubes of salt pork, onions and cream, and a crust of short pastry; *pompes au grattons*, with yeast-raised dough and pieces of salt pork; duck *à la Du Chambet*, served with cinnamon-scented apples and a sauce enriched with cubes of foie gras. All are succulent, earthy dishes which have contributed to the fame of the Hôtel de Paris at Moulins.

Rouergue could be split in two. The southern part, towards Millau, resembles the Midi and the Languedoc; the north, from Rodez to Conques, from the countryside of Marcillac with its red brick houses, vivid and rustic, as far as the highlands of the Aubrac, is a foretaste of the Auvergne. Shaded green forests, luxuriant foliage: in the lost valley of Conques, one of the most magnificent villages of the Auvergne, the traveler will re-experience the rich splendor of the region, first encountered at Murols and Saint-Nectaire.

This is still a region of hearty meals and rib-sticking dishes, where offal is in no way disdained. Many of the dishes that are said to be *auvergnat* in Paris actually belong to the Rouergue: the *florès* of Rodez, made from veal tripe; the dried hams of Naucelle; the *tripoux*, which are little, tied-up parcels of mutton tripe, braised in a tomato sauce over gentle heat; *estofinado*, made from dried cod cooked with potatoes; *fouace*, a cake flavored with orangeflower water. But the real wealth of the country, apart from the aforementioned *aligot*, which belongs equally to the Rouergue and the Auvergne, is the Roquefort.

The people of the Auvergne, solid and honest gourmands, are first and foremost hard workers. Many proprietors of cafes and lively brasseries in Paris today are former waiters and owners of *bois-charbons*, where they sold not only the means of heating but also the young red wine. Most of them came from the famous triangle Espalion-Estaing-Saint-Chély-d'Apcher. It is a harsh region, this Upper Rouergue, touching the nearby Auvergne on the vast plateau of Aubrac, crossed by *drailles*, paths made of dry stone. Many of its countrymen migrated, working day and night to earn their daily bread and, eventually, buy their own bistros. One such is Marcellin Cazes, who was a water carrier before he became the force behind the Brasserie Lipp on the Boulevard Saint-Germain. These citizens have been the most valiant ambassadors of their region. And of its wonderful dishes — *truffade*, *falette*, *tripoux* and *aligot* — which you eat with the horn-handled knife of Laguiole, and which sing with joy of the great land of the Auvergne.

DESSERTS

How sweet they are!

A SELECTION OF DECORATIVE *CONFISERIES* — "THISTLE" PRALINES
AND SWEET FRUIT AND ALMOND PASTES.

DESSERTS

How sweet they are!

NOT ONLY DO THE FRENCH GROW GRAPES FOR WINE-MAKING, BUT THEY
ALSO USE *RAISINS* IN ALL KINDS OF REGIONAL DISHES INCLUDING THE TASTY
ALSACE DESSERT *KUGELHOPF*.

Let's start with the cheeses. Brillat-Savarin deemed them the *premier des desserts*, the most important. But in France, cheeses in all their diversity ("a country with four hundred different cheeses will never die," promised Churchill during the debacle of 1940), remain a prelude to dessert.

The land of good things to eat, France does not ignore the appeal of sugar. The markets of eastern France feel the influence of central Europe, with Vienna at its hub, where cafes are meeting places. The town of Metz, for example, has one of the best chocolatiers in the whole country — Pierre Koenig, who exports his chocolate truffles, pralines and semisweet chocolate creams around the world — as well as a dozen or so top-quality *pâtisseries-salons de thé*. Strasbourg is obviously one of the most deliciously sweet towns in the world. Its specialties are many, starting with *kugelhopf*, *büeraweka* (a fruit loaf), fruity *Bettelmann* cake, and *schnecke*, known throughout the rest of France as *pain aux raisins*. Besides, many of the pâtisserie specialties of eastern France have spread to other parts of the country: the *meringue chantilly*, meringue with whipped cream, that is also found in Ile-de-France, for example; the *nid d'abeilles*, or bee's nest (a brioche dough sprinkled with sugar and filled with a custard cream), which finds its counterparts in the *tarte au sucre* of Artois and Picardy and the *tarte tropézienne* of the Var.

PREVIOUS PAGES: SNOW EGGS (top left, recipe page 232), MERINGUES
CHANTILLY (center left, recipe page 231), PRALINE BUTTER CREAM CAKE
(top right, recipe page 246) AND ORANGE LIQUEUR CRÊPES (bottom right,
recipe page 250), PHOTOGRAPHED IN THE ILE DE FRANCE.

PIERRE HUSSENOT/AGENCE TOP

Certain other regions have their own specialties, which rely on local resources: for example, in Brittany, *kouigh amann au miel*, prune-studded *far*, the rich butter cake known as *quatre-quarts*, and *galettes*, pastries made with salted butter. The *clafoutis* is now found everywhere, although it originated in the Limousin. The baba — is it a native of Lorraine? — becomes *savarin* when served in Paris, garnished with whipped cream.

Ice cream, introduced to the French court by Catherine de' Medici, who married the future Henri II, did not properly arrive in Paris until the following century, when Francesco Procopio opened the first cafe in Paris. This frozen treat — which became based on cream and eggs only around 1775 — and sorbets, made from all kinds of fruit, were an immediate hit. In the eighteenth century, Paris had 250 *limonadiers* selling ice creams during summer.

Since that time, the elaborately decorated and molded confections known as *bombes glacées* and similar preparations have vulgarized the use of iced desserts. Modern dietetics has endorsed the serving of sorbets — an ancient Chinese practice, passed on to the Persians and Arabs — which use neither eggs nor fats. Based on fruit pulp, preferably fresh, sorbets calmly follow the rhythm of the changing seasons.

Tarts, too, wed the fruits of all regions, all seasons. *Crêpes* are not necessarily Breton, as evi-

MILLE-FEUILLES, TARTE AUX MIRABELLES (TARTS WITH YELLOW PLUMS), *CHOUX A LA CHANTILLY* (CREAM PUFFS) AND *MOUSSE FRAISE* (STRAWBERRY MOUSSE), AS WELL AS *RELIGIEUSES* (LITTLE NUN CAKES) AND *ÉCLAIRES*, ARE SOME OF THE DELICIOUS PASTRIES YOU WILL FIND IN ANY FRENCH *PÂTISSERIE*.

THE FRENCH ARE VERY PARTICULAR ABOUT USING THE FRESHEST INGREDIENTS. THEY ARE DISCERNING CUSTOMERS AND TAKE TIME TO SELECT THE BEST PRODUCE.

denced by the very Parisian *crêpes Suzette*, delicately flavored with orange zest and dramatically flamed at the table. The dessert that finishes the meal should also be a feast for the eyes — hence the importance given to presentation. The great chefs have never been indifferent to this. Urbain Dubois, who was the chef of the Rocher de Cancale, then of the Café Anglais before exercising his talents in the service of Prince Orloff in Russia and William I in Germany, set down his rules of aesthetics in a work which has since become a classic, *La Cuisine Artistique*, dating from 1870 and predating by thirteen years his *Grand Livre des Pâtissiers et des Cuisiniers*.

A century later, Gaston Lenôtre, a pâtissier at Pont-Audemer, became the most famous caterer in the world; he understood, as did his predecessor Urbain Dubois, that if the dinner does not climax in dessert, even the finest cuisine will be a disappointment, and that the dessert will never be complete unless it is properly presented. His parades of elaborately constructed *pièces montées* borne by an army of white-hatted kitchen boys, a splendid array of ice creams and light and fruity sorbets, remain in the memory like living paintings worthy of Watteau. At the end of the twentieth century, French festivities — like those of the whole world — are indebted to Gaston Lenôtre for something of their sweet sparkle and a great deal of their magic.

FRUIT TARTS AND *GÂTEAUX*, BAKED DAILY, DECORATE THIS *PÂTISSERIE* WINDOW IN QUIMPER. REFLECTED IN THE GLASS IS THE STREET SCENE — THE OLD QUARTER OF TOWN WITH ATTRACTIVELY RESTORED HOUSES AND COBBLESTONE STREETS.

CATERING FOR EVERYONE'S TASTES, THIS SHOP IN DINAN, BRETAGNE IS A *BOULANGERIE, PÂTISSERIE* AND DELICATESSEN.

Aquitaine

LE NÈGRE
Flourless Chocolate Cake

Made with dark chocolate, butter and sugar this cake is served all along the Aquitaine coast from Bayonne to Bordeaux. Different families have different ways of preparing it, but the important thing is not to use flour, so that a very soft-textured cake rather like a baked mousse is achieved, served warm or cold, with custard cream.

7 oz (200 g) semisweet or bittersweet (plain) chocolate
7 oz (200 g) soft butter
1 cup (7 oz/200 g) sugar
4 eggs, separated

❖Preheat oven to 375°F (190°C). Butter an 8-in (22-cm) round cake pan. Break the chocolate up into small pieces and melt over hot water. Add the butter and stir with a spatula until smooth.
❖Add half the sugar to the egg yolks and whisk until the mixture is pale in color. Beat in the chocolate mixture. Beat the egg whites to soft peaks. Gradually add the remaining sugar, beating until the mixture is smooth and shiny. Fold gently into the chocolate mixture with a rubber spatula.
❖Pour the batter into the prepared pan and bake for 40 minutes or until a tester inserted in the center comes out clean.
❖Let the cake rest at room temperature for 10 minutes before turning it out of the pan. Serve warm, at room temperature or chilled.

SERVES 6

PETER JOHNSON

FLOURLESS CHOCOLATE CAKE

APRICOT PASTRY

PETER JOHNSON

Maine

JALOUSIES
Apricot Pastry

1 scant cup (7 oz/200 g) apricot jam
1¼ lb (600 g) puff pastry (recipe page 44)
To glaze:
1 egg yolk
1 tablespoon milk

❖Preheat oven to 425°F (215°C). Heat the jam in a small saucepan, then put it through a fine sieve to remove the skin of the fruit. Let cool. Roll out the puff pastry into two 8 x 3-in (20 x 8-cm) strips.
❖Lightly moisten a baking sheet and place one pastry strip on it. Spread with the jam to within ⅜ in (1 cm) of the edges. Place the second pastry strip on top, smooth side up (i.e., the side that was in contact with the work surface). Press down all around the edges so they will stick together. Make small knife cuts at ⅜-in (1-cm) intervals around the edges.
❖Beat the egg yolk and milk together and brush the surface of the pastry with the mixture; do not let the glaze run over the edges as this would keep the pastry from rising. With the point of a knife, make deep slanting cuts in the pastry ⅜ in (1 cm) apart and ¼ in (.5 cm) from the edges. Bake the pastry for 30 minutes or until golden brown. Transfer to a plate and serve warm.

SERVES 6

PUFF PASTRY WITH ALMOND FILLING

Orléanais

PITHIVIERS
Puff Pastry with Almond Filling

1¼ lb (600 g) puff pastry (recipe page 44)
For the filling:
5 oz (150 g) ground blanched almonds
1 cup (5 oz/150 g) powdered (icing) sugar
5 oz (150 g) soft butter
2 eggs
2 tablespoons dark rum
For the glaze:
1 egg yolk
1 tablespoon milk
2 tablespoons powdered (icing) sugar

❖Prepare the filling: mix the ground almonds and sugar in a small bowl. Cream the butter in a large bowl. Blend in the almond mixture, eggs and rum.

❖Preheat oven to 425°F (215°C). Cut the puff pastry into 2 equal parts and roll out into two 12-in (30-cm) circles, using a large plate or cake pan as a guide. Hold the knife very straight so that the pastry is not crushed, which would prevent it from rising evenly during baking.

❖Lightly moisten a baking sheet and lay one of the pastry circles on it. Spread with almond mixture to within ⅜ in (1 cm) of the edge. Place the second pastry disc on top of this, smooth side up (i.e. the side that was in contact with the work surface). Press firmly all around the edge of the pastry so that the two circles will stick together. Make small cuts in the edge of the *pithiviers* ⅜ in (1 cm) apart.

❖Prepare the glaze: beat the egg yolk and milk together and brush the mixture over the surface of the pastry; do not let it run over the edge, as this would prevent the pastry from rising as it bakes. Using the point of a knife, make very shallow curved cuts on the surface of the pastry, from the outside edge into the center.

❖Bake for 30 minutes. Sprinkle with powdered sugar and bake for 5 more minutes or until the surface is shiny and slightly caramelized. Transfer the pastry to a serving plate and serve warm.

SERVES 6

Bretagne

FAR
Warm Prune Tart

This is one of the most popular of Bretagne's desserts. It is served in different ways according to the region — plain in Saint Pol de Léon, filled with prunes at Quiberon, and with raisins at Brest.

11 oz (350 g) prunes
2 cups (16 fl oz/500 ml) milk
3 eggs
½ cup (4 oz/125 g) sugar
⅔ cup (2½ oz/75 g) all purpose (plain) flour

❖Soak the prunes in warm water to cover for 2 hours. Preheat oven to 400°F (200°C). Heat the milk in a small saucepan over gentle heat. Combine the eggs and sugar in a bowl and whisk until the mixture is pale in color. Whisk in the flour, then the milk.

❖Butter a 10-in (26-cm) deep-sided flameproof china tart plate. Drain the prunes and arrange in the plate. Cover with the batter and bake for about 45 minutes or until browned. Let the tart cool slightly. Serve warm from the baking dish.

SERVES 6

Bretagne

KOUIGH AMANN
Buttered Pastry

The Douarnenez region is the home of this cake, whose name means bread and butter.

7 oz (220 g) low-salt butter
10 oz (300 g) bread dough (page 41)
1 cup (7 oz/220 g) plus 2 tablespoons superfine (caster) sugar

❖Place the butter in a deep plate and work it with a fork until it is soft and the same consistency as the dough. Roll out the dough on a work surface into a square ⅜ in (1 cm) thick. Spread with butter to within ¾ in (2 cm) of the edges; sprinkle with 1 cup sugar. Fold the dough in thirds one way, then in thirds the opposite way. Roll it out as thinly as possible, being careful not to let any of the butter or sugar escape. Fold the pastry again, as before.

❖Butter a 10-in (26-cm) cake pan. Lay the dough in it and push down gently with your fingers, taking care not to break it. Start from the center and work outwards until the whole pan is covered with an even thickness of dough. Let rise for 30 minutes, preheating the oven to 425°F (200°C) after 10 minutes of rising. Bake the tart for 35 minutes, basting with the butter that rises to the surface during the last 15 minutes of baking.

❖Sprinkle the tart with the remaining 2 tablespoons sugar. Let cool slightly, then turn it out and serve.

SERVES 6

WARM PRUNE TART (left) AND BUTTERED PASTRY (right),
PHOTOGRAPHED IN BRETAGNE
PIERRE HUSSENOT/AGENCE TOP

BAKED CHERRY CUSTARD

Lorraine

BABA
Rum Baba

Finding the kugelhopf too dry for his taste, Stanislas Leszczynski had the idea of moistening it with Malaga wine. He christened the new dish "Ali Baba" in honor of his favorite book, the Thousand and One Nights. *Subsequently it became known simply as a* baba, *and the Malaga wine was replaced by rum.*

3 teaspoons sugar
¼ cup (2 fl oz/60 ml) warm water
1 envelope (½ oz/15 g) dry yeast
3 tablespoons milk
2 oz (60 g) butter
1 cup (4 oz/125 g) all purpose (plain) flour
2 eggs
3 pinches of salt
For the syrup:
¾ cup (6½ oz/200 g) sugar
1½ cups (12 fl oz/400 ml) water
6 tablespoons dark rum

❖Place 1 teaspoon sugar in a 1-cup (8-fl-oz/250-ml) measure. Add the warm water and stir until the sugar dissolves. Sprinkle the yeast over the surface and let stand in a warm place for about 10 minutes or until the mixture has risen almost to the top of the cup.
❖Meanwhile, heat the milk to lukewarm in a small saucepan. Work the butter with a wooden spoon until creamy. Sift the flour into a mixing bowl and make a well in the

Limousin

CLAFOUTIS
Baked Cherry Custard

The origin of the clafoutis *is not known, but both the Limousin and the Auvergne — where the very similar* millard *is made — claim this honor.*

1½ lb (750 g) ripe black cherries, not pitted
2 eggs
1 egg yolk
½ cup (4 oz/125 g) sugar
2½ oz (75 g) butter, melted
⅔ cup (2½ oz/75 g) all purpose (plain) flour
1 cup (8 fl oz/250 ml) milk
vanilla sugar

❖Preheat oven to 400°F (200°C). Wash, dry and stem the cherries.
❖Butter an ovenproof china or glazed earthenware mold large enough to hold the cherries in a single layer. Place the cherries in it. Combine the eggs and yolk in a bowl, add the sugar and whisk until the mixture is pale in color. Whisk in the butter. Sift in the flour and mix well, then mix in the milk. Continue beating until the batter is smooth, then pour over the cherries.
❖Bake for 40 minutes or until browned. Remove the *clafoutis* from the oven and sprinkle with vanilla sugar. Serve lukewarm, from the baking dish.

SERVES 6

RUM BABA

center. Add the eggs, salt, the remaining sugar, the milk and the yeast mixture to the well and mix. Add the butter and mix again. Knead the dough until smooth and elastic, lifting it as high as possible and letting it fall to force in as much air as possible.

❖Butter a 9-in (24-cm) baba mold and place the dough in it. Cover with a cloth and let rise until level with the edge of the mold, about 1 hour.

❖Preheat oven to 400°F (200°C). Bake the baba for 25 minutes.

❖Meanwhile, prepare the syrup: combine the sugar and water in a saucepan and bring to boil. Remove from heat and stir in the rum.

❖When the baba is baked, turn it out onto a serving plate. Prick it all over and spoon the syrup over, scooping up the syrup that runs down onto the plate and spooning it back over the cake until it is soaked all over. Refrigerate for at least 4 hours before serving.

SERVES 6

Ile de France

MERINGUES À LA CHANTILLY
Meringues Chantilly

In 1720, during his exile in Alsace, the former king of Poland Stanislas Leszczynski, a great gourmet, had the pastrycook Gasparini brought over from Switzerland. He created a cake which was called "meringue" after the Swiss village of Mehringen where he was born. As for the chantilly, it had been created earlier, in 1714, by a chef named Vatel who officiated in the château at Chantilly.

For the meringues:
4 egg whites
⅔ cup (5 oz/150 g) superfine (caster) sugar
⅔ cup (3½ oz/100 g) powdered (icing) sugar
For the chantilly:
2 cups (16 fl oz/500 ml) very cold heavy (double) cream
2 tablespoons superfine (caster) sugar

❖Make the meringues: preheat the oven to 225°F (110°C). Butter and flour a baking sheet. Beat the egg whites to soft peaks in a large mixing bowl. Gradually add ¼ cup (2 oz/60 g) superfine sugar and continue to beat until the mixture is smooth and shiny. Add the remaining superfine sugar and beat for another 2 minutes at low speed. Fold in the powdered sugar with a rubber spatula.

❖Transfer the meringue to a pastry bag fitted with a ¾-in (2-cm) fluted tip and pipe onto the prepared baking sheet in small domes or swirls as desired.

❖Bake the meringues for about 1 hour, without letting them brown. They should be ivory-colored; if they begin to brown, lower the heat. Remove the baked meringues with a metal spatula and let cool on a rack.

❖Prepare the chantilly: shortly before serving, whip the cream with an electric mixer until firm. Add the sugar and beat until the cream forms soft peaks.

❖Place the cream in a pastry bag fitted with a small smooth or fluted tip. Pipe it onto the flat side of one meringue and sandwich with a second meringue. Continue with the remaining meringues and cream. Serve at once.

MAKES APPROXIMATELY 16   *Photograph pages 222 – 223*

PETER JOHNSON

PRUNES COOKED IN WINE (top) AND ANGEVINE PEARS (bottom, recipe page 232)

Val de Loire

PRUNEAUX AU VIN
Prunes Cooked in Wine

2 lemons
1 vanilla bean (pod)
2 lb (1 kg) prunes
3 cups (24 fl oz/750 ml) red wine, such as Vouvray
1 cinnamon stick, 4 in (10 cm) long
⅓ cup (2½ oz/75 g) sugar

❖Wash the lemons and wipe dry. Remove the zest of each in a long strip; reserve the pulp for another use. Split the vanilla bean in two lengthwise.

❖Place the prunes in a large bowl and cover with the wine. Add the lemon zest, vanilla bean and cinnamon stick. Cover and let the prunes soak for 4 hours.

❖Drain the prunes and pour the wine into a large nonaluminum saucepan with the lemon zest, vanilla bean, cinnamon stick and sugar. Bring to boil over high heat, stirring until the sugar has dissolved. Add the prunes and poach gently for 10 minutes. Drain and set them aside. Boil the cooking liquid over high heat until reduced to about 1 cup (8 fl oz/250 ml) of syrupy, fragrant liquid. Pour this over the prunes and discard the lemon zest, cinnamon stick and vanilla bean. Let cool, then cover and refrigerate for 12 hours before serving.

SERVES 6

Anjou

POIRES BELLES-ANGEVINE
Angevine Pears

1 lemon
3 cups (24 fl oz/750 ml) red wine
1 cinnamon stick, 4 in (10 cm) long
½ cup (4 oz/125 g) sugar
4 large perfumed pears, about 7 oz (220 g) each

❖Wash the lemon and wipe dry. Remove the zest in a long strip; reserve the pulp for another use. Pour the wine into a large nonaluminum saucepan. Stir in the lemon zest, cinnamon stick and sugar. Bring to boil over high heat, stirring until the sugar dissolves.

❖Peel the pears, leaving them whole; do not remove the stems. Arrange on their sides in a flameproof deep-sided dish big enough to hold them without overlapping. Pour the wine mixture over them and poach for 20 minutes over gentle heat, turning often.

❖Drain the pears and set aside in a bowl. Boil the cooking liquid over high heat until reduced to about 1 cup (8 fl oz/250 ml) of fragrant syrup. Remove the lemon zest and cinnamon stick. Coat the pears with the wine syrup and let cool. Refrigerate for at least 2 hours before serving.

SERVES 4   *Photograph page 231*

Alsace

SOUFFLÉ AU KIRSCH
Kirsch Soufflé

5 tablespoons sugar
1 tablespoon cornstarch (cornflour) or potato flour
5 tablespoons milk
4 teaspoons butter
3 tablespoons kirsch
2 egg yolks
3 egg whites
pinch of salt

❖Preheat oven to 390°F (200°C). Butter the bottom and sides of a soufflé dish 6 in (16 cm) in diameter and 4 in (10 cm) deep. Sprinkle with 1 tablespoon sugar and turn the dish in your hands so that the sugar coats the entire inside surface.

❖Combine 2 tablespoons sugar, the cornstarch and the milk in a saucepan and beat briskly with a whisk. Place over moderate heat and bring just to boil, whisking constantly. As soon as the first bubbles appear, remove from heat and whisk in first the butter, then the kirsch and finally the egg yolks.

❖Combine the egg whites and salt in a bowl and beat until stiff. Add the remaining sugar and beat until smooth and shiny. Whisk a large tablespoonful of the whites into the soufflé base in the saucepan, then pour the contents of the saucepan over the remaining whites and fold together with a rubber spatula. Turn the mixture into the soufflé dish and bake for 25 minutes or until puffed and golden. Serve immediately.

SERVES 2

KIRSCH SOUFFLÉ

Ile de France

OEUFS À LA NEIGE
Snow Eggs

1 vanilla bean (pod)
1 qt (1 l) whole milk
8 eggs, separated
⅔ cup (5 oz/150 g) superfine (caster) sugar
For the caramel:
⅓ cup (3 oz/90 g) superfine (caster) sugar
3 tablespoons water

❖Split the vanilla bean lengthwise using a small knife. Place in a saucepan and add the milk. Bring to boil, then remove from heat, cover and let stand to infuse. Place the egg whites in a large bowl and the yolks in a large saucepan.

❖Sprinkle ⅔ of the sugar over the yolks, beating with a whisk or hand beater until the mixture is very pale in color. Beat in the hot milk. Place over low heat and cook, stirring constantly, until the custard coats the spoon. Remove from heat. Strain the mixture into a bowl and let cool, stirring from time to time.

❖Beat the egg whites until very stiff, then beat in the remaining sugar; continue beating until the mixture is the consistency of meringue. Bring several inches of water to boil in an 11-in (28-cm) sauté pan, then reduce the heat so that it barely simmers.

❖Dip a large, long-handled spoon into cold water, then scoop spoonfuls of the egg white from the bowl and place one by one into the simmering water; plunge the spoon into cold water beforehand so that the egg white will slide off easily. Turn each spoonful after 30 seconds and cook for 30 seconds on the other side. When the whites are cooked, use a skimmer to remove them from the water. Set on a wire rack that is covered with a cloth, not touching one another.

❖To serve, pour the custard into a bowl and pile the cooked egg whites on it in a dome shape. To prepare the caramel, cook the sugar and water in a saucepan over gentle heat to form an amber-colored syrup. Pour over the eggs in a thin stream and serve at once.

SERVES 6   *Photograph pages 222 – 223*

Bretagne

SORBET AUX FRAISES
Strawberry Water Ice

From May to July the whole of France enjoys the wonderfully sweet and fragrant fruit known as the strawberry. The most sought-after is the variety from Plougastel (Bretagne's "strawberry capital"), with its incomparable taste and flavor.

⅔ cup (5 oz/160 g) sugar
6 tablespoons water
13 oz (400 g) strawberries
1 tablespoon fresh lemon juice
To serve:
red fruits, such as strawberries, raspberries and/or red
   currants

❖Place the sugar in a saucepan, add the water and bring to boil. Remove from heat. Cool the syrup by plunging the bottom of the pan into cold water

❖Wash and drain the strawberries; remove the hulls. Put through the fine holes of a food mill (if you do not want the seeds in your sorbet) or puree in a blender or processor. Transfer the puree to a bowl and mix in the lemon juice and syrup.

❖Freeze the sorbet in an ice cream maker, following manufacturer's instructions. Serve in scoops in ice cream dishes, accompanied by fruits.

SERVES 4

Anjou

POIRIER D'ANJOU
Pear Cake

1 cup (8 oz/250 g) sugar
2 cups (16 fl oz/500 ml) water
1 vanilla bean (pod), halved lengthwise
2 lb (1 kg) large perfumed pears
3 oz (90 g) butter
¾ cup (6 fl oz/200 ml) milk
1⅔ cups (6½ oz/200 g) all purpose (plain) flour
2 teaspoons baking powder
2 eggs
2 tablespoons red currant jelly
3 tablespoons cointreau

❖Place ⅓ cup (90 g) sugar in a large saucepan. Add the water and vanilla bean and bring to boil over low heat. Halve, peel and core the pears. Place the pear halves in the boiling syrup and cook for 30 minutes or until just tender. Drain, reserving the syrup.

❖Preheat oven to 425 °F (215 °C). Melt the butter in a small saucepan and let cool slightly. Butter a 9-in (24-cm) cake pan. Combine the flour and baking powder in a food processor. Add the eggs, the remaining sugar, the butter and milk and blend to form a smooth batter. Pour into the cake pan. Cut each pear half vertically into slices ⅜ in (1 cm) thick and arrange on top of the batter in a rose pattern, starting from the center. Bake for 40 minutes or until a tester inserted in the center comes out clean.

❖Meanwhile, boil the syrup in which the pears were cooked over high heat until very thick and syrupy. Add the red currant jelly and boil for 1 minute more. Add the cointreau and remove from heat.

❖Coat the cake with this syrup and bake for another 5 minutes. Unmold onto a serving plate. Serve warm or cold.

SERVES 6

STRAWBERRY WATER ICE

PETER JOHNSON

PEAR CAKE

PETER JOHNSON

CHESTNUT MERINGUE

Savoie

MONT BLANC

Chestnut Meringue

*A mound of chestnut puree with whipped cream piled on top —
homage to Mont Blanc.*

4 lb (2 kg) chestnuts
1 qt (1 l) whole milk
1 vanilla bean (pod), halved lengthwise
¾ cup (6½ oz/200 g) sugar
1 cup (8 fl oz/250 ml) chilled heavy (double) cream
1 envelope vanilla sugar or 3 drops vanilla extract (essence)

❖Make a slash in the flat side of each chestnut. Bring a large saucepan of water to boil. Drop in the chestnuts and boil for 5 minutes. Drain and remove the outer shell and the brown inner skin. Pour the milk into a large saucepan, add the vanilla bean and bring to boil. Add the chestnuts. Cover and cook for 30 minutes, stirring from time to time.
❖Stir in the sugar and cook, stirring frequently, for about 30 minutes more or until the mixture forms a thick puree that comes away from the sides of the saucepan.
❖Put the puree through the fine holes of a food mill, held over a serving plate. Try not to break the vermicelli-like threads of chestnut if possible. Refrigerate for at least 2 hours.
❖At serving time, whip the cream with the vanilla sugar. Transfer it to a piping bag fitted with a small smooth or fluted tip and decorate the top and sides of the Mont Blanc. Serve immediately.

SERVES 6

Languedoc

GIMBLETTES D'ALBI

Albi Rings

Ring cookies used to form part of the decorations hung on olive branches on Palm Sunday. Nowadays they have become an everyday cookie.

2 tablespoons sugar
3 tablespoons warm water
1 envelope (½ oz/15 g) dry yeast
3 tablespoons milk
2 oz (60 g) butter
3¼ cups (13 oz/400 g) all purpose (plain) flour
3 eggs
grated rind of 1 lemon
2 oz (60 g) candied citron peel, diced
1 teaspoon orangeflower water
For the glaze:
1 egg yolk
1 tablespoon milk

❖Combine 1 teaspoon sugar and the warm water in a 6-oz (200-ml) glass and stir until the sugar dissolves. Sprinkle the yeast on top and mix it in. Let stand in a warm place for 10 minutes.
❖Heat the milk in a small saucepan. Add the butter and stir until it melts, then let cool slightly.
❖Sift the flour into a mixing bowl and mix in the remaining sugar. Make a well in the center and add the milk mixture, eggs, lemon rind, citron peel, orangeflower water and yeast mixture. Blend with a spatula, starting from the center and working out, until the dough becomes too thick to work with the spatula. Then knead with your hands for 10 minutes, lifting and letting the dough drop to the work surface frequently to incorporate as much air as possible. Roll the dough into a ball and return to the mixing bowl. Cover the bowl with a cloth and let the dough rise in a warm place for about 1½ hours or until it has doubled in volume.
❖Knead the dough for 2 minutes, then divide it into 1½-oz (40-g) pieces. Roll into small balls and push a hole into the center of each with your index finger dipped in flour. Rotate each ball on your finger to make a ring shape. Bring a large saucepan of water to a slow boil. Drop in the rings of dough and cook for about 30 seconds or until they puff up and rise to the surface. Lift out with a skimmer and arrange on a cloth.
❖Preheat oven to 400°F (200°C). Butter a baking sheet and arrange the rings on it. Beat the egg yolk and milk with a fork and brush each ring with the mixture. Bake the cookies for 20 minutes or until browned. Cool on racks before serving.

MAKES ABOUT 20 COOKIES

ALBI RINGS (right) AND SWEET BREAD (left)

PASTIS LANDAIS
Sweet Bread

5 tablespoons superfine (caster) sugar
3 tablespoons warm water
1 envelope (½ oz/15 g) dry yeast
2 oz (60 g) butter
2½ cups (10 oz/300 g) all purpose (plain) flour
3 pinches of salt
2 tablespoons anise liqueur
1 tablespoon orangeflower water
grated rind of 1 lemon
½ teaspoon vanilla extract (essence)
2 eggs, separated

❖Combine 1 teaspoon sugar and the warm water in a 6 oz (200 ml) glass and stir until the sugar dissolves. Sprinkle the yeast on top and mix it in. Let stand in a warm place for 10 minutes.
❖Melt the butter in a small saucepan and let cool.
❖Sift the flour into a mixing bowl and mix in the remaining sugar and the salt. Make a well in the center and add the liqueur, orangeflower water, lemon rind, vanilla, melted butter, egg yolks and yeast mixture to the well. Blend with a spatula, starting from the center and working out, until the dough becomes too thick to work with the spatula. Knead it with your hands for 10 minutes, lifting and letting the dough drop to the work surface frequently to incorporate as much air as possible. Return the dough to the bowl.
❖Beat the egg whites to soft peaks. Beat ⅓ into the dough to loosen it, then fold in the remaining whites in two portions. Cover the bowl with a cloth and let rise in a warm place for about 1½ hours or until doubled in volume.
❖Butter a 7-in (18-cm) charlotte mold. Place the dough in the mold and let rise for 45 minutes or until it reaches the top of the mold.
❖Preheat oven to 400°F (200°C). Bake the *pastis* for 45 minutes or until risen and browned.
❖Let cool for 10 minutes, then turn out onto a rack to cool.

SERVES 6

GÂTEAU DE NANCY
Nancy Cake

5 oz (150 g) semisweet or bittersweet (plain) chocolate
4 oz (125 g) butter
½ cup (4 oz/125 g) superfine (caster) sugar
4 eggs, separated
1 cup (3½ oz/100 g) ground almonds
1 level tablespoon potato starch (potato flour)
For serving:
2 tablespoons powdered (icing) sugar

❖Preheat oven to 375°F (190°C). Butter an 8-in (22-cm) cake pan. Melt the chocolate over hot water, add the butter and stir with a spatula until smooth. Let cool slightly.
❖Combine the sugar and egg yolks and whisk until pale in color. Beat in the chocolate mixture. Combine the

NANCY CAKE (bottom) AND ORANGE TARTLETS (top)

PETER JOHNSON

ground almonds and potato starch and stir in. Beat the egg whites to soft peaks and fold into the batter.
❖Pour the batter into the prepared pan and bake for 35 minutes or until a tester inserted in the center comes out clean.
❖Let the cake rest at room temperature for 10 minutes before turning it out onto a plate. Let cool completely. Sift the powdered sugar over it before serving.

SERVES 6

BARQUETTES D'ORANGES
Orange Tartlets

1½ cups (7 oz/200 g) blanched almonds
1 cup (7 oz/200 g) superfine (caster) sugar
9 tablespoons potato starch (potato flour)
3 tablespoons curaçao
2 oranges
4 egg whites
3 tablespoons granulated sugar

❖Preheat oven to 375°F (190°C). Butter 24 3-in (8-cm) oval tartlet molds (*barquettes*).
❖In a food processor, grind the almonds and ⅔ cup (5 oz/150 g) superfine sugar to a fine powder. Transfer to a mixing bowl. Sift in the potato starch and add the curaçao. Wash and dry the oranges and remove the rind with a lemon zester. Add the strips of rind to the bowl.
❖Beat the egg whites to soft peaks. Gradually add the remaining superfine sugar and continue beating to stiff peaks. Fold in the almond mixture.
❖Divide the dough among the prepared molds and flatten lightly with the back of a spoon to level the surface. Sprinkle granulated sugar over each tartlet.
❖Arrange the molds on a baking sheet and bake for 25 minutes or until browned. Let cool in the tins for 10 minutes before turning them out onto a wire rack to cool completely.

SERVES 6

PETER JOHNSON

VANILLA CUSTARD WITH CARAMEL SAUCE

Ile de France

CRÈME CARAMEL

Vanilla Custard with Caramel Sauce

This family dessert is sometimes made without the caramel, in which case it goes by the name of oeufs au lait *(eggs with milk).*

1 vanilla bean (pod)
1 qt (1 l) whole milk
¾ cup (6½ oz/200 g) sugar
½ teaspoon fresh lemon juice
2 tablespoons water
8 eggs

❖Preheat oven to 340°F (170°C). Split the vanilla bean in two lengthwise and place in a saucepan with the milk. Bring to simmer, then remove from heat. Cover and let stand to infuse.
❖Place half the sugar in a small saucepan. Add the lemon juice and water and bring to boil. Cook until an amber-colored caramel forms. Remove from heat and pour the caramel into a 2-qt (2-l) metal charlotte mold, soufflé dish or cake tin; it may also be divided among individual soufflé dishes. Quickly turn the mold in your hands so the caramel coats the bottom and sides.
❖Break the eggs into a large bowl and add the remaining sugar. Whisk until well blended, then whisk in the hot milk. Put the mixture into the mold through a fine sieve.
❖Place the mold in a bain-marie and bake for 1 hour (45 minutes for individual molds), or until the custard is set and a knife inserted in the center comes out clean.
❖Remove the *crème caramel* from the water bath and let cool. Unmold onto a plate and serve at room temperature or cold. If it is to be served cold, keep refrigerated until serving time, then plunge the bottom of the mold into hot water for 30 seconds before unmolding the custard.

SERVES 6 – 8

Bretagne

TARTE AUX FRAISES

Strawberry Tart

10 oz (300 g) sweet pastry (recipe page 246)
½ cup (6½ oz/200 g) raspberry jam
2 tablespoons water
2 lb (1 kg) strawberries

❖Preheat oven to 425°F (215°C). Butter a 10-in (26-cm) tart plate (flan tin). Roll out the pastry into a 12-in (30-cm) circle and line the plate with it. Line with parchment paper and fill with dried beans or pie weights. Bake the pastry for 15 minutes, then remove the beans and paper and bake until the bottom is golden, about 20 minutes. Cool the tart shell on a wire rack. (The shell may be prepared several hours in advance.)
❖An hour before serving time, combine the raspberry jam and water in a small saucepan and cook over low heat until the jam melts. Remove from heat and let cool. Wash, drain and hull the strawberries. Dry with paper towels and refrigerate.
❖Fifteen minutes before serving, arrange the strawberries in the pastry shell, pointed ends up. Coat with the cooled jam and serve.

SERVES 8

Alsace

TARTE AUX POMMES À L'ALSACIENNE

Alsatian Apple Tart

10 oz (300 g) sweet pastry (recipe page 246)
1 lb (500 g) Golden Delicious or pippin apples
4 egg yolks
⅓ cup (3 oz/90 g) sugar
1 envelope vanilla sugar or 3 drops vanilla extract (essence)
4 pinches of cinnamon
¾ cup (6 fl oz/200 ml) heavy (double) cream

❖Preheat oven to 425°F (215°C). Butter a 10-in (26-cm) deep tart plate (flan tin). Roll out the pastry dough into a 12-in (30-cm) circle and line the plate with it.
❖Peel, quarter and core the apples. Cut each quarter into 4 slices. Arrange evenly over the pastry in the form of a rose, starting from the outside and overlapping the slices slightly. Bake for 15 minutes.
❖Meanwhile, combine the egg yolks, sugar, vanilla sugar and cinnamon and beat well. Beat in the cream. Coat the apples with this mixture and bake for another 35 minutes or until the apples are tender. Serve warm.

SERVES 6

STRAWBERRY TART (top) AND
ALSATIAN APPLE TART (bottom)
PETER JOHNSON

Provence

TARTE AU CITRON
Lemon Tart

8 oz (250 g) sweet pastry (recipe page 246)
3 lemons
4 eggs
4 oz (125 g) butter
1 cup (7 oz/220 g) superfine (caster) sugar

❖Preheat oven to 425°F (215°C). Butter a 9-in (24-cm) tart plate (flan tin). Roll out the dough to an 11-in (28-cm) circle and line the tart plate with it. Line with parchment paper and fill with dried beans or pie weights. Bake for 15 minutes.

❖Meanwhile, prepare the filling: wash and dry lemons. Grate the rinds into a bowl. Halve the lemons and squeeze out the juice; pour ¾ cup (6 fl oz/200 ml) of the juice into the bowl. Separate 3 of the eggs. Combine the yolks and whole egg and beat with a fork. Place the whites in a larger bowl.

❖Melt the butter in a saucepan, add ¾ cup (6 oz/185 g) of the sugar and mix well. Add the egg yolk and lemon mixtures and cook over low heat, beating constantly, for 5 minutes or until the mixture thickens. Strain into a large bowl and let cool.

❖Remove the beans and paper from the tart shell and bake until browned, about 10 more minutes. Pour in the lemon filling. Beat the egg whites until very stiff, then beat in the remaining sugar to form a meringue. Spread the meringue evenly over the surface of the tart, using either a large spoon or a piping bag with plain tip. Return the tart to the oven for 10 to 15 minutes or until the meringue is golden. Let cool completely before serving.

SERVES 6   *Photograph page 4*

Provence

TOURTE AUX BLETTES
Swiss Chard Pie

13 oz (400 g) sweet pastry (recipe page 246)
1½ lb (800 g) Swiss chard greens (silverbeet)
2 eggs
½ cup (3½ oz/100 g) firmly packed brown sugar
2 oz (60 g) Edam, Gouda or Emmenthaler cheese, freshly and finely grated
⅔ cup (3 oz/90 g) currants
2½ oz (75 g) pine nuts
1 teaspoon grated lemon rind
freshly ground pepper
1 egg yolk
1 tablespoon milk

❖Preheat oven to 400°F (200°C). Butter an 8-in (22-cm) deep-sided ovenproof china pie plate. Divide the dough in two, one piece a little larger than the other. Roll out the larger piece into a 10-in (25-cm) circle and line the pie plate with it.

❖Wash the chard and place in a very large pot with the water still clinging to the leaves. Cover and cook over high heat for 5 minutes. Drain in a colander and let cool. Squeeze the chard between your hands to get rid of as much moisture as possible, then chop it coarsely.

❖Break the eggs into a mixing bowl and beat in the sugar with a fork. Add the cheese, chard, currants, pine nuts, lemon rind and pepper and mix well. Pour this filling into the pastry shell. Using a pastry brush, moisten the edge of the pastry, then lay the remaining pastry over the top of the filling and crimp the edges of the pastry to seal.

❖Beat the egg yolk and milk and brush the entire surface of the pie with this mixture. Bake for 45 minutes or until the crust is golden. Let the pie cool for 10 minutes before turning it out onto a wire rack. Serve at room temperature.

Provence

FOUGASSE
Provençal Fruit Loaf

Originally this "hearth-cake" was one of the thirteen Provençal Christmas desserts. In some areas it is called fouace, *in others* pompe *or* pogne.

Today you can buy it in any bakery all year round, either savory, filled with anchovies or bacon, or sweet and filled with candied fruit or sprinkled with coarsely crushed loaf sugar.

1 tablespoon superfine (caster) sugar
¼ cup (2 fl oz/60 ml) warm water
1 envelope (½ oz/15 g) dry yeast
7 tablespoons milk
4 cups (1 lb/500 g) all purpose (plain) flour
3 pinches of salt
3 tablespoons olive oil
1 tablespoon orangeflower water
6½ oz (200 g) mixed candied fruit and peel
1 egg yolk
1 tablespoon milk

❖Place the sugar in a 1-cup (250-ml) measure. Add the warm water and stir until the sugar dissolves. Sprinkle the yeast over the surface, stir in and let stand in a warm place for about 10 minutes or until the mixture has risen almost to the top of the cup. Meanwhile, heat 6 tablespoons milk to lukewarm in a small saucepan.

❖Sift the flour into a mixing bowl and make a well in the center. Add the salt, oil, orangeflower water, milk and yeast mixture to the well and mix. Knead the dough until it is smooth and comes away from your fingers. Cover with a cloth and let rise until doubled in volume, about 2 hours.

❖Preheat oven to 425°F (215°C). Chop the candied fruit and peel into ¼-in (.5-cm) cubes. Punch the dough down and knead in half the fruit. Form into a large figure 8.

❖Oil a baking sheet and place the dough on it. Arrange the remaining candied fruit and peel on top, pushing the pieces lightly into the dough. Let rise for 20 minutes.

❖Beat the egg yolk and 1 tablespoon milk and brush the dough with this mixture. Bake for about 30 minutes or until the *fougasse* has risen and browned. Let cool on a wire rack before serving.

SERVES 6

Bretagne

GALETTE BRETONNE
Rum and Butter Cake

2 oz (60 g) candied angelica, finely diced
3 tablespoons rum
5 oz (150 g) soft unsalted butter
⅔ cup (5 oz/150 g) superfine (caster) sugar
pinch of salt
2 cups (8 oz/250 g) all purpose (plain) flour
2 eggs
To glaze:
1 egg yolk
1 tablespoon milk

❖Preheat oven to 400°F (200°C). Butter a deep 9-in (24-cm) ovenproof china tart plate or quiche dish. Place the angelica in a small bowl, sprinkle with the rum and stir.
❖Cream the butter, sugar and salt until pale in color. Using a rubber spatula, stir in half the flour and the eggs, then the remaining flour and the rum-soaked angelica. Add any unabsorbed rum. Press the dough into the center of the tart plate and out to the edge, keeping the surface as smooth as possible.
❖Beat the egg yolk and milk together with a fork and brush over the surface of the _galette_. With the point of a knife, mark the surface with a grid pattern. Bake until browned, about 30 minutes. Turn out onto a rack to cool before serving.

SERVES 6

PROVENÇAL FRUIT LOAF (top) AND RUM AND
BUTTER CAKE (bottom)

PETER JOHNSON

PETER JOHNSON

CREAM MOLDS WITH FRUIT

Anjou

CREMETS
Cream Molds with Fruit

1½ cups (12 fl oz/400 ml) heavy (double) cream
2 egg whites
To serve:
superfine (caster) sugar
chilled heavy (double) cream
red fruits, such as strawberries, raspberries and/or
   red currants

❖Whip the cream until it forms soft peaks. Whisk the egg whites until stiff but not dry. Gently whisk together the two ingredients.
❖Line 4 small round or heart-shaped perforated molds with cheesecloth (muslin). Each should be large enough to hold a quarter of the mixture. Divide the mixture among them and fold the corners of the cheesecloth over the top. Set the molds on a plate and refrigerate for 3 hours.
❖Fold back the corners of the cheesecloth. Unmold each _cremet_ onto a dessert plate and remove the cloth. Serve with sugar to taste, cream, and fruits of your choice.

SERVES 4

NORMANDY COOKIES (top) AND CRISP HONEY COOKIES (bottom)

Normandie

SABLÉS NORMANDS

Normandy Cookies

These little shortbread cookies are also found in Bretagne, where they are made with low-salt butter and given an egg glaze.

1¼ cups (5 oz/150 g) all purpose (plain) flour
5 tablespoons superfine (caster) sugar
3 oz (90 g) soft butter
2 egg yolks

❖Sift the flour onto a work surface and mix in the sugar. Make a well in the center. Add the butter and egg yolks to the well and mix rapidly with your fingertips until all the ingredients are amalgamated. Roll the dough into a ball and let rest in a cool place for 1 hour.
❖Preheat oven to 375°F (190°C). Butter one large or two small baking sheets. Roll the dough out to a thickness of ¼ in (.5 cm) and cut into 1¼-in to 1½-in (3- to 4-cm) circles using a smooth or fluted round cutter.
❖Arrange the *sablés* on the baking sheet(s) and bake until just turning golden, about 10 minutes. Cool on a rack before serving. *Sablés* will keep for several weeks in an airtight tin.

MAKES APPROXIMATELY 20 COOKIES

Auvergne

CROQUANTS

Crisp Honey Cookies

These particularly crunchy little cakes are a specialty of Mauriac, a pretty little town in Cantal.

2 cups (8 oz/250 g) all purpose (plain) flour
6 tablespoons superfine (caster) sugar

3 tablespoons honey
8 oz (250 g) soft butter
2 eggs
To glaze:
1 egg yolk
1 tablespoon honey

❖Sift the flour onto a work surface and make a well in the center. Add the sugar, honey, butter and eggs and mix quickly with the tips of your fingers to form a smooth, stiff dough. Roll it into a ball and let rest in a cool place for 1 hour.
❖Preheat oven to 375°F (190°C). Butter one large or two small baking sheets. Roll the dough out on a lightly floured surface to a thickness of ¼ in (.5 cm). Cut into different shapes (leaves, hearts, wreaths, etc.) with cookie cutters. Arrange the cookies on the baking sheet(s). Beat the egg yolk and honey together and brush over the cookies. Bake until lightly browned, 15 minutes. Cool on a rack before serving.

MAKES APPROXIMATELY 15 – 25 COOKIES

Artois

TARTE AU SUCRE

Sugar Tart

⅓ cup (2½ oz/75 g) sugar
¼ cup (2 fl oz/60 ml) warm water
1 envelope (½ oz/15 g) dry yeast
6 tablespoons milk
2 cups (8 oz/250 g) all purpose (plain) flour
2½ oz (75 g) soft butter
2 egg yolks
6 pinches of salt
For the topping:
¾ cup (4 oz/125 g) firmly packed brown sugar
2 oz (60 g) butter

❖Place a teaspoonful of sugar into a 1-cup (250-ml) measure. Add the warm water and stir until the sugar is dissolved. Sprinkle the yeast onto the surface, stir to mix and let stand in a warm place for about 10 minutes or until the mixture has risen almost to the top of the cup.
❖Meanwhile, heat the milk to lukewarm in a small saucepan. Sift the flour into a mixing bowl and make a well in the center. Cream the butter in another bowl. Add the remaining sugar and beat until pale in color. Add the egg yolks, milk, yeast mixture and salt and mix well. Pour into the center of the flour and mix to form a smooth dough.
❖Place the dough on a work surface and knead for 10 minutes or until it is smooth and comes away from your fingers. Place it in a mixing bowl, cover with a cloth and let rise in a warm place for 2 hours or until doubled in volume.
❖Preheat oven to 425°F (215°C). Butter an 8-in (22-cm) cake pan. Punch the dough down and knead again for 5 minutes. Roll out into an 8-in (22-cm) circle and lay it in the cake pan. Sprinkle with the brown sugar and dot with the butter. Let rise to the top of the pan, about 20 minutes. Bake for about 30 minutes or until puffed and golden. Serve warm or at room temperature.

SERVES 6

Lorraine

TARTE AU FROMAGE BLANC
Cheese Tart

8 oz (250 g) sweet pastry (recipe page 246)
1 lemon
½ cup (4 oz/125 g) sugar
3 whole eggs
1 egg yolk
1 teaspoon all purpose (plain) flour
6 tablespoons heavy (double) cream or crème fraîche
1 lb (500 g) ricotta cheese, drained

❖Preheat oven to 400°F (200°C). Butter a 9-in (24-cm) deep-sided ovenproof china tart plate. Roll out the pastry into an 11-in (28-cm) circle and line the tart plate with it.
❖Wash and dry the lemon and grate the rind into a bowl. Add the sugar, the whole eggs, the yolk and the flour, and beat with a hand beater until the mixture turns pale in color. Add the cream and the drained cheese and continue beating until smooth.
❖Pour the filling into the pastry shell and smooth the surface with a spatula. Bake for 50 minutes or until the filling is puffed and golden. Let the tart cool before serving.

SERVES 6

Lorraine

GÂTEAU DE METZ
Metz Cake

4 eggs
1 cup (7 oz/200 g) superfine (caster) sugar
1 cup (4 oz/125 g) all purpose (plain) flour
1 scant cup (7 oz/200 g) heavy (double) cream or crème fraîche
4 oz (125 g) semisweet or bittersweet (plain) chocolate, grated

❖Preheat oven to 375°F (190°C). Butter an 8-in (22-cm) round cake pan.
❖Beat the eggs and sugar until the mixture is pale in color. Sift the flour and blend in. Add the cream and chocolate and mix well.
❖Pour the batter into the prepared pan and bake for 45 minutes or until a tester inserted in the center comes out clean.
❖Turn the cake out onto a rack and cool completely before serving.

SERVES 6

SUGAR TART (bottom left), CHEESE TART (bottom right) AND METZ CAKE (top)

PETER JOHNSON

241

PETER JOHNSON

CREAM HORNS (top) AND MADELEINES (bottom)

Lorraine

MADELEINES DE COMMERCY
Madeleines

Stanislas Leszczynski, Marie Leszcynska's cook, Talleyrand's cook Avice, and Mme Perrotin de Barmond's cook, Madeleine Paulmier — have all been credited with the invention of the madeleine. This "little shell of cake, so generously sensual beneath the piety of its stern pleating," as Marcel Proust described it, remains, however, the uncontested specialty of the small town of Commercy.

3 eggs
¼ cup (2 oz/60 g) superfine (caster) sugar
½ teaspoon orangeflower water
2 oz (60 g) soft butter
½ cup (2 oz/60 g) all purpose (plain) flour

❖Preheat oven to 375°F (190°C). Butter 20 to 24 madeleine tins, depending on size.
❖Combine the eggs and sugar and beat until the mixture is pale in color. Stir in the orangeflower water and butter. Sift in the flour and fold in gently.
❖Divide the batter among the molds, filling them ¾ full. Bake for 15 minutes or until the madeleines have risen and are lightly browned. Turn out and cool on a rack before serving.

MAKES APPROXIMATELY 24 MADELEINES

Auvergne

CORNETS DE MURAT
Cream Horns

2 oz (60 g) butter
2 egg whites
6 tablespoons superfine (caster) sugar
½ cup (2 oz/60 g) all purpose (plain) flour
1 tablespoon dark rum
For the filling:
2½ cups (20 fl oz/600 ml) very cold heavy (double) cream
1 envelope vanilla sugar or ¼ teaspoon vanilla extract
(essence)

❖Preheat oven to 375°F (190°C). Butter one large or two small baking sheets. Melt the butter in a small saucepan, then remove from heat and let cool.
❖Beat the egg whites with a fork until frothy. Mix in the sugar. Sift in the flour and stir, then beat in the butter and rum. Drop the batter by tablespoonfuls onto the baking sheet(s); it will spread out slightly to form small circles.
❖Bake for 8 to 10 minutes or until the pastry circles are just golden. Quickly form the hot wafers into cone shapes, inserting the point of the pastry into the neck of a bottle and it will hold its shape until it cools. Let cool completely.
❖At serving time, whip the cream and vanilla sugar to soft peaks. Spoon into a pastry bag filled with a small fluted tip and pipe into the cones.
❖The cream horns may be prepared several hours in advance, but should be served as soon as they are filled.

SERVES 6

Lorraine

MACARONS DE NANCY
Nancy Macaroons

At the time of the French Revolution, when the monastic orders were dispersed in 1792, some nuns found refuge at the home of a middle-class family in rue de la Hache, Nancy. To pay for their lodging they baked these little delicacies, and so great was their success that the nuns who began selling them became known as the "macaroon sisters."

⅔ cup (5 oz/150 g) superfine (caster) sugar
1⅓ cups (5 oz/150 g) ground almonds
2 egg whites
1 tablespoon powdered (icing) sugar

❖Mix the sugar and ground almonds in a mixing bowl. Add the egg whites and beat rapidly with a wooden spoon until well mixed. Cover the bowl and refrigerate for at least 2 and not more than 8 hours.
❖Preheat oven to 350°F (180°C). Lightly oil a baking sheet and line with waxed paper; oil the paper. Divide the dough into 16 balls, shaping them with wet hands. Arrange on the waxed paper and flatten into discs ¼ in (.5 cm) thick. Sift the powdered sugar over them.
❖Bake the macaroons for 15 minutes or until barely colored.
❖Place the waxed paper on a wet tea towel and let the macaroons cool completely. They will come away from the paper very easily.

MAKES APPROXIMATELY 12 MACAROONS

NANCY MACAROONS (center right), BEE'S NEST CAKE (bottom, recipe page 244)
AND ALMOND AND RAISIN CAKE (top, recipe page 244), PHOTOGRAPHED IN ALSACE
PIERRE HUSSENOT/AGENCE TOP

NID D'ABEILLES

Bee's Nest Cake

For the bread dough:
2 cups (8 oz/250 g) all purpose (plain) flour
3 oz (90 g) soft butter
1 egg
6 tablespoons warm milk
1 envelope (½ oz/15 g) dry yeast
2 tablespoons sugar
3 pinches of salt
For the glaze:
2 oz (60 g) butter
1 tablespoon honey
⅓ cup (3 oz/90 g) superfine (caster) sugar
3 oz (90 g) slivered (flaked) almonds
For the custard:
2 cups (16 fl oz/500 ml) milk
3 egg yolks
⅓ cup (3 oz/90 g) sugar
⅓ cup (1½ oz/50 g) all purpose (plain) flour
1 tablespoon kirsch

❖ Prepare the bread dough according to the recipe on page 41, adding the butter and egg with the milk. Let rise until doubled in volume, about 2 hours.

❖ Butter a deep-sided 10-in (26-cm) ovenproof china tart plate. Pat down the dough to its original volume and spread in the tart plate.

❖ Prepare the glaze: heat the butter and honey in a saucepan over gentle heat, stirring until melted. Mix in the sugar and almonds and remove from heat. Distribute this mixture evenly in teaspoonfuls over the dough. Let rise in a warm place until doubled in volume, about 30 minutes.

❖ Preheat oven to 400°F (200°C). Bake the cake for 25 minutes; if it seems to be browning too much, lower the heat to 375°F (190°C).

❖ Meanwhile, prepare the custard: bring the milk to boil in a small saucepan. In a large saucepan, whisk the egg yolks and sugar until pale in color. Add the flour and mix well. Whisk in the boiling milk. Place over medium heat and beat until the custard thickens; let it boil for another minute. Remove from heat and add the kirsch. Let cool, stirring from time to time.

❖ Let the cake cool for 5 minutes, then cover it with a sheet of foil and invert it onto a plate. Turn it back again onto a wire rack to cool completely. Cut horizontally into two halves, fill with the custard and serve.

SERVES 8   *Photograph page 243*

KUGELHOPF

Almond and Raisin Cake

Legend has it that a certain Kügel, a potter by trade, offered hospitality to the Three Wise Men on their way home from Bethlehem. By way of thanks, they are supposed to have made a special mold, the kugelhopf, and baked a cake in it.

The real story of this cake is not known, but it appears that Marie Antoinette brought it to France from Austria, and it has since become one of the glories of the Alsace cuisine.

6 tablespoons raisins
2 tablespoons kirsch
¼ cup (2 oz/60 g) superfine (caster) sugar
¼ cup (2 fl oz/60 ml) warm water
1 envelope (½ oz/15 g) dry yeast
6 tablespoons milk
4 oz (125 g) soft butter
2 cups (8 oz/250 g) all purpose (plain) flour
2 eggs
4 pinches of salt
For the mold:
1 tablespoon butter
2 tablespoons all purpose (plain) flour
2 tablespoons slivered (flaked) almonds
To serve:
1 tablespoon powdered (icing) sugar

❖ Wash the raisins under warm water, drain and place in a bowl. Sprinkle with kirsch.

❖ Place ⅓ of the sugar in a 6-oz (200-ml) glass. Add the warm water and stir until the sugar dissolves. Sprinkle the yeast over the surface and mix in. Let stand in a warm place for about 10 minutes or until the mixture is level with the rim of the glass.

❖ Meanwhile, warm the milk in a small saucepan. Work the butter with a spatula until creamy.

❖ Sift the flour into a mixing bowl. Make a well in the center and add the eggs, salt, remaining sugar, milk and yeast mixture and blend well. Add the butter and mix again. Turn the dough out onto a work surface and knead by hand, adding the raisins; lift the dough as high as possible and let it fall again to achieve maximum aeration.

❖ Butter and flour a 9-in (22-cm) kugelhopf mold. Turn it in your hands and shake it to remove excess flour; press the slivered almonds into the grooves of the fluting. Place the dough mixture into the mold. Cover with a clean towel and let rise for about 1 hour or until it is level with the rim of the mold.

❖ Preheat oven to 375°F (190°C). Bake the kugelhopf for 40 minutes or until golden brown. Turn it out onto a wire rack to cool, then transfer to a serving plate. Sprinkle with powdered sugar and serve.

SERVES 6   *Photograph page 243*

CASTANHET

Chestnut Cake

This cake was traditionally eaten with a glass of the local liqueur after chestnut-gathering in the Cévennes and the Ardèche.

2 lb (1 kg) chestnuts
2 oz (50 g) butter
2 eggs
⅔ cup (5 oz/150 g) superfine (caster) sugar
1 envelope vanilla sugar or 3 drops vanilla extract (essence)

❖ Make a slash on the flat side of each chestnut. Bring a large saucepan of water to boil. Drop in the chestnuts and boil for 30 minutes; drain. While still hot, remove the outer shell and the brown inner skin.

❖ Preheat oven to 400°F (200°C). Butter a 9-in (24-cm) cake pan. Put the chestnuts through the fine holes of a food mill.

Blend in the butter, using a wooden spoon. Whisk the eggs and sugar in a bowl until the mixture is pale in color. Blend in the chestnut puree. Pour into the prepared pan and bake for 30 minutes. Turn the cake out onto a serving plate. Dust the top with vanilla sugar. Let cool before serving.

SERVES 6

Limoges/Auvergne

GÂTEAU AU POTIRON
Pumpkin Cake

2 lb (1 kg) peeled and seeded pumpkin
3 eggs, separated
½ cup (4 oz/125 g) sugar
2 tablespoons dark rum
⅓ cup (1½ oz/50 g) cornstarch (cornflour)
¼ cup (1 oz/25 g) all purpose (plain) flour

❖Cut the pumpkin into ¾-in (2-cm) cubes and steam for 20 minutes or until very soft. Drain in a colander, then put it through the fine holes of a food mill or blend to a smooth puree in a food processor.
❖Preheat oven to 400°F (200°C). Butter a 9-in (24-cm) cake pan or mold. Combine the egg yolks and sugar and whisk until the mixture is pale in color. Stir in the rum and pumpkin puree, then the cornstarch and flour. Beat the egg whites until stiff and fold them gently into the mixture.
❖Pour the batter into the prepared pan and bake for 40 minutes.
❖Let the cake cool for 10 minutes in the pan, then turn out on a rack and cool completely before serving.

SERVES 6

PETER JOHNSON   PUMPKIN CAKE (top) AND CHESTNUT CAKE (bottom)

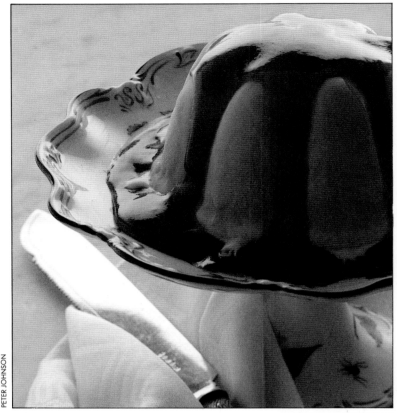

PETER JOHNSON

ICE CREAM PLOMBIÈRES

Lorraine

GLACE PLOMBIÈRES
Ice Cream Plombières

In 1858 Napoleon III met Cavour at Plombières-les-Bains. In honor of the visit, the keeper of a local eating-house invented this dessert, christened plombières, *or* glace plombières. *Today the name is also given to an ice cream made with candied fruits soaked in kirsch, which are added to an almond custard base.*

6 cups (48 fl oz/1.5 l) heavy (double) cream
1⅓ cups (7 oz/220 g) blanched almonds
1 cup (8 fl oz/250 ml) milk
10 egg yolks
1 cup (7 oz/220 g) sugar
½ teaspoon almond extract (essence)
¾ cup (8 oz/250 g) apricot jam

❖Bring 4 cups (32 fl oz/1 l) cream to boil in a saucepan. Remove from heat. Combine the almonds and milk in a food processor. Blend until the almonds are ground, then pour the mixture through a strainer into the cream in the saucepan.
❖Combine the egg yolks and sugar in a second saucepan and whisk until the mixture is very pale in color. Add the almond milk and cook over gentle heat, stirring constantly, until the custard coats the spoon. Remove from heat and add the almond extract. Let cool, stirring from time to time.
❖When the custard is completely cooled, whip the remaining cream until it forms soft peaks. Fold into the almond mixture. Pour into a large round or square mold and freeze until firm.
❖Meanwhile, heat the jam in a small saucepan. Force through a fine strainer and let cool.
❖Plunge the mold into hot water for 20 seconds; then unmold the ice cream onto a plate. Coat with the jam and serve immediately.

SERVES 8

UPSIDE DOWN APPLE TART

Orléanais

TARTE TATIN

Upside Down Apple Tart

The Tatin sisters ran a restaurant at Lamotte-Beuvron in Sologne at the beginning of this century. They created this tart, with its crusty golden pastry beneath a filling of soft caramelized apples. Being cooked upside down, it also goes by the name of tarte renversée *or* tarte à l'envers.

3 oz (90 g) soft butter
⅓ cup (3 oz/90 g) sugar
3 lb (1.5 kg) Golden Delicious or pippin apples
8 oz (250 g) sweet pastry (recipe below)

❖Preheat oven to 425 °F (215 °C). Grease a 9-in (24-cm) cake pan with ⅔ of the butter, then sprinkle over ⅔ of the sugar. Cut the apples in two, peel and core them, and arrange the halves upright, tightly packed in the cake pan. Sprinkle with the remaining sugar and the butter which has been cut into small pieces. Place the pan over medium heat and cook for 20 minutes or until a light caramel forms on the bottom.
❖Transfer the pan to the oven and bake for 5 minutes to cook the top surface. Remove from the oven.
❖Roll out the dough to a 10-in (26-cm) circle. Place over the cake pan and pass the rolling pin around the edge to remove the overhanging pastry. The dough will sink down the sides of the tin onto the top of the apples.
❖Return the pan to the oven and bake for 20 minutes or until the pastry is well browned. Invert the tart onto a serving plate and serve at once.

SERVES 6

PÂTE SUCRÉE

Sweet Short (Shortcrust) Pastry

For approximately 1 lb (500 g) pastry: *
4 oz (125 g) soft butter
⅓ cup (3 oz/90 g) superfine (caster) sugar
1 egg
2 cups (8 oz/250 g) all purpose (plain) flour
2 pinches of salt

❖Cream the butter and sugar until pale and fluffy. Add the egg and mix for 30 seconds. Add the flour and salt and mix until a smooth dough forms.
❖Place the pastry on a work surface and knead, pushing it out with the palm of the hand then reforming it into a ball, until the dough is smooth and elastic; this should take about 5 minutes. Wrap the ball of dough in plastic and refrigerate for at least 2 hours, preferably longer. Remove from the refrigerator 1 hour before using. Any leftover pastry can be stored in the refrigerator for 4 days or frozen.
❖The egg will prevent this pastry from becoming soggy, even when cooked directly with the filling. It may also be baked blind, in large or small pans, by covering the pastry with waxed or parchment paper and filling it with rice, dried beans or pie weights.

* *Makes enough to line two 9- to 10-inch (24- to 26-cm) pans.*

Ile de France

PARIS–BREST

Praline Butter Cream Cake

A Paris pastrycook was watching the Paris-to-Brest cycling race passing in front of his shop in 1891 when he had the idea of creating this cake, which is ring-shaped like a bicycle wheel.

13 oz (400 g) choux pastry (recipe page 247)
1 egg white
2 oz (60 g) slivered (flaked) almonds
For the filling:
1⅓ cups (11 oz/350 ml) milk
3 egg yolks
⅓ cup (3 oz/90 g) superfine (caster) sugar
½ vanilla bean (pod)
¾ cup (3 oz/90 g) all purpose (plain) flour
100 g powdered praline (see below)
3 oz (90 g) soft butter
2 tablespoons powdered (icing) sugar
For the praline:
2 oz (60 g) almonds, coarsely chopped
¼ cup (2 oz/60 g) sugar
3 drops lemon juice

❖Preheat oven to 425 °F (215 °C). Lightly oil a nonstick baking sheet. Place an 8-in (20-cm) plate in the center of it. Place the choux pastry dough into a pastry bag fitted with a plain ¾-in (1.5-cm) tip and pipe a circle of pastry around the edge of the plate. Remove the plate and pipe another circle of pastry inside the first one, then pipe a third circle overlapping the first two. Lightly beat the egg white with a fork until frothy and brush over the pastry. Scatter the slivered almonds over. Bake for 15 minutes, then lower the heat to 375 °F (190 °C) and bake for 15 minutes longer.
❖Meanwhile, prepare the filling: bring the milk to boil in a small saucepan. Combine the egg yolks, sugar and vanilla bean in a large saucepan and whisk until the mixture turns pale in color. Add the flour and mix again. Whisk in the boiling milk. Place over moderate heat and cook the custard, beating constantly, until it thickens. Let it boil for 1 minute, then remove from heat and let cool, stirring occasionally. When cool, add the praline and then the butter, beating by hand for 2 minutes. Refrigerate.
❖To make the praline: in a dry pan over medium heat,

lightly brown the almonds for 5 minutes. In a separate pan melt the sugar with the lemon juice to make a light caramel. Add the almonds and mix for 2 minutes until the caramel darkens. Pour onto a marble slab and let cool completely. Break the caramel and pound or grind to a fine powder.

❖Let pastry stand in the turned-off oven for 10 minutes with the oven door slightly ajar. Remove from the oven and let cool. Cut the pastry in two horizontally, a third of the way from the top; the bottom part, which is to be filled, must be higher.

❖Place the cooled filling in a pastry bag fitted with a fluted ¾-in (2-cm) tip. Fill the bottom of the pastry with the custard, letting it overlap the edges slightly. Replace the top third of the pastry. Sprinkle with powdered sugar and keep in a cool place until serving time.

SERVES 6   *Photograph pages 222 – 223*

PÂTE À CHOUX
Choux Pastry

For approximately 1 lb 10 oz (800 g) pastry:
1¼ cups (150 g) all purpose (plain) flour
1 cup (8 fl oz/250 ml) water
2 teaspoons sugar
1 teaspoon salt
3 oz (90 g) butter
5 eggs

❖Sift the flour into a large bowl. Combine the water, sugar, salt and butter in a saucepan over low heat and bring just to boil. Remove from heat. Pour in all the flour, stirring quickly with a wooden spoon.

❖Return the saucepan to the stove and stir over low heat for 1 minute longer to dry out the mixture. Remove from heat and beat in the eggs one at a time, completely incorporating each before the next is added. Once the last egg has been mixed in, stop stirring; this helps produce smooth, uniform puffs.

❖The finished pastry may be used immediately or wrapped in plastic and refrigerated for several days.

Provence

OREILLETTES
Pastry Puffs

Oreillettes *in Provence,* bottereaux *in Vendée,* bugnes *in Lyon,* frivolles *in Champagne,* merveilles *in Charentes,* guenilles *in Auvergne,* carquelin *in Savoie — all these are names for the fritters that are made all over France for Mardi Gras, Mid-Lent, Christmas, and at times of family celebration.*

2½ cups (10 oz/300 g) all purpose (plain) flour
3 eggs
1 oz (30 g) soft butter
grated rind of 1 orange and 1 lemon
1 teaspoon orangeflower water
3 pinches of salt
2 qt (2 l) peanut (groundnut) oil
To serve:
superfine (caster) sugar

❖Sift the flour onto a work surface and make a well in the center. Add the eggs, butter, grated rinds, orangeflower water and salt and mix with your fingertips, beginning from the center and working out. Then work the dough by pushing it away from you repeatedly with the flat of your hand until it is smooth and soft and comes away from your fingers.

❖Roll the dough into a ball, wrap in plastic and refrigerate for 4 hours.

❖Roll the dough out on a floured surface as thinly as possible. Cut into 3 x 1½-in (8 x 4-cm) rectangles. Heat the oil in a deep fryer to 375°F (190°C). Drop in the dough pieces in batches and fry until puffed and brown. Turn with a skimmer, remove and then drain on paper towels.

❖When all the pastries are cooked, pile them on a plate, sprinkling sugar over each layer. They should be served the day they are made.

MAKES APPROXIMATELY 20 – 30   *Photograph page 4*

Normandie

TERRINÉE
Caramel Rice Pudding

Also known as beurgoule *or* teurgoule, *the* terrinée *is a traditional dessert of Normandie. In the old days it was left to cook all night in the baker's oven.*

It is often served with a slice of fallue *— a kind of brioche — or with the Normandie version of* sablés.

2 qt (2 l) whole milk
⅔ cup (4 oz/125 g) short-grain rice
½ cup (4 oz/125 g) superfine (caster) sugar
4 pinches of cinnamon

❖Preheat oven to 175°F (80°C). Pour the milk into a saucepan and bring to boil. Let cool.

❖Mix the rice, sugar and cinnamon in a 4-qt (4-l) baking dish. Stir in the cooled milk. Bake uncovered for 6 hours without disturbing. When the *terrinée* is cooked, the rice will be covered with a thick, shiny brown skin which has a delicious caramel taste. Serve the pudding warm or hot.

SERVES 6

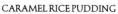
CARAMEL RICE PUDDING

GINGERBREAD

❖Bake for 40 minutes or until a tester inserted in the center comes out clean. Let cool for 15 minutes in the pan, then turn out onto a rack to finish cooling.
❖The gingerbread will keep for several weeks in an airtight tin.

SERVES 6

Pays Basque

GÂTEAU BASQUE
Basque Cake

In Itxassou and Sarre gâteau Basque is filled with black cherries in syrup and cherry jam rather than crème pâtissière.

4½ oz (140 g) butter
2 eggs
11 tablespoons superfine (caster) sugar
1 teaspoon vanilla extract (essence)
1 tablespoon dark rum
2¼ cups (9 oz/280 g) all purpose (plain) flour
1 teaspoon baking powder
2 pinches of salt
For the filling:
1 cup (8 fl oz/250 ml) milk
3 egg yolks
⅓ cup (3 oz/90 g) superfine (caster) sugar
¼ cup (1 oz/30 g) all purpose (plain) flour
1 tablespoon dark rum
1 teaspoon vanilla extract (essence)
For the glaze:
1 egg yolk
1 tablespoon milk

❖Melt the butter in a small saucepan over low heat, then let cool. Combine the eggs, sugar and vanilla and mix well. Blend in the butter and rum. Sift in the flour, baking powder and salt and stir until a soft dough forms. Refrigerate for 1 hour.
❖Meanwhile, prepare the filling: bring the milk to simmer in a small saucepan. Combine the egg yolks and sugar in a large saucepan and whisk until pale in color. Mix in the flour. Beat in the hot milk. Place the saucepan over moderate heat and cook the custard until it thickens, beating constantly. Let boil for 1 minute, then remove from heat and add the rum and vanilla. Let cool, stirring occasionally.
❖Preheat oven to 400°F (200°C). Butter a 10-in (26-cm) round cake pan. Divide the dough into two pieces, one a little larger than the other. Roll out the larger portion into a 9-in (24-cm) circle ⅜ in (1 cm) thick. Carefully line the cake pan with the dough, flattening it against the sides. Spread the custard on top and turn the edge of the dough circle back over the custard, but do not press down. Moisten the edge of the dough with a pastry brush dipped in cold water. Roll out the remaining dough into a 9-in (24-cm) circle and lower it into the pan to cover the custard.
❖For the glaze, beat the egg yolk and milk and brush over the top of the cake. Bake the cake for 40 minutes or until golden brown. Let cool before turning out of the pan. Let the cake rest at room temperature for a few hours before serving.

SERVES 8

Bourgogne

PAIN D'ÉPICES
Gingerbread

References to pain d'épices — a mixture of flours, honey and spices — are found throughout history. In France the most famous version today is that of Dijon, which has taken over from the success of the Rheims pain d'épices.

Its origins certainly go back to 1452, when Philippe Le Bon tasted a galette with honey and spices in Flandres and at once took into his service the man who had prepared it. So began a time of glory for Dijon, with the three feathers in its cap: mustard, cassis and pain d'épices.

½ cup (4 fl oz/125 ml) water
½ cup (4 oz/125 g) sugar
⅓ cup (4 oz/125 g) honey
2 cups (8 oz/250 g) all purpose (plain) flour
½ cup (2 oz/60 g) rye flour
2 teaspoons baking powder
grated rind of 1 orange
1 tablespoon cinnamon
1 teaspoon ground aniseed
½ teaspoon ground ginger
pinch of salt

❖Preheat oven to 375°F (190°C). Butter a 9-in (24-cm) square cake pan. Combine the water and sugar in a saucepan and bring to boil. Cook for 5 minutes over low heat. Remove from heat and stir in the honey.
❖Sift the two flours and the baking powder into a large mixing bowl. Mix in the orange rind, spices and salt. Make a well in the center, pour in the contents of the saucepan and stir for 5 minutes. Turn the batter into the prepared pan.

BASQUE CAKE
PIERRE HUSSENOT/AGENCE TOP

Ile de France

CRÊPES SUZETTE

Orange Liqueur Crêpes

Were these famous pancakes invented in 1896 at the Café de Paris *when the Prince of Wales visited in the company of a lady named Suzette, or in 1898 at the* Maire *restaurant? The mystery remains. As for their filling, some people maintain that mandarin oranges are indispensable; others prefer oranges.*

For the batter:
1 cup (4 oz/125 g) all purpose (plain) flour
2 cups (16 fl oz/500 ml) milk
2 eggs
1 tablespoon sugar
1 envelope vanilla sugar or 3 drops vanilla extract (essence)
1 tablespoon peanut (groundnut) oil
4 pinches of salt
For the garnish:
4 oz (125 g) soft butter
2 mandarin oranges
⅓ cup (3 oz/90 g) sugar
3 tablespoons cognac
6 tablespoons curaçao

❖ Make the batter: place the flour in a food processor. Add the milk, eggs, sugar and vanilla sugar, oil and salt and process until you have a smooth, liquid batter. Pour through a strainer into a bowl and let rest for 1 hour.
❖ Melt 1 oz (20 g) butter in a nonstick 8-in (22-cm) skillet, then pour it into a bowl. Using a small ladle, pour some batter into the skillet and tilt it so that the mixture spreads to cover the bottom. When it is golden on the bottom, about 40 seconds, turn the crêpe over with a spatula and cook for about 30 seconds longer.
❖ Ten minutes before serving, wash the mandarin oranges and wipe dry. Grate the rind finely into the skillet in which the crêpes were cooked. Halve the oranges and squeeze the juice into the skillet. Add the remaining butter, the sugar, 1 tablespoon cognac and 3 tablespoons curaçao and boil until a thick syrup forms, about 1 minute. Dip the crêpes into the syrup one by one, fold each in quarters and arrange on a large plate; keep warm. Drizzle with the syrup remaining in the skillet.
❖ Heat the remaining cognac and curaçao in a small saucepan. Bring the crêpes to the table. Pour the boiling alcohol mixture over them and ignite. Serve as soon as the flames subside.

SERVES 6   *Photograph pages 222 – 223*

Savoie

BISCUIT DE SAVOIE

Savoy Sponge

1 cup (8 oz/250 g) superfine (caster) sugar
7 eggs, separated
2 teaspoons vanilla extract (essence) or the grated rind of 1 lemon
1 scant cup (3½ oz/100 g) all purpose (plain) flour
¾ cup (3½ oz/100 g) potato starch (potato flour)
For serving:

1 tablespoon powdered (icing) sugar

❖ Preheat oven to 280°F (140°C). Butter and flour a 9-in (24-cm) round cake pan.
❖ Combine the sugar, egg yolks and vanilla and beat with an electric mixer at high speed until the mixture is pale in color and tripled in volume. Sift the flour and potato starch and fold in. Beat the egg whites to stiff peaks and fold quickly into the batter.
❖ Spread the batter in the prepared pan and bake for 50 minutes or until the cake is golden brown and a tester inserted in the center comes out clean.
❖ Turn off the oven and let the cake rest for 10 minutes in the oven with the door open, then turn out of the pan onto a wire rack to cool completely. Sprinkle with powdered sugar before serving.
❖ The sponge may be eaten as is or filled with chocolate cream, jam, pastry cream or custard. It can also be used as a base for any kind of charlotte.

SERVES 6

Savoie-Dauphiné

GRENOBLOIS

Grenoble Caramel Walnut Cake

10 oz (300 g) butter
8 oz (250 g) walnuts
6 eggs, separated
1 cup (7 oz/200 g) superfine (caster) sugar
3 tablespoons dark rum
1 teaspoon coffee extract (or 1 teaspoon instant coffee dissolved in 1 teaspoon water)
¾ cup (3 oz/90 g) dry breadcrumbs
For serving:
6 tablespoons sugar
6 tablespoons water
½ teaspoon fresh lemon juice
walnuts

❖ Preheat oven to 400°F (200°C). Butter a 9-in (24-cm) round cake pan. Melt the butter over low heat in a small saucepan and let cool. Finely chop the walnuts in a food processor.
❖ Combine the egg yolks with ⅔ cup (5 oz/150 g) sugar and whisk until the mixture doubles in volume and is pale in color, about 10 minutes. Fold in the butter, rum and coffee extract, then the breadcrumbs and walnuts.
❖ Beat the egg whites to soft peaks, then gradually add the remaining sugar and beat until smooth and shiny. Gently fold the egg whites into the walnut mixture. Pour the batter into the prepared pan and bake until browned, about 35 minutes.
❖ Meanwhile, combine the 6 tablespoons sugar, water and lemon juice in a small saucepan and bring to boil. Cook until a dark caramel forms.
❖ Turn the cake out onto a serving plate. Pour the caramel over and decorate with walnuts. Let cool completely before serving.

SERVES 8

SAVOY SPONGE (top) AND GRENOBLE
CARAMEL WALNUT CAKE (bottom)
PETER JOHNSON

GLOSSARY

ANCHOVIES, SALTED OR IN OIL: salted anchovies are fresh anchovies preserved in brine. They are sold by weight. Anchovies in oil are salted anchovies separated into fillets, rinsed, drained and marinated in oil. They are sold in tins or jars.

ANISE LIQUEUR: a liqueur flavored with star anise, much appreciated in the South of France, where it flavors many desserts.

ARAIGNÉE: this long-legged crab — hence its name, spider crab or *maia squinado* — is caught in the Mediterranean and Atlantic, especially in Aquitaine and the Basque region. Its firm, fine-textured and delicate flesh is much appreciated.

ARMAGNAC: a spirit, distilled from wine, which is produced in a defined area of Gascogne — essentially within the *départment* of Gers. The region is divided into three areas of production: Bas-Armagnac, which produces a first-class brandy; Ténéraze, with its fragrant brandies; and Haut-Armagnac, where the brandies are less well defined. Armagnac is labeled *"monopole," "selection"* or *"trois etoiles"* (three stars) if it has been aged for at least a year; "VO" (very old), "VSOP" (very superior old pale) or *"réserve"* after at least four years of aging; and "extra," *"napoléon," "vieille réserve"* (old reserve) or *"hors d'âge"* when aged for more than five years. Armagnac is excellent for drinking at the end of a meal, and is also used in many main dishes and desserts to add strength and aroma.

ARTICHOKE: the large Breton artichoke is always eaten cooked, while the small purple artichoke of Provence is superb whether cooked or not — like the little *poivrade* artichokes that are munched raw.

BAGUETTE: this is the most familiar form of French bread. It is a long, crusty stick weighing 8 oz (250 g), most commonly prepared with bleached white flour.

BASIL: this herb has symbolized Mediterranean cuisine since the invention of *pistou*. There are several varieties, with smaller or larger leaves and with a more or less pronounced flavor. A decorative purple basil is also available.

BEANS: Broad bean: known for thousands of years, broad beans are most particularly appreciated in all the southern parts of France. Fresh in summer and autumn, they are sold in shells enclosing between five and ten beans of a green color, covered with a skin which must be removed before eating them, raw or cooked. Dried broad beans are also available; they must be soaked before cooking, like other dried beans.

Haricots verts: French green beans are cultivated mostly in the Val de Loire and in Provence, and are eaten from late spring until late fall. Several sizes are available, from thick to extra thin; the thinnest beans are considered the tastiest.

Flageolets: these beans are found ready to be shelled in all markets during late summer and in the fall. Out of season, they can be purchased dried, and should then be soaked for around 12 hours before cooking. These pretty beans, of a delicate green color, can be replaced by any other shelled white beans — navy beans, for example.

BOUQUET GARNI: a combination of herbs and flavorings tied together and used to flavor stocks and simmered dishes. The basic composition includes thyme, bay leaf and parsley, but according to the region and the type of dish, it might also include celery stalks, branches of fennel, leek leaves, orange rind.

BROUSSE DE BREBIS: as the name implies, this is a ewe's milk cheese. It comes fresh in a hemispherical shape, drained in wicker baskets or, today, in plastic cartons. The cheese is white, soft, very mild and flavorful. It is just as delicious in savory preparations (stuffings, tarts) as in desserts (cakes, mousses, charlottes).

BUTTER: a very important ingredient in French cuisine, particularly delicious when farm-made from unpasteurized milk. Most often it is sold in pasteurized form. It is important to differentiate unsalted butter from *demi-sel* or lightly salted butter, a Breton specialty. The best unsalted butters come from Normandie, Charentes and Deux-Sèvres.

CALVADOS: a spirit distilled in Normandie from cider. It is very good used in cooking, and excellent for adding an apple flavor to cakes and pastries. In Bretagne and Normandie a *"café-calva"* is served: the calvados comes with the coffee, and is either drunk after it or poured into the hot coffee before drinking.

CANTAL: a cheese with 45% fat, produced in Auvergne from cow's milk. It is semisoft and comes in the form of a cylinder about 16 in (40 cm) in diameter and 16 in (40 cm) high, weighing about 40 kg. The greyish crust hides a pale-colored cheese, firm and somewhat crumbly, its flavor slightly biting.

CAYENNE PEPPER: a fine red powder often known simply as "cayenne", made from the dried and powdered fruits of the cayenne pepper. These slender, long, pointed and very hot fruits are known as "bird peppers" in the Antilles.

CHEESES: the varieties of French cheese are by now too numerous to mention. Some of them are used mainly as the final addition to a dish; Gruyère or Parmesan, for example, is simply grated over pasta or rice or used in various stuffings. Others, however, are an integral part of a recipe — for example, in Savoie *comté* cheese is used in the celebrated local soufflé and in chicken dishes (see recipes). We should also note the many regional recipes using *beaufort*, goat cheese, *tomme* (made with cow's, goat's or ewe's milk depending on the region) or roquefort (a ewe's milk cheese with veins of blue mold that develop during the aging process).

COCKLE: a pale-shelled mollusk found in the Mediterranean, Baltic and American Atlantic. They can be eaten raw or cooked.

COGNAC: a spirit, distilled from wine, which is made in the area around Cognac, a town in Charentes. Cognac is labeled *"trois étoiles"* (three stars) if it has aged for at least two years; "VO" (very old), "VSOP" (very superior old pale) or *"réserve"* after at least five years of aging; and "extra," *"napoléon"* or *"vieille réserve"* (old reserve) when aged for more than seven years. Cognac is an excellent drink for the end of a meal; it is also used to add aroma to numerous main dishes and desserts. *"Fine champagne"* or liqueur cognac is a blending of the first two cognac vintages (*Grande Champagne* and *Petite Champagne*), containing at least 50% *Grande Champagne*.

CRAYFISH: there are numerous varieties of this little freshwater crustacean, which looks like a miniature lobster. The most famous, and the tastiest (with flavor like a lobster), is the crayfish *à pattes rouges*, with red claws. Unfortunately it is becoming more and more rare in our rivers and is most often imported or farmed.

CRÈME FRAICHE: a mature cream with a nutty, slightly sour tang. It can be made mixing two tablespoons of cultured buttermilk with two cups heavy cream; cover and let stand at room temperature until thick or leave overnight. Stir cream, then cover and refrigerate to thicken it further.

CRÉPINE: caul fat, a very thin membrane with veins of white fat which covers the internal organs of the pig. Used to wrap terrines and pâtés, it must always be soaked in warm water before use, to soften.

CROUTONS: small slices of bread fried in butter or oil, or simply toasted.

EMMENTHALER: a firm cheese, with 45% fat, prepared from cow's milk in the Franche-Comté or Savoie. It comes as enormous wheels 32 in (80 cm) in diameter and 10 in (25 cm) high, weighing as much as 180 lb (90 kg). The crust is smooth and yellow, the cheese mild and fruity, with large holes.

FAISSELLE: a fresh cow's milk cheese, solid in a *faisselle* (hence its name), a sort of colander in which the cheese drains.

GARLIC: it is important to differentiate the new season type from garlic that has been stored. The former appears in the markets around the end of spring and is available until the end of summer; it has a white or purplish bulb and a long stalk. The peeled garlic clove is white, mild and fruity, easy to digest (because the germ has not developed) and aromatic. As it dries, its flavor becomes stronger and more noticeable. Garlic braids can be kept for a whole year in a cool, dry place. After fall, the soft green germ, or shoot, starts to develop in the heart of the cloves. It is indigestible and should be removed, either after the clove of garlic is cut in half or just before it is eaten cooked whole.

GOOSE FAT: this is the fat from inside the goose, melted and then strained. Sold in jars and tins, it is very popular in the cuisine of the southwestern regions. Once used, it may be strained and stored in the refrigerator in a tightly sealed container for about one month. Take care; goose fat quickly becomes rancid.

GUINEA FOWL: this bird has tender flesh with a flavor resembling pheasant.

HAM, COOKED (*jambon cuit*): also known as *jambon de Paris*. Boned and cooked in water, it is traditionally prepared in most *charcuteries*. When the leg of pork is left whole with the bone in, it is called ham on the bone (*jambon à l'os*) or York ham. In both cases the meat must be pale pink and lean, and there must be no sign of moisture. This type of ham is generally served as is, in slices, for first course. It is also one of the most popular sandwich fillings.

HAM, UNCOOKED (*jambon cru*): The best known is certainly Bayonne ham, but every region has its local version, known as *jambon de pays*. Some uncooked hams are smoked. Uncooked ham is eaten as is for a first course, but it also contributes its incomparable flavor to many cooked dishes.

HERBES DE PROVENCE: a blend of dried herbs including thyme, rosemary, bay leaf, savory and lavender.

LANGOUSTINES: these little marine crustaceans – called *scampi* by the Italians and *gambas* by the Spaniards – are fished almost all year round along the Atlantic coast. The tail, from 10 to 15 in (15 to 30 cm) in length, has delicate flesh; the long pincers are almost without flesh. The langoustine's hue of pink, brick or salmon, marked with the finest of lines – showing its years – changes little in cooking.

MALAGA RAISINS: large black grapes dried as a bunch. They are very moist, sweet and flavorsome.

MARC: after the grapes have been pressed for making wine, a solid mass of skins, seeds and stems remains; this is distilled into alcohol known as *marc*. Different wine-growing areas produce *marcs* of different flavors — for example, *marc de Bourgogne* and *marc de Champagne*.

MUSHROOMS, CULTIVATED: white or pink *champignons de Paris* are available all year round. They must always be selected very fresh, with the caps firmly attached around the stalks. The white ones are a uniform ivory color, the pink ones a pinkish-brown. Both tiny and very large mushrooms are excellent; the small ones are used in sautés and gently simmered dishes, while the large ones are often stuffed.

MUSHROOMS, WILD: gathered in the fields and in woods, these mushrooms appear in French markets in spring and fall. Among the best known and most widely used are *cèpes* (boletus mushrooms or *porcini*, of which many varieties exist), the apricot-colored *girolles* (perhaps better known as

chanterelles), morels, blewits, *pleurotes* (which these days are cultivated), *craterelles* (sometimes called in France "trumpets of death"), and of course truffles (q.v.) They are often expensive and sometimes scarce, and are most often served as a vegetable, sautéed briefly with garlic or shallots and sometimes with cream added. But they also add a wonderful flavor to all sorts of stews and simmered dishes. Abroad, and in France too, when out of season, they are often replaced by dried mushrooms.

MUSTARD: Dijon mustard, or strong mustard is a pungent, aromatic mustard, smooth-textured and highly-colored, prepared with white wine. This is mostly used in cooking. There are numerous other varieties of mustard, for the most part served as condiments to accompany cold meats or vegetables and in the making of all sorts of vinaigrettes. *Meaux* mustard is made with coarsely crushed seeds, which accounts for its characteristic texture. It is mainly used as a condiment.

NEW SEASON ONIONS: fresh onions, round or elongated, with green stalks, sold in spring and summer. They may be eaten raw or cooked, and are distinguished by their sometimes pungent flavor.

OIGNONS GRELOTS: small pickling onions, round or oval in shape and about ½ to ¾ in (1 to 1.5 cm) in diameter, principally used as a vegetable accompaniment.

OLIVE OIL: extra virgin or first cold-pressing olive oil is derived from the first crushing of the olives, by mechanical means and not steam. This oil is natural, pure, fruity and unrefined and it is the ideal oil for salads as well as for cooking.

OLIVES: green or black, olives are always treated in brine before being sold. They are sold in brine, or marinated in oil with flavorings, loose or in jars. Niçoise olives are very small olives, macerated in oil and flavorings and prepared in the Nice region.

OYSTERS: true oysters are flat, but the deep ones called *gryphaea* or "Portuguese oysters" are mollusks belonging to the same family. Flat oysters have yellow flesh and a nutty flavor that is sweet rather than savory. The only variety still in existence is the *belon*, which takes its name from the Belon River in which these oysters were once fattened. They are also cultivated in the north of the *département* of Finistère. Flat oysters, with deep green shells and flesh that is almost colorless, are also found at Cancale, Bouzigue and Arcachon.

As for the deep variety, they came to France by accident: in 1868 a Portuguese boat carrying oysters to England lost its cargo off Arcachon. The oysters, which were still alive, reproduced and multiplied. Thus the Portuguese oyster, with its deep, long and narrow shell, was established in France.

The flesh of the oyster is more or less green according to the amount of time it has spent in the breeding park, where it feeds on the plankton that give it its unusual color. The *claires* ("pales") as their name indicates, are very light green in color, having spent only one month in the river basin; the *fines de claires* remain in the basin for three months, so they are greener and have a fuller flavor. As for the *spéciales*, which can stay in the basin for up to two years, they are best of all — a consistent green color, plump and delicate.

Belon and Portuguese oysters are classified by numbers: the 000 and 00 varieties are rare, very large and with a fatty flesh. Those numbered 0 and 1 are large, while no. 2s are medium-sized and no. 3s small. Finally there are the "butterflies," very small Portuguese oysters.

PÂTE À PAIN OR *PÂTE LEVÉE*: bread dough. This may be made at home, and it freezes very easily. In France it can be bought ready-prepared from the bakery, for making bread, all kinds of savory or sweet tarts, and cakes such as brioches, babas, kugelhopf, etc.

PÂTE BRISÉE: short pastry made from flour, butter, salt and water or milk. This is the simplest of French pastries, elastic and firm rather than delicate. Being fairly impermeable, it can be used for sweet or savory tart bases without precooking. It may be enriched with eggs, which make it still firmer.

PÂTE SABLÉE: flour, butter, eggs, sugar, salt and water. This is a delicate, very crumbly pastry which must be worked as little as possible. It is very rich, and is excellent for sweet tarts and cookies. For an even richer flavor, ground almonds may be added.

POIVRE MIGNONETTE: also known as "steak pepper". It is more or less finely crushed peppercorns, and may be white, black or a mixture of the two.

PORK BELLY: also known as *lard maigre*, lean lard. It is sold fresh, *demi-sel* (that is, salted; this must be parboiled before cooking), or smoked (salted, then smoked, and eaten raw or, more frequently, cooked).

PORK CAUL: can be replaced by thin slices of fatty bacon.

PORC DEMI-SEL OR *PORC SALÉ*: nearly all cuts of pork, such as shoulder, sparerib, rump, belly, flank, tail, feet, ears, etc, are salted. In the south, salted pork belly is referred to as *petit salé*. The salting is done with a pickling brine of salt, sugar, water and saltpeter, either by immersion or by injection with multiple needles. Salting times vary from one to six days; the longer the time, the saltier the meat will taste. Meat that has been salted for one day requires simply a rinse under running water; if it has been salted for several days, however, it should be soaked for 12 hours in several changes of water. If you do not have time to do this, you can blanch it for about 15 minutes in boiling salted water, then rinse it before cooking.

Meat can be salted at home, by rubbing it with coarse sea salt (flavored with thyme, rosemary, bay leaf or crushed peppercorns if you wish) and then keeping it buried in additional coarse sea salt in the refrigerator, where it will keep for six days. You must take care that it is always covered with salt; if the salt dissolves, add more. Rinse off the salt under running water and leave the meat to soak, or else blanch it before using.

PORK RIND: this must be trimmed of all fat and blanched before using, particularly in slow-simmered dishes. It gives a marvelous syrupy, slightly gelatinous consistency to the sauce base.

PRALINE: almonds cooked in caramel. Once cooked, the mixture is spread on a marble slab and cooled, then crushed to powder.

QUATRE-ÉPICES: a blend of spices used in France for many years to flavor meat terrines, pâtés and all kinds of charcuterie products. It is made of equal quantities of powdered white pepper, nutmeg, cloves and ginger. According to the end use, chili, cinnamon or mace may also be added.

RICE: Camargue, a small, long-grained rice grown in the Camargue. It is delicate and perfumed. Long-grain, the type of rice used when preparing boiled rice or pilaf. The grain is long and off-white in color. Short-grain, a type of rice with short, white grains, used in desserts because of its sticky properties.

SAUSAGES: there are two different types of sausage. Dry ones are eaten as is, thinly sliced — with drinks before dinner, as a first course in sandwiches, with baguette or coarse country bread accompanied by butter and gerkins, and so on. Cooking sausages are made from ground meat and fat, either alone or with truffles or pistachios added; they may be smoked or unsmoked. They must always be pricked several times with a fork before being slowly poached in barely simmering water for about 20 minutes.

SHALLOTS: there are two varieties: pink shallots, simply called shallots, and the grey type. The former are more common and more frequently used; they are a pinkish-brown color and much less aromatic and milder in flavor than the grey variety. The latter are greyish-brown in color and are covered by several thick layers of skin.

STOCK: used to poach fish fillets, prepare a *blanquette de veau* or poach pieces of beef suspended by a string, but just as important for cooking rice or making a soup. Stocks prepared from bouillon cubes or flavorings extracts are not perfect substitutes. If you have a little time to spare, make your own stocks. They can be frozen in 6 tablespoon (100 ml) portions in plastic bags.

TOMATO PUREE: tomatoes, cooked and reduced to a lightly concentrated puree. It is sold in cardboard packs. A flavorful natural product, it has many very practical uses.

TRUFFLE: There are two kinds of truffle, white and black. The white or Piedmontese truffle is rare in France; it grows under oaks and linden trees in winter, at a depth of 2 to 20 in (5 to 50 cm) beneath the ground, and looks rather like a large potato ranging from grey to ocher in color. It is superb and very delicate. The black truffle, called the "black diamond" of cooking, is certainly better known. This black tuber, which can measure up to 6 in (15 cm) in diameter, is covered with little pyramidal warts; it grows spontaneously and ripens throughout the winter and up to early spring underneath oak, ash and hazel trees. Today black truffles are cultivated in the Vaucluse and Périgord areas in plantations of truffle-producing oak trees. Fragrant and delicious, they form the basis of many special-occasion dishes. Out of season and abroad they are to be found bottled or tinned.

VANILLA SUGAR: superfine (caster) sugar flavored with natural vanilla (in which case it is called vanilla sugar) or artificial vanilla (in which case it is called vanillin sugar, vanillin being a synthetic vanilla flavoring). It can be bought in 15 lb (7.5-kg) envelopes in packs of five or ten. If you are unable to find it, you can make it yourself: ½ cup (4 oz/125 g) sugar, add 1 tablespoon powdered vanilla or a vanilla bean split in two. Keep this in an airtight jar for several months; more vanilla may be added as desired.

VENTRÈCHE: pork belly, salted, seasoned and formed into a roll. It should be cut into thin slices, like *poitrine fumée*. Most commonly used in the southwest.

VERMOUTH: a fortified wine, 18% alcohol, flavored with aromatic herbs. It may be red or white, dry or sweet. The dry white vermouth is the one most commonly used in cooking.

VINAIGRETTE: this sauce is a mixture of oil and vinegar or lemon juice, with the possible addition of salt and pepper. It is traditionally used to dress green salads but also for all kinds of *crudités*, vegetables, fish and cold meats. Various other ingredients may be added, such as chopped shallots, onions or fresh herbs, crushed garlic, crumbled anchovy fillets, chopped hard-cooked egg, *tapenade*, or various kinds of mustard. Different types of oil and of vinegar may be used — walnut, hazelnut, olive or peanut (groundnut) oil, wine vinegar, cider vinegar or flavored vinegar.

VINEGAR: obtained by a fermentation process that changes the alcohol of a wine into acetic acid. It is most often made with red or white wine, but can also be based on champagne or cider. Wine vinegar can be flavored with tarragon, basil, garlic, shallots, berries, etc.

WHELKS: they generally have a brownish or greyish shell and are found on both sides of the Atlantic Ocean although the North American variety is much larger.

PROVENCE
THE BEAUTIFUL
COOKBOOK

AUTHENTIC RECIPES FROM THE REGIONS OF PROVENCE

Barthelasse Sautéed Chicken (recipe page 376)

AUTHENTIC RECIPES FROM THE REGIONS OF PROVENCE

PROVENCE
THE BEAUTIFUL
COOKBOOK

RECIPES AND FOOD TEXT BY
RICHARD OLNEY

REGIONAL TEXT BY
JACQUES GANTIÉ

FOOD PHOTOGRAPHY BY
PETER JOHNSON

STYLED BY
JANICE BAKER

SCENIC PHOTOGRAPHY BY
MICHAEL FREEMAN

HarperCollinsPublishers

First published in USA 1993
by Collins Publishers San Francisco.
Reprinted in 1993; 1998; 1999

Produced by Weldon Owen Inc.
814 Montgomery Street
San Francisco, CA 94133 USA
Phone (415) 291 0100 Fax (415) 291 8841

Chairman: Kevin Weldon
President: John Owen
General Manager: Stuart Laurence
Co-Editions Director: Derek Barton
Publisher: Jane Fraser
Senior Editor: Anne Dickerson
Editorial Assistant: Jan Hughes
Copy Editor: Sharon Silva
Proofreader: Jonathan Schwartz
Translator: Barbara McGilvray
Production: Stephanie Sherman, Mick Bagnato
Design: Tom Morgan, Blue Design
Production Assistant: Jennifer Petersen
Design Concept: John Bull, The Book Design Company
Photography Editor: Sandra Eisert
Map: Kenn Backhaus
Illustrations: Diana Reiss-Koncar
Index: Frances Bowles
Assistant Food Stylists: Cara Hobday, Liz Nolan,
    Amanda Biffin
Photographic Assistants: Robert White, Miriam Miller

Library of Congress Cataloging-in-Publication Data:

Provence, the beautiful cookbook : authentic
    recipes from the regions of Provence / recipes
    and food text Richard Olney ; regional text
    Jacques Gantié ; food photography by Peter
    Johnson ; styled by Janice Baker ; scenic
    photography by Michael Freeman.
        p.   cm.
    Includes index.
    ISBN 0-00-255154-3 : $45.00
    1. Cookery, French—Provençal style.
    2. Cookery—France—Provence. 3. Provence
    (France)—Description and travel.
    I. Olney, Richard. II. Grantié, Jacques.
    TX719.2.P75P76   1993
    641.59449—dc20   93–55
                                            CIP
        ISBN 0-06-757598-6 (pbk.)

Printed by Toppan in China

A Weldon Owen ◆ Production

*Endpapers: Romanesque statues adorn a facade in Aix en
Provence.*

*Pages 256-257: The sweeping valleys of Alpes-de-Haute-
Provence are some of the most tranquil and least populated
regions of Provence.*

*Right: The Camargue is the French Wild West: home to
fighting bulls, wild horses and the gardians, French cowboys.*

*Pages 262-263; left to right: Gratin of Mashed Potatoes and
Garlic with Cheese (recipe page 430), Turnip Gratin
(recipe page 455).*

*Pages 266-267: A charming, unpretentious fishing village
along the Riviera, Cassis offers a quiet harbor, excellent
seafood restaurants and celebrated local white wines.*

At Domaine Tempier, Bandol, from left to right: Macédoine of Fruits in Bandol Wine (recipe page 490), Creamy Lemon Custard (recipe page 492)

CONTENTS

A palette of warm, Mediterranean ochers and yellows pervades Provençal art and architecture.

PROVENCE: CUISINES OF THE SUN

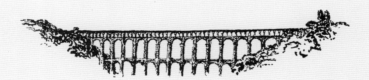

Those who look at Provence in a distant and detached way no doubt find it a single region with no precise definition. Yet this is a profoundly false impression. Provence is not one but many regions, and those who care to explore its depths and discover its secrets, who seek to understand its culinary truths, will speak of "the Provences," in the same way as the historian or the geographer approaches this amazing southeastern corner of France.

The plural, in fact, appropriately defines these lands of the sun, which do not allow themselves to be tamed easily. Nor is it a simple matter to know their flavors. This is a region whose personality is revealed only to those who take the time to pursue it: to those prepared to take their taste as a leisurely stroll, who know that the garden's treasures are not to be devoured but rather looked at, conversed with, gathered with love and then eaten in relaxed enjoyment.

There is no question, then, that there are Provences, plural. The Provence of the high country where the mistral blows, icy and biting at times, after it has swept along the valley of the Rhône, is not the Provence of the dazzling white coves between Marseilles and Cassis. Nor is it that of the peaceful hills of the Var, the ochers of the Esterel or the villages perched high on the Alpes-Maritimes where culinary traditions have their origins among mountains and valleys and where the bright, popular accents of Italian influence are seen.

Of course, the country air is the same, from melodious Vaucluse to the Lubéron, from Digne to Les Baux-de-Provence, from the golden dreams of Saint-Tropez to Nice, Cannes, Menton. To pause at each is like visiting different members of the same family.

And if Provence wants more attention, it has only to extract from beneath its oaks, its walnut and chestnut trees up in the hinterland, around Aups or between Ventoux and the Lubéron, its rich storehouse of truffles, brought here from the Balkans or from the Middle East first by the Romans and later by the Italians of the Renaissance.

In Provence, cooking is an artist's affair. Neither too much shadow nor too much sun. Neither excessive colors nor dominant flavors. In such conditions, with *la joie de vivre* everywhere, the culinary treasures of Provence become eloquent. This character is reflected in thick soups that whet the appetite and yet are the simplest concoctions in the world: served cold at midday—fish soup, tomato soup, crab soup—or in more robust versions in the evening—broad (fava) bean soup, squash soup, green bean soup. Great classics such as *aïoli, bouillabaisse, brandade de morue* (creamed salt cod)*, bourride* (fish soup with *aïoli*), a variety of daubes, and *pot-au-feu* echo the same eloquence.

So, too, do *pan bagnat,* in which the classic *niçois* ingredients of tomato, olives, sweet peppers (capsicums), young broad beans and so on are sandwiched between

Although the French Riviera is now the mecca of fashionable society, there are still quiet streets perfect for an afternoon stroll.

269

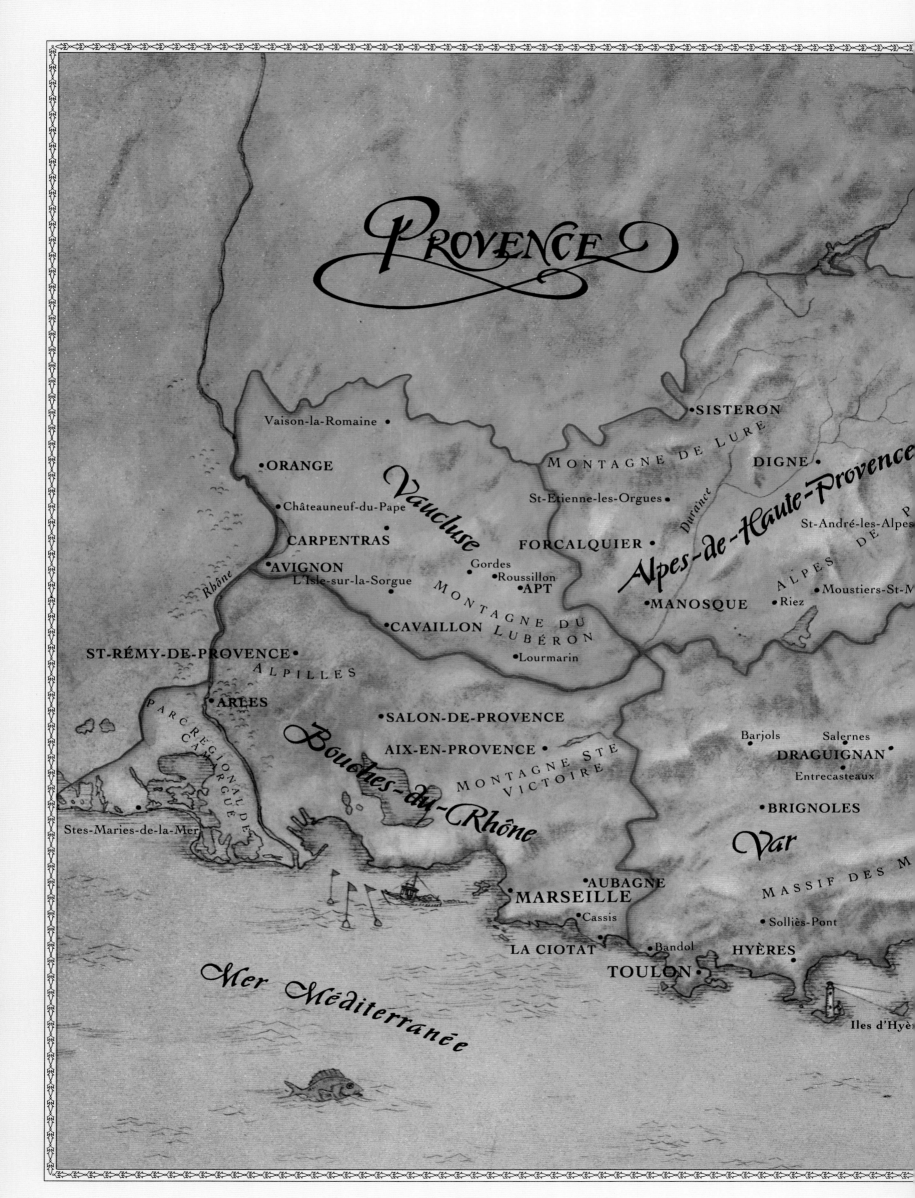

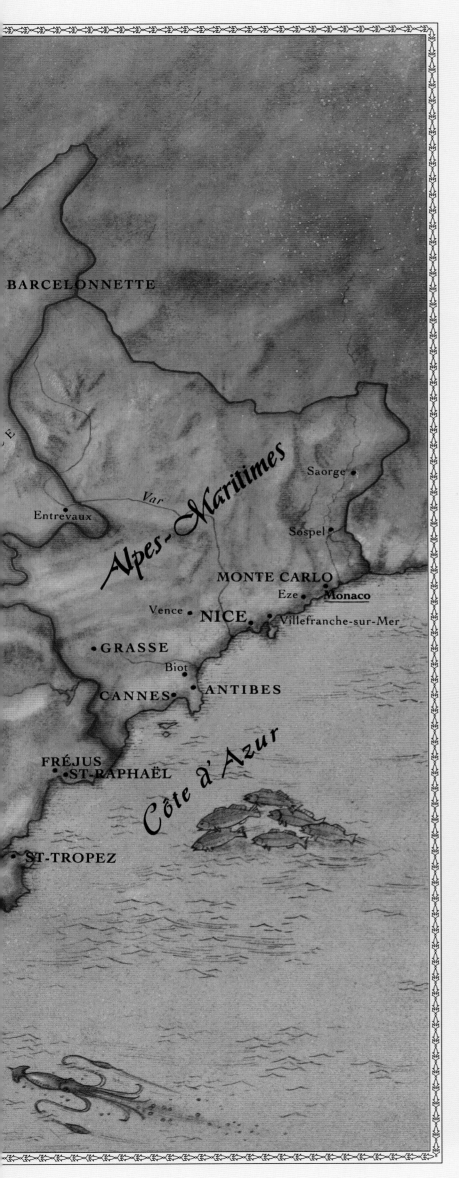

halves of French bread, and with the *casse-croûte,* or snack, known in the *niçois* dialect by its Italian name *merenda,* which is put together from next to nothing—toasted bread rubbed with garlic, *tapénade* or *anchoïade,* or even *panisses,* those *bonnes pâtes* made from chick-pea flour that have given their name to one of Marcel Pagnol's heroes. Although these may sound like foods for the famished, they are in fact the first rays of the cuisine of the sun.

As we approach the end of the century, notable chefs, some of whom work in Provence, have realized the importance of these simple preparations and have turned them into fashionable and delicious "back-to-the-country" food. In days gone by these providential morsels provided a treat for the peasants; today it is well-heeled gourmets who go into raptures over them, with no thought of ever laboring in fields! Without knowing it they are emulating the Countess de Sévigné, who wrote enthusiastically in a letter of 1694: "These partridges fed on thyme and marjoram . . . the white, sweet figs, muscat grapes like edible grains of amber that would certainly make the head swim if one were to eat them indiscriminately. . . . What a life, my dear cousin!"

The Provences have their distinctive moods and personalities, however. Writers and artists who have celebrated the south of France have discovered for us, as only poets can, their differences and hidden truths. Jean Giono, Marcel Pagnol, Alphonse Daudet, Colette, Zola, Matisse, Picasso, Signac, Cocteau, Dufy, Cézanne and Van Gogh were unerring in their words and their colors, and it was no uncertain country they evoked when they took the time to live and create in Aix, Manosque, Arles, Nice or Saint-Tropez.

The balmy weather of the Côte d'Azur attracts street musicians and people watchers to seaside cafés throughout the year.

271

Outdoor restaurants of Old Nice welcome patrons enjoying the summertime pleasures of the Côte d'Azur.

272

Likewise, the chefs of Provence, and before them the mothers of families who spent hours, or even days preparing soups, terrines, fritters and daubes, have always been able to find the correct proportions, experiment with flavorings and gauge quantities of the products of the sun according to whether they live on a hillside, in the depths of the valley, in a village atop a mountain or in the shelter of a fishing port.

But while places and people have their importance, it is when hunger calls and we sit down at the table that we uncover special idiosyncrasies of these golden lands and what constitutes the common language spoken throughout Provence. It is the language of the joy of cooking, a language that demands the use of *une pointe d'ail*—that is to say, "a touch of garlic"—the minute amount that clings to the tip of the knife.

It also demands that dishes be flavored with an olive oil that comes, if possible, from one of the last remaining independent presses in Maussane, Oppède, the Rouret, Contes, Nyons, Cucuron or another of the sacred places where people still process the olives grown on their own land. Sometimes it will be a light oil for cooking, and by all means a fruity one for salads. Once upon a time the aptly named, although today to some extent forgotten, *olivade* was the commonest of all family celebrations. The peasants marked the festivities by making *aïoli,* or by crushing garlic and anchovies onto chunks of bread steeped in virgin olive oil and toasting them over the fire.

And it demands that the dishes of the sun be enriched, in moderation, of course, with aromatic herbs whose use is limited only by the need not to be so

The church bell tower is the centerpiece of Bargemon, a quaint village perched in the austere countryside of northeastern Var.

The Alpes-Maritimes backcountry is home to timeless hamlets where old traditions endure.

273

aggressive as to "kill" a dish. Rosemary, basil, bay leaf, fennel, mint, marjoram, thyme and saffron all provide intelligent company when wisely used.

While Provençal cooking enraptures poet and traveler alike, it does not put on airs. Indeed, from the Alps to the Mediterranean it is often dubbed the "poor man's cuisine." This is exactly what gives it strength and imagination. Other regions of France possess more obvious wealth and traditions, and to the eyes of the world are seen as the culinary power brokers and custodians of the science of taste. They will keep you at the table for hours. Here, impetuous winds (the mistral off the water and the *tramontana* from the north), a burning sun, dry earth and the brisk, choppy sea have dictated other, more immediate rituals and knowledge.

Provence, before it became a pacific territory to be conquered only by the tourist, experienced much unhappiness and many invasions in the course of its history. It learned from such excursions to nourish its men and women to live long and to live on little.

In the old days, when knowledge and communication were passed on by word of mouth, families got together to share bread on their return from the fields or the hills, and on various important occasions. One such celebratory gathering centered around the *gros souper,* or "big supper," held on December 24. It called for not only thirteen round bread loaves placed in the center of the table, but also for thirteen desserts—the array a symbol of Christmas in Provence—including raisins, figs, almonds, walnuts, pears, apples and nougats.

A Provençal count wrote the following description of *un gros souper* early in the nineteenth century: "First, the 'raito,' a kind of hash of cod or eel, different species of fish,

The colorful maze of twisting streets, narrow windows and wrought iron lampposts give the old town quarter of Nice its characteristic charm.

The café is an intrinsic part of Provençal life; here couples enjoy afternoon refreshments while taking in the scenes of Marseilles.

Grasse, known as the perfume capital of France, has had distilleries since the 16th century; here a worker prepares fresh rose petals for the extraction vat.

grilled, and raw artichokes, cardoons, celery and various kinds of vegetables make up the first course. The first tablecloth is removed and then the *calenos* are set down; these consist of cakes, dried fruits, jams, biscuits and sweetmeats. The dessert may be more or less sumptuous according to the family's affluence. But cakes, dried fruits and chestnuts are always present. Nor are the wines and liqueurs forgotten."

Alas, today such venerable culinary customs and day-to-day formalities have largely disappeared. Despite their absence, however, the gourmand inheritance has not been wasted. Indeed, this cuisine has developed into one of the lightest in the world: an art of good living that inspires our daily diet and that a handful of great chefs in the kitchens of the finest restaurants in Provence and on the Côte d'Azur interpret and export in their individual ways. These masters have given a new style and new clothes to the ancient recipes. But their imagination, which characterizes the cuisine of the sun and the gastronomy of the south, has not brought an end to simple ideas. Provence has provided these artists and the rest of us with the foundations of a cultural inheritance.

ALPES-MARITIMES

ALPES-MARITIMES

S ome call *niçoise* cooking "cuisine of the poor," or at worst an Italian cuisine and at best an Italo-*niçoise* one. What happens to this sunny, spirited table in the Alpes-Maritimes, where we are no longer quite in Provence and not yet in Piedmont or Lombardy, the area's neighboring Italian regions, that makes people pay such scant regard to its originality and traditions?

The end of the century is fast approaching and it is becoming increasingly difficult to gain recognition and respect for the culinary traditions of the Nice region. It is as if there were a European movement absorbing this delicious idiosyncracy into a more general concept of Provençal cuisine or Mediterranean cuisine, even though today the area clearly functions as a school in the development of French taste and gastronomy.

And yet when we speak of this *département* in far southeastern Provence, of its sea, hills and mountains, these very *niçoises* traditions are the only ones we can rely on: the traditions of a county that was tied to France back in 1860. History's invasions here met plenty of obstacles. The highlands of Nice, Grasse and Menton, made up of mountain passes and valleys (Roya, Tinée, Vésubie, Var) were coveted, in succession, by the Greeks, the Romans, the Genoese, the Savoyards, the Piedmontese, and the Sardinians. These invaders did not try to put down lasting roots in this mountainous and hostile country, where mules followed the "salt route" between the fifteenth and the nineteenth centuries, transporting the precious commodity along the

Previous pages: The medieval village of Peillon captures the rosy glow of a Mediterranean sunset. Left: A part of France only since 1860, the old section of Nice retains its distinctly Italian character.

peaks that connected Nice with Tende, passing through the villages of Lucéram, Sospel, Lantosque and Saorge.

This hilly country is somewhat secluded, but it lights up as soon as one begins climbing around the many villages that cling to its peaks or to the sides of *baous* (the Provençal term for *rocks*): Bonson, Saint-Jeannet, Peillon, Gattières, Gourdon, Cabris, Saorge, Marie, Sainte-Agnès, Utelle. In fact it was here, where carefully tended plots cling to rocky cliffs, that kitchen-garden cuisine originated: a family-based and fiercely independent style of cooking that has laid down its flavors over the centuries.

It is a cuisine of contrasts, spontaneous and subtle, much like the land itself, which moves into a rapid ascent while still in view of the sea and boldly plays at mountains. In these gallant hills in days gone by, the women of the house transformed the family plots into countless bastions of the products of the sun.

Family kitchen gardens were, in effect, closed, sacred places that established the reputation of this so-called poor cuisine. All that came out of them in those early days were a few goat's milk products; the only fat was contributed by the solitary pig that many families possessed up to the beginning of the present century. Yet it was a complex and aromatic cuisine, rich in its own way, and above all a cuisine of patience.

The mountain area begins very close to Nice. In these tiny hilltop heavens we find, not far from the olive—the king of Provence trees—and the fig, the legendary plants that nourish the Mediterranean: vegetables, the region's chief treasures.

The vegetables too are "poor." There is the onion, the heart of the *pissaladière,* a tart garnished with anchovies and black olives. Chick-peas are used to make the famous *socca,* a large, flat cake cooked (in olive oil, naturally) in a hot wood-fired oven, and still served today, cut into

The quiet life is enjoyed by the locals in Alpes-Maritimes, the less populous, vast back-garden of the French Riviera.

golden slices, on the streets that surround the vegetable markets of picturesque Nice and Menton.

Then there are the more sun-drenched vegetables, such as corn, served as polenta if you wish, or tomatoes, which first appeared here in the mid-fifteenth century. And one must not forget broad (fava) beans (the young ones, *févettes,* consumed raw); the renowned zucchini (courgette), the pale green Cinderella of the kitchen garden that is indispensable to a ratatouille (eaten just warm, of course) or prepared as a gratin or fritters; or the sweet pepper (capsicum); artichoke; fennel or eggplant (aubergine). And finally there is Swiss chard (silverbeet), most notably used in a sweet tart scented with orange flower water or brandy called *tourta de blea,* one of the most famous desserts in the county of Nice.

Those who seek to rediscover the tastes and traditions of earlier times love the miracle products that illuminate a particular cuisine. In the Alpes-Maritimes these roles are filled by the inevitable, ever-present garlic (in the old days it was a custom in Nice for people to throw whole cloves into the fire on the Festival of Saint Jean, to guard against bad luck); fennel, sage, rosemary, thyme and the famous *balico* ("basil"), pounded in a mortar with garlic, Parmesan and olive oil to make *pistou.* Even the salad here asserts its individuality, in a lively mixture of escarole, lettuce, curly endive (chicory), arugula (rocket) and other greens called *mesclun.*

Of course Italy is close by, and the *niçois* region also embraces influences from Piedmont and the Ligurian coast. Ravioli, *gnocchi, capellini,* and *tortellini* are part of the local culinary history, as evidenced by the giant ravioli banquet prepared for the Stacada, a historic festival organized every four years in Breil-sur-Roya north of Menton. Ravioli, however, are almost an everyday dish. They are, in fact, the ubiquitous *raïlolas* seen at country feasts in the *niçois* highlands, although these days one can no longer guarantee that they are *cousus main,* that is, handmade.

As has been explained, the history of the county of Nice is not a closed one. An illustration of this is the presence of stockfish, or *estocaficada,* the most surprising of all popular dishes. Its strong smell is its best defense against democratization. And yet it comes from afar. It is the cod of the Atlantic peoples, the haddock of the Scandinavians.

In the nineteenth century, Mediterranean navigators took their olive oil in barrels to Norway, and, so they would not have to come home with empty boats, accepted in exchange cases of smoke-dried haddock, which the Scandinavians called stick fish. The French sailors might just as well have called it money, for once they reached the port at Nice or Villefranche, they used the stockfish to pay their *camalous,* the dockers who unloaded the cargo. Then it was up to local cooks to soak this foreign fish for over a week and restore it to life and a kind of unobtrusive charm with red sweet peppers (capsicums), garlic, onions, tomatoes, potatoes and the small black olives—*piccholines*—so typical of the Nice region. The *niçois* writer Louis Nucera evokes this culinary devotion thus: "The grandmother is camped by her stove. For a week this conspiracy has kept her laboring here, for that is how long the stockfish has been soaking in constant changes of water . . . saucepans, stew pot, sauté pan and steamer surround the cook. All these play a role in the preparation and separate cooking processes." And so the famous Nice *ragoût* was born, a classic dish for Friday, traditionally a meatless day, and one whose memory is still rigorously

Originally named for the cane surrounding its marshes, Cannes, now famous for its international film festival, is dubbed the French Beverly Hills.

protected in Nice by an association of purists set up in 1905 called *L'estocaficada*.

This then is a Provençal cuisine, certainly, but one that sits on the fringe of other cuisines. The cuisine *du pays nissart*, as it is called, is so closely linked to the work of the grandmothers of earlier times that a former mayor of Nice, Jacques Médecin, decided one day to pay homage to them. He wrote *The Cuisine of the County of Nice*, which is still used as a reference for its 300 recipes. In it are tastes and words that only truly sing when they are expressed in the *niçois* dialect: *lou pietch* (stuffed veal), and the *bagna cauda* (a fondue of Piedmont origin) over which, again in the words of Louis Nucera, "the grandmother keeps watch; at the merest hint of steam she would feel herself disgraced." Then there are *porchetta*, stuffed suckling pig, admittedly of central Italian origin; *trule*, a sausage made with herbs; *merda de can, gnocchi* rolled by hand, filled with chard and strewn with Parmesan; and, finally, the all-too-rare *poutine*, minute baby fish that can only legally be caught between Antibes and Menton during a forty-five-day period from February to April, thanks to an imperial charter dating back to the time of Sardinian rule before 1860.

So it is not the Nice of the Promenade des Anglais, the casinos or the town houses of the middle-class suburb of Cimiez that speaks to the culinary heart. It is instead the town painted in Italian colors, the cottage industries, and the narrow streets of Old Nice. It is not so far removed after all from the town Raoul Dufy painted, at times just a simple outline seen through a window between a row of palms and the seashore.

Finally, the people of Nice do not have to go far to survey their vine plantings or to find the right accompani-ment, if required, for their popular dishes. The Bellet vines on the hills next to the Var plain belong to a pocket-sized winery of roughly 150 acres (about sixty hectares) that recently celebrated its fiftieth year, although its vines go back more than five centuries. It is a vineyard so precious that at the time of the French Revolution, when all the village names containing reference to religion had to be changed, the inhabitants of Saint-Roman (of Bellet) chose the name of Bacchus! The vine growers here between Château de Crémat and Château de Bellet, with their subtle reds and wonderfully fine whites, continue to resist the concrete that is steadily creeping up from the valleys.

And if we are talking about the real Provence, we must go up to Villars sur Var in the hills, where the microscopic realm of M. Sassi, Clos Saint-Joseph, officially attached to the Côtes de Provence, is conducting its own resistance, with less than eight acres (three hectares)!

The abundance of local blessings almost forbids the suggestion the *niçoise* cuisine is a cuisine of the poor. Nonetheless it is true that these days the authentic eating places, restaurants offering genuine *niçoise* cuisine, can almost be counted on the fingers of one hand.

But even if the guardians of the temple are disappearing one by one, we still have the memory of this cuisine, and on a larger scale this time. The Alpes-Maritimes have the first Museum of Culinary Art, between Nice and Saint-Paul-de-Vence at Villeneuve-Loubet. The famous Auguste Escoffier Museum is named for one of the most innovative French chefs of the late nineteenth and early twentieth century— the creator of peach Melba—who was born here in 1846 and went on to conquer Paris, Monte Carlo, Lucerne, Rome and London (first at the Savoy and later at the Carlton).

SOUPS AND STARTERS

Mixed spices create a splash of color and texture in an open market in Moustiers-Ste-Marie.

SOUPS AND STARTERS

In Provence traditions are tenacious. Although the midday meal is now called *déjeuner* instead of *dîner,* in the villages and in family life it is still the main meal of the day. For those whose days are composed of long hours of physical labor—farmers, vineyardists, masons— a morning break at 8:30, called *le casse-croûte matinal,* is usual; it consists of charcuterie, cheese, bread and red wine, often supplemented by cold flat omelets, *pan bagnat* or another easily transportable local specialty.

Except for special occasions, supper is a light meal, usually soup followed by cheese and a fruit. When the soup is an unthickened broth, it is poured over semidry slices of bread, called *croûtes,* or "crusts," which may have been first anointed with olive oil. Many soups—indeed, some of the best—are simple combinations of finely cut-up vegetables or shredded greens boiled in water or broth and poured over crusts. Recipes for soups often finish with the phrase *Trempez votre soupe,* which might be translated "Soak your sop," and which means "pour the soup over slices of bread placed in a soup tureen," a reminder that originally *soupe* was the piece of bread over which one poured a hot liquid.

Provençal cooking is home cooking. The inventions of professional cooks "in the Provençal mode" never ring true. Stocks, *demi-glace* and sauce bases are unknown to the Provençal housewife or to the men who gather in country cabins to roast hunted birds or to boil a *bouillabaisse* over an open fire. When it is available, leftover *pot-au-feu* broth is the base for many soups and it enrichens daubes, braised vegetables or rice. For this reason, *pot-au-feu* is presented at the beginning of the soup section. The term, *pot-au-feu,* applies both to the pot and to the food prepared in it. A traditional *pot-au-feu* is a large, deep earthenware pot with slightly bulging sides and a slightly rounded bottom. Sizes vary, but an average pot holds ten quarts (10 l), is ten inches (25 cm) deep and measures nine inches (23 cm) in diameter at the brim. Any large, heavy, deep pot can replace it; enameled ironware *pot-au-feu* pots are manufactured.

When the kitchen contains no meat broth, the Provençal cook does not wring his or her hands in despair. Instead, water, wine or vegetable cooking liquid is substituted; chick-pea cooking liquid is especially admired. Plain water is better than that tainted by bouillon cubes.

Chick-peas, hardly eaten elsewhere in France, are adored in Provence, but in the entire repertory of Provençal cuisine only two "recipes" occur. Chick-peas are prepared as a salad, normally a first course but many willingly transform a chick-pea salad into a whole meal, preceding it with olives and *saucisson,* radishes or seasonal crudités. Leftover chick-peas are puréed with their cooking liquid to make a wonderful soup, accompanied with a dish of little croutons fried in olive oil.

The Provençal table is an intimate reflection of the seasons, of the native passion for raw things, be they from the sea, the uncultivated hillsides or the kitchen garden, and for freshly cooked vegetables, accompanied by olive

Previous pages, left to right: Marinated Fennel (recipe page 288), Stuffed Tomatoes and Zucchini (recipe page 316)

oil and lemon or vinegar. This is never more evident than in the luncheon starters, replete with tastes and textures that cannot be translated into recipes.

From September through April, a selection of sea urchins, *vioulets,* mussels, a half dozen different clamlike bivalves (*praires, coques, palourdes, clovisses, vernis, dattes de mer,* as well as clams, transplanted from the western Atlantic) and several varieties of oysters, all alive, frequently opens a meal. The small, purple-quilled Mediterranean sea urchins, whose saffron-red corals also transform scrambled eggs, fish soups and fish sauces, are the sweetest and most delicate of all urchins. *Vioulets,* primitive, amorphously shaped creatures that fix themselves to the seabed, go by the particularly appropriate Latin name microcosmus. It describes the incredible deep seascape of plant and animal life adhering to the *vioulets'* wrinkled, leathery exteriors. When cut open, these rough cases expose a heart of tender, yellow flesh with an exquisite lemony sea flavor. They are worshipped on the coast between Marseilles and Toulon and practically unknown elsewhere.

The Provençal gardener plants broad (fava) beans each year in October with the dream of being able to eat raw baby *fèves,* or *févettes,* for the new year. The ground nearly always freezes and the first *fèves* do not appear until March. At the raw-eating stage, the pods, warm green, velvety and firm to the touch, are about six inches (15 cm) long and the beans are the size of a little fingernail. A platter heaped high with unshelled broad beans is placed at table and everyone goes to work, shelling. They are eaten *à la croque-au-sel,* each bean first dipped in salt (it is sometimes necessary to moisten it on the tip of the tongue to make the salt cling), and often accompanied with slices of raw ham (prosciutto) from the Alpes-de-Haute-Provence (*jambon de montagne*) or from Bayonne, Corsica or Parma. Rustic bread (*pain au levain*) and cold, unsalted, unpasteurized butter complete the perfection.

Tender, chokeless artichokes appear in November, disappear with the first freezes and come back in February to remain throughout the spring. They are called *poivrade* and are served raw, with pepper mill, salt, vinegar and olive oil at table. Each person prepares a vinaigrette, in the hollow of a tilted plate, in which to dip, first the leaves, then the quartered heart.

Cultivated green asparagus from the Vaucluse (northern France prefers white, Provence prefers green) are around from the end of February until the end of May; they are perfect in March and April. The best of all come from Nice, and are never seen outside of the Alpes-Maritimes. They are only about six inches (15 cm) long, with dark purple tips and an intense flavor with an edge of the sea. Asparagus stalks are peeled, tied in bundles, boiled in salted water until the stalks are barely tender, and served hot or warm, folded in a napkin. The Provençaux have heard of hollandaise but do not consider the possibility of eating asparagus without olive oil. Cruets of oil and vinegar are at table. Individual asparagus plates have a well to one side in which to prepare a vinaigrette, or a normal dinner plate is tilted, the far side propped on a knife or fork, as for the raw artichokes. Asparagus is eaten with one's fingers: dip and bite, dip and bite; it is a ritual celebration.

April is the month of wild asparagus. At the same time that the hillsides turn violet with the blossom of wild thyme, fragile shoots, never more than an eighth of an inch (3 mm) thick, spring from the bases of unsightly, prickly wild asparagus plants. They are collected when eight to ten inches (20–25 cm) long and, in the kitchen, are snapped at the point where the tip turns tender. The tips are rapidly sautéed in olive oil and beaten into eggs to make a *drooly* or *baveuse* (rolled omelet). The flavor is the wild essence of asparagus, the center of the omelet is the voluptuous sauce.

Sweet, orange-red–fleshed melons from Cavaillon, in the Vaucluse, and Hyères, in the Var, begin their summer career the end of May. They are eaten with salt and pepper and, as in Italy, accompanied by slices of raw ham, sliced less thinly than across the border. In the fall, fresh figs escort the ham.

In late June and early July, green almonds appear at the lunch table. They look like green apricots, their still-tender shells, beneath the green, future black husk, easily cut through with a knife; the whitish skin of the nut itself is peeled off to reveal a milk-white, tender-crisp almond of wonderful delicacy. Coarsely chopped green almonds are also added to omelets, salads and myriad desserts.

Tomatoes are in their glory in July and August. A tomato salad can be anything. It is often scattered with black olives, anchovy fillets, sweet onion rings, fresh basil leaves, served in combination with a cucumber salad, or it may be simply fanned-out tomato slices, sprinkled with salt, pepper, olive oil and a few drops of vinegar. In whatever form, it is one of the openers of nearly every summer luncheon.

The only rule seriously respected in Provence is that tomatoes be freshly picked and very firm, with a green blush at the stem ends still visible. Completely ripened tomatoes are reserved for cooking. Throughout the summer, small, tender green beans, topped, tailed, rapidly boiled and served hot with olive oil and lemon sections, provide a delicious luncheon opener. Cauliflower florets, broccoli (stems peeled and sliced), spinach and Swiss chard (silverbeet) are served in the same way.

Garlic reigns as the most essential ingredient in Provençal cooking.

Sweet Pepper Salad

SALADE DE PIMENTS DOUX
Sweet Pepper Salad

Large red, yellow or green sweet bell peppers, grilled, peeled and seeded, are a precious addition to any of the salads invented anew each day in Provence. Choose evenly formed peppers; twisted or crumpled shapes are difficult to peel. This salad can be enriched with a latticework of anchovy fillets and a scattering of black olives.

2 lb (1 kg) large bell peppers (capsicums)
1 clove garlic
large pinch of coarse salt
freshly ground pepper
1 tablespoon Provençal herb vinegar (see glossary)
¼ cup (2 fl oz/60 ml) olive oil
1 sweet white onion, thinly sliced into rings, or 5 or 6
    young green shallots (see glossary) or green (spring)
    onions, sliced
fresh basil sprigs, including leaves and flower buds

◉ Prepare a fire in a charcoal grill or preheat a broiler (griller) or electric grill. If using a broiler or electric grill, arrange the peppers on a baking sheet. (Line the baking sheet with aluminum foil to make clean-up easy.) Place the peppers on the grill rack or under a broiler and grill, turning several times, until the skins are blistered and irregularly charred on all sides, 20–30 minutes. Place the grilled peppers on a plate and enclose the plate in a plastic bag with the open end folded beneath the plate. Let stand for 30 minutes; the steam will loosen the skins. Working over a bowl to collect any juices, pinch the skins to loosen them from the core and pull them off. Discard the core, tear each pepper into 3 or 4 sections and slip off the clinging seeds with your fingers. Pass all the juices through a small sieve to remove the seeds. Set aside.
◉ Arrange the pepper sections, peeled sides up and side by side touching, on a platter. In a mortar pound together the garlic, salt and pepper to taste to form a paste. Stir in the vinegar, the reserved pepper juices and, finally, the olive oil.
◉ Spoon the sauce evenly over the peppers and scatter the onion rings over the surface. Tear the basil leaves into fragments and crumble the flower buds. Scatter over the top.

SERVES 4

ALPES·DE·HAUTE·PROVENCE

PÂTES AUX HERBES
Herb Pasta

An alpine bouquet of green things, wild and cultivated, this pasta is never twice the same, for it depends upon what is available at the moment. Young dandelions, purslane and any other wild salad greens are good elements. In spring when the young shoots are tender, a discreet amount of winter savory is good. Basil and cultivated marjoram flower buds and leaves, lemon balm (melissa), arugula (rocket), hyssop, parsley, sorrel, celery leaves and green (spring) onions can be filled out with spinach or Swiss chard (silverbeet).

large pinch of coarse salt
4–5 oz (125–150 g) mixed fresh herbs and salad greens, chopped (see recipe introduction)
about 3 cups (12 oz/375 g) all-purpose (plain) flour
2 eggs
3–4 tablespoons (4 fl oz/125 ml) tepid water
1 tablespoon olive oil
Parmesan cheese and grater, unsalted butter and pepper mill for serving

◉ In a mortar pound together the salt and herbs and greens to form a paste. Put 2 cups (8 oz/250 g) of the flour into a mixing bowl and make a well in the center. Add the contents of the mortar and the eggs to the well and stir with a fork, moving outward to absorb the flour progressively and adding, if necessary, a bit of warm water or more flour to form a soft but coherent, sticky dough.

◉ Thickly flour a work surface and turn the dough out onto it. Knead repeatedly: turn it in the flour, push with the heel of your hand to stretch it, fold it, turn it in the flour, give it a quarter turn, push it again and so forth—push, fold, flour, turn. The greens progressively release their liquid, absorbing more flour. When the dough is silken and no longer sticky but still supple (it must be soft enough to be easily rolled out by hand), form it into a ball, cover it with a towel and leave to rest for 1 hour.

◉ Scrape the work surface clean, flour it again and roll out the dough about ⅛ in (3 mm) thick, turning it over (flip it or roll it up on the rolling pin) on the floured surface two or three times as you work. Cut it into strips about 1½ in (4 cm) wide and cut across the strips into squares.

◉ Bring a large pot filled with salted water to a boil. Add the oil. Toss the squares loosely in your hands to rid them of excess flour and drop them in the boiling water. When the water returns to a boil, adjust the heat to maintain a gentle boil and cook, stirring regularly with a wooden fork, until tender, about 6 minutes.

◉ Drain and serve in warmed soup plates. Offer cheese, butter and pepper at the table.

SERVES 4

Herb Pasta

287

MARINADE DE FENOUIL
Marinated Fennel

*Split celery hearts, trimmed; whole or quartered young artichokes
(see glossary); sections of the white parts of leeks; cauliflower florets
or cultivated mushrooms (quartered if large) can be prepared,
separately or in combination, in the same manner as the fennel.
Peeled, seeded, and chopped tomatoes and plumped currants or
raisins may be added with a pinch of sugar and a dash of cayenne.*

2 lb (1 kg) fennel bulbs
bouquet garni (see glossary)
½ lb (250 g) pickling onions
4 cloves garlic, crushed
pinch of fennel seeds
pinch of coriander seeds
½ teaspoon peppercorns, coarsely crushed
salt
5–6 tablespoons (3 fl oz/80 ml) olive oil
juice of 1 lemon
½ cup (4 fl oz/125 ml) dry white wine

▦ Remove the outer stalks of the fennel bulbs. Slice off the
remaining tough stalk ends at an angle; reserve any feathery,
green leaves. Split the bulbs into quarters lengthwise.
▦ Place the bouquet garni in a flameproof earthenware casserole (preferably) or in a saucepan. Arrange the fennel quarters,
onions and garlic in the pan, wasting no space. Scatter over the
dry seasonings. Pour over the oil, lemon juice, white wine and
enough water just to immerse the contents. Bring to a boil,
cover and cook at a gentle boil until the fennel is tender but still
firm, about 25 minutes.
▦ Discard the bouquet garni and pour the contents of the pan
into a terrine or deep serving dish. Let cool and serve at room
temperature or cover and chill before serving. Chop the
reserved fennel leaves and scatter over the top before serving.

SERVES 4   *Photograph pages 282–283*

SALADE FRANCILLON
À LA TAPÉNADE
Mussel and Potato Salad
with Tapénade

*The cooked potatoes must be peeled and sliced while they are still
hot, in order to absorb the flavor of the mussels' cooking liquid.
Protect your hands from burns by cradling the potatoes in a folded
towel as you handle them.*

2 lb (1 kg) mussels, opened with white wine over heat
    (see glossary)
1 lb (500 g) small, firm yellow-fleshed potatoes
3 or 4 young green shallots (see glossary) or green (spring)
    onions, thinly sliced
FOR THE VINAIGRETTE:

1 tablespoon Provençal herb vinegar (see glossary)
salt and freshly ground pepper
3 tablespoons *tapénade* (recipe follows)
¼ cup (2 fl oz/60 ml) olive oil

▦ Prepare the mussels as directed, reserving the cooking liquid
in a bowl and placing the shelled mussel meats in a salad bowl.
Meanwhile, place the potatoes in a saucepan filled with salted
water, bring to a boil and boil until just done, about 30 minutes.
Drain and peel while hot. As soon as each potato is peeled, slice
it into the bowl containing the mussels' cooking liquid.

▦ When the potatoes are cool, drain them (the mussels' liquid
can be reserved for soup) and join them to the mussels. Then
add the shallots or green onions.
▦ To prepare the vinaigrette, in a small bowl stir together the
vinegar and salt and pepper to taste. Then stir in the *tapénade*
and, finally, the olive oil. Pour the vinaigrette over the salad
ingredients, toss and serve.

SERVES 4

TAPÉNADE
Caper and Black Olive Spread

Tapeno is Provençal for "capers." Reboul, author of La cuisinière
provençale, *writes that* tapénade *is a creation of his friend,
Meynier, chef at La Maison Dorée in Marseilles during the last
century (others claim that it was known to the ancient Greeks).
In addition to the ingredients listed below, Meynier's recipe contains
marinated tuna, English mustard and Cognac; it contains no garlic.
Serve* tapénade *at room temperature spread onto individual croutons,
or mashed with hard-cooked egg yolks to stuff hard-cooked egg
whites, or mounded in small, seeded tomatoes, and so on. It is also
a delicious accompaniment to roast lamb.*

1⅔ cups (½ lb/250 g) Greek-style black olives, pitted
½ cup (3½ oz/100 g) capers, rinsed and well drained
3 salted anchovies, rinsed and filleted (see glossary)
pinch of Provençal mixed dried herbs (see glossary)
pinch of coarse salt
freshly ground pepper
2 cloves garlic
4–5 tablespoons (2–3 fl oz/60–90 ml) olive oil

▦ Combine the olives, capers and anchovies in a food processor fitted with the metal blade and purée. In a mortar pound
together the herbs, salt, a generous grind of pepper and the
garlic to form a paste. Add the olive mixture and work together, turning the pestle and adding olive oil, a little at a time,
until the mixture is the consistency of a thin paste.

SERVES 6

TROUCHA
Swiss Chard or Spinach Omelet

*Most omelets in Provence are flat and the eggs play a secondary
role, binding together the main ingredients. The Niçois believe this
omelet, la troucha, to be uniquely theirs. In Nice it is made with
Swiss chard greens. Frédéric Mistral, the Provençal poet, placed
troucha in the Vaucluse, where it is made with spinach. The
Marseillais and the Toulonnais willingly mix spinach and chard,
often adding a few chopped sorrel leaves and a couple of chopped
anchovy fillets.*

5–6 tablespoons (3 fl oz/90 ml) olive oil
1 clove garlic, finely chopped
1 lb (500 g) Swiss chard (silverbeet) greens or spinach,
    parboiled, squeezed dry and chopped (see glossary)
salt and freshly ground pepper
4 eggs
1 tablespoon unsalted butter, chilled and diced

▦ Warm 2 tablespoons of the olive oil in a frying pan over
medium heat. Add the garlic and, when it begins to sizzle, add
the chopped greens and salt and pepper to taste. Toss or stir
with a wooden spoon for 2–3 minutes. Remove from the heat.
▦ Combine the eggs, salt and pepper to taste and butter in a

On the bar of Le Caveau de la Tour de l'Isle, L'Isle-sur-la-Sorgue, clockwise from left: Swiss Chard or Spinach Omelet, Mussel and Potato Salad with Tapénade, Tapénade Stuffed Eggs

mixing bowl. Break up the eggs with a fork, whisking only enough to mix the whites and yolks. Add the greens, stirring and beating with the fork at the same time to disperse the heat throughout the mass of eggs.

▨ Select an omelet pan measuring 11 in (28 cm) at the top and 8 in (20 cm) at the bottom. Warm 3 tablespoons olive oil in the pan over high heat, rotating the pan to coat the sides with oil. Pour in the egg mixture and stir, or swirl, the mixture with the back of the fork without touching the bottom or sides of the pan. Smooth the surface with the fork, cover the pan and lower the heat for a minute or so.

▨ When the omelet begins to set, unmold it from the pan by first jerking the pan back and forth to loosen the omelet and then turning it out onto a lid. Add another tablespoon olive oil to the pan, return the omelet browned side up and turn the heat up for about 20 seconds to finish the cooking. Alternatively, finish the omelet without turning it out by slipping it under a hot broiler, removing it when it is no longer liquid at the center but not quite firmly set. Slide onto a serving platter and serve, hot or tepid, cut into wedges.

SERVES 4

PROVENCE

Soupe au Pistou
Provençal Vegetable and Basil Soup

This soup migrated from Genoa to Provence during the last quarter of the 19th century. The pounded garlic and basil mixture, called pistou *("pestle") has not changed, but a century ago the soup itself was comprised of only potatoes, beans, tomatoes and pasta. It contained practically no liquid, and recipes warned the reader of the danger of its sticking and burning.*

Many cooks find it easier to mix the pistou *into the soup before serving it at table, but the beauty of a handsome mortar in the center of the table and the pleasure of seasoning one's soup to taste are then lost. If the guests season their soup to taste, twice as much* pistou *will be required than for a soup seasoned in the kitchen.*

2½ qt (2.5 l) water
1 piece red- or yellow-fleshed winter squash, about 1 lb
   (500 g), peeled, seeded and cut into ½-in (12-cm) cubes
1 lb (500 g) fresh white (*coco*) shell beans or half cranberry
   and half white shell beans, shelled (see glossary)
large bouquet garni (see glossary)
salt
1 lb (500 g) potatoes, peeled, quartered lengthwise, and
   thickly sliced crosswise
2 sweet white onions, thinly sliced
2 leeks, including the tender green parts, thinly sliced
3 tomatoes, peeled, seeded and coarsely chopped
½ lb (250 g) carrots, peeled, split lengthwise and thickly sliced
5 oz (150 g) green beans, trimmed and cut into ½-in
   (12-mm) lengths
2 small zucchini (courgettes), coarsely diced
large handful of short macaroni or broken spaghetti

FOR THE *PISTOU:*

large pinch of coarse salt
freshly ground pepper
4 large cloves firm, crisp garlic
large handful of fresh basil leaves and flower buds
about 2 oz (60 g) Parmesan cheese
about ¾ cup (6 fl oz/180 ml) olive oil

◙ Pour the water into a large saucepan and add the squash, shell beans, bouquet garni and salt to taste. Bring to a boil,

Mixed Salad with Garlic Croutons

reduce the heat to medium-low, cover and cook at a gentle boil for 20–30 minutes. Add the potatoes, onions, leeks, tomatoes and carrots, return to a boil, cover and cook at a gentle boil for about 30 minutes longer. Add the green beans, zucchini and pasta and cook for about 15 minutes longer (note that in a soup the pasta should not be al dente).

◙ While the soup is cooking, prepare the *pistou*. Place the salt, pepper to taste, garlic and basil in a mortar and pound with a wooden pestle until everything is reduced to a liquid paste. Grate in some of the cheese, then pound and turn the mixture until it is a stiff paste. Dribble in some of the olive oil, turning the paste all the while until it becomes liquid again. Add more cheese, then more oil and so forth, until you are satisfied with the quantity. Precise measures are of no importance. Scrape the pestle clean with a tablespoon and place the mortar and spoon at the table.

◙ Remove and discard the bouquet garni from the soup pot and place the pot on the table. Ladle out generous servings of the soup and let each guest season his or her own with *pistou* to taste—normally, a scant tablespoon of *pistou* to each full soup plate. Reheat the soup before a second service.

SERVES 6

On a terrace in Lourmarin, Provençal Vegetable and Basil Soup

MESCLUN AUX CHAPONS
Mixed Salad with Garlic Croutons

Mesclun means "mixture." A Niçois mesclun is basically a mixture of young dandelion leaves, wild and cultivated arugula (rocket) and any number of fragile, just-sprouted, untransplanted lettuces. To these may be added fragments of chervil and watercress, purslane, "wild" chicory (a bitter, elongated green leaf that in Provence is also cultivated) and radicchio (red chicory); basil and chopped hyssop are welcome additions. Throughout Provence mesclun is priced in the markets by the hecto, which is equal to 100 grams, or roughly 3½ ounces—an honest portion for two people. Use whatever you can find and don't worry about missing elements.

The best bread for the croutons is a large, firm-crumbed sourdough loaf that is several days old. The slices should be grilled over dying embers, or otherwise, until the surfaces are dry and crisp but hardly colored.

The salad greens should be absolutely dry; many of the leaves are too small or too fragile to support the rough treatment of a salad basket. Instead they must be picked out of the rinsing water by handfuls, shaken vigorously, spread out on a towel, rolled up and, then rolled up again, tightly, in the opposite direction.

salt
freshly ground pepper
1 tablespoon Provençal herb vinegar (see glossary)
5 tablespoons (3 fl oz/80 ml) olive oil
5 or 6 young green shallots (see glossary) or green (spring) onions, thinly sliced
½ lb (250 g) *mesclun* (see recipe introduction)
2 large slices semidry bread, about ¾ in (2 cm) thick, lightly grilled, rubbed on both sides with garlic and cut into cubes
2 hard-cooked eggs, shelled and coarsely chopped

▨ In the bottom of the salad bowl, combine salt and pepper to taste. Add the vinegar, stir, then add the olive oil and stir again. Stir in the shallots, then cross the salad utensils over the dressing to minimize contact between the vinaigrette and greens.

▨ Pile the *mesclun* on the vinaigrette, scatter over the garlicky croutons and the chopped eggs and present at table. Toss at the last moment, with splayed fingers for the most perfect toss, or repeatedly with the salad service, turning, lifting and tossing.

SERVES 4

TOURTE DE BLETTES À LA NIÇOISE
Swiss Chard Pie

Provençal pastry dough (see anchovy-and-onion tart on
    page 303)
2 lb (1 kg) Swiss chard (silverbeet) greens, parboiled,
    squeezed dry and chopped (see glossary)
2 eggs
½ cup (2 oz/50 g) freshly grated Parmesan cheese
salt and freshly ground pepper
1 tablespoon olive oil

◙ Prepare the pastry dough and chill for about 1 hour. Preheat
an oven to 350°F (180°C).
◙ In a mixing bowl combine the chard, eggs, cheese and salt
and pepper to taste. Using your hands, mix thoroughly.
◙ Lightly oil a round baking sheet 10 in (25 cm) in diameter.
Divide the pastry in half. Roll out half of dough and line the
baking sheet as directed in anchovy-and-onion tart (recipe
page 303), allowing the edges to overhang slightly. Mound the
chard filling in the center and spread it to the edges. Roll out the
remaining pastry and transfer it to the top of the pie. Trim the
edges, if necessary, before pinching the top and bottom pastries together and rolling them up on the edge of the dish to form
a rim. Crimp with a floured thumb or the back of the tines of
a fork. Using the tips of pointed scissors held at an angle, snip
the pastry's surface 4 or 5 times to create steam vents. Brush the
surface and the rim of the pastry lightly with the olive oil.
◙ Place in the oven and bake until golden, about 30 minutes.

SERVES 4

CRESPÈU AUX COURGETTES
Zucchini Omelet

Throughout Provence flat omelets are commonly called crespèu
*(Provençal culinary scholar René Jouveau claims this designation
should, rightfully, be reserved for flat bacon or potato omelets).
When available, a handful of peeled, tender green almonds,
coarsely chopped, are a lovely addition to the omelet.*

about ¾ lb (375 g) small, firm zucchini (courgettes)
salt
5–6 tablespoons (3 fl oz/90 ml) olive oil
3 eggs
freshly ground pepper
large pinch of fresh flower buds and tender leaves of sweet
    marjoram, finely chopped
1 tablespoon unsalted butter, chilled and diced
¼ cup (1 oz/30 g) freshly grated Parmesan cheese

◙ Preheat a broiler (griller). Remove the stem and flower ends
of the zucchini. Depending upon their size, cut them crosswise in thirds; if they are large split them in half lengthwise
first. Pass them through the medium blade of a *mouli-julienne*
or a food processor fitted with the shredding disk. Layer the
shredded zucchini in a mixing bowl, sprinkling each layer
generously with salt, and leave for 30 minutes. Then pick up
the mass and squeeze repeatedly between both hands to rid
it of its water.
◙ Warm 2 tablespoons of the olive oil in a frying pan over high
heat. Add the zucchini and toss often, stirring and breaking it
up with a wooden spoon when necessary, for 2–3 minutes.
Remove from the heat.

◙ Combine the eggs, pepper to taste, marjoram and butter in
a bowl and break up with a fork, whisking only enough to mix
the whites and yolks. Add the sautéed zucchini, stirring and
beating with the fork at the same time to disperse the heat
throughout the mass of eggs.
◙ Select an omelet pan measuring 11 in (28 cm) at the top and 8 in

Top to bottom: Zucchini Omelet, Swiss Chard Pie

(20 cm) at the bottom. Warm the remaining 3 tablespoons olive oil in the pan, rotating the pan to coat the sides. Pour in the zucchini mixture and stir, or swirl, the mixture with the back of the fork without touching the bottom or sides of the pan. Smooth the surface with the fork, cover the pan and lower the heat for a minute or so. Sprinkle with the cheese, taking care that none touches the sides of the pan (lest it stick) and push the pan beneath the hot broiler until the cheese is melted and the center is no longer liquid but not quite firm. Slip the omelet onto a round platter and serve, hot or tepid, cut into wedges.

SERVES 4

SALADE D'ENCORNATS

Squid Salad

Small squid, if sautéed very rapidly, are meltingly tender and delicate. If overcooked, they toughen and must, then, be braised for a relatively long period to become tender again.

2 tablespoons olive oil
2 lb (1 kg) small squid, body pouches 4–6 in (10–15 cm) long, cleaned and body pouches cut crosswise into rings ½ in (12 mm) wide (see glossary)
salt and freshly ground pepper

FOR THE VINAIGRETTE:

2 garden-ripe tomatoes, peeled, seeded and cut into large dices
fine salt
pinch of coarse salt
freshly ground pepper
1 small clove garlic

1 tablespoon Provençal herb vinegar (see glossary)
the reduced squid cooking liquid
1 tablespoon chopped fresh flat-leaf (Italian) parsley
¼ cup (2 fl oz/60 ml) olive oil

Heat the olive oil in a large frying pan over high heat. Add the squid rings and tentacles and salt and pepper to taste. Toss and stir for no more than 1 minute, or until the squid have released an abundant amount of liquid and the flesh has firmed up, losing its translucent cast and turning opaque. Using a slotted spoon, transfer the squid to a salad bowl. Reduce the cooking liquid over high heat to 1–2 tablespoons of light syrup. Pour into a bowl and reserve.

To prepare the vinaigrette, sprinkle the tomato pieces with fine salt and place them on an overturned drum sieve or a wire rack to drain for 30 minutes. Chop them, quite finely, but not to a purée. In a mortar pound together the coarse salt, freshly ground pepper to taste and garlic to form a paste. Slowly stir in the vinegar, reduced squid liquid, tomatoes, parsley and, finally, olive oil. Pour over the squid, toss and serve.

SERVES 6

Clockwise from top: Provençal Fish Soup (recipe page 296), Squid Salad, Marinated Sardine Paupiettes, Mussel Soup

BOUCHES·DU·RHÔNE

PAUPIETTES DE SARDINES EN MARINADE

Marinated Sardine Paupiettes

Fish merchants in Provence put out signs advertising sardines de l'aube ("dawn sardines"), which means they were netted that morning. Very fresh sardines are bright eyed, stiff and arched, with steely blue glints.

2 lb (1 kg) fresh sardines
salt

FOR THE MARINADE:

1 carrot, peeled and thinly sliced
1 onion, thinly sliced
2 cloves garlic, crushed
1 small celery stalk with leaves
1 bay leaf

1 fresh thyme sprig
large pinch of fennel seeds
10–12 peppercorns
10–12 coriander seeds
2 cups (16 fl oz/500 ml) dry, acidulous white wine such as
    Sauvignon or Muscadet

◉ Rub the sardines gently under running water to scale them. Cut off the heads. Slit the abdomens, gut them and, using fingertips and a knife tip, pry the fillets free from the central bone, pinching it off at the tail. Leave the fillets attached at the tail and the length of the back. Rinse the sardines and pat them dry between layers of paper towels. Lay the sardines out, skin side down. Sprinkle lightly with salt, then roll each up from head to tail and pierce it with a wooden toothpick to hold the roll in place. Arrange the *paupiettes* on a tray or large platter, sprinkle well with salt on all sides and let stand for 3 hours.
◉ Combine all the ingredients for the marinade in a saucepan. Bring to a boil, reduce the heat, cover and cook at a gentle boil for 10 minutes. Remove from the heat and let cool.
◉ Sponge the *paupiettes* dry with paper towels and arrange them, side by side, in a terrine or deep, straight-sided dish. Discard the celery stalk, bay leaf and thyme sprig and pour the cold marinade over the sardines. Cover and refrigerate for a couple of days before serving.

SERVES 6

PROVENCE

SOUPE AUX MOULES

Mussel Soup

This recipe uses mussels that have been opened in a fragrant mix of wine and herbs.

2 lb (1 kg) mussels, opened with white wine over heat, shelled
    and immersed in a little of the cooking liquid (see glossary)
4 tablespoons (2 fl oz/60 ml) olive oil
1 sweet onion, finely chopped
1 leek, including the tender green parts, thinly sliced
3 garden-ripe tomatoes, peeled, seeded and coarsely chopped
large pinch of saffron threads or a knife tip (⅛–¼ teaspoon)
    of powdered saffron
2 or 3 short lengths wild fennel or a large pinch of fennel
    seeds pounded to a powder in a mortar
the mussels' decanted cooking liquid plus enough water to
    measure 4 cups (32 fl oz/1 l)
salt
4 egg yolks
freshly ground pepper
4 semidry slices bread, rubbed with a garlic clove

◉ Prepare the mussels as directed.
◉ Warm 2 tablespoons of the olive oil in a heavy saucepan over low heat. Add the onion and leek and cook gently until softened but not colored, 10–15 minutes. Add the tomatoes, saffron and fennel, raise the heat and stir for a few minutes. Add the mussels' cooking liquid–water mixture and cook at a gentle boil until the flavors are well blended, about 20 minutes. Taste for salt and remove from the heat.
◉ In a small bowl mix the egg yolks with the remaining olive oil and grind in pepper to taste. Drain the mussels and add the liquid to the egg mixture. Stir the egg mixture into the broth with a wooden spoon, return the saucepan to low heat and continue stirring until the broth barely coats the spoon, about 8–10 minutes; it must not boil. Remove and discard the fennel stalks and stir in the mussels just to heat through.
◉ Place a garlic-rubbed bread slice in each soup plate and ladle the soup into the bowls.

SERVES 4

AïGO BOUIDO
Garlic Broth

Aïgo bouido (or boulido) means "boiled water." This broth has given its name to the popular folk saying Aïgo bouido sauvo la vido—*"It saves your life." It is particularly recommended as a palliative to gastronomic or bacchic excesses. After straining the broth, eggs are sometimes poached in it. Or the hot broth can be whisked into 2 or 3 beaten egg yolks, with or without the addition of grated cheese. A branch of fennel can replace the sage, and some cooks add a strip of dried orange peel.*

6 cups (48 fl oz/1.5 l) water
salt
2 bay leaves
1 small fresh sage sprig
10–12 cloves garlic
4–5 tablespoons (2–3 fl oz/60–80 ml) olive oil
8 thin slices semidry bread
¾ cup (3 oz/100 g) freshly grated Gruyère or Parmesan cheese

◉ In a saucepan over high heat, combine the water, salt to taste, bay, sage, garlic and 2 tablespoons of the olive oil. When the water boils, reduce the heat, cover with the lid ajar and simmer for 15 minutes. Discard the herbs and pass the broth and the garlic through a sieve.
◉ Place 2 bread slices in each soup plate. Sprinkle the remaining 2–3 tablespoons olive oil and the cheese evenly over the slices. Reheat the broth and pour it over the bread.

SERVES 4

SOUPE DE VERMICELLE AUX TOMATES
Tomato Soup with Angel's Hair Pasta

In France the commercial pasta known elsewhere as angel's hair or capelli d'angelo *is called* vermicelle. *Any small soup pasta can be substituted for it in this soup, however. If you prefer to purée the soup before adding the pasta, the tomatoes need not be peeled. When this soup is made without the pasta, it is poured over bread slices that have first been anointed with olive oil and then sprinkled with cheese; in Toulon, this soup is garnished with little fried sausages and called* rate-rate.

3 tablespoons olive oil
1 onion, finely chopped
1 lb (500 g) garden-ripe tomatoes, peeled and coarsely chopped
1 clove garlic, crushed
1 bay leaf
salt
4 cups (32 fl oz/1 l) water or vegetable broth such as chick-pea, lentil, white bean, leek, or potato, boiling
large handful of angel's hair pasta
freshly ground pepper

◉ Warm the olive oil in a flameproof earthenware casserole or heavy saucepan over low heat. Add the onion and cook gently until softened and lightly colored, about 10 minutes. Add the tomatoes, garlic and bay and season to taste with salt; the amount of salt will depend upon whether you are using water or broth. Raise the heat and cook, stirring, for a couple of minutes. Pour in the boiling water or broth and boil lightly for 4–5 minutes.
◉ Add the pasta and cook for 10 minutes longer. Season to taste with pepper and serve.

SERVES 4

SOUPE DE POISSONS
Provençal Fish Soup

A good Provençal fish soup is infused with an exquisite essence of the sea. On the Mediterranean coast, the soup must include a large selection of rockfish fry, varying from less than 1 inch (2.5 cm) to more than 2–3 inches (5–7 cm) in length, and miniature versions of all the fish traditionally used in a bouillabaisse *(see recipe on page 313).*

FOR THE PASTA:
about 1½ cups (6 oz/180 g) bread (hard) flour
large pinch of salt
¼ teaspoon powdered saffron
1 egg
1 tablespoon olive oil
FOR THE SOUP:
¼ cup (2 fl oz/60 ml) olive oil
½ lb (250 g) onions, chopped
½ lb (250 g) leeks, including the tender green parts, thinly sliced
5 or 6 cloves garlic, crushed
3 lb (1.5 kg) Mediterranean soup fish or small, gutted rock-fish plus heads and carcasses from sliced or filleted white-fleshed fish such as cod, snapper and whiting, gills discarded
1 thick slice conger eel, about ½ lb (250 g), cut into small pieces
1 monkfish (anglerfish) head, chopped, or 1 thick slice monkfish, flesh and backbone cut into small pieces
small handful of coarse sea salt
1 or 2 cayenne peppers or other hot (chili) peppers
2 large sprigs fresh thyme
2 bay leaves
3 or 4 fennel stalks, each about 6 in (15 cm) long or a large pinch of fennel seeds
1 lb (500 g) garden-ripe tomatoes, coarsely chopped, or 1 can (15 oz/400 g) Italian chopped tomatoes with juice
2 cups (16 fl oz/500 ml) white wine
8 cups (64 fl oz/2 l) water, boiling
1 lb (500 g) small, lively crabs such as blue swimmers or sand crabs
large pinch of saffron threads or ½ teaspoon powdered saffron
salt

◉ First, prepare the pasta dough. While it is resting, put the soup on to cook, and while it is cooking, roll out and cut the pasta.
◉ For the pasta, put ¾ cup (3 oz/90 g) of the flour, the salt and saffron into a mixing bowl. Stir with a fork, then make a well in the center. Add the egg and olive oil to the well. Using the fork, stir from the center outward to incorporate as much flour as possible. Next, mash and work the mixture until it begins to pull together, sprinkling over a little additional flour as necessary to create a fairly soft, supple dough.
◉ Flour a work surface and turn the dough out onto it. Knead with your knuckles, continuously folding the dough and sprinkling it with more flour if it is sticky, until it is a smooth, consistent texture. Form it into a ball, cover with a folded towel and let rest for 1 hour.
◉ If you are using a hand-crank pasta machine, cut the dough in half and, using the heel of your hand, press one half on a floured surface to flatten it as much as possible. Turn it over and press again, then pass it slowly through the machine's rollers set at the maximum (kneading) width. Flour the dough again on both sides, fold the ends inward to meet and fold again to make four thicknesses. Flatten again with the heel of your hand and pass it again through the rollers set at the maximum width. Fold in half and pass again, if necessary (the fewer times it is passed, the better it will be; pasta that is folded and passed repeatedly through the machine loses its attractive rustic texture and fresh egg flavor). Without folding the dough, pass it through the rollers two or three times more, diminishing the

Left to right: Tomato Soup with Angel's Hair Pasta, Garlic Broth

thickness each time and finishing at the next to last "notch," or thickness. Hang the dough sheet over a broomstick suspended between two chairbacks until it is dry but still supple to the touch, about 30 minutes. Repeat with the other dough portion. Cut the dough sheets crosswise into 2-in (5-cm) lengths and pass each piece through the *tagliatelli* (the narrowest) cutter on the pasta machine. Sprinkle the cut pasta with flour and toss the pasta loosely with spread fingers to prevent it from sticking together before cooking.

◙ To roll out the pasta by hand, flatten it with the heel of your hand on a floured work surface, sprinkle flour over and roll it out, as thinly as possible, with a rolling pin, turning it over from time to time and sprinkling with flour when necessary to prevent sticking. Hang it over a broomstick to dry for 30 minutes, then return it to the floured work surface. Flour the surface of the pasta, roll it up loosely from one side to the center and then from the other side to the center. Using a large knife, cut the rolled pasta crosswise into ¼-in (6-mm) widths. Slip the knife blade, backside to the center, beneath the cut pasta and lift up to unroll it. With the side of your hand, lift the sections of cut pasta from the knife, spread them out lengthwise and cut across into approximately 2-in (5-cm) lengths. Sprinkle with flour and toss to prevent the pasta from sticking together.

◙ To prepare the soup, warm the olive oil in a large, heavy (8–10 qt/8–10 l) saucepan or stockpot over medium heat. Add the onions, leeks and garlic and stir for 4–5 minutes until softened; do not permit them to color. Throw in all of the fish, the salt, cayenne peppers and all the herbs. Cook for 10 minutes or so, stirring and crushing the contents with a wooden spoon. Add the tomatoes and continue to stir until the tomatoes break

up and begin to boil, about 5 minutes. Add the wine, raise the heat, and stir until the contents come to a full boil. Pour in the boiling water and stir to amalgamate the contents. Throw in the crabs and adjust the heat to maintain a gentle boil. Cover with the lid slightly ajar and cook for a few minutes. Remove from the heat.

◙ Three or four at a time, transfer the crabs to a mortar and crush and pound them with a wooden pestle until they are reduced to a coarse, broken-up purée. Spoon them back into the pot and pound the others. When all the crabs have been crushed, wash out the mortar with a ladle of broth and pour it back into the pot. Return the pot to the heat and continue to cook the soup gently until all the flavors have been drawn out by the liquid, about 40 minutes.

◙ Remove the pot to a work surface. Pass 2 or 3 ladlefuls of the soup through a sieve placed over a large bowl, pushing and pressing with the pestle to extract all the liquid and flavor. Discard the dry paste of shells and debris from the sieve and begin again, picking out and discarding the herbs as they turn up. When all the soup has been passed, clean out the soup pot and rinse the sieve, taking care to remove any tiny bones that may be caught in the mesh. Place the sieve over the pot and pour all of the liquid through it again; shake the sieve gently but do not stir the contents. Discard the fine purée that collects in the sieve. Add the saffron to the soup pot and reheat.

◙ While the soup is reheating, fill a saucepan with water, add salt to taste and bring to a boil. Add the noodles and cook until tender, no more than 2 minutes, then drain and add to the soup. Ladle into heated soup plates and serve.

SERVES 6–8   *Photograph pages 294–295*

BOUCHES-DU-RHÔNE/VAR

SOUPE DE FAVOUILLES

Crab Soup

Favouille is the Provençal name for the little Mediterranean green shore crab whose shell is only about 2–3 in (5–7 cm) wide. The same crab is found in Venice, where it is cultivated for eating, like the soft-shell blue crabs in America, at the time of molting. The distinctive peppery taste of the favouille *is considered indispens-*able to the complex flavor of a soupe de poissons *(recipe on page 296) or a* bouillabaisse *(recipe on page 313).*

3 tablespoons olive oil
1 large, sweet white onion, sliced
½ lb (250 g) leeks, including the tender green parts, thickly sliced
5 or 6 cloves garlic, crushed
about 2 dozen small, lively crabs such as blue swimmers or sand crabs
2–3 tablespoons marc de Provence (see glossary) or Cognac
½ cup (4 fl oz/125 ml) dry white wine

1 lb (500 g) garden-ripe tomatoes, coarsely chopped
large bouquet garni, including a fennel stalk (see glossary)
salt
a few grains cayenne pepper
6 cups (48 fl oz/1.5 l) water, boiling
large pinch of saffron threads
2 or 3 slices semidry bread, lightly toasted, rubbed on both
    sides with garlic and cut into cubes

◉ In a large, heavy sauté pan over medium heat, warm the olive oil. Add the onion, leeks and garlic and stir for 4–5 minutes until softened; do not permit them to color. Throw in the crabs and stir until they have begun to turn red on all sides. Add the brandy and, a minute later, the white wine and tomatoes. Bring to a rapid boil, stirring all the while. Add the bouquet garni, salt to taste and cayenne and cook, stirring, until the tomatoes have begun to disintegrate and the crabs are completely red, about 5 minutes. Remove from the heat.
◉ Three or four at a time, transfer the crabs to a mortar and crush and pound them with a wooden pestle until they are all reduced to a coarse, broken-up purée. Spoon them back into the pan and pound the others.
◉ Transfer the contents of the sauté pan to a saucepan (to avoid excess reduction) and add the boiling water. Bring to a boil, cover with the lid ajar and cook at a gentle boil for about 15 minutes. Remove and discard the bouquet garni.
◉ Pass 2 or 3 ladlefuls of the soup through a fine-mesh sieve placed over a large bowl, pushing and pressing with the pestle to extract all the liquid and flavor. Discard the dry paste of shells and debris and begin again. Repeat until all of the soup has been forced through the sieve. Add the saffron to the broth, reheat it and serve accompanied with a dish of garlic croutons.

SERVES 4

P R O V E N C E

POT-AU-FEU À LA PROVENÇALE

Provençal Pot-au-Feu

A Provençal pot-au-feu *is distinguished by the presence, in addition to the usual beef cuts, of a lamb shank (*béquet*), which lends complexity to the flavor and softness to the texture of the broth. The famous gastronome Austin de Croze, writing in 1928, claims that it is obligatory to accompany a Provençal* pot-au-feu *with a warm chick-pea salad. He is often quoted but rarely respected.*

1 pig's foot (trotter)
3 lb (1.5 kg) boned beef shank (shin), in a single piece
1½ lb (750 g) beef short ribs
1 lamb shank (shin) on the bone, about 1½ lb (750 g)
1 large beef marrow bone, about 1½–2 lb (750 g–1 kg), tied
    in cheesecloth (muslin)
½ cup (4 fl oz/125 ml) dry white wine
handful of coarse salt
1 large onion stuck with 2 whole cloves
1 whole head garlic
large bouquet garni (see glossary)
1 lb (500 g) young, tender carrots, peeled
1 lb (500 g) small, crisp turnips, peeled
2 lb (1 kg) leeks
6 slices semidry bread
coarse sea salt, capers and gray, unrefined black olives, if
    available, for serving

◉ Place the pig's foot in a saucepan, add cold water to cover and bring to a full boil. Drain, rinse under cold water, drain again and set aside.
◉ Using kitchen twine, tie the beef shank and short ribs together in a compact package. In a traditional earthenware

pot-au-feu or a deep, heavy saucepan with a capacity of about 10 qt (10 l), arrange all of the meats, including the pig's foot, so that no space is wasted but they are not packed tightly. Pour in cold water to cover the meat by about 2 in (5 cm) and place the pot over low to medium heat, protected from the direct flame by a flame-tamer. Bring slowly to a boil; this should require nearly 1 hour. As gray scum rises to the surface, skim it off continually. When the water begins to boil, add the wine and continue to skim.
◉ Add the salt, clove-studded onion, head of garlic and bouquet garni. Continue to skim until the liquid approaches a boil again. Cover with a lid slightly ajar and adjust the heat, repeatedly if necessary, so that a bare simmer is maintained. Cook for 2 hours. Check the pot from time to time; the liquid should never boil.
◉ After 2 hours add the carrots and the turnips and continue to simmer. Meanwhile, remove the dark green tops from the leeks and slit the upper leaf part; wash well and tie the leeks into a bundle. When the carrots and turnips have been cooking for 30 minutes, add the leeks and cook for 30 minutes longer.
◉ The *pot-au-feu* should be ready about 3 hours after it was first brought to a boil. Pierce the beef shank with a trussing needle or sharp skewer to see if the shank is tender (it requires the longest cooking of all the meats).
◉ Skim the excess fat from the surface of the broth. Discard the onion, head of garlic and bouquet garni, and put the pig's foot aside to be added to a salad another day. Remove the marrow bone from its wrapping and slip the marrow out onto a plate. Spread the marrow on the bread slices and place 1 slice in each soup plate.
◉ Serve the broth directly from the pot, leaving the meats and vegetables in the broth to keep them hot. Snip the strings from the meats and carve them, cutting only as much as you think may be eaten. The remainder will be easier to slice thinly for a *mironton* (recipe on page 152) when cold. Arrange the cut meats on a platter. Snip the string from the leeks and arrange the leeks and all the other vegetables around the meats. Pour some broth into a small pitcher or bowl and place on the table for those who wish to moisten their meats. Offer the sea salt, capers and olives at the table as well. When the meal is finished, remove the meat from the broth, wrap well and refrigerate.

SERVES 6

Provençal Pot-au-Feu

HOURTÊTE
Kitchen Garden Soup

Hourtête, which means "little garden," is no doubt as old as Provence; the recipe was first published in Le cuisinier Durand, *the earliest Provençal cookbook and still one of the best. The author, Charles Durand, was born in 1766; his career was mainly divided between Nîmes and Marseilles and spanned the Ancien Régime, the Revolution, the Napoleonic era and the reigns of Louis XVIII, Charles X and Louis-Philippe.*

6 cups (48 fl oz/1.5 l) water or broth
salt, if using water
5 oz (150 g) spinach leaves, stemmed, tightly rolled up and finely sliced
5 oz (150 g) Swiss chard (silverbeet) greens, tightly rolled up and finely sliced
5 oz (150 g) sorrel leaves, stemmed, tightly rolled up and finely sliced
small handful of celery leaves, chopped
small handful of fresh chervil sprigs, chopped
1 clove garlic
1 sweet white onion, thinly sliced
4 egg yolks
freshly ground pepper
thin slices semidry baguette
3–4 tablespoons (2 fl oz/60 ml) olive oil

◙ In a saucepan over high heat, add salt, if desired, and bring the water or broth to a boil. Add the spinach, chard, sorrel, celery, chervil, garlic and onion and boil gently for about 15 minutes.

◙ In a small bowl, break up the egg yolks with a fork and grind over pepper to taste. While stirring constantly, add a small ladleful of the hot soup. Remove the saucepan from the heat and let stand for a couple of minutes. Using a wooden spoon, stir in the egg mixture. Return the saucepan to low heat and continue to stir until the soup just begins to coat the spoon thinly, 8–10 minutes; it must not boil.

◙ Place the bread in a soup tureen or divide among individual soup plates and dribble with the olive oil. Ladle the soup over the bread and serve.

SERVES 4

OMELET AUX TOMATES
Tomato Omelet

5 tablespoons (3 fl oz/80 ml) olive oil, or as needed
1 sweet white onion, halved and thinly sliced
¼ lb (125 g) Italian sweet peppers or other sweet peppers (capsicums), cut in half lengthwise, seeded, deribbed and thinly sliced crosswise
2 cloves garlic, crushed
2 garden-ripe tomatoes, peeled, seeded and coarsely chopped
salt
cayenne pepper
5 eggs
freshly ground black pepper

◙ Warm 2 tablespoons of the olive oil in a wide, heavy frying pan over low heat. Add the onion and peppers and cook, stirring occasionally with a wooden spoon, until soft but not colored, about 15 minutes. Raise the heat and add the garlic,

tomatoes, salt to taste and a discreet dash of cayenne. Toss the contents of the pan repeatedly until the tomatoes begin to break up and boil, about 5 minutes. Turn the heat to low and simmer for about 15 minutes, stirring from time to time. Raise the heat to high once again and toss to evaporate any remaining liquid. Empty the tomatoes onto a plate and leave until completely cooled.

◙ In a mixing bowl combine the eggs and a pinch of salt. Grind over some black pepper and break up the eggs with a fork, whisking enough only to mix the whites and the yolks. Stir in the cooled tomato mixture.

◙ Select an omelet pan measuring 11 in (28 cm) at the top and 8 in (20 cm) at the bottom. Warm 3 tablespoons olive oil in the pan over high heat, rotating the pan to coat the sides with oil. Pour in the egg mixture and stir, or swirl, the mixture with the back of the fork without touching the bottom or sides of the pan. Gradually working around the circumference of the omelet, lift the edges with the fork tip, tilting the pan each time to permit the liquid egg on the surface to run beneath the underside.

◙ When the omelet begins to set, unmold it from the pan by first jerking the pan back and forth to loosen the omelet and then turning it out onto a lid. Add another tablespoon olive oil to the pan, return the omelet browned side up and turn the heat up for about 20 seconds to finish the cooking. Alternatively, finish the omelet without turning it out by slipping it under a hot broiler, removing it when it is no longer liquid at the center but not quite firmly set. Slide onto a serving platter and serve, hot or tepid, cut into wedges.

SERVES 4

OEUFS À LA TRIPE
Eggs in Onion Sauce

2 tablespoons unsalted butter
1 lb (500 g) sweet white onions, thinly sliced
salt
1 tablespoon all-purpose (plain) flour
1 cup (8 fl oz/250 ml) milk
freshly ground pepper
whole nutmeg
⅛ teaspoon powdered saffron dissolved in 1 tablespoon boiling water
6 hard-cooked eggs, shelled and quartered
chopped fresh flat-leaf (Italian) parsley for garnish

◙ Melt the butter in a heavy saucepan or sauté pan over low heat. Add the onions and salt to taste, cover and cook, stirring often with a wooden spoon until the onions are very soft but not colored, at least 30 minutes.

◙ Sprinkle the flour over the onions, stir around, and slowly add the milk, stirring all the while. Raise the heat to medium-high and continue stirring until a boil is reached. Reduce the heat to low and cook gently for another 30 minutes, stirring often.

◙ Grind over some pepper and scrape in a hint of nutmeg. Stir in the dissolved saffron and add the eggs, stirring carefully to avoid breaking them up. Heat through.

◙ Turn the mixture into a preheated serving dish and sprinkle with parsley.

SERVES 4

In a Lourmarin garden, clockwise from top: Kitchen Garden Soup, Tomato Omelet, Eggs in Onion Sauce

BOUCHES·DU·RHÔNE
SOUPE TÔT FAITE
Fast Soup

Also called soupe vite facho *and a refreshing change from the usual long-cooked potato-and-leek soup. Here, the vegetables are finely cut and boiled only briefly.*

1½ lb (750 g) potatoes
6 cups (48 fl oz/1.5 l) water
salt
1 lb (500 g) leeks, including the tender green parts, thinly sliced
4 slices semidry bread

2–3 tablespoons olive oil
freshly ground pepper

▦ Peel the potatoes, cut in half lengthwise and then slice each half into 3 or 4 lengthwise slices. Now thinly cut the slices crosswise. Set aside.
▦ In a saucepan over high heat, combine the water, salt to taste, potatoes and leeks. Bring to a boil and boil until the potato slivers are easily crushed against the side of the saucepan with a wooden spoon, about 20 minutes.
▦ Place 1 bread slice in each soup plate. Sprinkle with olive oil to taste and then grind pepper over the top. Ladle the soup over the bread and serve.
SERVES 4

Fast Soup

Anchovy and Onion Tart

PISSALADIÈRE

Anchovy and Onion Tart

Pissaladière *takes its name from* pissalat, *a traditional Niçois preparation of fish fry, salted and placed under a weight for a week before being sieved into a purée to be used as a seasoning (the same preparation, in the Bouches-du-Rhône, is called* melet). *Today salt anchovies nearly always replace the* pissalat. *Cooks in Provence often buy bread dough from the baker to roll out for their* pissaladières. *Some knead a bit of olive oil into it first; others prefer to use a butter-and-flour short crust or a Provençal olive-oil pastry dough. The best onions for a* pissaladière *are large, freshly dug, sweet white onions, which have a high water content.*

FOR THE PROVENÇAL PASTRY DOUGH:

2 cups (8 oz/250 g) all-purpose (plain) flour
large pinch of salt
1 egg
¼ cup (2 fl oz/60 ml) olive oil
¼ cup (2 fl oz/60 ml) lukewarm water
additional flour for rolling out dough

5 tablespoons (3 fl oz/80 ml) olive oil
3 lb (1.5 kg) sweet white onions, thinly sliced
3 or 4 cloves garlic
salt
1 bay leaf
1 fresh thyme sprig
8 salt anchovies, rinsed, filleted and mashed (see glossary)
¾ cup (4 oz/125 g) black olives
freshly ground pepper

◉ To prepare the dough, place the flour and salt together in a mixing bowl and stir together with a fork. Add the egg, olive oil and water. Mix first with the fork and then knead in the bowl with your knuckles until you have a soft, consistent dough. Form into a ball and leave in the bowl. Cover with a folded towel and let stand at kitchen temperature for about 1 hour before rolling out.

◉ Warm 3 tablespoons of the olive oil in a flameproof earthenware casserole or a heavy sauté pan over very low heat. Add the onions, garlic, salt to taste and herbs. Cover and cook over the lowest possible heat for about 1 hour, stirring occasionally with a wooden spoon. The onions must not color. If the cooking vessel is right and the heat low enough, they will be absolutely white and purée-soft after an hour of cooking. Remove from the heat and remove and discard the bay leaf and thyme sprig. Stir in the anchovies.

◉ Preheat an oven to 350°F (180°C). Lightly oil a large, round or rectangular heavy baking sheet. Flour a work surface and place the dough on it. Flatten the dough with your hand, then sprinkle it with more flour. Roll it out thinly to the approximate size and shape of the baking sheet. Drape the pastry around the rolling pin and transfer it to the sheet. Press it gently onto the bottom and sides of the sheet. Roll the edges under to form a rim. Crimp all around the edge with the side of your thumb, repeatedly dipping it in flour so it is not sticky. Prick the surface of the pastry here and there with the tines of a fork, then spread the onion mixture over the pastry. Push the olives into it, one by one, half buried and regularly distributed. Brush the rim of the pastry with a little of the remaining 2 tablespoons of olive oil, then sprinkle a bit more over the surface of the onions.

◉ Place in the oven and bake until the rim of the pastry is golden and crisp, about 30 minutes. Remove from the oven and grind over some pepper.

SERVES 6

CAVIAR D'AUBERGINE

Eggplant Spread

The spread is best served warm, as an hors d'oeuvre accompanied with warm toasts and chilled white or rosé wine.

3 elongated eggplants (aubergines), about 1½ lb (750 g) total weight
2 cloves garlic
pinch of coarse salt
2 salt anchovies, rinsed and filleted (see glossary)
freshly ground pepper
fine salt

4–5 tablespoons (2–3 fl oz/60–90 ml) olive oil

◉ Preheat an oven to 350°F (180°C).
◉ Prick the eggplants several times and place them in a shallow baking dish. Bake until the flesh is very soft when pierced with a knife tip, about 45 minutes. Remove from the oven and, when cool enough to handle, split the eggplants in half. Using a spoon scrape the flesh onto a plate. Discard the skins and mash the flesh to a coarse purée with a fork.
◉ In a mortar pound together the garlic and coarse salt to form a paste. Add the anchovies, grind in pepper to taste and pound again. Empty the contents of the plate into the mortar and turn with the pestle, slowly adding the olive oil until the mixture is a loose, spreadable consistency. Add fine salt to taste.

SERVES 4

bouquet garni (see glossary)
3 tablespoons olive oil
1 onion, thinly sliced
1 leek, including the tender green parts, thinly sliced
1 carrot, peeled and diced
2 cloves garlic, crushed
½ lb (250 g) Swiss chard (silverbeet) greens, shredded
salt
freshly ground pepper

◈ Place the lentils in a bowl, add cold water to cover and let stand for 2–3 hours.
◈ Drain the lentils and place in a flameproof earthenware casserole or an enamelware pot. Add water to cover, bring to a boil and boil for 5 minutes. Drain, return the lentils to the pot and pour in the boiling water.
◈ Add the bouquet garni, cover and simmer over low heat while you prepare the rest of the soup.
◈ In a saucepan over low heat, warm the olive oil. Add the onion, leek and carrot and cook gently until softened, about 15 minutes. Add the garlic, chard and salt to taste. Raise the heat and cook until the chard softens and its juices evaporate, about 5 minutes. Add the contents of the saucepan to the lentils and continue to simmer until the lentils are tender, about 1 hour. Season with salt, grind in some pepper and serve.

SERVES 6

ALPES-MARITIMES

POTAGE PRINTANIER
Spring Soup

Broad beans for soup should be more mature than those eaten raw, with each bean about the size of a thumbnail. The flesh should be a clear green and the beans should not have begun to turn starchy. At this stage, the peel on each bean is slightly tough and bitter and must be removed, but the flesh beneath should be tender and not hard to the touch. Petite green peas can be substituted or added.

8 cups (64 fl oz/2 l) water
salt
3 young, tender artichokes, trimmed, halved lengthwise, chokes removed if necessary and thinly sliced (see glossary)
10 oz (300 g) new potatoes, peeled and diced
½ lb (250 g) Swiss chard (silverbeet) greens, tightly rolled up and finely sliced
5 oz (150 g) young green shallots (see glossary) or green (spring) onions, sliced or chopped
2 or 3 fresh winter savory sprigs, tied together
2 lb (1 kg) young broad (fava) beans, shelled and each bean peeled
2 eggs
2 tablespoons olive oil
freshly ground pepper
Parmesan cheese for serving

◈ Pour the water into a large saucepan, add salt to taste and bring to a boil. Add the artichokes, potatoes, chard, shallots or onions and savory. Cover with the lid slightly ajar and cook at a gentle boil for about 15 minutes. Add the broad beans and cook until they are meltingly tender but still intact, about 10 minutes.
◈ Remove and discard the savory bouquet. In a small bowl combine the eggs and olive oil. Grind in pepper to taste and beat with a fork until blended. Stir in a small ladleful of the broth. Remove the pan from the heat and stir in the egg mixture. Serve at once, with a wedge of Parmesan and a grater on the side.

SERVES 6

Top to bottom: Spring Soup, Lentil Soup, Eggplant Spread

ALPES-MARITIMES

SOUPE DE LENTILLES À LA NIÇOISE
Lentil Soup

Tiny, speckled lentils, called lentilles vertes *or* lentilles du Puy, *are the best. They must be carefully sorted over by pouring small quantities at a time onto a plate from which they are shifted to a bowl. It is rare not to discover one or two tiny bits of gravel—very unpleasant to bite into if overlooked.*

1 cup (6 ½ oz/200 g) lentils, preferably *lentilles vertes* (see glossary)
8 cups (48 fl oz/2 l) water, boiling

GAYETTES/CAILLETTES À LA VAUCLUSIENNE
Vaucluse Pork Crépinettes

The name of this dish is thought to derive from the Provençal word
gaio, meaning "pork sweetbreads," which were, no doubt, once
included in its composition along with the heart, spleen and lungs of
the pig. It is nearly always served at room temperature.

¼ lb (125 g) each pork liver, poultry livers and salt pork
  (green bacon), finely chopped or passed through the
  medium blade of a meat grinder
½ lb (250 g) sausage meat (see glossary)
1 lb (500 g) spinach, parboiled, squeezed dry and chopped
  (see glossary)
1 onion, finely chopped and sautéed in 1 tablespoon olive
  oil until soft but not colored
persillade made with 2 cloves garlic (see glossary)
large pinch of Provençal mixed dried herbs (see glossary)
salt, freshly ground pepper and ground allspice
2 eggs
about 2 oz (60 g) caul, soaked briefly in tepid water with a
  dash of wine vinegar and drained (see glossary)
fresh sage leaves or small sprigs
about ½ cup (4 fl oz/125 ml) water

▣ In a large bowl combine all the ingredients except the caul,
sage and water, adding salt, pepper and allspice to taste. Using
your hands, mix thoroughly, squeezing the mixture repeatedly
between your fingers.
▣ Preheat an oven to 400°F (200°C). Stretch the caul out on a
work surface and cut it into 5-in (13-cm) squares. Moisten your
hands in water and form balls of the meat mixture the size of
a small orange. Wrap each ball in a square of caul and flatten the
ball slightly with the palm of your hand. Turn it over so the
pleat is on the bottom and press a sprig or leaf of sage on top.
▣ Pour the water into the bottom of a shallow baking dish.
Arrange the balls, side by side and touching but not crowded,
in the dish. Place in the oven and bake until the surfaces are
nicely colored and the caul is transformed into a beautiful
golden brown lace, about 30 minutes. Serve at room temperature.

SERVES 4

BEIGNETS
Fritters

Mixed fritters are always more amusing than a single element.
Other vegetable possibilities are little green (spring) onions, thin
slices of zucchini (courgette) and eggplant (aubergine), zucchini or
other squash flowers, parboiled green beans or cauliflower florets
and precooked salsify. Live mussels, removed from their shells at
the last minute, and raw, peeled shrimp make lovely fritters.

FOR THE BATTER:

1 cup (4 oz/125 g) all-purpose (plain) flour
salt and freshly ground pepper
2 eggs, separated
1 tablespoon olive oil
¾ cup (6 fl oz/180 ml) warm beer

2 or 3 small squid, cleaned (see glossary)
3 oz (100 g) fresh cultivated mushrooms, whole if small and
  quartered if larger

6 small or 4 medium young, tender artichokes, trimmed,
  quartered if small or cut into eighths if medium and
  chokes removed if necessary (see glossary)
1 tablespoon finely chopped mixed fresh herbs such as
  parsley, chives, and tarragon or hyssop or marjoram
juice of ½ lemon
1 tablespoon olive oil
salt and freshly ground pepper
about 8 cups (64 fl oz/2 l) corn oil or peanut oil
8 young, tender sorrel leaves, stems snipped close to leaf
handful of tiny bouquets of fresh flat-leaf (Italian) parsley
  leaves
2 cups (16 fl oz/500 ml) tomato sauce, heated (see glossary)

▣ In a mixing bowl whisk together the flour, salt and
pepper to taste, egg yolks, oil and beer, moving from the
center of bowl outward and whisking only long enough
to produce a smooth batter. Cover with a plate and rest
for 2 hours at room temperature. Just before using, in a

separate bowl whisk the egg whites until they hold limp peaks and fold them gently into the batter.

◉ Pull the wings off the squid pouches. Cut the upper part of the pouches into rings about ⅓ in (1 cm) wide and split the pouch tips in two. Using paper towels sponge the squid pieces dry, including the tentacles. Assemble them in a bowl with the mushrooms and the artichokes. Sprinkle the herbs, lemon juice, olive oil and salt and pepper to taste over the top, toss and marinate at room temperature for about 30 minutes. Toss 2 or 3 times.

◉ Following the directions for deep-frying in the glossary, heat the corn or peanut oil in a large pan. Add a few pieces of the squid, mushrooms and artichokes to the batter, turning them around so that all are perfectly coated. Hold the bowl next to the vessel of hot oil and, using a fork, lift each batter-coated piece, pausing above the bowl for a couple of seconds to allow excess batter to fall off. Then slip it into the oil from just above the surface. Do not crowd the fritters in the hot oil. After a

couple of minutes, when the floating fritters are golden at the edges, turn each over in the oil, nudging it from underneath with a rounded knife tip or similar instrument. Unless you are working with an electric fryer with a built-in thermostat, you may want to turn the heat up or down from time to time. When the fritters are beautifully colored on both sides—after 3–4 minutes—lift and drain them as directed.

◉ When all of the marinated elements are fried, pick up the sorrel leaves, one at a time by the stem end, dip each into the batter and then slip it into the oil and fry until golden. Remove and drain as for the other ingredients. When all of the sorrel has been removed from the fryer, drop the parsley leaves into the oil and stand back; there will be an explosive crackling for 1–2 seconds and they are done. Remove the parsley to paper towels. Scatter the parsley over the fritters and serve with the tomato sauce on the side.

SERVES 4

PROVENCE

OMELETTE BAVEUSE AUX ASPERGES

Asparagus Omelet

Rolled omelets in Provence are reserved for special garnishes—wild-asparagus tips, truffles, sea urchin corals, mussels, sea anemones—all of which are especially succulent bathed in the saucelike interior of an omelette baveuse. Visually beautiful omelets can be prepared any size, but a perfect rolled omelet, sufficiently moist inside, is difficult to prepare with more than 4 or 5 eggs. If serving more than two people, it is wiser to make two or more omelets—each requires about one minute's preparation from the time the eggs are poured into the pan to the time they are rolled onto the platter. The following recipe is designed for readers who have no access to wild asparagus. Asparagus, prepared in the same way, are also delicious incorporated into scrambled eggs.

½ lb (250 g) asparagus
4–5 tablespoons (2–3 fl oz/60–80 ml) olive oil
4 eggs
1 tablespoon unsalted butter, chilled and diced
salt and freshly ground pepper

◉ Cut off any tough asparagus stalk ends and peel each stalk to the point at which the skin becomes tender. Slice each spear, on the bias, into slivers varying in thickness from ¼ in (6 mm) at the tender tip end to ⅛ in (3 mm) at the stalk end. Bring a saucepan filled with salted water to a boil. Plunge the slivers into the boiling water and, as soon as the water returns to a boil, drain them.

◉ Warm 1 tablespoon of the olive oil in a sauté pan over high heat. Add the asparagus slivers and sauté for a few seconds. Remove from the heat.

◉ In a mixing bowl combine the eggs, butter and salt and pepper to taste. Break up the eggs with a fork, whisking enough only to mix the whites and yolks. Add the asparagus, stirring and beating with the fork at the same time to disperse the heat immediately throughout the mass of eggs.

◉ Select an omelet pan measuring 11 in (28 cm) at the top and 8 in (20 cm) at the bottom. Warm 2 tablespoons olive oil in the pan over high heat, rotating the pan to coat the sides with oil. Pour in the egg mixture and stir, or swirl, the mixture with the back of the fork without touching the bottom or sides of the pan. Gradually working around the circumference of the omelet, lift the edges with the fork tip, tilting the pan each time to permit the liquid egg on the surface to run beneath the underside.

◉ When the omelet begins to set, begin rolling the omelet at the handle side of the pan, lifting the edge with the side of the fork and folding it over. Fold again, pull the pan toward yourself, tilting it sharply to cradle the omelet at the far side, over the heat. Press the outer edge of the omelet against the rolled mass with the fork tines and hold the pan, still at an angle, over the heat for a few seconds to color the underside. Roll the omelet out onto a warmed platter, seam side down and golden side up, by partially inverting the pan.

SERVES 2

Asparagus Omelet

308

In the park of the Château de Lourmarin, Scrambled Eggs with Tomatoes and Basil

BROUILLADE AUX TOMATES

Scrambled Eggs with Tomatoes and Basil

2 tablespoons olive oil
1 clove garlic, finely chopped
1½ lb (750 g) garden-ripe tomatoes, peeled, seeded and
    coarsely chopped
salt
1 bay leaf
10 eggs
¼ cup (2 oz/60 g) unsalted butter, chilled and diced
freshly ground pepper
handful of fresh basil leaves, torn into fragments at the last
    minute

◈ Warm the olive oil in a flameproof earthenware casserole over low heat. Add the garlic and, before it begins to color, add the tomatoes, salt to taste and bay leaf. Raise the heat slightly until the tomatoes are heated through and bubbling, then lower it and cook, uncovered, stirring occasionally with a wooden spoon, until all the liquid evaporates, about 10–15 minutes. Remove from the heat and remove and discard the bay leaf.

◈ In a mixing bowl, combine the eggs, a pinch of salt, butter and freshly ground pepper to taste. Break up the eggs with a fork, whisking only enough to mix the whites and yolks. Place the pan holding the tomatoes over medium-high heat and pour in the eggs. Stir constantly, scraping the sides and bottom of the pan with the wooden spoon, until the mixture begins to form a thick cream.

◈ Remove from the heat, add the basil and continue stirring as the eggs continue to absorb heat from the pan. Serve directly from the pan.

SERVES 4

Ratatouille

PROVENCE

RATATOUILLE

Ratatouille is especially interesting to prepare in large quantity at the height of summer when all of the vegetables are at their best and usually in great abundance. It is a refreshing cold summer luncheon starter and the flavors meld and improve after a couple of days. Serve it hot with grilled or roast lamb, pork, veal or poultry, or mix it into scrambled eggs.

about 1 cup (8 fl oz/250 ml) olive oil
2 lb (1 kg) onions, coarsely cut
2 lb (1 kg) firm, glossy, elongated eggplants (aubergines), thickly sliced and then cut into large cubes
2 lb (1 kg) red, yellow and green sweet peppers (capsicums), halved lengthwise, seeded, deribbed and cut into squares
2 lb (1 kg) garden-ripe tomatoes, peeled, seeded, and coarsely cut
1 head garlic, cloves separated and peeled
handful of coarse sea salt

large bouquet garni, including 3 bay leaves and several fresh
    thyme sprigs (see glossary)
2 lb (1 kg) small, firm zucchini (courgettes), quartered
    lengthwise and thickly sliced crosswise
freshly ground pepper
fresh basil leaves

◙ Warm half of the olive oil in an 8–10-qt (8–10-l) stockpot
over low heat. Add the onions and cook gently until softened
but not colored, about 10 minutes. Stir occasionally with a
wooden spoon as you begin to cut up and progressively add all
the other vegetables, with the exception of the zucchini. Add
the salt and stir gently, scraping the bottom of the pot, until the
vegetables begin to release their liquid. Raise the heat to
medium and bring the liquid to a boil. From the time the onions
were added to the pot to the moment the boil is reached, 45
minutes to 1 hour should elapse.
◙ Bury the bouquet garni beneath the vegetables, reduce the
heat to maintain a light, bubbling simmer and cover with the
lid slightly ajar. After about 30 minutes, add the zucchini,
forcing it beneath the liquid's surface with the back of the
wooden spoon. Simmer for another 45 minutes to 1 hour, or
until all of the vegetables are meltingly tender.
◙ The vegetables must now be drained and their juices
reduced. The most practical way to do this is to place a large
colander with legs inside a large (12 in/30 cm in diameter),
heavy sauté pan. Pour the contents of the pot (slowly and away
from yourself, to avoid splattering) into the colander. Let drain
for a couple of minutes, then prop the colander over the empty
stockpot to continue draining.
◙ Place the juices over high heat, bring to a boil, and then
reduce the heat to maintain a gentle boil. Place a platter beside
the stockpot and, from time to time, move the colander to the
platter to empty newly drained juices from the pot into the
reducing liquid. About 1 hour will be required for the juices to
reduce to a deep, mahogany-colored syrup with a foamy boil.
Toward the end of the reduction, survey the pan constantly,
stirring often, and remove it from the heat the moment the
foamy boil begins to subside into a staccato bubble.
◙ Return the vegetables to their cooking pot, remove the
bouquet garni and pour in the reduced juices, scraping the pot
clean. Gently stir the vegetables until all are evenly coated with
the reduced juices. Turn them into a large dish to cool.
◙ Grind over some pepper and stir several spoonfuls of the
remaining olive oil into the cooled vegetables. Unless the dish
is meant to be consumed at a single sitting, spoon only as much
as you think necessary for the meal into a smaller serving dish
before adding a few more drops of olive oil to the surface. Tear
basil leaves into fragments and scatter them over the top.
Tightly cover the remainder and refrigerate.

SERVES 10–12

VAUCLUSE

BROUILLADE AUX TRUFFES
Scrambled Eggs with Truffles

*The northernmost section of the Vaucluse consists of a small enclave
within the department of the Drôme. Here, the villages of Valréas
and Richerenches are important truffle centers. The black truffle
season begins around the first of December, the truffles are best in
January and February and, then, the season is over. Eggs are a
perfect vehicle for the truffles' magic perfume. The eggs are cooked
in a* bain-marie, *a heavy saucepan placed on a low tripod in a
larger saucepan that is filled with water to about the level of the
eggs in the smaller pan. To gauge the amount of water necessary,
assemble the pans and the tripod in advance, pour water into
the larger pan until it reaches the correct level and then
remove the smaller pan.*

1 clove garlic, cut in half
3 oz (100 g) black truffles, brushed and sliced
⅓ cup (3 oz/100 g) unsalted butter, chilled and diced
10 eggs
salt
freshly ground pepper

◙ Rub the inside surfaces of a mixing bowl with the cut surface
of a half clove of garlic. Add the truffles and half the butter.
Break in the eggs, cover the bowl with a plate and leave for 30
minutes for scents and flavors to intermingle.
◙ Assemble the *bain-marie* as described in the recipe introduction and remove the small pan. Bring the water in the larger pan
to a boil and lower the heat so the water is hot but distinctly
beneath a boil. Rub a wooden spoon with the remaining half
clove of garlic. Sprinkle salt and pepper to taste over the eggs
and beat very briefly with a fork. Pour the egg mixture into the
smaller saucepan, wiping the bowl clean, and place the pan on
the tripod in the hot water. Stir the eggs with the garlic-rubbed
spoon, adjusting the heat when necessary to prevent the water
from boiling. At first, nothing seems to happen, but when,
finally, the eggs begin to thicken, it happens very rapidly. Stir
more rapidly at this point, removing the pan for a moment
from the water if you fear losing control. As the eggs begin to
turn into a thick, but easily pourable cream, remove the pan
from the water, add the remaining butter and continue stirring
for a few minutes. The amount of time necessary to cook the
eggs will vary, depending upon the cooking vessel. The longer
they take, the better their texture, however.
◙ Serve directly from the saucepan onto a warm—but not
hot—plate.

SERVES 4

Scrambled Eggs with Truffles

ALPES·MARITIMES

RAÏOLA
Ravioli

In Provence ravioli are made from daube, leftover or prepared especially for that purpose the previous day. The meat should be removed from its braising liquid while still warm. The reheated braising liquid is the sauce, and old women are known to guard jealously the "secret" of their ravioli sauces. Benoit Mascarelli, author of La table en Provence *(1946), writes, "We have seen old Niçois weep at the mere sound of the lovely name 'Raïola'!" In Nice ravioli stuffing typically contains chard (silverbeet) greens, and often a poached and puréed lamb's brain lends suavity.*

double recipe pasta dough made without saffron (see
 Provençal fish soup on page 296

FOR THE STUFFING:

1 tablespoon olive oil
1 onion, finely chopped
¼ lb (125 g) Swiss chard (silverbeet) greens or spinach,
 parboiled, squeezed dry and finely chopped (see glossary)
½ cup (1 oz/30 g) fresh bread crumbs
2–3 tablespoons daube braising juices, chilled to jellied state
 (see Provençal daube on page 376)
½ lb (250 g) braised beef from daube, chilled, finely chopped
¼ cup (1 oz/30 g) freshly grated Parmesan cheese
1 egg
freshly ground pepper
whole nutmeg
salt

about 2 cups (16 fl oz/500 ml) daube braising juices
few drops olive oil
½ cup (2 oz/60 g) freshly grated Parmesan cheese

◘ Prepare the ravioli several hours in advance so that, at the last minute, you only have to boil them and put on the braising juices to simmer. First prepare the pasta dough and let it rest for about 1 hour.

◘ To make the stuffing, warm the olive oil in a flameproof earthenware casserole or a heavy sauté pan over low heat. Add the onion and cook over low heat until softened but not colored, about 15 minutes. Add the greens and cook, stirring with a wooden spoon, for several minutes. Add the bread crumbs and a chunk of jellied daube braising liquid and simmer, stirring, until no

Top to bottom: Spinach Dumplings, Ravioli

liquid remains, about 5 minutes. Remove from the heat and stir in the chopped meat. Add the cheese, egg, grind over some pepper and, using the blade of a paring knife, scrape in a bit of nutmeg. Mix thoroughly and taste for salt. (In the past this stuffing was pounded to a purée and passed through a sieve. If you prefer a fine purée, you can assemble the stuffing up to this point and pass it briefly in a food processor fitted with the metal blade).

◘ Divide the pasta dough in half. On a floured work surface, roll out 1 dough portion as thinly as possible into a rectangle. Roll out the second portion into a rectangle of approximately the same size. On one, arrange teaspoonfuls of the stuffing, spacing them at 1-in (2.5-cm) intervals on all sides. Using a pastry brush dipped in water, moisten the areas between the rows of stuffing. Transfer the second rectangle to rest on top of the first and, using a stick ¼ in (6 mm) wide, press firmly between the rows to seal the dough sheets together. Using a pastry cutting wheel or a knife, cut along the middle of the sealed rows to separate the ravioli. Place them, side by side and not touching, on floured towels until ready to be cooked.

◘ Heat the braising juices in a saucepan and maintain at a simmer. Bring a saucepan filled with salted water to a boil and add the olive oil. Plunge the ravioli into the boiling water and boil until tender, 6–7 minutes. Pour a ladleful of hot braising juices into a warmed deep serving dish or oven dish and, using a spider or a large, flat slotted spoon, remove the ravioli, a few at a time, each time reposing the spoon on a folded towel to drain them before slipping them into the dish. Ladle additional braising juices over each layer of ravioli and sprinkle with some of the cheese. Cover the dish and hold in a warm place for 3–4 minutes before serving in warmed soup plates.

SERVES 4

ALPES·DE·HAUTE·PROVENCE

CAILLETTES GAVOTTES
Spinach Dumplings

½ lb (250 g) *brousse* (see glossary) or ricotta cheese
1 lb (500 g) spinach, parboiled, squeezed dry and chopped
 (see glossary)
salt and freshly ground pepper
persillade made with 1 clove garlic (see glossary)
2 eggs
about 2 cups (8 oz/250 g) all-purpose (plain) flour
2 cups (16 fl oz/500 ml) tomato sauce, heated (see glossary)
½ cup (2 oz/60 g) freshly grated Parmesan cheese
¼ cup (2 oz/60 g) unsalted butter

◘ In a mixing bowl and using a fork, mash together the *brousse*, spinach, *persillade,* eggs and salt and pepper to taste. Slowly add 1 cup (4 oz/125 g) of the flour, first stirring and then mixing and kneading with your hands until the mixture is firm but still supple, adding more flour as needed to achieve correct consistency. Cover with a towel and leave to relax for 1 hour.

◘ Thickly flour a work surface. Using the palms of your hands, roll pieces of the mixture on the surface into thick, elongated logs about 1 in (2.5 cm) in diameter. Cut each log into 2½-in (6-cm) lengths to form the dumplings. Roll the dumplings in the flour again, flouring the cut ends.

◘ Preheat an oven to 450°F (230°C). Bring a large pot filled with salted water to a boil. Drop in the dumplings. When the water returns to a boil, adjust the heat to maintain a gentle boil and cook for 15–20 minutes. Using a spider or a large slotted spoon, remove the dumplings to a platter. Layer half the dumplings in a gratin dish of a size just to contain them. Ladle half of the tomato sauce over the top, sprinkle with half of the cheese, and scatter over shavings of the butter. Repeat the layers.

◘ Place in the oven and bake until the sauce begins to bubble and the cheese melts, 6–7 minutes.

SERVES 4

One-Eyed Bouillabaisse

BOUILLABAISSE BORGNE

One-Eyed Bouillabaisse

For a bouillabaisse d'épinards *or* épinards à la marseillaise, *omit the tomatoes and the dried orange peel. Add 2 lb (1 kg) spinach, parboiled, squeezed dry and chopped (see glossary), to the saucepan with the onion and leeks and cook as directed before combining with the other ingredients. For a* bouillabaisse de petits pois, *omit the tomatoes and the dried orange peel and add 2 lb (1 kg) small green peas, shelled, with the potatoes.*

4–5 tablespoons (2–3 fl oz/60–80 ml) olive oil
½ lb (250 g) leeks, white and tender green parts, thinly sliced
1 sweet white onion, thinly sliced
4 cloves garlic
2 or 3 garden-ripe tomatoes, peeled, seeded and coarsely chopped
salt and cayenne pepper
large pinch of saffron threads
large bouquet garni, including a fennel stalk and a strip of dried orange peel (see glossary)
6 cups (48 fl oz/1.5 l) water, boiling
1 lb (500 g) potatoes, peeled, sliced ¼ in (6 mm) thick and rinsed
4 eggs
4 thin slices semidry bread, rubbed with a garlic clove

◉ Warm 3 tablespoons of the olive oil in a flameproof earthenware casserole or a heavy saucepan over low heat. Add the leeks and onion and cook, stirring occasionally, until softened but not colored, 10–15 minutes. Add the garlic, tomatoes, salt to taste, a suspicion of cayenne and the saffron. Raise the heat and cook for 5 minutes longer, shaking the pan and stirring the contents.
◉ Add the bouquet garni, the boiling water and potatoes. Return to a boil, adjust the heat to maintain a gentle boil, cover and cook until the potatoes are easily crushed against the side of the pan, 25–30 minutes. Remove from the heat.
◉ One at a time, break the eggs into a saucer and slip each egg into the soup so it floats on top. Cover the pan and leave the eggs to poach until the whites are opaque, 2–3 minutes.
◉ Place a bread slice in each soup plate. Dribble a little of the remaining olive oil over each slice. Using a slotted spoon remove a poached egg to each bread slice, then ladle the potatoes and broth directly from the cooking vessel into the bowls.

SERVES 4

In Roussillon, from top to bottom: Chick-pea Salad, Niçois Salad

PROVENCE

SALADE DE POIS CHICHES
Chick-pea Salad

Chick-peas are sensitive to hard water with a high calcium content. In the country, rainwater can be collected in pails in the open, away from trees and rooftops. In cities, the best solution is to use a neutral bottled mineral water; the most commonly used brand in Provence is Volvic. Chick-peas may require from 1½–3 hours or more cooking time, depending upon whether they are from this year's harvest or older and on the quality of the water. It is the custom to prepare more than are needed for the salad to make certain that some remain for a soup.

3¾ cups (1½ lbs/750 g) dried chick-peas
about 4 qt (4 l) neutral mineral water
1 large carrot, peeled and cut into thirds
1 onion stuck with 2 whole cloves
1 fresh thyme sprig
1 bay leaf
salt

FOR THE TABLE:

1 sweet white onion, finely chopped, or a handful of young
    green shallots (see glossary) or green (spring) onions,
    finely sliced
3 or 4 cloves garlic, finely chopped
bouquet of fresh flat-leaf (Italian) parsley, finely chopped
cruets of olive oil and vinegar
salt and pepper mill

⊞ Place the chick-peas in a bowl and pour over 1 bottle (1 qt/1 l) of slightly warmed mineral water. Let stand overnight.
⊞ Drain the chick-peas, put them into a flameproof earthenware casserole or an enameled ironware pan and pour in a bottle of cold mineral water. Bring to a boil, cover and cook at a gentle boil for about 30 minutes. Meanwhile, bring the remaining mineral water to a boil.
⊞ Drain the peas and return them to the cooking vessel. Add the carrot, onion, herbs, salt to taste and enough boiling mineral water to immerse the peas by about 1½ in (4 cm). Bring back to a boil, adjust the heat to cook at a gentle simmer, cover and cook until tender—intact but easily crushed. If, while cooking, the water level seems low, add more boiling mineral water. If the chick-peas become tender more quickly than expected, remove from the heat and reheat just before serving.
⊞ Remove and discard the carrot, onion and herbs. Serve the chick-peas hot, directly from the cooking vessel, using a spider or a slotted spoon. The table condiments—chopped onion, garlic and parsley—may be arranged in neat piles on a single plate or served in individual dishes. Each person seasons to taste with the condiments, olive oil, vinegar, salt and pepper. If the olive oil is freshly pressed, thick and cloudy, it is a great moment; if not, it is still wonderful. The explosion of perfume as the olive oil contacts the hot chick-peas is intoxicating.

SERVES 8

ALPES·MARITIMES

SALADE NIÇOISE
Niçois Salad

One of the principles of a salade niçoise is that it contain no cooked vegetables. A handful of shelled young broad (fava) beans or trimmed and thinly sliced baby artichokes (see glossary), tossed in lemon juice and drained, may be added. Pan bagnat is salade niçoise enclosed in a bread roll, left to soak for a while and eaten as a sandwich. In this case the tomatoes, eggs and anchovy fillets should be chopped and the olives pitted.

1 small cucumber
1 clove garlic, cut in half lengthwise
salt
3 barely ripened tomatoes, cored and cut into wedges
2 Italian green sweet peppers or other sweet peppers
    (capsicums), seeded, deribbed and thinly sliced crosswise
3 or 4 young green shallots (see glossary) or green (spring)
    onions, including the tender green parts, thinly sliced
2 hard-cooked eggs, shelled and quartered lengthwise
4 or 5 salt anchovies, rinsed and filleted (see glossary)
handful of black olives
handful of fresh basil leaves
freshly ground pepper
5–6 tablespoons (3 oz/90 ml) olive oil

◙ Peel the cucumber and cut it in half lengthwise. Scoop out the seeds, then cut crosswise into thin slices. Layer the slices in a bowl, sprinkling each layer with salt. Let stand for 30 minutes, then squeeze out excess liquid and sponge the slices dry.

◙ A wide, shallow dish permits the most attractive presentation. Rub the dish all over with the cut surfaces of garlic. Scatter the cucumber, tomatoes, peppers, shallots, eggs, anchovy fillets and olives casually but artfully into the dish. Tear the basil leaves into fragments and scatter over the surface. Present the dish at table. Sprinkle on salt and grind over pepper to taste. Pour the olive oil in a fine stream back and forth over the surface. Toss and serve.

SERVES 4

PROVENCE

RISSOLES
Deep-fried Savory Pastries

Rissoles are deep-fried ravioli, one of the many inspired ways of giving new life and a fresh look to leftovers. They can be made from any pastry or pasta dough, and the variety of possible stuffings is limited only by one's imagination. Instead of forming them into square ravioli, they are often cut into circles, stuffed, moistened around the edges, folded and sealed, by pressing with fingertips, into half-moons.

2 tablespoons olive oil
1 onion, finely chopped
¼ lb (125 g) fresh cultivated mushrooms, finely chopped
salt and freshly ground pepper
whole nutmeg
small pinch of Provençal mixed dried herbs (see glossary)
persillade made with 1 clove garlic (see glossary)
about 1 teaspoon fresh lemon juice
½ lb (250 g) leftover roast chicken, boned, skinned and
    finely chopped
3 tablespoons *tapénade* (recipe on page 288)
3 egg yolks
double recipe pasta dough made without saffron (see
    Provençal fish soup on page 296)

corn oil or peanut oil for deep-frying
2 cups (16 fl oz/500 ml) tomato sauce, heated (see glossary)

◙ Warm the olive oil in a heavy frying pan over low heat. Add the onion and cook over the low heat until soft but not colored, about 10 minutes. Add the mushrooms and raise the heat to high. Season to taste with salt and pepper and scrape in a suspicion of nutmeg. Add the herbs and toss or stir with a wooden spoon until the liquid from the mushrooms evaporates and the mixture is nearly dry. Add the *persillade* and stir around until you can smell the characteristic odor of frying garlic and parsley. Add a few drops of lemon juice, stir and remove from the heat.

◙ In a mixing bowl, stir together the mushroom mixture and chicken and leave to cool a bit. Add the *tapénade* and egg yolks and beat with the wooden spoon to mix well. Cover and chill the mixture to firm it up.

◙ While the filling is chilling, prepare the pasta dough and let it rest for about 1 hour.

◙ On a floured work surface, roll out 1 dough portion as thinly as possible into a rectangle. Roll out the second portion into a rectangle of approximately the same size. On one rectangle, arrange 2 teaspoonful mounds of the chicken mixture, spacing them 2 in (5 cm) apart on all sides. Using a pastry brush dipped in water, moisten the areas between the rows of stuffing. Transfer the second rectangle to rest on top of the first. Using your fingertips or the side of your hand, press firmly between the rows to seal the dough sheets together. Using a pastry cutting wheel or a knife, cut along the middle of the rows into 2-in (5-cm) squares. You can hold them for a while, spread out on floured towels, or fry them immediately.

◙ Following the directions for deep-frying in the glossary, heat the oil in a large pan. Slip a few of the pasta squares into the hot oil. Do not crowd the pan. Fry them, turning them over in the oil, until crisp and golden, about 5 minutes. Drain and keep warm as directed. Repeat with the rest of the squares.

◙ Serve the *rissoles* hot, accompanied with the tomato sauce.

SERVES 4

Deep-fried Savory Pastries

315

ANCHOÏADE
Anchovy Spread

An anchoïade, or anchoyade—or, in Marseilles, a quichet—was, in the past, a ritual performance. It was described by 19th-century Marseillais chef Caillat as the hors d'oeuvre de rigueur for every country lunch (déjeuner champêtre). Each person had slices of semidry bread and small pieces of fresh bread. Anchovy fillets were bathed in a plate of olive oil and laid on the dry bread, while the pieces of fresh bread were repeatedly dipped in the olive oil, pressed, sponged and rubbed on the anchovy fillets, then eaten. Finally, when the semidry crust was impregnated with disintegrated anchovy and olive oil, it was grilled over embers and eaten. In Nice, sauce provençale froide, or anchovy aïoli, is called anchoïade.

½ cup (4 fl oz/125 ml) olive oil
1 teaspoon Provençal herb vinegar (see glossary)
10–12 salt anchovies, rinsed and filleted (see glossary)
freshly ground pepper
1 semidry baguette, cut crosswise into quarters, then split in
    half lengthwise and surfaces dried in the sun or in a slow
    oven
3 or 4 cloves garlic

◉ Warm the olive oil, vinegar and anchovies in a flameproof earthenware casserole or heavy sauté pan over the lowest possible heat. The anchovies should not cook, but will melt in contact with the warmth. Grind in pepper to taste and stir to mix. Rub the dried cut surfaces of bread with the garlic cloves and spread them with the oil-anchovy mixture. Leave for 1 hour or so until the bread is thoroughly saturated.
◉ Meanwhile, prepare a fire in a charcoal grill or preheat a broiler (griller). Place the bread slices on a grill rack over dying embers or under the broiler (griller) and grill first on the crust side and then on the anchovy spread side. Serve hot.

SERVES 4

BAGNA CAUDA
Raw Vegetables with Hot Anchovy Sauce

Crudités—raw vegetables—are among the commonest of spring and summer Provençal lunch openers. Often they are simply served with cruets of olive oil and vinegar and salt and pepper. Or they may be accompanied by aïoli (see glossary), pistou (recipe on page 290) or tapénade recipe on page 288). Bagna cauda is an import from Piedmont, by way of Nice, now embraced by all of Provence. A Piedmont bagna cauda contains much more butter and, often, chopped or sliced white truffles.

SUGGESTED VEGETABLES:

Italian sweet peppers or other sweet peppers (capsicums),
    split lengthwise into quarters
Belgian endive (chicory/witloof), split lengthwise into
    quarters
celery hearts, split lengthwise into quarters
fennel bulb hearts, split lengthwise into quarters, or sliced
    radicchio (red chicory) leaves
small romaine (cos) leaves
young green shallots (see glossary) or green (spring) onions
radishes with leaves attached
cauliflower florets
crisp young cucumbers with undeveloped seeds, peeled and
    split lengthwise into quarters
carrots, peeled and split lengthwise into quarters
tender, young artichokes, tough outer leaves removed

4 firm, crisp cloves garlic
pinch of coarse salt
¾ cup (6 fl oz/180 ml) olive oil
2 tablespoons unsalted butter
12 salt anchovies, rinsed, filleted and chopped (see glossary)
bread for serving

◉ Arrange a selection of the suggested vegetables on attractive platters.
◉ In a mortar pound together the garlic and salt to form a paste. Place the paste in a small, flameproof earthenware casserole or enameled ironware casserole over low heat. Add the olive oil, butter and anchovies and stir with a wooden spoon until all the ingredients are melted together to form a sauce.
◉ At the table, place the pan over a spirit lamp or on a hot plate at low heat. Surround it with the platters of vegetables. Guests should take care to stir the sauce with each vegetable piece they dip into it and to hold a piece of bread nearby to collect dribbles when transporting the vegetable from the sauce to their mouths.

SERVES 4

PETITS FARCIS
Stuffed Tomatoes and Zucchini

Leftover braised or roasted meat is often used to prepare these stuffed vegetables. They are no less good as a starter when prepared without meat and are, then, also an appropriate garnish for grilled or roasted meats. As recently as 25 years ago, in the village streets of Provence on a Sunday morning one could see children carrying large trays of stuffed tomatoes and zucchini to the baker to be put into the ovens when the last batch of bread came out. Today, most households have ovens and few bakers still burn wood fires.

4 tomatoes, about 5 oz (150 g) each
salt
4 zucchini (courgettes), about 5 oz (150 g) each
6 tablespoons (3 fl oz/90 ml) olive oil
1 onion, finely chopped
¼ lb (125 g) sausage meat (see glossary)
¼ lb (125 g) boneless lean lamb, finely chopped
freshly ground pepper
pinch of Provençal mixed dried herbs (see glossary)
persillade made with 1 clove garlic (see glossary)
1 cup (2 oz/50 g) fresh bread crumbs
¼ cup (1 oz/30 g) freshly grated Parmesan cheese
1 or 2 eggs
dried bread crumbs

◉ Preheat an oven to 350°F (180°C).
◉ Cut a slice from the top of each tomato. Using a teaspoon, scoop out the flesh from the center of the tomato; discard the seeds and liquid but reserve the flesh. Salt the inside of each tomato and place the tomatoes, upside down, on a wire rack to drain.
◉ Remove the stem end and a sliver from the flower end of each zucchini. Cut each zucchini in half lengthwise and empty the halves with a melon baller, taking care not to cut too close to the walls. Reserve the flesh. Fill a large pot with water and bring to a boil. Slip the emptied zucchini halves into the pot and boil until the flesh is slightly softened but not cooked, 6–7 minutes. Remove them carefully with a slotted utensil, placing them, cut surface down, on a towel to drain.
◉ Chop the reserved zucchini and tomato flesh. Heat 2 tablespoons of the olive oil in a frying pan over low heat. Add the onion and cook until soft but not colored, about 10 minutes. Add the chopped zucchini and tomato and salt to taste and cook, stirring and tossing, for about 15 minutes, or until very soft and reduced, but not browned.
◉ Turn the cooked vegetables out into a mixing bowl. Add the meats, pepper to taste, herbs, *persillade,* fresh bread crumbs and

*Top to bottom: Raw Vegetables with Hot
Anchovy Sauce, Anchovy Spread*

Parmesan; mix thoroughly. Add 1 egg and a spoonful or so of the olive oil and mix with your hands. If the stuffing seems too dry, mix in another egg. Taste for salt.

✦ Arrange the tomato and zucchini shells in a shallow baking dish of a size to just hold them without touching (or, if easier, bake them in separate dishes). Sprinkle each with a little salt and then dribble with a thread of olive oil. Using a teaspoon, distribute the stuffing evenly among the vegetables, pressing gently with the back of the spoon to force it into place. Sprinkle the surfaces with dried bread crumbs and then dribble a thread of olive oil back and forth. Pour a little water into the bottom of the dish. Place in the oven and bake until the surface of the stuffing is golden and the vegetables are somewhat wrinkled and shrunken. Serve hot, warm or at room temperature.

SERVES 4 *Photograph pages 282–283*

BALLOTTES À LA NIÇOISE
Niçois Croquettes

This is a typical home-kitchen, all-purpose stuffing. Any leftover roast or braised meat or poultry can be used or the leftovers can be replaced by sausage meat (see glossary), ground lamb or beef or a combination. Semidry bread crumbs, soaked in milk and squeezed dry, often replace the potatoes. The little balls can simply be floured, without being breaded, and fried, or they can be poached, drained, spread in a gratin dish, sprinkled with grated cheese, covered with tomato sauce and passed for 10 minutes in a hot oven. These croquettes can also be fried in a frying pan in olive oil to a depth of about ¼ in (6 mm), shaking the pan gently to turn them around and over.

2 potatoes, about 6 oz (185 g), peeled
½ lb (250 g) leftover *pot-au-feu*, finely chopped
    page 299
persillade made with 1 clove garlic (see glossary)
3 or 4 young green shallots (see glossary) or green (spring)
    onions, finely chopped

Niçois Croquettes

salt and freshly ground pepper
3 or 4 eggs
all-purpose (plain) flour
dried bread crumbs
vegetable oil for deep–frying
2 cups (16 fl oz/500 ml) tomato sauce, heated (see glossary)

▦ Place the potatoes in a saucepan filled with salted water, bring to a boil and boil until just done, about 30 minutes. Drain, transfer to a plate and, using a fork, mash while still hot. Combine the mashed potatoes in a bowl with the meat, *persillade*, shallots, salt and pepper to taste and one of the eggs. Using your hands, mix thoroughly. If the mixture seems very stiff, add another egg.

▦ Sprinkle a tray or large platter with flour. Beat 2 eggs in a soup plate. Open several thicknesses of newspaper on a work surface and sprinkle thickly with bread crumbs. With moist hands, form the meat mixture into balls the size of large walnuts, placing them in a single layer on the flour as they are formed. Sprinkle more flour over the tops and roll the balls around, shaking or rotating the tray or platter, until well floured on both sides. Put several at a time into the eggs, rotate, rolling them around again, until they are well coated with the egg. Using a teaspoon, remove them, one by one, to the crumbs. Sprinkle more crumbs over the tops and roll them around with your hands in the crumbs. Leave them in the crumbs, sprinkled with more crumbs, to dry for 1 hour or so.

▦ Following the directions for deep-frying in the glossary, heat the oil in a large pan. Toss the balls in your hands to shake them free of loose crumbs and them slip them into the hot oil. Do not crowd the pan. Fry them, turning them over in the oil, until crisp and golden, about 4–5 minutes. Drain and keep warm as directed. Repeat with the remaining balls.

▦ Serve the croquettes hot, accompanied with tomato sauce.

SERVES 4

TERRINE DE GIBIER À PLUME
Game Bird Terrine

Wild duck, pheasant, partridge and woodcock are all wonderful elements in a game terrine, as are European wild rabbits or American cottontails. Farmed mallard ducks can be very good. Be sure the birds include the hearts, livers and gizzards. Use whatever is available, supplementing it, if necessary, with domestic duck or rabbit. Truffles are always a welcome addition.

2 game birds, or more if they are small, cut into pieces (see
    recipe introduction for suggestions)

FOR THE BROTH:

1 onion, coarsely chopped
1 carrot, sliced
1 bay leaf
1 fresh thyme sprig
broken-up bird carcasses
salt

5 oz (150 g) poultry livers
1 lb (500 g) sausage meat (see glossary)
¼ lb (125 g) pork back fat, chilled and cut into ¼-in (6-mm)
    dice
¼ lb (125 g) shank (shin) end of raw ham such as prosciutto,
    finely chopped
1 onion, finely chopped and cooked in 1 tablespoon olive oil
    until soft but not colored
large pinch of coarse salt
2 cloves garlic
1 cup (2 oz/60 g) fresh bread crumbs
large pinch of Provençal mixed dried herbs (see glossary)
¼ cup (2 fl oz/60 ml) marc de Provence (see glossary) or
    Cognac

At La Tourtine vineyard, Domaine Tempier, Game Bird Terrine

3 eggs
salt, freshly ground pepper and ground allspice
thin sheets of fresh pork back fat
boiling water as needed

◉ Remove the flesh from the pieces of game bird, set aside with the hearts, livers and gizzards. Discard the skins. Chop or break up any awkwardly shaped pieces of carcass.

◉ To prepare the broth, place the onion, carrot, bay and thyme in the bottom of a saucepan and arrange the carcass pieces on top. Cover generously with cold water and bring to a boil. Skim off any scum and froth and add salt to taste. Adjust the heat to maintain a simmer, cover with a lid slightly ajar and simmer for 2 hours. Strain, return to the saucepan and boil gently until reduced to about ½ cup (4 fl oz/125 ml); skim off any fat. Set aside.

◉ Cut the birds' breast meat into ¼-in (6-mm) dice. Chop the remaining flesh coarsely and place in a food processor fitted with the metal blade. Add the hearts, the fleshy lobes of the gizzards, the livers and the extra poultry livers. Process to a smooth purée.

◉ Combine all the meats and the cooked onion in a large mixing bowl. In a mortar pound together the coarse salt and garlic to form a paste. Add and mix in the bread crumbs, then add the reduced broth and stir to form a paste. Add the contents of the mortar to the mixing bowl, along with the herbs, brandy, eggs and salt, pepper and allspice to taste. Using your hands mix thoroughly.

◉ Preheat an oven to 325°F (165°C). Line a terrine, or more, depending upon size, with sheets of pork fat, pressing them firmly against the sides and bottom of the terrine(s). Pack the mixture, large spoonfuls at a time, into the terrine(s), pressing into place so as to leave no air pockets. Press a sheet of fat over the surface(s) and cover the terrine(s) with a lid or with aluminum foil.

◉ Place the terrine(s) in a large pan in the oven and pour in boiling water to reach halfway up the sides of the terrine(s). Place in the oven and bake small terrines (4 cups/16 fl oz/1 l) for about 1 hour and larger ones, depending upon their size, for up to 2 hours. They are done when the juices run clear, or when a trussing needle, thrust into the heart of the terrine, comes out quite warm to the touch.

◉ A terrine must be cooled under a weight to render the body compact for neat slicing. The weight should not exceed 1 ½–2 lb (750 g–1 kg). Place the terrine(s) on a tray, lest any juices overflow. Remove the lid(s), place a sheet of foil over the surface(s) and then stiff cardboard cut to the inside dimensions of the terrine(s). Place the weight, or weights, on top—tinned goods are practical for this purpose. When cooled, cover and refrigerate the terrine(s). The flavor will improve with 2 or 3 days ripening. If a terrine is to be kept, uncut, for more than a few days, melted lard should be poured over the surface to seal it. A partially consumed terrine should be protected from contact with air by a sheet of plastic wrap pressed to the cut surface.

SERVES 10

ALPES-DE-HAUTE-PROVENCE

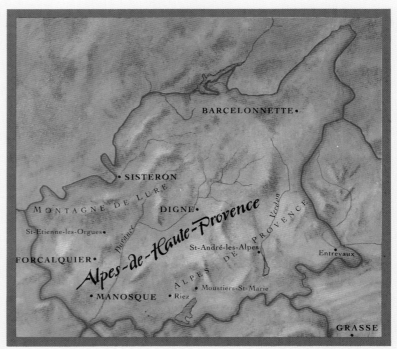

ALPES-DE-HAUTE-PROVENCE

The people of the Alpes-de-Haute-Provence live at the crossroads. These are the hinterlands, a Provence far from the Mediterranean, a sprawling area that stretches from the Italian border to the Montagne de Lure and the Vaucluse Mountains and encompasses the Mercantour National Park and the Verdon region. It is balanced between two lakes, Serre-Ponçon and Sainte-Croix, and is crossed by the Durance, a river once tumultuous and exuberant, which provided the route for invaders and for flocks moving to new pastures. Frédéric Mistral called it "one of the three evils of Provence."

This *département,* laced with hills and valleys, is the least tamed and most solitary of the region, its culinary customs seem a little more uncivilized than those in other parts of Provence.

The valleys of the Ubaye, the Bléone, the Jabron and the Durance, all the stories of the plateaus of Valensole and Forcalquier and Albion lead to uncharted territory. The first person to penetrate it was Jean Giono, writer of the stars, the man from Manosque, lord of Contadour, a hamlet of the Commune of Redortiers to the north of Banon. It was to Contadour, late one summer in 1935, that he led an expedition of citizens enamored of open spaces and frugal living. The author of *Regain* and *Collines* portrayed better than anyone else has done the rough, secretive, tormented peasants who inhabited a cold land beneath the purest of skies.

Previous pages: Still one of the most remote regions in Provence, the peaceful valleys of Alpes-de-Haute-Provence glow with blooming lavender in the summer. Left: Grand Canyon du Verdon, one of France's natural wonders, spans 12½ miles (21 km) in length and is 5,000 feet (1,500 m) deep.

The locals of Entrevaux find a quiet place in the shade and catch up on the day's events.

The way of life of the people in these parts still reflects Giono's Provence. Nor is it so very different from the one portrayed in another literary genre by Pierre Magnan, prominent author of local detective novels, who was born in Manosque and whose main character answers to the charming name Superintendent Laviolette. She, too, symbolizes a land of light where astronomers and all those who search for the stars come flocking. No doubt this explains, although only in part, why winter evenings by the fire with friends seem longer here than in other places.

In this special region, the thread that leads out of the labyrinth is the Durance. The river (which locals refer to as *la rivière* rather than *le fleuve,* thus more readily representing it as a female character) serves in its own way to bring together the culinary customs of the area, simply because the people have always moved along its banks, from the Dauphiné to the Rhône region. Another great writer from the south, Avignon-born Henri Bosco recalls the beneficial properties of the water of the Durance: " . . . water that makes the chick-pea, tomato, celery, asparagus, eggplant (aubergine) and bean grow as they grew in the Garden of Eden; water that will cook you a leek in ten minutes, water you don't just drink, you sip it and savor it; water without which all these or-

Here they make the golden *crespèu,* the omelet of the sun; they butcher the pig; they bake leg of lamb in the oven with potatoes; and around Barcelonnette, they eat a soup made with eggless pasta shells known as *crouzets.* In earlier days fish, which remain the magic of the Durance, even came back up the river, in boats, of course, and cooks prepared the anchovies, sardines and cod in spicy tomato sauces.

That said, the Alpes-de-Haute-Provence is nevertheless first and foremost a region of wild herbs that go into making magic soups, of little scrubland birds and of spelt, the poor man's corn that was highly valued in medieval times and is today making a return, this time to the most sophisticated tables. Although many foods are being rediscovered that are outside the reach of tourists, travelers will, no doubt, remember the cheese from Banon, wrapped in its chestnut leaf steeped in brandy and left to ferment, or covered in dried savory leaves and immersed in marc. Of course they will certainly also recall scrambled eggs with truffles, albeit not always served with due respect in the restaurants of the great far south. And they will remember the lamb, but only on the condition that it be the wonderful lamb from the Sisteron region, delicious at Easter and used in particular to prepare *le gigot aux olives,* leg of lamb roasted with olives, or *les côtelettes grillées à la braise,* tender lamb cutlets grilled over charcoal.

For color, finally, we have lavender, known as blue gold. There is indeed a Provence of lavender. The plant flourishes in summer on the high plateaus around Albion, the Montagne de Lure and Valensole, and plunges down to the hills of Grasse in the Alpes-Maritimes and the ocher Maures Mountains in the Var, on its way to join the Mediterranean.

Each year on August 15 a festival is held in Digne-les-Bains to celebrate lavender. The honored plant has had its share of misfortune, though; it is forced to share its empire with a hybrid, *lavandin.* The latter first appeared in the thirties, and now it is threatened by highly profitable artificial oils and essences.

The blue of the plateaus is a symbol of the inland paradise of the Alpes-de-Haute-Provence, a paradise that constitutes an obligatory route among pinnacles and orchards, an azure land where the legends, like the cooking, simmer for a long, long time among the stones of the country houses.

Much of the 20,000 acres of lavender harvested annually in Provence is reserved for the essence used in perfume and cosmetics, while the rest is dried to make sachets.

chards, kitchen gardens and the gardens full of apricot, peach, cherry and plum trees would be nothing but a desert of stones and rosehips."

In the end we must listen to the writers who throughout their lives have remained attached to their native soil. Paul Arène was another man of the Durance, born in Sisteron. He called himself Jean des Figues because he swore he was born at the foot of a fig tree, and rechristened his hometown Canteperdrix, because at that time (in the nineteenth century) it was still one of the last kingdoms of that delicate game bird, the *bartavelle* or "rock partridge."

Between the hills and the plains, however, cooking habits change. In the north and at high altitudes, cooks favor walnut oil, and in the old days lard and pork fat were used.

FISH AND SHELLFISH

Restaurant seafood displays lure diners along the Côte d'Azur.

FISH AND SHELLFISH

A Provençal fishmonger's display of the catch brought in at dawn to the village fishing ports is a wondrous thing, for its fresh beauty if not for its abundance. In fact, only single—or very few—specimens of the most noble varieties may be present: *loup de mer* (Mediterranean sea bass), *daurade royale* (gilt-head bream), *sar, denti, pageot* (other Mediterranean breams), *pagre* (red porgy, the only Mediterranean bream to have crossed the Atlantic) and *chapon de mer* (large red rascasse or scorpionfish) are likely to be in attendance. The latter, because of the firmness of its flesh, its thick, short, round body and its large head, which forms a single cavity along with that of the body, is the most wonderful of all fish for stuffing and baking. It need not be sewn up; it sits neatly on its belly and arrives at the table looking very grand. There may also be *mostelle* (also called *mustelle* or *moustelle* and, in English, fork beard, whose silken flesh probably has no equivalent outside of the Mediterranean); *murène* (moray eel); and little *rougets de roche* (red mullets), which require three or four for each serving and may be limited to only a dozen or two for sale. Usually there is also a pile of fish labeled *bouillabaisse* that can furnish no more than two or three clients. Whatever its composition, this pile always includes beautiful, spiky *rascasses,* both red and black; multicolored, striped splashed and speckled *rouquiers* and *lucrèces* (both wrasses); and *vives* (weavers) and often *rascasses blanches* (star gazers). *Grondin* (gurnard), *St.-Pierre* (John Dory), *congre* (conger eel), *baudroie* (monkfish or anglerfish) and the scuttling, furious *favouilles,* or green shore crabs, (called, for that reason, *enragées*) are sold separately to complete the *bouillabaisse.*

Sometimes a freshly caught thirty-inch (75-cm) *loup de mer* appears. It is rarely displayed for more than a few minutes before a proud client takes off with the prize at

This poissonnerie in the Alpes-de-Haute-Provence has fresh fish trucked in from the coast daily.

Previous pages, clockwise from top left: Provençal Crayfish (recipe page 353), Stuffed Squid (recipe page 342), Sautéed Shrimp (recipe page 342)

The fish mongers usually have a pile of fresh fish labeled bouillabaisse; this mixture provides the key ingredients to the celebrated fish stew.

come loose from the carapaces. They are done at this point and should be removed before drying out.

Fish nomenclature in America is a slippery thing. Depending on the locality, a single fish may be known by a number of different names or different fish may be known by the same name. This is more troublesome for the scholar than for the cook, since the fish that move in this confusion can all receive the same treatments in the kitchen. America's answer to the *loup de mer* is the striped bass. The Mediterranean breams find their equivalents in America's porgies (red porgy, scup, pinfish, sheepshead). Red snapper, red drum, black sea bass, kingfish, weakfish, spot and many others can receive the same treatments, usually baked or grilled, as the breams; they may also be used in the famous fish stews of Provence. The thick-lipped wrasses always present in a *bouillabaisse* are represented in America by the tautog (blackfish, chub) and the cunner. Any of the fish known as ocean perch, rockfish or redfish are good choices for the fish stews, as is grouper, when available. Sea robin represents the gurnards.

The fish market is a daily event on Quai des Belges in the old port of Marseilles.

breath-taking cost. (At the other extreme of the price scale, it is possible to feed four with stiff, arched, brightly glinting sardines, freshly netted, for very little money.) The *loup,* fresh from the sea, intact, unscaled and grilled over incandescent wood embers—about forty minutes for a six pound (3-kg) fish that will serve six people—embodies all of the poetry and the beauty of Provence and the Mediterranean. As it grills, the scales and the skin weld together, forming a charred, protective sheath, detached from the flesh. The fish is presented at the table in its blackened armor. The sheath is cut along the back, next to the fin bones, the length of the abdomen and at the tail and at the head. It is then lifted off like a lid to reveal miraculously white flesh sparkling in its own juices. It is seasoned by the sea. Salt and pepper cannot improve it and lemon will dull its clear sweetness.

Other large fish may be poached, grilled or baked whole and presented at the table to admiration and great expectation among the guests. In Provence, the fish most often presented in this way are sea bass, the various breams (porgies) and gray mullet. In America, among the many possibilities, red snapper, black sea bass and tautog should certainly be added to the list.

Also to be savored unseasoned (unscaled and ungutted—the scales are scraped off at table and the liver and other innards form the sauce) are the little *rougets de roche,* grilled for no more than a couple of minutes on each side, and one-pound (500-g) langoustes, or spiny lobsters, each an individual portion. The langoustes are grilled whole for about fourteen minutes and split in two at the moment of serving. When first put on the grill, they want to curl up their tails, but after a couple of turns the tails can be spread out. After a minute or two the legs begin to

329

BOUCHES·DU·RHÔNE

THON AUX ARTICHAUTS À LA MARSEILLAISE
Tuna with Artichokes

This is one of the many Marseillaise *variations on the theme of* bouillabaisse. *It is sometimes accompanied by* aïoli *(see glossary) or* rouille *(see* bouillabaisse *on page 362).*

1½ lb (750 g) tuna steak, skinned

FOR THE MARINADE:

freshly ground pepper
⅛ teaspoon powdered saffron
1 bay leaf
2 or 3 fresh thyme sprigs
3 cloves garlic
3 tablespoons olive oil

5 tablespoons (3 oz/80 ml) olive oil
3 young, tender artichokes, trimmed, halved lengthwise, chokes removed if necessary and sliced (see glossary)
salt
1 large onion, finely chopped
2 large tomatoes, peeled, seeded and coarsely chopped
3 oz (100 g) sorrel, stemmed and chopped
3 cups (24 fl oz/750 ml) water, boiling

8 slices baguette, partially dried in a warm oven and then rubbed with a garlic clove

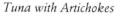 The natural structure of a tuna steak divides it neatly into quarters with a cross-shaped bone at the center. Quarter the steak, discard the bones and cut each quarter in half. Put the tuna pieces into a large bowl. For the marinade, grind some pepper over the tuna, then sprinkle with saffron. Add the bay leaf, thyme sprigs and garlic and pour the olive oil. Using your hands, toss all the ingredients together until the tuna pieces are evenly colored with saffron and coated with oil. Leave to marinate at room temperature for 1 hour.

◾ Warm 2 tablespoons of the olive oil in a large sauté pan. Add the artichokes, sprinkle with salt to taste and sauté over high heat until lightly colored, about 5 minutes. Set aside.

◾ Warm the remaining 3 tablespoons olive oil in a large saucepan. Add the onion and cook gently until softened but not colored, about 10 minutes. Raise the heat and add the tomatoes and sorrel. Using a wooden spoon stir regularly until they begin to break up, about 10 minutes. Then add the reserved artichokes and the tuna and all of its marinade, wiping the bowl clean. Stir around for a minute, pour in the boiling water and add salt to taste. Boil gently until the fish is tender, about 15 minutes.

◾ Using a large skimming spoon, transfer the tuna and artichoke slices (and anything that comes with them) to a heated platter. Place 1 or 2 slices garlic-rubbed bread in each soup plate and ladle some broth over them. Serve the tuna and artichokes at the same time, or after the broth has been consumed, accompanied with more broth.

SERVES 4

Tuna with Artichokes

PROVENCE

ÉCREVISSES À LA NAGE

Crayfish in Court Bouillon

This recipe should be shared with friends who don't mind eating with their fingers.

FOR THE COURT BOUILLON:

2 cups (16 fl oz/500 ml) water
2 cups (16 fl oz/500 ml) dry white wine
1 carrot, peeled and thinly sliced
1 onion, thinly sliced
3 cloves garlic, crushed
1 bay leaf

several fresh thyme sprigs
bouquet of flat-leaf (Italian) parsley stems and leaves
salt
4 dozen crayfish

◉ Combine all of the ingredients for the court bouillon in a large saucepan. Bring to a boil and cover with a lid ajar. Cook at a gentle boil for 30 minutes. Add the crayfish, stir them around, cover and cook, stirring a couple of times if all of the crayfish are not completely immersed, until the shellfish are tender, 8–10 minutes.

◉ Serve immediately, either from the saucepan or poured into a large bowl. Or, if you prefer, leave the crayfish to cool until tepid or at room temperature before serving.

SERVES 4

ESTOCAFICADA

Stockfish Niçois

Estocaficada is as sacred to the Niçois as is bouillabaisse *to the Marseillais. Stockfish is salt cod that is dried until it is stiff as a board. It must be sawn into pieces and requires at least 4–5 days soaking with repeated changes of water before it can be put to cook. In Nice, the cleansed and salted cod guts are sold separately and need only be soaked overnight before being used. If you are unable to find stockfish intestines, don't despair; a dimension may be lost but the dish will still be wonderful. Finally, if you cannot find stockfish, salt cod may be used, with a radical reduction in cooking time, and the result will be good, if less than sublime.*

½ cup (4 fl oz/125 ml) olive oil, plus olive oil for serving
1 large onion, finely chopped
½ lb (250 g) leeks, including the tender green parts,
    thinly sliced
2 large sweet red peppers (capsicums), seeded, deribbed
    and cut into long, narrow strips
4 cloves garlic, chopped
2 lb (1 kg) stockfish, soaked (see recipe introduction),
    skinned, picked over to remove bones and coarsely
    shredded or cut up
3 oz (100 g) stockfish intestines, soaked overnight
    and chopped
½ cup (4 fl oz/125 ml) marc de Provence (see glossary)
    or Cognac
4 lb (2 kg) tomatoes, peeled, seeded and coarsely chopped
large bouquet garni (see glossary)
2 lb (1 kg) new potatoes, peeled and quartered
1 cup (5 oz/150 g) black olives
persillade made with 1 clove garlic (see glossary)
3 salt anchovies, rinsed, filleted and mashed to a purée
    (see glossary)

◙ Warm the ½ cup (4 fl oz/125 ml) olive oil in a large, heavy sauté pan over medium-low heat. Add the onion, leeks and peppers and cook, stirring rapidly with a wooden spoon, until softened and beginning to color, about 20 minutes. Add the garlic, stockfish and intestines and stir with a wooden spoon for 1 minute. Pour in the brandy and stir in well. Empty the contents of the pan into a large, flameproof earthenware casserole or enameled ironware pan.
◙ Return the sauté pan to high heat, add the tomatoes and stir until they begin to boil. Empty the sauté pan into the casserole, stir the contents and tuck in the bouquet garni. Bring slowly to a boil, cover with the lid slightly ajar and simmer for 2 hours.
◙ Place the potatoes in a saucepan and add salted water to cover. Bring to a boil and boil until barely tender, about 20 minutes. Drain the potatoes and add them to the stew along with the olives.
◙ Then, 20 minutes later, stir in the *persillade* and anchovies. Simmer for 5 minutes longer and serve, accompanied with olive oil at table.

SERVES 6

TIAN DE CARPENTRAS

Gratin of Salt Cod with Mixed Greens

For Frédéric Mistral, the Provençal bard, the tian de Carpentras *is the real* tian, *the "gratin of gratins." Parboiled chopped purslane and finely shredded sorrel leaves can add a touch of mystery.*

3 eggs
½ cup (2 oz/60 g) freshly grated Parmesan cheese
½ cup (4 fl oz/125 ml) plus 3 tablespoons olive oil
2 cups (16 fl oz/500 ml) milk
salt and freshly ground pepper
whole nutmeg
½ lb (250 g) spinach, parboiled, squeezed dry and chopped
    (see glossary)
½ lb (250 g) Swiss chard (silverbeet) greens, parboiled,
    squeezed dry and chopped (see glossary)

332

Top to bottom: Stockfish Niçois, Gratin of Salt Cod with Mixed Greens

persillade made with 3 or 4 cloves garlic (see glossary)
1 lb (500 g) salt cod, poached and flaked (see glossary)
4 hard-cooked eggs, shelled and cut in half lengthwise
8 salt anchovies, rinsed and filleted (see glossary)
coarse dried bread crumbs

◙ Preheat an oven to 350°F (180°C). In a mixing bowl whisk the eggs briefly, then whisk in the cheese, the ½ cup (4 fl oz/ 125 ml) olive oil and milk. Season to taste with salt and pepper and scrape in a little nutmeg. Add the chopped greens, *persillade* and cod and, using a wooden spoon, stir well.

◙ Rub a 6-cup (48-fl oz/1.5-l) gratin dish with olive oil and spread the cod mixture in it. Embed the egg halves cut side up, in the mixture, to create a surface design. Press crossed anchovy fillets over each egg half. Sprinkle on bread crumbs generously, then dribble on the 3 tablespoons olive oil in a thread, forming a crisscross pattern.

◙ Place in the oven and bake until no depression remains at the center and the surface is nicely colored, 35–40 minutes. Serve immediately.

SERVES 4

MAQUEREAUX À LA
MARINADE CHAUDE

Mackerel in Hot Marinade

This is often served as a starter, but preceded by a simple salad and followed by cheese, it provides a satisfying lunch. Accompanied with a young red wine such as Bandol served quite cool, the mackerel is very much at home.

2 lb (1 kg) small mackerels, cleaned and heads removed
salt and freshly ground pepper
6 tablespoons (3 fl oz/90 ml) olive oil

Along the harbor in Cassis, from top to bottom: Salt Cod in Caper Sauce, Mackerel in Hot Marinade

mixing bowl. Sprinkle with salt, grind over some pepper and add 1 tablespoon of the olive oil. Toss with your hands to coat the fish evenly with the oil and seasoning. Arrange the fish in a gratin dish and put it into the oven for 10 minutes.

◫ Meanwhile, put the remaining oil, the chili peppers, bay leaves and garlic in a saucepan. Place it over high heat and, when the garlic begins to sputter and turn golden, add the vinegar.

◫ Remove from the heat and pour the contents of the saucepan over the hot mackerel. Serve at once.

SERVES 6

VAR

CAPILOTADE À LA FAÇON DE SIGNES
Salt Cod in Caper Sauce

The principle of a capilotade *is the same as that of salt cod in red wine (recipe on page 336)—to simmer fried salt cod briefly in a sauce. Tomato sauce, with or without the addition of black olives, chopped anchovy fillets or* persillade, *often replaces these sauces in dishes called* à la provençale, à la niçoise *or* camarguaise. *The addition of* vin cuit, *a sweet dessert wine made from dark grapes, to a* capilotade *originates in the village of Signes, inland from Toulon and Bandol.*

FOR THE SAUCE:

3 tablespoons olive oil
1 onion, finely chopped
1 leek, including the tender green parts, thinly sliced
¼ cup (2 fl oz/60 ml) Provençal herb vinegar (see glossary)
3 tablespoons all-purpose (plain) flour
3 cups (24 fl oz/750 ml) water
persillade made with 2 cloves garlic (see glossary)
bouquet garni (see glossary)
⅔ cup (3 oz/100 g) capers, rinsed and drained
½ cup (4 fl oz/125 ml) *vin cuit* or Port

1½ lb (750 g) salt cod, soaked and cut into 4 equal pieces (see glossary)
all-purpose (plain) flour
¼ cup (2 fl oz/60 ml) olive oil
freshly ground pepper

◫ To prepare the sauce, warm the olive oil in a heavy saucepan over low heat. Add the onion and leek, cover and sweat until they are softened and simmering in their own juices, about 10 minutes. Uncover, raise the heat and stir with a wooden spoon until the liquid evaporates and the onion and leek begin to turn color and stick to the pan, about 1 or 2 minutes. Add the vinegar and stir until it completely evaporates, 1–2 minutes. Sprinkle the flour evenly over the top and stir for 1 minute. Add the water, slowly at first, stirring all the while. Add the *persillade* and the bouquet garni and bring to a boil. Adjust the heat to a very gentle boil and cook for about 40 minutes, stirring occasionally.

◫ Add the capers and the *vin cuit* and keep at a gentle boil until the sauce has reduced to the right consistency and the taste of alcohol has disappeared, another 10–15 minutes.

◫ Meanwhile, coat the cod pieces with flour, shaking off any excess flour. Heat the olive oil in a frying pan over medium-high heat. Add the fish and fry, turning once, until lightly colored, a couple of minutes on each side. Remove the fish pieces to paper towels to drain.

◫ Place the cod pieces in a flameproof serving dish and grind over some pepper. Pour the sauce over the fish and place over medium heat. Simmer for 10 minutes and serve.

SERVES 4

2 dried cayenne chili peppers or other dried chili peppers
2 bay leaves
6 cloves garlic, crushed in their peels
3 tablespoons Provençal herb vinegar (see glossary)

◫ Preheat an oven to 450°F (230°C). If the mackerel are no longer than 6 in (15 cm), leave them whole. If they are longer than that, cut into 2-in (5-cm) lengths. Put the fish into a

MORUE EN RAYTE

Salt Cod in Red Wine Sauce

Morue en rayte is a traditional Christmas Eve dish in the Var. It is claimed that the sauce was introduced into Provence by the Phocaean sailors who founded Marseilles in 600 B.C., but it has probably only been around since tomatoes came into popular usage in the 19th century.

FOR THE SAUCE:

3 tablespoons olive oil
2 large onions, coarsely chopped
3 tablespoons all-purpose (plain) flour
3 cups (24 fl oz/750 ml) young, tannic red wine
2 cups (16 fl oz/500 ml) water
1 lb (500 g) tomatoes, coarsely chopped
large pinch of fennel seeds
large bouquet garni (see glossary)
salt
¾ cup (4 oz/125 g) black olives
2 tablespoons capers, rinsed

1½ lb (750 g) salt cod, soaked and cut into 4 equal pieces (see glossary)
all-purpose (plain) flour
¼ cup (2 fl oz/60 ml) olive oil
1 tablespoon chopped flat-leaf (Italian) parsley

◼ To prepare the sauce, warm the olive oil in a heavy saucepan over low heat. Add the onions and cook until softened but not colored, about 10 minutes. Sprinkle evenly with the flour, stir with a wooden spoon, raise the heat and add the wine, slowly at first, stirring all the while. Add the water, tomatoes, fennel seeds and bouquet garni. Salt lightly and bring to a boil, stirring. Adjust the heat to a simmer or very gentle boil and cook, uncovered, until the sauce is reduced by approximately two thirds, a couple of hours or more.

◼ Discard the bouquet garni. Pass the sauce through a fine-mesh sieve into a bowl, pressing it with a wooden pestle to extract all the liquid. Return it to the saucepan, add the olives and capers and taste for salt. Simmer gently while preparing the fish.

◼ Coat the pieces of cod with flour, shaking off any excess flour. Heat the olive oil in a frying pan over medium-high heat. Add the fish and fry, turning once, until lightly colored, a couple of minutes on each side. Remove the fish pieces to paper towels to drain.

◼ Ladle some of the sauce into a flameproof earthenware casserole or other heavy pot and place the fried fish pieces on top. Pour over the remaining sauce. Warm to a simmer over medium heat and simmer gently for 10 minutes. Sprinkle with the parsley and serve.

SERVES 4

Salt Cod in Red Wine Sauce

MORUE À LA BÉNÉDICTINE

Brandade with Potatoes

Brandade is poached salt cod, beaten over low heat with progressive additions of hot olive oil and hot milk until a supple and consistent purée is formed. Puréed garlic is usually added and, less often today, chopped truffles. According to anecdotal history, morue à la bénédictine is so named because a monastery near Marseilles, having only a small quantity of prepared brandade in the kitchen, received, unexpectedly, the visit of monks from a neighboring monastery. The genial cook boiled up a vast quantity of potatoes and incorporated them into the brandade; the guests were ravished and carried away the recipe.

1 lb (500 g) potatoes, peeled
1½ lb (750 g) salt cod, soaked (see glossary)
persillade made with 2 cloves garlic (see glossary)
freshly ground pepper
1 cup (8 fl oz/250 ml) milk, heated
½ cup (4 fl oz/125 ml) olive oil, plus olive oil for top
dried bread crumbs

◼ Place the potatoes in a saucepan. Add water to cover and bring to a boil. Cook until tender when pierced, about 30 minutes.

◼ Meanwhile, poach the cod as directed in the glossary. While it is still hot, flake the flesh, picking out any small bones, and purée it in a food processor fitted with the metal blade or pound it in a mortar.

◼ Preheat an oven to 400°F (200°C). Drain the potatoes and place in a bowl. Mash them and then add the puréed cod and *persillade*. Grind over some pepper. Using a wooden spoon, stir in the hot milk and olive oil, small quantities at a time and alternately, beating when the mixture becomes loose enough. When all of the liquid has been added, the mixture should be very supple but not quite pourable.

◼ Rub a 6-cup (48-fl oz/1.5-l) gratin dish with olive oil. Spread the potato-cod mixture in it and smooth the surface. Sprinkle the crumbs over the top and then dribble over a thread of olive oil. Place in the oven and bake until the surface is colored, 10–15 minutes. Serve hot.

SERVES 4

Top to bottom: Brandade with Potatoes, Salt Cod and Leeks

LA QUINQUEBINE CAMARGUAISE

Salt Cod and Leeks

Adapted from Vieilles recettes de cuisine provençale *by Chanot-Bullier, this preparation can, if one likes, be transformed into a gratin with the addition of bread crumbs and a thread of olive oil.*

3 tablespoons olive oil
2 lb (1 kg) leeks, including the tender green parts, thinly sliced
½ cup (4 fl oz/125 ml) water, boiling
salt
2 tablespoons all-purpose (plain) flour
2 cups (16 fl oz/500 ml) milk
persillade made with 2 cloves garlic (see glossary)

2 salt anchovies, rinsed, filleted and chopped (see glossary)
1½ lb (750 g) salt cod, poached and flaked (see glossary)
freshly ground pepper
whole nutmeg
¾ cup (3 oz/100 g) freshly grated Gruyère or
   Parmesan cheese

◈ Warm the olive oil in a heavy sauté pan over medium-low heat. Add the leeks and cook, stirring with a wooden spoon, until they are softened and begin to color, about 20 minutes. Add the water, salt very lightly and simmer until the water evaporates completely and the leeks begin to stick to the pan, 8–10 minutes. Sprinkle the flour evenly over the top, stir well and add the milk slowly, stirring all the while. Stir in the *persillade* and simmer gently for 15 minutes.
◈ Stir in the anchovies and the cod and simmer for 10 minutes. Grind over some pepper and scrape over a bit of nutmeg. Stir in the grated cheese and taste for salt. Simmer for a couple of minutes longer and serve directly from the sauté pan.

SERVES 4

RAIE À LA PROVENÇALE

Provençal Skate

Because of their eccentric shape, two small skate wings will fill a large frying pan. For this reason, they must be cooked in relays or in two large pans.

4 small skate wings, about 7 oz (220 g) each, or large wings skinned and cut into sections (see skate in caper sauce on page 88)
salt and freshly ground pepper
all-purpose (plain) flour
¼ cup (2 fl oz/60 ml) olive oil

FOR THE SAUCE:

small pinch of coarse salt
freshly ground pepper
1 clove garlic
3 salt anchovies, rinsed and filleted (see glossary)

1 tablespoon chopped fresh flat-leaf (Italian) parsley
2 cups (16 fl oz/500 ml) tomato sauce (see glossary)

❖ Preheat an oven to 450°F (230°C). Season the skate wings with salt and pepper and coat them with flour, shaking off any excess flour.

❖ In a frying pan over medium-high heat, warm the olive oil. Add the skate wings to the hot oil and fry for about 4 minutes on each side, adjusting the heat when necessary to achieve a light, golden surface. The wings are ready when a sharp skewer or trussing needle meets with little resistance at the thickest parts. Transfer to a gratin dish large enough to hold the wings in a single layer.

❖ To prepare the sauce, in a mortar pound together the salt, pepper to taste, garlic, anchovies and parsley to form a paste. In a saucepan, bring the tomato sauce to a boil and stir in the paste from the mortar. Pour the sauce over the skate.

❖ Place in the oven and bake until the sauce is bubbling, 8–10 minutes. Serve immediately.

SERVES 4

2 bay leaves
pinch of Provençal mixed dried herbs (see glossary)
5 oz (150 g) sorrel leaves, stemmed, tightly rolled up
   and thinly sliced
salt
2 lemons, peeled, thinly sliced and seeded
½ cup (4 fl oz/125 ml) dry white wine

▦ Using a sharp-pointed paring knife, pierce the surface of the tuna steak in 8 places between the rings of flesh. Slip an anchovy fillet into each slit.

▦ Preheat an oven to 325°F (165°C). Rub the bottom of a casserole whose circumference is only slightly larger than that of the tuna steak with 1 teaspoon of the olive oil. Line it with half of the lettuce leaves and place half of the tomato slices on top. Scatter over half the carrots and onion slices, 1 bay leaf and a small pinch of the dried herbs. Press half the shredded sorrel on top, sprinkle with salt and 1 tablespoon of the olive oil. Place half the lemon slices on top and then the tuna steak. Top with the remaining lemon slices, then the remaining tomatoes, carrots and onions. Sprinkle with the remaining dried herbs, add the remaining bay leaf and press the remaining sorrel over the top. Sprinkle with salt and dribble over the remaining olive oil. Sprinkle with the white wine and cover with the remaining lettuce leaves.

▦ Cover, place in the oven and bake until the flavors are melded, about 1 hour and 10 minutes. Lift off and discard the surface lettuce leaves before serving.

SERVES 4

B O U C H E S · D U · R H Ô N E

SOLE À LA MARINIÈRE, MOUTARDE DES PÊCHEURS

Fisherman's Sole with Fisherman's Sauce

Marius Morard, a 19th-century Marseillais chef, recounts his discussions with an old fisherman, who tells him, "In Marseilles, all fishermen are cooks, but we don't make such a fuss about it as you professionals. Here's the way we prepare a sole. We call it la solo dei pescadou (fishermen's sole). We wash it and clean it in sea water . . ."

FOR THE SAUCE:

pinch of coarse salt
freshly ground pepper
2 cloves garlic
2 hard-cooked egg yolks
1 tablespoon tarragon mustard
½ cup (4 fl oz/125 ml) olive oil

salt
2 soles, 8–10 oz (250–300 g) each, cleaned and skinned
1 tablespoon olive oil
coarse dried bread crumbs

▦ Prepare a fire in a charcoal grill. To prepare the sauce, in a mortar pound together the coarse salt, pepper to taste and garlic to form a paste. Add the egg yolks and pound again to a paste. Add the mustard and turn with the pestle until a smooth paste forms. Slowly incorporate the olive oil, adding it in a fine thread to the side of the mortar, stirring all the while with the pestle.

▦ Salt the soles to taste and then rub them with the olive oil. Coat them with bread crumbs on all sides. Place on the grill rack over hot coals and grill for 7–8 minutes on each side. Serve hot with sauce on the side.

SERVES 2

Clockwise from top left: Fisherman's Sole with Fisherman's Sauce, Tuna Chartreuse, Provençal Skate

B O U C H E S · D U · R H Ô N E

THON À LA CHARTREUSE

Tuna Chartreuse

This preparation is thought to derive from Carthusian monks famed for their production of Chartreuse liqueur. Some cooking authors add the liqueur to the recipe in an abortive attempt to justify its name.

1 thick slice of tuna, about ½ lb (750 g) and 1¼ in (3 cm)
   thick, skinned
8 salt anchovies, rinsed and filleted (see glossary)
3 tablespoons olive oil
1 head leafy lettuce
2 large, garden-ripe tomatoes, peeled, seeded and sliced
2 carrots, about 5 oz (150 g) total weight, peeled and
   thinly sliced
1 large onion, thinly sliced

PROVENCE

COQUILLES SAINT-JACQUES À LA PROVENÇALE

Provençal Sea Scallops

If you can find scallops with the golden roe still attached, buy them for this simple dish.

2 tablespoons olive oil
12 sea scallops, each cut in half across the grain and well dried
salt and freshly ground pepper
1 tablespoon unsalted butter
persillade made with 1 clove garlic (see glossary)
½ lemon

Warm the olive oil in a nonstick frying pan over high heat. Season the scallops with salt and pepper to taste. Add to the pan and sauté for not quite 1 minute on each side. Add the butter and, when it foams, add the *persillade*. Toss or stir for a few seconds, squeeze over a bit of lemon juice and serve immediately.

SERVES 4

PROVENCE

THON À LA RÉMOULADE

Grilled Tuna with Rémoulade Sauce

The sauce called rémoulade *today is usually mustard, anchovy essence and chopped pickles, capers and fines herbes stirred into a mayonnaise. Traditionally it is made with hard-cooked egg yolks. The anonymous author of* Le cuisinier méridional *(1855) gives two recipes for* rémoulade, provençale *and* languedocienne. *Only the Languedoc* rémoulade *contains mustard.*

1 tuna steak, about 1½ lb (750 g) and 1 in (2.5 cm) thick, skinned

FOR THE MARINADE:

pinch of Provençal mixed dried herbs (see glossary)
1 tablespoon dry white wine
½ lemon
1 teaspoon olive oil

FOR THE RÉMOULADE:

pinch of coarse salt
freshly ground pepper
1 clove garlic
1 tablespoon chopped shallots

Provençal Sea Scallops

A beach along the Bouches-du-Rhône coast, Grilled Tuna with Rémoulade Sauce

1 tablespoon chopped fresh flat-leaf (Italian) parsley
1 tablespoon capers, rinsed and squeezed dry
1 salt anchovy, rinsed and filleted (see glossary)
3 hard-cooked egg yolks
1 uncooked egg yolk
½ cup (4 fl oz/125 ml) olive oil
1 teaspoon fresh lemon juice

salt and freshly ground pepper
2 teaspoons olive oil

◾ Place the tuna steak in a shallow bowl. For the marinade, add the herbs, white wine, a few drops of lemon juice and olive oil to the fish. Marinate for 1 hour or so, turning it over and around in the marinade 2 or 3 times.
◾ To prepare the *rémoulade,* in a mortar pound together the salt, pepper, garlic, shallot and parsley to form a paste. Add the capers and anchovy and pound again to a paste. Add the hard-cooked egg yolks and pound and stir with the pestle to a smooth, homogenous paste. Stir in the raw egg yolk and turn with the pestle for a few moments. Slowly add the olive oil in a fine trickle to the side of the mortar while stirring vigorously with the pestle. Stir in the lemon juice. Set aside.
◾ Prepare a fire in a charcoal grill. Drain the tuna steak and pat it dry with paper towels. Season on both sides with salt and pepper and rub the olive oil over all the surfaces. Place the tuna steak on a well-oiled grill rack over hot coals and grill turning once, until tender, counting 6–7 minutes per side. Use a large, wide spatula to turn the steak and to remove it from the grill. Serve at once with the *rémoulade* on the side.

SERVES 4

CREVETTES GRISES À LA PERSILLADE

Sautéed Shrimp

Medium-sized shrimp in Provence are sold precooked—plunged alive into boiling salted water for 1 minute, drained and cooled. They are called bouquets. *The only shrimp found alive in the market are the tiny (average 1½ inches/4 cm from head to tail)* crevettes grises, *pale grayish, semitransparent shrimp with fragile, parchmentlike shells. Giant shrimp, averaging 8 inches (20 cm) from tip to tail, are called* gambas *and are sold raw but not alive; they are grilled, whole and unshelled, over hot coals for a couple of minutes on each side and served with a* remoulade *sauce (recipe on page 340).*

3 tablespoons olive oil
¾ lb (375 g) live *crevettes grises* or small shrimp (prawn) tails
  in the shell
salt and freshly ground pepper
persillade made with 1 clove garlic (see glossary)
1 lemon

◙ Warm the olive oil in a large, sharply slant-sided frying pan over high heat. Add the shrimp and salt and pepper to taste and sauté, tossing the shrimp repeatedly in the air, until they turn pale pink, 1 minute; count 2 minutes for shrimp tails. Add the *persillade,* toss again, squeeze over a few drops of lemon juice and serve. As with fried whitebait, everything is eaten (if shrimp tails have been substituted, they are shelled at table).

SERVES 4   *Photograph pages 326–327*

RAIE, SAUCE AUX CAPRES

Skate in Caper Sauce

The flesh of skate wings is melting and voluptuous. At table, it separates like magic from the tender, gelatinous bones when the tines of an overturned fork are drawn down the length of the bones.

1½ lb (750 g) skate wings, skinned and cut into 3–4-oz
  (100–125-g) sections if large
4 cups (32 fl oz/1 l) water
½ cup (4 fl oz/125 ml) white wine vinegar
salt

FOR THE SAUCE:
2 egg yolks
1 tablespoon plus 2 cups (16 fl oz/500 ml) water
1 tablespoon fresh lemon juice
1 tablespoon olive oil
freshly ground pepper
3 tablespoons unsalted butter
2 tablespoons all-purpose (plain) flour
salt
3–4 tablespoons (1½ oz/45 g) capers, rinsed and drained

◙ Arrange the skate wings or wing sections, thin parts overlapping, in a large, heavy sauté pan. In a saucepan combine the water, vinegar and salt to taste and bring to a boil. Pour it over the skate, place the sauté pan over the heat and again bring the liquid to a boil. Cover the pan tightly and remove from the heat. Hold, covered, until the sauce is ready.
◙ To prepare the sauce, in a small bowl combine the egg yolks, the 1 tablespoon water, the lemon juice, olive oil and pepper to taste with a fork. Set aside. In a saucepan, melt the butter over low heat. Add the flour and stir with a wooden spoon until the mixture begins to bubble, a couple of minutes. With a whisk in hand, pour the 2 cups (16 fl oz/500 ml) water into the saucepan, whisking at the same time. Season to taste with salt, raise the heat and continue whisking until the sauce boils. Remove it from the heat and leave to cool for a minute. Whisk in the egg yolk mixture and return the pan to low heat. Turn with the whisk or stir with the wooden spoon until the sauce thickens slightly, about 3 or 4 minutes. It must not boil. Stir in the capers.
◙ Using a flat, perforated skimming spoon, transfer the skate pieces to a heated serving platter, draining as well as possible. Sponge up any liquid that appears in the platter with a paper towel. Ladle a bit of sauce over the fish. Serve the rest of the sauce in a heated bowl.

SERVES 4

ENCORNETS FARCIS

Stuffed Squid

Here are three distinctive stuffings for squid; prepare the one that appeals. Because the squid mantles, or pouches, shrink in cooking, they should be loosely packed with stuffing. Leave a ½-in (12-mm) space at the opening; tack the top sides of the pouches closed with a trussing needle and kitchen string, pulling the ends of the string together, tying and clipping.

FOR THE ANCHOVY–BREAD CRUMB STUFFING:
1 tablespoon olive oil
1 onion, finely chopped
the squids' tentacles and wings, chopped
salt
2 tomatoes, peeled, seeded and chopped
1½ cups (3 oz/90 g) fresh bread crumbs
persillade made with 2 cloves garlic (see glossary)
2 salt anchovies, rinsed, filleted and chopped (see glossary)
freshly ground black pepper and cayenne pepper
2 eggs

◙ To prepare the anchovy–bread crumb stuffing, warm the olive oil in a sauté pan over low heat. Add the onion and cook until softened but not colored, about 10 minutes. Raise the heat, add the tentacles and wings and salt to taste and sauté until the liquid the squid gives off evaporates, 2–3 minutes. Add the contents of the pan to a mixing bowl. Add the tomatoes, bread crumbs, *persillade,* anchovies, black and cayenne peppers to taste and a bit more salt. Mix together loosely, add the eggs and, using your hands, mix thoroughly.

FOR THE RICE STUFFING:
¾ cup (4 oz/125 g) long-grain white rice
1 tablespoon olive oil
1 onion, finely chopped
the squids' tentacles and wings, chopped
salt and freshly ground pepper
1 teaspoon fresh marjoram flower buds and leaves, finely
  chopped
1 tablespoon chopped fresh flat-leaf (Italian) parsley

◙ To prepare the stuffing, bring a saucepan filled with water to a boil. Add the rice and parboil for 15 minutes. Drain into a sieve and rinse under cold running water. Drain again and let stand for 15 minutes.
◙ Warm the olive oil in a sauté pan over low heat. Add the onion and cook until softened but not colored, about 10 minutes. Raise the heat, add the tentacles and wings and sauté until the liquid the squid gives off evaporates, 2–3 minutes. Add the contents of the pan to a mixing bowl with all the remaining ingredients. Using a fork mix thoroughly but gently so as not to break up the rice grains.

Skate in Caper Sauce in the old port of La Ciotat

FOR THE SPINACH-MUSSEL STUFFING:

4 tablespoons olive oil
1 onion, finely chopped
the squids' tentacles and wings, chopped
1 lb (500 g) mussels, opened with white wine over heat
  (see glossary)
2 garlic cloves, finely chopped
1 lb (500 g) spinach, parboiled, squeezed dry and chopped
  (see glossary)
½ cup (1 oz/30 g) fresh bread crumbs
freshly ground pepper
whole nutmeg
2 eggs
salt

◙ To prepare the spinach-mussel stuffing, warm 1 tablespoon of the olive oil in a sauté pan over low heat. Add the onion and cook until softened but not colored, about 10 minutes. Raise the heat, add the tentacles and wings and sauté for 1 minute. Add about ½ cup (4 fl oz/125 ml) of the decanted mussels' cooking liquid and simmer until the liquid is reduced by about two-thirds, about 10 minutes. Set aside.

◙ Heat the remaining 3 tablespoons of olive oil in a sauté pan over medium-high heat. Add the garlic and, when it begins to sizzle, add the spinach and sauté, stirring with a wooden spoon for a minute or so. Add about ¼ cup (2 fl oz/60 ml) of the mussels' cooking liquid and stir until it is absorbed, just a few minutes. Stir in the bread crumbs and remove from the heat to cool partially.

◙ Shell the mussels. In a mixing bowl combine the onion-squid mixture, the shelled mussels and the spinach mixture.

Grind over some pepper and scrape over nutmeg. Add the eggs and, using your hands, mix thoroughly. Taste for salt.

FOR THE SQUID:

4 squid, ½–¾ lb (250–315 g) each, cleaned (see glossary)
3 tablespoons olive oil
1 onion, finely chopped
salt
4 tablespoons marc de Provence (see glossary) or Cognac
persillade made with 2 cloves garlic (see glossary)
3 salt anchovies, rinsed, filleted and chopped (see glossary)
2 tablespoons capers, rinsed, squeezed dry and chopped
½ cup (4 fl oz/125 ml) dry white wine

◙ Stuff the cleaned squid with one of the stuffings, following the directions in the recipe introduction.

◙ In a heavy sauté pan, warm the olive oil over low heat. Add the onion and cook gently until softened but not colored, about 10 minutes. Raise the heat, add the stuffed squid and salt to taste. Shake the pan back and forth, rolling them around, until the flesh has contracted firmly around the stuffing and has turned opaque. Pour over the brandy and ignite with a long-handled match. Shaking the pan, scatter over the *persillade,* anchovies and capers. Roll the squid around by shaking the pan, or turn them around and over with a wooden spoon. When flames die add the wine. Cover the pan tightly and cook over the lowest possible heat for 1 hour, shaking the pan from time to time.

◙ Clip and remove the strings and serve directly from the sauté pan, spooning some of the cooking juices over each squid.

SERVES 4   *Photograph pages 326–327*

DAURADE AU FOUR
Provençal Baked Porgy

1 large onion, cut in half and thinly sliced
4 or 5 cloves garlic, thinly sliced
4–5 tablespoons (2–3 fl oz/60–80 ml) olive oil
1 porgy (bream), red snapper or similar fish, about 4 lb
    (2 kg), cleaned
salt and freshly ground pepper
large pinch of Provençal mixed dried herbs (see glossary)
1 lb (500 g) tomatoes, peeled, seeded and sliced or cut
    into wedges
⅔ cup (3 oz/100 g) black olives
2 green Italian sweet peppers or other sweet peppers (capsi-
    cums), seeded, deribbed and cut into long, narrow strips
½ cup (4 fl oz/125 ml) dry white wine

◼ Preheat an oven to 400°F (200°C).
◼ Mix the sliced onions and garlic together. Rub the bottom of a large gratin dish with 1 tablespoon of the olive oil and scatter over half of the onion-garlic mixture. Season the fish inside and out with salt and pepper to taste and the mixed herbs. Place the fish in the gratin dish and rub it inside and out with olive oil, turning it around and over. Scatter the remaining onion-garlic mixture over the fish and then pile the tomatoes on top, smothering the fish. Scatter the olives and pepper strips over and around the fish and sprinkle salt over the surface. Dribble the remaining olive oil in a thread back and forth over the surface. Pour the wine into the bottom of the dish. If the fish's tail is not quite contained in the dish, fold a piece of aluminum foil around it to prevent its charring.
◼ Place in the oven and bake for about 40 minutes, basting a couple of times after the first 20 minutes. Test for doneness with a trussing needle or sharp skewer. Serve directly from the gratin dish, moving the vegetables to the side before serving in the same way as for the grilled fish (recipe follows). Accompany each portion with some vegetables and juices.

SERVES 4

DAURADE GRILLÉE
Grilled Fish

Red porgy, scup, sheepshead, black sea bass, red snapper, and the like are suitable for grilling. Unless the fish is grilled in its scales (in which case it makes no sense to marinate it), a hinged, double-faced fish grill is indispensable for turning the fish over on the grill. The cooking time for a large fish is judged by the fish's back at its thickest point, counting about 10 minutes per inch (2.5 cm). If a skewer inserted at the thickest point meets little resistance, or if the first spine of the dorsal fin can be easily pulled out with its attached bone, the fish is done. It needs no sauce, but olive oil and lemon wedges, green sauce (recipe on page 359), pistou (recipe on page 290) or tapénade (recipe on page 288) are all pleasant accompaniments. If neither fresh wild fennel nor dried fennel stalk is available, substitute a pinch of ground fennel seeds.

1 fish, 3–4 lb (1.5–2 kg), cleaned
fresh wild fennel stalks plus a handful of chopped, feathery
    leaves or, if out of season, sections of dried fennel stalk
freshly ground pepper
¼ cup (2 fl oz/60 ml) olive oil

1 tablespoon *pastis* such as Pernod 51 or Ricard
½ lemon
salt
several fresh thyme branches, stems tied together to
    form a brush

◼ Score the fish on each side two or three times, slicing shallowly crosswise on the bias, and place the fish in a large shallow oval dish. Stuff a bundle of fennel stalks, cut or bent to the right length, into the body and head cavity. If the season is right, sprinkle chopped fennel leaves over the fish, taking care to force a certain amount into the slits in the flesh.
◼ Grind some pepper over the fish, then sprinkle inside and out, first with the olive oil and then with the *pastis*. Squeeze over a bit of lemon juice and, using your hands, rub the fish gently all over.
◼ Leave the fish to marinate while preparing a solid bed of coals with good depth. They should be slightly on the decline before putting the fish to grill, with a film of white ash masking the ardent embers. Meanwhile, turn the fish over a couple of times, spooning over the marinade.
◼ Open out the fish grill and arrange 2 or 3 lengths of fennel stalk on one side. Salt the fish and place it on top, head at the hinge, and lay more fennel stalks on the fish before closing the grill. Reserve any marinade in the dish.
◼ Place the fish over the coals and turn it over every 4 or 5 minutes. Once it is turned, begin basting with the remaining marinade by dipping the bundle of thyme into it and dabbing it over the surface of the fish. The fish should be done after 25–30 minutes (see recipe introduction).
◼ Open the grill and slip the fish onto a serving platter, discarding the outside branches of fennel. At table, cut to the bone along the lateral line; slit the skin next to the fins and all the length of the back and from the abdomen to the tail. Then cut across and lift up serving portions with a spatula.

SERVES 4

BAUDROIE À LA PROVENÇALE
Provençal Monkfish

Monkfish is sold cleaned and skinned. When filleted, the fillets at the thickest part of the body are nearly round and can be sliced into neat, firm medallions.

1½ lb (750 g) monkfish (anglerfish), filleted and cut into
    slices ¾ in (2 cm) thick
salt and freshly ground pepper
all-purpose (plain) flour
¼ cup (2 fl oz/60 ml) olive oil
¾ cup (¼ lb/125 g) black olives
2 cups (16 fl oz/500 ml) tomato sauce, heated (see glossary)

◼ Preheat an oven to 350°F (180°C). Season the fish slices with salt and pepper to taste. Coat them with flour and toss them in your hands or in a sieve to shake off excess flour.
◼ Warm the olive oil in a large sauté pan or frying pan over medium heat. Add the fish slices and fry, turning once until golden, about 3 or 4 minutes on each side. Using a slotted utensil remove to paper towels to drain briefly, then arrange in a gratin dish. Scatter the black olives over the top, filling up any empty spaces. Pour the tomato sauce evenly over the fish.
◼ Place in the oven and bake until the sauce is bubbling, about 15 minutes. Serve immediately.

SERVES 4   *Photograph pages 346–347*

Top to bottom: Provençal Baked Porgy, Grilled Fish

BAUDROIE BOURGEOIS

Monkfish Durand

This is adapted from a recipe by famed chef Charles Durand, published in the early 19th century. It differs from his Bouil-Abaïsse à la Nimoise in that the latter contains a variety of fish "such as red mullets; half-cooked eels, soles, pageaux, dorades and langouste tails."

Monkfish liver is the sea's answer to foie gras. It has the same, voluptuous, velvety texture, is delicious simply sautéed and served with lemon sections and is a very useful element in stuffings and sauces.

FOR THE BROTH:

1 onion, thinly sliced
1 carrot, peeled and thinly sliced
1 bay leaf
1 fresh thyme sprig
stems from a bouquet of fresh flat-leaf (Italian) parsley
monkfish (anglerfish) head and backbone, chopped up
salt
1 cup (8 fl oz/250 ml) dry white wine

½ cup (4 fl oz/125 ml) olive oil
2 leeks, about 5 oz (150 g), including the tender green parts,
    thinly sliced
2 lb (1 kg) filleted monkfish, cut into about 8 equal pieces
persillade made with 1 clove garlic (see glossary)
the monkfish liver, no larger than ¼ lb (125 g)
3 egg yolks
freshly ground pepper
large handful of ½-in (12-mm) crustless croutons, fried in
    olive oil until golden and crisp

To prepare the broth, put the vegetables and the herbs in the bottom of a saucepan and place the fish head and backbone on top. Pour in water to cover and season to taste with salt. Bring to a boil and skim off any froth and scum. Reduce the heat, cover with the lid ajar and simmer for 15 minutes. Add the wine, return to a boil and simmer for 15 minutes longer. Strain the broth through a fine-mesh sieve. Set aside.

Choose a heavy sauté pan or saucepan of a size just to contain the monkfish fillets placed side by side. Warm 3 tablespoons of the olive oil in the pan over low heat. Add the leeks and cook gently, stirring occasionally, until softened but not colored, about 10 minutes. Arrange the pieces of fish atop the leeks, sprinkle the *persillade* over the top and pour in enough of the reserved broth to cover. Bring to a boil and add the liver. Adjust the heat to simmer. Remove the liver when it has firmed up but still remains pink inside, after about 5 minutes. Cook the monkfish for 15 minutes in all.

Meanwhile, in a mortar reduce the liver to a paste. Add the egg yolks and the pepper to taste and stir with the pestle until the mixture forms a smooth, consistent cream. Add the remaining olive oil in a fine trickle to the side of the mortar, stirring constantly with the pestle. The sauce should be quite thick, like a mayonnaise.

When the fish is done, remove the pan from the heat and, using a slotted spoon, transfer the pieces of fish to a warmed deep serving dish. Stir a ladleful of the cooking liquid into the mortar and add the contents of the mortar to the remainder of the cooking liquid, stirring with a wooden spoon. Return the pan to low heat and stir constantly until the sauce thickens slightly and coats the spoon, 8–10 minutes; it must not boil.

Hold a sieve over the fish and pour the sauce into it, moving the sieve back and forth to coat the fish pieces evenly. Stir the sauce in the sieve to help it pass (some of the chopped parsley will cling to the fish and the rest will remain behind in the sieve). Scatter over croûtons and serve.

SERVES 4

SARDINES FARCIES AUX ÉPINARDS

Sardines Stuffed with Spinach

The presentation of the stuffed and rolled sardines, their tails in the air and the dish cloaked in golden crumbs, is startling and beautiful.

18 fresh sardines
6 tablespoons (3 fl oz/90 ml) olive oil
1 onion, finely chopped
persillade made with 1 clove garlic (see glossary)

Clockwise from top: Monkfish Durand, Stuffed Porgy with Crab Sauce (recipe page 349), Sardines Stuffed with Spinach, Provençal Monkfish (recipe page 345)

2 lb (1 kg) spinach, parboiled, squeezed dry and chopped
  (see glossary)
salt and freshly ground pepper
whole nutmeg
2 hard-cooked eggs, chopped
dried bread crumbs

◙ Rub each sardine gently under running water to remove the scales. Cut off the head, slit the abdomen all the way to the tail, gut the fish and carefully pry the rib cage and spine loose with your fingertips and a knife tip. Pinch off the bone near the tail. Leave the fillets attached at the back and tail so that the sardine opens out into a kite shape.

◙ Preheat an oven to 425°F (220°C). Warm 3 tablespoons of the olive oil in a sauté pan over low heat. Add the onion and cook gently until softened but not colored, about 5 minutes. Raise the heat, add the *persillade* and stir around with a wooden spoon. Add the spinach and cook, stirring, over high heat for a minute or so. Add salt to taste, grind over some pepper and scrape over a bit of nutmeg. Stir well and remove from the heat.

◙ Spread half the spinach mixture in an oval 8-cup (48-fl oz/2-l) gratin dish. Stir the eggs into the other half. Lay the sardines out, skin side down. Spoon some stuffing onto the head end of each, roll the sardine up and push it into the bed of spinach in the gratin dish, tail in the air. Place the sardines side by side and touching so they hold their shape. Sprinkle bread crumbs generously over the top and dribble on the remaining 3 tablespoons olive oil in a thread, forming a crisscross pattern.

◙ Place in the oven and bake until the crumbs are golden, 20–25 minutes. Serve immediately.

SERVES 6

Herb-Stuffed Fish

VAR

DAURADE FARCIE À LA SANARYENNE

Stuffed Porgy with Crab Sauce

This recipe is adapted from one published in 1928 by Austin de Croze, author of Les plats régionaux de France; *it is signed and dated "Mme. Natte, 1886, Sanary." Sanary is a small fishing port between Bandol and Toulon, perhaps the prettiest and most charming in all the region. The crabs in the original recipe are the local* favouilles, *or green shore crabs. Blue swimmers, in their soft-shelled phase, may replace hard-shelled crabs.*

FOR THE STUFFING:

1 tablespoon olive oil
1 small onion, finely chopped
¼ lb (125 g) fresh cultivated mushrooms, finely chopped
salt and freshly ground pepper
whole nutmeg
2 tablespoons chopped fresh flat-leaf (Italian) parsley
1 lb (500 g) mussels, opened with white wine over heat
   (see glossary)
2 hard-cooked eggs, chopped

FOR THE SAUCE:

the mussel's cooking liquid
⅓ cup (3 fl oz/80 ml) dry white wine
1 lb (500 g) small, lively crabs (see recipe introduction)
2–3 tablespoons tomato sauce (see glossary)

1 porgy (bream), about 4 lb (2 kg), cleaned
salt and freshly ground pepper
¼ cup (2 fl oz/60 ml) olive oil
½ cup (4 fl oz/125 ml) dry white wine
tender shoots and feathery leaves of wild fennel

◉ To prepare the stuffing, in a frying pan warm the olive oil over low heat. Add the onion and cook until softened but not colored, about 10 minutes. Add the mushrooms and raise the heat. Add salt and pepper to taste and scrape over a hint of nutmeg. Toss and stir until the liquid the mushrooms release evaporates, about 5 minutes. Add the parsley and sauté for a few seconds, until the odor of cooking parsley fills the air. Transfer the pan's contents to a mixing bowl. Remove the mussels from their shells, reserving their cooking liquid. Stir the mussels and eggs into the mushroom mixture. Set aside.
◉ To prepare the sauce, combine the mussels' cooking liquid and the white wine in a saucepan. Bring to a boil, throw in the crabs, cover and cook, stirring the crabs around from time to time, for 6–7 minutes. Empty into a sieve placed over another saucepan. Remove the crabs, two or three at a time, to a mortar, and pound until broken up, coarse and crumbly. Transfer to a food processor fitted with the metal blade, add 2–3 tablespoons of their cooking liquid and process to a coarse purée. Using the wooden pestle, press the purée through a fine-mesh sieve, small quantities at a time, each time discarding the debris of shells that collects in the sieve. Combine the crab purée, the crabs' cooking liquid and the tomato sauce in a saucepan and set aside.
◉ Preheat an oven to 375°F (190°C). Stuff the fish with the mussel mixture and truss it with skewers and kitchen string as directed in herb-stuffed fish (recipe follows). Season the fish on both sides with salt and pepper. Place it in an oiled gratin dish and dribble the olive oil evenly over the top. Pour the wine into the dish.
◉ Place in the oven and bake for 45–50 minutes, basting often after the first 15 minutes. Begin to test for doneness with a trussing needle or sharp skewer after 40 minutes.
◉ While the fish is cooking, reduce the crab sauce at a light boil to a very light-bodied consistency. Transfer the fish to a heated platter (Mme. Natte suggests that it be placed on a bed of fresh fennel) and remove the skewers and string. Add the fish's cooking juices to the sauce. Return the sauce to a boil and reduce, if necessary. Pour it into a warmed bowl. Serve the fish in the same way as for the grilled fish (recipe on page 345). Pour some of the sauce over both the fish and the stuffing.

SERVES 4   *Photograph pages 346–347*

VAR

CHAPON FARCI AUX HERBES

Herb-Stuffed Fish

FOR THE STUFFING:

1 teaspoon olive oil
the fish's liver or a monkfish (anglerfish) liver
1 cup (2 oz/60 g) fresh bread crumbs
½ lb (250 g) spinach, parboiled, squeezed dry and chopped
   (see glossary)
½ lb (250 g) Swiss chard (silverbeet) greens, parboiled,
   squeezed dry and chopped (see glossary)
handful of sorrel leaves, stemmed and finely shredded
persillade made with 1 clove garlic (see glossary)
2 or 3 green (spring) onions, chopped or thinly sliced
salt and freshly ground pepper
2 eggs

1 scorpionfish, about 4 lb (2 kg), cleaned
¼ cup (2 fl oz/60 ml) olive oil
1 yellow onion, thinly sliced
2 cloves garlic, thinly sliced
fresh thyme sprigs and fennel stalk pieces
2 lemons, thinly sliced crosswise
½ cup (4 fl oz/125 ml) dry white wine

◉ To prepare the stuffing, in a small frying pan, warm the olive oil over low heat. Add the liver and cook until it firms up, about 1 minute. Transfer it to a mortar and pound to a purée. Add the bread crumbs and mix together, wiping up all the liver. Transfer the liver mixture to a mixing bowl. Add the spinach, chard, sorrel, *persillade,* and green onions and season to taste with salt and pepper. Mix together, add the eggs and, using your hands mix well, squeezing the mixture repeatedly between your fingers. Taste for seasoning.
◉ Preheat an oven to 375°F (190°C). Stuff the fish, pushing the stuffing well into the head, which, with the abdomen, should form a single cavity. Close the cavity with small, sharp skewers (lengths of bamboo skewer are practical); lace kitchen string back and forth, crossing like a bootlace, and then tie.
◉ Rub the bottom of a large gratin dish with olive oil and scatter the yellow onion, garlic, thyme sprigs and fennel pieces over it. Season the stuffed fish with salt and pepper to taste and pose it in the gratin dish. If the tail is not contained with the dish, wrap it in aluminum foil. Dribble the olive oil evenly over the surface. Arrange a row of lemon slices, slightly overlapping, along the entire length of the fish, from head to tail. Pour the white wine into the bottom of the dish.
◉ Place in the oven and bake for 45–50 minutes, basting often after the first 15 minutes. Begin to test for doneness with a sharp skewer or trussing needle after 40 minutes.
◉ Remove the skewers and string and serve at table in the same way as for the grilled fish (recipe on page 345). Pour a spoonful of pan juices over each serving and place a spoonful of stuffing to the side.

SERVES 6

PROVENCE

GRENOUILLES À LA PROVENÇALE

Provençal Frogs' Legs

40 pairs frogs' legs
6 tablespoons (3 fl oz/90 ml) olive oil
juice of ½ lemon
½ cup (2 oz/60 g) all-purpose (plain) flour
salt and freshly ground pepper
persillade made with 2 cloves garlic (see glossary)

◙ Place the frogs' legs in a shallow bowl. Add a few teaspoons of the olive oil and the lemon juice and toss and turn the legs a couple of times. Marinate at room temperature for 1 hour.
◙ Dry the frogs' legs on paper towels. Put the flour in a paper bag, add the frogs' legs, close the bag and shake well. Transfer the legs to a sieve and shake off the excess flour.
◙ Warm the remaining olive oil in a large, nonstick sauté pan over high heat. Add the legs and sauté until golden, 8–10 minutes. Season to taste with salt and pepper and remove to a warmed platter.
◙ Throw the *persillade* into the hot oil remaining in the pan for a couple of seconds. Pour the oil and *persillade* over the frogs' legs and serve immediately.

SERVES 4

PROVENCE

PETITE FRITURE

Fried Whitebait

In Provence petite friture *is composed mainly of sardine and anchovy fry* (poutine), *tiny, grayish transparent fish varying from 1 inch (2.5 cm) to 2½ inches (6 cm) in length. Whitebait, from more northerly waters, is thought to contain a large percentage of herring fry. Poutine and whitebait, in any case, look alike, taste alike and are treated in the same way. In the minds of many, petite friture is vacation food, to be enjoyed with a bottle of chilled Cassis white wine on the terrace of a seaside restaurant to break up a day at the beach. See the glossary for more information on deep-frying.*

⅔ cup (3 oz/90 g) all-purpose (plain) flour
salt, freshly ground black pepper and cayenne pepper
1 lb (500 g) whitebait
about 8 cups (64 fl oz/2 l) corn oil or peanut oil
handful of small bouquets of fresh flat-leaf (Italian)
    parsley leaves
2 lemons, cut in half

◙ The fish should be fried in three or four batches. Preheat an oven at its lowest setting to keep the first batches warm. Lay out several thicknesses of newspaper covered with paper towels on which to drain the fried fish. Prepare a platter covered with a large folded napkin on which to place them after draining. Put the flour and salt, black pepper and cayenne pepper to taste in a large paper bag. Close it and shake it to mix the flour and seasonings together.
◙ In a large pot or a deep-fat fryer, heat the oil to 375°F (190°C), or until it sizzles at contact when a small, floured fish is thrown in. While the oil is heating, throw a handful of whitebait into the paper bag, close it and shake it well. Remove the fish to a large sieve (leaving behind as much flour as possible). Hold the sieve over a sheet of newspaper and shake it, tossing the fish to rid them of all excess flour. (The flour that is shaken free can be returned to the paper bag.)
◙ When the oil is hot enough, empty the sieve into the oil and stir the fish around in the oil with a fork. A minute later, when the fish are crisp and light gold, remove them, using a slotted spoon, to the paper towels. Prepare another handful of fish in the paper bag, shake off excess flour and add them to the hot oil. Transfer the drained fish to the folded napkin, put the platter in the oven, and so forth until the last batch is fried.
◙ After the last of the fish are removed, add the parsley to the hot oil and remove it as soon as it is crisp. Drain for a second, then scatter it over the fish. Surround with lemon halves and serve, covered with the napkin fold.

SERVES 4

Provençal Frogs' Legs

Top to bottom: Toulon-Style Whiting Fillets, Fried Whitebait

VAR

MERLAN À LA TOULONNAISE
Toulon-Style Whiting Fillets

Toulon is famous for its mussels. Any preparation of fish in sauce
à la toulonnaise *is nearly certain to be garnished with mussels,*
to which are often joined black olives.

1 lb (500 g) mussels, opened with white wine over heat
    (see glossary)
2 cups (16 fl oz/500 ml) tomato sauce prepared without salt
    (see glossary)
salt and freshly ground pepper
4 whiting fillets, about 1 lb (500 g) total weight
all-purpose (plain) flour

¼ cup (2 fl oz/60 ml) olive oil

◼ Reduce the mussels' decanted cooking liquid over high heat
to about ⅓ cup (3 fl oz/90 ml). Taste for salt. If it is exces-
sively salty, add only as much of the reduced liquid as necessary to the tomato sauce to salt it correctly. Heat the tomato
sauce and hold it at a simmer while preparing the fish fillets.
◼ Season the fillets with salt and pepper. Cover them
with flour, shaking off any excess flour. Warm the olive
oil in a large frying pan over medium-high heat. Add the
fillets and fry, turning once, until lightly colored, 3–4 minutes on each side. Remove to paper towels to drain, then
arrange on a warmed platter.
◼ Shell the mussels. Add them to the simmering tomato
sauce and pour over the fillets. Serve immediately.

SERVES 4

PROVENCE

ENCORNETS À LA PROVENÇALE

Provençal Squid

This preparation is often called à l'americaine, in emulation of lobster (homard) à l'americaine. It is better suited to squid than to lobster. When octopus is prepared like this, with longer cooking, black olives are added at the end and it becomes poulpe à la niçoise. *A rice pilaf (recipe on page 449), with or without saffron, is an ideal accompaniment.*

3 tablespoons olive oil
1 onion, finely chopped
2 lb (1 kg) squid, cleaned and pouches cut into rings 1 in (2.5 cm) wide (see glossary)
salt, freshly ground black pepper and pinch of cayenne pepper
¼ cup (2 fl oz/60 ml) marc de Provence (see glossary) or Cognac
½ cup (4 fl oz/125 ml) dry white wine
1 lb (500 g) tomatoes, peeled, seeded and coarsely chopped
2 cloves garlic, finely chopped
bouquet garni (see glossary)

▦ Warm the olive oil in a heavy sauté pan over low heat. Add the onion and cook until softened but not colored, about 10 minutes. Raise the heat, add the squid and stir with a wooden spoon until the liquid the squid gives off evaporates, 2–3 minutes. Season to taste with salt and black and cayenne peppers. Add the brandy and ignite with a long-handled match. When the flames die add the wine and reduce by about half, about 10 minutes.
▦ Add the tomatoes, garlic and bouquet garni and bring to a boil. Adjust the heat to a simmer and cover with the lid ajar. After 30 minutes if the sauce is too abundant, remove the lid and raise the heat slightly to maintain a simmer. If when the squid is tender (45–50 minutes in all), the sauce is still too abundant, remove the squid to a plate and reduce the sauce over high heat, stirring with a wooden spoon. Put the squid back into the sauce to serve.

SERVES 4

BOUCHES·DU·RHÔNE

CATIGOT À LA CAMARGUAISE

Eel in Red Wine

Eels are sold alive. To kill an eel, run the point of a sharp knife through the brain. To skin it, cut the skin around the base of the head, grasp the head with a towel and pull off the body skin with pliers; it peels off like a glove. Cut off the head and gut the eel.

3 tablespoons olive oil
1 onion, chopped
1 large, garden-ripe tomato, peeled, seeded and coarsely chopped
1 eel, about 2 lb (1 kg), skinned, cleaned and cut into 3-in (7.5-cm) lengths (see recipe introduction)
salt
bouquet garni including a strip of dried orange peel and 1 dried cayenne chili pepper or other dried chili pepper (see glossary)
8–10 cloves garlic
1 cup (8 fl oz/250 ml) dry red wine

boiling water as needed
freshly ground pepper
1 tablespoon chopped fresh flat-leaf (Italian) parsley

▦ Choose a heavy sauté pan of a size just to contain the eel pieces side by side. Warm the olive oil in the pan over medium heat. Add the onion and when it begins to color lightly, in a few minutes, add the tomato. Stir well and raise the heat. Add the eel, salt to taste, bouquet garni and garlic cloves. In a separate pan, bring the wine to a boil. Pour it over the eel and add enough boiling water just to cover the eel. Boil, uncovered, turning the eel around and over from time to time, until tender, about 20 minutes.
▦ Grind over some pepper and remove from the heat. Discard the bouquet garni and sprinkle with the parsley. Serve on warmed plates.

SERVES 4

PROVENCE

ÉCREVISSES À LA PROVENÇALE

Provençal Crayfish

¼ cup (2 fl oz/60 ml) olive oil
1 carrot, peeled, thinly sliced lengthwise and then cut
    across into tiny dice
1 onion, finely chopped
1 small celery heart, finely diced
large pinch of Provençal mixed dried herbs (see glossary)
1 dried bay leaf, crumbled, or fresh bay leaf, finely chopped
salt and freshly ground black pepper
4 dozen crayfish
¼ cup (2 fl oz/60 ml) marc de Provence (see glossary) or Cognac

½ cup (4 fl oz/125 ml) dry white wine
3 tablespoons tomato sauce (see glossary)
large pinch of cayenne pepper
persillade made with 2 cloves garlic (see glossary)

◼ Warm the olive oil in a large, heavy sauté pan over low heat. Add the carrot, onion, celery, herbs, bay leaf and salt and black pepper to taste. Stir with a wooden spoon, cover the pan and sweat over the lowest possible heat for about 15 minutes, stirring occasionally.
◼ Raise the heat to high, add the crayfish and stir briskly until they begin to turn red. Add the brandy and ignite it with a long-handled match. Stir, shaking the pan, until the flames die. Add the wine, tomato sauce and cayenne, cover tightly and cook over medium heat, shaking the pan regularly, until the shellfish are tender, 8–10 minutes. Scatter over the *persillade* and serve.

SERVES 4   *Photograph pages 326–327*

Top to bottom: Grilled Mussel Skewers, Clam and Spinach Gratin, Blanquette of Snails

TIAN DE PALOURDES AUX ÉPINARDS

Clam and Spinach Gratin

In Provence carpet shells, or palourdes, *are used for this gratin. It is also often prepared with mussels.*

2 lb (1 kg) little neck or cherrystone clams, opened with
   white wine over heat, as for mussels (see glossary)
4 tablespoons (2 fl oz/60 ml) olive oil

1 clove garlic, finely chopped
2 lb (1 kg) spinach, parboiled, squeezed dry and chopped
   (see glossary)
2 tablespoons all-purpose (plain) flour
about 1 cup (8 fl oz/250 ml) milk
freshly ground pepper
whole nutmeg
salt
dried or semidried bread crumbs

◙ Cook the clams as directed. Remove the clams from the cooking liquid and strain the liquid. Set the liquid and clams aside. Preheat an oven to 375°F (190°C).

354

Warm 3 tablespoons of the olive oil in a sauté pan over medium heat. Add the garlic, disperse it with a wooden spoon and, when it begins to sizzle, add the spinach. Stir regularly until the spinach begins to stick to the pan. Sprinkle over the flour and stir for a minute. Slowly add the clams' decanted cooking liquid, stirring constantly, then add all or part of the milk, depending upon the quantity and the saltiness of the clams' juices. Bring to a boil, adjust the heat to a simmer and cook, uncovered, until slightly thickened, about 15 minutes, stirring from time to time. Grind over some pepper and scrape over some nutmeg. Taste for salt (it will probably need none). Stir in the clams. Spread the mixture in a 6-cup (48-fl oz/1.5-l) gratin dish. Sprinkle with bread crumbs and dribble over the remaining 1 tablespoon olive oil.

Place in the oven and bake until the sauce is bubbling and the surface is nicely colored, about 20 minutes. Serve hot.

SERVES 4

BOUCHES·DU·RHÔNE

PETITS-GRIS EN MATELOTE

Blanquette of Snails

The common striped garden snail, or petit gris *(Helix aspersa), is the type most often eaten in Provence. Before being cooked,* petits-gris *are starved for a week or so in a cool, dark place, kept in a bucket tightly covered with a screen or an overturned mason's sifter. They are then "disgorged": put into a basin with a large handful of salt and about half a bottle of vinegar, stirred around regularly for 30 minutes, thoroughly rinsed, plunged into boiling water for 5 minutes, drained, refreshed under cold water and twirled out of their shells with a small, two-pronged fork or a nutpick. A court bouillon (see crayfish in court bouillon on page 331) is strained over them and they are simmered, with the lid ajar, for 2 hours. At this point, they are ready for use in other recipes. Many people content themselves with cooking the disgorged snails in their shells and serving them with* aïoli *(see glossary).*

If you are obliged to use canned snails, it is best to first freshen their flavor by draining them, rinsing them and then simmering them gently for 30 minutes in a half recipe for court bouillon. If using canned snails, cut the number in half; they are twice the size of garden snails.

½ lb (250 g) pickling onions, peeled
3 tablespoons unsalted butter
salt
pinch of sugar
½ lb (250 g) fresh button mushrooms or quartered
   larger caps
juice of 1 lemon
¼ cup (2 fl oz/60 ml) water
80–100 garden snails, cooled in the court bouillon
   (see recipe introduction)
2 tablespoons all-purpose (plain) flour
2 cups (16 fl oz/500 ml) of the snails' court bouillon
3 egg yolks
freshly ground pepper
whole nutmeg
1 tablespoon chopped fresh flat-leaf (Italian) parsley
handful of ½-in (12-mm) croûtons cut from firm-crumbed,
   semidry bread, crusts removed, sautéed in olive oil until
   crisp and golden

Put the pickling onions in a saucepan of a size just to contain them in a single layer. Add ½ tablespoon of the butter, a pinch of salt, the sugar and just enough water to cover barely. Bring to a boil and cover with a lid ajar. Simmer for about 10 minutes, shaking the pan occasionally. If the water has not completely evaporated, remove the lid, turn up the heat and shake the pan gently until no water remains and the onions begin to cook in the butter. Set aside.

In another saucepan combine the mushrooms, ½ tablespoon of the butter, salt to taste, half the lemon juice and the water. Cover and bring to a boil over high heat. Boil for a few seconds, then set aside.

Strain the snails, saving the court bouillon. Put the snails and court bouillon aside separately.

Melt the remaining 2 tablespoons butter in a heavy saucepan over low heat. Add the flour and cook while stirring for 1 minute or so. Add 2 cups (16 fl oz/500 ml) of the snails' court bouillon all at once, whisking briskly at the same time. Raise the heat and continue whisking until the sauce boils. Adjust the heat to a simmer and cook for 15 minutes, stirring occasionally.

Strain the mushrooms, reserving the cooking liquid in a small bowl. Stir the strained mushrooms, the onions and snails into the simmering sauce and remove from the heat. Add the remaining lemon juice and the egg yolks to the bowl containing the mushrooms' liquid. Grind over some pepper, scrape over a bit of nutmeg and beat with a fork. Using a wooden spoon, stir the sauce into the saucepan with the snails. Reduce the heat to low and stir until the mixture thickens slightly, a few minutes; it must not boil.

Pour the snails and their sauce into a warmed deep platter, sprinkle with the parsley, scatter over croutons and serve.

SERVES 6

VAR

BROCHETTES DE MOULES À LA TOULONNAISE

Grilled Mussel Skewers

Slender, sharp-pointed bamboo skewers about 12 in (30 cm) long are ideal for these brochettes, which can also be cooked in a broiler (griller). Save the mussels' cooking liquid for use in a sauce or a soup.

1 slice lean salt pork (green bacon), about ¼ lb (125 g) and
   ½ in (12 mm) thick, cut into lardoons (see glossary)
2 lb (1 kg) large mussels, opened in white wine over heat,
   strained and shells discarded (see glossary)
freshly ground pepper
dried oregano
1 tablespoon olive oil
dried bread crumbs

Prepare a fire in a charcoal grill.

Place the lardoons in a saucepan half filled with cold water and bring to a rolling boil. Drain, rinse in cold running water, and pat dry with paper towels.

Place the lardoons in a mixing bowl and add the mussels. Grind over some pepper, crumble over a little oregano and dribble over the olive oil. Using your hands toss the mussels and lardoons until evenly coated with oil and seasoning.

Thread the mussels and lardoons onto skewers, alternating them; they should be touching but not crowded. Spread a layer of bread crumbs on a tray. Roll each skewer in the crumbs until evenly coated.

Place the skewers on a grill rack over hot coals and grill for 2 minutes on each side. Serve hot.

SERVES 4

VAR/BOUCHES·DU·RHÔNE

POULPE EN DAUBE

Octopus Daube

*A large octopus (pieuvre) may take as long as four hours'
cooking to become tender and is usually first beaten to help
it along. On the coast near Toulon, one often sees divers in
their outer-space costumes, heaving large octopus repeatedly
against the rocks. The octopus will be cooked in salted water
and whatever wild aromatic things grow within reach—thyme,
bay, fennel—and eaten hot with vinegar and oil. Sublime. In
Toulon octopus daube is accompanied with a mortar of aïoli
and diners mix the two sauces together at table.*

3 tablespoons olive oil
1 large onion, chopped
2 lb (1 kg) small octopus, weighing less than 1 lb (500 g)
    each, cleaned and hood and tentacles cut into 1-in
    (2.5-cm) squares or lengths
salt
¼ cup (4 fl oz/60 ml) marc de Provence (see glossary)
    or Cognac
2 tomatoes, peeled, seeded and coarsely chopped
8–10 cloves garlic
bouquet garni including fresh fennel stalks and 1 dried
    cayenne chili pepper or other dried chili pepper
    (see glossary)
1 cup (8 fl oz/250 ml) dry red wine
boiling water as needed

▨ Warm the olive oil in a flameproof, earthenware casserole
or heavy sauté pan over low heat. Add the onion and cook
until softened but not colored, about 10 minutes. Add the
octopus and salt to taste and raise the heat to medium. The
octopus will throw off some liquid; cook until nearly all the
liquid disappears. Add the brandy and ignite with a long-
handled match. Stir with a wooden spoon until the flames
subside. Add the tomatoes, garlic and bouquet garni and
cook, stirring, until the tomatoes begin to break up and boil,
about 10 minutes.
▨ Bring the red wine to a boil in a saucepan, pour it over the
octopus and add enough boiling water to cover. Cover with
the lid ajar and simmer for 1 hour. If the cooking juices are
abundant, remove the lid, raise the heat slightly to adjust to
a simmer and continue cooking, stirring occasionally, until
the octopus is tender, about 2 hours in all for small octopus.
The cooking liquid should be mostly reduced, coating the
pieces of octopus. Serve hot.

SERVES 4

BOUCHES·DU·RHÔNE

LE GRAND AÏOLI

*Aïoli or "garlic-oil," is garlic mayonnaise. The word also desig-
nates the ritual celebration of poached salt cod, boiled vegetables,
hard-cooked eggs and a selection of garden snails, sea snails,
periwinkles, mussels, octopus and other seafoods. When it is
complete, it is called Le Grand Aïoli. Everything is served warm,
simply because it is impossible to get it all onto the table hot.*

aïoli (see glossary)
2 lb (1 kg) salt cod, soaked and poached (see glossary)
6 beets (beetroots), wrapped individually in aluminum foil
    and baked at 350°F (180°C) until tender, 45–60 minutes
6 sweet potatoes, baked at 350°F (180°C) until tender,
    about 45 minutes
6 new potatoes, boiled in salted water until just tender,
    about 30 minutes

1 lb (500 g) small carrots, boiled in salted water until just
    tender, 10–15 minutes
1 lb (500 g) green beans, parboiled in salted water for
    5–10 minutes
6 young, tender artichokes, trimmed (see glossary) and
    boiled in salted water until tender, about 20 minutes

Left to right: Octopus Daube, Le Grand Aïoli

2 small heads cauliflower, separated into florets and
　parboiled in salted water for 2–3 minutes
12 garden-ripe plum (Roma) tomatoes, peeled
octopus daube (preceding recipe)
6 hard-cooked eggs, shelled

◉ Prepare the *aïoli* in a mortar and place the mortar in the
middle of the table. Surround it with platters on which all of
the remaining elements, except the octopus, are arranged
decoratively. Serve the octopus hot from its cooking vessel.
Its sauce mingles wonderfully with the *aïoli*.

SERVES 6

Top to bottom: Bourride, Poached Striped Bass or Mullet with Green Sauce

BOUCHES·DU·RHÔNE

BOURRIDE

A bourride usually contains monkfish (anglerfish) plus one or two other varieties—skate wings or any of the fish recommended for bouillabaisse. Ask your fish merchant to save the heads (gills discarded) and filleted carcasses, broken up or chopped with a cleaver. The cartilaginous monkfish backbone, rich in gelatin,

should be cut into small pieces. In the south of France the demand for monkfish heads, which contain abundant flesh and flavor, is so great they are now offered for sale.

FOR THE BROTH:

1 leek, thinly sliced
1 onion, thinly sliced
1 small celery stalk, thinly sliced
3 cloves garlic, crushed

1 bay leaf
1 fresh thyme sprig
stems from a bouquet of fresh flat-leaf (Italian) parsley
strip of dried orange peel
3 or 4 short lengths fennel stalk or large pinch of
    fennel seeds
fish heads and carcasses, gills discarded, chopped up
salt
2 cups (16 fl oz/500 ml) dry white wine

3 lb (1.5 kg) white-fleshed fish (see recipe introduction),
    cut into slices about 1 in (2.5 cm) thick or into 1-in
    (2.5-cm) fillet sections
aïoli (see glossary)
4 egg yolks
slices of baguette partially dried in the sun or in a
    warm oven

◙ To prepare the broth, place leek, onion, celery, garlic, bay leaf, thyme sprig, parsley stems and orange peel in the bottom of a saucepan and arrange the fish heads and carcasses on top. Pour in water to cover and add salt to taste. Bring to a boil and skim off any froth or scum. Reduce the heat, cover with the lid ajar and simmer for 15 minutes. Add the wine, return to a boil, then reduce the heat and simmer for 15 minutes longer. Strain the broth through a fine-mesh sieve.

◙ Arrange the fish pieces, side by side, in a large sauté pan. Pour in enough broth to cover and bring to a boil. Adjust the heat so the broth barely simmers, cover with a lid slightly ajar and simmer for 5 minutes. Cover tightly, turn off the heat and leave to steep for 5 minutes. Using a slotted utensil remove the fish to a warmed platter. Reserve the liquid in the pan.

◙ Put half of the *aïoli* into a mixing bowl. Add the egg yolks and whisk until blended. Slowly add the fish cooking liquid, whisking all the while. Pour the mixture into a saucepan, place it over low to medium heat and stir constantly with a wooden spoon until it acquires a light, creamy consistency and coats the back of the spoon, 8–10 minutes; it must not boil or it will break up.

◙ Place 1 or 2 bread slices in each soup plate. Pour some of the *aïoli* cream into a warmed soup tureen or serve it directly from the saucepan, pouring it over the bread in the soup plates. Serve the fish in the same plates with more cream poured over, accompanied by the remaining *aïoli*.

SERVES 4

P R O V E N C E

LOUP DE MER OU MULET POCHÉ, SAUCE AUX HERBES

Poached Striped Bass or Mullet with Green Sauce

It makes no sense to attempt poaching relatively large fish without the proper equipment. Poaching a fish that is wrapped in cheesecloth (muslin) or a towel in a makeshift vessel is messy and, with all possible care, it still risks being damaged before ending up on its serving platter. You need a fish kettle, or poaching pan, with a perforated rack on which the fish is placed. Although not essential, a thermometer that clips to the inside of the pan is convenient, for a poached fish should never boil: the ideal poaching temperature is about 185°F (85°C).

Some cooks prefer to prepare a white wine court bouillon for pouring over the fish. In the case of a very fresh sea bass, the court bouillon only masks the exhilarating, clean taste of the flesh. For the same reason, with a sea bass you may prefer to serve only olive oil in place of the sauce.

FOR THE SAUCE:
1 clove garlic
large pinch of coarse salt
freshly ground pepper
1 tablespoon capers, rinsed and drained
3 salt anchovies, rinsed, filleted and chopped (see glossary)
handful of chopped fresh flat-leaf (Italian) parsley
½ lb (250 g) spinach, parboiled, squeezed dry and chopped
    (see glossary)
handful of fresh bread crumbs
2 hard-cooked egg yolks
1 egg yolk, uncooked
1 tablespoon Provençal herb vinegar (see glossary)
about 6 tablespoons (3 fl oz/90 ml) olive oil

1 striped bass or mullet, about 4 lb (2 kg), gutted but
    not scaled
handful of coarse sea salt

◙ To prepare the sauce, in a mortar pound together the garlic, coarse salt and pepper to taste to form a paste. Add the capers and anchovies and pound again to a paste. Progressively add all the remaining ingredients, except the olive oil, and pound, stir and beat until the mixture is smooth and homogenous. Add the olive oil in a fine trickle to the side of the mortar, turning the mixture at the same time with the pestle. Set aside.

◙ Place the fish on a rack, lower it into a poaching pan, pour over water to cover by a generous inch (3 cm) and add the salt. Place the pan over medium heat atop two burners until the water approaches the simmering point or the temperature registers 185°F (85°C). Adjust the heat to very low and control it by keeping the pan's lid ajar; the water must not boil. Hold the kettle at this controlled heat for 20 minutes, then remove it from the heat and leave it, covered, for another 20 minutes. Lift the rack from the water and place it, at an angle, on top of the pan to permit the fish to drain for 1–2 minutes. Gently slip the fish onto its platter.

◙ Remove the skin from the top surface before presenting the fish at table: Using a small, sharp-pointed knife, slit the skin from the top of the head to the gill and the length of the back and underside, slitting closely to either side of the dorsal and anal fins and prying them free along with the tiny bones attached to them. Slit the skin at the base of the tail and carefully peel it free from the flesh, removing at the same time the pelvic and pectoral fins and their attached bones. Do not try to turn the fish over to remove the skin from the other side; it will remain in the platter after the service. Without displacing the fish, sponge the platter clean with paper towels or a tea towel.

◙ To serve, use a sole fillet knife or other medium-sized, supple-bladed, sharp-pointed knife and a spatula or wide palette knife. Have ready an empty platter on which to place the carcass after the top fillets have been served. With the knife tip, cut to the bone the entire length of the lateral line, a more or less curved line, running from the top of the gill to the center of the tail, which corresponds to the path of the spinal column. Slice, crosswise, to the bones, dividing each fillet in two to create individual servings. Slip the blade of the knife into the lateral cut and ease it, at an angle, beneath the section of fillet to be dislodged. Remove the serving to a plate with the spatula (the abdominal quarter will not provide as neat a serving as the rest). When the top fillets are served out, slip the knife tip beneath the spinal column near the base of the tail, slit the skin and lift the tail carefully to free the skeleton from the underlying fillets, holding them in place with the blade of the knife as the skeleton and head are detached from the rest. Move the carcass to the empty platter (don't forget to serve the cheeks to an honored guest) and serve the remaining fillets in the same way as the others. Serve the green sauce on the side.

SERVES 6

PROVENCE

FILETS DE MULET AUX FINES HERBES

Mullet Fillets with Fines Herbes

Other fish of approximately the same size can be treated in the same way.

FOR THE BROTH:

1 onion, chopped
2 cloves garlic, crushed
pinch of fennel seeds
flat-leaf (Italian) parsley sprigs
1 bay leaf
1 fresh thyme sprig
heads and carcasses of the mullets, gills discarded, chopped up
salt
1 cup (8 fl oz/250 ml) dry white wine

2 tablespoons olive oil
3 or 4 shallots, finely chopped
1 tablespoon finely chopped flat-leaf (Italian) parsley mixed
    with chopped fresh wild fennel leaves, if available
2 mullets, about 1½ lb (750 g) each, cleaned and filleted
salt
½ cup (4 fl oz/125 ml) dry white wine
3 egg yolks
juice of ½ lemon

Marseilles-Style Mussels

freshly ground pepper
whole nutmeg

◉ To prepare the broth, put the onion, garlic and herbs in the bottom of a saucepan and place the fish heads and carcasses on top. Pour in water to cover barely and add salt to taste. Bring to a boil and skim off any froth and scum. Reduce the heat, cover with a lid ajar and keep at a gentle boil for 15 minutes. Add the wine, return to a boil, then reduce the heat and simmer for another 15 minutes longer. Strain, return the broth to the saucepan over high heat and boil until reduced by half. Set aside.

◉ Choose a sauté pan of a size just to contain the fillets side by side. Smear the bottom with 1 tablespoon of the olive oil. Scatter the shallots and parsley over the bottom and place the fillets on top. Sprinkle with salt and pour in the wine. If it does not completely immerse the fillets, add some of the strained broth. Bring to a boil, cover the pan tightly, reduce the heat as low as possible and cook for 5 minutes. Remove from the heat and let stand, tightly covered, to steep for 3–4 minutes longer.

◉ Transfer the fillets to a heated serving platter and add their poaching liquid to the strained broth. In a bowl combine the egg yolks, lemon juice and the remaining tablespoon olive oil. Grind over some pepper and scrape over a bit of nutmeg. Whisk briefly and then whisk in a ladleful of the broth. Stir the egg mixture into the broth with a wooden spoon and place over medium-low heat. Stir until the sauce coats the spoon, about 5 minutes. It must not boil.

◉ Pour the sauce over the fillets and serve immediately.

SERVES 4

BOUCHES·DU·RHÔNE

MOULES À LA MARSEILLAISE

Marseilles-Style Mussels

Clams can also be prepared in this way.

2 lb (1 kg) mussels, opened over heat with white wine
  (see glossary)
4 tablespoons (2 fl oz/60 ml) olive oil
1 onion, finely chopped
2 large tomatoes, peeled, seeded and coarsely chopped
persillade made with 2 cloves garlic (see glossary)
salt and freshly ground pepper
dried bread crumbs

◉ Cook the mussels as directed. Remove the mussels from the cooking liquid and snap off and discard one shell from each. Place the mussels in their half shells in a gratin dish. Arrange in two layers, with the bottoms of the top layer reposing on the edges of those below so all the mussels will receive some sauce. Strain the mussel cooking liquid and set aside.

◉ Preheat an oven to 450°F (230°C). Warm 3 tablespoons of the olive oil in a large pan over low heat. Add the onion and sauté until soft but not colored, about 10 minutes. Raise the heat, add the tomatoes and *persillade* and sauté until the tomatoes break up and are boiling, about 6–7 minutes. Add the mussels' decanted cooking liquid and reduce, at a gentle boil, to the consistency of a sauce, about 10 minutes. Taste for salt and grind over some pepper.

◉ Spoon the sauce over the mussels, then sprinkle with bread crumbs. Dribble over the remaining 1 tablespoon olive oil. Place in the oven and bake until the sauce is bubbling and the crumbs are golden, 8–10 minutes. Serve immediately.

SERVES 4

Left to right: Baked Grouper, Sardine Paupiettes, Mullet Fillets with Fines Herbes

Mérou à la Provençale

Baked Grouper

Monkfish (anglerfish) or any large fish with firm, relatively boneless flesh that is sold cut up can be prepared in this way.

salt
4 large, garden-ripe tomatoes, peeled, seeded and cut into
    slices ½ in (12 mm) thick
¼ cup (2 fl oz/60 ml) olive oil
1½ lb (750 g) grouper fillets without skin, cut into 4 slices
    1 in (2.5 cm) thick
freshly ground pepper
¼ cup *tapénade* (recipe on page 34)
persillade made with 2 cloves garlic (see glossary)
dried bread crumbs

◙ Salt the tomato slices on both sides and lay them out on an overturned drum sieve or wire rack to drain for 30 minutes. Place them on a cotton towel or on paper towels to sponge off excess liquid.
◙ Preheat an oven to 375°F (190°C). Choose a gratin dish of a size just to contain the fish slices side by side and rub it with 1 teaspoon of the olive oil. Line the dish with half of the tomato slices. Season the fish slices on both sides with salt and pepper to taste and arrange them atop the tomatoes. Spread some *tapénade* on each fish slice, scatter over the *persillade* and press the remaining tomato slices on top. Sprinkle with salt and bread crumbs and dribble on the remaining olive oil in a thread, forming a crisscross pattern.
◙ Place in the oven and bake until the crumbs are golden, about 25 minutes. Serve hot.

SERVES 4

Paupiettes de Sardines à la Niçoise

Sardine Paupiettes

Zucchini bear male and female flowers. The fruitless male flowers are picked and sold immediately, before they wilt, in the Provençal morning markets. Usually they are dipped in batter and deep-fried.

4 tablespoons (2 fl oz/60 ml) olive oil
1 large sweet white onion, halved and thinly sliced
4 cloves garlic, thinly sliced
8 fresh sardines, cleaned and filleted
salt and freshly ground pepper
16 sorrel leaves, stemmed
16 freshly picked zucchini (courgette) blossoms, stems cut
    off at base
6 tablespoons (3 fl oz/90 ml) dry white wine

◙ Preheat an oven to 400°F (200°C). Rub the bottom of a gratin dish with 1 teaspoon of the olive oil. Mix together the onion and garlic and scatter half of the mixture in the dish. Season the sardine fillets with salt and pepper. Roll up a fillet in each sorrel leaf. Slip each sorrel package into a zucchini blossom, folding the pointed petal tips over each other to enclose the package.
◙ Arrange the stuffed blossoms side by side in the gratin dish. Scatter the remaining onion-garlic mixture over the top and dribble with the remaining olive oil. Sprinkle the wine over the top and cover the dish loosely with a sheet of aluminum foil.
◙ Place in the oven and bake for about 10 minutes. Turn off the oven and leave the covered dish in the cooling oven for 15 minutes, or in another warm place before serving.

SERVES 4

BOUILLABAISSE

The original bouillabaisse was a collection of unsold fish from the day's catch, boiled by fishermen over seaside bonfires in diluted sea water perfumed with the wild herbs that grew within reach. Today, the musts and must-nots of preparing bouillabaisse *are so numerous and so contradictory that one should be prepared to break rules at will. The water in the following recipe can be replaced by a fish broth made of heads and filleted carcasses; on the Mediterranean coast, many people prepare a saffronless fish soup (recipe on page 296) with which to moisten a bouillabaisse. Natives of* bouillabaisse *country are unanimous in their conviction that without* rascasses *(scorpionfish),* bouillabaisse *cannot exist, and they are scornful of Parisians, who add* langoustes, *or lobsters, to their* bouillabaisses; *the* Marseillais *disapprove of the* Toulonnais *habit of adding mussels and potatoes and purists are horrified at the notion of adding pastis (the purpose of which is, simply, to reinforce the fennel flavor if fennel stalks are missing). The Martigaux add tiny cuttlefish, whose ink sacks open up, turning the broth black; it is called* la bouillabaisse noire.

Count four or five varieties of firm, white-fleshed fish—monkfish (anglerfish) plus any of those listed in the chapter introduction; if these are in short supply, supplement with halibut, hake or cod. Large fish should be filleted and cut into serving sections; small fish should be cleaned but left whole. The rapid boil, characteristic of bouillabaisse, *may leave the fish looking a bit ragged; the rough treatment is necessary to create the liaison between olive oil and broth, which is one of the dish's most-admired qualities.*

6 lb (3 kg) mixed fish (see recipe introduction)
1½ lb (750 g) potatoes, peeled and quartered

FOR THE MARINADE:

¼ teaspoon powdered saffron
¼ teaspoon ground fennel seeds
¼ cup (2 fl oz/60 ml) olive oil
2 tablespoons *pastis* such as Pernod 51 or Ricard

FOR THE *ROUILLE:*

2 dried cayenne chili peppers or other dried chili peppers
3 cloves garlic
large pinch of coarse salt
large pinch of fresh bread crumbs
¼ teaspoon powdered saffron dissolved in 1 tablespoon
    boiling water

1 egg yolk, at room temperature
1 cup (8 fl oz/250 ml) olive oil, at room temperature

¼ cup (2 fl oz/60 ml) olive oil
1 large onion, finely chopped
2 leeks, including the tender green parts, thinly sliced
3 cloves garlic
1½ lb (750 g) tomatoes, peeled, seeded and coarsely chopped
large bouquet garni including a strip of dried orange peel (see glossary)
large pinch of saffron threads
salt
boiling water as needed
1 lb (500 g) small, lively crabs such as blue swimmers or sand crabs
baguette slices, partially dried in the sun or in a warm oven

◉ Spread the fish and potatoes out on a large platter. To marinate them sprinkle with the saffron and fennel seeds, then with olive oil, turn them all around until evenly coated with oil and colored with saffron. Sprinkle over the *pastis*, turn around again and leave for 1 hour or so. Cover with another platter or with plastic wrap.

◉ To make the *rouille*, in a mortar, pound the chili pepper to a powder. Add the garlic and coarse salt and pound to form a paste. Add the bread crumbs and dissolved saffron and again pound to a paste. Stir in the egg yolk with the pestle until completely integrated. Mount the *rouille* in the same way as an *aïoli* (see glossary), adding the olive oil in a trickle to the side of the mortar. Set the *rouille* aside.

◉ Warm the olive oil in a large, heavy pot over low heat. Add the onion and leeks and cook gently until softened but not colored, about 15 minutes. Add the garlic, tomatoes, bouquet garni, saffron and salt and raise the heat to high. Cook, stirring with a wooden spoon, until the tomatoes are broken up and boiling, about 10 minutes.

◉ Add the potatoes, place the fish on top and empty in all of the marinade. Pour in boiling water to cover and bring to a boil over high heat. Boil, uncovered, for 5 minutes, then throw in the crabs, gently displacing the pieces of fish to immerse the crabs completely. Continue to boil for 10 minutes.

◉ Stir 2–3 tablespoons of the boiling broth into the *rouille* to loosen it. Remove and discard the bouquet garni. Remove the fish, potatoes and crab to a warmed serving platter. Place 1 or 2 bread slices in each soup plate and dab some *rouille* on top. Ladle the broth over the bread slices. Serve the fish, crabs and potatoes in the same plates, with a little more broth poured over the top. Pass the remaining *rouille*.

SERVES 8

BOUCHES·DU·RHÔNE

PETITS-GRIS À L'AIXOISE
Aix-Style Stuffed Snails

For stuffed snails, it is convenient to have a snail service: metal or other ovenproof plates with round depressions in which to place the snails before heating them, special snail clamps with which to pick them up at table and small, two-pronged forks with which to remove each snail from its shell. This is done over a piece of bread that will collect the spilled, melted stuffing as well as any remaining in the shell, emptied over the bread when the snail is removed. One tucks the snail into one's mouth along with a bite of the anointed bread.

6 dozen garden snails

FOR THE STUFFING:

pinch of fennel seeds
large pinch of coarse salt

freshly ground pepper
whole nutmeg
3 cloves garlic
2 or 3 shallots, chopped
3 salt anchovies, rinsed and filleted (see glossary)
7 oz (220 g) raw beef marrow (see glossary), chopped
5 tablespoons (3 fl oz/80 ml) olive oil
juice of ½ lemon

◉ Prepare the snails as directed in the introduction for *blanquette* of snails (recipe on page 355). Remove the snails from their shells and cook them as directed in court bouillon; drain and set aside. Rinse and dry the shells and set aside as well.

◉ Preheat an oven to 500°F (260°C).

◉ To make the stuffing, in a mortar pound the fennel seeds to a powder. Add the salt, grind in some pepper and scrape in a bit of nutmeg. Add the garlic and shallots and pound to a paste. Add the anchovies and again pound to a paste. Add the marrow and pound well. Work in the olive oil and lemon juice until smooth and consistent. (Alternatively, transfer the marrow and mortar mixture to a food processor fitted with a metal blade and process until smooth, then mix in the olive oil and lemon juice.)

◉ Put a snail into each shell, twirling it in a spiral. Pack each shell's opening with stuffing, smoothing the surface. Arrange the snails on snail plates—or side by side on a shallow baking dish or dishes—with the stuffed surfaces facing straight up and heat in the oven for a few minutes until the stuffing is bubbling furiously.

◉ Serve immediately. If the snail service is lacking, place all of the snails in the middle of the table. Each person will take one at a time with a teaspoon and remove it from the shell with a cocktail fork or a nutpick.

SERVES 6

Aix-Style Stuffed Snails

VAUCLUSE

VAUCLUSE

I f the Bouches-du-Rhône is the region of the singsong accent, if the Alpes-de-Haute-Provence are the most solitary in appearance, if the Var knows how to hold its counsel and the Alpes-Maritimes how to cultivate their diverseness, the Vaucluse is indisputably the most elegant and most courted of all Provençal territories.

Here we have villages that capture the fullness of the light (Gordes, Roussillon, Ménerbes, Bonnieux), while others seek the discretion of the shadows (Lourmarin, Mirabeau). We have such opera and theater towns as Avignon and Orange whose lives seem to be one continuous festival, and others like Apt or Cavaillon, intellectual or industrious. But throughout this region, where tomatoes are charmingly called love apples and every village has its citizenry nicknames (slug-eaters, gourd-eaters, herring-suckers, tart-gluttons), where aromatic plants grow and venerable vines and olive trees flourish, where truffles reveal their secrets and vegetables blaze with color, there is a talent for cooking.

The people of the Vaucluse know how to cook and live on very little, as they do everywhere in Provence. They know how to use the things that enabled peasants of the past to toil under a relentless sun out on the *restanques* "terraced fields," or gave them hope at the end of the day on their return from the fields: an anchovy, a tomato, some olives, an onion, a clove of garlic, and, of course, a little bread. Bread once upon a time was cooked on a wood fire, long before the days of large restaurants

Previous pages: Provençal architecture is as diverse as the landscape; here, in the countryside near Gordes, is a characteristic farmhouse known as a mas. Left: The excellent acoustics inside Senanque, a 12th century Cistercian abbey, are perfectly suited to the Gregorian chants, performed here every summer

with gastronomic bakeries all choosing to make their own bread, as they do today. Onion bread, thyme bread, olive bread, walnut bread, Roquefort bread, garlic bread, pepper bread all existed in Apt and Cavaillon, and it is no surprise that a Baker's Museum has been opened in Bonnieux, in the heart of the Lubéron mountain area.

Just as there are Provences, there are Vaucluses. The Vaucluse of the plains is like a royal route: the Vaucluse *comtats* of Orange, Avignon, Cavaillon, Carpentras. It is a region whose towns are rich in history: Orange, the Roman gateway to Provence, where the honey, truffles and olives flourish. Avignon, city of the popes, with its palace-fortress and an unfinished bridge over the Rhône, which, legend has it, was built by a young shepherd. Cavaillon, melon capital and commercial center from time immemorial. Carpentras, with its truffles and its caramels. Vaison-la-Romaine, L'Isle-sur-la Sorgue, birthplace of René Char, one of the great French poets. And Châteauneuf-du-Pape, for which everyone will have something of a soft spot, because its name almost epitomizes the appellation of the Côtes du Rhône wines. Thirteen types of vine are nourished in this soil, all planted from vigorous stocks to resist the onslaught of the mistral. This is the place where the wine blends with the sun, even though it is at Suze-la-Rousse in the Drôme, a little farther north, that the University of Wine has been established.

The Vaucluse of the mountains is instantly summed up by the luminous Lubéron, a place Parisians, foreigners, artists, writers, actors and politicians start squabbling over as soon as summer comes. It is a region coveted by the *tout-Paris,* the chic Provence of the weekend house, although thirty years ago in Gordes, one of the most famous of the Lubéron villages, you would not have found ten telephones.

Oppède-le-Vieux, Ménerbes, Lacoste with the Marquis de Sade's château, Bonnieux, Gordes and the

Carpentras, famous for its truffles, is one of the most important agricultural centers in France.

Cistercian abbey at Senanque, Roussillon with its ocher cliffs each has its special attraction. In Lourmarin Albert Camus, winner of the Nobel Prize for Literature, died in 1960. In a neighboring cottage lived Henri Bosco, the Lubéron's leading writer (although he was born in Avignon), who wrote: "In this deserted countryside you wonder who cultivates the land. You can saunter about all the livelong day in vain, you never see a soul … these bare open fields between the cultivated valley areas and the meager pastures of the Lubéron guard closely the secrets of these men who ask of them nothing more than a bit of stunted corn and some tart wine."

Those secrets appear to sleep still, in the land of the *bories,* traditional dry-stone houses of the south. Solidly constructed vaulted buildings without a trace of mortar and neither windows nor chimneys, they are refuges against a demented wind, once used to shelter animals or to catch rainwater, or simply heaps of stones removed from fields destined for cultivation. *Bories* are part of the history and legend of this place, used by residents and artists alike: The painter Vasarély had one in Gordes set up as a studio and meditation room.

But the Lubéron is not merely a source of inspiration and special light. It has lost nothing of its colors and flavors, and even if it lacks a cuisine in the proper sense of the word, here too they know how to use and combine the magic of herbs and olive oil, prepare the vegetables that are so valuable for gratins, and make soups fit for a feast. The most robust and popular of these, prepared in all the best kitchens, is the one made with spelt, a noble variety of wheat that was used in the old days for soaking the scraps from a leg of lamb.

As recently as the eighteenth century the wealth of the lower Lubéron was not calculated in country houses or weekenders, but in *banastes* (large wicker baskets) full of beans gathered between Cavaillon and Pays d'Aigues (the Durance River country, from Merindol to Mirabeau). Pertuis was the undisputed bean capital, and its influence was described by Paul Arène, a Provençal writer of the nineteenth century: "Pertuis was sowing its beans. In the town the good citizens sat out in the fresh air and remarked as they watched the moving red and white dots: 'If the rains come in time, France will not be short of beans this year.'" Neighboring Cavaillon contributed its *faiou* beans to this bounty, while in more recent years Cadenet added their red *cocos* (haricot beans).

Finally, Vaucluse means the sweet things of life. There are the jams and preserved fruits from Apt, which were known to the Romans but were truly launched by the Avignon popes (in 1343, Clement VI had a personal "esquire of preserves"). Around 1860 a local confectioner popularized the caramels of Carpentras to the point of flooding the English market, adding to the traditional mixture of white and brown sugars the syrup from fruit preserves and a touch of mint for flavor. This golden age of caramels lasted until the 1950s. Then there are the *papelines* of Avignon, confections of sugar and fine chocolate. According to legend it was their liqueur, made with herbs from the Ventoux, that enabled the people of Avignon to beat cholera in 1884.

At the beginning of the twentieth century, the melons of Cavaillon experienced a period of considerable popularity. They are red- or white-fleshed, sweet and heavy fruits, with some weighing as much as thirty-five pounds (fifteen kilos). The smaller melons are known as Americans, and all of them are used in the making of the Apt fruit preserves. In 1869, Frédéric Mistral expressed his surprise that

Throughout Vaucluse there are clusters of small villages clinging to the hills, each retaining its own unique characteristics, festivals and traditions.

"gourmets eat the Cavaillon melons only with salt."

Here, too, as in the Alpes-de-Haute-Provence, we find honey, gathered by people known locally not as apiarists or beekeepers, but as bee shepherds, because they maintain the practice of moving their charges around the hills as shepherds do their flocks, searching for the perfumes of lavender, thyme or rosemary.

Finally, there are truffles, for which Carpentras still has the largest market in Provence, active between autumn and spring. Every Friday on the Cours des Platanes, the *rabasses*, as the local truffles are called, are weighed on Roman scales. Everything is done with an air of mystery, particularly transactions between the solitary lord of truffles, the *rabassaire* ("truffle picker"), and the purchaser. These precious fungi are tucked into omelets or scrambled eggs (the Provence *brouillade*), cut into strips as a simple yet impressive embellishment to a soup or a salad, or, more simply still, cooked whole buried in ashes. The wonderful brown or black truffle (not the white summer Saint Jean truffle), dug out of the side of the Lubéron, Ventoux, or Lure mountain, is such a precious possession that it is a magnet for secrets and legends.

Meats, Poultry and Game

Sausage, both fresh and cured, can be found in the neighborhood charcuteries of Provence.

MEATS, POULTRY AND GAME

The most important meat production in Provence is that of yearling lamb, called either *mouton* or *agneau,* from the Alpes-de-Haute-Provence. The commercial center is Sisteron. Anyone in Provence will tell you that *agneau de Sisteron* is known to be the best in France. Although beef and veal are not farmed in Provence, the consumption of beef is greater than that of lamb. Veal is less admired than either, unless it be in the useful shape of a breast to contain a stuffing from which emanate all of the flavors of the region. Everyone loves roast kid (*chevreau; cabri*), which is eaten, if not on Easter day, just before or just after when the kids are severed. From the end of March into May, the butchers display them, hung whole, wrapped with their caul, in which they will be roasted. In its infinite charcuterie disguises, the pig—*le cochon*—is present at all Provençal tables at practically every meal.

Guinea fowl and Muscovy duck (*canard de Barbarie*) are popular and both are often farmed on a small scale locally and offered for sale in the morning open-air markets. Rabbit, usually raised in home hutches, is often consumed in the form of a *gibelotte.* When sautéed tomato or some tomato sauce is added to a *gibelotte,* it is called *chasseur;* if winter savory replaces the thyme, it is called *lapin au pebre d'aï.*

In autumn wild boar and hare excite Provençal passions. Boar (*sanglier*) is increasingly rare on the market. Not so long ago, in November and December, one often saw this majestic beast, hanging whole and bristling,

The Provençal butcher takes as much care with the cutting, trimming and presentation of his meats as the chef does with his preparation.

Previous pages: The grounds of Château d'Ansouis. From left to right: Rabbit in Spicy Sauce (recipe page 398), White Wine Rabbit Stew (recipe page 387)

372

Most French game can be found in Provence where hunting is a popular sport.

water. They are poached for a quarter of an hour before being hung, steaming, in the front of the shop. In the homes, they are gently grilled and usually served with mashed potatoes.

Of all the local charcuterie, the most glamorous is *andouillettes* prepared *tirées à la ficelle,* chitterling sausages "drawn with string." In this preparation, twisted loops of intermingled, marinated and seasoned strips of pig's gut and long, slender strips of back fat are rolled in *persillade,* pulled with a string into lengths of large sausage casing, and then tucked in at the ends and simmered for hours in a stock or court bouillon. *Andouillettes* are served grilled, with puréed or fried potatoes, accompanied with Dijon mustard.

Entrevaux boasts its local specialty, secca de boeuf, *a type of dried salt beef delicious when eaten with olive oil and lemon juice.*

in front of a butcher shop with a sign indicating the date it would be cut up. For a week to follow, the butcher took orders, and the boar was then cut up and dispatched in a few hours' time. Young boar (*marcassin*) is subtle and delicate and treated like venison or lamb: leg or saddle roasted pink, the rib chops grilled semirare, the shoulder cut up and braised with red wine, like a *boeuf bourguignon* or an Avignon daube. The hare is prepared *en civet* ("with its blood"), exactly like a *gibelotte* but with red wine replacing the white and, just before serving, the sauce thickened with the blood. Like an egg-yolk binder, the sauce must not be allowed to boil after the blood is added, lest it break. By unanimous consent, an old Châteauneuf-du-Pape is the ideal companion to a *civet.* Both wild rabbit and hutch rabbit are also often prepared *en civet.*

In the villages, butchers double as *charcutiers* and each also has a daily specialty of some hot preparation to take out. A favorite take-out in the Bouches-du-Rhône and the Var is *pieds et paquets,* whose origins are in Marseilles, where it competes, with *bouillabaisse,* for supremacy of pride. *Pieds et paquets* are lamb trotters and small packages of lamb stomach stuffed with chopped lean salt pork (green bacon), lamb tripe and *persillade.* They are prepared in exactly the same way as *tripe à la marseillaise.* Butchers also offer them raw, with the packages stuffed and ready to be cooked.

Tuesday, for many butchers, is *boudin* or "blood sausage" (black pudding) day, when the long, narrow sausage casings are filled with a *soupe* of blood and stewed onions and then looped and twisted into garlands of sausages that are immersed in a cauldron of hot

PROVENCE

BLANQUETTE D'AGNEAU
Lamb Blanquette

Milk-fed lamb or kid is most often prepared in a blanquette, which is a traditional Easter dish. The following recipe is adjusted for yearling lamb. Accompany with boiled new potatoes or pilaf.

1 lamb shoulder with bone, cut into 8 equal pieces, about 3 lb (1.5 kg)
2 carrots, peeled
1 yellow onion stuck with 2 whole cloves
large bouquet garni (see glossary)
salt
½ lb (250 g) pickling onions
1 tablespoon unsalted butter
pinch of sugar
5 oz (150 g) fresh button mushrooms, quartered if large
juice of 1 lemon
4 egg yolks
freshly ground pepper
whole nutmeg

◙ In a large saucepan arrange the pieces of meat, carrots, yellow onion and bouquet garni so that they may be immersed in a minimum of liquid; do not crowd. Pour in water to cover, add salt to taste and bring slowly to a boil. Skim off any froth and scum. Adjust the heat to maintain a light simmer, cover with the lid ajar slightly and cook for 1½ hours.
◙ Meanwhile, put the pickling onions in a small saucepan of a size to contain them in a single layer. Add half of the butter, the sugar, a pinch of salt and enough water almost to cover them. Bring to a boil, reduce the heat to low, cover and simmer

Top to bottom: Leg of Lamb Braised with Garlic, Lamb Blanquette

for about 8 minutes. Remove the lid, raise the heat and cook, shaking the pan gently, until all the liquid evaporates and the onions are glazed and yellowed, about 5 minutes. Set aside.
◙ In another small saucepan, combine the mushrooms, the remaining ½ tablespoon butter, half of the lemon juice, a pinch of salt and about 3 tablespoons water. Bring to a boil, cover and boil for less than 1 minute. Remove from the heat and set aside.
◙ Remove the saucepan containing the meat from the heat. Discard the carrots, the onion stuck with cloves and the bouquet garni. Add the glazed onions to the meat. Drain the mushrooms' cooking liquid into a bowl and add the mushrooms to the meat. Add the remaining lemon juice and the egg yolks to the mushrooms' liquid. Grind over some pepper and scrape over some nutmeg. Beat with a fork until blended and, using a wooden spoon, stir the mixture into the saucepan. Return to low heat, stirring gently and continuously until the sauce coats the spoon, about 10 minutes. It must not boil. To serve, transfer the lamb and sauce to a warmed serving dish.

SERVES 4

VAUCLUSE

GIGOT À LA CAVAILLONNAISE
Leg of Lamb Braised with Garlic

Braised leg of lamb, for which there are many formulas, is an old-fashioned Provençal favorite rarely encountered today. Have your butcher prepare the leg for braising.

FOR THE LARDOONS (see glossary):

pinch of coarse salt
freshly ground pepper
pinch of Provençal mixed dried herbs (see glossary)
1 clove garlic
1 tablespoon chopped fresh flat-leaf (Italian) parsley
3 oz (100 g) pork back fat, cut into lardoons

1 leg of lamb, about 6 lb (3 kg), pelvic bone removed, leg bone shortened and fat trimmed
8 salt anchovies, rinsed and filleted (see glossary)
1 tablespoon olive oil
1 bay leaf
24 cloves garlic, unpeeled
½ cup (4 fl oz/125 ml) dry white wine
3 tomatoes, peeled, seeded and coarsely chopped
1 cup (5 oz/150 g) black olives

◙ Preheat an oven to 400°F (200°C).
◙ To prepare the lardoons, in a mortar pound together the coarse salt, pepper, herbs and garlic to form a paste. Mix in the parsley. Add the lardoons and mix well until they are evenly coated with the mixture.
◙ With the tip of a small, sharp-pointed knife, pierce the leg repeatedly, on the bias and with the grain. Open the slits with your finger and force in, as deeply as possible, the lardoons and anchovy fillets, alternating between the two.
◙ Rub the leg with the olive oil and place it in an oval ovenproof casserole with a tight-fitting lid. Put the casserole, uncovered, into the oven for 30 minutes. Reduce the oven temperature to 300°F (150°C). Add the bay leaf, garlic, wine and tomatoes, cover and cook for 2 hours, turning the leg several times in its juices. Add the olives and cook until the lamb is tender, another 15 minutes.
◙ Taste the sauce for salt. Transfer the leg to a warmed platter and surround it with the garlic and the olives and a bit of the pan sauce. Serve the remaining sauce in a warmed bowl alongside.

SERVES 8

Lamb and Artichoke Stew

RAGOÛT D'AGNEAU AUX ARTICHAUTS

Lamb and Artichoke Stew

Pilaf, fresh noodles or potatoes are all perfect accompaniments. Little new potatoes, boiled in their skins, can be peeled and added to the stew 10 minutes before serving to simplify things.

3 tablespoons olive oil
1 slice lean salt pork (green bacon), about 3 oz (100 g), cut into lardoons (see glossary)
1 lamb shoulder including shank, about 3 lb (1.5 kg), boned, trimmed of fat and cut into 1½–2 in (4–5 cm) pieces
salt
1 large tomato, peeled, seeded and coarsely chopped
4 cloves garlic, crushed
1 cup (8 fl oz/250 ml) white wine
bouquet garni (see glossary)
4 young, tender artichokes, trimmed, quartered and chokes removed if necessary (see glossary)
½ lb (250 g) pickling onions

◉ Warm 2 tablespoons of the olive oil in a heavy sauté pan over medium heat. Add the lardoons and sauté until colored on all sides, about 10 minutes. Remove them to a plate. Add the lamb pieces to the pan, sprinkle with salt and sauté until nicely colored on all sides, about 20 minutes.

◉ Drain the fat from the pan. Add the tomato, garlic and white wine and raise the heat to high. Stir and scrape the pan bottom with a wooden spoon to dissolve any browned bits. Add the bouquet garni, reduce the heat to low, cover and simmer gently for 1 hour.

◉ Meanwhile, warm 1 tablespoon olive oil in a large, flame-proof earthenware or enameled ironware casserole over low heat. Add the artichokes and the onions and salt lightly. Cover and sweat over very gentle heat, shaking the pan from time to time, for 20 minutes. Add the reserved lardoons and pour in the contents of the sauté pan. Cover and continue to simmer over very low heat until the artichokes and the meat are tender, another 20–30 minutes.

SERVES 4

PROVENCE

DAUBE À LA PROVENÇALE
Provençal Daube

Everyone agrees that a daube, one of Provence's most revered dishes, should be prepared strictly according to tradition. But traditions vary from one village to another and from one family to another. Some prepare it with white wine, some with red and others insist that a daube must not contain vegetables.

FOR THE LARDOONS (see glossary):

pinch of coarse salt
2 cloves garlic
pinch of Provençal mixed dried herbs (see glossary)
2 tablespoons chopped fresh flat-leaf (Italian) parsley
1 piece pork back fat, ¼ lb (125 g), cut into lardoons

4 lb (2 kg) boneless beef shank (shin), cut into 3 oz (100 g) pieces
2 tablespoons olive oil
3 cups (24 fl oz/750 ml) dry red wine
1 pig's foot (trotter), about 1 lb (500 g), split in half lengthwise
¼ lb (125 g) pork rind
1 slice lean salt pork (green bacon), about 5 oz (150 g), cut crosswise into sections ½ in (12 mm) wide
2 carrots, peeled and chopped
2 onions, chopped
3 cloves garlic, chopped
1 oz (30 g) dried cèpes, soaked in cold water to cover for 30 minutes, drained, stem ends trimmed and finely chopped
1 lb (500 g) tomatoes, peeled, seeded and coarsely chopped
⅔ cup (3 oz/100 g) black olives, pitted
salt
large bouquet garni, including strip of dried orange peel (see glossary)
½ cup (4 fl oz/125 ml) marc de Provence (see glossary) or Cognac
broth or water, plus any leftover roasting juices
1 lb (500 g) macaroni

⊞ To prepare the lardoons, in a mortar pound together the salt, garlic and herbs to form a paste. Mix in the parsley, add the lardoons and mix until each lardoon is well coated with the mixture. Using a small, sharp-pointed knife, pierce each piece of meat 2–3 times, with the grain, and force a lardoon into each slit. Save any leftover lardoons and seasoning.
⊞ Put the meat pieces into a bowl, add the olive oil and red wine and marinate at room temperature for 4 hours, turning the meat around in the marinade several times.
⊞ In a saucepan place the pig's trotter, pork rind and salt pork and add water to cover. Bring to a boil, drain and rinse well. Cut the pork rind into 1-in (2.5-cm) squares.
⊞ In a large bowl mix together the pork rind, salt pork pieces, carrots, onions, garlic, cèpes, tomatoes and olives. Put a layer of the pork rind mixture in the bottom of an earthenware vessel, preferably a *daubière,* or a heavy pot. Place the pig's trotter halves on top and finish the layer with pieces of the larded meat. Sprinkle to taste with salt. Continue layering the pork rind mixture and the meat pieces, embedding the bouquet garni in the middle and finishing with the rind mixture. Pour over any red wine marinade remaining in the bowl, the brandy and almost enough broth to immerse the contents.
⊞ Cover and place over medium-low heat, protected by a flame-tamer. Bring to a boil (this will take about 1 hour) and adjust the heat to very low to maintain only a murmur at the liquid's surface for about 6 hours. Skim off, as well as possible, all the fat. (If, toward the end of skimming, you spoon up juices with the fat, empty the skimming spoon into a bowl and refrigerate the bowl; when the fat solidifies, it can be lifted off and discarded and the jellied juices returned to the leftover daube.)
⊞ Preheat an oven to 400°F (200°C).
⊞ Bring a large pot filled with salted water to a boil. Add the macaroni and cook according to the package instructions,

10–15 minutes for most types of macaroni. Drain well and empty the macaroni into a gratin dish. Spoon over some of the daube's cooking juices and put into the oven for a few minutes until the juices are bubbling.
⊞ Serve the daube directly from its cooking vessel, accompanied with the macaroni.

SERVES 8

VAUCLUSE

POULET SAUTÉ À LA BARTHELASSE
Barthelasse Sautéed Chicken

La Barthelasse is an island in the Rhône River, between Avignon and Villeneuve-lès-Avignon. In the last century, it was a favorite rendezvous for Sunday lunch, when residents of both towns flocked to the restaurants there to eat poulet à la Barthelasse.

1 frying chicken, about 2½ lb (1.2 kg), cut into serving pieces
salt and freshly ground pepper
¼ cup (2 fl oz/60 ml) olive oil
¼ cup (2 fl oz/60 ml) dry white wine
persillade made with 2 cloves garlic (see glossary)

⊞ Season the chicken pieces with salt and pepper to taste. Warm the olive oil in a sauté pan over medium-high heat. Put all the pieces in the pan except the breasts. Sauté, turning the pieces, for 15 minutes. Add the breasts and sauté until all the pieces are nicely colored on both sides, about 10 minutes longer. Add the wine, moving the chicken pieces around and scraping the pan bottom with a wooden spoon until the browned bits dissolve.
⊞ Add the *persillade,* turn the pieces around and, when the characteristic odor of cooking parsley and garlic fills the air, serve directly from the pan.

SERVES 4   *Photograph page 258*

BOUCHES·DU·RHÔNE

AILLADE DE VEAU
Veal and Garlic Stew

Stews with abundant garlic garnish are favorite Provençal fare. The garlic cloves remain intact but collapse into a sweet purée in the mouth.

1½ lb (750 g) stewing veal, cut into 1½-in (4-cm) pieces
salt and freshly ground pepper
3 tablespoons olive oil
2 tablespoons dried bread crumbs
½ cup (4 fl oz/125 ml) white wine
1 lb (500 g) tomatoes, peeled, seeded and chopped
16 cloves garlic
double recipe pasta dough made without saffron, cut into noodles (see Provençal fish soup on page 42)

⊞ Season the pieces of veal with salt and pepper to taste. Warm the olive oil in a sauté pan over medium heat. Add the veal and brown until colored on all sides, about 30 minutes. Remove the meat to a plate.
⊞ Add the crumbs to the pan and stir well. Pour in the wine and deglaze the pan, stirring and scraping the pan bottom with a wooden spoon until all the browned bits dissolve. Add the tomatoes, garlic and a pinch of salt and cook for 10 minutes. Put the meat and its juices into the sauce, reduce the heat to very low, cover and simmer until the meat is tender, about 45 minutes.
⊞ Fill a large saucepan with salted water, bring to a boil and add the noodles. Parboil for about 2 minutes and drain. Stir the noodles into the sauce, simmer for a few minutes longer and serve.

SERVES 4

Overlooking the village of Gordes, from left to right:
Provençal Daube, Veal and Garlic Stew

Clockwise from top: Camargue Veal Rib Tips, Shoulder of Lamb on a Bed of Potatoes, Camargue Lamb Stew

ÉPAULE D'AGNEAU À LA BOULANGÈRE

Shoulder of Lamb on a Bed of Potatoes

Epaule (or gigot) à la boulangère is so named because, traditionally. it was prepared in a baker's oven after the last batch of morning's bread was removed.

1 tablespoon unsalted butter
2 lb (1 kg) potatoes, peeled and thinly sliced but unrinsed

2 large onions, thinly sliced
about 1 cup (8 fl oz/250 ml) broth or salted water
1 lamb shoulder, including shank, about 3 lb (1.5 kg)
pinch of Provençal mixed dried herbs (see glossary)
salt and freshly ground pepper
1 tablespoon olive oil

◙ Preheat an oven to 375°F (190°C).
◙ Butter a large baking dish. In a saucepan combine the potatoes and onions. Pour in the broth to immerse them barely. Bring to a boil, stirring with a wooden spoon to prevent them from sticking. Pour them into the baking dish. Smooth the surface and bake for 20 minutes.
◙ Trim any superficial fat from the shoulder. Sprinkle it with the herbs, salt and pepper and rub the surfaces with the olive oil.

Place the shoulder on the bed of onions and potatoes. Bake for 30 minutes, basting 2 or 3 times with the baking juices. Turn the oven off and leave the baking dish in the oven for 20 minutes before removing.

▣ Carve the lamb in the kitchen and arrange the slices atop the potatoes and onions. Pour over any carving juices.

SERVES 4

PROVENCE

CÔTELETTES D'AGNEAU AU GRIL

Grilled Lamb Loin Chops

Grilled lamb is best pink all the way through, neither rare nor well done. Thick pieces of meat give the best results. The bed of coals should have good depth and a veil of white ash masking its intensity.

4 lamb loin chops, each about 3 in (7.5 cm) thick, at room temperature
2 cloves garlic
pinch of Provençal mixed dried herbs (see glossary)
freshly ground pepper
1 tablespoon olive oil
salt

▣ Prepare a fire in a charcoal grill.
▣ With a sharp knife, remove all the visible fat, including the sheath of back fat, from the chops. Take care not to separate the apron from the loin. Rub the sawn bone surfaces repeatedly with the garlic cloves, smearing the resulting purée over the meat's surface. Sprinkle lightly with the herbs and grind some pepper over all the surfaces. Wrap the apron around the chop and fix it in place with a sharpened rosemary branch or a 4-in (10-cm) length of bamboo skewer. Rub the chops all over with the olive oil. The chops have five sides: the two cut sides, the fillet, the filet mignon and the bone surface, around which the apron is wrapped.
▣ Salt the chops and place them on the grill rack. Grill them for 3–4 minutes on each side, the two cut surfaces first. When all the sides are colored, leave the chops, bone surface down, facing the dying coals, for 8–10 minutes.

SERVES 4

BOUCHES·DU·RHÔNE

TENDRONS DE VEAU À LA GARDIANE

Camargue Veal Rib Tips

Like boeuf à la gardiane, *this is a Camargue cowboys' stew. A saffron-flavored pilaf is a good accompaniment.*

3 tablespoons olive oil
2 lb (1 kg) veal rib tips
salt
½ lb (250 g) pickling onions
3 cloves garlic, crushed
¼ lb (125 g) fresh cultivated mushrooms, finely sliced
pinch of Provençal mixed dried herbs (see glossary)
1 tablespoon all-purpose (plain) flour
1 cup (8 fl oz/250 ml) dry white wine
1 lb (500 g) tomatoes, peeled, seeded and coarsely chopped
⅔ cup (3 oz/100 g) black olives
⅔ cup (3 oz/100 g) green olives, blanched for a few seconds in boiling water and drained

▣ Warm the olive oil in a large sauté pan over medium heat. Salt the rib tips, add to the pan and brown until well colored on all sides, about 15 minutes. Remove to a plate. Add the onions, garlic and mushrooms, sprinkle with the herbs and salt to taste and turn up the heat. Shake the pan and stir the contents with a wooden spoon until the mushrooms' liquid evaporates. Sprinkle the flour over the top, reduce the heat and cook, stirring, for 1–2 minutes.
▣ Pour in the white wine and deglaze the pan, stirring and scraping the pan bottom with a wooden spoon. Add the tomatoes, bring to a boil and slip the meat and its juices into the sauce. Reduce the heat to low, cover and simmer for 1¼ hours. Add the olives and simmer until the meat is tender, 15 minutes longer.

SERVES 6

BOUCHES·DU·RHÔNE

GARDIANE D'AGNEAU

Camargue Lamb Stew

This is Provence's answer to Irish stew, simple and satisfying.

2 tablespoons olive oil
1 lb (500 g) neck chops, superficial fat removed
4 cloves garlic, crushed
1 lb (500 g) russet potatoes, peeled and thinly sliced
1 bay leaf
salt
boiling water as needed

▣ Warm the olive oil in a sauté pan over medium heat. Add the chops and cook, turning once, until colored on both sides, about 10 minutes.
▣ Add the garlic, potatoes, bay leaf and salt to taste and pour in boiling water to cover barely. Reduce the heat to very low, cover and simmer until the potatoes begin to fall apart to thicken the sauce, about 1 hour.

SERVES 4

Grilled Lamb Loin Chops served with potatoes au gratin

GIGOT RÔTI À LA PROVENÇALE

Roast Leg of Lamb

A leg of lamb should always be carved at table. The ritual ceremony adds an important dimension to the pleasure taken in the meal. To carve, hold the leg end with the other end resting on the platter. Carve away from yourself, at a sharp bias, nearly parallel to the bone, lifting off thin slices, first from the rounded, fleshy part of the leg, then from the leaner muscle to the other side and, finally, slice off small pieces of meat from the leg end. Each has a different flavor and degree of doneness. Serve a slice of each to each guest.

pinch of coarse salt
freshly ground pepper
pinch of Provençal mixed dried herbs (see glossary)
41 firm cloves garlic
pinch of fine salt
1 tablespoon dry white wine
1 leg of lamb, about 6 lb (3 kg), leg bone unsawn and pelvic
   bone boned out, at room temperature
1 tablespoon olive oil
mirepoix (see glossary)
3 cups (24 fl oz/750 ml) dry red wine

▨ In a mortar pound together the coarse salt, pepper to taste, herbs and 1 garlic clove to form a paste. Stir in the white wine.
▨ Trim off any superficial fat from the lamb leg. With a small, sharp-pointed knife, cut several deep slits in the leg, on the bias and with the grain. Open up each slit with your finger and, with a teaspoon, insert some of the herb mixture. Smear any remaining mixture over the meat's surface. Rub the leg all over with the olive oil, cover with plastic wrap and leave to marinate at room temperature for 1 hour or so.
▨ Meanwhile, prepare the *mirepoix* and combine in a small saucepan with the wine. Bring to a boil and simmer, uncovered, until reduced by two thirds, or to about 1 cup (8 fl oz/250 ml). Pass the reduced wine through a sieve, pressing the vegetables with a wooden pestle to extract all the liquid.

Roast Leg of Lamb

▨ Preheat an oven to 400°F (200°C). Put the leg in a shallow, oval ovenproof dish. Place in the oven and roast for 10 minutes. Reduce the oven heat to 350°F (180°C); 20 minutes later reduce the heat to 325°F (160°C). When the leg has been in the oven for 45 minutes, turn the oven off and leave the leg to rest, in the oven, for 20 minutes (if your oven is very hermetic, open the oven door for a couple of minutes to cool it down).
▨ While the leg is resting, in a small saucepan combine the garlic cloves with water to cover and the fine salt. Bring to a boil and simmer for 15 minutes. Drain, reserving the cooking water. Combine the cooked garlic cloves and the red wine reduction in a small saucepan and gently reheat.
▨ Transfer the leg of lamb to a heated serving platter. Place the roasting pan on the stove top over high heat and deglaze it with some (or all, depending on what remains) of the garlic cooking liquid, scraping the pan bottom with a wooden spoon until all the browned bits dissolve. Add it to the wine reduction and bring to boil.
▨ Pour the boiling wine reduction into a warmed bowl. At table after carving, add the juices from the carved leg to the bowl. Ladle the juices and garlic cloves over the slices of lamb on each serving plate.

SERVES 8

GRILLADE DE BOEUF À LA PROVENÇALE

Provençal Grilled Beef

Panfried steak is shunned in Provence. Steaks are grilled over hot coals and many feel that grilled beef can achieve its perfect expression only if it is finished with anchovy. Fruit woods, grapevine stock and broom are the woods preferred for preparing the embers; olive wood makes a wonderful, long-lasting bed of coals. The butcher's cut (l'onglet; le morceau du boucher), also known as hanging tender or bloody skirt, is especially favored. It is composed of a single muscle joining the flanks inside the body. When pared of all external fat and nervous tissue, it falls into two elongated oval strips, 2½–3 inches (6–7.5 cm) thick, the juiciest and most flavorful of all grilling cuts.

freshly ground pepper
1 butcher's cut, 1½ lb (750 g), trimmed (see recipe introduction)
2 teaspoons olive oil

FOR THE SAUCE:

small pinch of coarse salt
2 cloves garlic
2 salt anchovies, rinsed and filleted (see glossary)
3 tablespoons olive oil
1 tablespoon chopped fresh flat-leaf (Italian) parsley

▨ Grind the pepper over the steak, rub it with olive oil and marinate at room temperature for 2 hours. To prepare the sauce, in a mortar pound together the salt and garlic to form a paste. Add the anchovies and pound again to a paste. Stir in the olive oil with the pestle, and then stir in the parsley with a spoon. Set aside.
▨ Prepare a fire in a charcoal grill. When the flames have died and the coals are glowing, place the steak on the grill rack and grill the steak, turning 3 or 4 times, 8–10 minutes.
▨ Transfer the steak to a carving board and slice it thinly, on the bias, without displacing the slices of meat. Slip the sliced steak, in its original form, onto a warmed platter. Pour over any juices that have escaped in carving. Spoon on the sauce the length of the steak.

SERVES 4

Along the backroads of the Vaucluse, Provençal Grilled Beef

Top to bottom: Sausages in Rice, Roast Pork with Olives and Anchovy, Grilled Pork Chops with Piquant Sauce

BOUCHES·DU·RHÔNE

SAUCISSES À LA MÉNAGÈRE

Sausages in Rice

8 fresh pork link sausages
1 leek, including the tender green parts, finely chopped
1½ cups (8 oz/250 g) long-grain white rice

salt and cayenne pepper
large pinch of saffron threads
3 cups (24 fl oz/750 ml) water, boiling

◙ Separate the sausages and prick each several times with a trussing needle or sharp skewer. Pour only enough water into the bottom of a sauté pan to form a film. Add the sausages and cook over low heat, shaking the pan and turning the sausages,

382

until the water evaporates and the sausages are lightly browned on all sides in their own fat, about 10 minutes. Remove the sausages to a plate.

▣ Add the leeks to the pan with the sausage drippings and cook, stirring, over low heat until softened, about 10 minutes. Add the rice, salt and cayenne pepper to taste and the saffron. Stir with a wooden spoon over low heat until the rice turns milky and opaque in appearance, about 5 minutes. Add the boiling water, stir once, cover tightly and simmer over very low heat for 10 minutes. Remove the lid, lay the sausages on top of the rice, re-cover and cook until the rice is tender, about 12 minutes longer.

SERVES 4

V A R

RÔTI DE PORC À LA TOULONNAISE

Roast Pork with Olives and Anchovy

In Provence sage is nearly always associated with pork. The sage must be fresh, as dried sage has a musty flavor.

1 section of pork loin, about 3 lb (1.5 kg), boned without
    separating the loin and the tenderloin
salt and freshly ground pepper
persillade made with 1 clove garlic (see glossary)
8 salt anchovies, rinsed and filleted (see glossary)
⅔ cup (3 oz/100 g) black olives, pitted and chopped
several fresh sage sprigs
½ cup (4 fl oz/125 ml) dry white wine

▣ Preheat an oven to 450°F (230°C). Lay out the boned loin, back side down. Sprinkle with salt and pepper to taste and then with the *persillade*. Distribute the anchovy fillets and chopped olives along the sides of the tenderloin. Roll up the loin, tie it and, on the fat surface, pierce the flesh at regular intervals with the tip of a sharp knife. Insert tiny sprigs or single, larger leaves of fresh sage into the slits. Sprinkle the roast with salt and place in a roasting pan.

▣ Place in the oven and roast for 10 minutes. Reduce the oven temperature to 325°F (160°C). Begin basting regularly with the drippings after 30 minutes. After 45 minutes, spoon most of the fat out of the roasting pan, add a few spoonfuls of the wine and continue basting, every 3–4 minutes, adding more wine to the pan if it begins to dry up. After about 1¼ hours, the roast will be nicely glazed.

▣ Remove the pork to a carving board, snip the strings and carve into slices ⅓ in (8 mm) thick. Lay the slices, overlapping, on a heated serving platter. Pour over the carving juices and the basting juices from the roasting pan.

SERVES 6

V A R

BÉQUETS AU FOUR

Baked Lamb Shanks

The unpeeled garlic cloves are squeezed and spread on bread at table. After long cooking, they are transformed into a sweet purée.

4 lamb shanks, about 1 lb (500 g) each
salt
pinch of Provençal mixed dried herbs (see glossary)
1 tablespoon olive oil
16 garlic cloves, unpeeled

2 carrots, peeled and cut into 1-in (2.5-cm) pieces
2 onions, coarsely chopped
½ cup (4 fl oz/125 ml) dry white wine

▣ Preheat an oven to 400°F (200°C).
▣ Sprinkle the shanks with salt and herbs and rub them with olive oil. Place in a roasting pan and roast for 30 minutes.
▣ Remove the shanks from the oven and reduce the oven temperature to 300°F (150°C). Transfer the shanks to a lidded oven casserole and add the garlic, carrots and onions. Sprinkle with a little salt. Pour off the fat in the roasting pan and place the pan over high heat. Pour in the wine and deglaze the pan, scraping the pan bottom with a wooden spoon until all the browned bits dissolve. Pour the deglazing juices over the contents of the casserole and cover.
▣ Place in the oven and bake until the shanks are tender, about 1½ hours.

SERVES 4 *Photograph pages 384–385*

P R O V E N C E

CÔTES DE PORC, SAUCE HACHÉE

Grilled Pork Chops with Piquant Sauce

Sauce hachée—"chopped sauce"—is such a wonderfully descriptive name that it is a pity to lose it. Today, it is called sauce piquante, *but only the name has changed.*

FOR THE SAUCE:

1 tablespoon olive oil
1 onion, finely chopped
salt and cayenne pepper
1 tablespoon all-purpose (plain) flour
1 cup (8 fl oz/250 ml) broth or water
persillade made with 1 clove garlic (see glossary)
2 or 3 shallots, finely chopped
2 or 3 fresh cultivated mushrooms, finely chopped
6 tablespoons (3 fl oz/90 ml) red wine vinegar
1 tablespoon capers, rinsed and chopped
2 salt anchovies, rinsed, filleted and mashed (see glossary)
4 sour gherkins, finely chopped

4 pork chops, each about 1 in (2.5 cm) thick
2 teaspoons olive oil
24 fresh sage leaves
salt and freshly ground pepper

▣ Prepare a fire in a charcoal grill. To prepare the sauce, warm the olive oil in a saucepan over low heat. Add the onion and sauté over low heat until softened and lightly colored, about 10 minutes. Add salt and cayenne pepper to taste and the flour and stir well. Raise the heat to medium-high. Slowly pour in the broth or water, whisking constantly. Continue to whisk until the mixture comes to a boil. Reduce the heat to a gentle simmer.

▣ In a small saucepan over high heat, combine the *persillade,* shallots, mushrooms and vinegar. Bring to a boil and simmer gently until nearly dry, just a few minutes. Then pour the mushroom mixture into the broth mixture. Add the capers, anchovies and gherkins, stir well and hold over very low heat.

▣ Rub the pork chops with the olive oil. Press 3 sage leaves onto each side of each chop. Season to taste with salt and grind over some pepper. Place on the grill rack over dying embers. Grill until cooked, about 5 minutes on each side.

▣ Reheat the sauce, if necessary, and serve with the pork chops.

SERVES 4

GRILLADE DES MARINIERS
Braised Beef Slices with Anchovy

This was once a specialty of the riverside bistros frequented by the Rhône river sailors, who called it la grillade, *not because the meat was grilled but because it was cut into slices like a* grillade.

3 lb (1.5 kg) boneless beef shank (leg), cut into slices ⅓ inch (8 mm) thick
2 bay leaves
large pinch Provençal mixed dried herbs (see glossary)
6 tablespoons (3 fl oz/90 ml) olive oil
4 cloves garlic, finely chopped
1 lb (500 g) sweet white onions, coarsely chopped
½ cup (4 fl oz/125 ml) dry white wine
¼ cup (2 fl oz/60 ml) Provençal herb vinegar (see glossary)
¼ cup (2 fl oz/60 ml) marc de Provence (see glossary) or Cognac
salt and freshly ground pepper
3 tablespoons capers, rinsed, squeezed dry and chopped
6 sour gherkins, chopped
3 salt anchovies, rinsed, filleted and mashed (see glossary)

▨ In a large bowl sprinkle the beef slices with the herb mixture and then turn them around with the 3 tablespoons of the olive oil and the bay leaves. Leave to marinate at room temperature for 3–4 hours.
▨ In a bowl mix together the garlic and onions. In another bowl stir together the wine, vinegar and brandy. Put a layer of the onion-garlic mixture in the bottom of a flameproof earthenware *daubière* or a heavy pot. Top with a layer of meat slices and then more of the onion-garlic mixture. Sprinkle 2–3 tablespoons of the wine mixture over the top and season to taste with salt and pepper. Continue layering, tucking the bay leaves in a middle layer and finishing with a layer of the onion-garlic mixture. Add any remaining wine mixture and marinade. Cover tightly and cook over very low heat for 2 hours.
▨ Add the capers and gherkins, swirl the pot and cook for 2 hours longer. Add the mashed anchovies, swirl the pot and leave to simmer for a few minutes. Sprinkle over the remaining 3 tablespoons olive oil and serve directly from the pot.

SERVES 8

ÉPAULE D'AGNEAU À LA VENAISSINE
Braised Stuffed Lamb Shoulder

A boned lamb shoulder, when laid out flat on a work surface, has four irregular corners, recalling the map of France. After pressing the stuffing in place, bring opposite corners to meet, tacking them with a trussing needle and kitchen string. Tie a length of string around the circumference and then, with a good yard (meter) of string, at least four times vertically around to form a melon shape.

1 whole lamb shoulder including shank about, 3 lb (1.5 kg), boned and trimmed of fat
pinch of Provençal mixed dried herbs (see glossary)
2 tablespoons olive oil
1 cup (8 fl oz/250 ml) dry white wine
1 cup (2 oz/60 g) fresh bread crumbs
persillade made with 1 clove garlic (see glossary)
2 oz (60 g) lean salt pork (green bacon), chopped
1 egg
salt and freshly ground pepper
mirepoix (see glossary)

▨ Sprinkle the boned shoulder lightly on both sides with the herbs. Place it flat in a dish. Pour over ½ cup (4 fl oz/125 ml) of the wine and about 2 teaspoons of the olive oil. Marinate for 2–3 hours at room temperature, turning the shoulder over a couple of times.
▨ Preheat an oven to 400°F (200°C). In a bowl, combine the bread crumbs, *persillade,* salt pork, egg and 1 tablespoon of the olive oil. Season lightly with salt, grind over some pepper and mix thoroughly.
▨ Drain the shoulder, reserving the marinade, and pat it dry with paper towels. Spread the crumb mixture on the shoulder and press it on firmly; tie it up as directed in the recipe introduction. Rub with the remaining 1 teaspoon olive oil.

Left to right: Braided Stuffed Lamb Shoulder, Braised Beef Slices with Anchovy, Baked Lamb Shanks (recipe page 383)

Sprinkle the tied lamb with salt and place in a small, ovenproof frying pan or a round baking dish.

◙ Place in the oven and roast for 40 minutes. Meanwhile, prepare the *mirepoix* in the bottom of a heavy saucepan of a size just to contain the shoulder. Place the shoulder on top. Pour off the fat from the roasting pan and place the pan on the stove top over high heat. Pour in the marinade and the remaining ½ cup (4 fl oz/125 ml) wine and deglaze the pan, scraping the pan bottom with a wooden spoon until all the browned bits dissolve. Pour the deglazed pan juices over the lamb shoulder. Cut a sheet of parchment (kitchen) paper to the dimensions of the saucepan, smear one side lightly with olive oil, and place, oiled side down, over the meat. Cover with a lid and simmer,

over very low heat until tender when pierced with a trussing needle, about 1 hour.

◙ Preheat an oven again to 400°F (200°C). Carefully clip and remove the strings from the shoulder and return it to its roasting pan. Strain the braising juices through a sieve, pressing the vegetables with a wooden pestle to extract all the liquid. Remove any fat from the surface, if necessary, and pour the juices over the shoulder. Place in the oven and baste every couple of minutes until the surface is glazed, 10–15 minutes.

◙ With a wide spatula, transfer the shoulder to a heated platter. Pour the juices into a warmed bowl and pass at the table. Cut the shoulder into wedges to serve.

SERVES 4–6

From left to right: Boiled Beef Gratin, Stuffed Pork Chops

HACHIS AU GRATIN

Boiled Beef Gratin

Leftover beef from pot-au-feu *(recipe on page 299) should be cooled out of its broth, enclosed in plastic wrap and refrigerated. When cold, a gelatinous cut, like leg of beef, is very firm and can be thinly*

sliced easily or cleanly chopped. Try also boeuf à l'arlésienne, *thin slices of broiled beef overlapping in a gratin dish, sprinkled with a* persillade, *covered with a layer of hot ratatouille (recipe on page 56) and put into a 400°F (200°C) oven for 10 minutes.*

3 tablespoons olive oil
1 onion, finely chopped
1 lb (500 g) *pot-au-feu* beef (recipe on page 310), chilled, thinly
   sliced, cut into narrow strips and chopped

persillade made with 2 cloves garlic (see glossary)
salt
1 cup (8 fl oz/250 ml) tomato sauce (see glossary)
freshly ground pepper
whole nutmeg
2 lb (1 kg) russet potatoes, peeled and quartered
¼ cup (2 oz/60 g) unsalted butter, chilled and diced
handful of dried bread crumbs
2 tablespoons freshly grated Parmesan cheese

◉ Warm 2 tablespoons of the olive oil in a heavy saucepan over low heat. Add the onion and cook gently until soft but not colored, about 5 minutes. Add the chopped meat, raise the heat and stir with a wooden spoon for a couple of minutes. Add the *persillade* and the tomato sauce, stir, bring to a boil, reduce the heat to low and simmer gently for 10 minutes. Grind over pepper and scrape over a bit of nutmeg.

◉ Meanwhile, place the potatoes in a saucepan with lightly salted water just to cover. Bring to a boil, cover and boil until just tender, about 30 minutes. Drain them into a sieve placed over a bowl, saving their water. With a wooden pestle, push them, without turning the pestle, through the sieve back into their saucepan. Add the butter and some of their cooking water, grind over some pepper and stir but do not beat with a wooden spoon. Continue to add cooking water and to stir until the mixture is quite fluid—almost pourable. This may use up all of the cooking liquid.

◉ Preheat an oven to 350°F (180°C). Spread the meat–tomato sauce mixture in the bottom of a 6-cup (48-fl oz/1.5-l) gratin dish or other baking dish. Spread the potato purée evenly on top. Drag the tines of a fork back and forth across the surface to create a textured design. In a small bowl stir together the bread crumbs and cheese and sprinkle evenly over the potato layer. Dribble the remaining 1 tablespoon olive oil in a fine thread over the top, forming a crisscross pattern.

◉ Place in the oven and bake until golden, about 20 minutes.

SERVES 4

PROVENCE

Côtes de Porc Farcies à la Provençale
Stuffed Pork Chops

Wild mushrooms can be substituted for cultivated; prepared with cèpes, these chops are sumptuous.

FOR THE STUFFING:

1 tablespoon olive oil
1 onion, finely chopped
2 oz (60 g) fresh cultivated mushrooms, finely chopped
small pinch of Provençal mixed dried herbs (see glossary)
persillade made with 1 clove garlic (see glossary)
a few drops of lemon juice
salt, freshly ground pepper, and freshly scraped nutmeg
handful of fresh bread crumbs
1 egg

4 double-rib pork chops, trimmed of fat except for thin layer
    of back fat
salt and freshly ground pepper
2 tablespoons olive oil
2–3 tablespoons dry white wine

◉ To prepare the stuffing, warm the olive oil in a frying pan over low heat. Add the onion and cook gently until softened but not colored, about 10 minutes. Add the mushrooms, raise the heat and sauté until nearly all the liquid released from the mushrooms evaporates, about 5 minutes. Add the herbs, *persillade,* lemon juice and salt, pepper and nutmeg to taste.

Empty into a bowl and let cool for a few minutes. Add the bread crumbs and egg and, using your hands, mix thoroughly.

◉ Using a small, sharp-pointed knife, pierce the back of each chop deeply, ¾ in (2 cm) from the spine end to ¾ in (2 cm) from the tip, to form a pouch. Divide the stuffing equally among the pouches and stuff them. Close each opening with a pair of crossed toothpicks. Season the chops to taste with salt and pepper.

◉ Warm the olive oil in a heavy sauté pan over medium heat. Add the chops and brown, turning once, over moderate heat, 7–8 minutes on each side. Cover and cook over very low heat until the chops are tender, about 45 minutes. Turn the chops in their juices several times; if the juices appear to be drying up, add some of the wine once, or as often as necessary.

◉ Serve the chops with cooking juices spooned over the top.

SERVES 4

PROVENCE

Saupiquet de Lapin
Rabbit in Spicy Sauce

In the villages and countryside of Provence, literally half the population has rabbit hutches. Gibelotte and saupiquet are favorite and often-prepared dishes. Cookbooks not destined to be read by native Provençaux often substitute chicken—rabbit is better.

1 rabbit, about 3½ lb (1.7 kg), with liver
pinch of Provençal mixed dried herbs (see glossary)
2 bay leaves
3 cloves garlic, unpeeled, plus 1 clove, peeled
freshly ground pepper
½ cup (4 fl oz/125 ml) olive oil
salt
½ cup (4 fl oz/125 ml) dry white wine
pinch of coarse salt
1 clove garlic
4 salt anchovies, rinsed and filleted (see glossary)
2 tablespoons capers, rinsed and squeezed dry
1 tablespoon finely chopped fresh flat-leaf (Italian) parsley
⅔ cup (3 oz/100 g) black olives, pitted and coarsely chopped

◉ Cut the rabbit into 8 pieces: 2 forelegs; 2 hind legs; the saddle cut in two, kidneys left attached; and rib cage split in two.

◉ Place the rabbit pieces in a bowl and sprinkle with the Provençal herbs. Add the bay, unpeeled garlic, pepper to taste and 3 tablespoons of the olive oil. Toss together, cover and marinate in the refrigerator for several hours or overnight.

◉ Preheat an oven to 350°F (180°C). Spread the rabbit pieces and their marinade in a shallow oven dish. Place in the oven and roast until the rabbit is tender, 45 minutes, turning the pieces at regular intervals. After 20 minutes, baste from time to time with 2 or 3 tablespoons of the wine, never letting the dish become dry.

◉ Meanwhile, in a small frying pan over high heat, sauté the liver in a few drops of olive oil until slightly firmed up but still rare. Remove from the heat and set aside.

◉ In a mortar pound together the coarse salt, pepper to taste and the peeled garlic to form a paste. Add the anchovies and the capers and continue to pound to a paste. Add the liver, pound to a paste, and stir in the remaining olive oil (about 5 tablespoons/3 fl oz/80 ml) slowly with the pestle. Finally, stir in the parsley and olives. Transfer the mixture to a small, flameproof earthenware casserole and warm over very low heat; it should not cook.

◉ Transfer the rabbit pieces to a warmed platter. Discard the bay leaves and garlic and stir the roasting juices into the warmed anchovy-caper sauce. Spoon the sauce over the rabbit to serve.

SERVES 4 *Photograph pages 370–371*

BOUCHES·DU·RHÔNE

GRAS-DOUBLE À LA MARSEILLAISE

Tripe à la Marseillaise

Whether pieds et paquets or beef tripe is prepared this way, it is one of the great dishes of Provence. Beef tripe is sold partially precooked. In some countries, it is sold "bleached," which makes it tasteless and useless. Buy it unbleached in ethnic neighborhoods and, if possible, include a mixture of all four stomachs: blanket, honeycomb, bible and reed. Bible tripe, so-named because of its bible page–thin, ripply extensions, is the loveliest of all. Boiled potatoes are excellent with this dish.

1 pig's foot (trotter), split in half lengthwise
2 leeks, white and tender green parts, thinly sliced
2 onions, coarsely chopped
10 oz (300 g) carrots, peeled and thinly sliced
1½ lb (750 g) tomatoes, peeled, seeded and coarsely
    chopped
3 cloves garlic
large pinch of Provençal mixed dried herbs (see glossary)

2½ lb (1.25 kg) tripe, cut into strips ¾ in (2 cm) by 4 in (10 cm)
salt
bouquet garni, including a strip of dried orange peel
    (see glossary)
⅓ cup (3 fl oz/80 ml) marc de Provence (see glossary)
    or Cognac
about 2 cups (16 fl oz/500 ml) dry white wine

◉ Place the split pig's foot in a saucepan and add water to cover. Bring to a boil, drain and rinse in cold running water. Drain again and set aside.
◉ Mix together all the vegetables, garlic and the dried herbs and put a handful of the mixture in the bottom of a large earthenware pot or other large pot. Place the trotter halves and a handful of the tripe on top. Sprinkle with salt. Repeat the layers, sprinkling each one with salt and burying the bouquet garni in the middle. Finish with a layer of vegetables. Add the brandy and enough white wine just short of immersing the contents.
◉ Place a flame-tamer between the pot and the heat source, cover and bring slowly to a boil, counting about 1 hour. Simmer over very low heat for at least 7 or 8 hours.
◉ Slowly rewarmed and simmered for an hour the following day, the tripe is even better.

SERVES 4

Tripe à la Marseillaise

The entry to Château d'Ansouis, Jellied Daube

DAUBE EN GELÉE

Jellied Daube

A daube's intoxicating, dense harmony of flavors is even more clearly defined when served in its jelly than when hot. At lunch on a hot summer's day, a green salad is the perfect accompaniment. A daube is often prepared specially to be served cold. This recipe assumes about half of the daube is left over.

leftover daube in its cooking pot (recipe on page 122)
fresh flat-leaf (Italian) parsley bouquets, black olives and
  tomato sections

◎ While the daube is still warm, drain off all the cooking liquid. Put a spoonful onto a small metal dish and chill it in the coldest part of the refrigerator (but not the freezer). If the spoonful does not set to a firm jelly, pour the cooking juices into a saucepan and reduce over high heat to the correct consistency when a spoonful is tested.

◎ Discard the bouquet garni, pressing it between 2 spoons to recuperate the juices. Bone the trotter and cut the flesh into small pieces. In a mixing bowl (preferably metal, which facilitates unmolding) of a size to contain the solids and the cooking liquid without excessive leftover space, distribute the pieces of beef, trotter, rind and salt pork evenly. Pour over the cooking liquid, leave to cool, cover and refrigerate until the following day.

◎ To unmold, first loosen the rim of jelly from the bowl by running the tip of a small knife around the edge. Then immerse the bowl very rapidly, almost to the level of its contents, in hot water. Place it on a towel, place an overturned round platter on top and turn the platter and the mold over together. Surround the unmolded daube with parsley bouquets, tomato sections and black olives. Present it at table before slicing, then slice and serve the slices with the aid of a spatula.

SERVES 4

FARCI BRAISÉ

Braised Stuffed Breast of Veal

Here, the stuffed veal breast is slowly braised in the oven and then served with the pan juices.

3 lb (1.5 kg) veal breast, stuffed with stuffing of choice
   (recipes on page 406)
1 tablespoon olive oil
salt
mirepoix (see glossary)
1 bay leaf
½ cup (4 fl oz/125 ml) dry white wine
2 cups (16 fl oz/500 ml) broth, boiling

◙ Preheat an oven to 400°F (200°C).
◙ Smear the surface of the stuffed breast with the olive oil and sprinkle with salt to taste. Place it in a shallow roasting pan and roast for 30 minutes, basting with the pan juice after 15 minutes. Remove from the oven and turn the oven down to 325°F (160°C).
◙ Meanwhile, prepare the *mirepoix* and spread it in the bottom of an oval ovenproof casserole of a size to contain the breast. Add the bay leaf and place the meat atop the *mirepoix*. Drain off any fat in the roasting pan and place the pan over medium-high heat. Pour in the wine and deglaze the pan, scraping the pan bottom with a wooden spoon until all the browned bits dissolve. Pour the deglazing juices and the boiling broth over the meat. Cut a sheet of parchment (kitchen) paper to the dimensions of the casserole, smear one side lightly with olive oil and place the paper, oiled side down, on top of the meat. Cover the casserole and place in the oven 1½ hours. Remove the casserole from the oven and increase the heat to 400°F (200°C).
◙ Put the breast back into the roasting pan. Pass the braising juices through a sieve; press the solids firmly but do not purée them into the juices. Put the juices into a small saucepan and bring to a boil. Move the saucepan half off the heat, adjusting the heat to maintain a very light boil on one half of the surface, until a skin forms on the still side, collecting the fat. Ladle some of the fatless juice from the boiling side of the pan over the stuffed breast and place it in the oven. Keep a small bowl and a tablespoon beside the saucepan to skim off the fatty skin from time to time, pulling it to the edge of the pan with the side of the spoon. Baste the meat often, either with the juices in the roasting pan or with fat-free juices from the saucepan. When no more fat collects on the still side of the saucepan, remove the pan from the heat.
◙ When the surface of the veal breast presents a glistening, bronzed surface, after about 20 minutes, remove it to a heated platter and snip the strings. Pour the remainder of the sauce into a warmed bowl. Present the glazed breast at table, then slice.

SERVES 6

BOEUF À LA PROVENÇALE

Sautéed Boiled Beef

Similar rapid sautés can be made from other well-cooked meats (but not from rare roasts, which turn tough with this treatment). Potatoes, pasta and rice are good accompaniments.

3 tablespoons olive oil
1½ lb (750 g) tomatoes, peeled, seeded and coarsely chopped
salt
persillade made with 1 clove garlic (see glossary)
1 lb (500 g) *pot-au-feu* beef, chilled and cut into ¾-in (2-cm)
   cubes (recipe on page 299)
⅔ cup (3 oz/100 g) black olives
several fresh basil sprigs with flower buds
freshly ground pepper

◙ Warm the olive oil in a sauté pan over high heat. Add the tomatoes, sprinkle with salt to taste, and add the *persillade*. Sauté to evaporate the tomatoes' juices as rapidly as possible.
◙ Add the beef cubes, reduce the heat to low, cover and simmer for 10 minutes. Add the olives, cover and simmer until heated through and flavors are blended, 3–4 minutes.
◙ Just before serving tear the basil leaves into fragments and crumble the flower buds. Add the leaves and buds to the pan. Grind over some pepper, stir the sauce and serve.

SERVES 4

ALOUETTES SANS TÊTE; PAUPIETTES DE BOEUF À LA PROVENÇALE

Provençal Beef Birds

Charles Durand's all-purpose stuffing (see poached stuffed breast of veal, page 406) can replace the stuffing used here. Red wine often replaces white wine in the sauce for this dish. Serve with boiled potatoes, mashed potatoes, pilaf or macaroni.

2 lb (1 kg) beef rump
FOR THE STUFFING:
½ lb (250 g) lean salt pork (green bacon), chopped
the chopped beef trimmings
persillade made with 3 garlic cloves (see glossary)
salt and freshly ground pepper

¼ cup (2 fl oz/60 ml) olive oil
1 onion, finely chopped
½ cup (4 fl oz/125 ml) dry white wine
2 tomatoes, peeled, seeded and chopped
salt
bouquet garni (see glossary)
1 cup (8 fl oz/250 ml) broth or water
⅔ cup (3 oz/100 g) black olives

◙ Cut the beef into 12 slices ⅓ in (8 mm) thick and about 3 in (7.5 cm) by 4 in (10 cm). Reserve the trimmings and chop them. Flatten the slices of meat slightly with the side of a heavy knife blade or a meat mallet.
◙ In a bowl mix together thoroughly all of the stuffing ingredients, including salt and pepper to taste. Separate the mixture into 12 equal portions. Cut twelve 1-foot (30-cm) lengths of kitchen string. Place a portion of the stuffing near a narrow end of a meat slice and roll up the slice. Loop the string around the middle of the rolled slice, then cross it and loop it lengthwise around the roll. Finish up with a double knot. Clip off the excess string and tuck the ends of the meat roll in to make a neat package. Repeat with the remaining stuffing and meat slices.
◙ In a heavy sauté pan of a size to contain the rolls without crowding, warm the olive oil over medium heat. Add the rolls and brown lightly on all sides, about 15 minutes. Add the onion and keep turning the meat regularly until the onion is lightly colored, about 5 minutes. Pour in the white wine and deglaze the pan, moving the meat around and scraping the pan bottom with a wooden spoon. Add the tomatoes, salt, bouquet garni and almost enough broth to cover the meat. Bring to a boil, reduce the heat to low, cover, and simmer, turning the meat regularly in its sauce about 1¼ hours. Add the olives and continue simmering until the rolls are tender, about 1¼ hours longer. When ready, the beef birds should be richly glazed and very little sauce should remain.
◙ Clip and remove the strings. Place on a warm platter and serve.

SERVES 6

Clockwise from top: Braised Stuffed Breast of Veal, Provençal Beef Birds, Beef and Potato Stew, Sautéed Boiled Beef

BOEUF À LA GARDIANE

Beef and Potato Stew

This is the traditional beef stew of the gardians, horsemen, or cowboys, who guard the bulls and horses of the Camargue.

2 tablespoons olive oil
2 lb (1 kg) stewing beef (leg or chuck), cut into 1¼ in (4 cm) cubes
salt
1 slice lean salt pork (green bacon), about ¼ lb (125 g), cut crosswise into finger-thick sections
1 large onion, chopped
3 cloves garlic, crushed
boiling water as needed
bouquet garni including a strip of dried orange peel (see glossary)
1 lb (500 g) russet potatoes, peeled and sliced ¼ in (6 mm) thick
⅔ cup (3 oz/100 g) black olives
freshly ground pepper

◨ In a heavy sauté pan over medium heat, warm the olive oil. Add the beef pieces and brown on all sides, shuffling them around with a wooden spoon. This should take about 15 minutes. Season to taste with salt, add the salt pork and stir occasionally until lightly colored, about 6 minutes. Add the onion, lower the heat and stir regularly.

◨ When the onion is lightly browned, after about 5 minutes, add the garlic, pour in 1 cup (8 fl oz/250 ml) boiling water and deglaze the pan, scraping the pan bottom with the wooden spoon until all the browned bits dissolve. Tuck the bouquet garni into the center, pack in the potatoes, sprinkle with salt and add more boiling water until the potatoes are nearly covered. Cover tightly and cook over the lowest possible heat until the meat is tender and the potatoes are falling apart, 2½–3 hours.

◨ A few minutes before serving, stir in the olives and grind over the pepper.

SERVES 4

391

ALPES·MARITIMES

ESTOUFFADE À LA NIÇOISE

Niçois Braised Beef

The presence of tomato and black olives place this stew in the south of France. It is a recipe type that exists under different names all over France. If, for instance, the white wine is replaced by red, the tomato sauce is eliminated and the olives replaced by little onions, it becomes a boeuf bourguignon.

1 slice lean salt pork (green bacon) 5 oz (150 g) cut into lardoons (see glossary)
4 tablespoons (2 fl oz/60 ml) olive oil
1 lb (500 g) onions, coarsely chopped
2 lb (1 kg) stewing beef, cut into 3-oz (100-g) pieces
salt
2 tablespoons all-purpose (plain) flour
2 cups (16 fl oz/500 ml) dry white wine
½ cup (4 fl oz/125 ml) tomato sauce (see glossary)
bouquet garni (see glossary)
broth or water as needed
5 oz (150 g) fresh cultivated mushrooms, quartered
⅔ cup (3 oz/100 g) black olives
freshly ground pepper

▨ Place the lardoons in a saucepan, add water to cover and bring to a boil. Drain immediately, rinse in cold water and dry. Set aside.
▨ In a large sauté pan over medium-low heat, warm 2 tablespoons of the olive oil. Add the lardoons and color very lightly on all sides, about 7 minutes. Remove them to a dish and add the onions to the pan. Cook over medium-low heat until softened and beginning to color, about 10 minutes. Turn them into a sieve placed over a bowl to collect the oil. Add 1 tablespoon of the remaining oil and the oil from the onions to the sauté pan. Add the beef pieces and brown over medium heat on all sides, salting them as they are turned, about 15 minutes. Sprinkle the flour over the meat and continue to turn the meat pieces until the flour is lightly browned. Return the onions to the pan and stir well. Pour in the wine and deglaze the pan, scraping the pan bottom with a wooden spoon until all browned bits dissolve. Add the tomato sauce, the bouquet garni and enough broth just to immerse the meat. Bring to a boil, reduce the heat to low, cover and simmer, until the meat is tender, 2½–3 hours.
▨ While the meat is cooking, warm the remaining 1 table-spoon oil in another sauté pan over high heat. Add the mush-rooms and salt to taste. Sauté until lightly colored and their liquid is reabsorbed. Set aside.
▨ Remove the meat pieces to a plate and pour the contents of the sauté pan into a sieve placed over a bowl. Return the meat to the sauté pan, add the reserved lardoons, mushrooms and olives. Grind over some pepper and cover the pan to keep its contents warm.
▨ Squeeze and discard the bouquet garni and press the sauce through the sieve, puréeing the onions. Put it into a saucepan of a size just to contain it, bring to a boil and hold, half off the heat, at a light boil to one side. Skim the still side with a spoon occasionally until no more fat rises. Pour the sauce into the pan holding the meat. Bring to a boil and simmer for 10 minutes before serving.

SERVES 4

An 18th century home on a hillside vineyard in the Var,
Niçois Braised Beef

PAIN DE VEAU À LA PROVENÇALE
Provençal Veal Loaf

Other chopped leftover meats or ground uncooked meats may be added if the necessary quantity of cooked veal is lacking. The sorrel leaves melt in cooking, leaving a delicate, veined pattern on the surface of the unmolded loaf.

1 lb (500 g) roasted or braised veal, finely chopped
2½ cups (5 oz/150 g) fresh bread crumbs, moistened with a few tablespoons of hot milk
persillade made with 1 clove garlic (see glossary)
pinch of Provençal mixed dried herbs (see glossary)
3 eggs
salt, freshly ground pepper and freshly scraped nutmeg
1 tablespoon unsalted butter, softened
8–10 large sorrel leaves, stemmed
boiling water as needed
2 cups (16 fl oz/500 ml) tomato sauce, heated (see glossary)

▣ Preheat an oven to 350°F (180°C).
▣ In a mixing bowl combine the meat, moistened bread crumbs, *persillade,* herbs, eggs and salt, pepper and nutmeg to taste. Using your hands mix well.
▣ Grease a 6-cup (48-fl oz/1.5-l) charlotte mold with the butter. Line it with sorrel leaves, pressing their top surfaces firmly against the buttered bottom and sides of the mold. Fill the mold carefully, to avoid displacing the leaves (or refrigerate the mold first to set the butter and hold the leaves in place). Smooth the surface and tap the bottom of the mold against a work surface to settle the contents. Place the mold in a larger, deep oven dish and add boiling water to reach halfway up the sides of the mold. Place in the oven for 45 minutes. Remove from the oven and from the oven dish and leave to settle for 10 minutes.
▣ To unmold, place a round platter upside-down over the mold; using a folded towel, grasp the edges of the platter and the ears of the mold and invert the platter and mold together. Lift off the mold. Pour a ribbon of hot tomato sauce around the loaf and serve, accompanied with the remaining sauce in a bowl.

SERVES 4

ROUELLE DE VEAU À L'ANCHOIS
Veal Shank with Anchovy

Fresh egg noodles, parboiled, drained and tossed with butter are a good accompaniment to the veal shank.

1½ lb (750 g) veal shank, boned
4 salt anchovies, rinsed, filleted and cut in half crosswise (see glossary)
3 tablespoons wine vinegar
3 tablespoons olive oil
salt
about ½ cup (4 fl oz/125 ml) dry white wine
persillade made with 1 clove garlic (see glossary)
1 teaspoon grated orange zest

▣ With a small, sharp-pointed knife, pierce the meat repeatedly, with the grain, on both sides and slip a half anchovy fillet into each slit. Put the meat into a large bowl and sprinkle over

the vinegar and 1 teaspoon of the olive oil. Marinate for 4 hours at room temperature, turning it around two or three times.
▣ Drain the meat and pat it dry with paper towels. Warm the remaining olive oil in a heavy saucepan of a size just to contain the meat with ease. Put the meat in the pan, salt lightly, cover and cook over very low heat, turning it regularly. Watch the meat carefully. At first, it will release some of its own liquid and

Top to bottom: Veal Shank with Anchovy, Provençal Veal Loaf

begin to simmer before the liquid evaporates and the meat begins to color in the oil. Tease the cooking along, adding a couple of spoonfuls of the wine each time the pan becomes dry. It will be ready in about 1½ hours. Remove the meat to a heated serving platter. Slice and keep warm.

▣ Simmer the juices over medium-low heat until the pan is dry and the juices have turned solid and are adhering to the pan bottom. Pour off the fat and deglaze the pan with a few spoonfuls of the wine, scraping the bottom with a wooden spoon to dissolve all browned bits. Pour these juices over the meat. Mix together the *persillade* and orange zest and sprinkle on top.

SERVES 4

395

Braised Stuffed Duck with Olives

CANARD FARCI AUX OLIVES
Braised Stuffed Duck with Olives

FOR THE STUFFING:

3 oz (100 g) *brousse* (see glossary) or ricotta cheese
1 egg
1 tablespoon olive oil
1 onion, finely chopped
the duck heart, liver and fleshy lobes of the gizzard, cut into
    small pieces
pinch of coarse salt
1 clove garlic
½ cup (1 oz/30 g) fresh bread crumbs
1 lb (500 g) Swiss chard (silverbeet) greens, parboiled,
    squeezed dry and chopped (see glossary)
dried oregano flowers, salt and freshly ground pepper and
    freshly scraped nutmeg

1 duck, about 4 lb (2 kg)
1 teaspoon olive oil
salt
mirepoix (see glossary)
¼ cup (2 fl oz/60 ml) dry white wine
2 cups (16 fl oz/500 ml) broth, boiling
⅔ cup (3 oz/100 g) green olives in brine, parboiled for
    1 minute and drained
½ lemon

◆ To prepare the stuffing, combine the cheese and egg in a
mixing bowl and mash together well with a fork. Warm the
olive oil in a small frying pan over low heat. Add the onion and
cook until softened but not colored, about 10 minutes. Add the
heart, liver and gizzard and cook, stirring, until they turn gray,

just a few minutes. Remove from the heat.
◆ In a mortar pound together the coarse salt and garlic to form
a paste. Stir in the bread crumbs.
◆ Add the onion mixture, the crumb-garlic mixture and the
chard to the mixing bowl. Crumble over dried oregano flowers
to taste, then season with salt, pepper and a few scrapings of
nutmeg. Using your hands mix thoroughly.
◆ Preheat an oven to 450°F (230°C). Remove the wishbone
from the duck as directed for roast chicken with anchovies
(recipe on page 150). Cut off the wing tips at the second joint;
cut the tips in two at the first joint. Cut the neck into short
sections. Set these pieces aside. Stuff the abdomen of the duck
with the chard mix and sew up or skewer closed. Truss the duck
with kitchen string. Rub it with the olive oil and sprinkle all over
with salt. Put into a roasting pan, breast side up, with the neck
and wing tip pieces. Wrap the bone tip of each drumstick with
a fragment of aluminum foil to prevent its charring.
◆ Place in the oven and roast for 35–40 minutes, basting often
with the pan juices after the first 15 minutes. Remove from the
oven and reduce the oven temperature to 300°F (150°C).
◆ Meanwhile, prepare the *mirepoix* and spread it on the bottom
of an oval Dutch oven or other heavy pot with a lid of a size just
to contain the duck.
◆ Remove the foil drumstick wrappings and place the duck on
the *mirepoix,* scattering the wing and neck pieces around the
bird. Pour off all the fat from the roasting pan and place the pan
on the stove top over high heat. Pour in the wine and deglaze
the pan by scraping the pan bottom with a wooden spoon until
all browned bits dissolve. Pour the deglazing juices and the
boiling broth over the duck. Lightly oil a piece of parchment
(kitchen) paper cut to the dimensions of the casserole and
place, oiled side down, on top of the duck. Cover and braise in
the oven for 1 hour. Remove from the oven. Raise the oven
temperature to 375°F (190°C).

Transfer the duck to a shallow, oval oven dish. Pour the braising juices through a sieve placed over a small saucepan, pressing the *mirepoix* with a wooden pestle to extract all the liquid. Bring the juices to a boil, then move the saucepan half off the heat, adjusting the heat to keep a gentle boil on the heated surface. Ladle some of the fat-free juices from the boiling side over the duck and put it into the oven. When a skin forms on the still surface in the saucepan, pull it to the side with the edge of a spoon and remove it. Continue cleansing the sauce and basting the duck in this manner until no more fat rises to the surface in the saucepan. Add the olives to the saucepan.

When the duck is richly glazed, after about 20 minutes, remove it to a warmed platter. Snip and remove the trussing strings. Pour the juices from the oven dish into the saucepan. Sharpen the mixture with a squeeze of lemon juice. Pour the sauce and the olives into a heated bowl. Carve the duck and ladle some of the juices and olives over each serving.

SERVES 4

VAR

POULET FARCI EN CRAPAUDINE
Baked Stuffed Chicken

FOR THE STUFFING:

¼ lb (125 g) *brousse* (see glossary) or ricotta cheese
2 tablespoons olive oil

1 egg
½ lb (250 g) spinach, parboiled, squeezed dry and chopped (see glossary)
handful of fresh bread crumbs
¼ cup (1 oz/30 g) freshly grated Parmesan cheese
persillade made with 1 clove garlic (see glossary)
salt, pepper and freshly scraped nutmeg

1 chicken, about 3 lb (1.5 kg)
1 tablespoon olive oil
salt and freshly ground pepper

To prepare the stuffing, combine all the ingredients in a mixing bowl. Using your hands, mix thoroughly.

Preheat an oven to 450°F (230°C). Split, flatten and remove the breastbone from the chicken as directed for chicken grilled with Provençal herbs (recipe on page 151). Using your fingertips and starting at the neck, gradually loosen the skin from the breasts and legs, being careful not to tear it. With one hand, introduce the stuffing, small quantities at a time, between the skin and the flesh, distributing and molding it from outside with the other hand. Truss the chicken with chicken string. Rub it with the olive oil and sprinkle with salt and pepper. Place the bird, breast side up, in a round, shallow baking dish of a size to just hold the chicken, and roast for about 10 minutes. Reduce the oven temperature to 350°F (180°C) and continue to roast, without turning, until juices run clear when pierced at the thigh joint, about 40 minutes. Baste the bird with the pan juices two or three times during the last 30 minutes of roasting.

To serve, move the chicken to a carving board and carve in the same way as for the grilled chicken.

SERVES 4

Baked Stuffed Chicken

POULET À LA VAUCLUSIENNE
Vaucluse-style Chicken

1 chicken, about 3 lb (1.5 kg), trussed
salt and freshly ground pepper
1 tablespoon olive oil
2 oz (60 g) lean salt pork (green bacon), diced
1 onion, finely chopped
½ cup (4 fl oz/125 ml) dry white wine
1 lb (500 g) tomatoes, peeled, seeded and coarsely chopped
⅔ cup (3 oz/100 g) black olives
1 elongated eggplant (aubergine), about ¼ lb (250 g)
all-purpose (plain) flour
vegetable oil as needed

❖ Remove the breast bone from the chicken as directed for roast chicken with anchovies on page 396. Season the chicken with salt and pepper to taste. Put it into a deep, oval flameproof casserole or Dutch oven with the olive oil and salt pork and place over medium-low heat. Move the ingredients around in the pan, cover and uncover it, turn the chicken and stir the pork for 10–15 minutes. Add the onion and keep stirring. When the onion is lightly colored, raise the heat, add the wine, and stir and move the contents. Add the tomatoes and salt. When the tomatoes begin to fall apart and boil, after about 10 minutes, cover and reduce the heat to low. Cook, gradually turning the chicken completely around in the juices over the next 45 minutes. Stir in the olives at the end of the cooking period.
❖ Meanwhile, slice the eggplant into rounds ¼ in (6 mm) thick. Salt them on both sides.
❖ Remove the chicken from the casserole; clip and remove the trussing strings. Carve the bird and arrange the pieces and slices in a warmed deep platter or large earthenware gratin dish. Pour the contents of the casserole over the chicken and keep warm.
❖ In a large frying pan over medium-high heat (375°F/190°C), pour in vegetable oil to a depth of ½ in (12 mm). Sponge the eggplant slices dry with paper towels. Coat them with flour, shaking off any excess. When the oil is hot, slip the slices into the pan. Fry, turning once, until golden brown, about 2–4 minutes on each side. Remove to paper towels to drain.
❖ Arrange the eggplant slices around the chicken and serve.

SERVES 4

POULET AU RIZ À LA PROVENÇALE
Chicken Pilaf

A pilaf is the perfect way to dispose of the giblets, necks and wing tips that remain after trussing birds for roasting. Livers should be sautéed rapidly, kept pink and added only a moment before serving. This is a perfect family meal.

¼ cup (2 fl oz/60 ml) olive oil
1 frying chicken, about 3 lb (1.5 kg), cut into serving pieces
salt and freshly ground pepper
1 onion, finely chopped
1 sweet red pepper (capsicum), seeded, deribbed, cut into
   ½-in (12-cm) strips wide and then cut crosswise into squares
1½ cups (8 oz/250 g) white long-grain rice
⅛ teaspoon powdered saffron
small pinch of cayenne pepper
persillade made with 1 clove garlic (see glossary)
2½ cups (20 fl oz/625 ml) water, boiling
2 large tomatoes, peeled, seeded and coarsely chopped

❖ Warm the olive oil in a large, heavy sauté pan over medium-high heat. Season the chicken pieces with salt and pepper to taste. Put all the chicken pieces except the breasts in the pan. Sauté, turning the pieces, for 10 minutes. Add the breasts and sauté until all the pieces are nicely colored on both sides, about 10 minutes longer. Transfer the chicken pieces to a plate.
❖ Pour most of the oil from the sauté pan into a large frying pan and reserve it. Add the onion and the pepper to the sauté pan and stir them around over low heat until softened. Add the rice, salt to taste, saffron and cayenne and stir with a wooden spoon until the rice turns opaque, about 5 minutes. Stir in the *persillade,* pour in the boiling water, stir once, and place the chicken pieces on top. Pour over any juices that have drained from the pieces, cover the pan tightly and cook over very low heat until the rice is tender and the chicken is cooked, about 25 minutes.
❖ Meanwhile, heat the leftover oil in the frying pan. Add the tomatoes and a pinch of salt and sauté over high heat until most of their liquid evaporates. After the rice and chicken mixture has cooked for 15 minutes, spread the tomatoes over the surface without disturbing the contents. Recover and continue cooking until done.

SERVES 4

GIBELOTTE DE LAPIN
White Wine Rabbit Stew

In the last century, a gibelotte often included an eel, skinned, cut up and sautéed with the rabbit. The pieces of eel were then held aside until the rabbit was nearly done and then simmered for a few minutes in the sauce.

1 rabbit, about 3½ (1.7 kg), with liver
salt and freshly ground pepper
3 tablespoons olive oil, plus a few drops
1 slice lean salt pork (green bacon), about ¼ lb (125 g), cut into
   lardoons (see glossary)
1 large onion, coarsely chopped
3 cloves garlic, crushed
3 tablespoons all-purpose (plain) flour
¼ cup (2 fl oz/60 ml) marc de Provence (see glossary) or Cognac
2 cups (16 fl oz/500 ml) dry white wine
boiling broth or water (as needed)
bouquet garni (see glossary)
1 lb (500 g) small new potatoes, peeled

❖ Cut the rabbit into 8 pieces: 2 forelegs; 2 hind legs; the saddle cut in two, kidneys left attached; and rib cage split in two.
❖ Season the rabbit pieces with salt and pepper. Warm the 3 tablespoons olive oil in a large sauté pan over medium heat. Add the rabbit pieces and tuck the lardoons into the empty spaces. Turn the lardoons regularly, either by shaking the pan or by flipping them over with a knife tip or a fork. When the rabbit pieces are all colored on one side and turned, after about 20–30 minutes, add the onion. Displace the contents of the pan by pushing, nudging and stirring with a wooden spoon until the onion is softened and beginning to color, about 10 minutes.
❖ Add the garlic, sprinkle the flour evenly over the top and turn the rabbit pieces over. Continue to move and displace everything for a couple of minutes, then pour over the brandy.
❖ Turn, stir and scrape the pan bottom. If it flames, keep stirring. Pour over the wine and continue to stir and scrape until it comes to a boil. Tuck the bouquet garni into the middle and pour over enough broth or water to immerse the rabbit pieces. Cover and simmer at very low heat for 45 minutes. After 15 minutes, add the potatoes, one by one, here and there, making certain they are completely immersed in the sauce.
❖ A minute before serving, remove any visible fat from the sauce's surface. Cut the liver into small pieces and sauté it for a few seconds in a few drops of olive oil. Scatter the pieces over the surface of the dish. Serve directly from the sauté pan.

SERVES 4   *Photograph pages 370–371*

Sunset vista from Bonnieux, from left to right: Vaucluse-style Chicken, Chicken Pilaf

BROCHETTES D'ABATS
Brochettes of Mixed Meats

In the south of France, the word brochette, *unless qualified, means a skewer of mixed lamb offal. Some cooks like to include cubes of tender meat from the leg or the loin. Whatever the mixture, everyone adores it. It is practical to skewer the meats an hour or so ahead of time and leave them to marinate at room temperature. Saffron-flavored pilaf and Provençal baked tomatoes (recipe on page 427) are typical and ideal accompaniments.*

2 slices lean salt pork (green bacon), about ¼ lb (125 g) and
    ½ in (12 mm) thick, cut into lardoons (see glossary)
large pinch of coarse salt
freshly ground pepper
pinch of Provençal mixed dried herbs (see glossary)
2 cloves garlic
2 tablespoons olive oil
2 lamb hearts, trimmed of fat and arterial tubes, quartered
    lengthwise and then each quarter halved crosswise
2 veal kidneys, halved lengthwise, trimmed of fat and then
    each half cut into ¾-in (2-cm) pieces
fresh rosemary, optional

◈ Place the lardoons in a saucepan and add water to cover. Bring to a boil, drain and refresh under cold running water. Drain again and pat dry with paper towels; set aside.
◈ In a mortar pound together the coarse salt and freshly ground pepper, herbs and garlic to form a paste. Stir in the olive oil with the pestle and empty the mortar into a large mixing bowl. Wipe out the mortar with a handful of meat pieces. Add

them to the mixing bowl, along with all the other meat pieces. Turn the mixture all around with your hands, until meat and marinade are intimately intermingled.
◈ Count your pieces ahead of time to portion them equally among the skewers. You will have 4 heart pieces, probably 5 lardoons and 6 or 7 kidney pieces per skewer. Thread them onto the skewers, more or less alternately, touching but not packed. Lay them on a platter or a tray, pour over any marinade left in the bowl and hold until the fire is ready.
◈ Prepare a fire in a charcoal grill. Place the skewers on the grill rack over glowing coals and grill, turning every couple of minutes, for 8–10 minutes. If fresh rosemary is available, throw a handful of leaves or a couple of branches onto the coals a few seconds before removing the brochettes (do not use dried rosemary—it will blaze up instead of smoking).

SERVES 4

PINTADE AUX CHOUX
Guinea Fowl with Cabbage

The classic is partridge with cabbage. Guinea fowl replaces partridge out of the game season. Old pheasants are treated in the same way. For the poaching sausage, select a pork sausage, coarsely ground and well-seasoned but not smoked.

1 large savoy cabbage
salted boiling water as needed
1 guinea fowl, about 3 lb (1.5 kg), trussed
1 tablespoon olive oil
salt and freshly ground pepper
2 slices lean salt pork (green bacon), about ¼ lb (125 g) each
2 large onions, coarsely chopped
¼ cup (2 fl oz/60 ml) dry white wine
1 poaching sausage, ½ lb (250 g), pricked in several places
large bouquet garni (see glossary)
½ lb (250 g) carrots, peeled and cut into slices ¾ in (2 cm)
    thick
about 2 cups (16 fl oz/500 ml) broth, boiling

◈ Preheat an oven to 450°F (230°C). Remove and discard the dark green, outer leaves from the cabbage. Quarter the cabbage vertically and cut out the core from each quarter. Trim off visible thick ribs and then coarsely shred the quarters. Pack them into a large saucepan and pour in salted boiling water to cover. Cook at a gentle boil for 10 minutes. Drain into a colander, refresh the cabbage beneath cold running water and then squeeze to extract as much liquid as possible.
◈ Rub the guinea fowl with the olive oil and sprinkle all over with salt and pepper. Put into a Dutch oven or other oval roasting dish, breast side up. Place in the oven and roast for 20 minutes. Remove from the oven and reduce the oven temperature to 300°F (150°C).
◈ Meanwhile, place the salt pork in a saucepan and add water to cover. Bring to a boil over high heat and drain. Rinse under cold running water and drain again; set aside.
◈ In the bottom of a heavy oval pot, scatter a handful of the parboiled cabbage and all of the onions. Place the guinea fowl on top, breast side up. Place its roasting pan on the stove top over high heat. Pour in the wine and deglaze the pan by scraping the pan bottom with a wooden spoon until all the browned bits dissolve. Pour the deglazed juices over the bird. Tuck a slice of salt pork alongside each side of the bird. Place the poaching sausage along one side and the bouquet garni along the other. Scatter the carrots around the bird. Cover everything with the remaining cabbage, pressing it into place, and pour over just enough boiling broth to cover barely.
◈ Cover and place in the oven until the bird is very tender, about 2 hours. The bird will have given most of its goodness to the cabbage, but that is what is wanted. Remove the sausage

Guinea Fowl with Cabbage

Left to right: Brochettes of Mixed Meats, Provençal Quail Pilaf

and salt pork after the first hour, then put them back in to warm up 10 minutes before removing the pan from the oven.

▣ Put the bird on one plate and the sausage and salt pork on another; keep warm. Place a large sieve over a large saucepan and pour the cabbage and juices into it. Mound the cabbage in the center of a warmed platter. Put the saucepan over high heat and boil to reduce the juices to ½–⅔ cup (4–5 fl oz/125–150 ml).

▣ Using poultry shears cut the bird into quarters; discard the trussing strings. Slice the sausage thickly and cut the salt pork slices in half; distribute around and on top of the cabbage. Pour the reduced juices over the top.

SERVES 4

PROVENCE

CAILLES AU RIZ À LA PROVENÇALE

Provençal Quail Pilaf

4 quail
4 tablespoons (2 fl oz/60 ml) olive oil
1 onion, finely chopped
1½ cups (8 oz/250 g) long-grain white rice
small pinch of Provençal mixed dried herbs (see glossary)
1 bay leaf

salt
3 cups (24 fl oz/750 ml) broth, boiling
freshly ground pepper
½ cup (4 fl oz/125 ml) dry white wine
¼ cup (2 fl oz/60 ml) tomato sauce (see glossary)

▣ Using poultry shears, split each quail down the back. Open the birds out flat, skin side up, and flatten them with your hand. Set aside.

▣ Warm 1 tablespoon of olive oil in a flameproof earthenware casserole or heavy sauté pan over low heat. Add the onion and sauté gently until softened, about 10 minutes. Add the rice, mixed herbs and bay, salt lightly and stir with a wooden spoon until the rice turns milky and opaque, about 5 minutes. Pour in the boiling broth, stir once, cover tightly and cook over very low heat for 25 minutes.

▣ As soon as the rice is covered, heat the remaining 3 tablespoons olive oil in a sauté pan over medium heat. Season the quail with salt and pepper and place in the pan. Cook, turning once, until nicely colored, 5–6 minutes on each side.

▣ Place the quail on top of the cooking rice and cover tightly again. Place the sauté pan over high heat. Pour in the wine and deglaze the pan by scraping the pan bottom until all browned bits dissolve. Boil until reduced by half, then stir in the tomato sauce and simmer for a couple of minutes.

▣ When the rice and quail are ready, pour the sauce over the quail. Serve directly from the pan.

SERVES 4

Clockwise from top left: Gratin of Pork and Beans, Pork and Red Wine Stew, Pork Cutlets with Tapénade

V A R

CIVET DE PORCELET

Pork and Red Wine Stew

A civet, strictly speaking, is a meat stew, the sauce of which is thickened at the last minute with the animal's blood. Civet de porcelet, which is a popular specialty in Provençal country auberges, is usually a simple pork and red wine stew. If you are able to obtain pork blood, mix ½ cup (4 fl oz/125 ml) of the blood with the anchovy-garlic mixture in the following recipe, stir some of the sauce into it and, off the heat, stir it into the stew. Stir over low heat until the bright red color of the blood turns chocolate brown; it must not boil or the sauce will break.

2 lb (1 kg) boneless pork shoulder butt or blade, cut into
    2-in (5-cm) pieces
3 cups (24 fl oz/750 ml) dry red wine
4 tablespoons (2 fl oz/60 ml) olive oil
pinch of Provençal mixed dried herbs (see glossary)

1 slice lean salt pork (green bacon), ¼ lb (125 g), cut into
    lardoons (see glossary)
fine salt
½ lb (250 g) yellow onions, coarsely chopped
2 tablespoons all-purpose (plain) flour
4 tablespoons marc de Provence (see Glossary) or Cognac
1 bay leaf
1 fresh sage sprig
½ lb (250 g) pickling onions
1 teaspoon unsalted butter
pinch of sugar
⅔ cup (3 oz/100 g) black olives
pinch of coarse salt
freshly ground pepper
1 clove garlic
2 salt anchovies, rinsed and filleted (see glossary)

▓ In a bowl combine the meat, wine, 1 tablespoon of the olive oil and the herbs. Mix well and marinate in the refrigerator several hours or overnight.

402

◩ Drain and dry the meat pieces. Warm 2 tablespoons of the olive oil in a heavy sauté pan over medium-low heat. Add the lardoons and sauté until lightly colored but not crisp, about 10 minutes. Remove to a plate. Add the meat pieces to the same pan. Season to taste with fine salt and brown over medium heat. When the pieces are turned to brown the second side, add the yellow onions. Sauté until the onions are lightly colored, about 10 minutes. Add the flour, stir around for a couple of minutes, then add the brandy and marinade. Raise the heat and deglaze the pan, scraping the pan bottom with a wooden spoon until all the browned bits dissolve. Add the bay leaf and sage and bring to a boil. Reduce the heat to low, cover and simmer and cook until the meat is tender, about 1½ hours.

◩ Meanwhile, in a small saucepan combine the pickling onions, butter, sugar, a pinch of fine salt and enough water almost to cover the onions. Bring to a boil, cover and simmer over low heat for 8 minutes. Remove the lid, raise the heat and cook until the liquid evaporates and the onions begin to color. Put them aside with the lardoons.

◩ Remove the pieces of meat from the sauce and discard the bay leaf and sage. Empty the sauté pan into a sieve placed over a bowl to catch the liquid. Put the meat back into the sauté pan and add the lardoons, pickling onions and olives. Cover and set aside. Pass the sauce through the sieve, puréeing the onions. Pour the sauce into a small saucepan, bring to a boil and move half off the heat. Adjust to a light boil on half the surface and allow a skin of fat to form on the still surface. Pull the skin to the side of the pan with a spoon and remove it; repeat until no more fat appears.

◩ Pour the sauce over the meat, onions and olives. Return the sauté pan to low heat, cover and simmer gently for 15 minutes.

◩ In a mortar pound together the coarse salt, pepper to taste, garlic and anchovies to form a paste. Stir in the remaining 1 tablespoon olive oil. Stir the garlic mixture into the stew and serve.

SERVES 4

VAUCLUSE

TIAN DE HARICOTS
Gratin of Pork and Beans

If fresh white shell beans (cocos; see glossary) are available, substitute 4 lb (2 kg) shell beans in their pods for the dried beans. Cook them in salted boiling water, with the same aromatic elements, for 30–40 minutes before joining them to the meat.

1¾ cups (¾ lb/350 g) small dried white beans such as Great Northerns
1 carrot, peeled
1 onion stuck with 2 whole cloves, plus 1 large onion, thinly sliced
bouquet garni including 1 fresh sage sprig (see glossary)
boiling water as needed
salt
2 teaspoons olive oil
¼ lb (125 g) lean salt pork (green bacon), diced
1½ lb (750 g) boneless pork shoulder butt or blade
freshly ground pepper
2 tomatoes, peeled, seeded and coarsely chopped

◩ Place the beans in a large bowl. Add water to cover and let stand for several hours or as long as overnight. Drain the beans, empty them into a large saucepan and add cold water to cover abundantly. Bring to a boil and boil gently for 10 minutes. Drain the beans, return them to the saucepan and add the carrot, onion stuck with cloves and the bouquet garni. Pour over boiling water to cover by about 1 in (2.5 cm). Bring to a boil, reduce the heat to low, cover and simmer until nearly but not quite done, about 45 minutes. Season to taste with salt.

◩ Meanwhile, warm the olive oil and salt pork in a heavy saucepan over medium heat. Season the pork shoulder or blade with salt and pepper and add it to the pan. Color the meat on all sides, about 20 minutes. Add the sliced onion and continue to cook, stirring and turning the meat, until the onion is lightly colored, about 10 minutes. Add the tomatoes, raise the heat and cook until they begin to fall apart and boil, 5–10 minutes. Reduce the heat to low, cover and simmer until the beans are ready.

◩ Preheat an oven to 350°F (180°C). Transfer the meat to a large, deep oven dish, preferably earthenware. Drain the beans, reserving their liquid. Remove and discard the carrot, the onion stuck with cloves and the bouquet garni. Add the beans and about 1 cup (8 fl oz/250 ml) of their liquid to the sauce in the saucepan, stirring and pouring around the piece of pork. Add enough additional beans' cooking liquid to immerse all the ingredients. Put the dish in the oven and, as soon as the surface is bubbling, reduce the oven temperature to 300°F (150°C). Stir the beans a bit every 20 minutes or so, immersing the skin that forms on the surface. Add more cooking liquid from time to time; the beans should never dry out. Bake until beans are tender, about 1½ hours.

SERVES 4

PROVENCE

ESCALOPES DE PORC À LA TAPÉNADE
Pork Cutlets with Tapénade

Because they take up so much space, breaded cutlets for more than two servings must be prepared either in relays or in two large frying pans at the same time.

4 pork loin cutlets, each about ⅓ in (8 mm) thick
salt and freshly ground pepper
4 tablespoons (3 oz/90 g) *tapénade* (recipe on page 288)
½ cup (2 oz/60 g) freshly grated Parmesan cheese
2 eggs
½ teaspoon olive oil
semidried bread crumbs
peanut oil or corn oil for frying
1 lemon, quartered

◩ Press the cutlets firmly with the side of a large knife blade to flatten them slightly. Sprinkle on both sides with salt and pepper. Spread 1 tablespoon *tapénade* on one side of each cutlet. Cover and chill to firm up the *tapénade*.

◩ Assemble side by side: a plate spread with half the grated cheese; a soup plate in which the eggs, olive oil and a few drops of water have been beaten with a fork; and an opened newspaper spread abundantly with bread crumbs. Place a cutlet, *tapénade* side up, on the bed of Parmesan. Sprinkle some of the remaining Parmesan on top, pressing it in lightly with the palm of your hand. Transfer the cutlet to the beaten eggs, spoon some of the egg over the top and lift the cutlet rapidly to the bread crumbs. Sprinkle crumbs generously over the top and press on gently. Repeat with the remaining cutlets and leave the cutlets on the bed of crumbs to dry for 1 hour or so before frying.

◩ In a large frying pan over high heat, pour in oil to a depth of ½ in (12 mm). Slip in the cutlets and turn down the heat to medium or medium-low if necessary to prevent the cutlets from browning too rapidly. When they are golden around the edges, turn them by piercing, near the edge of the cutlet, with a single tine of a long-handled, two-pronged fork. When both sides are golden and crisp, after about 8 minutes, use a spatula to transfer them to paper towels to drain. Serve accompanied with the lemon quarters.

SERVES 2

POULET AUX ANCHOIS

Roast Chicken with Anchovies

This is adapted from Le cuisinier méridional *(1855). The original recipe is for a spit-roasted bird turned before open flames.*

FOR THE STUFFING:

2 oz (60 g) lean salt pork (green bacon), finely chopped
3 salt anchovies, rinsed, filleted and finely chopped (see glossary)
1 oz (30 g) *brousse* (see glossary) or ricotta cheese
3 tablespoons finely chopped fresh flat-leaf (Italian) parsley
3 tablespoons finely chopped shallots
freshly ground pepper

1 chicken, about 3 lb (1.5 kg)
1 tablespoon olive oil
salt and freshly ground pepper

❋ Combine all the ingredients for the stuffing in a bowl. Using a fork mash together very thoroughly.

❋ To make the eventual carving of the bird easier, remove the wishbone: Carefully pull the neck skin over the breast to expose the flesh. With a small knife tip, slit the flesh against the contours of the wishbone, freeing the vertex at its attachment to the breastbone. Hook your finger at the angle of the bone and pull it loose from its attachment at the wing joints.

❋ Preheat an oven to 450°F (230°C). Using your fingertips and starting at the neck, gradually loosen the skin from the breasts and the legs, being careful not to tear it. With one hand, introduce the stuffing, small quantities at a time, between the skin and the flesh, distributing and molding it from outside with the other hand. Truss the chicken with kitchen string. Rub it with the olive oil and sprinkle with salt and then grind over some pepper.

❋ Place the bird in a roasting pan, breast side up, and roast for about 10 minutes. Reduce the oven temperature to 350°F (180°C) and continue to roast, without turning, until the juices

salt and freshly ground pepper
all-purpose (plain) flour
¼ cup (2 fl oz/60 ml) olive oil
1 small onion, finely chopped
½ cup (4 fl oz/125 ml) dry white wine
1½ lb (750 g) tomatoes, peeled, seeded and coarsely chopped
persillade made with 1 clove garlic (see glossary)
⅔ cup (3 oz/100 g) black olives
fresh basil leaves

◙ Season the chicken pieces with salt and pepper, then coat with flour, shaking off any excess. In a large sauté pan over medium heat, warm the olive oil. Put all the pieces in the pan except the breasts. Sauté, turning the pieces, for 10 minutes. Add the breasts and sauté until all the pieces are nicely colored on both sides, about 10 minutes longer. Reduce the heat to low, cover and cook for 10 minutes.

◙ Transfer the chicken pieces to a warmed platter; keep warm. Add the onion to the pan and stir it around with a wooden spoon. When it begins to color, pour in the wine. Raise the heat to high and deglaze the pan, scraping the pan bottom with a wooden spoon until the browned bits dissolve and the wine is almost completely reduced. Add the tomatoes and salt to taste and continue to cook over high heat, shaking the pan and stirring, until their excess liquid evaporates. A couple of minutes before removing from the heat, add the *persillade* and olives.

◙ Just before serving, tear some basil leaves into small fragments and stir them into the sauce. Pour the sauce over the chicken pieces and serve.

SERVES 4

POULET GRILLÉ AUX HERBES DE PROVENCE

Chicken Grilled with Provençal Herbs

Young guinea fowl, pigeons (squabs) and quail are prepared in the same way. Guinea fowl requires the same cooking time as chicken; pigeons are done in 15–18 minutes and quail in 12–15 minutes.

1 frying chicken, about 3 lb (1.5 kg)
pinch of Provençal mixed dried herbs (see glossary)
salt and freshly ground pepper
1 tablespoon olive oil

◙ Cut off the wing tips from the chicken at the second joint. Using poultry shears, split the back, from tail to neck, cutting along one side of the neck. Cut along the other side of the neck to remove the neck and a section of the spine to the mid-back. Open the chicken out, skin side facing up. Press hard on the breastbone to fracture it and the rib-cage structure. Turn the chicken over and pull out the breastbone. Turn it over once again, skin side up. Using a small knife tip, pierce the skin of the abdomen between the thigh and the tip of the breast, to each side, and force the drumstick up to push its tip through the slit to the underside.

◙ Prepare a fire in a charcoal grill and position the grill rack about 4 in (10 cm) from the coals. Season the chicken with the herbs and salt and pepper to taste and rub all the surfaces with the olive oil. Place on the grill rack and grill for about 35 minutes, turning several times. When the skin side is facing the coals, watch it carefully as the skin chars easily and rapidly. Most of the grilling, once the skin is golden brown, should be done skin facing up.

◙ Present the bird on a carving board. To carve the chicken, split it the length of the breast and slit the skin from around the thighs to the back. It will fall into quarters.

SERVES 4

Clockwise from top: Roast Chicken with Anchovies, Provençal Sautéed Chicken, Chicken Grilled with Provençal Herbs

run clear when pierced at the thigh joint, about 40 minutes. Baste the bird with the pan juices two or three times during the last 30 minutes of roasting. Carve at table.

SERVES 4

POULET SAUTÉ À LA PROVENÇALE

Provençal Sautéed Chicken

Chicken sautéed with tomatoes is a recurrent theme in Provençale cuisine. Often the chicken is sautéed more briefly and finishes cooking in the tomato sauce.

1 frying chicken, about 3 lb (1.5 kg), cut into serving pieces

FARCI BOUILLI
Poached Stuffed Breast of Veal

This first stuffing is a simplified adaptation of a recipe by Charles Durand. He recommends the addition of chopped truffles and writes that it can be used to stuff all kinds of poultry or breasts of veal or lamb, poached or braised. Remove the marrow from the sawed sections of marrow bone using a knife tip. Each recipe makes enough stuffing for a 3 lb (1.5 kg) veal breast.

STUFFING 1

½ lb (250 g) each spinach, Swiss chard (silverbeet) greens
   and sorrel leaves, stemmed and finely chopped
5 oz (150 g) veal, chopped
¼ lb (125 g) lean salt pork (green bacon), chopped
3 oz (100 g) raw beef marrow (see glossary)
pinch of coarse salt
2 cloves garlic
handful of chopped fresh flat-leaf (Italian) parsley
1 teaspoon finely chopped fresh tarragon
2½ cups (5 oz/150 g) fresh bread crumbs
3 oz (100 g) shank end of raw ham such as prosciutto, cut
   into ⅛-in (3-mm) dice
1 slice pork back fat, 2 oz (60 g), cut into narrow strips and
   then diced
3 eggs
salt, freshly ground pepper, ground allspice and freshly
   scraped nutmeg

◙ Layer the chopped spinach, chard and sorrel leaves together in a bowl, salting the layers well. Let stand for 30 minutes. Squeeze the leaves dry and set aside.
◙ Combine the veal, salt pork and marrow in a food processor fitted with the metal blade and process to a purée. Set aside.
◙ In a mortar pound together the coarse salt and garlic to form a paste. Mix in the parsley, tarragon and bread crumbs.
◙ In a mixing bowl combine all the ingredients, including salt, pepper, allspice and nutmeg to taste. Using your hands mix thoroughly until the mass is absolutely homogenous.

STUFFING 2

Trimmed and finely sliced young artichokes are often added to this typical stuffing from Nice. In season, tender, peeled broad (fava) beans can replace or be added to the peas. Sometimes, shelled hard-cooked eggs, tips removed, are placed end to end at the heart of the stuffing so that each slice contains a round of yellow and white at its center.

½ lb (250 g) sausage meat (see glossary)
½ lb (250 g) ground veal
1 lb (500 g) Swiss chard (silverbeet) greens, parboiled,
   squeezed dry and chopped (see glossary)
¼ cup (3 oz/90 g) long-grain white rice, parboiled for
   15 minutes, drained and rinsed
1 large handful of shelled small green peas
   (about 1 lb/500 g unshelled)
persillade made with 1 clove garlic (see glossary)
½ cup (2 oz/60 g) freshly grated Parmesan cheese
pinch of Provençal mixed dried herbs (see glossary)
2 eggs
salt and freshly ground pepper

◙ Assemble all the ingredients, including salt and pepper to taste, in a mixing bowl. Using your hands mix thoroughly until all the elements are evenly incorporated.

FOR THE VEAL:

To ready a breast of veal for stuffing, slice the ribs and backbone section free of the flesh. Using your fingertips and a knife tip, open the two layers of muscle separated by a fatty membrane. (If you like, ask your butcher to prepare the breast for stuffing.) Stuff the pouch loosely with stuffing, fold the flaps over to enclose it and sew together with looped stitches at intervals of 1–1½ in (2.5–4 cm).

A poached stuffed breast of veal can be treated in the same way as a pot-au-feu: the broth served as a first course, poured over crusts of bread, with grated cheese on the side. In this case, ⅛ teaspoon powdered saffron enhances the soup. Often the broth is reserved for another use and a tomato sauce accompanies the poached breast. Or the stuffed breast is removed from its broth, cooled completely, cut into thin slices and served cold with tapénade *(recipe on page 288)*

1 veal breast, 3 lb (1.5 kg), stuffed with stuffing of choice
   (preceding recipes)
2 whole cloves
2 onions
3 carrots, peeled and cut into sections
3 cloves garlic, crushed
bouquet garni (see glossary)
handful of coarse sea salt

◙ Place the stuffed breast in a heavy oval pot. Stick the cloves into 1 of the onions. Surround the breast with the onions, carrots, garlic and bouquet garni. Pour in water to cover and add the salt. Bring slowly to a boil and skim off any scum and froth. Adjust the heat to maintain a gentle simmer and cover with the lid slightly ajar. Simmer for 2 hours.
◙ Clip and remove the strings before serving, either hot or cold.

SERVES 6

BOEUF MIRONTON À LA PROVENÇALE
Beef in Onion Sauce

Mironton (or miroton) is a great classic, a symbol of fulfilling, rustic, family food. Sometimes a few filleted salt anchovies are mashed and added to the sauce.

4 tablespoons olive oil
10 oz (300 g) onions, finely sliced
2 tablespoons all-purpose (plain) flour
2 cups (16 fl oz/500 ml) *pot-au-feu* broth (recipe on page 45)
2 tablespoons Provençal herb vinegar (see glossary)
persillade made with 1 clove garlic (see glossary)
1 bay leaf
1 fresh thyme sprig
salt
1 lb (500 g) *pot-au-feu* beef, chilled and thinly sliced
   (recipe on page 299)
1 tablespoon capers, rinsed
freshly ground pepper
dried bread crumbs

◙ Warm 3 tablespoons of the olive oil in a saucepan over medium-low heat. Add the onions and cook, stirring, until lightly colored, about 10 minutes. Add the flour and cook, stirring, for 1 minute. Add the broth and vinegar, stirring. Add the *persillade,* bay leaf and thyme and bring to a boil, stirring. Adjust the heat to low and simmer for 20 minutes. Season to taste with salt.
◙ Preheat an oven to 350°F (180°C). Layer half of the beef slices, overlapping, in a gratin dish. Grind some pepper, scatter some capers and pour some sauce over the top. Repeat the layers, ending with sauce. Sprinkle with crumbs and dribble the remaining tablespoon of oil in a thin thread back and forth over the top. Put into the oven and bake until the sauce is bubbling and the surface is lightly browned, 15–20 minutes.

SERVES 4

Top to bottom: Beef in Onion Sauce, Poached Stuffed Breast of Veal

VAR

PAQUETS DE LAPIN AU FOUR
Roast Rabbit Packages

The upper part of a rabbit doesn't lend itself to this preparation; save it for a stew. Any potato gratin is a good accompaniment.

2 hind legs and the saddle, cut in half, of 1 rabbit
1 tablespoon olive oil
4 fresh winter savory sprigs
2 bay leaves
2 cloves garlic, crushed
freshly ground pepper
½ lemon
salt
about ½ oz (15 g) caul, soaked briefly in tepid water with a
    dash of wine vinegar and drained (see glossary)

◈ In a bowl combine the rabbit pieces, olive oil, savory, bay and garlic. Grind over some pepper, squeeze over a few drops of lemon juice and toss with your hands. Marinate at room temperature for 1 hour or so, turning everything around a couple of times.

◈ Preheat an oven to 400°F (200°C). Discard the bay leaves and garlic. Salt the rabbit pieces and press a sprig of savory onto each. Lay the caul out flat on a work surface. Cut it into 4 squares, each measuring 6–8 in (15–20 cm). Wrap a piece of rabbit with its savory sprig in each caul square.

◈ Place a small wire rack in the bottom of a shallow oven dish. Place the rabbit packages on top, pleat side of the caul facing down. Roast until the caul has melted and browned into a lovely lacework, 20–25 minutes.

SERVES 4

PROVENCE

POULET AUX QUARANTE GOUSSES D'AIL
Chicken with 40 Cloves of Garlic

A classic, Provençal method for preparing roast chicken.

1 roasting chicken, about 4 lb (2 kg), cut into serving pieces
    with thighs and legs separated
salt and freshly ground pepper
½ lb (250 g) cloves firm, crisp garlic, unpeeled
2 bay leaves or 2 or 3 fresh thyme sprigs
1 fresh savory sprig
½ cup (4 fl oz/125 ml) olive oil
large bouquet garni (see glossary)

◈ Season the chicken pieces to taste with salt and pepper. Put them in a mixing bowl with the garlic, loose herbs and olive oil. Using your hands mix well. Cover and leave to marinate at room temperature for 1–2 hours.

◈ Preheat an oven to 300°F (150°C). Discard the herbs from the marinade (or incorporate them into the bouquet garni). Place the bouquet garni in the middle of an ovenproof earthenware casserole. Arrange the chicken pieces and garlic cloves around the bouquet, neither packed nor with wasted space. Empty over any remaining oil from the marinade, cover tightly (if the lid is not tight fitting, first place a sheet of heavy aluminum foil over the casserole before pressing the lid in place) and bake until the chicken is tender, about 1¾ hours.

◈ Serve directly from the casserole.

SERVES 6

Roast Rabbit Packages

In Lourmarin, Vaucluse, Chicken with 40 Cloves of Garlic

PROVENCE

RIS DE VEAU BRAISÉS AUX ARTICHAUTS

Veal Sweetbreads Braised with Artichokes

Sweetbreads should be plump and full in appearance, white, with a slight pink cast, moist and glistening. Whatever the final preparation of the sweetbreads, the preliminary steps are the same. First soak the sweetbreads in repeated changes of cold water for 12–24 hours. Then place them in a large saucepan, cover generously with cold water, bring to a boil over medium-low heat and hold beneath the boil for 15 minutes. Drain, plunge into a basin of cold water and, when cool enough to handle, pull off and discard all visible fat, gristly tubes and membrane. The fine, interior membranes, which hold together the lobular structure, should be left intact.

mirepoix (see glossary)
4 young, tender artichokes, trimmed, quartered and chokes
   removed if necessary (see glossary)

2 lb (1 kg) veal sweetbreads, soaked, boiled and cleaned (see
   recipe introduction)
bouquet garni (see glossary)
salt
¼ cup (2 fl oz/60 ml) dry white wine
freshly ground pepper

▣ Prepare the *mirepoix* in a large, flameproof earthenware casserole or heavy sauté pan. Place the artichokes, sweetbreads and bouquet garni on top and sprinkle with salt. Cover and sweat over very low heat, turning everything over a couple of times, for about 10 minutes.
▣ Sprinkle the wine over the top. Lightly oil one side of a sheet of parchment (kitchen) paper cut to the dimensions of the pan and place over the sweetbreads oiled side down. Cover with a lid and simmer over very low heat for 45 minutes. Turn the sweetbreads and artichokes over halfway through the cooking, and, if moisture is lacking, add a couple spoonfuls of boiling water or white wine.
▣ Serve directly from the pan.

SERVES 4

410

VAUCLUSE

FOIE DE VEAU À LA MOISSONNEUSE

Harvesters' Calf's Liver

Foie à la moissonneuse, *which also often made with lamb's liver, is essentially the same as the Venetian specialty,* fegato di vitello alla veneziana. *It is said to have been a favorite dish of the wheat harvesters in the Vaucluse in the last century.*

5 tablespoons (3 fl oz/80 ml) olive oil
1 lb (500 g) large sweet white onions, halved and sliced paper-thin
1 bay leaf
1 fresh thyme sprig
persillade made with 3 cloves garlic (see glossary)
salt
½ cup (4 fl oz/125 ml) red wine
¾ lb (375 g) calf's liver
freshly ground pepper
all-purpose (plain) flour
2 tablespoons red wine vinegar

▨ Warm 2 tablespoons of the olive oil in a large, flame-proof earthenware casserole or heavy sauté pan over very low heat. Add the onions, bay, thyme, *persillade* and salt to taste. Cover and sweat, stirring a couple of times, for about 45 minutes. At this point, the onions will have cooked in their juices without coloring. Remove the lid, turn up the heat slightly and permit them to color lightly, stirring regularly with a wooden spoon. Add the wine, bring to a boil and simmer, uncovered, over low heat, until reduced to the consistency of a sauce, about 15 minutes. Grind over some pepper.

▨ Cut the liver into slices about ½ in (12 mm) thick, then cut each slice into 1-in (2.5-cm) squares. Season the squares with salt and pepper. Coat them with flour and then toss them in a sieve to rid them of any excess flour.

▨ Warm the remaining 3 tablespoons olive oil in a large sauté pan. Add the liver squares and sauté them, tossing and stirring, until slightly firmed up but still rare, no more than a couple of minutes.

▨ Add the liver pieces to the onion sauce. Pour the vinegar into the sauté pan over high heat. Deglaze the pan by scraping the pan bottom until all the browned bits dissolve. Stir the deglazing juices into the onion sauce and serve.

SERVES 4

Harvesters' Calf's Liver

411

BOUCHES-DU-RHÔNE

BOUCHES-DU-RHÔNE

hen a river meets the sea everything becomes possible. The ancient love story between the Rhône and the Mediterranean seems to have given birth to the multitude of contrasts we find in this peaceful and whimsical *département*. It lies among the dry stones of the Alpilles, the Valley of the Durance, the *étangs* of the Camargue, the luminous Aix country, the mingled beauty and ugliness of Marseilles and the last remaining coves around Cassis.

Marseilles represents a concentration of the most marked features of Mediterranean civilization. The *ville* is open, colorful, secret, excessive and often impossible for the visitor. This is a city that never loses sight of the Provençal traditions without which it would simply be a community like any other, but at the same time the door is always open to influences and flavors filtering in from elsewhere. And the port of Marseilles? "It is the market France offers to the vendors of the vast world," wrote Albert Londres in *Marseille porte du Sud* (Marseilles, Gateway of the South).

It is a matter of both fragrance and color, a characterization epitomized by the local *bouillabaisse. Lou bouiabaisso* means "when this boils, turn down the heat!" This simple dish has more than once lost its soul in third-rate restaurants in the port area and along the coast, and its composition is a subject of debate, not to say war, between purists and heretics. These days in Marseilles it is also the subject of a charter, and we still find it on the

Previous pages: The poppy fields and picturesque mountains outside Aix-en-Provence inspired Picasso to spend his final years here. Left: A fisherman pulls fish from his net in Marseilles, the largest port in the Mediterranean.

The intricately carved cloisters of the Cathedral of Saint-Trophîme in Arles, erected between the twelfth and fourteenth centuries, provide exquisite examples of both Romanesque and Gothic architecture.

family table in a form dictated by the various rock fish brought into port by the little local fishing boats known as *pointus.* It comes flavored, of course, with saffron, which in days gone by was brought from the Orient; sometimes it is accompanied with pasta or even sprinkled with grated cheese and includes among its ingredients a lobster or *muscardins,* those little cuttlefish whose sacs spread ink to make the soup black. There are as many variations as there are moods.

Now we turn to the undeniable king of Marseilles cuisine, who also reigns well beyond these boundaries: on the hills of Aubagne, in the countryside around Aix and alongside the Alpilles, in a magic triangle between Salon-de-Provence, Arles and Saint-Rèmy. Along the little Mediterranean coves known as *calanques* where the blue sea sparkles and in the open country lashed by the mistral, this sun king is called garlic. It flavors every dish, invites itself to every table. You will find it in plaits on the butchers' stalls along the Cours Belzunce, on trestles in little Provence markets, hanging in kitchens within the cook's reach, or a few cloves carefully preserved in the huts along the seashore. Certainly the cuisine of Provence and the cooks of Marseilles have no exclusive rights when it comes to the use of garlic. But this extraordinary plant, which arrived several thousand years ago from Central Asia, is part of the legend and of the landscape in Provence. It can revive the most tasteless of cuisines, and its beneficial properties are legion.

Reinvigorating, diuretic and antiseptic garlic is believed to cure colds, arthritis, cholesterol and melancholy, as well as prolong life. Provençal writer Jean Giono speaks in *Le hussard sur le toit* (The Hussar on the Roof) of this heaven-sent garlic that must be harvested before the peak of the hot season. So it is perfectly normal that the people of Provence should use and abuse this sun king, which has its local capital in Piolenc. Chefs these days offer it on their menus almost reluctantly: It is "sweet garlic" that flavors their dishes, not the robust and formidable variety that, according to the

great cook Curnonski, obliges anyone who has eaten it "to use only indirect speech"!

Thus garlic is omnipresent, in all sorts of ways, in the cuisine of Provence. It is the indispensable companion of spring lamb in the Alpilles, and is immortalized in *aïoli,* the garlic sauce that, according to the poet Frédéric Mistral, heats up the body and bathes the soul in rapture.

Here, in the Bouches-du-Rhône more than in other places happiness is built on very little. On basil, for example, which responds perfectly to olive oil, appearing in a *soupe au pistou* or teaming up with a couple of red mullet happened on from the catch of the day. Or on the sea urchins, so memorably sketched by Raoul Dufy, which are the true fruits of the Mediterranean, to be eaten raw with a drop of lemon juice. *Panisses,* poor man's pancakes made from chick-pea flour, speak of Greek and Roman civilizations. These same chick-peas are preferred eating for traditionalists on Palm Sunday, as a way of remembering the great famines of the fifteenth century. Then there is *pieds et paquets,* a dish of sheep tripe that is part of the culinary heritage of Marseilles, as are *navettes,* elongated boat-shaped cookies for Candlemas, traditionally made from November through Easter.

It may appear as if Marseilles is dictating the rules for a whole *département.* But the Bouches-du-Rhône does not live under the thumb of the city. Marcel Pagnol's Provence also passes through Aubagne, the land of the *santons* (clay figures for the Christmas crib) and the rock-anchored village of Cassis, with its coves, and its white wine pressed from terrace-grown vines. Mistral wrote that "it sparkles like some limpid diamond and tastes of the rosemary, the mist and the myrtle that envelop our hills." Here, too, they have their *bouillabaisse,* or rather, around La Ciotat, their *choupin,* a chunk of bread that fishermen at sea in days of old dipped into a fish bouillon, a sort of ragout seasoned with a few onions and a bit of vinegar.

The Provence of Aix has a totally different style from

that of Marseilles. Here the tone was set in the sixteenth century by middle-class traders, men of influence and magistrates who invested in land and established country houses and mansions that were all front, the better to maintain the secrecy of their affairs. Aix-en-Provence is a city of water; in evoking its fountains the poet Jean Cocteau said of it: "A blind man would think it is raining, but were he able to see into his cane as in a mirror, he would behold the blue fountains singing the glory of Cézanne." It is a city of art and architecture, with its Archbishop's Palace, its grand town houses, its squares and parks with their air of melancholy.

The great impressionist painter Paul Cézanne spent his youth here, walking the paths of the Sainte-Victoire Mountain so dear to the people of Aix, and painting, as did Renoir, the mineral landscape and harsh light of this enchanting mountain. The renowned writer Émile Zola, an unrepentant gourmand, recited poems there as he nibbled *calissons,* the city's famed pastries made from home-grown almonds, preserved melon and fruit syrup, or fished for crayfish.

According to the celebrated nineteenth-century cook Auguste Escoffier, Zola "loved freshly caught sardines seasoned with pepper and salt, sprinkled lightly with olive oil and grilled over vine embers, then arranged on an earthenware plate rubbed with garlic, and coated with a *persillade* made with the local Aix oil. . . . He was also fond of a *blanquette* of milk-fed lamb *à la Provençale* served with saffron noodles, of scrambled eggs with cheese and thinly sliced white Piedmont truffles, of risotto with small birds and black truffles, and of the famous polenta with white truffles that was also dear to the heart of the Emperor Napoleon."

And there are other moods still. There are those of the Camargue, land of many waters, where the stones to build the characteristic farmhouses known as *mas* have come down from the quarries of the Alpilles; where there are ponds and marshes, white horses and black bulls, and an internal sea (the Vaccarès). It is a threatened area with a secret vegetation, a domain of dead wood that tourists seldom attempt to penetrate. For a big celebration in these parts, a bull might be basted with spicy oil and roasted all night on a spit, or perhaps *la gardiano,* a hearty ragoût prepared with shoulder of lamb and potatoes, will be put on to cook.

Here we have the moods of La Crau and its stony spaces, of Salon-de-Provence, where Nostradamus lived and wrote a *Treatise on Preserves and Cosmetic Making,* after the manner of *mères de famille* at the time. It was in Salon where, at the beginning of the century, everyone was something of an olive oil merchant, selling to Parisians and "people from the north" who liked their oil more fresh than fruity (sacrilege!).

The bright sunlight Mistral wrote about is the sun of the Arles and Alpilles region. Its rays are never so pure as in Maillane, the town where Mistral was born, and where he lived in a home named the House of the Lizard. This is the heart of Provence, a place of poetry and the cradle of the Provençal language. Here, as in Fontvieille where the memory of Alphonse Daudet and his famous mill is preserved, in Maussane-les-Alpilles and in the Baux where Van Gogh transformed the olive trees into burning, tortured creatures, the land is harsh, and it is a crazy wind that whistles through the reeds of Vallabrègues bearing legends.

In Arles the wind calms down, and all the world knows that this, the earliest of the Roman colonies, which later became a capital port, a city of sailors, is where the knowing Provence draws on its memories to rediscover its heritage. Here are the Musée Arlaten, repository of regional folklore and costume, the amphitheatre, the cemetery and the walks of the Alyscamps painted by Gauguin. This is a country of golden hues and flame colors that, of course, has its distinguishing culinary features.

The joy of the market garden is present in eggplants (aubergines) *à la boumiano,* the new season's broad (fava) beans, or purslane. We still find the sailors' traditional *fricot,* a stew of beef, onions, oil, anchovies and, of course, garlic simmered together in a clay *toupin.* Garlic is also present in the local Arles sausage. Nothing has been lost, not even the little white vineyard snails that are still enjoyed *à la suçarelle* (noisily sucked out their shells, without the aid of a fork) with onion, tomato, parsley, garlic and anchovies. The goat cheeses, flavored with thyme or bay leaf, are also known by a very Camargue name: *guardians.* And again, these Provençals of the Rhône delta make use of what is at hand in a simple and instinctive cuisine. For fruity wines (especially whites), which express in their own way the joy of being in Provence, they need look no further than the Côteaux des Baux or the Côteaux d'Aix.

The Provençaux are serious about boules, *their sport of choice and will gather in the village square at any opportunity to practice it.*

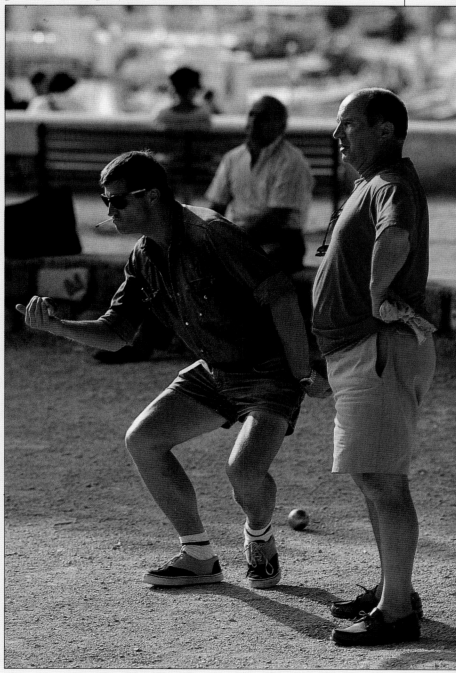

VEGETABLES AND GRAINS

Fresh red peppers and eggplant are basic to many Provençal summer recipes.

VEGETABLES AND GRAINS

Fresh green shallots resemble green onions yet their flavor is more complex and intense.

The several cuisines of Provence and Italy find a philosophical common ground in their treatment of vegetables and grains. Nowhere are these dietary staples treated with greater respect, variety or wit, always with a direct and uncomplicated clarity of flavor and often in similar styles. Not surprisingly, the similarities are most marked in the cooking of Nice, which has been part of France only since 1860. Except for brief occupations by France under Louis XIV and twenty years under the Convention and Napoléon, Nice belonged to the house of Savoy for five centuries and was part of the kingdom of Piedmont and Sardinia. Its history is reflected in its treatment of vegetables and in its affection for pastas, gnocchi, polenta and rice. Only in Nice does a *rizotto* resemble that of Piedmont; elsewhere in Provence, a *rizotto* is a pilaf. Pilaf is dry; *rizotto* is wet.

Many of the preparations in this chapter are equally at home as starters and as garnishes to roasts. In Provence people like to savor single flavors or well-considered combinations of two flavors. Cluttered plates do not exist; a roast takes one garnish. A typical Provençal menu reserves a place apart for a vegetable service, between the first course and the main course. Mixed vegetable stew; any artichoke, eggplant (aubergine), zucchini (courgette) or mushroom preparation; stuffed vegetables; and most gratins are all admirable vegetable entrées. In April a dish of tender broad (fava) beans in *sauce poulette* (white sauce bound with egg yolks and flavored with mushrooms)

Previous pages: A terrace in Solliès-Pont. Clockwise from top left: Braised Artichokes (recipe page 443), Provençal Green Beans (recipe page 437), White Beans with Sausage and Salt Pork (recipe page 450).

The produce stand is often the first stop of the day dictating the direction of an entire menu.

Zucchini blossoms, a summer delicacy, add a splash of sunshine to the vibrant displays of vegetables.

with a pinch of finely chopped spring shoots of savory is exquisite savored alone. In May little peas braised with lettuce and onions are *de rigueur.*

Vegetables never take a back seat. Even as a garnish to a roast, the signature depends on the way the vegetables are treated. Roast beef is no different in Provence than in any other part of the world until it is escorted by an eggplant gratin, Provençal baked tomatoes or garlicky potatoes. Then, it is Provençal roast beef.

At the height of summer, the morning street markets, a riot of vegetable colors undulating in a dapple of light filtered through the shade of plane trees, bring to mind the reflected light of Provence on Renoir's blue and purple eggplant, red and yellow peppers, and tomatoes stroked with green at their stem ends. They spark memories and anticipation of cool wine and relaxed summer lunches shared with friends on vine-covered terraces, of well-being and ritual communion.

ARTICHAUTS FARCIS

Stuffed Artichokes

These stuffed artichokes will be best appreciated as a separate course.

4 large, young artichokes, trimmed (see glossary)
2 oz (60 g) raw ham such as prosciutto, chopped
persillade made with 1 clove garlic (see glossary)
2 oz (60 g) semidry bread, crusts removed, soaked briefly
 in water to cover, squeezed dry and chopped
1 egg
¼ cup (1 oz/30 g) freshly grated Parmesan cheese
salt and freshly ground pepper
4 tablespoons (2 fl oz/60 ml) olive oil
1 onion, chopped
2 tomatoes, peeled, seeded and chopped coarsely
1 bay leaf
1 fresh thyme sprig
½ cup (4 fl oz/125 ml) dry white wine

◉ Preheat an oven to 350°F (180°C).
◉ Fill a large saucepan with water and bring to a boil. Add the trimmed artichokes and boil for 7–8 minutes; drain well.
◉ Using a teaspoon, carefully pry free and pull out the tender leaves from the hearts of the artichokes; reserve. Pry out and discard the chokes. Chop the leaves and add them to a bowl with the ham, *persillade,* bread, egg, cheese and salt and pepper to taste. Mix well and stuff the artichokes, mounding the stuffing and molding the surface with an overturned tablespoon. Set aside.
◉ In a flameproof earthenware casserole or other shallow flameproof vessel of a size to hold the artichokes snugly, warm 2 tablespoons of the olive oil over low heat. Add the onion and cook gently until softened, about 10 minutes.
◉ Spread the tomatoes over the onions and sprinkle with salt to taste. Place the artichokes on top, tuck in the bay leaf and thyme sprig and dribble the remaining 2 tablespoons of olive oil over the surfaces of the artichokes. Pour the wine around the artichokes, cover and bake until tender, about 45 minutes. Remove the cover after 30 minutes to permit the surfaces to color and the pan juices to reduce.

SERVES 4

FÈVES À LA MÉNAGÈRE

Broad Beans in Poulette Sauce

In Provence broad beans are at their best in April, when winter savory is also sending forth its tender new shoots. The two are always allied.

2 tablespoons olive oil
1 onion, finely chopped
4 lb (2 kg) young, tender, thumbnail-sized broad beans
 (favas), shelled and each bean peeled
salt
1 fresh winter savory sprig
3 tablespoons water, boiling
3 egg yolks
2 tablespoons cold water
freshly ground pepper

Stuffed Artichokes

Left to right: Broad Bean Purée, Broad Beans in Poulette Sauce

◼ Warm the olive oil in a flameproof earthenware casserole or other heavy pot over low heat. Add the onion and cook gently until softened, about 10 minutes. Add the beans, savory and salt to taste; cover and cook, shaking the pan regularly, 4–5 minutes. Add the boiling water, cover and shake regularly for a few minutes longer until the beans are heated through.

◼ Combine the egg yolks and cold water in a small bowl and grind over some pepper. Whisk with a fork, then, using a wooden spoon, stir the mixture into the broad beans. Rotate the pan to swirl the contents gently and serve.

SERVES 4

Purée de Fèves

Broad Bean Purée

For a purée, broad beans should be somewhat larger than those prepared in a poulette sauce (see recipe on page 422). They must be quite firm and beginning to turn starchy, but still a bright, clear green color when skinned. Reject any that are beginning to turn yellow. Especially good as an accompaniment to roast lamb or pork.

4 lb (2 kg) large, tender broad (fava) beans, shelled and each bean peeled
1 large onion, coarsely chopped
2 or 3 fresh winter savory sprigs, tied together
salt and freshly ground pepper
½ cup (4 oz/125 g) unsalted butter, diced

◼ Fill a saucepan with salted water and bring to a boil. Add the beans, onion and savory and cook at a gentle boil until the beans are tender enough to purée, 10–15 minutes.

◼ Drain, reserving the cooking liquid; discard the savory and, using a wooden pestle, pass the beans and onion through a fine-mesh sieve back into the pan. Add a little cooking liquid when necessary to ease the passage. If the finished purée seems stiff, loosen it by stirring in more cooking liquid. Taste for salt and grind over a little pepper.

◼ Reheat over medium heat, stirring and beating constantly with a wooden spoon, until heated through. Remove from the heat, beat in the butter, and serve immediately.

SERVES 4

Left to right: Lentils in Red Wine, Lentil Purée with Celery

LENTILLES À LA PROVENÇALE
Lentils in Red Wine

If available, use the small greenish brown–speckled lentils called lentilles du Puy *or* lentilles vertes.

1½ cups (10 oz/300 g) lentils
1 tablespoon olive oil
5 oz (150 g) lean salt pork (green bacon), cut into ½-in (12-mm) dice
1 onion, thinly sliced
bouquet garni (see glossary)
2 cloves garlic
2 cups (16 fl oz/500 ml) broth or water
½ cup (4 fl oz/125 ml) dry red wine
½ cup (4 fl oz/125 ml) tomato sauce (see glossary)
salt and freshly ground pepper

▨ Place the lentils in a bowl and add water to cover. Let stand for several hours.
▨ Warm the olive oil in a large flameproof earthenware casserole or heavy pot over medium-low heat. Add the salt pork and cook until its fat begins to melt. Add the onion and cook, stirring occasionally, until softened and lightly colored, 8–10 minutes. Add the bouquet garni and garlic and pour in the broth or water, wine and tomato sauce. Bring to a boil, cover and reduce the heat to a simmer.
▨ Drain the lentils and put them into a saucepan. Cover generously with cold water and bring to a boil. Drain and empty them into the pan holding the wine mixture. Cover and simmer until the lentils are tender, 45–60 minutes, depending upon the quality and age of the lentils. Add a little boiling water if the lentils begin to dry out.
▨ Taste for salt and grind over some pepper before serving.

SERVES 4

PURÉE DE LENTILLES AU CÉLERI
Lentil Purée with Celery

Especially good as an accompaniment to guinea fowl or to small, furred or feathered game. If possible, use lentilles du Puy *or* lentilles vertes.

1½ cups (10 oz/300 g) lentils
bouquet garni (see glossary)
1 onion stuck with 2 whole cloves
1 carrot, peeled and cut in half
boiling water as needed
salt
¼ cup (2 oz/60 g) unsalted butter, diced
1 heart of celery, crisped in ice water and cut into small dice

▨ Place the lentils in a bowl and add water to cover. Let stand for several hours.
▨ Drain the lentils and put them into a saucepan. Cover generously with cold water and bring to a full boil. Drain and return them to the saucepan. Add the bouquet garni, onion and carrot. Pour in boiling water to cover by about 1 in (2.5 cm), cover and simmer until lentils are purée-tender, about 1 hour. Add salt to taste after 30 minutes.
▨ Drain, reserving the cooking water.
▨ Pass the lentils through a fine-mesh sieve, pressing them with a wooden pestle and adding a little of the cooking water from time to time to help them pass.
▨ Reheat over medium heat, stirring constantly with a wooden spoon. Remove from the heat and stir in the butter and celery. Taste for salt and serve at once.

SERVES 4

OIGNONS FARCIS

Stuffed Onions

As these stuffed onion sheaths cook, the enclosing seam melts and your guests may wonder how it was possible to stuff a seemingly whole, elongated onion without opening it up. A lovely separate course.

4 very large, sweet white onions, about 2 lb (1 kg) total weight, split in half lengthwise

FOR THE STUFFING:

chopped hearts of the parboiled onions
1 lb (500 g) spinach, parboiled, squeezed dry and chopped (see glossary)
½ lb (250 g) *brousse* (see glossary) or ricotta cheese
½ cup (2 oz/60 g) freshly grated Parmesan cheese
2 oz (60 g) raw ham such as prosciutto, chopped
pinch of finely chopped fresh marjoram
2 eggs
whole nutmeg
salt and freshly ground pepper

2 cups tomato sauce, heated (see glossary)
handful of freshly grated Parmesan cheese

◙ Bring a large pot filled with water to a boil and drop in the onions. Cook at a light boil for 20 minutes. Drain the onions and refresh in a basin of cold water.

◙ Drain the onions again and carefully pull them apart, layer after layer. Lay the layers out on towels. Chop the centers, whose sheaths are too small for stuffing, and place them in a mixing bowl. Add all the remaining stuffing ingredients, including a scrape of nutmeg and salt and pepper to taste. Using your hands mix thoroughly.

◙ Preheat an oven to 350°F (180°C). Pour enough of the hot tomato sauce into the bottom of a large gratin dish to form a thin layer. Place a heaping tablespoonful of stuffing on each of the onion layers, roll up and place them, seam sides down, in the gratin dish. They should be arranged side by side and touching but not packed too tightly. Pour over the remaining hot tomato sauce; the stuffed onions should be not quite immersed. Cover the dish loosely with aluminum foil, place in the oven and bake for 30 minutes.

◙ Remove the foil, sprinkle with cheese and bake until the onion rolls are tender and the sauce is bubbling, 15–20 minutes longer. Serve at once.

SERVES 4

Preheat an oven to 375°F (190°F). Salt the drained tomato halves again and grind over some pepper. Heat 3 tablespoons of the olive oil in a large frying pan over high heat. Add the tomato halves, cut side down, and fry until the liquid they give off evaporates and the pan contains a slightly caramelized residue. Reduce the heat, turn the tomatoes over and cook gently on the skin sides for a few minutes, shaking the pan to keep them from sticking.

Arrange the tomato halves, cut sides up, in a gratin dish just large enough to accommodate them. Return the frying pan to high heat, throw in the *persillade* and stir it around for a few seconds. Remove from the heat and add a large pinch of bread crumbs—enough to absorb the oil and juices from the pan. With a teaspoon, evenly distribute the *persillade*-crumb mixture among the tomato halves, gently forcing it into the seed pockets. Sprinkle crumbs over the surfaces and dribble evenly with the remaining 1 tablespoon olive oil.

Place in the oven and bake until the tomatoes have shrunken a little and the tops are browned, 10–15 minutes. The tomatoes will be fragile, so serve with a spatula.

SERVES 4

V A U C L U S E / B O U C H E S · D U · R H Ô N E

CHAMPIGNONS À LA BÉRIGOULE

Mushrooms Durand

In his seminal work on Provençal cookery, Charles Durand proposed this recipe for oronges *(Caesar's mushrooms,* Amanita caesarea*), which, in fact, are never better than when anointed with olive oil, seasoned with salt and pepper and grilled. The following preparation is best adapted to cultivated mushrooms.*

1 lb (500 g) large, firm, unopened fresh cultivated
    mushrooms, stem ends trimmed
2 cloves garlic
pinch of coarse salt
3 tablespoons olive oil
½ cup (4 fl oz/125 ml) dry white wine
salt
freshly ground pepper
2 tablespoons chopped fresh flat-leaf (Italian) parsley
2 salt anchovies, rinsed, filleted and chopped (see glossary)
dried bread crumbs

Gently force the stem of each mushroom, from one side, then from another, until it breaks off at the point where it joins the cap. Chop the stems.

In a mortar pound together the garlic and coarse salt to form a paste. Rub a little garlic paste inside each mushroom cap where the stem was broken off. Put the caps and chopped stems in a saucepan. Add 2 tablespoons of the olive oil, the wine and a pinch of salt. Bring to a boil over high heat, cover and simmer for 15 minutes, turning the mushroom caps over a couple of times.

Meanwhile, preheat an oven to 450°F (230°C). Transfer the mushroom caps to a gratin dish just large enough to accommodate them, hollow sides up and lightly touching. Grind over some pepper. Add the parsley and anchovies to the chopped stems and the juices in the saucepan and cook, uncovered, at a gentle boil until very little liquid remains. Spoon the mixture into the mushroom caps, sprinkle with the dried bread crumbs and dribble a few drops of the remaining olive oil over each cap.

Place in the oven until the crumbs have browned and the mushrooms are piping hot, about 10 minutes. Serve at once.

SERVES 4

In Bonnieux, Vaucluse, from left to right: Stuffed Onions, Provençal Tomatoes, Mushrooms Durand

V A R

TOMATES À LA PROVENÇALE

Provençal Tomatoes

Throughout Provence this is a beloved dish. In summer it appears at many tables daily, served separately or as a garnish to roast and grilled meats or poultry. There are slight variations: sometimes the bread is fresh, soaked, squeezed and chopped; sometimes the persillade *is not fried. This is the Toulonnaise version.*

8 firm, garden-ripe tomatoes
salt and freshly ground pepper
4 tablespoons olive oil
persillade made with 4 cloves garlic (see glossary)
semidried bread crumbs

Cut the tomatoes in half horizontally, to expose cross sections of the seed pockets. With your little finger, loosen the seeds in each pocket and give the tomato half an abrupt upside-down shake to empty it without damaging the flesh. Sprinkle the cut surfaces with salt and place the halves, cut surface down, on a wire rack for 30 minutes to drain.

GNOCCHI AUX POMMES DE TERRE

Potato Gnocchi

Potato gnocchi are often served with the braising juices from a daube or estouffade (recipe on page 290) or with tomato sauce (see glossary). They are also delicious served with pistou (recipe on page 393).

2 lb (1 kg) baking potatoes, peeled and cut into pieces
salt
whole nutmeg
1 egg
2 cups (8 oz/250 g) all-purpose (plain) flour
¼ cup (2 oz/60 g) unsalted butter, melted and kept warm
¾ cup (3 oz/100 g) freshly grated Parmesan cheese

▣ Fill a saucepan with salted water and add the potatoes. Bring to a boil and boil just until tender, about 20 minutes. Drain well and pass through a sieve, food mill or ricer into a mixing bowl.
▣ Season the potatoes with salt to taste and scrape over some nutmeg. Add the egg and work in the flour, progressively, to make a firm but still supple, workable dough. Using your knuckles, knead the dough in the mixing bowl until smooth, then transfer it to a floured work surface. Flour your hands well and, using your palms, roll out orange-sized sections of the dough into logs about ½ in (12 mm) thick. Cut the logs into 1-in (2.5-cm) lengths. Press the center of each piece with a floured thumb or forefinger, to form a hollow. Alternatively, place each piece on a fork, press and give the dough a quarter roll, leaving one side indented and the other decoratively striated by the tines of the fork.
▣ Bring a large saucepan filled with water to a boil. Working in batches to prevent the gnocchi from sticking together, drop a batch into the boiling water. As soon as the gnocchi rise to the surface, after about 3 minutes, remove them with a large, flat, perforated skimming spoon. Let drain for a few seconds

Potato Gnocchi

and then put them into a warmed deep serving dish. Repeat with the remaining gnocchi.
▣ When all the gnocchi are cooked, pour over the melted butter, sprinkle over the cheese and serve.

SERVES 6

TIAN À LA COMTADINE

Potato Gratin with Garlic

When this gratin accompanies a leg of lamb, the leg is placed directly on top of the potatoes to roast.

2 lb (1 kg) potatoes, peeled, thinly sliced and wiped dry
¼ cup (2 fl oz/60 ml) olive oil
12 cloves garlic
salt
1 bay leaf
boiling water as needed

▣ Preheat an oven to 350°F (180°C). In a mixing bowl toss together the potato slices and olive oil until all the slices are evenly coated. Spread half the slices in the bottom of a large, shallow 6-cup (48-fl oz/1.5-l) gratin dish, preferably earthenware. Distribute the garlic cloves evenly amongst the potatoes and sprinkle with salt. Add the bay leaf then top with the remaining potato slices. Pour over boiling water almost to cover, sprinkle with salt to taste and dribble over any oil remaining in the bowl.
▣ Place in the oven and bake until all the water is absorbed, 50–60 minutes. If the surface is well colored before then, cover loosely with aluminum foil to protect it from darkening further. Serve at once.

SERVES 4

BOULANGÈRE À L'OSEILLE

Potato Gratin with Sorrel

The acidity of the sorrel and the sweetness of the onions do wonderful things to potatoes. A perfect accompaniment to any roast.

2 tablespoons unsalted butter
5 oz (150 g) young sorrel leaves, stemmed, tightly rolled up and thinly sliced
salt
¾ cup (6 fl oz/175 ml) heavy whipping (double) cream
2 lb (1 kg) large potatoes, peeled and sliced lengthwise as thinly as possible, preferably with a mandoline
½ lb (250 g) sweet white onions, thinly sliced

▣ Preheat an oven to 350°F (180°C). Butter a 8-cup (64-fl oz/2-l) gratin dish.
▣ Melt 1 tablespoon of the butter in a sauté pan over low heat. Add the sorrel, sprinkle with salt to taste and cook for a few minutes, stirring with a wooden spoon, until the sorrel turns gray and begins to dissolve. Add the cream and simmer for a few minutes. Remove from the heat.
▣ Combine the potatoes (unrinsed and undried) and onions in a saucepan. Season to taste with salt and pour over enough water almost to cover. Bring to a boil, shaking the pan and displacing the potatoes with a wooden spoon to prevent them from sticking to the bottom. Pour into the gratin dish and smooth the surface. Spread the creamed sorrel evenly on top.
▣ Place in the oven and bake until the potatoes are tender, about 1 hour. Serve immediately.

SERVES 4

Left to right: Potato Gratin with Garlic, Potato Gratin with Sorrel

POMMES DE TERRE SAUTÉES À LA PROVENÇALE

Provençal Sautéed Potatoes

These potatoes are delicious cooked in their skins, but the French never consider the possibility of eating potato skins, and peel them carefully at table before eating them.

3 tablespoons olive oil
1½ lb (750 g) small new potatoes
12 cloves garlic, unpeeled
salt
freshly ground pepper
1 tablespoon chopped fresh flat-leaf (Italian) parsley

❧ Warm the olive oil in a flameproof earthenware casserole or heavy sauté pan over low heat. Add the potatoes and garlic cloves and season to taste with salt. Cover and cook until the potatoes are tender, about 40 minutes. Shake the pan from time to time to turn the potatoes over. When removing the lid to check their progress, do not tilt it, and be sure to wipe it dry before putting it back in place.
❧ Just before serving, grind over some pepper, sprinkle with the parsley and toss the contents of the pan well.

SERVES 4

MOUSSELINE AU GRATIN

Gratin of Mashed Potatoes and Garlic with Cheese

A perfect accompaniment to grilled sausages of any kind— andouillettes, *blood sausages (black pudding), link sausages.*

2 lb (1 kg) potatoes, peeled and quartered
8 cloves garlic
salt
boiling water as needed
4 tablespoons (2 fl oz/60 ml) olive oil
½ cup (2 oz/60 g) freshly grated Parmesan cheese
3 eggs
freshly ground pepper
whole nutmeg

❧ Preheat an oven to 400°F (200°C). Combine the potatoes and garlic in a saucepan. Add a pinch of salt and enough boiling water just to cover. Cover and cook at a gentle boil until the potatoes are just done, about 30 minutes.
❧ Drain, saving the cooking water, and pass the potatoes and garlic through a fine-mesh sieve with the help of a wooden pestle. Using a wooden spoon, stir in enough of the cooking water to form a loose, not quite pourable purée.
❧ Smear a 6-cup (48-fl oz/1.5-l) gratin dish with olive oil. In a small bowl combine 2 tablespoons of the olive oil, half of the cheese, the eggs and a little of the cooking water. Grind over some pepper, scrape in some nutmeg and whisk together. Stir the oil mixture into the sieved potatoes. Pour into the gratin dish, sprinkle with the remaining cheese and dribble with the remaining 2 tablespoons olive oil.
❧ Place in the oven and bake until swelled and golden, 15–20 minutes. Serve hot.

SERVES 4–6   *Photograph pages 262–263*

PIMENTS DOUX AU GRATIN

Gratin of Sweet Peppers

Serve either as a course apart or as an accompaniment to a roast; especially good with lamb. The anchovies and olives provide good salty counterpoints to the sweetness of the peppers in this colorful dish.

2 large red sweet peppers (capsicums) and 2 large yellow sweet peppers

Left to right: Gratin of Sweet Peppers, Provençal Sautéed Potatoes

6 salt anchovies, rinsed, filleted and chopped (see glossary)
⅔ cup (3 oz/100 g) black olives, pitted and halved
persillade made with 1 clove garlic (see glossary)
salt and freshly ground pepper
4 tablespoons (2 fl oz/60 ml) olive oil
semidried bread crumbs

▨ Grill, peel and seed the sweet peppers as directed for sweet pepper salad (recipe on page 286). Cut them lengthwise into narrow strips; collect and reserve the juices that result from the grilling.

▨ Preheat an oven to 350°F (180°C). In a gratin dish mix together the peppers and their juices, anchovies, olives, *persillade,* salt and pepper to taste and 2 tablespoons of the olive oil. Spread evenly over the bottom of the dish. Sprinkle with enough bread crumbs to cover the ingredients so they are no longer visible. Dribble the remaining 2 tablespoons olive oil over the top.
▨ Place in the oven and bake until the top is browned, about 30 minutes. Serve immediately.

SERVES 4

PETITS POIS À LA MÉNAGÈRE

Peas Braised with Onions and Lettuce

The peas should be tender enough to be eaten raw with pleasure. Serve as a separate course.

1 small head leafy lettuce
1 fresh thyme sprig
bouquet of fresh flat-leaf (Italian) parsley sprigs
¼ lb (125 g) walnut-sized green (spring) onions,
    tops discarded
2 tablespoons water
4 lb (2 kg) small, young peas, shelled
¼ cup (2 oz/60 g) unsalted butter, chilled and diced
salt
pinch of sugar

▨ Remove the outer leaves from the head of lettuce. Wash, but do not dry, both the leaves and the heart. Enclose the thyme and parsley bouquet in the heart and tie as for a bouquet garni (see glossary). Place it in a small, flameproof earthenware casserole or heavy sauté pan. Scatter the onions around and add the water. Mix together the peas and butter and add to the pan. Sprinkle with salt to taste and the sugar and press the lettuce leaves over the surface.
▨ Cover the pan and sweat over very low heat until the peas are very tender, about 45 minutes. Remove the lettuce leaves and heart before serving.

SERVES 4

TIAN DE COURGETTES

Zucchini and Rice Gratin

Serve as a separate course, accompanied by tomato sauce, or with a roast.

4 tablespoons (2 fl oz/60 ml) olive oil
1 large onion, finely chopped
1 lb (500 g) zucchini (courgettes), thinly sliced
salt and freshly ground pepper
2 cups (16 fl oz/500 ml) milk
1 cup (2 oz/60 g) fresh bread crumbs
3 eggs
large pinch of fresh marjoram flower buds and leaves,
    finely chopped
¾ cup (3 oz/100 g) freshly grated Parmesan cheese
½ cup (3 oz/90 g) long-grain white rice

▨ Preheat an oven to 350°F (180°C). Smear a 6-cup (48-fl oz/1.5-l) gratin dish with olive oil.
▨ Warm 2 tablespoons of the olive oil in a frying pan over low heat. Add the onion and cook gently until softened but not colored, about 10 minutes. Add the zucchini and salt and pepper to taste and sauté for a couple of minutes. Remove from the heat.
▨ In a mixing bowl, pour 1 cup (8 fl oz/250 ml) of the milk over the bread crumbs. Add the remaining 2 tablespoons olive oil, the eggs, marjoram, about two thirds of the cheese and salt and pepper to taste. Beat or whisk until smooth. Stir in the onion-zucchini mixture and the rice and pour into the gratin dish. Smooth the surface and pour the remaining 1 cup (8 fl oz/250 ml) milk evenly over the top.
▨ Sprinkle with the remaining cheese and place in the oven. Bake until golden, about 1 hour. Serve hot.

SERVES 4

POMMES DE TERRE AU GRATIN

Potato Gratin

2 lb (1 kg) potatoes, peeled and cut into slices ⅛ in (3 mm) thick
boiling broth or water as needed
salt, if needed

432

Clockwise from top: Peas Braised with Onions and Lettuce, Potato Gratin, Zucchini and Rice Gratin

½ cup (2 oz/60 g) freshly grated Gruyère or Parmesan
  cheese, or a mixture
½ cup (4 fl oz/125 ml) heavy whipping (double) cream
2 eggs
whole nutmeg

◙ Preheat an oven to 350°F (180°C). Put the potatoes in a sauce-pan and pour in just enough boiling broth or water to cover. Season with salt, if using water, cover and simmer until the potatoes are nearly done, about 15 minutes. Remove from the heat.

◙ Combine half of the cheese, the cream and eggs in a bowl. Scrape in a bit of the nutmeg and whisk together until well blended. Pour the mixture into the potatoes, swirl the contents of saucepan, and then pour into a gratin dish. Smooth the surface and sprinkle over the remaining cheese.
◙ Place in the oven and bake until the surface is golden and the potatoes are set in a light custard, about 20 minutes. Serve immediately.

SERVES 4

VAUCLUSE

TRUFFES AU CHÂTEAUNEUF-DU-PAPE

Truffles in Red Wine

Fresh black truffles are in season in Provence during the months of December, January and February. They are best after the first of the year. In the truffle markets they are sold with soil adhering and must be brushed and washed before being used. Exported truffles are brushed and ready for use.

mirepoix (see glossary)
2 cups (16 fl oz/500 ml) dry red wine
8 tablespoons (4 oz/120 g) unsalted butter
1 tablespoon all-purpose (plain) flour
2 cups (16 fl oz/500 ml) broth, preferably *pot-au-feu* broth
½ lb (250 g) black truffles, brushed
salt and freshly ground pepper
1 tablespoon Cognac
8 slices baguette
1 garlic clove

❀ Combine the *mirepoix* and red wine in a saucepan and bring to a boil. Simmer, uncovered, until reduced to ¾ cup (6 fl oz/175 ml), about 45 minutes.
❀ Meanwhile, melt 1 tablespoon of the butter in a saucepan over medium-high heat. Stir in the flour until well blended, then slowly whisk in the broth and continue to whisk until a boil is reached. Reduce the heat and simmer gently for 30 minutes.
❀ Pour the red wine reduction through a fine-mesh sieve into the broth, pressing with the back of a spoon to extract all the liquid. Move the saucepan partially off the heat and adjust the heat to maintain a gentle boil on one side of the surface. Wait for 15 minutes, then remove the skin and fat from the still side by pulling it off with a spoon. Keep warm.
❀ Meanwhile, preheat an oven to 375°F (190°C). Butter a flameproof earthenware casserole or heavy sauté pan with 1 tablespoon of the butter.
❀ Peel the truffles and place the peels in a mortar. Pound to a purée; set aside. Cut the truffles into wedges and add them to the casserole. Salt lightly and grind over pepper generously. Sprinkle with Cognac, cover and place over the lowest possible heat for about 15 minutes—long enough to sweat only, not cook.
❀ Melt the remaining butter and brush it on both sides of the bread slices. Place them on a baking sheet, put them into the oven, and toast, turning once, until golden and crisp on the surfaces, just a few minutes. Stroke each slice once or twice on each side with the garlic clove. Stir the pounded truffle peels into the hot sauce, then pour the sauce over the truffles.
❀ To serve, place the bread slices on individual heated serving plates and spoon the truffles and sauce over the top.
SERVES 4

Truffles in Red Wine

Braised Belgian Endives

ENDIVES BRAISÉES

Braised Belgian Endives

Serve as a separate course or to accompany roasted or grilled veal or pork.

1½ lb (750 g) heads Belgian endive (chicory/witloof), bases
   trimmed and blemished leaves removed
salt
1 oz (30 g) raw ham such as prosciutto, cut into matchsticks
1 tablespoon unsalted butter, cut into small pieces

juice of ½ lemon
6 tablespoons (3 fl oz/90 ml) heavy whipping (double) cream

◉ Butter a flameproof earthenware casserole or heavy sauté
pan of a size to just hold the endives. Arrange them in the
casserole in a single layer. Sprinkle with salt to taste and
scatter over the ham. Place the butter fragments on top of
the endives. Cover tightly and place over very low heat to
sweat, checking from time to time and turning them over,
until very tender and colored on all sides, 50–60 minutes.
◉ Add the lemon juice and turn the endives around to coat
them evenly. Pour the cream over the endives, rotate the pan
to swirl the contents gently and serve.

SERVES 4

FENOUIL À LA NIÇOISE

Braised Fennel

The garlic is transformed, within its skin, into an irresistible purée, delicious spread on bread, on the fennel or on a slice of meat. Serve braised fennel on its own or as an accompaniment to any roast or grilled meat or fowl.

2 lb (1 kg) fennel bulbs
¼ cup (2 fl oz/60 ml) olive oil
1 head garlic, cloves separated and loose husk removed but unpeeled
salt
½ cup (4 fl oz/125 ml) dry white wine

◙ Remove and discard the outer blemished stalks from the fennel bulbs. Trim off the tubular stems, reserving the leaves, and split the bulbs in half lengthwise.

436

the fennel halves back onto their flat sides, cover and braise gently over very low heat for about 1 hour, adding a few drops of the remaining wine from time to time to keep the fennel from drying out. When finished, the fennel should be meltingly tender and the juices a rich brown color and slightly syrupy.

◉ Chop the reserved fennel leaves and sprinkle over the braised bulbs just before serving.

SERVES 4

Braised Fennel

VAUCLUSE/BOUCHES-DU-RHÔNE

HARICOTS BLANCS À LA VILLAGEOISE

White Beans with Sausage and Salt Pork

When fresh white shell beans (cocos; see glossary) are available, substitute them for the dried large Great Northerns. Shell 4 pounds (2 kg) cocos and boil them, with the same aromatic elements, for about 20 minutes before joining them to the bacon and sausage. Save leftover cooking water for soup or broth. The sausage should be the best large, fresh pork sausage you can find that is suitable for poaching. The sausage meat described in the glossary could be stuffed into a fresh, natural casing and used for this dish.

2½ cups (1 lb/500 g) dried Great Northern beans
bouquet garni (see glossary)
1 onion stuck with 2 whole cloves
1 carrot, peeled and cut in half
3 cloves garlic, unpeeled
boiling water as needed
salt
1 slice lean salt pork (green bacon), about ¾ in (2 cm) thick
2 tablespoons olive oil
1 onion, chopped
1 fresh poaching sausage, about 10 oz (300 g), pricked on all sides with a sharp skewer or trussing needle

◉ Place the beans in a bowl; add water to cover and let stand for several hours or overnight. Drain the beans and place in a saucepan. Cover abundantly with cold water, bring to a boil and boil for 10 minutes. Drain, return the beans to the saucepan and add the bouquet garni, whole onion, carrot and garlic. Pour in boiling water to cover by a good inch (2.5 cm), cover and simmer for 45 minutes. Salt the water to taste and continue to simmer until the beans are not quite done, another 15 minutes or so, depending upon their quality and age.

◉ Meanwhile, place the salt pork in a saucepan, add water to cover and bring to a boil. Drain immediately and rinse in cold water. Set the pork aside.

◉ Warm the olive oil in a flameproof earthenware casserole or other heavy pot over low heat. Add the chopped onion and cook until softened, about 10 minutes. Place the salt pork and the sausage on top. Drain the beans, saving the liquid; discard the whole onion. Empty the beans over the meats. Add enough of the cooking liquid to cover barely, cover and simmer until tender, about 40 minutes, adding more liquid if necessary to keep the beans from drying out. When the beans are ready, they should have absorbed nearly all of the liquid.

◉ Discard the bouquet garni and carrot. Remove the meats; cut the salt pork into wedges and slice the sausage. Scatter the wedges and the slices over the beans and serve from the pan.

SERVES 4   *Photograph pages 418–419*

◉ In a large, heavy sauté pan, warm the olive oil over medium-low heat. Place the fennel halves in the pan, cut sides down, and fill all the interstices with the garlic cloves. Sprinkle with salt to taste, cover and cook until the cut sides are a light golden brown. Turn the fennel halves, salt again, cover and lightly brown the other sides in the same way. It will take about 30 minutes to color the fennel.

◉ Uncover and pour about half of the wine over the fennel. Shake the pan gently until the liquid comes to a boil, turn

GRATIN DE CHOUFLEUR

Cauliflower Gratin

This is a Niçois gratin. Elsewhere in Provence, a cauliflower gratin often consists of parboiled florets covered with béchamel *sauce, sprinkled with cheese and baked until bubbling. The* béchamel *sauce can be enriched by whisking in a couple of egg yolks and a handful of grated cheese before pouring it over the cauliflower.*

1 unblemished white cauliflower, broken into florets and
    large florets split in half lengthwise
¼ cup (2 fl oz/60 ml) olive oil
salt and freshly ground pepper
whole nutmeg
½ cup (2 oz/60 g) freshly grated Parmesan cheese
handful of semidried bread crumbs

◉ Preheat an oven to 400°F (200°C). Fill a large saucepan with salted water and bring to a boil. Plunge the florets into the boiling water and cook until barely tender (when a knife tip still meets with slight resistance at the stem end of a floret), about 5 minutes. Drain well and toss the florets in a bowl with the olive oil.
◉ Spoon the florets into a gratin dish, arranging them snugly. Sprinkle lightly with salt, grind over some pepper, and scrape over a bit of nutmeg. Sprinkle with the Parmesan and then with the bread crumbs. Dribble over any olive oil remaining in the bowl.
◉ Place in the oven and bake until the surface is nicely colored, about 10 minutes. Serve hot.

SERVES 4

CAPOUNS NIÇOIS

Stuffed Cabbage Leaves

Swiss chard (silverbeet) leaves are often treated in the same way. Serve as a separate vegetable course or as a simple supper main course.

1 large savoy cabbage
FOR THE STUFFING:
1 large onion, finely chopped and cooked in 2 tablespoons
    olive oil until soft but not colored
½ cup (3½ oz/100 g) long-grain white rice, parboiled for
    15 minutes and drained
persillade made with 2 cloves garlic (see glossary)
5 oz (150 g) sausage meat (see glossary)
1 thick slice from shank end of raw ham such as prosciutto,
    chopped
½ cup (2 oz/60 g) freshly grated Parmesan cheese
pinch of Provençal mixed dried herbs (see glossary)
2 eggs
salt and freshly ground pepper
whole nutmeg

mirepoix (see glossary)
½ cup (4 fl oz/125 ml) tomato sauce (see glossary)
½ cup (4 fl oz/125 ml) dry white wine
broth as needed

◉ Discard any blemished outer leaves of the cabbage. Cut out a large cone at the base of the cabbage to remove the core and free the leaves. Carefully separate at least 8 perfect leaves, one by one, and trim the rib of each, slicing off excess thickness. Layer the leaves in a large saucepan, slowly pour over boiling water to cover, bring to a boil and, after a few seconds, carefully slip the contents of the saucepan into a large colander. Refresh the leaves under cold running water and lay them out, side by side, on cotton towels to drain.
◉ Split the heart of the cabbage lengthwise and cut out any remaining core; shred the halves coarsely and chop the shreds. Fill a saucepan with salted water and bring to a boil. Add the chopped cabbage and parboil for 5 minutes. Drain, refresh under cold running water and squeeze thoroughly dry. Place in a mixing bowl and add all the remaining stuffing ingredients, including salt and pepper to taste and a scrape of nutmeg. Using your hands mix thoroughly. Set aside.
◉ Preheat an oven to 325°F (165°C). Prepare the *mirepoix* in a large flameproof earthenware casserole or other heavy pot. Set aside off the heat.
◉ Place a handful of stuffing near the stem end on the inside surface of a cabbage leaf. Roll up the leaf a third of the way, fold the sides inward over the top and finish rolling. Place the package, seam side down, on the bed of *mirepoix*. Repeat with the remaining leaves and stuffing, arranging the packages snugly in the pan. Pour over the tomato sauce, the wine and enough broth to immerse the packages.
◉ Bring to a boil over medium heat, then cover and place in the oven. Bake until the cabbage packages are translucent, slightly wrinkled and are coated with the reduced sauce, about 1½ hours. Serve hot.

SERVES 4

AUBERGINES EN ÉVENTAIL

Eggplant Fans

Zucchini (courgettes) can be prepared in the same way, except that a dash of dry white wine should be added just after the seasonings and the cooking time should be shortened by 20 minutes. Both are as good as they are beautiful and provide perfect separate vegetable courses.

5 tablespoons (3 fl oz/80 ml) olive oil
2 large sweet white onions, cut in half lengthwise and
    thinly sliced
4 cloves firm, crisp garlic, sliced paper-thin
4 small, elongated eggplants (aubergines), about 5 oz
    (155 g) each
about 1½ lb (750 g) firm, garden-ripe tomatoes
small branches of fresh thyme and winter savory or a
    pinch of Provençal mixed dried herbs (see glossary)
3 bay leaves
pinch of coriander seeds
salt and freshly ground pepper

◉ Preheat an oven to 450°F (230°C). Smear a very large gratin dish (or use 2 dishes) with olive oil.
◉ Mix together the onions and garlic and spread half of the mixture in the bottom of the dish. Cut off the stem end and a sliver from the flower end of each eggplant. Cut each eggplant in half lengthwise symmetrically. Place the halves, cut side down, on a work surface. Beginning about ⅔ in (1.5 cm) from the stem end, cut each eggplant half lengthwise into slices ⅓ in (1 cm) thick. The uncut stem end will hold the slices together, creating intact fans.
◉ Slice the tomatoes in half lengthwise. Cut out the core at the stem end and place each half, cut side down, on a work surface. Cut into lengthwise slices ⅓ in (1 cm) thick. Slip 3 tomato slices in a row between each pair of eggplant slices and, each time an eggplant half is fully garnished, transfer it to the gratin dish using a wide spatula and holding the fan firmly together with your hand. Arrange the fans, packing gently, so that a minimum of space is lost. Scatter over the remaining onion-garlic mixture and tuck in the herbs here and there. Sprinkle over the coriander seeds and salt to taste

Clockwise from top: Eggplant Fans, Cauliflower Gratin, Stuffed Cabbage Leaves

and grind over some pepper. Dribble the olive oil evenly over all the fans. Cover with heavy-duty aluminum foil, pressing it firmly around the dish rim to keep it in place.

◉ Place in the oven and reduce the heat to 350°F (180°C). Cook until the eggplant is tender when pierced, about 1 hour.

Turn off the oven and leave the dish in the oven for 30 minutes before serving. If the oven is needed, remove the covered dish and place in a warm spot.

SERVES 4

CHICORÉE FRISÉE BRAISÉE

Braised Frisée

*This preparation is specifically intended to accompany roast lamb.
It is also good with roast veal or pork. Frisée is similar to chicory
(curly endive) which can be used here as a substitute.*

4 heads frisée, blemished leaves discarded and cored
handful of coarse salt
boiling water as needed
2 tablespoons olive oil
pinch of Provençal mixed dried herbs (see glossary)
persillade made with 1 clove garlic (see glossary)
1 tablespoon all-purpose (plain) flour
½ cup (4 fl oz/125 ml) broth, or as needed
deglazed roasting juices and carving juices

◻ Pack the frisée into a large saucepan, add the salt, and pour
over boiling water to cover. Bring to a boil and boil for a
couple of minutes. Drain, refresh under cold running
water, squeeze as dry as possible and chop.
◻ Warm the olive oil in a heavy saucepan over medium heat.
Add the frisée and cook, stirring with a wooden spoon, for a
few minutes. Sprinkle with the herbs and *persillade* and cook
a few minutes longer. Sprinkle with the flour and stir for
1 minute. Slowly stir in the ½ cup (4 fl oz/125 ml) broth.
Reduce the heat to very low, cover and cook, stirring occasionally, about 1¼ hours. If the frisée begins to dry out, add
a little boiling broth or water.
◻ Just before serving, stir in the roasting and carving juices.

SERVES 6

Spinach and Egg Gratin

ROUSSIN D'ÉPINARDS

Spinach and Egg Gratin

*Serve this as a separate vegetable course or as a family supper
main course.*

4 tablespoons (3 fl oz/80 ml) olive oil
1 onion, finely chopped
2 lb (1 kg) spinach, parboiled, squeezed dry and chopped
    (see glossary)
salt
persillade made with 1 clove garlic (see glossary)
1 tablespoon all-purpose (plain) flour
2 cups (16 fl oz/500 ml) milk
freshly ground pepper
whole nutmeg
4 hard-cooked eggs, shelled and halved lengthwise
semidried bread crumbs

◻ Preheat an oven to 375°F (190°C).
◻ Warm 2 tablespoons of the olive oil in a sauté pan over
low heat. Add the onion and cook until softened and lightly
colored, about 10 minutes. Add the spinach and continue to
cook, stirring regularly with a wooden spoon, until it exudes
no more moisture and begins to stick to the pan, about 5–10
minutes. Season to taste with salt, add the *persillade* and
sprinkle with the flour. Stir until the flour is no longer
visible. Over the next 30 minutes, add the milk, a little at a
time, stirring regularly.
◻ Smear a 6-cup (48-fl oz/1.5-l) gratin dish with olive oil. Grind
some pepper and scrape some nutmeg over the spinach. Stir
together and pour the mixture into the gratin dish. Push the
half eggs into the spinach so that the cut surfaces are at the
same level as the spinach mixture. Sprinkle the entire surface
with bread crumbs and dribble over the remaining 2 tablespoons olive oil in a thread, forming a crisscross pattern.
◻ Place in the oven and bake until the surface is golden, about
30 minutes. Serve at once.

SERVES 4

TIAN D'ÉPINARDS À LA COMTADINE

Spinach Gratin

*This rustic preparation, delicious with roast pork, is sometimes
sprinkled with flour in place of the bread crumbs.*

1½ lb (750 g) young, tender spinach leaves, stemmed and
    chopped
salt and freshly ground pepper
large handful of semidried bread crumbs
3 tablespoons (2 fl oz/60 ml) olive oil

◻ Preheat an oven to 450°F (230°C). Smear a large gratin dish
with olive oil.
◻ In a mixing bowl, toss the spinach with salt and pepper to
taste. Pack the spinach into the gratin dish, pressing it down
firmly. Sprinkle a thick layer of bread crumbs over the
spinach and then dribble on the olive oil in a thread, forming
a crisscross pattern.
◻ Put the dish in the oven, turn the heat down to 325°F
(165°C) and bake until the volume has reduced by more than
half and the surface is browned, about 1 hour. Serve at once.

SERVES 4

Left to right: Braised Frisée, Spinach Gratin

TOMATES FARCIES
À L'ANTIBOISE

Antibes-Style Stuffed Tomatoes

Serve as a separate vegetable course.

8 firm, garden-ripe tomatoes
salt
4 tablespoons (2 fl oz/60 ml) olive oil
1 onion, finely chopped
pinch of coarse salt
freshly ground pepper

Antibes-Style Stuffed Tomatoes

◼ Slice off the top quarter of each tomato. Scrape the flesh free from the skins of the top slices. With your little finger, loosen the seeds in the seed pockets and give the tomatoes an abrupt upside-down shake to empty them. Using a small, sharp-pointed knife, cut the walls of the seed pockets loose from the outside tomato walls and scoop out the centers of the tomatoes. Chop them, along with any flesh scraped from the top slices. Sprinkle the inside of the tomato shells with salt and turn upside down on a wire rack for 30 minutes to drain.

◼ Meanwhile, preheat an oven to 350°F (180°C). Smear a 6-cup (48-fl oz/1.5-l) gratin dish with olive oil.

◼ Warm 2 tablespoons of the olive oil in a small pan over low heat. Add the onion and cook until softened, about 10 minutes. Raise the heat to high, add the chopped tomato flesh and sauté briefly until it begins to fall apart. Remove from the heat.

◼ In a large mortar pound together the coarse salt, pepper, anchovies and basil to form a paste. Stir in 1 tablespoon of the remaining olive oil to loosen the mixture, then add the fresh bread crumbs. Mix well with the pestle and stir in the onion-tomato mixture and eggs.

◼ Stuff the tomato shells with the tomato-crumb mixture, mounding and molding the surfaces with an overturned spoon. Arrange the tomatoes in the gratin dish just large enough to accommodate them. Sprinkle with dried bread crumbs and dribble over the remaining 1 tablespoon olive oil.

◼ Place in the oven and bake until the tomatoes are tender and the tops are browned, about 30 minutes. Serve hot.

SERVES 4

2 cloves garlic
2 salt anchovies, rinsed and filleted (see glossary)
small handful of fresh basil leaves
1 cup (2 oz/60 g) fresh bread crumbs
2 hard-cooked eggs, shelled and chopped
dried bread crumbs

PROVENCE

ARTICHAUTS À LA BARIGOULE

Braised Artichokes

Whether or not, as some people believe, artichauts à la barigoule *were originally simply grilled artichokes, today they are always braised, sometimes stuffed with a mushroom* duxelles, *the classic sauté of finely chopped mushrooms, onion and parsley with a hint of lemon juice. These artichokes are wonderful as a course on their own.*

mirepoix (see glossary)
bouquet garni (see glossary)
12 egg-sized artichokes, trimmed and left whole, or 6
    medium-sized artichokes, trimmed, quartered and
    chokes removed if necessary (see glossary)
salt
¼ cup (2 fl oz/60 ml) olive oil
½ cup (4 fl oz/125 ml) dry white wine

◼ Prepare the *mirepoix* in a large flameproof earthenware casserole or nonreactive heavy sauté pan. Place the bouquet garni in the center and the artichokes all around, bottoms down if they are whole. Sprinkle with salt to taste, dribble the olive oil evenly all over the artichokes, and pour in the white wine.

◼ Cover and cook the artichokes very gently, turning them around and over two or three times and basting them, until they are tender and most of the liquid has evaporated, about 45 minutes. When serving, spoon the *mirepoix* and pan juices over the artichokes.

SERVES 4   *Photograph pages 418–419*

RAGOÛT D'ARTICHAUTS AUX PETITS POIS

Stew of Artichokes and Peas

In Nice this dish is known as petits pois à la niçoise. *Elsewhere in Provence it is called either* petits pois à la provençale *or the name given here. Similar preparations also exist in Italian cuisine.*

3 tablespoons olive oil
3 oz (100 g) salt pork (salt bacon), cut into ¼-in (6-mm) dice
12 egg-sized artichokes, trimmed and left whole, or 6 medium-sized artichokes, trimmed, quartered and chokes removed if necessary (see glossary)
½ lb (250 g) walnut-sized green (spring) onions, tops discarded
1 heart leafy lettuce enclosing a bouquet of fresh flat-leaf (Italian) parsley sprigs and 1 fresh thyme sprig, tied as for a bouquet garni (see glossary)
salt
4 lb (2 kg) small, young peas, shelled
¼ cup (2 fl oz/60 ml) water

▣ Warm the olive oil in a flameproof earthenware casserole or heavy sauté pan over medium-low heat. Add the salt pork, artichokes and onions, cover and cook, shaking the pan from time to time, until the contents are softened and just beginning to color, about 10 minutes.
▣ Add the lettuce bouquet, salt to taste, peas and water. Cover tightly and simmer over very low heat, shaking the pan occasionally, until the vegetables are tender, about 40 minutes. Serve immediately.

SERVES 4

TIAN DE COURGETTES AUX HERBES

Zucchini and Greens Gratin

There are countless variations on mixed-greens gratins in combination with other vegetables. Your imagination is the limit. They all escort roasts admirably and all can easily stand alone.

2 lb (1 kg) zucchini (courgettes)
salt
4 tablespoons (2 fl oz/60 ml) olive oil
3 oz (100 g) lean salt pork (salt bacon), cut into ¼-in (6-mm) dice
1 large sweet white onion, finely chopped
1 lb (500 g) Swiss chard (silverbeet) greens, parboiled, squeezed dry and chopped (see glossary)
large handful of sorrel leaves, stemmed, tightly rolled up and thinly sliced
persillade made with 3 cloves garlic (see glossary)
½ cup (2 oz/60 g) Parmesan cheese, grated
salt and freshly ground pepper
3 eggs

▣ Cut the zucchini into sections and shred them through a vegetable shredder fitted with the medium blade or in a food processor fitted with the shredding disk. Layer the zucchini on a plate, sprinkling salt between the layers, and let stand for 30 minutes. Squeeze dry and place in a mixing bowl.

▣ Meanwhile, preheat an oven to 350°F (175°C). Smear the bottom and sides of a 8-cup (64-fl oz/2-l) gratin dish with olive oil.
▣ In a small frying pan, warm 1 tablespoon of olive oil over very low heat. Add the salt pork and cook until lightly colored, about 10 minutes. Add the onion and cook, stirring with a wooden spoon, until soft and golden, about 15 minutes. Empty the salt pork and onion into the bowl holding the zucchini. Add the chard, sorrel, *persillade* and half of the Parmesan. Season to taste with salt and pepper and add the eggs. Using your hands mix thoroughly.
▣ Pack the mixture into the gratin dish. Smooth the surface and sprinkle the remaining cheese evenly over the top. Dribble on the remaining 3 tablespoons olive oil in a thread, forming a crisscross pattern. Place in the oven and bake until set and golden, about 40 minutes. Serve immediately.

SERVES 4

CHARLOTTE DE TOMATES

Gratin of Tomatoes and Potatoes

This rustic gratin is a perfect accompaniment to roast pork. A handful of pitted black olives can be scattered over the layer of potatoes.

1 lb (500 g) potatoes
4 tablespoons (2 fl oz/60 ml) olive oil
1 lb (500 g) onions, chopped
1 lb (500 g) firm, garden-ripe tomatoes, sliced
large pinch of fresh thyme leaves
1 teaspoon chopped fresh tarragon
salt and freshly ground pepper
whole nutmeg
dried bread crumbs

▣ Preheat an oven to 375°F (190°C).
▣ Fill a saucepan with salted water and bring to a boil. Add the unpeeled potatoes and boil until half-cooked, 15–20 minutes. Drain and, with your hand cradling the potato protected by a folded cotton towel, peel and then slice while still hot.
▣ Meanwhile, warm 2 tablespoons of the olive oil in a heavy pan over low heat. Add the onions, cover and cook, stirring occasionally with a wooden spoon, until soft, about 30 minutes.
▣ Smear the bottom and sides of a 6-cup (48-fl oz/1.5-l) gratin dish with olive oil. Line the gratin dish with half of the tomatoes. Sprinkle with a few thyme leaves, a pinch of tarragon, and salt and pepper to taste. Spread one third of the onions over the top. Layer the hot sliced potatoes on top, sprinkle with more thyme, tarragon, salt, and pepper and then scrape over a little nutmeg. Spread half of the remaining onions over the potatoes. Top with the remaining tomatoes, season with salt and pepper, and layer the remaining onions over them. Finally, sprinkle evenly with bread crumbs and dribble on the remaining 2 tablespoons olive oil in a thread, forming a crisscross pattern.
▣ Place in the oven and bake until golden and crisp, about 45 minutes. Serve hot.

SERVES 4

Top to bottom: Stew of Artichokes and Peas, Zucchini and Greens Gratin, Gratin of Tomatoes and Potatoes

444

Summer Rice

RIZOTTO D'ÉTÉ
Summer Rice

Parboiled little peas or rapidly sautéed sliced baby artichokes are also lovely added to this rizotto at the last minute. Round-grained Arborio rice from Piedmont is necessary for the success of this dish. Serve it as a separate course or, for a simple meal, as the main course.

mirepoix (see glossary)
2 cups (10 oz/300 g) Arborio rice
salt, if needed
about 5 cups (40 fl oz/1.2 l) broth or water, boiling
¼ lb (125 g) young, tender green beans, trimmed
¼ cup (2 oz/60 g) unsalted butter, chilled and diced
½ cup (2 oz/60 g) freshly grated Parmesan cheese

Prepare the *mirepoix* in a heavy saucepan. Add the rice and stir with a wooden spoon over low heat until all the grains are coated with oil and opaque. Season with salt if you will be adding water.

Over medium-low heat, add a ladleful of the boiling liquid and stir constantly until the rice is nearly dry. Continue adding the liquid in this manner, a ladleful at a time, until the rice is tender, 20–25 minutes.

Meanwhile, gather the green beans together and slice crosswise into ¼-in (6-mm) lengths. Fill a saucepan with water and bring to a boil. Add the green beans, boil for 1 minute until barely tender and drain.

Stir the green beans into the rice. The rice should be almost liquid but not quite pourable. It is usually necessary to add a little more liquid before removing it from the heat to achieve the correct consistency.

Off the heat, stir in the butter and the cheese. Spoon onto hot plates to serve.

SERVES 4

POLENTE À LA NIÇOISE
Polenta Baked with Tomato Sauce

A memory of Nice's attachment to the kingdom of Piedmont. Serve as a first course, in place of a vegetable course, or as a main course.

4 cups (32 fl oz/1 l) water
salt
1½ cups (8 oz/250 g) coarse cornmeal
boiling water if needed
3 cups (24 fl oz/750 ml) tomato sauce, heated (see glossary)
¾ cup (3 oz/100 g) freshly grated Parmesan cheese

In a saucepan bring the water to a boil and add salt to taste. Holding the cornmeal well above the saucepan, sprinkle it into the water in a slow stream while stirring constantly with a wooden spoon. Lower the heat to maintain a gentle boil and stir constantly until the cornmeal is thick and pulls away form the sides of the pan, at least 30 minutes. Add small amounts of boiling water if the cornmeal becomes too thick to stir before that time (if you have helpers, keep stirring for another 20 minutes).

Lightly oil a marble slab or a large tray with olive oil and turn the polenta out onto it. Using a spatula moistened in cold water, quickly spread it out to a thickness of ½ in (12 mm) or less. Let cool completely, then cut into approximately 2-in (5-cm) squares.

Preheat an oven to 350°F (180°C). Pour a little hot tomato sauce into the bottom of a 8-cup (64-fl oz/2-l) gratin dish to form a thin layer. Place half of the polenta squares on top of the sauce, slightly overlapping them. Cover with half of the remaining tomato sauce and sprinkle with half of the Parmesan cheese. Arrange the remaining polenta squares on top, pour on the remaining sauce and sprinkle with the remaining cheese.

Place in the oven and bake until the sauce is bubbling and the cheese is lightly colored, about 30 minutes. Serve immediately.

SERVES 4–6

Polenta Baked with Tomato Sauce

PILAF DE RIZ

Rice Pilaf

In most of Provence this is called rizotto. It is a perfect accompaniment to brochettes of mixed meats; grilled, peeled and seeded peppers; and most dishes in sauce, simple ragouts and blanquettes *in particular. Depending upon the dish it escorts, it can often be enhanced by the addition of a pinch of saffron at the same time that the salt is added.*

2 teaspoons olive oil
1 onion, finely chopped, or, preferably, a handful of young
    green shallots, sliced
2 cups (10 oz/300 g) long-grain white rice
salt
4 cups (32 fl oz/1 l) broth or water, boiling
2 tablespoons unsalted butter, chilled and diced

◉ Warm the olive oil in a flameproof earthenware casserole or a heavy saucepan over low heat. Add the onion or shallots, cover, and sweat until softened, about 10 minutes. Add the rice and salt to taste and stir constantly until the rice is opaque. Add the boiling liquid, stir once, cover tightly and cook over very low heat until the grains are tender, about 20 minutes.
◉ Remove from the heat. Add the butter and toss the rice with 1 or 2 forks to incorporate the butter gently and to loosen the grains without damaging them. Serve immediately.

SERVES 4

POMMES PAYSANNE

Provençal Potato Casserole

Serve this as a supper main course.

5 oz (150 g) lean salt pork (green bacon), cut into lardoons
    (see glossary)
2 tablespoons olive oil
5 oz (150 g) small pickling onions
1 clove garlic, crushed
bouquet garni (see glossary)
2 tomatoes, peeled, seeded and coarsely chopped
1½ lb (750 g) small new potatoes, peeled, or larger potatoes,
    peeled and quartered
about 2 cups (16 fl oz/500 ml) broth or water, boiling
salt, if needed
1 tablespoon chopped fresh flat-leaf (Italian) parsley

◉ Preheat an oven to 350°F (180°C).
◉ Place the salt pork in a saucepan, add water to cover and bring to a boil. Drain and rinse in cold water. Pat dry with paper towels.
◉ Warm the olive oil in a flameproof casserole or Dutch oven over medium-low heat. Add the salt pork and when it begins to color lightly, add the onions. Shake the pan often until the onions are lightly colored, about 10 minutes. Add the garlic, bouquet garni and tomatoes and increase the heat. Stir until the tomatoes begin to break up, about 10 minutes.
◉ Add the potatoes, just enough boiling broth or water to cover them and salt if using water. Bring back to a boil, cover and place in the oven. Bake until the potatoes are tender, about 30 minutes.
◉ Remove from the oven, sprinkle with parsley and serve.

SERVES 4

Left to right: Rice Pilaf, Provençal Potato Casserole

TIAN DE COURGE

Squash Gratin

Serve as a separate vegetable course or to accompany veal, pork or rabbit, grilled or roasted.

4 tablespoons (2 fl oz/60 ml) olive oil
½ lb (250 g) leeks, including the tender green parts,
    thinly sliced
1½ lb (750 g) winter squash such as Hubbard or pumpkin,
    peeled and diced
salt
2 tablespoons water
½ cup (4 fl oz/125 ml) heavy whipping (double) cream
2 eggs
½ cup (2 oz/60 g) freshly grated Parmesan cheese
freshly ground pepper
whole nutmeg
semidried bread crumbs

🔲 Heat 2 tablespoons of the olive oil in a flameproof earthenware casserole or heavy sauté pan over low heat. Add the leeks and cook gently until beginning to dissolve, 10–15 minutes. Add the squash, salt and water and cook, stirring often with a wooden spoon, until the squash has reduced almost to a purée, about 30 minutes. Remove from the heat.
🔲 Meanwhile, preheat an oven to 375°F (190°C). Smear a 6-cup (48-fl oz/1.5-l) gratin dish with olive oil.
🔲 In a small bowl, whisk together well the cream, eggs, half of the Parmesan cheese, pepper to taste and some scraped nutmeg. Stir the egg mixture into the squash, then empty the contents of the pan into the gratin dish. Sprinkle the surface evenly with the remaining cheese and then with a thin layer of bread crumbs. Dribble the remaining 2 tablespoons olive oil over the surface in a thread, forming a crisscross pattern.
🔲 Place in the oven and bake until golden, about 30 minutes. Serve hot.

SERVES 4

HARICOTS VERTS À LA PROVENCALE

Provençal Green Beans

Small, tender green beans, 3–4 inches (7.5–10 cm) long, are best for sautéing. Larger beans should be snapped in two and parboiled before being sautéed. In place of the bread crumbs, add a couple of peeled, seeded and chopped tomatoes and sauté them until their liquid evaporates.

¼ cup (2 fl oz/60 ml) olive oil
4 cloves garlic, unpeeled, crushed
1 lb (500 g) small, tender green beans, trimmed
salt and freshly ground pepper
handful of semidried bread crumbs, prepared without crusts

🔲 Warm the olive oil in a large frying pan over medium-high heat. Add the garlic cloves and, when they begin to sizzle and color, add the beans. Cook, tossing repeatedly, for 4–5 minutes. Season to taste with salt and grind over some pepper. Add the crumbs and toss or stir with a wooden spoon only until the crumbs are crisp and begin to color.
🔲 Serve directly from the pan onto heated plates.

SERVES 4   *Photograph pages 418–419*

Squash Gratin

PROVENCE

CHAMPIGNONS AU GRIL

Grilled Marinated Mushrooms

Saffron milk caps (Lactarius deliciosus), *called* champignons des pins, safranés *or* lactaires délicieuses, *flood the markets of Provence in late autumn. Healthy specimens about 2 inches (5 cm) in diameter are wonderful treated in this way. The stems must be removed to permit the mushrooms to lie flat on the grill; they can be reserved for other preparations. Cultivated mushrooms may be grilled in the same way.*

2 cloves garlic
pinch of coarse salt
freshly ground pepper
pinch of Provençal mixed dried herbs (see glossary)
1 tablespoon chopped fresh flat-leaf (Italian) parsley
2 tablespoons olive oil
juice of ½ lemon
1 lb (500 g) large, firm, unopened fresh mushrooms
    (see recipe introduction), stemmed

◈ In a mortar pound together the garlic, salt, pepper and dried herbs to form a paste. Stir in the parsley, olive oil and lemon juice and transfer to a large mixing bowl. Add the mushroom caps and mix with your hands, turning the mushroom caps around in the marinade until they are well coated on all sides. Leave to marinate for 30 minutes, turning them or tossing a couple of times.

◈ Meanwhile, prepare a fire in a charcoal grill. When the fire is ready, arrange the mushrooms on the grill rack over hot coals and grill, turning once, until nicely colored and visibly shrunken from their original size, 7–8 minutes on each side. Serve immediately.

SERVES 4

PROVENCE

CHAMPIGNONS SAUTÉES À LA PROVENÇALE

Provençal Sautéed Mushrooms

Although this recipe is written for fresh cultivated mushrooms, chanterelles are a delicious alternative.

3 tablespoons olive oil
¾ lb (375 g) small fresh cultivated mushrooms, stem
    ends trimmed
salt and freshly ground pepper
persillade made with 1 clove garlic (see glossary)
1 lemon

◈ Warm the olive oil in a large frying pan over high heat. Add the mushrooms and sauté, tossing repeatedly in the air or stirring with a wooden spoon, for 3 or 4 minutes. Season to taste with salt and pepper and add the *persillade*. Continue to sauté for 1 minute or so, or until the scent of frying *persillade* fills the air.

◈ Squeeze over a few drops of lemon and serve.

SERVES 4

Provençal Sautéed Mushrooms

Grilled Marinated Mushrooms

AUBERGINES AU GRIL

Grilled Eggplant

Even simpler than this preparation and equally delicious are whole small eggplants (one per person) grilled over coals until purée-tender and served with salt, pepper and olive oil at table.

4 elongated eggplants (aubergines), about 2 lb (1 kg)
   total weight
salt
freshly ground pepper
olive oil

◈ Cut off the stem ends and split the eggplants in half lengthwise. Using a small, sharp-pointed knife, cut a criss-cross pattern in the flesh, taking care not to cut all the way through to the skin. Salt the cut surfaces and leave for 30 minutes.

◈ Meanwhile, prepare a fire in a charcoal grill. When the fire is ready, sponge the eggplant halves dry with paper towels. Grind pepper over the cut surfaces and then sprinkle with olive oil. Place cut side down on the grill rack over hot coals and grill until marked with golden brown lines from the grill. Turn skin side down and grill until the flesh is very tender when tested near the stem end, about 15 minutes, total cooking time.

SERVES 4

◈ In a large frying pan with sharply slanted sides and rounded bottom edges, warm the olive oil over high heat. Add the zucchini and salt and pepper to taste and sauté for 3–4 minutes, shaking the pan constantly and tossing the zucchini into the air regularly (stir with a wooden spoon if you fear tossing, but the result is not the same).

◈ Add the *persillade,* continue to toss for 1 minute and serve.

SERVES 4

In a vineyard in Vaucluse, from left to right: Grilled Eggplant, Potatoes with White Wine and Olives Provençal Sautéed Zucchini

PROVENCE

COURGETTES SAUTÉES À LA PROVENÇALE

Provençal Sautéed Zucchini

Serve this as a garnish to grilled or roasted meats. It is also very good tossed with pasta, grated cheese and butter.

¼ cup (2 fl oz/60 ml) olive oil
1 lb (500 g) zucchini (courgettes), thinly sliced
salt and freshly ground pepper
persillade made with 2 cloves garlic (see glossary)

PROVENCE

GRATIN DE NAVETS

Turnip Gratin

As an accompaniment to roast duck or pork, this gratin is especially good mingled with the roasting juices.

2 lb (1 kg) young, crisp turnips, peeled and cut into slices
  ¼ inch (6 mm) thick
3 tablespoons unsalted butter
thin slices semidry bread
salt and freshly ground pepper
½ cup (2 oz/60 g) freshly grated Parmesan cheese

◈ Bring a saucepan filled with salted water to a boil. Add the turnip slices and boil until tender, 15–20 minutes.

◈ Meanwhile, preheat an oven to 325°F (165°C). Butter a deep 6-cup (48-fl oz/1.5-l) gratin dish with 1 tablespoon of the butter and line it with bread slices.

◈ Drain the turnip slices and spread a layer of them over the bread slices. Salt lightly, grind over some pepper and sprinkle with some of the Parmesan. Add another layer of bread slices, and then turnip slices, and again season and sprinkle with cheese. Repeat the layers until all ingredients are used, finishing with a layer of turnips seasoned with salt and pepper and sprinkled with Parmesan.

◈ Cut the remaining 2 tablespoons of butter into small pieces and scatter over the top. Place in the oven and bake until golden and the turnips begin to melt, about 40 minutes. Serve immediately.

SERVES 4   *Photograph pages 262–263*

VAR

ÉTUVÉE DE POMMES DE TERRE AUX OLIVES

Potatoes with White Wine and Olives

Effortless and delicious, with grilled lamb chops, for instance.

1½ lb (750 g) potatoes, peeled and quartered or cut into
  large cubes
3 or 4 shallots, thinly sliced
2 cloves garlic, crushed
salt
3 tablespoons olive oil
½ cup (4 fl oz/125 ml) dry white wine
⅔ cup (3 oz/100 g) black olives, pitted if desired

◈ Combine all of the ingredients in a flameproof earthenware casserole or heavy sauté pan. Cover and simmer over low heat until the potatoes are tender, about 40 minutes. Serve immediately.

SERVES 4

SPAGHETTI AUX ANCHOIS

Spaghetti with Anchovies

The exhilarating, fresh flavor of this sauce depends on rapid execution. The larger the frying pan in which the tomatoes are sautéed, the more rapid will be the evaporation of their juices. The dish requires only about 10 minutes to prepare.

¾ lb (375 g) spaghetti
5 tablespoons (3 fl oz/80 ml) olive oil
6 salt anchovies, rinsed and filleted (see glossary)
4 cloves garlic
1 lb (500 g) tomatoes, peeled, seeded and coarsely chopped
salt
⅔ cup (3 oz/100 g) black olives, pitted

Artichoke Gratin

freshly ground pepper
handful of fresh basil leaves, torn into small fragments at the last minute
freshly grated Parmesan cheese and unsalted butter for serving

◙ Bring a large saucepan filled with salted water to a boil. Following the package directions, add the spaghetti so that it is ready just as the tomatoes are cooked.
◙ Pour 2 tablespoons of the olive oil into a large, flameproof earthenware casserole or heavy sauté pan. Lay out the anchovy fillets, side by side, in the oil and place the pan over the lowest possible heat. The anchovies will melt in the warm oil; they should not fry.
◙ Meanwhile, in a large frying pan, warm the remaining 3 tablespoons olive oil over high heat. Add the garlic cloves and, when they begin to sizzle but before browning, add the tomatoes and salt to taste. Toss the tomatoes until their liquid evaporates, about 5 minutes; the tomatoes should not cook to a purée. Add the olives and empty the frying pan into the pan with the anchovies. Grind over some pepper and stir in the basil.
◙ Drain the spaghetti and add to the anchovy sauce. Toss together with fork and spoon. Serve into heated pasta dishes or soup plates, accompanied with a dish of Parmesan and a dish of butter for diners to add as desired.

SERVES 4

TIAN D'ARTICHAUTS

Artichoke Gratin

Enclosed in a crisp golden sheath, these meltingly tender pale artichoke slices must be eaten as a separate course to be appreciated fully.

6 young, tender artichokes, trimmed, split in half lengthwise, chokes removed if necessary, and finely sliced lengthwise (see glossary)
6 tablespoons (3 fl oz/90 ml) olive oil
2½ cups (5 oz/150 g) fresh bread crumbs
3 oz (100 g) lean salt pork (green bacon), diced
persillade made with 2 cloves garlic (see glossary)
1 bunch tender green (spring) onions, including the tender green parts, finely sliced
salt and freshly ground pepper
2 eggs
½ cup (4 fl oz/125 ml) milk

◙ Preheat an oven to 400°F (200°C).
◙ Dry the sliced artichokes in a cotton towel or between paper towels and toss them in a bowl with 2 tablespoons of the olive oil.
◙ In a large bowl, combine the bread crumbs, salt pork, *persillade,* onions and salt and pepper to taste. In another, smaller bowl beat together the eggs, milk and 2 tablespoons of the olive oil until well blended. Add to the crumb mixture and stir together thoroughly.
◙ Smear the bottom and sides of a 6-cup (48-fl oz/1.5-l) gratin dish with olive oil. Spread half the crumb mixture in the bottom of the dish; spread the sliced artichokes evenly over the surface. Spread the remaining crumb mixture on top, smoothing the surface. Drizzle with the remaining 2 tablespoons olive oil.
◙ Place the dish in the oven and turn the heat down to 325°F (165°C).
◙ Bake until crisp and golden, about 1 hour. Serve hot.

SERVES 4

Spaghetti with Anchovies

457

COURGETTES AU GRATIN

Zucchini Gratin

Serve as a separate course.

3 tablespoons olive oil
1 onion, finely chopped
2 salt anchovies, rinsed, filleted and chopped (see glossary)
1½ lb (750 g) small, firm zucchini (courgettes), diced
salt and freshly ground pepper
persillade made with 1 clove garlic (see glossary)
⅔ cup (3 oz/100 g) black olives, pitted
3 hard-cooked eggs, shelled and chopped
dried bread crumbs

◉ Preheat an oven to 400°F (200°C). Smear a 6-cup (48-fl oz/ 1.5-l) gratin dish with olive oil.
◉ Warm 2 tablespoons of the olive oil in a frying pan over low heat. Add the onion and cook until softened, about 10 minutes. Add the anchovies and, as they begin to melt, add the zucchini. Cook over low heat, stirring regularly with a wooden spoon, until the zucchini are quite tender, about 15 minutes.
◉ Salt lightly and grind over pepper generously. Stir in the *persillade,* olives and eggs and spread in the gratin dish. Sprinkle bread crumbs over the top and dribble on the remaining 1 tablespoon olive oil.
◉ Place in the oven and bake until golden, about 20 minutes. Serve immediately.

SERVES 4

PAPETON D'AUBERGINES

Molded Eggplant Pudding

A quaint legend claims that one of the 14th-century Avignon popes, recently arrived from Rome, reproached the local cooks for their lack of finesse. To prove his worth, one Avignon cook created a divine eggplant dish in the form of a pope's tiara, which definitively converted the pope to la cuisine avignonnaise. *Serve as a separate course.*

3 lb (1.5 kg) elongated eggplants (aubergines)
salt
olive oil as needed
5 eggs
1 cup (8 fl oz/250 ml) milk
⅛ teaspoon powdered saffron dissolved in 1 tablespoon
    boiling water
boiling water as needed
3 cups (24 fl oz/750 ml) tomato sauce, heated (see glossary)

◉ Cut off the stem ends from the eggplants. Slice 2 or 3 lengthwise slices ⅓ in (8 mm) thick from the center of each eggplant. Using a sharp-pointed knife tip, crosshatch the left-over sides. Salt the slices and the sides and leave in a colander to drain for 30 minutes. Sponge dry with paper towels.
◉ Preheat an oven to 350°F (180°C). In a large frying pan, pour in olive oil to a depth of ¼ in (6 mm) and place over medium heat. Slip the eggplant slices, a few at a time, into the hot oil and fry, turning once, until golden on both sides, about 10 minutes. Add more oil as needed. Remove to paper towels to drain. Then fry the crosshatched sides in the same manner and drain on paper towels.
◉ Scrape all the flesh from the crosshatched sides into a bowl and mash to a purée with a fork. Add the eggs and a pinch of salt and whisk together. Then whisk in the milk and the

dissolved saffron until thoroughly incorporated. Set aside.
◉ Line a 6-cup (48-fl oz/1.5-l) savarin mold (circular mold with a well) or other round mold with the eggplant slices, overlapping them slightly and pressing firmly into place. The tips should extend beyond the outer rim and the central well. Pour in the custard mixture and fold the extending tips over the surface.
◉ Place the mold in a large oven pan and pour in boiling

Zucchini Gratin

water to reach halfway up the sides, to form a *bain-marie*. Place in the oven and bake until the surface of the custard is no longer liquid, about 40 minutes. Remove from the *bain-marie* and leave to settle for 10 minutes.

◙ To unmold, fold a kitchen towel lengthwise and place the mold on it. Place an overturned platter on top and grip the ridge of the mold, protected by the towel, using your finger-nails. While holding the platter firmly in place with your thumbs, turn over the mold and platter together. Lift off the mold. Pour a ribbon of tomato sauce around the outside of the *papeton* and pour the remainder into a heated bowl to serve alongside.

SERVES 6 *Photograph pages 460–461*

AUBERGINES FARCIES À LA PROVENÇALE

Provençal Stuffed Eggplants

Delicious with roast lamb or as a separate course. Often chopped mushrooms are cooked with the onion and, for a supper main course, chopped leftover lamb can be incorporated into the stuffing.

4 elongated eggplants (aubergines), about 1½ lb (750 g) total weight
salt
olive oil as needed
1 onion, finely chopped

2 tomatoes, peeled, seeded and coarsely chopped
pinch of coarse salt
1 clove garlic
2 salt anchovies, rinsed and filleted (see glossary)
½ cup (1 oz/30 g) fresh bread crumbs
1 tablespoon chopped fresh flat-leaf (Italian) parsley
small pinch of Provençal mixed dried herbs (see glossary)
freshly ground pepper
1 egg
dried bread crumbs

◙ Cut off the stem ends and split the eggplants in half lengthwise. Using a small, sharp-pointed knife, cut into the flesh all the way around each eggplant half. Cut at a slight bias, about ¼ inch (6 mm) from the edge, and be careful not to approach the skin. Using the knife tip, crosshatch the flesh within the border cut. Sprinkle the surfaces with salt and leave for

460

In a mortar pound together the coarse salt, garlic and anchovy fillets to form a paste. Add the fresh bread crumbs and mix well, wiping the mortar walls clean. Add the crumb mixture to the bowl, along with the parsley, herbs, pepper to taste and egg. Using your hands mix well. Taste for salt.

▣ Arrange the eggplant shells in a large gratin dish, hollow sides up, and stuff them with the eggplant mixture. Smooth the surfaces with the back of a spoon, sprinkle with dried bread crumbs and dribble with olive oil. Bake until the surfaces are crisp and golden, 20–25 minutes. Serve immediately.

SERVES 4

V A R

GRATIN D'AUBERGINES
Eggplant Custard Gratin

This can only stand alone, as a separate vegetable course; it is exquisite.

3 elongated eggplants (aubergines), about 1½ lb (750 g) total
    weight, cut lengthwise into slices ½ in (12 mm) thick
salt
olive oil as needed
1 onion, finely chopped
2 cloves garlic, finely chopped
1 lb (500 g) tomatoes, peeled, seeded and coarsely chopped
¼ lb (125 g) *brousse* (see glossary) or ricotta cheese
2 eggs
½ cup (2 oz/60 g) freshly grated Parmesan cheese
½ cup (4 fl oz/125 ml) heavy whipping (double) cream
freshly ground pepper
fresh basil leaves

▣ Sprinkle the eggplant slices on both sides with salt, spread them out on a tray and leave for 30 minutes. Sponge dry with paper towels.

▣ In a large frying pan, pour in olive oil to a depth of ¼ in (6 mm) and place over medium heat. Fry the eggplant slices, in batches, in the hot oil until golden and tender at the stem ends, turning once, about 10 minutes. Add more oil to the pan as needed. Remove and drain on paper towels. Pour off any oil.

▣ Preheat an oven to 450°F (230°C). In the same frying pan, warm 2 tablespoons olive oil over low heat. Add the onion and cook gently until softened, about 10 minutes. Add the garlic, tomatoes and salt to taste and increase the heat to high. Toss until the moisture from the tomatoes evaporates, about 15 minutes. Set aside.

▣ In a mixing bowl break up the *brousse* or ricotta cheese and the eggs with a whisk. Add half of the grated cheese, cream, and salt and pepper to taste and whisk to the consistency of a pourable cream.

▣ Line a 6-cup (48-fl oz/1.5-l) gratin dish with about half of the eggplant slices in a single layer, pressing them in place. Grind over some pepper. Tear basil leaves into fragments and scatter over the eggplant. Sprinkle lightly with half of the remaining grated cheese and then spread over the tomato mixture. Arrange the remaining eggplant slices on top in a single layer, pressing them firmly in place. If there are a few extra slices, press them on top. Pour over the cheese-egg mixture and smooth the top. Sprinkle with the remaining grated cheese.

▣ Place in the oven and immediately reduce the heat to 350°F (180°C). Bake until the custard surface is swelled and golden with no depression in the middle, about 30 minutes. Serve hot.

SERVES 4

Clockwise from top: Provençal Stuffed Eggplants, Eggplant Daube, Molded Eggplant Pudding, Eggplant Custard Gratin

30 minutes. Sponge dry with paper towels.

▣ Preheat an oven to 375°F (190°C). In a large frying pan, pour in olive oil to a depth of ¼ in (6 mm) and place over medium heat. Slip the eggplant halves into the pan, cut sides down, and fry until lightly colored. Turn skin side down and fry, adjusting heat as necessary, until the flesh is tender enough to be easily scooped out with a teaspoon, about 15 minutes. Remove to paper towels to drain.

▣ Pour off most of the oil from the frying pan. Reheat the oil remaining in the pan over low heat. Add the onion and cook gently until softened, about 10 minutes. Add the tomatoes and increase the heat to high. Toss until the moisture from the tomatoes evaporates, about 10 minutes. Empty the pan into a mixing bowl.

▣ Scoop the flesh from the eggplant halves into the bowl, leaving the ¼-in (6-mm) border of flesh near the skin intact.

VAR

PURÉE BLANCHE
White Purée

Nothing accompanies braised lamb, especially stuffed shoulder (recipe on page 384), better than this magical purée. Do not discard the leftover cooking water; it is a wonderful soup base. Add a few allspice berries to the peppercorns in your mill.

1 lb (500 g) small, crisp turnips
½ cup (4 oz/125 g) unsalted butter
1 lb (500 g) celeriac (celery root), peeled and cut into large cubes
salt
1 lb (500 g) potatoes, peeled and quartered if large
1 lb (500 g) onions, peeled and quartered
1 head garlic, cloves separated and peeled
freshly ground pepper

◙ Peel the turnips and quarter them if large. Fill a saucepan with water and bring to a boil. Add the turnips and boil until half-cooked, about 15 minutes. Drain well.
◙ In a heavy pan, melt 2 tablespoons of the butter over very low heat. Add the turnips, cover and cook, shaking and tossing occasionally, until tender, 20–30 minutes.
◙ Meanwhile, bring a large saucepan filled with salted water to a boil. Add the celeriac and boil for 15 minutes. Add the potatoes, onions and garlic and cook at a gentle boil until all the vegetables are tender, about 30 minutes. Drain in a colander, saving the cooking water.
◙ Using a wooden pestle, pass the turnips and their cooking butter and the boiled vegetables into a purée. If it is very stiff, add a bit of the reserved cooking liquid.
◙ Reheat the purée in a heavy saucepan over medium heat, stirring and beating constantly with a wooden spoon to prevent sticking. When it is heated through, remove from the stove.
◙ Grind some pepper over the top. Dice the remaining butter into small pieces and stir it into the purée. Serve at once.

SERVES 6

ALPES·MARITIMES

CÔTES DE BLETTE À L'ANCHOIS
Chard Ribs with Anchovy Sauce

To arrive at 1 pound (500 g) of chard ribs, you will need at least 4 pounds (2 kg) chard. After cutting the ribs free from the green leaves, parboil the leaves, refresh them under cold running water and squeeze them dry (see glossary). Enclose the ball of squeezed leaves in plastic wrap and refrigerate it for up to 3 or 4 days. Use it in innumerable Provençal stuffings, soups, omelets or gratins.

FOR THE COURT BOUILLON:

8 cups (64 fl oz/2 l) water
1 large onion, finely sliced
1 bay leaf
1 large fresh thyme sprig
stems from a bouquet of fresh flat-leaf (Italian) parsley
1 small dried cayenne chili pepper or other dried small chili pepper
1 tablespoon vinegar
salt

1 lb (500 g) Swiss chard (silverbeet) ribs, strings removed and cut into pieces 4 in (10 cm) long by 1 in (2.5 cm) wide
freshly ground pepper

pinch of coarse salt
2 cloves garlic
2 salt anchovies, rinsed and filleted (see glossary)
2 tablespoons olive oil
2 tablespoons all-purpose (plain) flour

◙ Combine all the ingredients for the court bouillon in a large saucepan and bring to a boil. Cover and cook at a gentle boil for 45 minutes.
◙ Strain, return the liquid to the saucepan and add the chard ribs. Boil for 10 minutes, then drain, reserving the liquid. Spread the chard pieces in a gratin dish and grind over the pepper.
◙ Preheat an oven to 400°F (200°C). In a mortar, pound together the coarse salt, garlic cloves and anchovies to form a paste.
◙ Heat the olive oil in a saucepan over medium-high heat. Add the flour and stir for a minute or so. Stir in the anchovy paste and pour in 3 cups (24 fl oz/750 ml) of the reserved court bouillon, whisking at the same time. Continue to whisk until a boil is reached. Lower the heat and cook, uncovered, at a simmer or very gentle boil for 20 minutes. Taste for salt.
◙ Pour the anchovy sauce through a sieve over the chard ribs. Put the dish in the oven and bake until the sauce is bubbling and the surface is lightly colored, about 20 minutes. Serve at once.

SERVES 4

VAUCLUSE

DAUBE D'AUBERGINES
Eggplant Daube

A sketchy version of this recipe was first published by René Jouveau in La cuisine provençale de tradition populaire, *1963. Its similarity to a traditional daube resides mainly in the choice of aromatic elements and, especially, in the presence of the dried orange rind.*

2 tablespoons olive oil
5 oz (150 g) lean salt pork (green bacon), cut into ⅓-in (8-mm) dice
2 large, sweet white onions, thinly sliced
5 oz (150 g) carrots, peeled and thickly sliced
1 lb (500 g) tomatoes, peeled, seeded and coarsely chopped
3 cloves garlic, crushed
bouquet garni including a strip of dried orange peel (see glossary)
2 lb (1 kg) firm, young eggplants (aubergines), cut into ¾-in (2-cm) cubes
½ cup (4 fl oz/125 ml) dry white wine
salt
freshly ground pepper
1 tablespoon chopped fresh flat-leaf (Italian) parsley

◙ Warm the olive oil in a flameproof earthenware casserole or other heavy pot over medium heat. Add the salt pork and fry gently, stirring occasionally with a wooden spoon. As the salt pork begins to color, add the onions and carrots. Cook over low heat until the onions are soft, about 15 minutes.
◙ Add the tomatoes, garlic and bouquet garni. Spread the eggplant cubes on top and pour in the white wine. Sprinkle with salt to taste and raise the heat so that the contents of the pan begins to bubble. Cover, reduce the heat to low and simmer gently until the eggplant is tender, about 1 hour.
◙ Drain off the liquid from the casserole into a small saucepan. Bring the liquid to a boil and reduce over medium-high heat to about ½ cup (4 fl oz/125 ml). Grind pepper over the eggplant and pour the reduced juices over the top. Swirl the contents of the pan to mix lightly, sprinkle with the parsley and serve.

SERVES 4   *Photograph pages 460–461*

Left to right: White Purée, Chard Ribs with Anchovy Sauce

Spring Vegetable Stew

ESTOUFFADE PRINTANIÈRE

Spring Vegetable Stew

A lovely dish, served either on its own or as an accompaniment to roast lamb. The broad beans should be freshly picked, about thumbnail size, clear green when peeled and tender enough to be eaten raw.

several leaves tender, leafy lettuce
2 tablespoons olive oil
4 young, tender artichokes, trimmed, quartered and chokes
  removed if necessary (see glossary)
½ lb (250 g) walnut-sized green (spring) onions,
  tops discarded
12 cloves garlic, preferably new garlic, unpeeled
bouquet garni (see glossary)
salt
2 tablespoons water
4 lb (2 kg) young, tender broad (fava) beans, shelled and
  each bean peeled

freshly ground pepper
2 tablespoons unsalted butter, chilled and diced
a few fresh savory leaves, finely chopped and mixed with a
  pinch of chopped fresh flat-leaf (Italian) parsley

⊞ Rinse the lettuce leaves but do not dry. Roll up the leaves into a tight cylinder and thinly slice crosswise. Set aside.
⊞ Warm the olive oil in a flameproof earthenware casserole or heavy sauté pan over low heat. Add the artichokes, onions, garlic and bouquet garni. Sprinkle with salt to taste and spread the lettuce over the top. Cover tightly and cook over very low heat, shaking the pan occasionally, until the lettuce is "melting" and the artichokes are tender yet firm, about 40 minutes.
⊞ Add the water and the broad beans, cover and raise the heat slightly to create steam. Shake to intermingle the contents of the pan. When the broad beans are heated through, after 5 or 6 minutes, grind over some pepper and remove from the heat.
⊞ Swirl in the butter and sprinkle the savory-parsley mixture over the top. Serve at once.

SERVES 4

BRANDADE DE HARICOTS

White Bean Brandade

The anchovies here replace poutargue—*salted tuna or mullet roe, pressed and dried—which is more traditional in this dish from Marseilles. Often served as a starter, these simmered white beans are also delicious as an accompaniment to roast lamb or pork.*

2½ cups (1 lb/500 g) dried Great Northern beans
1 cup (8 fl oz/250 ml) olive oil
about ½ cup (4 fl oz/125 ml) milk, heated
freshly ground pepper
6 salt anchovies, rinsed, filleted and chopped (see glossary)
juice of ½ lemon
salt
handful of small croutons, fried in olive oil until crisp
   and golden

◉ Prepare the dried beans as directed for white beans with sausage and salt pork (recipe on page 437) but simmer them with the bouquet garni, whole onion, carrot and garlic until tender enough to be puréed, about 1½ hours.
◉ Drain the hot beans, discard the aromatics and, using a wooden pestle, pass the beans through a fine-mesh sieve back into the saucepan. Place the saucepan over very low heat. Stir and beat the purée with a wooden spoon while adding the olive oil in a trickle (or ask someone else to trickle while you beat). Do not add all of the oil if the consistency of the purée is reasonably supple. Beat in only enough of the milk for the purée to remain very supple without being pourable. Grind over some pepper abundantly, then stir in the anchovies and lemon juice.
◉ Taste and adjust seasonings with salt and pepper. Empty the purée into a heated deep platter and scatter the croutons over the top. Serve immediately.

SERVES 4–6

FEUILLES DE CÉLERIS À LA MÉNAGÈRE

Celery Gratin Durand

Charles Durand, author of the first Provençal cookbook, suggests preparing purslane leaves in the same way as the celery in this recipe.

2 bunches celery
3 tablespoons olive oil
2 salt anchovies, rinsed, filleted and chopped (see glossary)
salt and freshly ground pepper
whole nutmeg
¼ lb (125 g) semidry bread, crusts removed
1½ cups (12 fl oz/375 ml) milk
3 egg yolks
¼ cup (1 oz/30 g) freshly grated Parmesan or Gruyère cheese
1 tablespoon unsalted butter, cut into small pieces

◉ Remove the tough outer stalks from the celery bunches and trim the root ends. Cut the bunches across, just below the leaf-branch joints. Remove the leaves and set aside. (Put the leaf branches and tough outer stalks aside for use in bouquets garnis.) Slice the stalk bunches crosswise into 3 or 4 sections.
◉ Fill a saucepan with salted water and bring to a boil. Add the sliced stalk bunches and the reserved leaves and parboil them for 10 minutes. Drain and, when cool enough to handle,

squeeze tightly in a towel to rid of excess moisture. Chop the leaves and stalks.
◉ Preheat an oven to 400°F (200°C). Heat 2 tablespoons of the olive oil in a sauté pan. Add the chopped celery and anchovies, season lightly with salt, grind over some pepper, and scrape over a bit of nutmeg. Cover and cook over very low heat, stirring occasionally with a wooden spoon, for 10 minutes.
◉ Meanwhile, break the bread into a small saucepan and pour in the milk. Bring to a boil and simmer over medium heat for 10 minutes. Pour the bread mixture into the sauté pan, stir well and simmer, stirring regularly, until the mixture is consistent but still quite loose, just a few minutes. Remove from the heat.
◉ Smear a 6-cup (48-fl oz/1.5-l) gratin dish with olive oil. In a small bowl, combine the egg yolks, the remaining 1 table-spoon olive oil and a couple tablespoons water. Using a fork beat together until blended. Then, using a wooden spoon, stir the egg mixture into the celery mixture. Pour into the gratin dish and smooth the surface. Sprinkle with the cheese and distribute butter fragments evenly over the top.
◉ Place in the oven and bake until the surface is slightly colored, about 10 minutes. Serve at once.

SERVES 4

Left to right: White Bean Brandade, Celery Gratin Durand

VAR

VAR

There is no doubt that the Var region is a bit too timid. That character trait is about the only thing we can find to explain a culinary identity that is caught between two terrains, less marked than the Nice region in the Alpes-Maritimes with its very special accents, or than the endless conversation Provençal cuisine conducts between the Bouches-du-Rhône, the Alpes-de-Haute-Provence, and the Vaucluse.

Yet the dishes that flourish on the hills overlooking the Lavandou or the islands of Hyères, in the hanging villages of the high country or around the approach to the Verdon, or in the heart of Saint-Tropez, definitely have a family connection with the other tastes of Provence. The Var is at the crossroads between the flavors of the sea with their hint of Italy and the influences of Provence's interior.

Here again *bouillabaisse* (with a variant from Toulon called *revesset* containing spinach, Swiss chard [silver beet] or perhaps sardines), *bourride,* and *anchoïade* or *aïoli* are the basis of the culinary scene along the seaboard. Olive oil (this is France's foremost oil-producing district, with six million olive trees) and vegetables play a major part, and as soon as you start climbing around the hills you will discover mushrooms (the tiny orange-red *sanguins* or the delectable *grisets*), tiny snails and game.

While the recipe for *lapin en paquets* ("rabbit in parcels") is still treasured in Brignoles, few of its inhabitants recall *pistoles de Monsieur,* the name given in memory of Gaston d'Orléans to plums that had been dried and

Previous pages: A quiet cove in St. Tropez is sheltered from the thousands of tourists who flock here in the summer. Left: This bucolic setting is near Draguignan, named after the dragon that was said to have terrorized the area in the fifth century.

469

flattened like the ancient gold coins called *pistoles.*

Even though little birds have become a rarity (and their capture is forbidden), Barjols retains its larks *à la barjolaise,* roasted in olive oil. And every four years, in January, the fatted ox is still paraded through this town full of springs and fountains, for the name-day festival of Saint Marcel. The animal is cut up and its tripe distributed, and everyone dances in celebration of *Fête des Tripettes.*

The Var is an area that stands apart from the rest of Provence, an area of the *caillette* (tripe); of pork sweet-breads, fresh liver and bacon; beef and lamb daubes; of *pieds et paquets* and artichokes *à la barigoule;* of *tians* that are named for the local earthenware pot in which they are cooked; of fritters and stuffings. It is sweet, quiet yet agitated, as if it were harking back to the Saracens who in the eighth century lay in ambush in the Maures Forest. It is also luminous, as evidenced in the ochers of the Esterel Mountains scoured once upon a time by legendary bandits like Gaspard de Besse. And it is a bit temperamental as well. Saint-Tropez proves that. Courted and beseiged by the world at large, she jealously preserves the memory of her painters and writers, of Dunoyer de Segonzac, Matisse, Bonnard, Signac, Colette.

This Var depends increasingly on its hanging villages— Fayence, Tourtour, Bargemon, Salernes, Montauroux, Entrecasteaux, Cotignac, Mons, Seillans—to defend its reputation as an unspoiled *département;* and on its golden islands (Port-Cros, for example, or Porquerolles, where two quality vineyards remind us that in the past this was a paradise of vines and market gardens) to act as a link between the Mediterranean and Provence.

This discussion would be woefully incomplete if it failed to bring together the food and wine of the Var, as happens with Bordelais and Beaujolais. The conquest of the vine in the Var is one of the most amazing of French victories. And the artist's palette represented by the wine areas, which at times is a highly complex one, fits well with the moods of Provençal cuisine.

Winemakers all over the world arrange the course of history to their own advantage and delve back into furthest antiquity to explain the nobility of their vintages. Here they do the same. For example, the supporters of the small Bandol appellation go back to the sixth century B.C.

Wine production is one of the Var's major industries and the vineyards of Bandol produce wine rated among the best in Provence.

to pick up the trail of the Greek navigators who searched the length of the coast between Saint-Cyr and Bandol for trading posts to organize bartering. They were welcome navigators indeed, who set about teaching the men of Gaul how to dress vines and make wine. We will take their word for it, even if historical accuracy sometimes suffers in the process, and imagine the wine contained in the amphora that are still found in wrecks between Marseilles and Antibes: two cities which were already at that time cornerstones of the corn-vine-olive trilogy so essential to Mediterranean civilization.

Wine and food. The partnership is beyond question. The contribution of traditional and imported grape varieties to the development of Provençal recipes is well known. Syrah, the oldest of them all, was brought in by the Romans and known for its powerful aroma. Also prized are the enduring fruitiness of the old Grenache, the sweetness of Cinsault, the luster and vigor of the rich but less known Tibouren, the sturdiness of the now-discarded Carignan brought across from Spain, and lastly, the variety that must "see the sea," the Mourvèdre, king of the Bandol vines, established on the hot, calcareous hills around Le Beausset, the Castellet and La Cadière d'Azur.

Two appellations reign at the table, Côtes de Provence and Bandol, expressing the richness of the Var's vineyard. Sometimes, in a show of Provence solidarity, they are backed up by the neighboring vineyards of Cassis, Palette, or the Côteaux d'Aix, or even the tiny Nice vineyard of Bellet. And one must not forget the recent rise to prominence of Côteaux Varois, a young, new appellation among these wines of the sun.

The rosé thrives in the company of a rack of lamb or a vegetable dish, alongside a ratatouille or an *aïoli* or certain kinds of fish. We know, of course, that it is no longer the rough wine so badly cultivated twenty years ago in overheated cellars by careless wine makers.

The red, blended with the very Bordeaux Cabernet Sauvignon grapes, is suited to game from the hills, the wild boar that run in the old Maures forests and the open country of the northern Var. But there is no doubt it goes equally well with a beef daube, a *caillette* or a garlicky leg of lamb. The whites (based on Clairette, Semillon, Ugni Blanc and Rolle grapes, depending upon the region) are marvelous with porgy (sea bream) or John Dory baked in the oven and simply drizzled with olive oil.

One could name dozens of areas that produce exceptional wines. Only the ones that are basic to the history of the Côtes de Provence are mentioned here: the Ott Estates, belonging to that great family who came from Alsace in 1896, to teach the people of Provence how to nourish the soil, cultivate the vine and create a great wine. At Beausset, at Taradeau in the heart of the Var, at La Londe les Maures where the Clos Mireille vines grow on a level with the Mediterranean, the family continues its reign, producing model rosés, whites and reds.

These Var wines follow the rhythm of the seasons and comfort a peasant gastronomy that does not neglect its traditions: game in autumn, truffles in the Aups region from November to March. Listen to this miller from Tourtour at the beginning of the twentieth century describing a meal with which he consumed a couple of bottles of local wine (the quotation is abbreviated here): "I order artichoke served raw and moistened with my fragrant virgin oil. Before me a stemmed glass is filled with a rosé wine brought from Carcès. The maidservant sets on the table a huge red casserole in which there simmers a rabbit cooked in the Brignoles style, *en paquetons.*

Narrow alleyways and compact dwellings typify the Provençal village, built to confrom to the confines of the terrain.

Another maidservant puts down a white china sauce jug with the cooking juices in it, and brings a flask from Tourves in which a red wine dances in the sun. . . . Then in an avalanche, thrush barded with bacon, stuffed with juniper berries and browned in the oven, two long skewers of small birds . . . and larks prepared as they do them in Barjols . . . pork *caillettes* and slices of lamb's liver dressed with sauce and capers and strewn with chopped garlic

The medieval village of Seillans is known for its perfume and flower production.

and parsley. . . . I like to eat my crayfish and my snails *à la suçarelle* . . . scrambled eggs with truffles, and potatoes browned in oil and accompanied by fillets of anchovy. I serve the wine of Pontevès when the *pignins aux saucissettes* (small sausages) arrive. . . . The excellent cooked wine of Entrecasteaux is already finished when the brandy, this gem from Lorgues, is poured for us."

Fortunately people no longer eat like that these days—on pain of dying of happiness! But the Haut Var goes on dispensing its products of the sun. The honey that flourished from the sixteenth century around the Brignoles and Draguignan region is still produced in the hives and honey farms that crowd the villages of Lorgues, Taradeau, Thoronet, Montfort sur Argens, Comps, Trigance, Aups. There is honey perfumed with rosemary, *mille fleurs* honey and lavender honey taken from along the border between the villages of the Verdon and the Alpine plateaus of Haute Provence.

Then there is black gold. Truffles. One of the undisputed capitals of the truffle is Aups, village of fountains. The truffles are gathered in the hills by the *caveurs,* who dig around the roots of the truffle oaks—when the wild boar or poachers don't get there before them—assisted by their special dogs, pigs, or flies.

The market here is as famous as the one at Carpentras in Vaucluse, and every Thursday between November and March, at market time, baskets are filled with truffles. Or rather, the papers containing the precious truffles are unfolded in the back rooms of the cafes, and it is negotiation time: time for the peasants to conduct their secret negotiations with the brokers, who weigh each fragrant jewel to the nearest gram and pass over wads of banknotes in silence.

Thus the Var, though virtually never out of sight of the Mediterranean, lives the best of its Provençal life in the secret of its small towns.

DESSERTS

The finest Provençale goat cheeses often come from small, independent farms.

DESSERTS

Provençal desserts are, first of all, cheeses and fresh fruits. A favorite dessert, adored by children, is fresh *brousse,* unsalted ewe's milk curdled by the addition of rennet and sold in perforated molds while still draining. It is usually sprinkled with sugar and a few drops of orange flower water, but salted, and with a veil of pepper, its sweetness and subtlety are better thrown into relief. *La brousse du Rove,* west of Marseilles, is famous in the region. Barjols, in the upper Var, is a large producer of *brousse* and other ewe's milk cheeses.

Except in the Alps, Provençal cheese production is limited to cheeses made from ewe's or goat's milk, mainly the latter. The little disks of ewe's milk cheese called *tommes de Camargue* or *tommes arlésiennes,* exquisite when a week old, have a well-deserved reputation, but the production is so low that they can be found only in the immediate region. The goat cheeses of Banon, in the Alpes-de-Haute-Provence, either wrapped in chestnut leaves or presented with sprigs of fresh savory stuck to their surfaces, travel farther than most (they are easily found in Paris).

Throughout Provence, along the country roads, hand-painted signs at the entrances to properties announce farmers' goat cheeses for sale. The finest cheeses often come from these small producers; they are at their best after two weeks' cellaring, drained on straw mats and turned daily. The Provençaux have a special affection for their goat cheeses, but they do not hesitate to complete their cheese platters with cheeses from farther afield: Reblochon, Saint-Nectaire, Gorgonzola and Gruyère are amongst the favorites. An old Châteauneuf-du-Pape, Palette or Bandol is often uncorked for the cheese service.

The most famous of Provençal desserts are the ritual thirteen desserts of the Christmas Eve supper, a Lenten but abundant meal composed of such rustic fare as *aïgo bouido,* celery sticks with *anchoïade,* snails with *aïoli,* salt cod or eel in sauce, chick-pea salad and vegetable gratins. The thirteen desserts include almonds, hazelnuts (filberts) and walnuts; dried figs, dates, raisins and prunes; bananas, oranges, tangerines, pears and grapes hung in the attic, withered and concentrated; candied almonds and fruits, quince paste and *calissons d'Aix* (glazed little diamonds of fruit-flavored almond paste); black and white nougats. *Nougat noir* (unskinned almonds and honey, boiled until dark and cooled under a weight between sheets of rice paper) and *pompe à l'huile,* a sweetened bread dough biscuit, are obligatory elements.

These desserts are always accompanied by *vin cuit,* a sweet red wine made by vineyardists at the time of the grape harvest. They reduce unfermented must, drawn from the vats, in huge cauldrons heated over wood fires to concentrate the grape sugars. Then they ferment the must in barrels until the high sugar content arrests the fermentation (commercial and homemade *vins cuits* are often doctored by the addition of brandy). The rather dry

Previous pages: A Roman bridge, Montagne du Lubéron. From top to bottom: Peach and Bread Pudding (recipe page 485), Apricot Tart (recipe page 488).

pompe à l'huile is transformed when broken and dipped into a glass of authentic, aged *vin cuit*.

Many simple sweet things are traditionally eaten on specific religious holidays. Village saints' days are celebrated with *oreillettes,* sweetened noodle dough rolled out into small ovals, slit, twisted into ear shapes and deep-fried. In Nice, fried ribbons of the same dough are called *ganses* and, in Arles, the ribbons are loosely tied and named *bugnes; ganses* and *bugnes* are both associated with carnival celebrations.

For Twelfth Night, January 6, bakers prepare crowns of sweet brioche, garnished with candied fruits and each enclosing a token, originally a dried broad (fava) bean. Friends gather to share a *gâteau des rois* and the recipient of the token is crowned king. For Candlemas, February 2, nearly everyone in Provence eats crêpes, but in Marseilles, Candlemas is celebrated with little boat-shaped sweet cookies called *navettes.* Sweet fritters are for Mardi Gras and Ash Wednesday, and *brassadeaux,* bracelets of sweetened egg dough, first poached and then baked like bagels, are reserved for Easter.

Because the Provençal meal usually ends with a simple fruit dessert, quality and freshness are essential.

White cherry blossoms dot the valleys of Provence in the spring yeilding ripe, delicious fruit in the summer.

PROVENCE

OREILLETTES
Carnival Fritters

Oreillettes, shaped like ears, *are but one name for these fritters, which might also be called* ganses *("ribbons") and* bugnes *("knotted ribbons"). In fact, no matter what the shape, these fritters are called* bugnes *in Arles,* ganses *in Nice and* oreillettes *throughout Provence. They are sometimes simply small rectangles, about 1½ in (4 cm) by 3 in (4 cm), or larger rectangles with slits cut inside the borders.*

about 3 cups (12 oz/375 g) all-purpose (plain) flour
salt
2 tablespoons granulated sugar
2 eggs, beaten
¼ cup (2 oz/60 g) unsalted butter, at room temperature
¼ cup (2 fl oz/60 ml) dark rum
8 cups (64 fl oz/2 l) peanut oil or corn oil
confectioners' (icing) sugar

▦ In a mixing bowl stir together 2 cups (8 oz/250 g) of the flour, the salt and granulated sugar. Make a well in the center and add the eggs, butter and rum. Stir with a fork, working from the center outward to gather in all the flour progressively. Sprinkle over more of the flour as needed to create a supple dough. Knead the dough in the bowl, using your knuckles and sprinkling over a little more of the flour as needed to reduce stickiness. When the dough is smooth, form it into a ball in the bowl, cover the bowl with a towel and leave to rest for 1 hour.
▦ Line a baking sheet with a thin cotton towel and sprinkle with flour. To make "ears" pinch off apricot-sized pieces of dough and roll out into oval shapes ⅛ in (3 mm) thick. Alternatively, divide the dough in half and roll out each portion ⅛ in (3 mm) thick. Using a pastry cutter, cut out ovals about 4½ in (11 cm) long by 3 in (7.5 cm) wide. Cut 2 lengthwise slits within each oval, equidistant from the edges and from each other, to form 3 bands of attached dough. Lift the two outer bands up toward the center. Push one band through the far slit as you pull the other band in the opposite direction. Press the bands slightly to flatten them.
▦ To make knotted ribbons, divide the dough in half and roll out each portion into a long rectangle ⅛ in (3 mm) thick and about 8 in (20 cm) wide. Cut the rectangles into strips ¾ in (2 cm) wide and 8 in (20 cm) long. Loop each strip to form a loose knot in the middle, pulling gently at the ends to fix it.
▦ Following the directions for deep-frying in the glossary, heat the oil in a large pan. Working in small batches, slip the shapes into the hot oil; do not crowd the pan. After 1 minute turn the fritters in the oil. When they are uniformly golden, after about 2 minutes, lift them out with a slotted utensil and place on paper towels to drain briefly.
▦ Transfer to a large platter lined with a napkin. Sprinkle generously with confectioners' sugar. Serve hot.

SERVES 6

PROVENCE

TIAN DE LAIT
Provençal Custard

This is the ancestor of all set custards. Serve it hot, tepid or cold, accompanied with little cookies (biscuits).

4 cups (32 fl oz/1 l) milk
1 cup (8 oz/250 g) sugar

4 whole eggs plus 6 egg yolks
¼ cup (2 fl oz/60 ml) dark rum

▦ Preheat an oven to 300°F (150°C).
▦ Pour the milk into a saucepan and warm over medium heat. Stir in the sugar and continue to stir until a boil is

Carnival Fritters

almost reached, then remove from the heat. Leave to cool for a few minutes.

🔸 In a mixing bowl whisk together the whole eggs and egg yolks. Slowly add the milk, whisking constantly. Whisk in the rum. Pour into an earthenware oven dish. Place in the oven and bake until the custard is no longer liquid at the center—the timing depends upon the size of the dish and the depth of the custard—30–40 minutes. Test for doneness by touching the center with your fingertip; it should be firm.

SERVES 8

Photograph pages 478–479

Clockwise from top left: Provençal Pumpkin Pie; Sabayon with
Muscat de Beaumes-de-Venise (recipes page 480); Swiss Chard,
Apple and Raisin Pie; Provençal Custard (recipe page 476)

TOURTE DE BLETTES

Swiss Chard, Apple and Raisin Pie

The ingredients are surprising, but this sweet Niçois chard pie rarely fails to seduce. The original dough was bread dough, kneaded with sugar and egg. Some cooks add sliced bananas and others jellies or jams. A sweetened spinach tart is traditional in the Vaucluse; if chard is unavailable, substitute spinach.

Ingredient proportions vary for the pastry, which is called pâte sablée *and is the most commonly used pastry in Provence today for sweet tarts and pies. This recipe makes enough dough for one 9- or 10-in (23- or 25-cm) double-crust pie.*

FOR THE CRUMBLY PASTRY:

2 cups (8 oz/250 g) all-purpose (plain) flour
¼ cup (2 oz/60 g) sugar
pinch of salt
½ cup (4 oz/125 g) unsalted butter, at room temperature
2 eggs, beaten with a fork until just amalgamated

pinch of unsalted butter
2 eggs
1 tablespoon olive oil
½ cup (4 oz/125 g) granulated sugar
½ cup (2 oz/60 g) freshly grated Parmesan cheese
⅓ cup (2 oz/60 g) pine nuts
⅓ cup (2 oz/60 g) raisins soaked in ¼ cup (2 fl oz/60 ml)
   dark rum several hours or overnight
1 lb (500 g) Russet, pippin or Golden Delicious apples,
   quartered, cored, peeled and sliced or diced at last minute
1 teaspoon grated lemon zest
2 lb (1 kg) Swiss chard (silverbeet) greens, parboiled,
   squeezed dry and chopped (see glossary)
freshly ground pepper
whole nutmeg
confectioners' (icing) sugar

◈ To prepare the pastry, in a mixing bowl stir together the flour, sugar and salt. Make a well in the center and add the butter and eggs to the well. Stir, mix and mash rapidly with a fork to form a coherent mass. Turn out onto a floured work surface and knead briefly. Form the dough into a ball, enclose it in plastic wrap and refrigerate for 2 hours before rolling it out.

◈ Preheat an oven to 350°F (180°C). Use the butter to grease a 10-in (25-cm) deep pie plate. Divide the pastry dough into 2 portions, one portion slightly larger than the other.

◈ On a lightly floured work surface, roll out the larger dough portion into a round about ⅛ in (3 mm) thick. Drape the pastry around the rolling pin and transfer it to the prepared dish. Press the pastry lightly against the bottom and sides of the dish; leave the edges overhanging the rim.

◈ In a mixing bowl whisk together the eggs, olive oil, granulated sugar and cheese until well mixed. Add the pine nuts, raisins and any remaining liquid, apples, zest and chard. Grind over some pepper, scrape over some nutmeg and mix thoroughly. Empty the mixture into the pastry-lined plate, and smooth the surface.

◈ Roll out the remaining pastry and transfer it to the top of the pie. Trim the edges to overhang the rim of the dish by about ½ in (12 mm), then pinch the top and bottom layer together and roll them up onto the edge of the dish to form a rim. Crimp with a floured thumb or the back of the tines of a fork. Using the tips of pointed scissors held at an angle, snip the pastry's surface 4 or 5 times to create steam vents.

◈ Place in the oven and bake for 40 minutes, checking the color after 30 minutes. If very light, turn the oven up to 400°F (200°C) for the last 10 minutes.

◈ Remove from the oven and sprinkle generously with confectioners' sugar. Serve tepid, preferably, or at room temperature.

SERVES 6

SABAYON AU MUSCAT DE BEAUMES-DE-VENISE

Sabayon with Muscat de Beaumes-de-Venise

Nice claims sabayon *as its heritage from Piedmont. Made with Muscat de Beaumes-de-Venise, it belongs to the Vaucluse.*

½ cup (4 oz/125 g) sugar
4 egg yolks
¾ cup (6 fl oz/180 ml) Muscat de Beaumes-de-Venise

◈ Choose a small, heavy saucepan in which to make the *sabayon*. Place a tripod in a larger saucepan, pose the smaller pan on the tripod and pour water into the larger pan until the smaller pan is immersed by half. Remove the smaller pan and bring the water to a near boil. Adjust the heat to low. In the smaller pan whisk together the sugar and egg yolks until creamy. Whisk in the wine and set the saucepan on the tripod in the hot water. Whisk until the *sabayon* is thick, foamy and has more than doubled in volume, about 10 minutes. Raise the heat somewhat, if necessary, remembering that the water should not boil.
◈ Serve either directly from the saucepan or pour into small, individual serving dishes or sherbet glasses and cover and chill before serving.

SERVES 4   *Photograph pages 478–479*

TARTE DE POTIRON

Provençal Pumpkin Pie

In Provençal cuisine, squash is usually reserved for soups or savory gratins. This sweet tart is probably a fairly recent addition to the Provençal repertory, for there is no sign of it in cookbooks of the last century. Pumpkins and Hubbard squashes are generally larger than what is needed for this recipe; they are, however, sometimes sold by the piece in markets.

½ recipe crumbly pastry (recipe on page 479)
¼ cup (2 oz/60 g) plus pinch of unsalted butter
1½ lb (750 g) pumpkin or Hubbard squash, cut into pieces, seeds and fibers discarded, peeled and diced
2 tablespoons all-purpose (plain) flour
3 eggs
1 tablespoon orange blossom water
3 tablespoons dark rum
1 teaspoon grated lemon zest
1 teaspoon grated orange zest
½ cup (4 oz/125 g) granulated sugar
handful of toasted almonds, coarsely chopped
confectioners' (icing) sugar

◈ Make the pastry and chill for 2 hours.
◈ Melt the ¼ cup (2 oz/60 g) butter in a large, heavy sauté pan over very low heat. Add the squash, cover and cook, stirring often with a wooden spoon, until the pieces are falling into a purée, 40–45 minutes. Uncover and cook, stirring, for a few minutes longer to permit excess humidity to evaporate. Sprinkle with the flour and stir in well. Remove from the heat and let cool.
◈ Preheat an oven to 350°F (180°C). Use the pinch of butter to grease a 10-inch (25-cm) pie plate. On a lightly floured work surface, roll out the pastry dough into a round about ⅛ in (3 mm) thick. Drape the pastry round around the rolling

pin and transfer it to the pie plate. Press the pastry lightly against the bottom and sides of the plate, then trim and crimp the edges.
◈ In a mixing bowl whisk together the eggs, orange blossom water, rum, grated zests and granulated sugar. Whisk in the pumpkin and stir in the almonds. Pour into the pastry-lined plate and smooth the surface.
◈ Place in the oven and bake until a toothpick inserted in the middle comes out dry, 45–50 minutes. Remove from the oven and sprinkle with confectioners' sugar. Serve tepid, preferably, or at room temperature.

SERVES 6   *Photograph pages 478–479*

NAVETTES DE LA CHANDELEUR

Marseilles Candlemas Cookies

These cookies (biscuits) are also called navettes de Saint-Victor *because they are traditionally sold in the square in front of the church of Saint-Victor in Marseilles on Candlemas day.*

1 teaspoon active dry yeast
2 tablespoons lukewarm water
about 4 cups (1 lb/500 g) all-purpose (plain) flour
pinch of salt
¼ cup (2 oz/60 g) unsalted butter, at room temperature
1 cup (8 oz/250 g) sugar
2 whole eggs
3 tablespoons orange blossom water
grated zest of 1 lemon
1 teaspoon olive oil
1 egg yolk beaten with 1 tablespoon water

◈ In a small bowl dissolve the yeast in the lukewarm water and let stand until creamy, about 10 minutes.
◈ Meanwhile, in a large mixing bowl stir together 3 cups (12 oz/375 g) of the flour and the salt. Make a well in the center. In another bowl mash together the butter and sugar until soft and crumbly. Beat in the whole eggs, dissolved yeast, orange blossom water and grated zest. Empty the egg mixture into the flour well and stir with a fork, working from the center outward to gather in all the flour progressively. Sprinkle over more of the flour as needed to create a firm but supple dough. Knead the dough in the bowl, using your knuckles and sprinkling over a little more of the flour as needed to reduce stickiness. When the dough is smooth and no longer sticky, form it into a ball in the bowl, cover with a towel and leave to rest in a warm place for at least 30 minutes or for up to 1 hour.
◈ Rub a large baking sheet with the olive oil. Turn the dough out onto a floured work surface and cut it into 3 equal portions. Using your hands, roll each portion into a log about 1 in (2.5 cm) thick. Cut each log crosswise into pieces about 2½–3 in (6–7.5 cm) long. You should have about 30 pieces in all. Roll each piece between your palms, tapering the ends, into a boat shape. Place the boats on the baking sheet, spacing them about 1½ in (4 cm) apart. Cover with a towel and leave in a warm place for 2 hours. They will rise somewhat in this time but will not have doubled.
◈ Meanwhile, preheat an oven to 375°F (190°C). Using a razor blade, make a slit the length of each boat and about one-third its depth. Using a pastry brush, paint the surface of each boat with the yolk-water mixture.
◈ Place in the oven and bake until light brown, about 25 minutes. Remove to a wire rack to cool.

MAKES ABOUT 30 COOKIES

Marseilles Candlemas Cookies

CLAFOUTIS
Cherry Pudding

Culinary historians will tell you that clafoutis *belongs to the Limousin. As far as the natives of the Gapeau river valley are concerned,* clafoutis *belongs to them. Until a few years ago, and for as long as anyone can remember, the Gapeau valley was famous for producing the first cherries in France. The wholesale distribution center was Solliès-Pont. On the first of April, the entire valley lay beneath a blanket of white cherry blossoms, and, a month later, the small, black, sweet* cerises de Solliès *appeared in markets all over Europe. Today, the cherry orchards have been replaced by housing developments and prefabricated villas.*

2 tablespoons unsalted butter
1 lb (500 g) small black cherries, stemmed but not pitted
½ cup (4 oz/125 g) plus 2 tablespoons granulated sugar
4 eggs
small pinch of salt
½ cup (2 oz/60 g) all-purpose (plain) flour
1 cup (8 fl oz/250 ml) milk
¼ cup (2 fl oz/60 ml) kirsch
confectioners' (icing) sugar

◙ Preheat an oven to 400°F (200°C). Grease a shallow 10-in (25-cm) porcelain or earthenware oven dish with ¼ in (3 cm) sides with 1 tablespoon of the butter.
◙ Spread the cherries in a tight layer in the bottom of the dish. In a mixing bowl whisk together the ½ cup (4 oz/125 g) granulated sugar, the eggs and salt until well blended. Sift in the flour, stirring at the same time with the whisk. Whisk in the milk and kirsch. Pour the mixture over the cherries. Cut the remaining 1 tablespoon butter into shavings and scatter over the surface. Sprinkle with 2 tablespoons confectioners' sugar.
◙ Place in the oven and bake until the surface is golden, about 25 minutes. Remove from the oven and immediately sprinkle with additional confectioners' sugar. Serve lukewarm.

SERVES 6

FIGUES AU VIN ROUGE
Dried Figs in Thyme and Red Wine Syrup

This unusual melding of flavors recalls all the scents of the Provençal garrigue.

1 lb (500 g) dried figs
2 fresh thyme sprigs, tied in a piece of cheesecloth (muslin)
¼ cup (3 oz/90 g) honey
red wine as needed

◙ Put the figs in a saucepan and embed the cheesecloth package in their midst. Dribble the honey over the top and pour in red wine to cover generously. Bring to a boil, reduce the heat to low, cover and simmer for 1 hour.
◙ Using a slotted spoon, remove the figs to a serving dish. Discard the thyme package.
◙ Boil the liquid gently until reduced by half and syrupy, about 20 minutes. Pour the syrup over the figs.
◙ Serve tepid or cover tightly and chill before serving.

SERVES 4

Cherry Pudding

Dried Figs in Thyme and Red Wine Syrup in the kitchen of Domaine Tempier

Apple Tart

TARTE AUX POMMES

Apple Tart

Provençal fruit tarts are always of an exemplary simplicity. Their goodness depends upon the quality of the fruit and the quality of the pastry. The subtle flavor of the honey produced around the lavender fields of the northern Var lends an attractive nuance to this tart.

½ recipe crumbly pastry (recipe on page 479)
pinch of unsalted butter
1 lb (500 g) Russet, pippin or Golden Delicious apples
½ cup (4 oz/125g) sugar
about ¼ cup (3 oz/90 g) Provençal lavender honey if available, or thyme or rosemary honey

▨ Make the pastry and chill for 2 hours.
▨ Preheat an oven to 350°F (180°C). Use the butter to grease a baking sheet. On a lightly floured work surface, roll out the pastry into a round about ⅛ in (3 mm) thick. Drape it around the rolling pin and transfer it to the prepared baking sheet. Roll up and crimp the edges to shape a free-form circular tart shell with a rim ⅛–¼ in (3–6 mm) high. Using a floured thumb or the back of the tines of a fork, to form an attractive rim.
▨ Split the apples lengthwise and cut out the cores. Peel the halves, then cut each half crosswise into slices about ⅛ in (3 mm) thick. Arrange the slices, starting just inside the pastry rim, in concentric circles with both the slices overlapping and the circles overlapping. Sprinkle with the sugar.
▨ Place in the oven and bake until both the pastry and the apples are beautifully golden, 50–60 minutes.
▨ Meanwhile, put the honey in a small bowl and immerse the base of the bowl in hot water for a couple of minutes to render the honey more fluid.
▨ Remove the tart from the oven. Using a pastry brush, paint the apples immediately with honey. Slip the tart onto a platter and serve warm.

SERVES 6

TARTE AUX ABRICOTS

Apricot Tart

Apricots are one of the most important fruit crops of Provence. Small apricots with deep orange flesh and a distinct red blush on the skins are usually the most intensely flavored.

pinch of unsalted butter
½ recipe crumbly pastry (recipe on page 479)
1 lb (500 g) apricots, split in half and pitted
6 tablespoons (3 oz/90 g) sugar
6 tablespoons (4 oz/125 g) puréed apricot jam

▨ Preheat an oven to 375°F (190°C). Use the butter to grease a baking sheet.
▨ On a lightly floured work surface, roll out the pastry into a rectangle about ⅛ in (3 mm) thick. Drape it around the rolling pin and transfer it to the prepared baking sheet. Roll up and crimp the edges, to shape a free-form rectangular tart shell with a rim ⅛–¼ in (3–6 mm) high. Using a floured thumb or the back of the tines of a fork, form an attractive rim. Starting just inside the pastry rim, arrange the apricot halves, close together and skin sides down. Sprinkle with the sugar.
▨ Place in the oven and bake until both the pastry and the apricots are golden, about 40 minutes.
▨ Remove the tart from the oven and let stand for 15 minutes. In a pan, heat the apricot jam over low heat. Spoon the apricot jam thinly and evenly over the surface of the apricots. Serve the tart tepid or at room temperature.

SERVES 6   *Photograph pages 472–473*

VAUCLUSE

Pêches au Muscat de Beaumes-de-Venise

Peaches in Muscat de Beaumes-de-Venise

The village of Beaumes-de-Venise lies in the heart of the Comtat Venaissin, papal territory until the Revolution and a stone's throw from the vines of Châteauneuf-du-Pape. In recent years the fame of its liquorous amber wine, which owes its intense, exotic perfume to the Muscat grape, has spread around the world.

1½ lb (750 g) ripe yellow peaches, peeled and sliced
¼ cup (2 oz/60 g) sugar
1 cup (8 fl oz/250 ml) Muscat de Beaumes-de-Venise

❁ Put the sliced peaches into a deep serving dish. Crystal is attractive for throwing into relief the warm colors of the peaches and the wine. Sprinkle with the sugar and pour over the wine over the top. Cover tightly with plastic wrap and chill well before serving.

SERVES 4

PROVENCE

Compote d'Abricots

Apricot Compote

The kernels of the apricot pits lend a delicate bitter almond flavor. Accompanied with a creamy custard, this is a sumptuous dessert.

1½ lb (750 g) ripe but firm apricots
1 cup (8 fl oz/250 ml) water
1 tablespoon fresh lemon juice
1 cup (8 oz/250 g) sugar

❁ Halve the apricots. Crack half the pits with a nutcracker or a hammer and tie them up in a piece of cheesecloth (muslin).
❁ Combine the water and lemon juice in a saucepan. Stir in the sugar and leave to melt. Bring to a boil, reduce the heat and simmer until the liquid is clear, 2–3 minutes. Add the apricot halves and the package of broken pits and return to a boil. Remove from the heat and leave to cool.
❁ Using a slotted spoon, remove the apricot halves to a serving dish. Discard the pits. Boil the liquid gently until reduced by half and syrupy, about 15 minutes. Pour the syrup over the apricots.
❁ Leave to cool, cover tightly with plastic wrap and chill before serving.

SERVES 4

PROVENCE

Figues au Four

Baked Fresh Figs

Deep red–fleshed September figs are best for this dish. They should be picked at the moment cracks begin to appear on the skins.

1 lb (500 g) ripe figs
2 tablespoons green Chartreuse liqueur
¼ cup (3 oz/90 g) Provençal lavender honey, if available, or thyme or rosemary honey

❁ Preheat an oven to 450°F (230°C). Cut the figs in half lengthwise and arrange the halves closely in a gratin dish. Sprinkle the surfaces with the Chartreuse and dribble the honey over the top.
❁ Bake for about 7 minutes. Serve hot from the oven.

SERVES 4

In l'Isle-sur-la-Sorgue, clockwise from top: Peaches in Muscat de Beaumes-de-Venise, Baked Fresh Figs, Apricot Compote

POMPE DE NOËL

Sweet Christmas Bread

An alternative name for this bread is gibassier, *which is derived from the Provençal word* gibo, *meaning "bump." It refers to the bumps created by the slashes on the bread's surface. It is also known as* pompe à l'huile *because of the use of olive oil in the dough. In the Alpes-Maritimes,* pompes *are replaced by* fougassettes de Grasse, *smaller, oval breads made from a similar dough to which a pinch of saffron is often added.* Pompes de Noël *are traditionally broken and shared at the table.*

FOR THE SPONGE:

2 teaspoons active dry yeast
1 cup (8 fl oz/250 ml) lukewarm water
1 cup (4 oz/125 g) bread flour
about 4 cups (1 lb/500 g) bread flour

salt
6 tablespoons (3 oz/90 g) sugar
1 tablespoon grated orange zest
2 tablespoons orange blossom water
½ cup (4 fl oz/125 ml) olive oil

▨ To make the sponge, in a large bowl stir together the yeast and lukewarm water. Whisk in the flour to create an easily pourable batter. Cover the bowl tightly with plastic wrap and leave at room temperature for 24 hours.

▨ Put 3 cups (12 oz/375 g) of the flour into a large mixing bowl. Make a well in the center and add the salt, sugar, orange zest, orange blossom water, olive oil and the sponge. Stir with a fork, working from the center outward, until all the flour is incorporated. Thickly flour a work surface with the remaining flour. Turn the dough out onto the work surface and knead until elastic and no longer sticky, adding additional flour, a little at a time, if dough remains sticky. Form it into a ball, return to the mixing bowl, cover with a towel and let stand in a warm place until the dough has approximately doubled in volume, about 2 hours.

▨ Return the dough to the floured surface and punch it down. Knead hardly at all to avoid its becoming elastic and unworkable. Divide the dough into 3 equal portions. Flatten each portion as much as possible with the palm of your hand, turning it over repeatedly on the floured surface. Using a rolling pin, roll out each portion into a near round about ½ in (12 mm) thick.

▨ Transfer the dough rounds to 1 or more baking sheets. Using a razor blade, cut a circle about ¼ in (6 mm) deep (about half the thickness of the round) and ⅔ in (1.5 cm) in from the edge of the round. Then cut a checkerboard pattern within the circle, forming 1 in (2.5 cm) squares and again cutting about ¼ in (6 mm) deep. Cover with a towel and leave to rise in a warm place for 1 hour.

▨ Meanwhile, preheat an oven to 400°F (200°C). Place the loaves in the oven and bake until brown and crusty, 20–25 minutes. Remove to wire racks to cool.

MAKES 3 LOAVES 12 IN (30 CM) IN DIAMETER

TIAN DE PAIN AUX PÊCHES

Peach and Bread Pudding

Provence produces vast quantities of both white and yellow peaches. They are very different in flavor and texture, but either lends itself well to this preparation. If the peaches resist peeling, drop them into boiling water and drain immediately; the skins will then slip off effortlessly.

½ cup (4 oz/125 g) unsalted butter
¼ lb (4 oz/125 g) semidry bread, sliced and torn into pieces
handful of raisins, soaked in ½ cup (4 fl oz/125 ml) marc de Provence (see glossary) or Cognac for several hours or overnight
1½ lb (750 g) ripe peaches, peeled and sliced
3 eggs
½ cup (4 oz/125 g) sugar
3 cups (24 fl oz/750 ml) milk

488

Sweet Christmas Bread

⊞ Preheat an oven to 350°F (180°C). Butter a 6-cup (48-fl oz/ 1.5-l) gratin dish.

⊞ Melt ¼ cup (2 oz/60 g) of the butter in a sauté pan over low heat. Add the pieces of bread and cook gently, turning them around and over and adding more butter as necessary, until crisp and golden on all sides, 10–15 minutes.

⊞ Empty the bread into the gratin dish. Drain the raisins, reserving the brandy, and scatter the raisins over the bread. Add the peaches and move them around to disperse the peaches, raisins and bread evenly.

⊞ In a mixing bowl whisk together the eggs and sugar. Whisk in the milk and the reserved brandy. Pour the mixture evenly over the contents of the gratin dish.

⊞ Place in the oven and bake until the custard is set and the surface is lightly colored, about 40 minutes. Serve warm or at room temperature.

SERVES 4

Photograph pages 472–473

PROVENCE

POIRES AU VIN ROUGE

Pears in Red Wine Syrup

Peeled yellow peaches are also very good prepared this way, and a stunning sight if left whole and unpitted. Count half the cooking time.

6 slightly underripe Bartlett (Williams) pears, halved
    lengthwise, cored and peeled
strip of dried orange peel
piece of cinnamon stick
½ cup (4 oz/125 g) sugar
3 cups (24 fl oz/750 ml) red wine

❖ Arrange the pear halves in a large enameled ironware or stainless-steel pan. Tuck in the orange peel and cinnamon stick and sprinkle the sugar over the top. Pour in wine to cover and bring to a boil. Reduce the heat, cover and simmer for 1 hour.
❖ Using a perforated skimming spoon, remove the pear halves to a serving dish. Discard the orange peel and cinnamon. Boil the liquid gently until reduced by two thirds and syrupy, about 20 minutes. Pour the syrup over the pears.
❖ Leave to cool, cover tightly with plastic wrap and chill before serving.

SERVES 4

VAR

MACÉDOINE AU VIN DE BANDOL

Macédoine of Fruits in Bandol Wine

In late spring and early summer, this is a popular dessert on Provençal tables. If you prefer, the raspberries can be sieved and poured over the other fruits before adding the wine. The shells of green almonds are still unformed and can be removed by cutting into them with a knife. The skins are a tender white parchment that easily peel off. If green almonds are unavailable, a few slivered almonds can be scattered over the fruits, but not to the same effect.

½ lb (250 g) cherries, stemmed but not pitted
½ lb (250 g) small strawberries, stemmed
½ lb (250 g) raspberries
2 yellow or white ripe peaches, peeled and sliced
2 firm, ripe Bartlett (Williams) pears, quartered lengthwise,
    cored, peeled and cut into cubes
about ½ cup (3½ oz/100 g) sugar
about 30 green almonds, peeled
2 cups (16 fl oz/500 ml) young, deeply colored, tannic red
    wine

❖ Assemble all the fruits in a glass serving bowl. Sprinkle with the sugar and toss them gently together with splayed fingers. Leave to steep for 30 minutes.
❖ Toss in the almonds and pour the wine over the top. Cover tightly with plastic wrap and refrigerate for 2–3 hours before serving.

SERVES 6 *Photograph page 264*

Pears in Red Wine Syrup in a Vaucluse garden

CRÊPES

Crêpes are a favorite dessert in Provence. They are made in pans the size of dinner plates and receive no complicated treatments. A choice of jams (cherry and apricot are favorites), sugar, and, often, a bottle of génépi, a strong herbal liqueur, are placed at table. Each person flavors the crêpes to taste, spreading them with jam or sprinkling with sugar or génépi, or both, before rolling them up.

½ cup (2 oz/60 g) all-purpose (plain) flour
pinch of salt
4 eggs
1½ cups (12 fl oz/375 ml) milk
3 tablespoons unsalted butter
2 tablespoons marc de Provence (see glossary) or Cognac

▨ In a mixing bowl stir together the flour and the salt. Make a well in the center and add the eggs to the well. Whisk, working gradually from the center of the bowl outward, to incorporate the flour until no lumps remain. If the mixture begins to become pasty, add a little milk as you whisk. Slowly whisk in the milk, continuing to whisk until the batter is the consistency of light (single) cream. If the batter is not absolutely smooth, pass it through a sieve into another bowl. Melt the butter in a crêpe pan. A pan 9-in (23-cm) in diameter is traditional but any size will do. Pour the butter into the batter along with the brandy. Stir to mix.

▨ Using a cloth or a paper towel, wipe the crêpe pan to leave only a film of butter. Heat the pan over medium heat, then adjust the heat to medium-low. Give the batter a stir with a small ladle, lift the crêpe pan and pour in just enough batter to coat the bottom and edges of the pan, rotating the pan at the same time. The batter should sizzle on contact. Return the pan to the heat. When the surface of the crêpe is nearly dry and the edges turn golden and curl away from the pan (after 1–2 minutes), slip a round-tipped knife blade beneath the crêpe and flip it over. Or, using your fingertips, pick it up by the loosened edge and turn it over. A few seconds later, slip it onto a heated plate.

▨ Remove the pan from the heat for 2–3 seconds before adding batter for the succeeding crêpe. Give the batter a brief stir with the ladle each time before pouring. Do not butter the pan; the butter contained in the batter is sufficient lubrication. Stack the crêpes as they come out of the pan and serve while still warm.

SERVES 4

CRÈME AU CITRON

Creamy Lemon Custard

This custard is often flavored with orange blossom water, or locust (acacia) blossoms are infused in the hot milk. Lovely alone or as an accompaniment to fruits in red wine syrup, stewed apricots, and the like.

½ cup (4 oz/125 g) sugar
1 teaspoon cornstarch (corn flour)
6 egg yolks
3 thin strips lemon zest
2 cups (16 fl oz/500 ml) milk

▨ Prepare a large bowl of crushed ice, or of ice cubes with some water added. In a mixing bowl stir together the sugar and cornstarch. Place the egg yolks in another bowl.

▨ Fill a saucepan with cold water and empty it. Then add the lemon zest and milk to the pan, bring to a boil and remove from the heat.

▨ Add the egg yolks to the sugar mixture and whisk until pale yellow and the mixture falls in a lazy ribbon from the whisk, about 10 minutes. Remove the lemon zests from the milk and pour the milk slowly into the egg yolk mixture, whisking constantly at the same time.

Crêpes

◼ Pour the egg-milk mixture into a heavy saucepan over low heat. Stir with a wooden spoon in a figure-eight pattern, reaching all corners, until the custard thickly coats the spoon but well before there is any suggestion of a boil. This should take about 15 minutes.

◼ Remove from the heat, embed the saucepan in the bowl of ice and continue stirring until cooled. Pour the custard into 4 shallow bowls and chill before serving.

SERVES 4

Photograph page 264

POMMES AU MUSCAT DE BEAUMES-DE-VENISE

Apples Baked with Muscat de Beaumes-de-Venise

In Provence Russet apples (reinettes) are used for baking. Golden Delicious do not have as fine a flavor, but they share with Russets the virtue of holding together well during cooking.

¼ cup (2 oz/60 g) unsalted butter, at room temperature
⅓ cup (3 oz/90 g) plus 3 tablespoons sugar
1 teaspoon grated orange zest
4 large baking apples such as Russets, pippin or
    Golden Delicious
juice of ½ lemon
pinch of powdered saffron
½ cup (4 fl oz/125 ml) Muscat de Beaumes-de-Venise

◉ Preheat an oven to 325°F (165°C).
◉ Cream together the butter, ⅓ cup (3 oz/90 g) sugar and the zest. Core the apples, either with an apple corer or with a small, sharp-pointed paring knife, removing a ¾-in (2-cm) cylinder from stem end to flower end. Peel the top third of each apple and dip the peeled surfaces in lemon juice.
◉ Stuff the empty cylinders with the creamed mixture, spreading some on the peeled surfaces as well. Not all of it may be used at this point. Stand the apples up, side by side, in a porcelain or earthenware oven dish of a size to just hold them. Sprinkle a little saffron over the peeled surfaces and pour the wine into the bottom of the dish.
◉ Place in the oven and bake until tender when pierced, about 45 minutes, basting several times with the juices. As the filling empties out from the apples, add any leftover creamed mixture to the holes.

◉ Sprinkle the surfaces of the apples with 3 tablespoons sugar, raise the oven temperature to 450°F (230°C) and watch them closely. As soon as the sugar caramelizes, remove from the oven. Serve hot, tepid or at room temperature.
SERVES 4

GLACE AU MIEL

Honey Ice Cream

Honey lends a soft, seductive allure to ice cream, which may surprise those accustomed to sweetening with sugar.

2 cups (16 fl oz/500 ml) milk
5 egg yolks
½ cup (5 oz/155 g) herb honey such as lavender, thyme
    or rosemary
small pinch of salt
1 cup (8 fl oz/250 ml) heavy whipping (double) cream

◉ Prepare a large bowl of crushed ice, or ice cubes with some water added. Pour the milk into a saucepan and bring to a boil.
◉ Meanwhile, in a mixing bowl whisk together the egg yolks, honey and salt until the color lightens. Slowly pour in the hot milk, whisking constantly. Pour the mixture into a saucepan over low heat. Stir with a wooden spoon until the custard lightly coats the spoon, about 10 minutes.
◉ Remove from the heat, embed the saucepan in the bowl of ice and continue stirring until completely cooled. Stir in the cream and pass through a fine-mesh sieve into a bowl. Pour the custard into an ice cream freezer and freeze according to the manufacturer's instructions.
MAKES 1 QT (1 L); SERVES 4

Honey Ice Cream

*Apples Baked with Muscat de Beaumes-de-Venise in
the kitchen of Château d'Ansouis*

GLOSSARY

THE PROVENÇAL KITCHEN

Primordial to the Provençal kitchen is a marble mortar and a wooden pestle. The mortar should hold a minimum of four to five cups (32–48 fl oz/1–1.25 l) liquid; small apothecaries' mortars will not do. Ritual in the kitchen is as important to the cook as ritual at table is to the guests. Close to the heart of the Provençal cook is the simple gesture of smacking a garlic clove with the heel of one's hand, removing the loosened hull from the ruptured clove and, with abandon, tossing the garlic into a mortar. There it is pounded with a pinch of coarse sea salt, whose roughness helps reduce the garlic and salt, together, to a silken, liquid paste that no garlic press can approximate. A food processor can successfully replace a mortar and pestle in many instances, but an *aïoli* or a *pistou* made in a food processor is cottony and dry; the voluptuous texture and the fruit of the olive oil are destroyed.

The taste of Provence can never be complete without a bed of incandescent wood embers over which to grill foods. Even the *croûtes à l'ail*—slices of semidry bread, grilled, rubbed with garlic and dribbled with olive oil— so often served as an appetizer, along with olives and slices of raw-cured sausage *(saucisson sec),* are magical only when enhanced by the smoky caress of dying embers. A Provençal kitchen includes a table-height fireplace with a work-surface ledge in front. An outdoor barbecue for use in good weather is a welcome accessory, but a bonfire reduced to embers can serve as well. Heavy, welded cast-iron grills, preheated over the coals, are used for grilling meats, poultry and vegetables. Double-faced, heavy wire grills on legs, which can be turned over or upright, are used for fish whose fragile flesh easily sticks and tears if turned on a cast-iron grill; different sizes and forms exist, with swelled faces approximating the shape of sea bass or porgies (breams) and large, flat, double-faced grills designed to contain a dozen or two small fish—sardines or red mullets—that can be turned over with a single flip.

Much of the food of Provence is cooked in earthenware, which absorbs heat slowly and evenly and holds it for long; it also absorbs and holds flavors, which can subtly improve a dish on condition that its vessel always be used for similar types of preparations. The *poêlon,* an earthenware casserole shaped like a flattened sphere with a hollow handle, is constantly used (recipes begin, "Pour a *rasade* ["a large swallow"] of olive oil into a *poêlon,* smash a couple of cloves of garlic and throw them in . . ."). Gratins are prepared in a *tian,* a large, shallow earthenware dish, and boiled meats and poultry in a *pot-au-feu,* a large pot with bulging sides. Long-cooking stews go into a *daubière,* a potbellied vessel with a reduced evaporation surface; a daube prepared in anything else never tastes as good as a daube simmered for hours in a *daubière* in which, over the years, hundreds of daubes have simmered for thousands of hours. As in any kitchen, heavy sauce and sauté pans and good knives are essential. For chopping, the Provençal home cook uses a half-moon cutter, or *demi-lune,* the handle of which is held by both hands in order to rock the blade back and forth; the professional cook uses knives.

AÏOLI

The Provençaux often speak of *aïoli,* or garlic mayonnaise, as their "national" dish. The Marseillais believe that an *aïoli* should contain at least two cloves of garlic per person. In addition to the array of boiled and baked vegetables, poached salt cod and other preparations that compose the entire meal called *aïoli,* the mayonnaise is often served with room temperature or barely warm meats (roast leg of lamb or chicken, in particular), individual boiled vegetables, octopus stews and the like.

If possible, the garlic cloves should be fresh and crisp with no sign of a sprout or germ. If a tiny green sprout is visible, remove it from the heart of the clove before adding the clove to the mortar. The eggs and the olive oil should both be at room temperature and it is important always to add the oil—at first in a tiny trickle and then in a greater stream— interrupting the flow from time to time while continuing to turn the pestle. It is said the pestle should always be turned in the same direction (to know if this is true, one would have to break the rule, which makes no sense since it is easier to turn the pestle always in the same direction). If one person pours while another turns the pestle, the task is simplified.

To prepare *aïoli* for 6 persons, place a large pinch of coarse sea salt and 6–12 (fewer or more, to taste) firm, crisp garlic cloves in the mortar and pound to a paste. Add a large pinch (5 fingers) of fresh bread crumbs (without crusts, prepared in a blender or a processor) and pound and turn to a consistent paste. Then work in 2 egg yolks. Turn the mixture with the pestle for a minute or so before beginning to add 2 cups (16 fl oz/ 500 ml) olive oil. Pour it in at a slight trickle to the side of the mortar so that it is gradually incorporated into the mass by the movement of the pestle. As the sauce begins to thicken noticeably, the oil may be poured in a steadier flow, still to the side of the mortar. It should not become too stiff; after about half the oil has been added, add the juice of ½ lemon or 1 teaspoon water, continuing to turn the pestle. Keep adding oil and, if necessary, a bit of water until you have the desired quantity of sauce. You can add more or less oil.

To prepare a saffron *aïoli,* put a pinch of saffron threads into a small bowl, pour over 1 tablespoon boiling water, leave to cool and wipe out the bowl with the bread crumbs before adding them to the mortar.

To prepare a cold Provençal sauce *(sauce provençale froide),* rinse and fillet a couple of salt anchovies (q. v.)

and pound them to a paste with the garlic before adding the bread.

There is no reason for an *aïoli* to break up if it is prepared carefully; if the oil is too cool or added too rapidly this may happen. Pour the broken sauce into a bowl, clean out the mortar and start again with another egg yolk, adding the broken sauce slowly, a teaspoon at a time, to the side of the mortar, turning the pestle constantly.

ANCHOVIES see *salt anchovies.*

ARTICHOKES

An artichoke is a thistle-flower bud. It must be eaten at an undeveloped stage for, when it opens out into flower, it is the "choke" that becomes the purple blossom. Provençal recipes for artichokes are always for "young, tender artichokes," and the Provençal ideal is a violet artichoke the size of an egg in which the choke has not yet developed. The size of an artichoke, however, is not necessarily an indication of its age. The best artichokes are those that develop first at the summit of a stalk; if the whole length of the stalk is not cut, smaller artichokes of inferior quality spring from the lower leaf joints. Round globe artichokes, which in Provence are known as Brittany artichokes and which when mature are the size of a grapefruit, are wonderful if picked when the size of an orange, the choke still undeveloped. A young artichoke always has a stem that is thick in relation to the size of the artichoke itself (in Provence, the stems are peeled and cooked with the artichokes), and its contour, from the base of the leaves to their tips, describes a clean curve. Narrow, fibrous stems and an indented profile above the base are signs of advanced age.

The cut surfaces of artichokes discolor in contact with air and carbon steel. Keep at hand a bowl containing the juice of a lemon and use stainless-steel knives. Cut off the stem and remove the tough outer leaves, curving each backward and downward until it snaps free from the tender flesh at its base. Cut off the top third of the leaves of a young artichoke or about the top half from a fully developed artichoke. Hold the artichoke upside down and pare off the dark green surfaces, turning the artichoke in a spiraling fashion while keeping the knife more or less stationary. Turn it over and pare off the extremities of the outer leaves. Turn it around in the lemon juice and leave it in the bowl while preparing the others. Larger artichokes are often quartered for a stew or for deep-frying; the choke is then sliced free and the cut surface immediately rubbed with lemon. If the artichoke is to be sliced, it is first cut in half lengthwise, the choke cut out and the cut surface rubbed with lemon before each half is sliced and the slices tossed in the lemon juice.

BEEF MARROW

Beef marrow is taken from the thigh bone, or marrow bone, of beef. Ask your butcher to saw off the joint ends and to saw the bone into one- to two-inch (2.5–5-cm) lengths to facilitate prying the marrow out with a knife tip. Incorporated into stuffings, it lends a silken, velvety texture.

BOUQUET GARNI

A bouquet garni is a neatly tied bundle of herbs which, without disintegrating into the dish, imparts all of its flavors and is, at the same time, easily removed after cooking. The usual elements are thyme sprigs, bay leaf, parsley stems or, preferably, parsley root, and celery. Winter savory or dried orange peel is often included. For a large bouquet, a four- to five-inch (10–12-cm) section of leek green can be taken apart and reformed to enclose the package, sheathlike, before it is tied up, winding the string several times around and tying tightly.

BROUSSE

Except that this cheese is always made from sheep's milk, *brousse* is the same as Italian ricotta. Ricotta can always be substituted in recipes calling for *brousse.*

CAUL

In cooking, caul means pork caul. It is a fragile, transparent membrane, threaded with a pattern of veins of fat, that envelopes the intestines. Used as a protective and decorative covering for roasted or grilled meats, caul nourishes as the fat melts and is transformed into a golden brown, lacelike web.

COCOS

Cocos are fresh white shell beans. The beans are plump, almost round and, when cooked the texture is velvet smooth. Their green pods, or "shells," turn pale yellow when they mature. They appear on the Provençal market in July and persist until early November. Other fresh shell beans can be substituted. All shell beans are better fresh than dried—and more easily digested.

DEEP-FRYING

Olive oil cannot support the same high temperatures peanut or corn oil can, and, when used for deep-frying, it degrades rapidly; it is best reserved for shallow frying and used only once. For deep-frying, any relatively large kettle or saucepan will do. It should be tall enough so that it need not be more than half filled with oil and so that you can easily immerse the elements to be fried. If you are using a deep-fat fryer, the basket should be removed before frying batter-dipped foods. The most practical device for removing batter-dipped foods is a large, shallow wire spoon called a spider; next best is a shallow, slotted skimming spoon. Have ready a thick layer of newspapers with paper towels laid on top for draining the fried articles as they are removed from the oil. Also, preheat an oven to its lowest setting and have at hand a platter topped with a folded napkin in which the drained fried things will be placed and held in the warm oven while further batches are being cooked. Except in rare instances, 375°F (190°C) is, by common consensus, the correct frying temperature—the temperature is correct when a leaf of parsley crackles or a drop of batter sizzles at contact with the oil.

GAME BIRDS

In Provence hunters like to eat partridge *au bout du fusil,* that is, plucked, gutted and roasted the moment it is shot. As a general rule, game birds improve after hanging in their feathers for three or four days, either in a refrigerated room or, in winter, in an unheated room. They must be young to be tender; old birds are only good for braising. Supple beaks and breastbones, a pointed rather than rounded tip to the longest wing feather and delicate, thinly scaled feet are indications of youth.

Except for wild duck, game birds are barded for roasting by tying a thin sheet of pork back fat over the breast. They are roasted at high heat and kept underdone to be succulent. Those who complain that pheasant meat is dry and tasteless have always eaten it too fresh and overdone. A pheasant is roasted at 450°F (230°C) for 25 minutes; after 20 minutes, the bard is removed, the trussing strings clipped and the legs partially disjointed and opened out. Partridge and grouse are roasted for 18 minutes at the same temperature, and quail for 12 to 15 minutes.

Woodcock is not gutted, for the trail is clean; only the gizzard, because of its gravel sack, is not eaten. It is a self-trussing bird: After being plucked to the head, the skin is torn free of the neck and peeled from the head, taking the eyes with it. The heel joints of the legs are dislocated and crossed and locked yogalike. The head is drawn down to the side of the body and the drumsticks and body are transpierced by the long, needlelike beak near the thigh joint. The woodcock is barded and roasted for 15 minutes.

Because a duck's legs are so tightly wedged into the back of the body and because the breast meat of wild duck is best quite rare, the legs are still bloody when the breast is correctly cooked. After roasting, the legs of a wild duck are removed and grilled until the skin is crisp and the flesh no longer rare. The breast is carved thinly, served first, and the legs are served as a separate course, accompanied with a green salad. Count 15 to 20 minutes at 450°F (230°C) for mallard and 12 to 15 minutes for teal.

GREEN SHALLOTS see *shallots.*

HERBS

WILD: Provençal cooks divide the herb world into two categories, wild and cultivated. First, the wild herbs.

BAY *(laurier-sauce)* trees are, of course, planted, but they also reseed themselves and grow wild. Bay leaves are frequently used alone, to the exclusion of other herbs. Whereas recipes from other regions may call for a fraction of a bay leaf, Provençal recipes often call for two or three leaves. A bay leaf is always present in a bouquet garni. The fresh leaves are sometimes cut in two and strung on skewers between pieces of meat for grilling.

WILD FENNEL *(fenouil)* has a much stronger anise flavor than cultivated bulb fennel. It grows abundantly along roadsides or on other uncultivated lands, the stalks reaching a height of a yard and a half (1.5 m) or more before coming into flower in late summer. After the flowers have gone to seed, the stalks are cut and broken or bent to form bundles that are tied and used throughout the winter to flavor innumerable fish preparations. Fish merchants always keep a supply of dried fennel on hand and automatically stuff a bouquet into the body and head cavity of any large fish prepared for grilling or baking. In early spring the tender shoots and feathery leaves can be chopped and incorporated into a fish stuffing, and throughout the summer the green stalks and leaves are used to line fish grills or gratin dishes in which fish are to be baked.

WILD LAVENDER *(aspic)* is commonplace. A certain amount is often included in commercial mixtures of Provençal herbs (q. v.) destined for tourists; the flavor is too exotic for the Provençal palate.

OREGANO *(origan, marjolaine),* or wild marjoram, is known simply as *marjolaine.* It comes into flower in July when it is picked, tied into bundles and hung to dry; its perfume is improved by drying. Oregano enters into herb mixtures, but is so rarely used alone in traditional Provençal cuisine that it is commonly identified as "the pizza herb."

ROSEMARY *(romarin)* often grows so thickly as to form patches of tall, nearly impenetrable brush on the hillsides. It is a popular hedge in Provence, where it flowers year-round except for the hottest part of summer. In the Provençal air the scent is ravishing, but in cuisine it is overwhelming and hardly ever used. Rosemary thrown onto embers just before removing meats or poultry from the grill will flavor delicately and, if the rosemary is fresh, will not flame up.

THYME *(thym, farigoule, farigoulette)* covers the hillsides with its violet flowers in April, the best time to pick it for drying. For use in bouquets garnis, it is picked fresh as needed.

WINTER SAVORY *(sarriette de montagne, poivre d'âne, pebre d'ase, pebre d'aï)* flowers in July and August for picking and drying. The Provençaux have a special affection for savory, which nearly everyone knows as *pebre d'aï* ("garlic pepper"), a deformation of its real name, *pebre d'ase* or *poivre d'âne* ("ass's pepper"). Fresh sprigs of savory garnish the little Banon goat cheeses from the Alpes-de-Haute-Provence; tender early spring leaves are judged to be an indispensable presence with broad (fava) beans, and sprigs of savory often replace or accompany thyme in a bouquet garni.

CULTIVATED:

BASIL *(basilic)* comes in many forms—tiny leaf, large leaf, very large waffly leaf, purple flat leaf, purple frilly leaf. The purple basils are beautiful additions to salads. The large-leaf Italian basil has the most characteristic flavor and is the best for a *pistou*. In much of Provence, basil is used almost exclusively for *soupe au pistou;* Niçoise cooking finds other uses for it. It is good to have 8 or 10 plants in a kitchen garden. The budding flowers are as valuable as the leaves, but a basil plant should not be permitted to go to seed or it will die; when the budding flowers are too plentiful to be used, they should be pinched off and discarded.

CELERY, GARDEN *(céleri du potager)* is grown in all kitchen gardens. Its flavor is similar to but stronger than that of stalk celery; a single small branch with its leaf attached is all that is necessary for a bouquet garni. Those who have no kitchen garden ask their green-grocer for a stalk of celery; a bunch is always kept to the side, from which stalks are broken off to be offered to clients.

CHERVIL *(cerfeuil)* is always present in the salad mixture, *mesclun*. Its delicate, slight anise flavor is easily lost in most Provençal seasoning, however, and it is also difficult to grow in the meridional climate and soil.

CHIVES *(ciboulette)* are sometimes used in salads, but green (spring) onions and young green shallots (q. v.) are much more often used in the same way.

HYSSOP *(hysope)* is not widely used. The finely chopped leaves and the exquisite blue flowers have a slightly bitter, refreshing taste that can enhance many a salad.

LOVAGE *(livèche, ache de montagne)* is closely related to the celeries and its flavor is the same, but wilder. It can replace celery in a bouquet.

For certain Provençal preparations, a strip of DRIED ORANGE PEEL is required. Because most oranges now are treated to prevent their spoiling, rub them well under cold running water before removing the peel strip. Dry well in a towel and peel as thinly as possible to avoid taking any of the white, spongy part with the zest. Using a trussing needle—or darning needle—and some kitchen string, pass the peel strips onto the string and tie the two ends at two points to suspend the peels in the air without touching. A few days later, unstring them and store them for future use.

FLAT-LEAFED (ITALIAN) PARSLEY *(persil commun)*, among the most common cultivated herbs, is the only parsley seen in the gardens and markets of Provence. Its flavor, on condition that it be freshly picked, is much finer than that of curly parsley (although the latter may be substituted if the flat-leaf variety cannot be found). Parsley is a biennial, but because it bolts and goes to seed in its second year, it must be planted every year.

It grows easily from seed if the seeds are first soaked in water overnight, well drained and mixed with dry sand to facilitate the planting. Bolted plants should not be torn up and discarded. The plant remains alive for the remainder of the season, and the root, pulled up when needed, scraped and washed, is a precious addition to a bouquet garni, replacing advantageously the parsley stems usually called for.

SAGE *(sauge)* is rustic and perennial; the long, flowering stems should be cut back after flowering. A sprig of fresh sage is usually an element in a garlic broth *(aïgo bouido)* and fresh leaves are tucked into slits in a pork roast or simply stuck to the surface of pork chops to be grilled.

SWEET MARJORAM *(marjolaine cultivée)* flowers throughout spring, summer and autumn; with mild winters, it is a perennial. The buds, before they break into flower, have the most delicate, sweetest flavor; finely chopped, along with the tender leaves closest to the buds, they do something very nice to eggs, either simply scrambled or in an omelet, alone or with zucchini (courgettes), onions or artichokes; marjoram and garlic do nothing for each other. The flower bud stems should be picked regularly to encourage others to grow; tie them in bundles and dry them—marjoram is a valuable element in a dried herb mixture.

TARRAGON *(estragon)* is used occasionally by a Niçois cook. Except for the other fines herbes—parsley, chervil and chives—it does not mix well with other herbs.

LARDOONS
Commonly cut from slices of lean salt pork (q. v.) or pork back fat, usually measuring ⅓–½ in (8–12 mm) wide, cut from pork slices of an equal thickness.

LENTILLES VERTES
These lentils, also known as *lentilles du Puy* for the city most famous for their production, are a small (less than half the size of the common blond or beige lentil) and a dark speckled brownish green. They hold their shape in cooking and their flavor is the finest of all lentils.

MARC DE PROVENCE
Marc is brandy made by distilling the grape pulp after the grapes have been pressed and the wine drawn off. Marc de Provence is usually aged in oak barrels for two or three years before being put into bottles.

MIREPOIX
A *mirepoix* is an aromatic base for many braised meat, fish or vegetable preparations. To prepare, warm 1 tablespoon olive oil in a saucepan over very low heat. Add 2 carrots, peeled and finely chopped; 1 large onion, finely chopped; 1 small celery stalk, finely chopped; pinch of Provençal mixed dried herbs and salt to taste. Cover and sweat, stirring occasionally, for 30 minutes.

MUSHROOMS see *wild mushrooms.*

MUSSELS
A simple bistro version of mussels *à la marinière—* mussels opened over heat with aromatics and white

wine—is used to prepare mussels for any number of dishes. They are also delicious served as they are: both the mussels in their shells and their liquid ladled into soup plates (in this case add 1 tablespoon unsalted butter and a generous grinding of pepper to the pan before placing it over the heat). To prepare, fill a large bowl or other vessel with cold water and add a handful of salt and the mussels. Let stand for 30 minutes. Discard any mussels with broken shells. Scrub, scrape or rub against the surfaces of the other mussels to remove loose adherences; barnacles, however, are harmless. Pull out the "beard," which is lodged near the hinge of the bivalve, and then press each mussel between a thumb and forefinger, to make certain it is alive. The resistance will be noticeable. Rinse well and place the mussels in a large, two-handled stew pot with a tight-fitting lid. Add 3 cloves garlic, crushed; 1 small onion, finely chopped; 1 bay leaf; 2 or 3 fresh thyme sprigs; 2 tablespoons chopped fresh flat-leaf (Italian) parsley; and ½ cup (4 fl oz/125 ml) dry white wine. Cover and place over high heat. As the wine approaches a boil (after 1 minute or less), begin shaking the pan, holding the lid and handles firmly together with a folded towel or kitchen gloves. After 2–3 minutes, remove the lid; if most of the mussels are gaping, remove the pot from the heat; if not, replace the lid and shake over high heat for a few seconds or as much as 1 minute longer. Pour the contents into a colander placed in a large bowl. Line a sieve with a dampened cloth or several layers of dampened cheesecloth (muslin) and filter the liquid through the sieve into another bowl. Remove the mussels from their shells, collecting them in a small bowl. Any mussels that are closed tightly should be discarded. Any mussels that are open only a crack can be opened fully by slipping a knife blade between the shells until it touches the muscle; these are often the fleshiest and juiciest mussels. Discard the shells and aromatic debris in the colander.

OLIVE OIL

The best olive oils are called "extra-virgin, first cold-pressing." The quality of a Provençal table depends very much upon the quality of the olive oil. Wine merchants often make a point of keeping superior olive oils in stock. The new year begins with wonderfully fruity, still cloudy new oil and it is first tasted poured over hot slices of semidry bread grilled over wood coals. It is also especially admired poured abundantly over hot chick-peas, seasoned at table with freshly ground pepper, vinegar, chopped shallots, garlic and parsley.

OLIVES

Dishes of olives are always present at the beginning of a Provençal midday meal. Black olives are puréed for the multipurpose *tapénade* (recipe on page 288), and olives, both black and green, garnish many a salad and sauce. By mid-October, the green olives are full size; they ripen irregularly on a single tree and from one tree and one variety to another. By mid-December, most are black. Black olives can be picked well into January.

The first home olive preparation of the season is called *olives cassées* ("broken olives") or, more correctly but more rarely, *olives écachées* ("crushed olives"): Between mid-October and mid-November, the green olives are picked, each is tapped lightly with a wooden mallet to break the skin and they are soaked in a large basin of water, changed at least once daily, for 9 or 10 days before being put into a stoneware jar and covered with an aromatic brine. To judge the necessary quantity of brine, drain off the olives' soaking water, put them into the stoneware jar and add enough water to immerse them generously. Put this quantity of water into a saucepan, add one tenth of its weight in coarse sea salt (⅓ cup/3 oz/100 g per 4 cups/32 fl oz/1 l) and, to each quart (l), a couple of segments of dried fennel stalk (or a large pinch of fennel seeds), a strip of dried orange peel, a large pinch of coriander seeds, and a couple of bay leaves. Bring to a boil, boil for 5 minutes, leave to cool and pour the cold brine through a sieve over the drained olives. Cover the jar with a plate. *Olives noires en saumur,* which are more often a mixture of green, half-ripened violet and black olives, are pricked with pins that have been pushed through a slice of cork, soaked in water for 10 days like the *olives cassées,* drained and put into the same cold brine. Both are ready to eat 5 or 6 days later and will keep well for a couple of months.

The traditional method of preparing *olives à la picholine* (and they certainly taste the best) is first to soak freshly picked green olives in a thick, but pourable paste of wood ashes for 5 or 6 days or until the bright green color turns olive green and, when cutting into one, the flesh of the olive can be felt to separate more easily from the pit. Hardwood ashes are the best (olive wood is wonderful); they burn more completely to a fine white ash, which should be passed through a sieve before being mixed with water. While soaking, the ashes slowly settle to the bottom of the basin and the olives settle in the water to the top; ashes and olives should be stirred gently together with a wooden spoon a couple of times daily. When they are removed from the paste of ashes, the olives should be thoroughly rinsed in several waters and put to soak in a basin of water like the others, with regular changes, for 9 or 10 days, after which they are put into exactly the same brine. They are less bitter and will hold longer than the others.

Best of all are the completely ripened, very black olives picked, preferably, after the first freeze. They will have lost much of their bitterness while ripening and are simply layered in a jar, heavily salted, tossed, drained and resalted daily for 5 or 6 days, then drained and transferred to a wicker basket placed on a platter, resalted and tossed several times daily until no more liquid drains from them—8 or 9 days in all, often less. Black olives that have begun to wither on the tree often drain hardly at all. If visible salt clings to the olives' surfaces, they can be briefly rinsed and well drained; if not, put them directly into an earthenware or stoneware container with a few bay leaves, a couple of sprigs of thyme, grind over pepper generously and pour over enough olive oil to keep them well coated, turning them around at least daily. Begin eating them 3 or 4 days later. Some varieties are sweeter or fleshier or have thinner skins than others; the preferred variety in the region of Toulon for this treatment is called, locally, *caillon* or *caillonne.* Note that, despite the abundance of salt with which they have been treated, black olives prepared in this way are never salty; the salt all runs off with the liquid it has drawn from the olives.

PARSLEY, GARLIC AND PERSILLADE

For information on parsley, see *herbs.* To chop parsley without making a mess, the leaves must be absolutely dry. To easily control the chopping, the leaves should remain attached to the stems. A parsley branch forks into three leaf stems of which the central stem is the longest: pinch off the central stem from each branch and form a tight bouquet at the base of the leaves, fold the outer leaves under, fixing the mass tightly against the chopping board with fingertips and slice the parsley into fine threads. Discard the stems (or save them for a bouquet garni) and chop through the threads if you want a finer cut.

To peel garlic without crushing it when whole cloves or fine slices are required, cut off the root-end tip, place the flat side of a large knife blade, sharp edge directed away from you, on the clove of garlic and tap it firmly but gently with the heel of your hand. The skin will be ruptured and will lift off easily; unless the tap carried too much force, the clove will remain intact. Cloves to be crushed, chopped or pounded can be smacked more vigorously, simply with the heel of your hand or using a knife blade. *Persillade*—flat-leaf (Italian) parsley and garlic, first chopped separately and, then, together—is a recurrent theme in Provençal cooking. Practically anything *"sauté à la provençale"* is first sautéed in olive oil, then sautéed for a minute or so with a *persillade* and, usually, finished with a few drops of lemon juice. The garlic for a persillade should be chopped very finely: First slice it paper-thin, then chop it repeatedly, gathering it together in a mound with the knife blade and chopping through it again before assembling it with the parsley and rechopping. A normal portion of *persillade* is 2 tablespoons of finely chopped flat-leaf (Italian) parsley chopped with 1 clove of finely chopped garlic.

PROVENÇAL HERB VINEGAR see *vinegar.*

PROVENÇAL MIXED DRIED HERBS

Commercial mixtures of dried Provençal herbs usually contain too many herbs, including rosemary, lavender and sage, and usually smell musty. If you are able to collect your own herbs and dry them, a good mixture is composed of thyme, oregano, savory and marjoram, in descending proportions. When the bundles are dry, store them in paper bags, stapled or covered over with other paper bags to protect them from dust without enclosing them in an airtight atmosphere, until autumn when all of the herbs have been picked and dried. Crumble the bunches between gloved hands, whirl the crumbles, small batches at a

time, in a food processor, pass the processed herbs through a sieve with the help of a gloved hand, put them into jars and store them. A wonderful seasoning for stuffings, marinades, sausage meat and pâtés, grilled meats and poultry, or to replace a bouquet garni if you are in a hurry or have no fresh herbs at hand.

SAFFRON

Saffron, the condiment, is the dried stigma—a mara thread—of the autumn-blooming purple saffron crocus. The stigmas of well over five thousand blossoms are said to be necessary to produce one ounce (30 g) of saffron. Its luminous color and captivating scent and taste are essential to many Provençal preparations. It is expensive, but a little goes a long way.

SALT ANCHOVIES

These prepared anchovies are a cornerstone of Provençal cuisine. They cannot be replaced by canned anchovies in oil, which have a harsh flavor and are always too salty. Freshly netted anchovies appear in abundance on the market in May, when they rise by the millions from the depths of the sea to the surface to spawn, and recur at intervals throughout the summer. To preserve them in salt, first spread a layer of coarse sea salt on a large tray. Split the abdomen of each anchovy with your finger or the tip of a small knife, then pinch off the head at the back and pull it forward, drawing out the guts at the same time. Discard the heads and guts. Layer the anchovies on the salt and sprinkle another layer of salt over them; leave them for 3 or 4 hours, then remove them to paper towels to sponge them dry. If you like, you can sprinkle them lightly with Provençal mixed dried herbs (q. v.) before beginning to pack them, in alternate layers, with coarse salt into a stoneware or wide-mouthed glass jar. Begin and end with a layer of salt. The layers of salt should be quite thick, about ½ in (12 mm), and the single layers of anchovies should be very closely packed in, side by side, head to tail, and curved to marry the inside surface of the jar. Place a weight made of nonreactive material—a water-filled, flat-bottomed bottle, for instance, whose circumference is slightly smaller than that of the jar—on the salt surface and keep in a cool place for several days. The salt will draw more liquid from the anchovies and partially dissolve to create a brine. Remove the weight and carefully skim off any traces of oil floating on the surface of the brine, then cover the jar and store in a cool place.

To prepare salt anchovies for use, they may or may not have to be soaked for some time to desalt them, depending upon the length of time they have been salted down. Anchovies that have been in salt for no more than a few months need only be carefully rinsed. Gently rub them under cold running water to remove clinging salt crystals and any remaining scales. Pry the fillets free from the spinal structure with fingertips; remove traces of fin bones from the edges, rinse again and lay out on paper towels with other towels pressed atop to sponge the fillets dry. The longer the anchovies remain in salt, the firmer, drier and saltier their flesh becomes. Those that have been in salt for a couple of years or more may have to be soaked in a bowl of cold water for a quarter of an hour, not only to desalt them partially, but also to render the flesh pliable enough to fillet them neatly. After being cleaned up and rinsed, they may need to be soaked again to get rid of salt—a taste will tell. Anchovies used during the first year after salting are the best. Salt anchovies are commonly available at Italian grocers and in fancy food shops. The recipes in this book simply specify "salt anchovies, rinsed and filleted;" the above message should alert you as to whether they must be soaked before and after. A recipe that calls for "2 salt anchovies, rinsed and filleted" means 4 fillets.

SALT COD
Called *morue* in French, fresh cod is roughly filleted, the spinal bone removed before and then the fillets are salted. Normally, if soaked for 24 hours, salt cod is ready to use. Depending upon its origin and the length of time it has been in salt, this can vary 12 to 36 hours. Check with your merchant about soaking time when buying salt cod. The best cod comes from the thickest part of the tail section, neither the abdomen nor the end of the tail. Cut it into sections and put it to soak in a colander immersed in a large basin of cold water, changing the water several times over the period of soaking; it will have whitened and doubled in bulk when it is ready to be cooked.

To poach soaked salt cod, put it into a large pan with a bay leaf and a sprig of fresh thyme, cover it abundantly with cold water, bring to a boil, cover the pan tightly and remove from the heat. Leave it in its poaching liquid for 10 minutes, or more if the piece or pieces are more than one inch (2.5 cm) thick.

SALT PORK
Called green bacon in Britain, salt pork is lean bacon that has been salted but not smoked.

SAUSAGE MEAT
Simply seasoned sausage meat is an important ingredient in pâtés, terrines and meat stuffings. Many commercial sausage meats contain more fat and filler than meat. To make your own basic sausage meat, select 2 pounds (1 kg) pork without bones with a ratio of about two parts lean meat to one part fat. A side, belly, shoulder or blade cut is appropriate. Cut the pork into large sections and sprinkle on all sides with coarse salt. Place them in a nonmetallic container (tray or large gratin dish), cover with plastic wrap and let stand overnight. Discard the liquid, rinse the pieces well, drain them and dry in a cloth towel or with paper towels. Cut them up and pass them through the medium blade of a meat grinder into a bowl. Season generously with pepper, a few grains of freshly pounded or ground allspice and a hint of freshly scraped nutmeg. Sprinkle Provençal mixed dried herbs (q. v.) and ¼ cup (2 fl oz/60 ml) dry white wine over the top and mix thoroughly with your hands. Fry a small lump in a few drops of olive oil and salt to taste.

SHALLOTS
Milder in taste than the onion, shallots are members of the same family. The two most common types of shallot are pink and gray and they are usually about the size of a walnut. Young green shallots resemble green (spring) onions, except that the thin bulbs, which grow in clusters, are each covered with a brown husk. When the root tip is cut off and the husk removed, the white flesh and green leaves look very much like green onions. The flavor of green shallots is more complex and more intense but, if unavailable, green onions can be substituted.

SORREL
A green, leafy plant, sorrel has a distinctive acidity and flavor popular as a seasoning for Provençal dishes. It is easy to grow, perennial and should be picked regularly to encourage the formation of young leaves. Old leaves are dark in color and have an acrid taste; they should be rapidly parboiled and drained before use. Young leaves are a light, tender green and may be used raw, with discretion, in salads.

SPINACH AND SWISS CHARD (SILVERBEET)
Spinach or chard are first parboiled, refreshed, squeezed and chopped before adding to any number of Provençal stuffings, gratins or omelets. Except for the small tender leaves at the heart of the plant, spinach should be stemmed: with the stem pulled backward, fold the surface of the leaf upon itself, tearing out the central vein. Spinach needs abundant washing, usually at least three waters, before it is completely rid of clinging soil. After each washing, the leaves should be lifted loosely from the water to a colander, leaving the soil behind in the basin.

The variety of chard most common in the markets has large leaves, often 20 inches (50 cm) from stem end to tip and 10 inches (25 cm) wide, with fleshy white ribs that can be 3 in (7.5 cm) wide at the base. Each leaf is laid flat on a chopping board and the rib is cut away from the green parts before they are washed separately. The ribs are peeled, cut into sections, parboiled and treated like cardoon; only the green parts are treated like spinach. Small-leaf chard is stemmed in the same way as spinach.

To parboil spinach or chard, pack the leaves into a large saucepan, add a handful of coarse salt, place the saucepan over high heat and pour over boiling water (slowly, with the spout of the tea kettle close to the surface of the leaves, to avoid splashing) to cover. Using a wooden spoon immerse the leaves repeatedly in the water as it returns to a boil. Turn them around a couple of times in the boiling water and then pour into a colander. Run cold water over to cool, gather the leaves together in both hands and squeeze them several times, firmly, between cupped hands to form a well-drained, compact mass. To chop, place the ball on a chopping board, flatten it slightly, slice it thinly, give the mass a quarter of a turn and slice through it again.

SQUID

Available in various sizes, squid appear in a number of Provençal dishes, including stuffed with a variety of savory mixtures. To clean a squid, pull the head and clinging innards free from the body pouch. Pull out and discard the transparent quill-like cartilage from the pouch. Squeeze out the small beak from the mouth at the base of the tentacles and, using scissors, cut away the eyes. Using your fingers, clean out the pouch under cold running water. Discard everything except the tentacle-head portions and the body pouches with their attached wings. If you prefer, rub or peel off the brownish violet skin; it is harmless. Rinse all the squid parts well. Split the heads and tentacles into two parts. Cut the pouches as directed in individual recipes.

TOMATOES

Full-flavored, garden-ripe tomatoes are available in Provence from July through September. The rest of the year peeled canned tomatoes from Italy are the best choice. To peel fresh tomatoes, core them, removing a small cone from the stem end of each and, using a sharp knife tip, slit the skin in the form of a cross at the flower end. Slip the tomatoes, a few at a time into a large saucepan of boiling water and remove them immediately. Grasp each skin tip at the cross between thumb and knife blade and pull the skins toward the stem end. To seed them, cut each tomato in half horizontally, to expose cross sections of the seed packets. Loosen the seeds in each packet with your little finger and give the tomato half a good shake. To coarsely chop a tomato, place the halves, cut side down, on a chopping board, slice through each two or three times, give it a quarter turn and slice again to produce large dice.

TOMATO SAUCE (COULIS)

In culinary language, *coulis* means purée. A century ago, it meant a reduced meat sauce base. In America it is often believed to indicate specifically a purée of raspberries or other fruit. In Provence a *coulis* is a purée of tomatoes. Wonderful tomato sauce can be made from fresh tomatoes, garden ripened, only during the summer. Unless you put up your own tomatoes, peeled and chopped, canned plum (Roma) tomatoes from Italy *(polpa di pomodoro)* are the best out-of-season substitute. There is no need to peel fresh tomatoes since the peels will be left behind when the sauce is

puréed. The reason for seeding them is to get rid of excess liquid and to shorten the cooking-reduction process; a fresh flavor depends on the sauce being reduced to the right consistency as rapidly as possible. The size of the pan is important; the larger the evaporation surface, the more rapid the reduction. The following proportions will produce 3–4 cups (24–32 fl oz/750 ml–1 l) of sauce.

Warm 3 tablespoons olive oil in a large, heavy saucepan or sauté pan. Add 1 onion, chopped, and cook over low heat until softened but not colored, about 10 minutes. Add 4–5 lb (2 kg) tomatoes, seeded and coarsely chopped; 3 garlic cloves, crushed; 1 bay leaf; 1 parsley root or a tied bundle of parsley stems; and salt to taste. Turn up the heat and stir and crush the tomatoes regularly with a wooden spoon until they are bathed in their liquid and beginning to boil. Reduce the heat to maintain a very light boil, cover with a lid ajar, and cook for about 40 minutes. Discard the bay leaf and parsley root or stems and pass the sauce through a food mill or through a sieve, pressing with a wooden pestle. If the sauce seems too thin, return it to its pan and reduce for a few minutes over medium heat, stirring all the while.

In small quantities, good tomato sauces can be made very rapidly and they are often the best: Join 2 or 3 tomatoes, cut up; 1 small onion, chopped; 1 clove garlic, crushed; 1 bay leaf; large pinch of salt; and 1 tablespoon water in a saucepan. Place over high heat, crush, stir and boil until reduced, about 15 minutes, then purée the sauce. Alternatively, in a large frying pan, heat 2 tablespoons olive oil and 1 clove garlic, crushed, over high heat. Before the garlic begins to brown, add 2 or 3 tomatoes, peeled, seeded and coarsely chopped; add salt and pepper to taste and sauté, tossing the tomatoes repeatedly in the air, for 3–4 minutes. Scatter over fresh basil leaves, torn into fragments, toss once or twice more and remove from heat. Do not purée.

For another simple yet excellent sauce, cut 2 or 3 tomatoes in half lengthwise. Cut a V at the stem end of each half to remove the core, place each half, cut side down, on a chopping board and slice very thinly (⅛ in/3 mm). Give the tomato half a quarter turn and slice thinly through the slices. In a large frying pan, heat 1 small onion, chopped, and 1 clove garlic, crushed, in 2 tablespoons olive oil over high heat. Before the onion and garlic begin to brown, add the tomatoes, pinch of Provençal mixed dried herbs and salt and pepper to taste and sauté over high heat, shaking the pan and tossing repeatedly, for a few minutes, or until the sauce has lost its liquid. The presence of tomato peel when the tomato is finely cut up is not troublesome.

TRUFFLES

The white Piedmont truffle doesn't exist in France. Black truffles, sometimes called *truffes du Périgord* (after the most important truffle-producing center in France), are seen in season from late November until late February. January and February truffles are usually the ripest and richest in flavor. The upper Vaucluse and the upper

Var are also known for their fine black truffles. Like mushrooms, truffles are parasitic fungus growths. They grow underground, usually near oak or hazelnut roots, and are searched out with trained dogs or pigs. Their penetrating, unique scent and flavor are the passion of all who taste them. Fresh truffles are flown to America. They are always expensive. If you can only find preserved truffles, purchase those sterilized with very little liquid, usually a bit of Cognac or Madeira, in glass jars. Truffles immersed in the water in which they have been boiled and packed in cans have very little flavor.

VINEGAR

The acetic bacteria that transform wine into vinegar are aerobic; they can live and propagate only in the presence of oxygen. They form a white veil, or flower, on the surface of the wine over which air should circulate freely, but which should never be disturbed for, if immersed, the bacteria are drowned and fall, inert, to the bottom of the wine vessel, or *vinaigrier*. A four-quart (4-l) ceramic or stoneware vinaigrier, with a hole at the base into which is fitted a cork-tipped wooden spigot, will provide enough vinegar for most kitchens. A bottle of good, unpasteurized wine vinegar should be poured in as a starter; then fill the *vinaigrier* three-quarters full with red wine, loosely cover and leave for several months at room temperature. It is a mistake to draw off small quantities of vinegar and to add wine frequently. Bottle ends of decanted or leftover wines and wine left in glasses at table should be saved in filled and corked bottles until the *vinaigrier* is partially emptied. It can then be refilled to the three-quarters mark by pouring in the wine through a long-necked funnel with the tip immersed in the remaining vinegar so as not to disturb the flower surface. The vinegar that has been drawn off can be turned into Provençal herb vinegar by macerating it for a month in a covered large stoneware jar containing bundles of thyme, oregano, winter savory and marjoram; a sprig each of rosemary and sage; several bay leaves and a few crushed, unpeeled cloves of garlic. Then strain it through a cheesecloth- (muslin-) lined funnel into bottles, cork them and lay them down. The vinegar will improve with bottle age.

A more serious *vinaigrier* can be fashioned from a small four-gallon (16-l) wine keg, first fitted with a wooden spigot and filled with water to soak for two or three days. When emptied, bore a hole for air circulation just beneath the top of the keg, diametrically opposite the spigot, and tack a piece of plastic screen over to keep out fruit flies. After filling the keg with starter and wine to the level of the air hole, cork the bunghole and keep it corked. Bore a hole in the bunghole cork and permanently fit it with a long-necked funnel that reaches to just below the spigot level. Except when filling the keg, keep the funnel covered with plastic wrap. This quantity of vinegar is best left undisturbed for some eight months before being drawn off to the spigot level. The loss by evaporation is quite dramatic; 14 three-cup (750-ml) wine bottles are required to fill the keg from spigot level to air-hole level and approximately eight bottles

of vinegar will be drawn off. The first batch of vinegar from a new *vinaigrier* is sometimes disappointing but, as the *vinaigrier* is broken in, the vinegar will progressively improve.

WILD MUSHROOMS

The mushroom most commonly encountered in the markets of Provence after the autumn rains (November is the richest month) are the saffron milk cap *(safrané, Lactarious delicious)*; two varieties of chanterelle *(griolles, Canthorellus cibarious,* and *chanterelle, Canthorellus infundibuliformis)*; the horn of plenty, also known as the trumpet of death *(trompette de la mort, Craterellus cornucopioides)* and the cèpes *(Boletus edulis)*. Rare, but perhaps the most exquisite of all, is Caesar's mushroom *(orange, Amanita caesaria)*. In May, both light and dark morels *(morille, Morchella)* appear, rarely in sufficient abundance to be seen in the market. There are many other edible mushrooms, but they are left to the collectors who, in theory, are supposed to check with a pharmacist for edibility before taking them home and sautéing them.

Saffron milk caps, chanterelles, horns of plenty and cèpes are usually sautéed in olive oil, seasoned with salt and pepper, finished with a *persillade* and, depending upon a personal taste, with a few drops of lemon juice, or, if the shape lends itself, marinated and grilled. Caesar's mushrooms are best simply anointed with olive oil, seasoned with salt and pepper and grilled. Morels are stewed gently in butter, seasoned and often finished with cream.

WINES OF PROVENCE

The wines and the food of a given region always seem to need each other for both to be thrown into perfect relief. The food of Provence is high-spirited, often with an edge of violence that, however joyous, can offend or destroy a delicate old Burgundy or an aristocratic Bordeaux. The native wines are exalted in its presence; their bouquets reflect the wild herbs and bramble of the hillsides and a rustic, solid structure refuses to be intimidated by the aggression of garlic, saffron or tomato. This is not to suggest that the most serious of Provençal wines will fail to evolve, to gain in complexity and elegance with age. A red Châteauneuf-du-Pape, Palette or Bandol will rise to unsuspected heights after 10, 15 or 20 years of bottle age, as the bouquets of wild herbs and fruits mellow into scents of undergrowth, humus, truffles and small game while retaining a suave fruit.

The best wines of France come from stony, arid soils, too poor to produce any other crop of value. Provence is no exception. In the Vaucluse, between Avignon and Orange, Châteauneuf-du-Pape, the most famous of Provençal wines and the largest single *Appellation d'Origine Contrôlée* (AOC) in France, with some eight thousand acres (3,200 hectares) of vines, produces an average of 13 million bottles of wine per year, nearly all red, about 75 percent of which are exported to all corners of the world. The landscape is unearthly: the vines rise from a sea of smooth, flattened, oval or round riverbed stones, varying in size from that of an egg to that of a human head, deposited there by prehistoric glaciers; no soil is visible. Until recently, red Châteauneuf-du-Pape could be made from any combination of 13 grape varieties, of which several are white. Because of its high sugar content and the intensity of its young fruit, some growers have leaned too heavily on Grenache, often to the exclusion of all the others. Pending legislation will limit the amount of Grenache that may be used and impose minimum percentages of Syrah, the Hermitage grape, and Mourvèdre, the dominant Bandol varietal.

Château de Beaucastel makes it a point of honor to use all 13 varieties. This property also produces an unusual and beautiful white Châteauneuf-du-Pape, principally from the Roussanne grape, which can age gracefully for 20 years or more. White Châteauneuf, steely structured, floral and honeyed, brings a new dimension to the local *caillettes* (pork crepinettes) and accompanies to perfection a *bourride,* a gratin of mussels and spinach or stuffed and braised squid. The black truffles from nearby Valréas and Richerenches are cooked in young red Châteauneuf and washed down with old Châteauneuf. Perhaps more than any other red wine, a Châteauneuf-du-Pape enjoys the assault of a blue cheese and it is an ideal companion to game in any form or to the richly aromatic daubes and *estouffades* of the region.

A neighboring appellation, Gigondas, produces a red wine from the same grape varieties, usually confined to Grenache, Syrah, Mourvèdre, Cinsault and Clairette, which, although similar in spirit, is rougher and more rustic and less apt to age; it is best when drunk at two, three or four years of age. From the same varietals, *Côtes du Rhône* and *Côtes du Rhône-*, hyphenated either with the word *Villages* or with a specific village name such as Cairanne, Valréas and so on—produce red, rosé and white wines of which the reds are usually the more interesting, often very good and reasonably priced. Rasteau produces a sweet apéritif or dessert wine from Grenache grapes, and Beaumes-de-Venise is known for its intensely perfumed, amber, sweet wine made from the Muscat grape, best served with a dessert or used in the confection of a dessert; sliced fresh peaches macerated in Muscat de Beaumes-de-Venise are delicious.

In the Bouches-du-Rhône, a few minutes drive from Aix-en-Provence, the tiny appellation Palette has long been recognized as one of the most distinguished of Provence. Almost the entire appellation is embraced by a single vineyard, Château Simone, whose proprietor, René Rougier, loyally vinifies his wines exactly as his father and grandfather did. The red, made from Cinsault, Grenache and Mourvèdre, is raised for two years in large oak tuns and passes its third year in barrels before being bottled; it profits immensely from being laid down for at least five or six years before being drunk. The rosé, made from the same grapes, is deep colored, the result of the grapes first macerating with the skins before being pressed and fermented, and is more muscular than most rosés; it lives in wood for a year before bottling. Two whites are made, mainly from Clairette; one, meant to be drunk young, is bottled six

months after the harvest to retain its fresh fruit, and the other is raised for two years in barrels, gaining in complexity and resistance to oxidation, and, like the red, it needs bottle age to open out fully. The Clairette, Ugni Blanc and Marsanne vines on the hillsides overlooking the fishing village of Cassis, 14 miles (23 km) east of Marseilles, produce a solid, stony, fruity white wine, the choice of the Marseillais for *bouillabaisse* or, for that matter, anything that comes from the sea. Cassis reds and rosés are less successful. From the Côteaux d'Aix-en-Provence, between Aix and Les Baux-de-Provence, the Domaine de Trévallon, with a microclimate too rude to plant traditional Provençal grape varieties, makes an astonishing red wine, big, rich and complex, from half Syrah and half Cabernet Sauvignon.

In the Var, the star is Bandol, an appellation encompassing eight villages whose hillsides, with the mountains behind, form a natural, protective amphitheater with the fishing village of Bandol at center stage. The grape varieties are Mourvèdre, Cinsault, Grenache, Syrah, Ugni Blanc and Clairette. Some white wine is made from the last two, but for the most part they go into the rosé, a pale, playful, spicy wine bottled in the spring following the harvest. For red Bandol—thanks mostly to the efforts of Lucien Peyraud, proprietor of the Domaine Tempier—legislation now imposes a minimum of 50 percent Mourvèdre, a late-ripening low producer, rich in tannins, intensely colored with exuberant flavors and antioxidant powers that ensure long life. Most bottlings at Domaine Tempier contain 70 to 80 percent Mourvèdre and one, from the old Cabassão vines on the lower half of the hillside rising to the village of Le Castellet, is 100 percent Mourvèdre and of a supreme elegance if given the chance to grow up. Red Bandol must pass a minimum of 18 months in wood before bottling; how much more depends on the natural evolution of the wine and on the discretion of the grower. At the apéritif hour, nothing is more at home with a *tapénade,* an *anchoïade* or with raw sea urchins than a Bandol rosé and a cool, young red Bandol served with *bouillabaisse* is a revelation; at 10 or 20 years of age, it will be happier with roasted or braised red meats or with a carefully selected cheese platter.

The Côtes de Provence appellation is scattered across all the Var. The rosé is a famous summer, seaside thirst quencher. Despite the inconsistency of soils and expositions, the rosés and the reds, because of more rigid disciplines than in the past, have greatly improved in recent years; many of the whites are innocuous, lacking in acidity.

Nice is proud of its Bellet, whose production is so limited that it is rarely encountered outside of the Alpes-Maritimes. In combination with traditional Provençal grape varieties, the specifically Niçoise Rolle (white), Folle and Braquet (both red) leave their mark on these light, tender, elegant wines. A *pissaladière* loves Bellet, red, rosé or white, drunk young and cool.

ACKNOWLEDGMENTS

Weldon Owen would like to thank the following people and organizations for their assistance in the preparation of this book:

Mme. Marie-Françoise Guichard, Patrick Benhamou, Wendely Harvey, Norman Kolpas, Tori Ritchie, Roger Smoothie, Richard Van Oosterhout, Fee-Ling Tan, Laurie Wertz, Dawn Low, Janique Poncelet, Jim Obata, Tara Brown, Sigrid Chase, Bruce Bailey, Pinnacle Publishing Services, Bob Firken.

The on-location photography team would like to thank the following for their contribution: Richard Olney; Jean Luc Villemot; Dixon Long and Ruthanne Dickerson; M. and Mme. François Peyraud and Mme. Lucie et M. Lucien Peyraud, Domaine Tempier;

Chateau d'Ansouis, residence of the De Sabran Ponteves family, M. Robert and Mme. Noelle Rocchi, Le Caveau de la Tour de L'Isle, L'Isle sur la Sorgue.

The photographer and stylist would like to thank the following for props provided for the studio photography in Sydney: Appley Hoare Antiques, Woollahra; The Bay Tree, Woollahra; Country Floors, Woollahra; Parterre Garden, Woollahra; Studio Haus, Double Bay; Les Olivades, Double Bay; In Residence, Paddington; John Normyle, Paddington; Gregory Ford, Paddington; The Art of Food and Wine, Woollahra; Alison Coates Flowers, Paddington; Country Furniture Antiques, Balmain; Accoutrement, Villeroy & Boch, Brookvale; Hale Imports for Pillivuyt, Brookvale; Sewita Marble, Silverwater.

ILLUSTRATION GUIDE

 This frieze was designed for the doors of the former priory of Notre-Dame-de-Salagon outside of Mane in Alpes-de-Haute-Provence. After falling to ruin when the monks abandoned it during the French Revolution, the church became a barn; its original artwork lay undiscovered for decades behind the bales of straw and farm equipment. Today the site is a center for study and research, with permanent exhibitions covering local history and botanical gardens.

The Aqueduc de Roquefavour in the Bouches-du-Rhône, was constructed from 1842 to 1847 by François  de Montricher to carry the waters of the Durance River to Marseilles. Built of hewn stones, it spans the Valley of the Arc and was designed to replicate the Roman Pont du Gard, an ancient aqueduct in Nîmes that has stood intact for almost two thousand years.

 Much of Provence is characterized by the way in which its *départements* celebrate water, from ancient Roman aqueducts, to innumerable sparkling fountains, recuperative spas and mineral-water baths that inspired the water worship of the early Gauls. Throughout Provence the sounds of trickling water lead to village squares where decoratively carved fountainheads provide a steady stream such as this one in Aspremont, Alpes-Maritimes.

The Carolingian antependium in Limans, Alpes-de-Haute-Provence, is an anonymous work of the early Middle Ages. Its monogram represents a combination of four Greek letters (chi, rho, alpha and omega) that form a cross signifying the beginning and end of all things in God. The letters, however, were used in the wrong order, leading to speculation that the artist did not understand their meaning.

 The famed Arc de Triomphe in Orange, Vaucluse, is the best preserved Roman arch in France. Built circa 20 B.C. to commemorate the campaigns of the II Legion, the monument is comprised of three archways and represents the force of Roman colonization. The decorative friezes and carvings depict Roman victories on land and sea and suggest Rome's triumph over ancient Gaul.

 Carved in the twelfth century, the figures on the doors of Saint-Trophime in Arles, Bouches-du-Rhône, depict Biblical lore and are characteristic of medieval Provençal sculpture. Perhaps the finest Romanesque church in Provence, it was built in dedication to Saint Trophime who was credited with having brought Christianity to France.

 This detail from a sarcophagus in the church of La Gayole in Brignoles, Var, was carved between A.D. 259 and 280 and is thought to be the most ancient funerary masterpiece in France. The stone sarcophagus, an example of early Roman Christian sculpture, was carved in Smyrna (the former name of Izmir, Turkey) and was brought to Brignoles in 1890.